Zooarchaeology, Second Edition

This book serves as an introductory text for students interested in the identification and the analysis of animal remains from archaeological sites. The emphasis is on animals whose remains inform us about the relationship between humans and their natural and social environments, especially site-formation processes, subsistence strategies, the processes of domestication, and paleoenvironments. Examining studies from all over the world, from the Pleistocene period up to the present, this volume is organized in a way that is parallel to a faunal study, beginning with background information, bias in a faunal assemblage, and basic zooarchaeological methods. A zooarchaeological Hypothetical Collection illustrates the fundamental methods for the collection of primary and secondary data that are applicable to zooarchaeology practice.

This revised edition reflects developments in zooarchaeology that have occurred during the past decade. It includes new sections on enamel ultrastructure and incremental analysis, stable isotopes and trace elements, ancient genetics and enzymes, environmental reconstruction, people as agents of environmental change, applications of zooarchaeology in animal conversation and heritage management, and a discussion of issues pertaining to the curation of zooarchaeological materials.

ELIZABETH J. REITZ is Professor of Anthropology at the Georgia Museum of Natural History, University of Georgia. Her work is based on the identification and interpretation of animal remains from coastal archaeological sites, particularly in South America, the Caribbean, and the southeastern United States. She is the co-author and co-editor of several volumes, as well as the author of more than 150 articles and book chapters.

ELIZABETH S. WING is Curator Emeritus at the Florida Museum of Natural History, University of Florida. The co-author of two books and author of many scholarly articles, she received the Fryxell Award from the Society for American Archaeology in 1996 for distinguished contributions to archaeology through interdisciplinary research. In 2006, Dr. Wing was elected to the National Academy of Sciences and received the President's Medal from the University of Florida.

Cambridge Manuals in Archaeology

General Editor
Graeme Barker, *University of Cambridge*

Advisory Editors
Elizabeth Slater, *University of Liverpool*
Peter Bogucki, *Princeton University*

Cambridge Manuals in Archaeology is a series of reference handbooks designed for an international audience of upper-level undergraduate and graduate students, and professional archaeologists and archaeological scientists in universities, museums, research laboratories, and field units. Each book includes a survey of current archaeological practice alongside essential reference material on contemporary techniques and methodology.

Books in the series

Clive Orton, Paul Tyers, and Alian Vince, POTTERY IN ARCHAEOLOGY
R. Lee Lyman, VERTEBRATE TAPHONOMY
Peter G. Dorrell, PHOTOGRAPHY IN ARCHAEOLOGY AND CONSERVATION, 2ND EDITION
A. G. Brown, ALLUVIAL GEOARCHAEOLOGY
Cheryl Claasen, SHELLS
Clive Orton, SAMPLING IN ARCHAEOLOGY
Steve Roskams, EXCAVATION
Simon Hillson, TEETH, 2ND EDITION
William Andrefsky, Jr., LITHICS, 2ND EDITION
James Conolly and Mark Lake, GEOGRAPHICAL INFORMATION SYSTEMS IN ARCHAEOLOGY
Andrew Chamberlain, DEMOGRAPHY IN ARCHAEOLOGY
A. M. Pollard, C. M. Batt, B. Stern, and S. M. M. Young, ANALYTICAL CHEMISTRY IN ARCHAEOLOGY

Zooarchaeology

SECOND EDITION

Elizabeth J. Reitz *University of Georgia*
Elizabeth S. Wing *Florida Museum of Natural History*

CAMBRIDGE
UNIVERSITY PRESS

CAMBRIDGE UNIVERSITY PRESS
Cambridge, New York, Melbourne, Madrid, Cape Town, Singapore,
São Paulo, Delhi, Dubai, Tokyo, Mexico City

Cambridge University Press
32 Avenue of the Americas, New York, NY 10013-2473, USA

www.cambridge.org
Information on this title: www.cambridge.org/9780521673938

First published 2008
Reprinted 2010 (twice)

A catalog record for this publication is available from the British Library.

Library of Congress Cataloging in Publication Data

Reitz, Elizabeth Jean, 1946–
Zooarchaeology / Elizabeth J. Reitz, Elizabeth S.Wing. – 2nd ed.
p.   cm. – (Cambridge manuals in archaeology)
Includes bibliographical references and index.
ISBN 978-0-521-85726-0 (hardback) – ISBN 978-0-521-67393-8 (pbk.)
1. Animal remains (Archaeology) – Identification – Handbooks, manuals, etc.
I. Wing, Elizabeth S.   II. Title.   III. Series.
CC79.5.A5R45   2007
930.1–dc22   2007019451

ISBN 978-0-521-85726-0 Hardback
ISBN 978-0-521-67393-8 Paperback

*Dedicated to our families and colleagues in appreciation
of their support and inspiration.*

CONTENTS

LIST OF FIGURES

LIST OF TABLES

PREFACE TO THE SECOND EDITION

When we were asked to prepare a second edition to *Zooarchaeology*, we anticipated that this would be relatively easy. We proposed to update the literature and work on sections that we or our colleagues found did not "work" in practice. We quickly realized, however, the truth of the statement that zooarchaeology is a dynamic field. We were surprised to find a few major changes in the traditional approaches in the field over the past 10 years and significant advances in archaeogenetic, isotopic, and incremental growth applications. A shift in research emphasis also has occurred. Whereas in 1999 many zooarchaeologists focused on biological and anthropological interpretations pertaining to economies and the history of animal domestication, today publications on environmental change, environmental reconstruction, and applied zooarchaeology constitute a large percentage of the literature. Advances in geochemical applications make it possible to develop holistic perspectives on the human–environment relationship, dissolving problematic distinctions among anthropology, archaeology, ecology, geology, human biology, and zoology. At the same time, after many years of functional interpretations, structural explanations have assumed a larger place in the literature. One of the most gratifying discoveries is the increase in important zooarchaeological studies published in peer-reviewed, international journals by scholars from beyond Europe and North America. This more broadly inclusive community of scholars is a good sign that zooarchaeology continues to be strongly international.

Thus, in preparing this second edition, we made major changes in sections in which the greatest advances have been made in the past decade. Chapters 3, 9, and 10 are substantially rewritten to incorporate new information and research trajectories. Chapter 8 required significant, though less extensive, modifications. We have included literature from 1999 through 2006, as well as inadvertent omissions from before 1999. These new references reflect the directions that the field of zooarchaeology has taken over the past decade. We believe these directions represent the future of the field. We repeat, however, our admonition from the first edition that theoretical interpretations are no better than the methods used to develop supporting data. It is as necessary to be well-grounded in the basics as it is to be guided by good theory.

There are some changes we did not make. As with the first edition, this edition is not intended to replace the many excellent biological references; works focused on single organisms or groups of organisms; methodological descriptions and reviews developed out of specific research needs; or regional archaeofaunal syntheses and theoretical treatments. The focus of the volume continues to be on topics of broadly global applications pertaining to major research trajectories. We do not advocate for or against methods or provide detailed descriptions of specific methods or outcomes. Students should recognize the importance of developing their own research designs, which will be implemented using appropriate methods obtained through their own review of the literature.

PREFACE TO THE FIRST EDITION

This volume is directed to all those interested in the recovery, identification, and analysis of animal remains from archaeological sites. Our intent is to review standard zooarchaeological methods and to suggest the circumstances under which they may be most successfully applied. Because we believe that a background in both anthropology and biology is important for a balanced approach to zooarchaeology, both relevant anthropological and biological information are reviewed. The exchange among archaeological, biological, ethnographic, and paleontological research is the important defining characteristic of the study of animal remains that links the following pages. The development of zooarchaeology owes much to an awareness of the importance both of ecological relationships on human behavior and of the human impact on the planet. Despite its diverse, interdisciplinary nature, zooarchaeology has three common research themes: (1) methodology; (2) continuity and change in human societies; and (3) biological relationships. These are the primary topics explored in this volume.

The animals emphasized include macrofaunal as well as some microfaunal organisms. The term "macrofauna" refers to large vertebrates and invertebrates. All vertebrate classes are included. These are mammals (Mammalia), birds (Aves), reptiles (Reptilia), amphibians (Amphibia), cartilaginous fishes (Chondrichthyes), and bony fishes (Actinopterygii). Invertebrates include primarily molluscs (Mollusca) and crustaceans (Crustacea). The term "microfauna" may refer to small members of these same classes, such as anchovies, or to small organisms, such as land snails or insects. The tissues reviewed include skeletal bone and teeth, mollusc shell, and exoskeleton (such as crab shell). Egg shell and keratinized tissue, such as hair, skin, and feathers, are not stressed here.

Our emphasis is on animals whose remains inform us about aspects of relationships between humans and their natural and social environments, especially site-formation processes, subsistence strategies, and paleoenvironments. Among these animals, those that offer food, shelter, transport, fuel, tools, ornaments, clothing, and social identity receive particular attention. We also explore material culture related to the procurement and husbandry of animals. Examples are primarily those illustrating modern human (*Homo sapiens sapiens*) uses of these animals. The time period is from the Pleistocene into the twenty-first century A.D.

The geographic range is global. Although examples are drawn from many parts of the world, we make no effort to provide regional surveys of zooarchaeological developments. Smith's (1995) review of the emergence of agriculture throughout the world provides regional surveys of both plant and animal data. His volume is a good place to obtain an overview of zooarchaeological knowledge in the context of broader archaeological research. Our intention is to review anthropological, biological, and ecological aspects of zooarchaeology from the wide variety of geographical settings in which zooarchaeology is practiced and to summarize, broadly, the diverse ways in which humans and animals interact.

The volume is organized in much the same way as a faunal study might be. Familiarity with the history of zooarchaeology and current research topics provides the intellectual background a zooarchaeologist should bring to the study of a specific faunal assemblage (Chapter 2). It is also important to be familiar with biological (Chapter 3) and ecological principles (Chapter 4) basic to the discipline. In Chapters 5, 6, and 7, three sources of bias in a faunal assemblage are reviewed, beginning with taphonomy and excavation procedures. Chapters 6 and 7 present some of the most basic zooarchaeological methods, using an archaeofaunal Hypothetical Collection to illustrate fundamental methods for collecting primary and secondary data. In the remaining chapters, animal remains are interpreted in terms of subsistence strategies (Chapter 8), domestication (Chapter 9), and human interactions with the environment (Chapter 10). The final chapter (Chapter 11) draws these threads together and considers future directions in the field.

This volume is not intended to replace the many excellent biological references available; works focused on single organisms or groups of organisms; methodological descriptions and reviews; regional archaeofaunal syntheses; or theoretical treatments. Extensive references are offered for each topic covered in the following pages. We urge readers to use these as guides to more detailed treatments of each subject. We hope to excite students to pursue their own interests in this diverse field so that they may share, with us, many hours of stimulating puzzlement.

ACKNOWLEDGMENTS

It is with deep gratitude that we acknowledge the contributions of the many people who helped to bring the first and second editions of this volume to completion. In particular, we appreciate the willingness of Graeme Barker, Laszlo Bartosiewicz, Don R. Brothwell, Anneke T. Clason, Dena F. Dincauze, Norman Herz, Stephen A. Kowalewski, Clark Spencer Larsen, William H. Marquardt, Arturo Morales Muñiz, Lynette Norr, Barnett Pavao-Zuckerman, Ann B. Stahl, and an anonymous reviewer to read all or portions of the manuscript. Richard G. Cooke, Simon J. M. Davis, Annie Grant, Laura Kozuch, Robert Newman, Nanna Noe-Nygaard, Wendell H. Oswalt, Paul W. Parmalee, Sebastian Payne, Irvy R. Quitmyer, and Melinda A. Zeder were particularly generous in helping to prepare the illustrations. Sarah M. Colley, Greg Cunningham, Elizabeth McGhee, Katherine E. Quitmyer, Dawn Reid, Donna Ruhl, Jaap Schelvis, Pamela Soltis, David W. Steadman, and Stephen R. Wing also provided invaluable assistance at critical times. Special thanks are extended to Max Reitz, Sylvia J. Scudder, Irvy R. Quitmyer, and the students in our zooarchaeology classes. We may not have followed all of the insightful suggestions offered, but we are grateful for the comments nonetheless. The volume is enhanced by the artistic contributions of Virginia Carter Steadman, Paloma Ibarra, Tina Mulka, Tara Odorizzi, Daniel C. Weinand, Molly Wing-Berman, and Wendy Zomlefer. The cover illustration was prepared by Molly Wing-Berman. Most of the graphics not attributed to these artists were prepared by Gisela Weis-Gresham, who once again demonstrates the value of good illustrations. We are grateful to the many individuals and presses who granted permission to use work previously published. We also appreciate the advice and support of Beatrice Rehl, Peggy M. Rote, Jessica Kuper, Frances Brown, and the Cambridge University Press staff. Through the generosity of Kitty Emery, the Florida Museum of Natural History provided essential support during the final preparation of the second edition. Finally, we thank the Florida Museum of Natural History, the Georgia Museum of Natural History, colleagues (among whom we number our students), and families for their patience and cooperation as we attempted to squeeze the field of zooarchaeology into a single volume.

Zooarchaeology

INTRODUCTION

Zooarchaeology refers to the study of animal remains excavated from archaeological sites. The goal of zooarchaeology is to understand the relationship between humans and their environment(s), especially between humans and other animal populations. Zooarchaeology is characterized by its broad, interdisciplinary character, which makes it difficult to write a review that adequately covers all aspects of the field. This diversity can be traced to the application of many physical, biological, ecological, and anthropological concepts and methods to the study of animal remains throughout the world by scholars with a wide range of theoretical interests and training.

ZOOARCHAEOLOGY, AN INTERDISCIPLINARY FIELD

Although animal remains, especially fossils, have intrigued the human mind for centuries, the first critical examinations of these remains were not conducted until the 1700s. Since then, zooarchaeologists have relied on combinations of the natural and social sciences, history, and the humanities for concepts, methods, and explanations. By tradition, many studies focus on zoogeographical relationships, environmental evolution, and the impact of humans on the landscape from the perspective of animals. Many zooarchaeologists pursue anthropological interests in nutrition, resource use, economies, residential patterns, ritual, social identity, and other aspects of human life involving animals or parts of animals. All of these topics are encompassed within modern zooarchaeology.

  Biological principles and topics are fundamental to zooarchaeology. Biological research includes exploration of extinctions and changes in zoogeographical distributions, morphological characteristics, population structure, the history of domestication, paleoenvironmental conditions, and ecological relationships of extant fauna using subfossil materials to provide historical perspective. Paleontologists explore these issues in deposits that predate modern humans. Many of these topics can be studied without reference to humans, although the human element is important (Weigelt 1989:62; Wintemberg 1919). Much archaeofaunal research continues to reflect biological interests, especially ecological ones.

The anthropological or historical orientation of archaeology is an important source of diversity in zooarchaeology. Many researchers practice archaeology as a subfield of anthropology and strive to achieve a holistic perspective on human biological and cultural behaviors (Willey and Sabloff 1974:12–16). Anthropological archaeologists have studied the cultural aspects of archaeological deposits under a succession of theoretical perspectives on the human–environment relationship, which contributes to the diversity of the field. In other academic traditions, archaeology is a separate discipline with strong ties to classics, economics, and history.

Another source of diversity in zooarchaeology lies in themes traditionally associated with specific regions of the globe or specific time periods (see Figure 1.1). Much research in Eurasia and northern Africa focuses on domestic animals within developing agricultural systems during the recent millennia. Researching the evolution of hunting behavior among early members of the human family dominates zooarchaeology in much of sub-Saharan Africa. Post-Pleistocene migratory patterns and the processes of human immigration are research themes in the Americas, Australia, and many Pacific islands. Research into the role of animals in the development of complex cultures is characteristic of other settings and other time periods.

Perhaps the greatest source of diversity in the field is the multidisciplinary background of zooarchaeologists. Despite an early debate over whether zoologists or anthropologists (Chaplin 1965; Daly 1969; Reed 1978; Thomas 1969) should study animal remains from archaeological sites, in reality, the person working with them may be trained in a number of fields. Zooarchaeologists may be anthropologists, paleontologists, archaeologists, biological anthropologists, zoologists, ecologists, forensic biologists, veterinarians, agricultural scientists, geographers, or geologists. Each field brings different perspectives, methodologies, and research goals to the study of animal remains.

WHAT'S IN A NAME?

This combined biological and anthropological background is reflected in disagreements over the name for the field. One of the first clear references to the field was by Lubbock (Avebury 1865:169), who used the term "zoologico-archaeologist" to refer to Steenstrup and Rütimeyer – Europeans who studied animal remains from archaeological sites. These scholars and this term influenced American zooarchaeology through Morlot (1861) and Wyman (1868a), among others. For example, the Danish term "kjøkkenmøddinger" (kitchen middens) appears in the title of one of Wyman's publications (1868a). Many nineteenth-century American studies refer to European research.

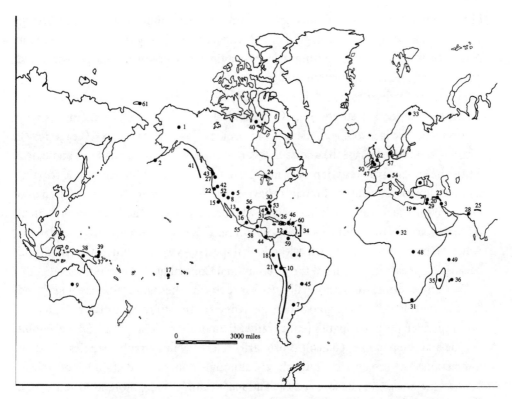

FIGURE 1.1. Locations mentioned in the text. 1. Alaska, USA; 2. Aleutians, Alaska, USA; 3. Ali Kosh, Iran; 4. Amazon Basin; 5. Anasazi, Colorado, USA; 6. Andes, western South America; 7. Argentina; 8. Arizona, USA; 9. Australia; 10. Ayacucho, Peru; 11. Black Sea; 12. Bonaire, The Netherlands Antilles; 13. Casa Grandes, Chihuahua, Mexico; 14. Cedar Key, Florida, USA; 15. Channel Islands, California, USA; 16. Chihuahuan Desert, USA and Mexico; 17. Cook Islands, Polynesia; 18. Ecuador; 19. Egypt; 20. Ein Mallaha, Isreal; 21. El Paraiso, Peru; 22. Emeryville, California, USA; 23. Fertile Crescent, southwest Asia; 24. Fort Michilimackinac, Michigan, USA; 25. Himalayas; 26. Hispaniola, Greater Antilles, Caribbean; 27. Hoko River, Washington, USA; 28. Indus Valley, Pakistan; 29. Jericho; 30. Kings Bay, Georgia, USA; 31. Klasies River mouth, South Africa; 32. Lake Chad, northern Africa; 33. Lapland; 34. Lesser Antilles, Caribbean; 35. Madagascar; 36. Mauritius, Indian Ocean; 37. New Britain, Melanesia; 38. New Guinea; 39. New Ireland, Melanesia; 40. northern Canada; 41. Northwest coast, North America; 42. Old Sacramento, California, USA; 43. Ozette Village, Washington, USA; 44. Panama; 45. Paraguay; 46. Puerto Rico; 47. Salisbury Plain, England; 48. Semliki Valley, Zaire; 49. Seychelles, Indian Ocean; 50. Somerset Levels, England; 51. southwest Florida, USA; 52. southwestern United States; 53. St. Augustine, Florida, USA; 54. Swiss Lake sites, Switzerland; 55. Teotihuacan, Mexico; 56. Texas, USA; 57. Troldebjerg, Denmark; 58. Uaxactun, Guatemala; 59. Venezuela; 60. Virgin Islands; 61. Wrangel Island, Russia; 62. York, England.

The modern derivatives, such as *zooarchaeology*, *zooarchéologie*, or *zooarchaeología*, are probably the most commonly used terms in the Americas and reflect the anthropological perspective of studying animal remains from archaeological sites for information about human behavior (Bobrowsky 1982b; Hesse and Wapnish 1985:3; Olsen and Olsen 1981). Although Lyman (1982) proposes that "zooarchaeology" be confined to studies of paleoenvironmental conditions, the term more often implies a cultural perspective rather than a zoological or ecological one (Mengoni 1988). Many workers trained in the Americas do emphasize the cultural aspects of animal remains over zoological ones and prefer to call themselves zooarchaeologists.

The term "archaeozoology" is commonly used by researchers working in Eurasia and Africa, and it emphasizes the biological nature of animal remains. Strictly interpreted, "archaeozoology" means "old zoology" or "paleontology" (Legge 1978). Although Bobrowsky (1982b) argues that "archaeozoology" subsumes both zoological and archaeological interests, it may be interpreted as the study of ancient animal remains without any relationship to human behavior (Hesse and Wapnish 1985:3; Olsen and Olsen 1981). The research of many people who prefer the term "archaeozoology" often is more biological than anthropological in nature. This name is widely recognized in the Americas both because many American faunal specialists work in Eurasia or Africa and because it appears in the title of the International Council of Archaeozoology (ICAZ).

Two other terms are occasionally used to describe the field: "ethnozoology" and "osteoarchaeology." Ethnozoology may be defined as the study of human/animal relationships from the participant's (emic) rather than from the observer's (etic) viewpoint (Vayda and Rappaport 1968:489). It primarily refers to ethnographic studies of extant interactions between humans and animals, although it once included studies of archaeological materials (e.g., Baker 1941; Cleland 1966; Gilmore 1946; Moreno-García 2004). The term "paleoethnozoology" might refer to the study of human behavior in the past using animal remains from archaeological sites, much as "paleoethnobotany" does for plants (Pearsall 2000).

Uerpmann (1973:322) defines "osteoarchaeology" as the study of animal bones from archaeological sites for their contribution to cultural and economic history. *Osteoarchaeology* appears in the title of Reed's (1963) influential article, although he uses *zooarchaeology* in the text. Osteoarchaeology implies that only vertebrate bone is studied (Olsen and Olsen 1981), and, hence, studies of invertebrates or of vertebrate structures, such as scales and teeth, might not be included. Most faunal analysts consider both vertebrates and invertebrates to be important evidence of site-formation processes, economies, and environmental conditions, so few use the term "osteoarchaeology" except in reference to the study of human osteology (e.g., Derevenski 2001).

The term "bioarchaeology" refers to the study of animal remains. In some academic traditions, bioarchaeology is a term that refers only to the study of human remains (e.g., Derevenski 2001; Larsen 1997). In others, bioarchaeology refers to all biological remains, human and nonhuman animals, as well as plants (Branch et al. 2005; Wilkinson and Stevens 2003:17). From this second perspective, zooarchaeology is a component of bioarchaeology, and, is ultimately, a discipline in environmental archaeology.

Although the discussion over a name seems trivial, and largely can be traced to the ways different languages handle compound words, it demonstrates that animal remains are sources of both biological and anthropological data (Bobrowsky 1982b; Chaplin 1965; Grayson 1979; Lawrence 1973; Lyman 1987; Ringrose 1993; Uerpmann 1973). In many ways, emphasis on either biological or anthropological questions reflects the variety of roles played by animals in human lives and the diversity of information provided by animal remains from archaeological sites – not all of which are pursued by every researcher. Depending on the specialist's training and interests, the nature of the archaeological deposit, and the research objectives of the project, faunal analysis may include all vertebrate and/or invertebrate classes, or focus only on one taxonomic group. Hair, horn, feathers, hide, scales, feces, blood residue, DNA, stable isotopes, trace elements, insects, mites, or egg shells recovered from archaeological contexts may be central to a faunal study, occasionally examined, or ignored altogether. Using animal remains, one may explore urbanization, bioturbation, nutrition, predator–prey relationships, settlement patterns, social boundaries, meat exchange, domestication, faunal successions, ritual, animal husbandry, or human-induced climate change. Such differences are reflected in the names applied to the field.

In essence, zooarchaeology and archaeozoology are alternate ways to view the same materials. It is not so much that the perspectives of anthropology, archaeology, biology, classics, ecology, geography, history, or the humanities dominate a study, but rather that they be integrated. An anthropological analysis of animal remains begins with a sound biological foundation, but we must always be aware of the human context of the materials studied. Hence, "zooarchaeology" is used throughout this volume. The field is strengthened by the diverse interests subsumed under this name, including some that are traditionally viewed as biological or historical. Most faunal analysts do not find these perspectives mutually exclusive. They recognize that humans respond to the same biological requirements governing the behavior of other organisms and that these responses influence cultural institutions. Humans alter the world around them, as do other organisms. At the same time, faunal assemblages reflect cultural systems from economic institutions to ideology. These must not be exclusive research perspectives (e.g., O'Connor 1996). The integration of all facets of animal remains enlivens the field and is fundamental to its intellectual health.

The biology/anthropology dichotomy has another facet that has an impact on the relationship between zooarchaeology and archaeology. Although zooarchaeologists recognized long ago that animal remains in archaeological sites are artifacts that passed through the "cultural filter" (Daly 1969; Legge 1978; Reed 1963:210; Uerpmann 1973), some archaeologists distinguish between "artifacts," which are modified by humans, and "ecofacts," which are culturally relevant nonartifactual materials (Binford 1964; Shackley 1981:1). To separate the consequences of human behavior from natural phenomena, it is critical that the *artifactual* nature (the cultural context) of animal remains be appreciated (Daly 1969; Legge 1978; O'Day et al. 2004). Biologists and paleontologists recognized the artifactual nature of unmodified as well as modified animal remains in archaeological contexts more quickly than did archaeologists (e.g., Weigelt 1989). Some animals are considered inedible. Others are important as sacrifices, but would never be eaten and their remains would not be used to make ordinary tools. In some cases, these classifications have little to do with the local abundance of the resource or its nutritional value, though they may have an ecological basis (Harris 1974). Even those animals present in a faunal assemblage without human intent reflect human behavior because hedgerows, attics, and gardens are important animal habitats. The animals, for whom human behaviors unintentionally create such habitats, offer a wealth of information about the built environment, though their usefulness as a source of information about the *natural* environment may be limited. As zooarchaeologists increasingly contribute to conservation management decisions, this cultural context needs to be recognized.

THE INTERACTION OF HUMANS AND ANIMALS: THE MANY USES OF ANIMALS

The primary purpose of zooarchaeological research is to learn about the interactions of humans and animals and the consequences of this relationship for both humans and their environments. Most animal remains are the result of complex human and nonhuman behaviors with resources in the environment, cultural perceptions of those resources, and the technological repertoire used to exploit them. On the one hand, exploration of change in human societies is one of the most common areas of zooarchaeological research, but many geological, biological, and historical factors may be responsible for such changes. On the other hand, stasis is a common feature in the zooarchaeological record. Explaining cultural change and continuity is complicated by those interactions, and it is important to consider the many uses of animals and the diverse paths over which animal remains travel to become part of the archaeological record. This is what Reed (1963) meant by the "cultural filter." Zooarchaeologists may find evidence of these uses hard to define, but doing so is an important component of zooarchaeological research.

One of the most fundamental uses of animals is to meet nutritional needs. This is the foundation of subsistence strategies and eventually of economic and other cultural institutions. Associating animal remains recovered from archaeological sites with nutrition is one of the primary goals of many zooarchaeologists. Some of these uses leave ambiguous archaeological evidence. For example, salt fish may leave little evidence for fish consumption at the recipient end of a trade network, and the purchase of meats from markets may be invisible at a residential site. Viscera, brains, and eggs are used for food but leave little evidence of their use. Antlers, often interpreted in terms of tools or ornaments, are ingested for medicinal purposes in many parts of the world today. Ethnographic observations, as well as coprolites (paleofeces), indicate that what is edible, and what is not, cannot be assumed (Price 1985; Sobolik 2007; Szuter 1988, 1994; Weir et al. 1988).

Much of an animal's carcass may be used for nonnutritional purposes. Wool, hair, and hide provide clothing, shelter, carrying devices, cordage, watercraft, traps, and other tools. Some elements may be used as tools after their food value is depleted, and others, such as a clam shell, may be more highly valued as raw material for tools and ornaments than as food. Oils, fats, gelatin, and glue are important by-products, but the activities related to extracting them may be difficult to distinguish from other processes (Mulville and Outram 2005; Schmid 1972:46–9). Manure may be used as fuel, building material, or fertilizer. Many of these uses leave little or no archaeological evidence. They are, however, important in the relationship between humans and the environment, as well as in the formation of the archaeological record.

Domestic animals are widely used as work animals. Their labor is important in trade and tilling fields, and they sometimes serve guard duty. We tend to think of dogs (*Canis familiaris*) in this role, but birds, such as the double-striped thick-knee (*Burhinus bistriatus*), (Reitz and Cumbaa 1983; Thomson 1964:816) and geese (e.g., *Anser anser*) provide alarms, too. Animals are used for hunting (dogs), gathering truffles (pigs [*Sus domesticus*]), and fishing (cormorants [Phalacrocoracidae]). Animals may be so valuable in these roles that they are not slaughtered until they are very old, if at all, and their remains may not be discarded in locations commonly excavated by archaeologists (e.g., Payne 1972a).

Animals are used to signify cultural attributes, such as social affiliation and belief systems. Symbolic associations may either mean that an animal is represented in a faunal assemblage for nonnutritional and nontechnological reasons, or mean that the animal is absent from the faunal assemblage even though it was culturally important. Many people keep animals as pets (Gade 1977; Redford and Robinson 1991; Serpell 1986, 1989). The animal, parts of the animal, or images of the animal may be kept so that the individual, household, or community will be associated with its special powers. Bones from a rabbit's foot (Lagomorpha) could be skinning refuse, but they might be from a charm. Cattle astragali may be gaming pieces, butchering refuse, or ritual sacrifices. Many ceremonies use animals to symbolize social structure and shared values.

REQUIREMENTS FOR THE STUDY OF ANIMAL REMAINS

The study of animal remains from archaeological sites requires a sound biological foundation. Without this background, the faunal study is, at best, incomplete and, at worst, inaccurate. Such knowledge begins with basic biological and ecological concepts. This includes skeletal biology and morphology of tissues, such as teeth, bone, shell, and crustacean exoskeleton usually recovered from archaeological sites. Taxonomic classifications, such as those in Table A1.1, are not static. Therefore, it is necessary to be familiar with current systematic classifications and the basis for those classifications.

It is important to be familiar with animal behavior and ecology, especially with those concepts related to predator–prey relationships, biogeography, ecosystems, population ecology, and the habits and habitats of the animals with which humans interact (Tchernov 1992a).

Components of a Study

Inadequate attention to the biological component of animal remains hampers interpretations of such data in terms of human behavior. All zooarchaeologists can cite cases where inattention to biological details undermines conclusions. For example, failure to know the zoogeographic history of Eurasian rats (*Rattus norvegicus* and *R. rattus*) may mean that the significance of these species if they are found in an archaeological sample deposited in the Americas prior to European colonization will go unrecognized. Our current understanding is that members of the genus *Rattus* were introduced into the Americas by European expansion (Armitage 1993). Therefore, a *Rattus* identified in the Americas means that the archaeological context was deposited after A.D. 1492, the rat was in an intrusive context, or the attribution is incorrect. Similar knowledge of the zoogeography of the turkey (*Meleagris gallopavo*) enabled the identification of an intrusive deposit in Egypt (Gautier 2005).

Consideration of site-formation processes and excavation procedures is equally important for an adequate interpretation of animal remains. The taphonomic history of a site may introduce or remove animal remains and is an important contributor to the final character of archaeological deposits. Human disposal patterns, the function and structure of the site, and archaeological techniques all have an impact on faunal composition.

The complexity of the relationship between humans and their environments requires pursuit of numerous lines of inquiry using techniques that do not mask or skew the evidence and that are appropriate to the research questions. Many zooarchaeological techniques originate in biology and geology. Additional techniques develop as the need arises and are then applied in other situations. All techniques have strengths and weaknesses that should be considered before they are applied to faunal studies.

After assessing the history of the assemblage and recording the biological data, researchers interpret the results using information from many sources. This is especially true when data can be subject to several interpretations. Support for each hypothesis should be derived from several lines of evidence (e.g., Kislev et al. 2004). This includes multiple faunal data sets, but also ethnographic analogy, modern experimental studies, and the cultural contexts of the materials. Ethnographic analogy is widely used in archaeology to broaden our horizons about the ways humans and animals interact and the consequences of those behaviors (Hudson 1993; Wylie 1985; Yellen 1977a: 4–5). Experimental and ethnoarchaeological studies contribute to our understanding of depositional, spatial, temporal, and social factors that might have an impact on archaeological deposits (Brain 1981; Gifford-Gonzalez 1989; Kroll and Price 1991). The cultural context of an assemblage is critical in the interpretation of archaeological data because activities involving animals are quite different depending on whether the context excavated is a temple, midden, house, storage structure, or kill site. Cultural institutions are involved in storage, resource control and exchange, warfare, wealth, kinship, and ritual aspects of animals. Additional information may come from petroglyphs, figurines, murals, written records, or other archaeological artifacts.

Terminology

Zooarchaeologists use a great many names and abbreviations (Casteel and Grayson 1977; Lyman 1994a). This large nomenclature creates confusion but some terms need to be defined in this volume. In the following presentation, a "specimen" is an isolated bone, tooth, or shell (Lyman 1994b; Shotwell 1958). The term "element" refers to a single complete bone, tooth, or shell. A "specimen" is either a complete bone, a tooth, or a shell or a portion thereof. If a specimen is complete, it is an "element," and if it is broken it is a "fragment of an element." This same concept may be applied to complete or broken molluscan valves and crustacean carapaces. Elements rarely are found in archaeofaunal samples; fragmentary specimens constitute most of an archaeofaunal sample. "Samples" contain multiple faunal specimens of various taxa that presumably had some relationship before excavation began. A sample is contained within an individual collection container from a unique archaeological provenience or context identified and segregated in the field. All samples from a single time period from a single site comprise a "collection." Many sites have multiple occupations of different time periods. These represent an "assemblage."

Systematic relationships are valuable tools in communicating clearly which species or other taxonomic levels are under discussion (Gentry et al. 2004). Scientific names, as well as their related common or vernacular names, are usually used by zooarchaeologists with precise meanings in mind. By following a standard systematic scheme, most zooarchaeologists understand what their colleagues mean in their choice of scientific and common names. Domesticated members of the family Bovidae, however, are an exception to this because common English terms are not directly related to taxonomy. Strictly speaking, only female members of the species *Bos indicus* and *Bos taurus* should be called cows, but the term is often used in reference to male bulls and castrated steers as well. However, the term "cattle" may be used to encompass all domestic members of this family, including neat cattle, such as goats (*Capra hircus*) and sheep (*Ovis aries*). In the following pages, the term "cattle" refers only to *Bos taurus, B. indicus*, and their hybrids. When other members of this family are meant, other terms are used.

CONCLUSIONS

Zooarchaeologists explore many exciting topics. One of these is the use of resources by human populations and the common threads that run through the diverse adaptations that humans and their animals made to different environments. Another is the integration of plant, animal, human, and geological evidence into a holistic understanding of the human past. Others explore animals in nonfood roles, such as raw materials and social identity. Biological research, especially that focusing on the evolutionary history of landscapes and animal populations, engages many zooarchaeologists. In the following chapters, we introduce the concepts on which such studies are based, the biological basis for zooarchaeological procedures and interpretations, the methods by which these are applied to animal remains from archaeological sites, and some of the interpretations that may be developed.

2

Zooarchaeological History and Theory

INTRODUCTION

Research does not occur in an intellectual vacuum. When developing research designs, scholars should be familiar with both the history of their discipline and the current theoretical climate in the field in which they work. Zooarchaeology is such a diverse field that it is impossible to do justice to its history on a global scale; therefore, our emphasis is on zooarchaeology in the context of anthropological archaeology, primarily in the United States. Despite regional variations, it is surprising how similar zooarchaeology is internationally. This may result, in part, from international networks and the focus on animal remains. It may also be that the biological background of many zooarchaeologists and the relative youth of the field are responsible for the many shared features (Horton 1986). Nevertheless, it is important that students review literature from their study locale to learn about zooarchaeological trajectories in that specific area. Obituaries and dedicatory reviews are good sources of information about the field and collegial networks.

Zooarchaeological research has two related goals: (1) to understand, through time and space, the biology and ecology of animals, and (2) to understand the structure and function of human behavior. To address these goals, theories and methods are drawn from a number of sources. The biological and physical sciences are one source. The second source is anthropology, particularly those methods and theories pertaining to the relationship of humans with their natural and social environments. A third source is archaeology itself, especially where anthropology and archaeology are separate disciplines. The role of zooarchaeology in biological and anthropological research, as well as the questions zooarchaeologists address, reflect shifts in prevailing research interests in these spheres.

ANTHROPOLOGICAL THEORY

Anthropological theories about the relationship between humans and the world around them are closely linked to the development of zooarchaeology. The relationship between environmental studies and anthropology is fundamental. Exploring environmental relationships is a major theme in anthropology. Concepts about the relationships among environment, subsistence, technology, human populations, and other aspects of cultural life may be broadly classified as environmental determinism, environmental possibilism, cultural ecology, ecological anthropology, and historical ecology (Crumley 1994; Ellen 1982; Hardesty 1977:1–17; Jochim 1981:5–10; Vayda and Rappaport 1968:479, 483). The ascendency of one or the other of these theories influences the study of animal remains in archaeological research.

Environmental Determinism

In the late nineteenth and early twentieth centuries, one of the most prevalent theories was that the environment caused cultural phenomena (Hardesty 1977:1–4; Jochim 1981:5–6; Moran 1979:24–33). Environmental determinists argue that environmental characteristics limit the development of material culture and technology. In extreme interpretations, the environment, especially climate, is said to dictate the level of cultural development achieved. Environmental factors may include topography, vegetation, or soil. Regardless of the identity of the causal agent, culture is viewed as a passive rather than an active agent, and cultural phenomena are explained by the environment in which they are found. Although this perspective does not preclude faunal studies (e.g., Fewkes 1896), most current zooarchaeological studies are conducted under other theories.

Environmental Possibilism

In contrast to the causal role proposed by environmental determinists, environmental possibilists argue that environments may permit certain cultural developments, but there are always cultural alternatives (Ellen 1982:21–32; Moran 1979:33–7). According to the possibilist position, the environmental role is a broadly limiting one explaining the absence of traits but not their presence (Kroeber 1939). Environmental possibilists argue that cultures act selectively, or even capriciously, on their environments but that the environment itself is passive. Kroeber (1939:205) notes that "no culture is wholly intelligible without reference to the noncultural or so-called environmental factors with which it is in relation and which condition it" (see also Harris 1968:339–40; Kroeber 1939:3). However, he also argues that historic and geographic research is relevant only because of an "archaeological preoccupation" with these concepts (Kroeber 1939:3). The limited role played by faunal remains in the early twentieth century is also related to the historical particularist approach advocated by Boas, who argues that cultures are individually unique phenomena that should be studied only in terms of their own histories (Harris 1968:274, 326).

From this perspective, faunal remains, subsistence strategies, and economics are of little interest. However, many of the cultural areas defined by environmental possibilists correspond to natural areas, with the relationship explained in terms of what a natural area would or would not permit. Cultural areas are often defined using extensive trait lists. Similar lists of traits are found in the archaeological literature. Lists of large-bodied mammals available in a given area are particularly common, but the archaeofaunal remains are not identified. These lists are considered to be an adequate study of animal use because of the assumption that people at a site naturally used the animals that were abundant near the site and that animals abundant near the site today were common when the site was occupied. In the absence of anthropological theories relevant to animal remains, most faunal research influenced by environmental possibilism focuses on biological issues. The results of faunal research are rarely published in anthropological sources. Zooarchaeology, as a social science, does not flourish under this theoretical perspective.

Cultural Ecology, Ecological Anthropology, and Human Ecology

A different perspective on the human–environment relationship is provided by cultural ecology (Ellen 1982:52–65; Hardesty 1977:8–10; Jochim 1981:7; Moran 1979:42–58, 1990). According to Steward (1955:31), cultures and environments are part of a total web of life. Each can be defined in terms of the other, with the environment playing an active, reciprocal role in human affairs rather than a determining or passive one. Steward (1955:30) urges cultural ecologists to study the processes by which cultural features are influenced by adaptations to the environment. He argues that resource utilization is more strongly related to the environment than to other cultural phenomena. Thus, characteristics associated with subsistence and economics, especially technological ones, constitute the cultural core. Secondary features are less strongly related to the cultural core and may be determined by purely historical factors. Steward advocates that attention should be paid to the resources of specific habitats in order to identify the subsistence and demographic patterns that influence political and social relationships.

Cultural ecology is often associated with studies of adaptive strategies and is distinguished from human ecology. In biological or human ecology, theoretical concepts derived from plant and animal ecology dominate efforts to describe, interpret, and predict the interaction between humans and their environments, with an emphasis on holistic, evolutionary, and systemic models (Bates and Lees 1996; Butzer 1990; Ellen 1982:66). These perspectives stress cultural behavior in both natural and social environments (Ellen 1982:73–9; Jochim 1979:9, 1981:4; Moran 1990; Vayda and Rappaport 1968:494). Ecological concepts, such as niche breadth, evolutionary ecology, and systems theory, are particularly important (Clarke 1972:30; Winterhalder and Smith 1992). Although some studies emphasize ecological populations (e.g., Moran 1979), others focus on networks and ecological systems (e.g., Geertz 1963) or economic, political, and other social dimensions (e.g., Bogucki 1988). A consequence of such studies is a holistic view of human life and an awareness of the complex, interactive relationship that exists among cultural systems, human populations, and the environments within which they operate. Historical ecology provides the temporal perspective of a changing landscape to studies of both structural and functional properties (Winterhalder 1994).

Cultural ecologists and ecological anthropologists do not interpret the relationship between humans and their environments as deterministic. Instead, the relationship is viewed as part of a dynamic process that may result in alternatives to specific behaviors or institutions (Jochim 1981:3–4). Cultural ecologists may focus on the adaptive relationship between humans and their environments, including subsistence strategies and reactions to environmental change. The selection and consequences of food acquisition and intake are based on a combination of cultural, environmental, and technological considerations. It was within this multidisciplinary, ecological framework that zooarchaeology has assumed a prominent role in archaeological research.

ZOOARCHAEOLOGY IN ARCHAEOLOGICAL RESEARCH

These anthropological theories have influenced the history of zooarchaeology. This section emphasizes the development of zooarchaeological research within archaeological research: on classification and descriptions in the nineteenth century, on cultural history in the early twentieth century, and on context and function into the twenty-first century. Although this review is organized chronologically, many research questions from earlier centuries guide modern zooarchaeological research, albeit with methods unheard of in earlier centuries (e.g., Albarella 2001; Evans 2003; Evans and O'Connor 2001; Hesse 1995; O'Connor 2000b; Roskams 2001; Wilkinson and Stevens 2003; Willey and Sabloff 1974; Zeder, Bradley, Emshwiller, and Smith 2006; Zeder, Emshwiller, Smith, and Bradley 2006).

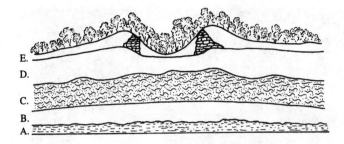

Section of shell-heap

A.   Original hardpan
B.   Echinus layer
C.   Fishbone layer
D.   Mammalian layer
E.   Modern deposits, including house-pit, and vegetable mold

FIGURE 2.1. Section of an Aleutian shell heap (modified from Dall 1877).

Classification and Description

After a period of speculation about the relationship between the environment and human society, scholars began purposefully gathering evidence to support or refute popular perceptions of natural history. It was during this time that scientific geology and Darwinian concepts of evolution developed. Archaeologists became somewhat more rigorous in their work and began to classify artifacts on the basis of factual descriptions (Daniel 1981; Willey and Sabloff 1974:42). Such interests dominated archaeology throughout the nineteenth century and into the early twentieth century.

Faunal studies were largely conducted by individuals with biological interests. Although most of these studies were descriptive, some foreshadowed future directions in zooarchaeology. One of these directions was interest in the historical association of humans with environmental change. Faunal remains from archaeological sites proved that humans had contact with extinct animals and demonstrated that changes had taken place in the geographical distributions of nonhuman species (e.g., Eaton 1898; Hay 1902; Loomis and Young 1912; Mercer 1897; Wyman 1868a, 1868b, 1875). In other cases, faunal remains defined chronological and stratigraphic changes in animal use. Lartet, for example, argued that the Upper Paleolithic should be divided into the Cave Bear, Woolly Mammoth and Rhinoceros, Reindeer, and Aurochs or Bison periods (Daniel 1981:63). A similar approach was taken by Dall (1877), who classified the strata of several Aleutian shell mounds using animal remains, the weapons by which these animals were obtained, and the utensils used to process them (Figure 2.1).

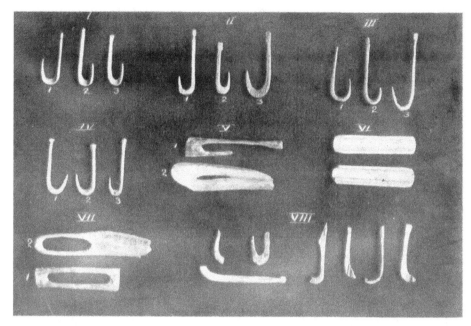

FIGURE 2.2. Fish hooks and the stages in their manufacture (Mills 1906:108). Reproduced from the collections of the Ohio Historical Society and used with their kind permission.

Some cultural interpretations were made. Sometimes the animal remains received more attention than did either the lithic or the ceramic artifacts. Swiss veterinarian Ludwig Rütimeyer influenced much of the future direction of zooarchaeology with his 1861 report on fish and early domestic animals at Swiss lake-dwellings (Clason 1973, 1986). Eaton's (1898) unquantified vertebrate and invertebrate species lists were accompanied by zoological and geological notes, a discussion of human remains, descriptions of worked faunal remains, observations on butchering habits and other modifications unrelated to tool manufacture, a suggestion that the shell mounds were occupied throughout the year, and a zoogeographical note about the extinct great auk (*Pinguinus impennis*). Mills (1904, 1906) described both modified and unmodified animal remains, estimated dietary contributions, discussed capture techniques, and reviewed food preparation methods in his reports (Figure 2.2). The work of Loomis and Young (1912) is particularly interesting because their vertebrate and invertebrate lists were quantified in terms of the number of individuals. Their paper included descriptions of the species recovered, hypotheses about their dietary importance based on frequency and butchering patterns, inferences about the season in which the site was occupied, and descriptions of modified animal remains. Although most of the animals in their shell middens were consumed, Loomis and Young (1912) observed that some probably were not.

Some early concerns with methods and the processes involved in the formation of these deposits are evident. Lartet demonstrated that species richness increases

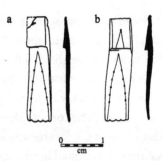

FIGURE 2.3. Bone objects from Burial A-2, Uaxactun, Guatemala. Originally identified as (a) small ornaments of bird bone
(Kidder 1947:57; Smith 1937: figure 8) are actually (b) unmodified
armadillo (*Dasypus novemcintus*) dermal bone. Used with the
kind permission of the Carnegie Institution of Washington.

considerably when the remains of small animals are studied (Clermont 1994). Although
his observations were not quantified, Wyman (1875) expressed interest in improving
analytical approaches.

Cultural History, Chronology, and Trait Lists

Early efforts to describe archaeological materials were followed by chronological and
methodological concerns (Daniel 1981; Dunnell 1986; Willey and Sabloff 1974). The
stratigraphic and stylistic interests that dominated archaeological research in the first
half of the twentieth century produced complex chronologies and cultural histories
based on descriptive typologies. The focus on cultural history and the prevailing environmental possibilist theories did not encourage archaeologists to study archaeological
materials deemed to be of little chronological significance (Barker 1985:4). Typically,
archaeological accounts included only those faunal remains associated with human
burials (e.g., Webb 1928) or those that were modified (e.g., Boekelman 1936, 1937). In
much of Europe and southwestern Asia, zooarchaeology was synonymous with the
study of domestic animals (Clason 1983, 1986). Reflecting the emphasis of archaeology
on nonbiological issues, most zooarchaeological papers are in biological rather than
anthropological publications. In those rare cases where animal remains were included
in archaeological reports, the attributions sometimes were inaccurate because people
familiar with animal remains were seldom consulted (Figure 2.3; Smith 1937).

Although archaeologists interested in chronology rarely incorporated faunal remains
in their studies, many biologists pursued the environmental information offered by these
remains. Zoologists were directed to archaeological materials for information about animal distributions, extinct forms, morphological change, and pathologies (Wintemberg
1919). Hargrave (1938) published a similar list 20 years later. Examples of this literature
are very common. For example, van Giffen studied fish remains from dwelling mounds
known as *terpen* in the Netherlands (Clason 1983, 1986). Many of these studies reported
associations of humans with extinct animals (e.g., Eddy and Jenks 1935; Miller 1929a,
1929b).

Some anthropological questions were considered. For example, in her report on the Emeryville avifauna, Howard (1929) reviewed both biological and cultural aspects of the materials. She discussed plant and animal communities around the site, provided a biological description of the bird remains, and considered modified specimens, exploitation of juvenile birds, hunting range, and evidence for year-round occupation of the site. Although he concentrated on biological issues, Baker (e.g., 1923, 1931, 1941) noted that some of the invertebrates he identified provided evidence for trade routes in the southeastern United States, and he interpreted vertebrate and invertebrate remains in terms of meat resources.

Growing methodological sophistication is reflected in papers addressing the importance of recovery techniques and curation of faunal remains. Weigelt's (1989) important taphonomic work, published in 1927, reflects this early concern with procedures. Several papers called attention to factors affecting preservation and urged recovery, retention, and study of all specimens (e.g., Wintemberg 1919). Hargrave (1938) urged his colleagues to save all faunal materials and to have them identified by a zoologist rather than be satisfied with wild guesses. Methodological concerns were reflected in notes about accurate identifications (Merriam 1928) and calls for measurements (Clason 1983). Howard (1929) also discussed archaeological recovery methods and provided illustrations that could be used to identify bird elements. She observed that although paleontologists might think that archaeological specimens were in good condition, most zoologists were unimpressed with these dirty, broken fragments (Howard 1929:311).

Context and Function

In the 1940s, archaeologists began to develop research interests requiring knowledge of the context and function that went beyond descriptive trait lists, chronology, and cultural history (Barker 1985:5; Daniel 1981; Willey and Sabloff 1974; Wilkinson and Stevens 2003:246–54). These studies showed a greater awareness of the information about cultural behavior and former lifeways that artifacts provide. During this period, Steward (1955) defined cultural ecology and Taylor (1948) proposed the conjunctive approach. Interest in cultural adaptations required considering the role that local plants and animals play in human endeavors. Although most biological and geological disciplines continued to make minor contributions to the research of conventional archaeologists, by the 1960s, they had assumed a significant place in ecologically oriented archaeological research.

Although functional and contextual concepts required systematic collection and analysis of faunal samples and anthropological rather than biological interpretations, many archaeologists still thought environmental data to be unimportant to the study of cultural phenomena. Much of the increase in faunal studies during this period was in unquantified descriptions. Often worked specimens would be described in the text, while unmodified materials appeared in a brief appendix or note (e.g., Hadlock 1943; Tyzzer 1943; Webb 1959), if at all. Unmodified faunal remains were often discarded.

However, a growing number of archaeologists wanted their faunal samples identified competently and quickly, and this caused a number of problems (Gilmore 1946; Taylor 1957). For most of this period, there were no zooarchaeological specialists. Most attributions were done by biologists or people with no formal training in archaeology. Yet, as anthropological interest in animal remains grew, biologists increasingly considered archaeological identifications an unmitigated drudge (Gilmore 1949:163) – an attitude not improved by the fact that archaeologists wanted a report as soon as possible (Gilmore 1949). By this time, most biologists specialized in single groups of animals. They could not do an integrated study of the archaeological materials, and most lacked an anthropological background for interpreting archaeological faunal remains in human terms. Trying to improve the situation, Gilmore (a biologist) provided biologists and archaeologists with examples of the information that could be obtained from animal remains by publishing similar articles in both *American Antiquity* (1946) and *Journal of Mammalogy* (1949). Gilmore (1946) recommended that archaeologists become involved in preparing reference collections, quite rare at the time, in order to appreciate the variety of information animal remains might provide.

Without a thoughtful research objective for the archaeological project, in general, and the faunal data, in particular, little could be expected from faunal studies other than lists. Taylor's (1948:7, 1972) definition of the conjunctive approach, the study of the interrelationships that exist within a culture, provided an important step forward. Taylor called for holistic studies of the relationship between people and their environment. To study human subsistence, Taylor (1948:188–9) advocated archaeologists collect adequate faunal samples and have them studied. He suggested that such studies be funded so that specialists would view archaeological studies as legitimate research rather than spare-time projects (Taylor 1948:200). He stressed the importance of publication and quantification (Taylor 1948:156, 169). Taylor's (1957) edited volume on the identification of what he called nonartifactual archaeological materials included chapters by Barbara Lawrence, Paul Parmalee, and Charles Reed, all of whom influenced zooarchaeology in the latter part of the twentieth century. It is probably significant that Gilmore and Taylor were colleagues (e.g., Gilmore 1947).

Campaign-style projects, such as those in Asia (e.g., Bate 1937; Braidwood and Braidwood 1982; Braidwood and Howe 1960; Hole et al. 1969), Mexico (Byers 1967), and Peru (Izumi and Sono 1963; Izumi and Terada 1972), contributed to the development of zooarchaeological specialists. Some of these projects began in the early part of the twentieth century, lasted for many years, and excavated large quantities of material. Project personnel included faunal specialists who worked as part of multidisciplinary teams, often in the field. There they had an opportunity to learn about the context of the faunal remains and provide advice about their treatment and recovery. The most important contribution of these projects may have been the training they provided for students who eventually became leaders in the field.

As a consequence of these developments, zooarchaeology became a recognized field with a greater role in archaeological studies. With this growth came concerns about site-formation processes, methods, and interpretation. Some of the most significant zooarchaeological reference collections and laboratories trace their roots to the mid-twentieth century (e.g., Chaplin 1965; Driesch 1991; Schibler and Chaix 1994). The impact of cultural and natural transformations on the archaeofaunal record became a greater concern (Byers 1951; Dart 1957; Efremov 1940) as did sampling issues (e.g., Parmalee 1957a, 1957b; White 1956). White (shown in Figure 2.4) published a series of important methodological papers (1952, 1953a, 1953b, 1954, 1955, 1956) based primarily on butchering marks and techniques. He is probably best known for introducing archaeologists to a technique used by paleontologists (e.g., Stock 1929) to estimate the minimum number of individuals (MNI), (White 1953a). Lawrence (1957) urged changing the emphasis from identification to interpretation so that the work would be more intellectually exciting and attractive. Meighan and his colleagues (1958a, 1958b) published a two-part series proposing a number of ecological interpretations that could be made using archaeological materials. Methods for studying dietary components and population size were proposed (e.g., Cook and Treganza 1947). Many of these topics remain important research themes in zooarchaeology.

RECENT ZOOARCHAEOLOGICAL RESEARCH THEMES

Cultural ecology and ecological anthropology theories dominate most of the recent archaeological research (Renfrew and Bahn 2004:37–42; Willey and Sabloff 1974:189). The focus of these studies is on adaptive aspects of behavior, especially subsistence strategies and economics, in order to study functional relationships between humans and their environments (Barker 1985:19–25; Butzer 1971; Dunnell 1986; Hesse 1995; Wilkinson and Stevens 2003:249–52). Recent archaeological research often incorporates interdisciplinary studies of human behavior, cultural adaptations, cultural change, and environmental processes. Often, explicit hypotheses test general laws about the interactions among humans economies, technologies, and environments, and guide this research (e.g., Clarke 1968:32–42; Jochim 1981). Ecological principles form the basis of these hypotheses and are tested with empirical archaeological evidence. The combination of ecological anthropology, processual explanations, and cultural resource management (salvage or rescue archaeology) changed the role of archaeofaunal materials in the direction advocated by Taylor. A second trend in recent archaeological research

FIGURE 2.4. Theodore E. White. Used with the kind permission of Robert W. Newman.

is the renewed interest in structural and ideological interpretations of human behavior and of animal remains.

Many zooarchaeological studies conducted after the mid-twentieth century are more analytical and anthropological than those that preceded them. Another consequence is a dramatic increase in the number of zooarchaeological studies. Two concepts that emerged in this period are particularly important for zooarchaeology. One is middle-range theory, which is based on observations of technology, subsistence, and settlement patterns in extant populations. The other uses ecological and economic models to examine strategic decisions in the acquisition and allocation of natural and social resources. These concepts share many ecological ideas (see Chapter 4) and are, in practice, not mutually exclusive. Biotic as well as abiotic data are central to such studies, and zooarchaeology has flourished under this paradigm.

Middle-Range Theory

Middle-range theory relies on empirical observations of the processes and principles responsible for the formation of the archaeological record in order to interpret, even predict, efficient human behavior and human relationships with the environment (Bettinger 1991:61–2; Binford 1977:6; Evans 2003; Grayson 1986; Raab and Goodyear 1984; Wilkinson and Stevens 2003: 252–53). Understanding the impact of these processes is fundamental to exploring cultural behavior because it is necessary to discriminate between the consequences of human activities and those caused by other processes, for example, to distinguish between cultural and noncultural faunal assemblages (e.g., Thomas 1971). Behavioral archaeology (Schiffer 1976) and ethnoarchaeology (Gould 1978; Mutundu 2005) provide important contemporary observations that may be applied to understanding the development of archaeological sites. Some of these actualistic studies test models based on Binford's (1980) distinction between highly mobile foragers and highly sedentary collectors as two ends of a continuum described by different combinations of settlement patterns and technologies.

Some of the most influential zooarchaeological studies published after 1960 developed from interest in site-formation processes with which middle-range theory is often equated (Bettinger 1991:77–82; Gifford-Gonzalez 1991; Kroll and Price 1991:310; Thomas 1986). This includes evaluations of sample sizes, methodologies, and taphonomy. Especially prominent is research into butchering and transportation decisions as these relate to the value placed on portions of an animal carcass and distances between kill/butchery sites and consumption sites (Figure 2.5; Thomas and Mayer 1983:Figure 188). These topics are not new to zooarchaeology (e.g., Wintemberg 1919), but they assume a more central role under this model.

Game Theory and Optimal Foraging Models

Game theory and optimality models facilitate study of the allocation of scarce resources in terms of costs and benefits (Clarke 1972; Jochim 1976:6–10, 1981:10–12). Cost might be time, effort, risk, or the energy expended. Benefits might be energy acquired, safety, or time saved. Linear programming is a mathematical modeling technique that permits researchers to play simulated economic games in which the best allocation of resources and the consequences of hypothetical choices can be evaluated (Coombs 1980; Keene 1981; Reidhead 1979). It can be used, for example, to identify a nutritionally satisfactory combination of foods or the role of labor minimization in subsistence decisions (e.g., Reidhead 1980). Game theories and optimality models provide the implicit, if not explicit, foundation of many zooarchaeological studies.

In game theory, decisions are based on budgets of resources, such as nutrients, prestige, raw materials, land, time, energy, or specialized knowledge. These decisions involve all aspects of behavior, including ones not directly related to food acquisition (Clarke 1968:43, 73, 85, 90; Earle and Christenson 1980). Decisions are patterned solutions that may have a variety of outcomes, such as reducing labor, maximizing acquisition

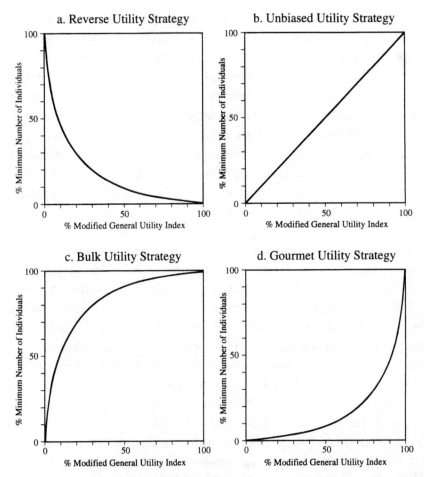

FIGURE 2.5. Four behavioral strategies predicted by middle-range theory. The reverse-utility strategy graph reflects the types of elements that would be found at a kill/butchery site at which elements with low utility would be abundant; elements with high utility would be under-represented because they were removed to consumption sites. The other three curves predict the types of elements that would be found at consumption sites based on three other utility strategies. The minimum number of individuals and the modified general utility index follow Binford (1978); see Chapter 7 in this volume for further discussion. Modified from Thomas and Mayer (1983:figure 188). (© American Museum of Natural History. Used with the kind permission of the American Museum of Natural History and David Hurst Thomas.)

of raw materials, or reducing risk (Clarke 1968:45–53, 1972). Clarke distinguishes between optimizer strategies and satisficer strategies. Optimizer strategies "try to get the best possible results given the conditions" (Clarke 1968:94). Satisficer strategies meet predetermined, but not optimal, levels. Satisficer strategies may be mixed or random-ized. A prudent satisficer strategy "aims at maximizing the minimum outcome (max-imin), or put another way, on minimizing the maximum risk (minimax)" (Clarke 1968:95).

Optimum foraging models characterize human diets based on the costs and benefits of search and pursuit (e.g., Ballbé 2005; Grayson and Delpech 1998; Hawkes and
O'Connell 1981; Madsen and Schmitt 1998; Outram 2004; Perlman 1980; Smith and
Winterhalder 1992; Thomas 1986; Wilkinson and Stevens 2003: 251–2; Winterhalder
1987; Winterhalder et al. 1988). Optimal foraging theorists argue that humans make
rational decisions to maximize the net rate of energy captured, measured usually in
calories, although other measures could be used (Bettinger 1991:84; Butler and Campbell 2004; Leech 2006; see also Jochim 1981:9–10). Optimal foraging encompasses topics
such as dietary choices, scheduling of foraging activities, and decisions about settlement and foraging locations (e.g., Winterhalder 1981). One of the most well-known
components of optimal foraging theory is diet breadth, which balances the abundance of resources, the amount of energy produced by each, the amount of energy
needed to search for and pursue each, and the amount of time required to process each
resource obtained against others. "Search time" is the time needed to find a species, and
"pursuit time" is the time required to capture a single animal of that species once it
is found. When search time is high, diet breadth may be high as well. However, when
pursuit time is high, the response may be specialization in order to manage time spent
(Winterhalder 1981). From the perspective of managing subsistence costs, a willingness
to use a wide range of common, fairly immobile resources may substantially reduce
the amount of time required to find and capture suitable ones. Patch choice, foraging
time, central-place theory, resource constraints, and carrying capacity are additional
important concepts incorporated into much of this research.

Another important group of theories focuses on site-catchment analysis, locational
analysis, and other types of landscape or regional analysis (Figure 2.6; Bettinger 1991:66;
Evans 2003; Gamble 1984; Higgs and Vita-Finzi 1972). This involves defining or predicting the areas or resources habitually exploited by inhabitants of a site. Gravity and
central-place models are intrinsic to much of this research (Crumley 1979). The gravity
model conceptualizes economic behavior between two centers, and the central-place
model specifies behavior among centers on a regional scale (Crumley 1979). These are
usually considered in terms of adaptive strategies and the distribution of energy or other
resources based on least effort.

Important steps in site-catchment analysis include defining a site's territory and
classifying the encompassed resources in terms of spatial and temporal variables (Roper
1979). Seasonal and daily cycles have an impact on the distribution of resources in
terms of time and space. These variables, in turn, influence the degree to which the
residential pattern is mobile or sedentary. They may influence the development of
economic exchanges with other communities and domestication of crops and animals.
Therefore, periodicity in resource availability and schedules for their use are important
components of territoriality. Differences in length of occupation, season of occupation,
and the use of animals are related to site function. For this reason, it is important to

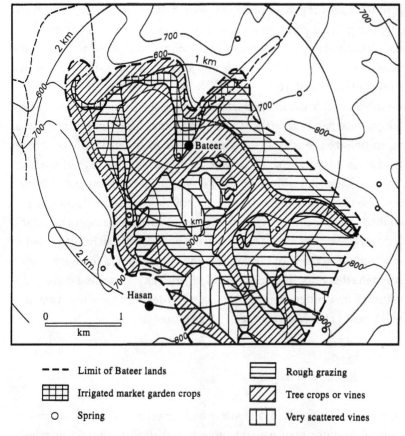

FIGURE 2.6. Catchment area of an Arab village. Modified from Higgs and Vita-Finzi (1972:31) and used with the kind permission of Cambridge University Press.

know if the site was a village, a residential base camp, or a specialized site, such as a hunt stand, burial ground, or shellfishing station.

Social Interpretations of Human Behavior

Because ecological and environmental studies emphasize functional and processual aspects of human behavior rather than social relationships or culture history, symbolic and structural interpretations have received less attention from zooarchaeologists and archaeologists alike (Leone and Potter 1988; Wilkinson and Stevens 2003:254–62). Nevertheless, human behavior is guided by political, religious, and other social objectives as well as by ecological and economic ones. Ideology, ritual, social identity, inequality, urbanization, colonialism, and other social mechanisms are important components of human behavior (e.g., Evans 2003; Hayden 2001). Evans (2003:6) argues that "work in several animal groups is showing that much behaviour is about establishing, maintaining, and even opposing social relationships." We can expect humans to express how they relate to each other and to their environments through animals and to manipulate their environments for social purposes. People are, after all, social animals living in a chemical, physical, and biological world.

The obvious symbolic and structural importance of animals cannot be ignored. Many theoretical developments, particularly those subsumed under the terms postprocessual or postmodern, emphasize the critical role animals play in the social life of human communities or examine human behavior in terms of native meaning (e.g., Hesse 1995; Hodder 1982, 1990; Miracle and Milner 2002; O'Day et al. 2004; Ryan and Crabtree 1995; Serjeantson 2000). Some of these studies are reactions to the reductionism or determinism implied when a culture is viewed solely as an adaptive strategy (Evans and O'Connor 2001:7, 217). Many aspects of the archaeological record can be attributed to social behavior, which is the fabric of the cultural filter (Reed 1963). These are among the critical phenomena that must be considered, along with environmental and ecological theory, nonhuman first-order changes, and second-order changes when evaluating evidence that will be used in applied contexts (Mulville 2005).

Heritage and Cultural Resource Management

Another important factor in the field of zooarchaeology after 1960 is the increase in heritage and cultural resource management projects and similar contract or salvage programs in many countries (Choyke 2004; Roskams 2001; Zeiler 2004). Frequently, these projects are brief, and data recovery is extremely limited. To develop competitive proposals with a theoretical basis, many contractors include subsistence, site function, seasonality, and economic studies in their research designs. To address such questions, environmental studies, including zooarchaeology, are needed. The funding made available by these projects contributed to a substantial growth in the field (e.g., Coy 1978, 1979). Although budgets and time schedules frequently do not permit thoughtful integration of zooarchaeological data with other findings about the site or region, the number of zooarchaeologists and the amount of research conducted expanded rapidly. This produced a vast amount of material, data, and literature for which arrangements for long-term curation must be made (Cram 2004; Lauwerier and de Vries 2004).

THREE FACETS OF MODERN ZOOARCHAEOLOGICAL RESEARCH

Zooarchaeology now embraces many research orientations. These can be roughly subdivided into methodological research, anthropological research, and biological research – results in one informs research in the others. Some are traditional zooarchaeological interests with roots in earlier centuries; others represent recent developments either in zooarchaeology or in related fields. Most stem from one of the theoretical paradigms reviewed in this chapter. All are featured in greater detail in subsequent chapters.

Methodological Research

The increased demands made on faunal data for explanations resulted in extensive methodological research. In part owing to the presence of specialists in zooarchaeology, increased use of quantification techniques, and the rigor required by the scientific method, most zooarchaeologists are concerned about biases in faunal data. The debate over whether zoologists or archaeologists should study animal remains can be seen as an early concern about how to obtain reliable results while maximizing interpretive potential. Considerable research is directed toward understanding the consequences of the abiotic and biotic processes that contribute to first-order changes (e.g., Lyman 1994c; Peacock et al. 2005). Second-order changes associated with excavation decisions and identification procedures are widely studied (e.g., Halstead et al. 2002; Outram 2001; Payne 1972b). Many faunal studies are highly quantitative and the numerous analytical methods must be evaluated (e.g., Grayson 1984; Jones 2004; Lyman 2003).

Anthropological Research

An increase in theoretical studies of the relationship between humans and animals is characteristic of recent zooarchaeological research (e.g., Byers et al. 2005). Much of this focuses on the causes for continuity and change in ecological and economic aspects of human behavior. Subsistence and economic research requires study of both the biological needs that diets meet and the strategies by which humans procure dietary components.

The biological aspects of subsistence include human nutritional requirements as well as the nutritional contributions of specific taxa. Human nutrition is more often studied by biological anthropologists, who examine human skeletal remains for evidence of nutritional diseases, demographic variables, and subsistence activities (e.g., Larsen 1997; White and Folkens 2005). Many zooarchaeologists use biochemical analysis of isotopic ratios and trace elements to study diets (e.g., Newsome et al. 2004). Some researchers study the nutritional value of specific taxa and translate meat weights and nutritional values into estimates of dietary contributions (e.g., Barrett 1993; De Negris and Mengoni Doñalons 2005; Parmalee and Klippel 1974).

Subsistence strategies are the target of much research. Subsistence strategies encompass procurement decisions and technologies; economic, political, and social institutions; and ritual activities. These studies include efforts to identify general subsistence patterns (e.g., Anderson 1988; Cachel 2000; Hoffecker et al. 1991; Loponte and Acosta 2004; Koike and Ohtaishi 1987; Plug 1987b); settlement patterns and catchment areas (e.g., Davidson 1983; Mengoni 1986; Mondini et al. 2004); and seasonal characteristics based on growth structures and age at death (e.g., Brewer 1987; Higham and Horn 2000; Landon 1993; Tomé and Vigne 2003). Many of these studies consider more than one aspect of subsistence and may use predictive models, such as niche breadth, energy flow, and foraging theory (e.g., Outram 2004; Tchernov 1992a, 1992b). Studies of subsistence technologies are common, especially of animal remains modified into tools, capture techniques, and butchering methods (e.g., Choyke 1987; Noe-Nygaard 1989; Olsen 1987; Rabett 2004; Yerkes 2005). Many of these rely on actualistic studies (e.g., Ioannidou 2003b), geochemical applications (e.g., Pechenkina et al. 2005), and archaeogenetics (e.g., Troy et al. 2001).

Exchange networks, political organization, kinship systems, and belief systems are studied in the context of subsistence systems or in their own right (e.g., Arndt et al. 2003; Miracle and Milner 2002). Such studies may consider trade both as a component of economic and political affairs and as a source of animal products (e.g., Barker 1987; Bowen 1992; Maltby 1994; Rowley-Conwy 2000). Social status and ethnic identity are additional active research avenues (e.g., Crabtree 1990; Lev-Tov 2004; Scott 2007). Humans associate food and animals with important symbolic attributes, and concepts of animals and the natural world reflect symbolic or structural relationships (e.g., Altuna 1983; Cooke 2004; Lauwerier 1993a; Levy 1995; Minc and Smith 1989).

Much zooarchaeological research involves the origin, spread, and health of domestic animals (e.g., Benecke 1987; Copley et al. 2004; Davies et al. 2005; Higgs and Jarman 1972; Renfrew 2000; Stahl and Norton 1987; Voigt 1987). These studies include the history of domestication, systematic research into the origin and development of domestic animals, the use of these by humans, and comparative studies of wild and domestic forms. Animal domestication in the context of emerging agricultural systems, complex societies, and urbanization is an important research avenue. Much of this work is informed by archaeogenetics (e.g, Bradley 2000; Zeder, Bradley, Emshwiller, and Smith 2006; Zeder, Emshwiller, Smith, and Bradley 2006).

Biological Research

Although the growth in zooarchaeological research reflects increased archaeological interest in anthropological explanations, biological aspects of archaeofaunal remains continue to be important. Biological research is a fundamental aspect of the

domestication of animals and the history of economically important breeds, especially where archaeogenetics and zooarchaeology are combined. Faunal remains offer
information about paleoenvironmental conditions and characteristics of nonhuman
populations (e.g., Avery 1987; Bobrowsky and Gatus 1984; Bocherens et al. 2000; Haynes
1987). One source of this information is obtained from the morphology of the species
involved (e.g., Avery 2004; Hernández et al. 1993; Iregren 1988). Evidence for the size,
weight, and health of the animals in a region indicates the conditions under which
animals lived (e.g., Luff and Bailey 2000). Alterations in morphological features suggest
environmental change, overexploitation, or domestication. Contributions in zoogeography and animal diversity demonstrate the association of humans with extinct fauna
and elaborate on range extensions and/or contractions (e.g., Anderson 1989; Graham
et al. 1981; Lauwerier and Zeiler 2001; Patton 2000; Steadman 1995). In many cases,
changes in biological aspects of animals in archaeological sites indicate environmental changes so that zooarchaeology contributes to historical ecology, conservation, and
natural resource management (e.g., Andrus et al. 2002b; Driver and Hobson 1992; Kislev
et al. 2004; Langemann 2004; Lyman 1996; Mulville 2005; Plug and Lauwerier 2004).

CONCLUSIONS

Smith (1976) argues that zooarchaeology suffers from what Leone (1972) called
"paradigm lag." While one group engages in ecological research, a second group
"twitches off" to compile descriptive species lists. A third group pursues biological
research. The first two groups trace their roots to the fundamental difference between
two anthropological concepts about the human–environment relationship: environmental possibilism and ecological anthropology. Archaeologists interested in descriptive or chronological questions still operate under the constructs of environmental
possibilism. This influence is evident in discussions where environmental aspects of
the archaeological record are but a thin cover for a basically descriptive study. In such
reports, faunal remains are just one more thing to list. When associated with projects
uncommitted to ecological studies, zooarchaeologists persist in producing laundry lists
(Clark 1972:ix).

   This deficiency cannot be attributed solely to qualitative or quantitative problems
but rather to a continuing interest in descriptive cultural history on the part of many
archaeologists. There is no particular reason why studies of cultural history, behavioral
adaptations, and social meaning are in opposition. As a holistic discipline, anthropologists should recognize that these are all part of the fabric of human life. Human behavior
is inherently flexible and subject to temporal and spatial variations reflecting both the
natural and social environment. However, rarely are good zooarchaeological studies
associated with highly focused cultural chronologies or studies of social relationships,

perhaps because archaeologists with such interests fail to communicate adequately with zooarchaeologists or to involve a zooarchaeologist at all. This is exacerbated by the overpowering influence of cultural resource management on field work. Animal remains recovered during small test excavations at a few sites along the route of a proposed highway that are summarily described, studied by an untrained member of the laboratory staff, included in reports printed in limited numbers, and filed do not contribute to sophisticated ecosystem, economic, or social analyses.

Significant research requires a long-term commitment to time-consuming data collection on a regional and interregional basis combined with truly collaborative research. To understand the use of resources by human populations and the common threads underlying the diverse adaptations made to different environments, it is necessary to integrate data from a number of different sources. These include botanical remains, human remains, vertebrate and invertebrate fauna, as well as physical and chemical properties of biological materials and the soils in which they are found. Social and historical interpretations, in particular, require that the archaeological context be thoroughly explained to the zooarchaeological staff. Only through integration of archaeological, biological, ethnographic, and geological data can we understand the human past. All parties must take the time to look at their data from a variety of perspectives and share their insights freely with collaborating scholars. In such a context, zooarchaeologists engage in meaningful anthropological and ecological research.

A background in the history of anthropological theory and the development of zooarchaeology is important because these are reflected in current zooarchaeological research. Zooarchaeology's role in archaeology and the questions zooarchaeologists address reflect shifts in prevailing theoretical perspectives. Many of today's philosophical and methodological debates are best understood from a historical perspective. Some methods, originally developed in the context of questions that are not popular today, have new applications. Some questions require the development of new techniques. In other cases, both the questions and the methods have endured. In subsequent chapters, these topics are revisited; beginning with the biological and ecological foundations of modern zooarchaeology.

3

Basic Biology

INTRODUCTION

"An ancient Chinese proverb has it that knowing the right names for things is the birth of wisdom" (Beck 1996:460). If not the birth of wisdom, at least this knowledge facilitates communication about the animals associated with archaeological sites. Much of what is known about human uses of animals is based on the survival of the durable tissues from those animals. The morphology of the surviving specimens must be sufficiently complete to retain the characteristics that allow identification of the element or portion thereof as well as the taxon (plural: taxa) represented. With this information, the role of a suite of animals in a society can be understood and the uses of these animals can be interpreted. This requires an extensive knowledge of taxonomy, anatomy, and ecology, the subjects of this chapter and Chapter 4.

Both taxonomy and anatomy trace their roots to ancient history. For example, circumstantial archaeofaunal evidence points to a practical understanding of anatomy by hunters. Some healed injuries found on specimens are not random; they occur on elements that protect the vulnerable heart and brain, indicating that hunters aimed at these organs (Noe-Nygaard 1975, 1989). Although these healed injuries show that hunters sometimes missed their target, it is clear that they knew where to aim. Hunters in the past had specific names for the animals they hunted and the animals' anatomy. Current scientific plant and animal classifications were codified and detailed knowledge of anatomy developed from this folk knowledge (Mayr 1982).

Zooarchaeological research is based on the types of animals represented in the sample and the body parts from which they are identified. Thus, familiarity with the principles of taxonomy and anatomical characteristics of hard tissues is necessary for competent identification and analysis. An exhaustive treatment of everything needed to reconstruct whole living animals and interpret them in terms of human behavior is not possible in a single chapter. Instead, a general biological background applicable to zooarchaeological work anywhere in the world is summarized here. The following discussion of taxonomic relationships and anatomical characteristics focuses on those attributes that typify specimens commonly found in archaeological samples. This general information should be augmented with details about the organisms found in the specific region being studied.

TAXONOMY

Zooarchaeologists use systematic nomenclature primarily for the identification of taxa recovered from archaeological sites. This should not be confused with taxonomic classification, which involves "*ordering of organisms into taxa on the basis of their similarity and relationship as determined by or inferred from their taxonomic characters*" (Mayr 1982:185; italics are Mayr's). Understanding the basics of taxonomic classification is fundamental to correct use. Correct taxonomic designations are essential for accurately interpreting archaeological remains and communicating results.

Modern scientific taxonomies are based on morphologies such as skin, fur, or feather, valve color, scale patterns, size, proportion, soft-tissue morphology, and genetic characteristics. Some morphological characteristics of hard tissues are intrinsic to taxonomic descriptions, whereas other hard-tissue anatomy is not part of the specific description although it corresponds to the evolutionary relationships on which taxonomic classifications are based.

Folk Taxonomy

Naming organisms is a fundamental characteristic of our linguistic past. Folk taxonomy examines the way people name organisms. Such taxonomies reveal people's concepts about animals, associations between different animals, and the source of introduced animals when they and their names are adopted together (Berlin 1992; Conklin 1972; Prummel 2001; Serjeantson 2000). Some folk taxonomies are the same as Linnaean classifications, others are more finely subdivided, and some combine organisms with quite different biological histories. Knowing which distinctions or combinations were made is essential to understanding economic and social systems.

The names used by people to identify animals are called common or vernacular names. These differ from one place to another and among languages. The names "perro," "hund," "allqu," "chichi," and "chien" all refer to the same biological organism, known in English as "dog." Different common names may be used for the same species, or the same common name may be used for different species even among speakers of the same language. For example, *Cervus elephus* is called "red deer" in Europe and either "elk" or "wapiti" in North America, whereas *Alces alces* is "elk" in Europe and "moose" in North America. An early chronicler in the Caribbean called sea turtles (Cheloniidae) "so excellent a fishe" (Carr 1986). In some parts of the southeastern United States, burrowing pocket gophers (*Geomys pinetus*), which create large sand mounds, are called "salamanders." This is thought to be a corruption of "sandy-mounder." This rodent should not be confused with amphibians that are also called salamanders (order Caudata), or with gopher tortoises (*Gopherus polyphemus*), both of which live in the same area as the pocket gopher.

Some folk classifications correspond closely with scientific classification for organisms that are economically important but use broad-category names for animals of little economic significance. The Fore people of the New Guinea Highlands classify all animals into a few higher categories, which are subdivided into lower categories. Many of these lower categories correspond directly to species defined using scientific nomenclature (Diamond 1966). Both the birds hunted for food and those of little economic value have folk taxonomic names that distinguish them and allow the Fore hunter to recognize the choice prey that are the object of the hunt. In contrast to the detailed classification used for economically important species and related forms, diverse and conspicuous animals with little economic value, such as butterflies, have only one higher category name.

Despite the potential for confusion, common or vernacular names are widely used when referring to organisms by biologists and the lay audience alike. However, common names lack the worldwide recognition needed for reporting scientific research. To increase clarity, lists of scientific and common names (e.g., American Ornithologists' Union 1983; Dickinson 2003; Nelson et al. 2004; Turgeon et al. 1998; Williams et al. 1989) and field guides, such as those sponsored by the Audubon Society or published in the Peterson field guide series, provide both scientific names and corresponding ("official") common names. Many of the taxonomic guides available through the World Wide Web enable searches using either the common or the scientific name. Throughout this book, we use the common name first, followed by the scientific name in parentheses. The scientific names used in the text are listed in phylogenetic order in Table A1.1.

Systematics

Although the concept of classification is old, the foundation of modern systematics is based on Linnaeus's *Systema Naturae* (1758). This scientific treatise was written in Latin, the international language at the time. The goals of the Linnaean system are that any single organism has one, and only one, valid name, and this name is not shared by any other organism. The hierarchical system Linnaeus envisioned is referred to as binomial (or binominal) nomenclature. Each taxonomic level is based on clearly defined species diagnoses describing similarities. Linnaeus included the variety, species, genus, order, and class in his nomenclatural hierarchy. Subsequently, many finer gradations were added. The most important levels continue to be the genus and species (a binomen), the family, order, class, phylum, and kingdom. Changes in the procedures and objectives of taxonomic research build on and modify the Linnaean system.

A species is defined as "*a reproductive community of populations (reproductively iso-lated from others) that occupies a specific niche in nature*" (Mayr 1982:273; italics are Mayr's). The species is the most important unit in whole-animal biology. The genus is a collection of species that share similar characteristics and are presumed to have a common phylogenetic origin, having evolved from a common ancestor (Mayr et al. 1953:48–9). All species in a genus occupy a similar niche, although one that is broader than that of a single species (Mayr et al. 1953). Higher taxonomic categories include increasingly broader groups of animals and more widely shared features.

The classification of animals is codified, and the procedures for making changes are subject to rules governed by the International Code of Zoological Nomenclature. As the taxonomy of groups of organisms is revised, the affiliations of species and genera or even higher levels of classification change, and this is reflected in name changes. Some groups of animals are more subject to changes than others as more is learned about them and their phylogenetic relationships are better understood. No single scheme is completely final, in part because studies of DNA (deoxyribonucleic acid) reveal relationships among animals that are not clear on morphological grounds alone. Latin or latinized forms (regardless of linguistic origin) persist as the primary basis for constructing or revising scientific names, therefore scientific names are subject to Latin rules of grammar. The genus name is usually a noun, and the species (or trivial name) is usually an adjective.

Scientific nomenclature is dynamic and changes are made even among the best-known groups of animals. A good example of this is found in Table 3.1. For many years, the class that includes ray-finned fishes was "Osteichthyes." In the sixth edition of *Common and Scientific Names of Fishes from the United States, Canada, and Mexico*, the American Fisheries Society finds that "Actinopterygii" is now the valid name for this class (Nelson et al. 2004).

The hierarchy in classification can be illustrated by an example of a taxonomic scheme for the stoplight parrotfish (Table 3.1; Nelson 1984). The stoplight parrotfish is known as "*Sparisoma viride* (Bonnaterre, 1788)." This binomen includes the genus and species (or trivial name). The first letter of the genus is capitalized, the species is lower case, and both are underlined or italicized. The name and date following the species is the name of the author (Bonnaterre) who first described the species and the date (1788) when this description was published. In the case of the stoplight parrotfish, the name and date are in parentheses because the first description of this species was under a different genus (*Scarus*) and the species name (*viridis*) agreed with the former genus name in gender. With subsequent study of more specimens, the alliance of *Scarus viridis* with members of the genus *Sparisoma* was determined (Winn and Bardach 1957), and the genus for this species was changed. At the same time, the trivial name (*viridis*) was also

Table 3.1. *The higher classification of the stoplight parrotfish* (Sparisoma viride), *with a brief list of the characteristics of each category, following Nelson (1984)*

Category	Taxonomy	Characterization
Phylum	Chordata	possess a notochord
Subphylum	Vertebrata	cranium, vertebrae, and bone and/or cartilage present
Superclass	Gnathostomata	jaw derived from gill arches present
Grade	Pisces	jawed aquatic vertebrates with gills and paired limbs, includes Chondrichthyes and Actinopterygii and two extinct classes; differing from the Tetrapoda, which includes four classes, Mammalia, Aves, Reptilia, and Amphibia
Class*	Actinopterygii	ray-finned fishes
Subclass		
Superorder	Acanthopterygii = Percomorpha)	anatomical features of the gills separate this superorder
Order*	Perciformes	dominant fish group
Suborder	Labroidei	includes the wrasses and parrotfishes, which have many osteological characteristics in common
Family*	Scaridae	all parrotfishes
Subfamily	Sparisomatinae	separates *Sparisoma* and two minor genera from *Scarus* and three minor genera
Genus*	*Sparisoma*	
Species*	*Sparisoma viride*	

Note: *Designates most important categories for zooarchaeology.

changed to *viride* to agree in gender with the new generic name. If the generic affiliation of a species is not changed, the author's name and the date of the original description are not in parentheses. The author or describer of the species is not always included in references to a species. The series of changes a scientific name undergoes is known as a synonymy.

It is possible to verify that the species named by Bonnaterre was the same as the species examined by Winn and Bardach because a type specimen is designated when a species is described. The original description is based on the type specimen, as are subsequent revisions. The type locality is the location where the type was found. In the case of the stoplight parrotfish, the type locality in the original description is simply "the Bahamas." At the time Bonnaterre described this animal, species were thought to be static entities that did not change through time or space, whereas today species are viewed as members of evolving populations. With the present emphasis on the population of the species, descriptions are now usually based on a series of specimens in addition to the type so that individual variation and sexual dimorphism can also be described. Type localities are much more detailed even though the stoplight parrotfish is common throughout the Bahamas.

The categories subspecies, variety, race, form, ecotype, and breed are used to describe variability within a species. The only one of these categories with formal taxonomic standing is the subspecies. This is defined as "a distinctive, geographical segment of a species, that is, it comprises a group of wild animals that is geographically and morphologically separate from other such groups within a single species" (Clutton-Brock 1999:42). The subspecies name follows the genus and species; the full name is called a trinomial. Breeds are variations within domesticated species. The distinction between a "subspecies" and a "breed" is that a subspecies is restricted to a geographic area and evolved through reproductive isolation, whereas a breed is the product of selection by people irrespective of geographic barriers (Clutton-Brock 1999:42 ff.). "Variety," "race," "ecotype," and "form" are all terms describing variability among populations of animals but are not part of a formal classification system. Categories below species can rarely be recognized in zooarchaeological remains.

A number of conventions are followed in the use of scientific names for animals. The specific endings are used to indicate levels in the hierarchy, for example, "-iformes" for order in fishes and birds, "-idae" for family, and "-inae" for subfamily. The family name may be transformed into a common name by dropping the ending "-ae" and putting the first letter of the name in lower case. So a parrotfish (Scaridae) is referred to as a scarid (plural: scarids). The terms "genus" and "species" are singular. Plural of "genus" is "genera," whereas plural and singular forms of "species" are the same. All names higher in the taxonomic hierarchy are plural.

It may be possible to attribute archaeological specimens to a genus but not to a species. In those cases, the generic name is followed by an abbreviation "sp." for species; "spp." indicates that more than one species is possible. Sometimes the abbreviation "cf." (from the Latin *confere*) is used to signify that the attribution of a species is not completely secure, but that the species in question is close to or compares with a particular species. In such a case, the name might be written: *Sparisoma* cf. *viride*. These abbreviations are not underlined or italicized. When the same genus is referred to within a page of a document, the name is spelled out completely the first time and can be abbreviated subsequent times. For example, having discussed *Sparisoma viride*, we may now make reference to *S. rubripinne*, which is a different species in the same genus. This form can be used only when there is no chance for confusion, that is, there are no other genera beginning with the same letter under discussion at this point in the text.

Scientific Literature

The scientific literature should be consulted to learn the key characteristics of a species and how that species fits into a phylogenetic classification scheme. This literature falls into four general types: (1) higher taxonomies with worldwide coverage; (2) regional or state checklists; (3) regional handbooks and identification guides; and (4) original taxonomic descriptions and revisions. Users of these references should be aware that the taxonomy in them may be out-of-date and that the choice of names and other information in them may not be the current consensus of scientific opinion.

Higher taxonomies organize major taxonomic units in phylogenetic order with the most primitive members of the group first and the most advanced last. The term "primitive" means that the taxonomic group is found earlier in the fossil record than more advanced organisms. Primitive organisms have features that are ancestral to later, derived ones (Wolff 1991:33–4). This does not mean the animals are inferior to later forms although they may be generalists rather than specialists. Many such publications include a description of the distinguishing characteristics of the higher categories. Higher taxonomies provide guidance for arranging families and species in scientific publications and museum collections (e.g., Abele 1982; Austin 1971; Brusca and Brusca 1990; Nelson 1984; Romer 1956; Simpson 1945; Vaught 1989). Within each class, organisms are usually arranged in phylogenetic order. However, classes are typically arranged either in ascending or descending order of complexity, that is, from molluscs to mammals or the reverse.

Checklists for regions of varying size include species of a taxonomic group, such as a class or phylum, usually listed in phylogenetic order. A series of lists is published by the American Fisheries Society for the United States and Canada and now includes volumes for fishes (Nelson et al. 2004), decapod crustaceans (Williams et al. 1989), and molluscs (Turgeon et al. 1998). These are simply lists of scientific names with authors and dates and the major locations where they occur, such as Atlantic, Pacific, freshwater, or terrestrial. *The List of North American Recent Mammals* (Miller and Kellogg 1955) also includes a full synonymy, type locality, and range for each subspecies but does not include common names or descriptions (see also Nowak [1991]). Some monumental works have worldwide coverage, such as the *Checklist of Birds of the World* (Mayr and Greenway 1962) begun by J. L. Peters and colleagues in 1931 and *Mammal Species of the World: A Taxonomic and Geographic Reference* (Wilson and Reeder 2005). These include synonymies, type localities, and ranges. Helpful references also are available through the World Wide Web, although these often are not peer-reviewed and users should know that they may trade accuracy for convenience when they use these sites.

Regional handbooks, biological surveys, and identification guides fit into the third type. They usually are arranged phylogenetically and include key characteristics by which each species can be identified as well as ecological information and distribution. They are usually well-illustrated (e.g, Clutton-Brock 2002). Some are so profusely illustrated, approaching 1,000 pages in length, that they cannot be considered handbooks; otherwise, they contain much the same type of information, although in greater detail (e.g., Abbott 1974; Böhlke and Chaplin 1968; Fischer 1978; Grant 1982). Biological surveys of animals in particular regions are often compiled with governmental support (e.g., Bailey 1931;

Baird 1857). Such surveys continue today, particularly in areas where the fauna is less well-known. These include volumes on the mammals of South America (Eisenberg 1989; Redford and Eisenberg 1992). Other surveys are done with a focus on rare and endangered species (e.g., Humphrey 1992).

Original taxonomic descriptions and revisions focus on single taxonomic groups, a family or genus, within a particular geographic range. These descriptions arrange genera and species alphabetically or phylogenetically. They may include complete synonymies, dichotomous keys, localities where specimens have been found, and descriptions of new species (e.g., Carleton and Musser 1989; Hershkovitz 1962; Hooper 1952; Howell 1938; McLean 1984; Schultz 1958). Comparable literature can be found for most regions and organisms.

Summary of Taxonomy

A taxonomic list of the animals referred to in this volume is listed in Table A1.1. Accuracy is vital for all scientific endeavors, and use of scientific names is an important means of precisely communicating a great deal of information to other researchers using only one or two words. It is important to determine the credentials of the individuals or committees proposing names, as well as to recognize that scientists often disagree about the interpretation of phylogenetic relationships provided by biological evidence. These disagreements are reflected in the scientific names that each scholar prefers. Thus, scientific nomenclature is not quite as stable and universal as Linnaeus anticipated. Nevertheless, correct use of current nomenclature is important because the name is associated with the characteristics of the animal's biology that were important to the people who used them in the past and are important to zooarchaeologists today. At the same time, folk taxonomy provides insight into the associations that people have with the animals and the meanings that animals have in human affairs.

ANATOMY

Just as taxonomy is an important tool in zooarchaeology, so too is anatomy. The anatomy of every species contains characteristics of its ancestry, as well as modifications for life in its environment. This information can help to attribute each archaeological specimen to a scientific taxon and to interpret the animal remains.

The bauplan (plural: baupläne) of an animal is the "structural range and architectural limits, as well as the functional aspects of a design" (Brusca and Brusca 1990:43). This concept aids in describing the capabilities and limitations of the structural and functional components of an entire organism or of an organ system such as the skeleton.

Both the form and the composition of hard tissue are critical for its function. Species that evolved as basic baupläne were modified to enable animals to move, eat, and reproduce in different niches. Many ancestral characteristics and adaptive modifications distinguish among classes of vertebrates and invertebrates and serve as the basis for identifying the specimens and animals represented in zooarchaeological materials.

Ancestral characteristics and adaptive modifications are reflected in the hard tissue of animals. Evolutionary processes may produce structures that are homologous or analogous. Evolved structures are homologous if they have the same origin. For example, the wing of a bird is homologous with the forelimb of a mammal. In some animals, the modification is so great that the homologous structure cannot be recognized without reference to intermediate stages in the evolution of the structure. Analogous structures are those that have a similar function but not the same evolutionary origin. For example, the legs of a mammal and those of a crab are analogous. Those interested in knowing more about the evolution of animals as represented in hard tissue should refer to texts on paleontology and comparative anatomy (e.g., Alexander 1994; Carroll 1987; Hildebrand 1982; Kardong 1995; Romer 1955; Vermeij 1987; Wolff 1991).

Higher taxonomic categories, such as phyla, have evolved along different trajectories and are distinct enough to be readily recognized by the composition and form of their hard tissue alone. The major types of hard tissue found in archaeological sites are from four phyla: (1) Chordata, (2) Arthropoda, (3) Mollusca, and (4) Echinodermata (Tables 3.2 and A1.1). Most of the hard tissues of animals (except exoskeletons of insects) owe their durability to the calcium compounds of which they are composed. Vertebrate (phylum Chordata subphylum Vertebrata) teeth and bones are composite materials consisting primarily of calcium phosphate in the form of hydroxyapatite and collagen. Echinoderm tests (phylum Echinodermata), found in such animals as sea urchins, are made of porous ossicles composed primarily of calcite (Brusca and Brusca 1990). The shells of molluscan snails and clams (phylum Mollusca) are primarily calcium carbonate, in the form of either calcite or aragonite, and organic conchiolin (Vermeij 1993). Crabs, shrimps, and lobsters (phylum Arthropoda subphylum Crustacea) have an exoskeleton made of a cuticle composed of chitin and protein mineralized by deposition of calcium carbonate (Brusca and Brusca 1990). Insects are also arthropods and have exoskeletons composed of chitin that is not mineralized. More details of the hard anatomies of these organisms can be found in Figures A2.1–A2.20.

In the vertebrate skeleton, hard tissues are composed of inorganic compounds, conferring rigidity and hardness, and organic material, conferring toughness, resiliency, and elasticity (Hildebrand 1982; Romer and Parsons 1977:150). The various constituents of the vertebrate skeleton are primarily hydroxyapatite (inorganic) and collagen (organic; Hildebrand 1982; Wolff 1991:196–7, 328–9). Tissues with the highest percentage of inorganic mineral, such as tooth enamel and dentine, have the greatest chance to survive in archaeological sites (Table 3.3). Keratin is a hard tissue composed of fibrous protein that

Table 3.2. *Classes most commonly found in archaeological contexts and characteristics of their most common remains*

Phylum	Class	Characteristic
Chordata	Mammalia	vertebrae complex and differentiated along the column; centrum usually with flat articulating surface (amphiplatyan); usually a differentiated tooth row with teeth that have roots that fit in alveoli (thecodont attachment); fused cranium in adult (Figures 3.1, 3.3, 3.6, and A2.2)
	Aves	vertebrae complex with differentiation along the column; saddle-shaped vertebral centra (heterocoelous); mouth sheathed with keratinized epidermal beak; skeleton modified for flight (Figures 3.15 and A 2.3)
	Reptilia	some differentiation along the column; vertebrae vary greatly though many have centra that are concave anterior, convex posterior (procoelous); in turtles the trunk vertebrae are fused to the shell; turtles have a keratinized beak; many reptiles, such as most lizards and snakes, have teeth anchored to the edge of the jaw (pleurodont attachment); rooted teeth anchored in sockets occur among the crocodilians (thecodont attachment) (Figures 3.1, 3.3, and (A 2.4–9)
	Amphibia	vertebrae of frogs and toads are reduced in number and are typically procoelous; tail vertebrae are fused into a single rod (the urostyle), and the ilium is greatly elongated; centra of salamanders are biconcave (amphicoelous) (Figures 3.1, 3.3, and A 2.10)
	Chondrichthyes	calcified centra biconcave and cylindrical (Figure 3.2a)
	Actinopterygii	vertebral centra biconcave (amphicoelous) except in gars (Lepisosteidae), which have centra convex anterior and concave posterior (opisthocoelous); vertebrae complex and differentiated along the column in advanced fishes; vertebrae simple, cylindrical, and undifferentiated along the column of primitive fishes (Figures 3.1, 3.2b, 3.3, and (A 2.11–13)
Echinodermata	Echinoidea	spines, exoskeletal test with tubercles for the attachment of spines, Aristotle's lantern (Figure 3.4)
Mollusca	Polyplacophora	chitons have eight shell plates (Figure A2.14)
	Gastropoda	typically with a coiled shell but also includes limpets and abalone as primitive members (Figure A2.15)
	Bivalvia	two valves hinged dorsally with hinge teeth (Figures (A 2.16–17)
	Scaphopoda	tubular shell open at both ends
Arthropoda	Maxillopoda	barnacles (subclass Cirripedia) have six calcareous plates that are usually attached to a substrate and four that open and allow filter feeding and reproduction
	Malacostraca	crabs, shrimps, and lobsters (subclass Eumalacostraca, order Decapoda) can be recognized by the chelipeds and other hard parts (Figures 3.8, 3.9, and (A2.18–20)

Table 3.3. *The relative percentage of organic and inorganic constituents of various hard tissues*

Tissue	Organic percentage	Inorganic percentage
bone	35	65
bone of young children	39	61
bone of middle-aged people	34	66
cow femur	33	67
antler	41	59
whale auditory bulla	14	86
tooth: cementum	35–40	65–70
tooth: dentine	20–25	75–80
tooth: enamel	0.5–4	96–99.5
mollusc shell	low	high
crustacean exoskeleton	variable	variable
crustacean gastrolith	3	97
fish otolith	0	100

Note: Data from Alexander (1994:37–9), Davis (1987:48), Lyman (1994c:72), and Travis (1960).

forms in the epidermis to produce nails, hooves, hair, baleen, and the "shell" covering the bony carapace and plastron of turtles. Keratin is preserved in archaeological deposits only under special circumstances. Cartilage contains even fewer inorganic compounds. It is a tough and dense connective tissue that is important because it is both elastic and compressible. Cartilage is important in the growth and development of vertebrate skeletons, but its survival in archaeological sites is extremely rare.

Size, shape, and structural density are other factors related to durability of hard tissue (Cruz 2005; Cruz and Elkin 2003; Lyman 1994c; Walker 1987:172). Although the decay of elements of the vertebrate skeleton is a complex and poorly understood process, it is likely that the ability of bone and teeth to survive is related to density and mineral content (O'Connor 2000b:25). In an effort to correlate the survivor potential of vertebrate elements and parts of elements in archaeological collections, numerous methods are used to measure the volume density (VD) or the bone mineral density of mammalian, avian, and fish elements (Dirrigl 2001; Elkin 1995; Ioannidou 2003a; Lam et al. 2003; Lyman 1984; Pavao and Stahl 1999; Stahl 1999; Symmons 2004; Zohar et al. 2001).

Structures that receive a lot of wear, such as teeth, or are subject to great forces, such as limb elements, are strengthened by their composition and their form. Because the form and the composition of structures relate to their function, these are discussed together. Familiarity with both form and function is an important aid in the study. The rest of this chapter reviews characteristics of the calcified tissues of the phyla most frequently encountered by zooarchaeologists in terms of form and function.

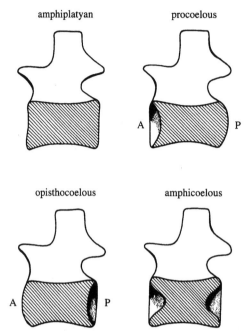

FIGURE 3.1. Vertebral types: *Amphiplatyan* is characteristic of mammals; *procoelous* is characteristic of some reptiles and amphibians; *opisthocoelous* is characteristic of other reptiles and amphibians; and *amphicoelous* is characteristic of cartilaginous and bony fishes except gars, which have opisthocoelous vertebral centra. One of the chief differences between procoelous and opisthocoelous vertebrae is that the anterior (A) face is concave in the procoelous vertebra and the posterior (P) face is concave in the opisthocoelous vertebra. Illustration modified from Romer (1956:224). Used with the kind permission of the University of Chicago Press.

CLASS DISTINCTIONS: VERTEBRATES

Living chordates of the subphylum Vertebrata, animals with backbones, are divided into six classes. In most vertebrates, the notochord, a simple cartilaginous rod that runs along the length of the body, is replaced by a series of articulated vertebrae. The six classes are (1) mammals, (2) birds, (3) reptiles, (4) amphibians, (5) cartilaginous fishes, and (6) bony fishes. These familiar animals are distinguished by the structure of their vertebrae, the attachment of their teeth, and other anatomical details (Table 3.2).

The vertebral centrum, the body of the vertebrae, and the way vertebrae articulate with one another are particularly distinctive and help to distinguish among vertebrate classes (Figure 3.1). With few exceptions, mammals have centra that are flat at each end. This is an amphiplatyan form. Birds have saddle-shaped vertebral centra. This is a heterocoelous form. Centra vary in reptiles and amphibians. Generally, the centra are concave at one end and convex at the other. In some taxa they are all concave and there are other variations. Those with the anterior end concave and the posterior end convex are procoelous forms. The opposite arrangement, anterior end convex and posterior end concave, is an opisthocoelous form. The vertebrae of turtles that lie within the carapace are fused to the neural bony plates of the carapace. Both bony and cartilaginous fishes (other than gars), which have vertebral centra that are concave at both ends, are amphicoelous forms. Gars are the exception because they have opisthocoelous vertebrae. Vertebrae of most bony fishes are distinguished from those of cartilaginous fishes by

FIGURE 3.2. Dorsal views of (a) a shark (Carcharhinidae) and (b) a primitive bony fish (tarpon, *Megalops atlanticus*) vertebra. Drawn by Wendy Zomlefer.

a   b

a thecodont   b pleurodont   c acrodont

FIGURE 3.3. Three of the basic types of tooth attachments: (a) thecodont, characteristic of mammals and crocodilians; (b) pleurodont, characteristic of most reptiles and amphibians; and (c) acrodont, characteristic of most bony fishes. Illustration modified from Edmund (1969:127).

having lateral spines, dorsal neural arches fused to the centra along the entire length of the column, and ventral haemal arches fused to the centra posterior to the body cavity. The neural arch provides a protective canal for the nerve chord, and the haemal arch surrounds the major blood vessel. Vertebrae of higher vertebrates also have lateral spines and a neural arch. The neural and haemal arches of cartilaginous fish vertebrae insert into dorsal and ventral foramina in the centra. These foramina persist in the calcified cartilaginous vertebral centra of sharks and their kin, as well as in those of primitive bony fishes (Figure 3.2).

Although vertebrae are usually very distinctive, some species do not clearly express the characteristics of their class. For example (Figure 3.2a and 3.2b), the vertebrae of cartilaginous fishes, such as sharks and rays (Chondrichthyes), are easily confused with those of some primitive bony fishes such as bowfin (*Amia calva*), tarpon (*Megalops atlanticus*), and bonefish (*Albula vulpes*). Lateral spines are present on the vertebrae of these primitive bony fishes, but they are very small. Neither these primitive bony fishes nor the cartilaginous fishes have bony or calcified neural or haemal arches fused to the centra.

Ancestral characteristics of each vertebrate class can be seen in the details of the tooth structure and attachment to the jaw and in the number and placement of teeth. Four basic types of tooth attachment are recognized among vertebrates (Figure 3.3; Romer 1956; Wolff 1991). Most mammals and crocodilians have teeth with roots that fit into alveoli in the upper and lower jaws, a type of attachment called thecodont (Figure 3.3). The teeth of most reptiles exemplified by snakes (Serpentes) and most lizards (Lacertilia), and frogs (Ranidae) among the amphibians, are anchored on a shelf along the edge of the dentary, premaxilla, maxilla, and/or pterygoid. This type of attachment is called pleurodont. The teeth of some bony fishes are attached to the dentary, maxilla, and vomer (prevomer), and sometimes to the palatines and pharyngeal bones by pedestals at their base. As teeth are lost, new ones erupt from below. This type of tooth attachment is called acrodont. Sharks and rays have multiple rows of teeth held to the mandibular cartilage of the jaws by collagenous fibers (Sharpey's fibers) that run into the dentine from the dermis.

Tooth replacement and tooth attachment differ among vertebrate classes. Most mammals have a deciduous and a permanent set of dentition (Hillson 2005:11), a condition described as diphyodont. The deciduous, or milk, teeth include incisors, canines, and premolars. Deciduous premolars sometimes superficially resemble the permanent molars and sometimes are called "deciduous molars" rather than "deciduous premolars." The eruption of the permanent dentition pushes the deciduous teeth out. Permanent molars erupt behind the premolars. The toothed whales, however, have only a single set of teeth and are monophyodont. Animals, such as reptiles and fishes, that replace their teeth continuously throughout their lives, have polyphyodont dentition.

CLASS DISTINCTIONS: INVERTEBRATES

Invertebrates have neither vertebrae nor teeth homologous with those of vertebrates. Those with hard tissues that are most commonly found in archaeological deposits are members of three invertebrate groups: (1) echinoderms, (2) molluscs, and (3) crustaceans. Characteristics other than tooth-like structures help to distinguish their hard parts. A few of the distinguishing characteristics are discussed here. Invertebrate taxonomy follows Brusca and Brusca (1990).

Of the six living classes of echinoderms, sea urchins, in the class Echinoidea, are most commonly found in archaeological sites (Table 3.2). Fragments of sea urchin test can be recognized by the pattern of knobs (Figure 3.4a) that are articulations for spines, as well as the spines themselves. Pieces of the Aristotle's lantern feeding complex are also identifiable (Figure 3.4b and 3.4c).

Molluscs usually are the most abundant invertebrates in archaeological sites (Figures A2.14–A2.17; Table 3.2) and of the molluscs, taxa from four classes are usually the most common. Polyplacophora, the chitons, cling to rocks with their broad ventral foot and are unique because they have eight dorsal shell plates. Bivalvia (Pelecypoda), the clams, have two valves hinged together. Scaphopoda, the tuskshells, have a tubular shell open at both ends. Gastropoda, the snails, usually have a single spirally coiled shell, but limpets are gastropods with conical shells. Some gastropods have calcareous opercula that they

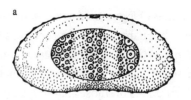

FIGURE 3.4. Sea urchin test and feeding complex: (a) a side view of the test showing its general shape: the oval portion provides an enlarged view of the surface texture; (b) an internal view of one of the five pyramids of the feeding complex known as Aristotle's lantern, which fit inside the test; and (c) an external view of Aristotle's lantern showing one pyramid and side views of two bracketing pyramids with the teeth seen on the ventral side. Drawn by Virginia Carter Steadman.

can close to protect the soft body parts within the coiled shell. Invertebrates in the class Cephalopoda, members of which have either no shell or a very reduced shell, such as octopus and squid, are unlikely to be found in archaeological deposits but are relished by many people today – a tradition that likely extends into the past.

Two arthropod classes, the Maxillopoda and Malacostraca (phylum Arthropoda, subphylum Crustacea), are found in archaeological sites (Table 3.2). The Maxillopoda include the barnacles, which are encrusting organisms that often come to a site attached to a hard substrate such as a mollusc shell. However, larger barnacles, such as goose barnacles (Lepadidae), are eaten today and probably were in the past as well. The barnacle specimens recovered from archaeological sites are from the calcareous plates within which the settled adult lives. The other important class, Malacostraca, includes shrimps, crayfishes, lobsters, and crabs in the order Decapoda (Figures A2.18–A2.20). Most crustaceans, such as shrimps, do not have hard tissues that survive, and it is likely that some were more important economically than their presence in archaeological sites suggests.

FUNCTIONS AND STRUCTURES OF HARD TISSUE

Hard tissues fulfill many functions that can be divided into the functional morphology of feeding, locomotion, and protection. Feeding structures primarily involve teeth but also include such analogous structures as crab and shrimp mandibles. Crustacean chelipeds have an active role in manipulating food. Locomotion involves the supporting structures of legs as well as the vertebral column. Protection comes in many forms but generally a hard shell-like structure, such as the vertebrate cranium, turtle shells, mollusc valves, barnacle shell plates, sea urchin tests, and egg shells, encases soft body parts. The structural composition and functional morphology of each of these is discussed with emphasis on those characteristics that are useful in archaeological studies.

Structures Used in Feeding

Structures used to capture and process food are often hardened with calcium compounds. Teeth are among the most dense tissues in the body. Toothed vertebrates include cartilaginous and bony fishes, reptiles (other than turtles) amphibians, and mammals. Structures that serve the functions of teeth in invertebrates are mandibles and chelipeds in crustaceans. The feeding complex of sea urchins, called "Aristotle's lantern," is equipped with teeth. Many molluscs other than bivalves have a radula with teeth. Radular teeth are very small but have some of the same adaptations to food consumption as are seen in vertebrates. One might anticipate finding radular teeth in the coprolites of people who ate snails.

Some vertebrates are edentate and lack teeth. Birds and turtles have heavily keratinized epidermal beaks that may be serrated and sharp to serve the functions of teeth. The keratinized beaks that cover the bones of the jaw rarely survive; however, the bones supporting the horny beak conform to its shape. Baleen whales (Mysticeti) are suspension feeders that strain their food out of plankton-rich water with keratinized baleen plates. Bony fishes that are suspension feeders have either tiny teeth or no teeth at all. Ant-eating mammals have few or no teeth and catch their prey with long sticky tongues.

Some birds and alligators (Alligatoridae) ingest stones called gastroliths to help grind up food in the digestive tract. These lithic gastroliths acquire a characteristic polish from this grinding action and look like shiny pebbles (Bottema 1975). These ingested gastroliths should not be confused with crustacean gastroliths, which are calcium carbonate deposits and are discussed later in this chapter.

Vertebrate teeth are complex structures consisting of a dentine core and an enamel crown (Figure 3.5; Hillson 2005:8). They are as hard as bone or substantially harder (Table 3.3). Cementum is a slightly softer bone-like material that forms on the outside surface of the roots and holds the tooth in place (Wolff 1991:327–8). Cementum is also found on the occlusal surfaces of some herbivore teeth. Some animals, cartilaginous and bony fishes particularly, have many teeth. Sharks may have as many as 34,000 teeth in a lifetime and 280 at any one time. This increases the chances of these teeth being preserved and subsequently found. Coupled with survivability, teeth have diagnostic characteristics useful for identification because they combine characteristics of the taxonomic

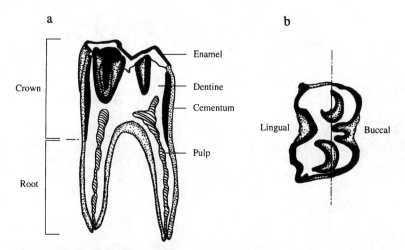

FIGURE 3.5. Right lower first molar of a cow (*Bos taurus*): (a) cross section and (b) occlusal view indicating the position of the cross section. The cross section shows a view of the lingual half. Drawn by Virginia Carter Steadman.

group to which the animal belongs with features that reveal adaptations for particular modes of feeding and other facets of the animal's life history. The internal structure of enamel, dentine, and cementum also may provide information about the mechanical stresses associated with feeding, seasonal cycles in food and growth, disease states, domestication history, and genetic properties (Burke and Castanet 1995; Sathe 2000).

Teeth within the tooth row often perform different tasks related to capturing, holding, and subdividing food and have different forms suited to these functions (Hillson 2005:13–19). Such differentiated dentition is called "heterodont." Typically, mammals have incisors with a single root and a simple crown, which are used in cutting or holding (Figure 3.6). Behind the incisors are canines, which also have single roots and simple, pointed crowns. They are used for piercing and holding. Following the canines in the tooth row are premolars with one or more roots and simple or complex crowns. Last in the tooth row are the molars, which usually have several roots and a complex crown. The molars and premolars are used for shearing, crushing, or grinding. Mammalian species have distinct numbers of these tooth types, which can be seen in a comparison of the upper dentition of several mammals (Figure 3.6). These characteristics are expressed in dental formulae, which are usually included with species descriptions (Hillson 2005:12; Nowak 1991). By convention, dental formulae are written using the first letter of the tooth followed by the number of that type of tooth in the upper and lower tooth row (White and Folkens 2005:128–30). For example, the dental formula for dogs is written: I 3/3 C 1/1 P 4/4 M 2/3. The number can be written as a superscript for upper teeth and a subscript for lower teeth (e.g., I^3 for upper third incisor or I_3 for lower third incisor). Some teeth grow into tusks, although these develop out of different types of teeth. Elephant tusks are incisors that grow throughout the animal's life. Male narwhals

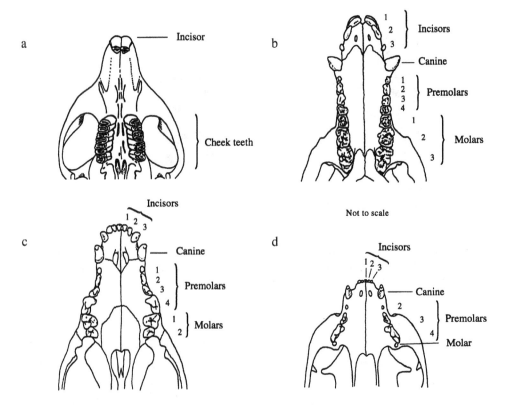

FIGURE 3.6. Different mammalian dental characteristics as seen in the upper dentition of (a) a herbivore (beaver, *Castor canadensis*) with one incisor and four cheek teeth, one of which is a premolar and three of which are molars, and a long diastema; (b) a herbivore-omnivore (pig, *Sus domesticus*) that is primarily a herbivore but will also eat animal tissue; (c) a carnivore (dog, *Canis familiaris*); and (d) a specialized carnivore (cat, *Felis catus*) with premolars specialized for shearing and a reduced number of teeth. (a) drawn by Virginia Carter Steadman; (b–d) from Ron Wolff (1991:367) and used with his kind permission. Figures are not drawn to the same scale.

(*Monodon monoceros*) have a single tusk that develops from the upper left incisor. The tusks of walrus (*Odobenus rosmarus*) are the upper canines.

Lower vertebrates also have characteristic arrangements of teeth. Some of these teeth are as differentiated as in mammals. Differentiated teeth are referred to as incisiform, caniniform, and molariform after their general shape and position. Incisiform and molariform teeth are found in the dentary of a porgy (Sparidae; Figure 3.7). They also perform many of the same functions as mammalian dentition.

Many mammalian teeth have roots that close when the tooth is fully erupted, while other mammalian teeth remain open. Once the root is closed, the tooth ceases to grow. Adult teeth with open roots are those that grow throughout the life of the animal. Examples of open-rooted teeth in adults are rabbit (Leporidae) and vole (tribe Microtini)

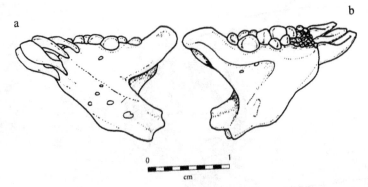

FIGURE 3.7. A porgy (Sparidae) dentary showing differentiation of teeth, including rounded molariform teeth and spatulate incisiform teeth. (a) is a lateral or labial view and (b) is a medial or lingual view. Reprinted from E. Roselló Izquierdo (1986:91) and used with her kind permission.

cheek teeth, rodent (Rodentia) incisors, and pig (Suidae) canines. These teeth continue to grow in height so the capacity to chew is not diminished even as the opposing teeth are worn down. Such teeth require use to maintain a functional height. If they are not used, they will grow unrestrained and misaligned so that normal wear is no longer possible.

Fish and reptile teeth become larger in all dimensions as the animal grows. This is accomplished by continual replacement of teeth rather than the elongation of the same tooth. Replacement occurs in two different ways: either by eruption of new teeth as older teeth are shed or by the migration of teeth toward the outer margin of the jaw as in cartilaginous fishes (Wolff 1991:329). In some mammals, such as manatees (*Trichechus manatus*) and elephants (Elephantidae), molars erupt sequentially – as the new ones emerge, they push the older worn molars to the front of the jaw where they are worn away.

Structures that are not technically teeth but function as teeth are usually denser than other body parts in order to withstand the pressures of feeding. Among these structures are the chelipeds and the mandibles of crustaceans. These structures are composed of chitin mineralized with calcium carbonate and are more heavily calcified than other parts of the exoskeleton. These heavily calcified parts are the ones that preserve best, such as the thick claws or chelipeds of the Florida stone crab (*Menippe mercenaria*; Figure 3.8). The dactyl and propodus of the cheliped, the crustacean body parts most frequently found in archaeological samples, are used for capturing and manipulating prey. The mandibles, used to process food, are also found in archaeological samples. Marine and freshwater crayfishes are represented by their mandibles in archaeological sites in South Africa and New Zealand (Leach and Anderson 1979). As with crayfishes and crabs, the exoskeletal element of shrimps that appears to be most durable is the

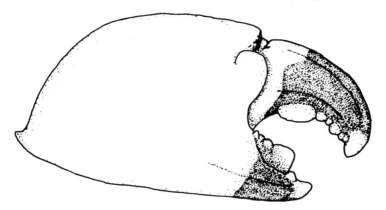

FIGURE 3.8. A Florida stone crab (*Menippe mercenaria*) cheliped showing rounded cusps for crushing invertebrates. The top portion is the movable dactyl and the bottom portion is the propodus. Modified from G. J. Vermeij (1987:162). Reproduced with the kind permission of Princeton University Press.

mandible. The right and left mandibles of shrimps (*Penaeus* sp.) have delicate projections (Figure 3.9a) that do not usually survive under archaeological conditions, so the archaeological specimens appear somewhat differently (Figure 3.9b).

The Aristotle's lantern of sea urchins is a complex apparatus composed of calcium carbonate (Figure 3.4; Brusca and Brusca 1990:468–9, 808). This apparatus is composed of five triangular-shaped plates called pyramids (Figure 3.4b internal view). Each pyramid has a canal that accommodates a tooth. The five-pointed teeth superficially resemble rodent incisors and function in much the same way. These teeth continue to grow at their internal ends as the external ends are worn down by use.

Functional Morphology of Feeding

General modes of feeding, such as crushing, grinding, shearing, piercing, and suspension feeding, are accomplished in similar ways across different phylogenetic groups. These feeding actions are responses to similar problems that have been met through evolutionary adaptations. The structure of teeth and many other elements are related to feeding behaviors. Adaptive modifications related to the mode of feeding, combined with the retention of basic ancestral characteristics, make the elements associated with feeding particularly diagnostic. Although teeth are often the first line of attack on food, other structures also are involved in feeding, such as claws and chelipeds. Likewise, structures used in feeding also may be used for other functions.

In general, animals are broadly classified as herbivores, carnivores, and omnivores, although few animals are exclusively one or the other. Herbivores consume primarily plant foods. If these plants are primarily grasses, the animals are grazers; if they consume

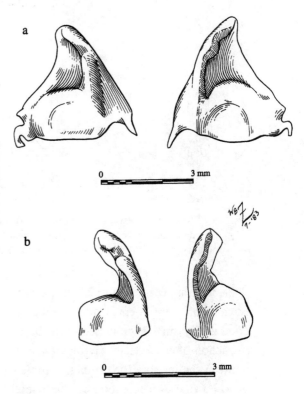

FIGURE 3.9. Left and right shrimp (*Penaeus* sp.) mandibles: (a) as they appear in a reference specimen; and (b) as they appear from an archaeological deposit. The left mandible is on the left side of the page. Only the hardest portion of the chewing surface is illustrated. Drawn by Wendy Zomlefer. Used with the kind permission of Irvy R. Quitmyer.

primarily woody vegetation, the animals are called browsers. Herbivores confront food sources that wear teeth down at a rapid rate and need considerable processing before the nutrients are available. Carnivores consume meat primarily. Compared to plant tissue, animal tissue is relatively soft and requires less processing for digestion. However, the food itself is often quite mobile, and carnivores must be able to capture and hold their prey as they consume it. Omnivores eat both plant and animal tissues and must be able to process coarse vegetation as well as animal tissues that may be tough (e.g., insect exoskeletons) or mobile.

Many variations on these themes exist. Some animals are classified as fish-eaters (piscivores), fruit-eaters (frugivores), insect-eaters (insectivores), or they are suspension feeders and may lack teeth altogether. Animals that eat carrion are called scavengers. These animals may have adaptations for defending food rather than for catching it. Some animals have special adaptations for consuming nectar, pollen, or blood.

Crushing molluscs, crabs, sea urchins, and coral to extract their soft body parts within requires particularly hard, opposable surfaces that can break through protective shells. Teeth modified for crushing can be seen in such widely different aquatic animals as eagle rays (Myliobatidae), porgies (Figure 3.7), drums (Sciaenidae), and porcupinefishes (Diodontidae). Some crab chelipeds have similar rounded cusps that also are used for crushing invertebrates with hard shells (Figure 3.8; Vermeij 1977).

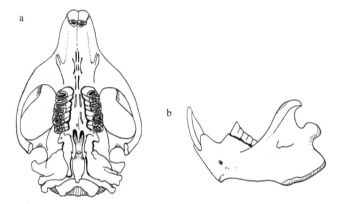

FIGURE 3.10. A beaver (*Castor canadensis*) skull: (a) a ventral view of the skull showing the paired incisors, the long diastema, the cheek teeth with complex folded enamel; and (b) a lateral or labial view of the mandible. Drawn by Virginia Carter Steadman.

Plant eating is accomplished with a combination of tooth types. Teeth used to cut or chisel off plant fibers or other food particles usually are in the front of the mouth. Food is then further processed in the back of the mouth with the grinding or crushing action of cheek teeth. Herbivores, such as the beaver, have a space, or diastema, between the incisors (or canines, if present) and the cheek teeth (Figure 3.10). This provides an area where food can be manipulated. Grinding plant fibers also requires a hard surface, preferably one with multiple plates of enamel. A high-crowned (hypsodont) tooth, or a tooth that continues to grow, allows for grinding hard and abrasive plant material throughout life. Herbivore teeth also have grinding surfaces formed into ridges, lophs, or cusps. Lophodont teeth are found in rodents and odd-toed ungulates (Perissodactyla). Even-toed ungulates (Artiodactyla) have crescent-shaped cusps, a form called selenodont. Teeth adapted for plant grinding are seen in some members of seven mammalian orders: kangaroos (Macropodidae), rabbits, rodents, elephants, manatees, perissodactyls, and artiodactyls.

A similar arrangement of incisor-like teeth in front and a grinding mechanism in back is found in many fishes. The beak (dentary and premaxilla) of parrotfishes is used to scrape coral, and pharyngeal grinding mills in the throat crush the coral to expose the soft animal and plant tissues within (Figure 3.11). Comparable dentition is seen in drums, which have grinding teeth on some pharyngeal arches, and in porgies with molariform teeth on the dentary and premaxilla (Figure 3.7). Members of these families need to crush the protective valves of molluscs.

Omnivores, including humans, typically have several different kinds of teeth (Figure 3.6b). In addition to primates, bears (Ursidae), raccoons (Procyonidae), and pigs (Suidae) are omnivores and share similar dentition. This includes broad incisors for cutting, moderate to large canines for capturing and holding, and low-crowned teeth with cusps formed into peaks (bunodont) on premolars and molars for crushing or grinding.

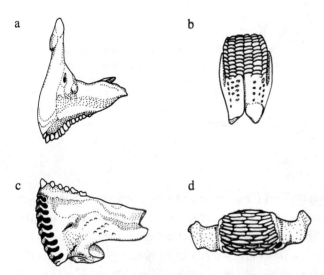

FIGURE 3.11. Stoplight parrotfish (*Sparisoma viride*) jaws and pharyngeal grinding mills: (a) lingual view of the right premaxilla; (b) ventral view of the paired upper pharyngeal grinding mills, anterior at the top; (c) lingual view of the right dentary; and (d) dorsal view of the lower pharyngeal grinding mill, anterior at the bottom. Drawn by Virginia Carter Steadman.

Holding and piercing a food item before swallowing it is accomplished by simple pointed teeth. Many pointed conical teeth are also curved with the points directed backward, an additional assurance that the captured animal will not escape. The reduction of the food for absorption takes place mainly in the gut of carnivores that feed in this fashion. Sharp, pointed teeth are common among fishes, such as groupers (Serranidae) and snappers (Lutjanidae); reptiles, such as snakes and crocodilians (Crocodylia); and mammals, such as toothed whales (Odontoceti) and porpoises (Delphinidae). Some pointed teeth are specialized to deliver venom by injection, as in pit vipers (Viperidae). The fangs may be raised when the snake is striking or lowered when its mouth is closed.

Shearing flesh to reduce it to smaller packages requires blade-like teeth. Such teeth are characteristic of carnivorous animals, whether they live on land or in the water. Many members of the mammalian order Carnivora have pairs of large, laterally compressed, blade-like carnassial teeth (P^4 and M_1) for shearing flesh (Figure 3.6c and 3.6d). Some of the most highly adapted flesh-eating animals are fishes such as barracudas (Sphyraenidae) and mackerels (Scombridae). Blade-like teeth with serrated edges are even more effective in cutting flesh. Renowned flesh eaters, such as the Komodo monitor or Komodo dragon (*Varanus komodoensis*; Auffenberg 1981), the white shark (*Carcharodon carcharias*), and piranhas (*Serrasalmus* spp.), have serrated blade-like teeth (Figure 3.12).

Suspension feeding, also called filter feeding, sustains some of the largest animals, such as baleen whales, as well as small animals, such as anchovies (Engraulidae) and clams. This manner of feeding involves filtering water to retain suspended small organisms

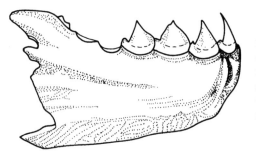

FIGURE 3.12. A lateral view of the left dentary of a piranha (*Serrasalmus* sp.). Notice the serrated, blade-like teeth and the three pedestals along the posterior edge of the dentary where teeth are missing. Drawn by Virginia Carter Steadman.

such as phytoplankton and zooplankton (Sanderson and Wassersug 1993). Suspension feeding requires specialized structures to take in sufficient water and to strain out the organisms for consumption. Whales feed by ramming their open mouths through the water. Organisms suspended in the water are filtered out by baleen plates, also known as whale bone. Baleen plates are keratinized rods that hang down on either side of the tongue from the upper jaw. The tongue pushes the water out through the baleen plates thereby straining out the suspended organisms and leaving a mouth full of krill (small crustaceans) and other plankton. Anchovies are efficient suspension feeders that pass the strained water out through the gills. Anchovies and other ram feeders tend to be fast swimmers with streamlined bodies and long jaws (dentary and premaxilla) with small or no teeth. Some birds, such as flamingoes (Phoenicopteridae) and some ducks (Anatidae), strain suspended food particles by pushing water out of their mouths past keratinized lamellae on the edges of their beaks. Many invertebrates are suspension feeders. Barnacles catch food particles passing in the flow of water over their cirri. Most bivalves feed by generating a water current within the mantle and gleaning suspended food particles with specialized structures called ctenidia (Brusca and Brusca 1990).

Some teeth are highly specialized and are used for activities such as courtship displays, in addition to feeding. For example, enlarged canines in male baboons (*Papio* spp.), cats, pigs, and llamas (*Lama glama*) are used for sexual combat and display.

These adaptations are evolutionary modifications of feeding mechanisms by organisms in very different taxonomic groups. This is called convergent evolution. For example, blade-like teeth evolved independently among carnivorous fishes, reptiles, and mammals. Convergence, in this case, occurred as a result of the similarity of the challenges of feeding on flesh and the genetic potentials of organisms to adapt to cutting flesh by the evolution of opposing sets of laterally compressed teeth with sharp points, broad bases, and some with serrated edges.

Although these general forms of dentition seem simple, the range of variation within them is great. Ancestral differences between animals and degrees of the expression of some of these adaptations are responsible for this variation. The characteristics of dentition are of practical use in the process of zooarchaeological identification. The tooth types help to determine the class to which the animal belongs as do the number of teeth and their shape. The adaptations to feeding further define the range of possibilities within an animal class. Similar variation exists in different modes of locomotion.

Structures Used in Vertebrate Locomotion

Two important structural tissues used by vertebrates for locomotion are cartilage and bone. Cartilage serves an important role in connective tissue and protects the ends of many skeletal elements; however, it is rarely present in archaeological materials. During development of individual vertebrates from juvenile to adult, most elements become progressively more ossified as cartilage is replaced by bone. Some cartilaginous tissues become highly calcified as, for example, the vertebral centra of cartilaginous fishes. These have the appearance of other vertebrate bones, although their microscopic structure and development is different. What follows is largely a description of bone development in mammals (for a description of bone development and structure in birds, see Higgins 1999).

Bone that forms indirectly by replacing a cartilage model is called endochondral, or cartilage-replacement, bone. Bone that forms directly in connective tissue of the epidermis is called membrane or dermal bone. This classification reflects the developmental history of bones. Each of these may occur in all classes of vertebrates or in different parts of a skeleton. No evolutionary progression from simple to complex tissue is implied by these classifications. It is not possible to tell from simply looking at an element whether the bone is of dermal or endochondral origin (Kardong 1995:173).

Bone differs in the way it forms and its histological appearance (Enlow and Brown 1956, 1957, 1958). Bone types may be classified as (1) immature or woven bone; (2) primary vascular, including lamellar and acellular bone; (3) secondary lamellar or Haversian bone; and (4) nonvascular (Lyman 1994c:72–8; White and Folkens 2005:43–6). No evolutionary developmental sequence is suggested by this classification either. The immature bone matrix, or woven bone, has randomly oriented collagen fibers. Although woven bone is characteristic of very young elements it is also found in injured elements in the early stages of healing (White and Folkens 1991:20). Primary and secondary lamellar bone has fibers arranged parallel to the axis of the element and is typically found in long bones of adult mammals. Many modern bony fishes have acellular bone in which the cells die and the spaces they leave are filled with bone mineral. In such acellular elements, bone is added incrementally at the edge (Enlow and Brown 1956, 1957, 1958; Wheeler and Jones 1989).

Mature bone structure of many long bones has both an outer layer of compact or cortical bone, which appears dense, and an inner region of cancellous or trabecular bone that appears porous or spongy. The exact composition varies depending among classes and among species within classes. Compact bone makes up the outer surface of most elements, leaving an interior medullary cavity that is partly filled by cancellous bone and, in life, is the site for marrow. Cancellous bone, often found at the ends of elements interior to the compact bone, has a pattern of trabeculae or bony struts that gives it strength and at the same time makes it lighter than compact bone. The periosteal membrane that surrounds the elements secretes layers of cortical bone. Bone continues to be remodeled from both the inner and outer surfaces to adjust to growth, use, and repair. The attachment of muscles to bone and the force applied by those muscles initiates a response in the bone to develop a larger more robust surface for muscle attachment and a thicker shaft. The heaviest and densest elements are manatee (*Trichechus manatus*) ribs, composed entirely of compact lamellar bone. Other extremely dense elements are the otic capsules of dolphin, which are composed predominantly of compact bone in a reticular pattern (Enlow and Brown 1956, 1957, 1958). Those skeletons and parts of skeletons that are predominantly compact bone are consequently more dense and more durable in archaeological deposits.

Functional Morphology of Vertebrate Locomotion

All modes of locomotion require coordination between muscles, nerves, and skeletal structure. To function effectively during locomotion, the skeletal structure must bear the weight of the animal and receive the forces of the attached muscles and the animal in motion. These forces leave their impression on the skeleton and are seen as muscle attachment scars on the elements in the absence of the muscles. Thus, the entire skeleton, as well as individual elements, is shaped by the mode of locomotion.

The primary modes of locomotion for vertebrates are swimming, digging, walking, running, hopping, and flying. Animals are adapted to varying degrees for these activities. Moles (Talpidae) spend their lives underground digging and display extreme modifications for this way of life. Dogs, however, dig to bury food or to expose cool soil in which to lie but do not display special modifications for this activity. Some of the adaptations for particular locomotion are described here with emphasis on only the full development of these adaptations.

The earliest vertebrate form of locomotion is swimming. This is achieved through undulation of the body by action between trunk muscles and the vertebral column such as is found in fishes. The driving power for swimming is the lateral sweep of the tail, back and forth. Efficiency and speed is achieved by a broad flat tail or caudal fin that pivots at its base and is accompanied by a streamlined body. Some fishes that swim particularly fast, such as the mackerels, have broad lateral spines and shortened, interlocking caudal vertebrae that stiffen the tail so it is more effective for propulsion. Members of each of the higher vertebrate classes have returned to the water and adapted secondarily to swimming. This secondary adaptation involves undulation of the trunk, either from side-to-side or up and down, accompanied by paddling and steering with

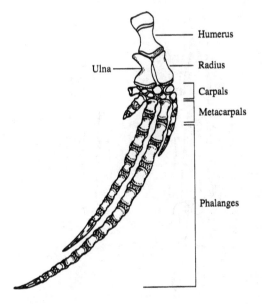

FIGURE 3.13. Elements in the right front flipper of a whale (Cetacean). Drawn by Virginia Carter Steadman.

the limbs. Higher vertebrates that returned to aquatic life are found among mammals (whales [Cetacea], seals [Pinnipedia], and sirenians [Sirenia]), birds (penguins [Sphenisciformes] and petrels [Procellariiformes]), and reptiles (turtles [Testudines], crocodilians, and snakes). Some of these, such as whales and sirenians, are completely bound to life in the water. They have many adaptations for swimming, including flippers or fin-like forelimbs (Figure 3.13); the only vestige of the hindlimb is the reduced pelvic girdle. Power for swimming is achieved through the undulation of the body in an up-and-down direction. Sea turtles and seals retain four feet as flippers, permitting locomotion on land. The upper forelimb element, the humerus, of these aquatic animals is usually short, heavy, and has a large deltoid process for muscle insertion. The femur is generally short and broad with large processes for attachment of other muscles. The skeletal elements of the flipper are generally straight, relatively long, and without complex articulations. Many of the other swimming animals have webbed hindfeet, for example otters (*Lontra canadensis*), ducks, and frogs.

The vertebral column tends to be more differentiated among terrestrial animals than among aquatic ones. The vertebrae along the column of cartilaginous fishes differ little. In most bony fishes, the vertebrae are divided into two regions: (1) the anterior trunk region and the (2) posterior tail or caudal region. Higher vertebrates that have returned to aquatic life have less differentiation along the vertebral column than their terrestrial ancestors. The vertebrae of terrestrial animals must support their weight and are consequently more differentiated. The amount of distinction among the vertebrae is also different depending on the form of locomotion. In tetrapods, the trunk is differentiated into a neck, sacral, and caudal region. Mammals typically have cervical, thoracic, lumbar, sacral, and caudal vertebrae. Adaptations for flight in birds include fused sections of the vertebral column.

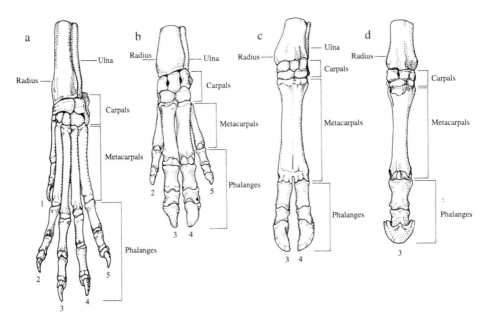

FIGURE 3.14. Elements in digitigrade (a and b) and unguligrade (c and d) left feet: (a) dog (*Canis familiaris*), (b) pig (*Sus domesticus*), (c) cow (*Bos taurus*), and (d) horse (*Equus caballus*). Numbers correspond to the digit; that is, 1 is digit 1. Only the distal ends of the radius and ulna are shown. Figures are not drawn to the same scale. Drawn by Virginia Carter Steadman.

Some of the adaptations for swimming seen in the humerus are also evident in animals that dig. Limb elements are short and powerful with large surfaces for muscle attachments. This similarity between the adaptations for swimming and digging results from the greater forces required to move through the dense medium of water and soil. A digger's foot is, however, quite different from an aquatic animal's flipper. The front feet of moles, armadillos (*Dasypus novemcinctus*), pocket gophers (Geomyidae), and other digging animals have relatively large toes with strong claws.

Locomotion on land ranges from walking to running and hopping. Along this spectrum, the adaptations for speed are elongation of the limb elements, including the metacarpal and metatarsal elements, accompanied by fusion and reduction in the number of elements in the foot. Many generalists, such as humans, bears, and raccoons, walk on the entire sole of the foot. This involves the carpal, tarsal, metacarpal, and metatarsal elements, as well as the phalanges. This type of locomotion is called plantigrade. The first stage in adaptations for running is seen in members of the dog and pig families, which have moderately elongated metapodia that are reduced in number to facilitate walking on their toes (Figure 3.14a and 3.14b). This is a form of locomotion called digitigrade. Animals that run particularly fast are well-represented among the ungulates. They tend to have long, straight limb elements with the radius and ulna fused and the fibula significantly reduced. The metapodia either are reduced to a single element through the fusion of two metapodia (numbers three and four of the basic five-toe pattern), as in deer (Cervidae), cattle, goats, and sheep (Bovidae) (Figure 3.14c), or lack

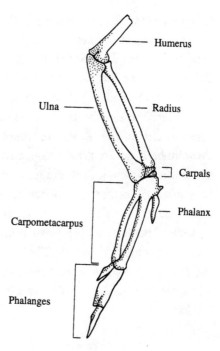

Humerus

Ulna

Radius

Carpals

Phalanx

Carpometacarpus

Phalanges

FIGURE 3.15. Elements in the right wing of a bird. Only the distal end of the humerus is shown. Drawn by Virginia Carter Steadman.

all but the third metapodium, as in horses (Equidae; Figure 3.14d; Wolff 1991:258–9). Although the functional number of metapodia is reduced they may be accompanied by vestigial metapodia that lie on either side of the functional members. Accompanying the reduction in the numbers of elements of the foot and elongation of the metapodia is a shift from the weight being borne on the entire foot (plantigrade) to only the tips of the central toe or toes (unguligrade). This shift also gives added length to the limb and, consequently, a longer stride that increases speed.

Hopping is achieved with many of the same adaptations developed for speed in running. The limb elements are elongated, and the number of elements in the foot is reduced. The major difference in hopping is that this adaptation is restricted to the hindlimb; the forelimb is shorter and is usually used for balance and manipulation. Kangaroos, kangaroo mice (Heteromyidae), rabbits, as well as frogs and toads (Anura) are consummate hoppers.

Flight is a highly complex mode of locomotion requiring specialized adaptations of the entire body. Development of wings adapted for flight by bats (Chiroptera) and birds followed different routes. The wing among bats is composed of a flight membrane supported by greatly elongated elements of the forelimb. The humerus, radius, and phalanges are very long but the ulna is greatly reduced. In birds, the wing skeleton, which controls the position of the flight feathers, is highly modified from the ancestral forelimb (Figures 3.15, A2.3). Some elements of the manus (forefoot) are fused, which reduces the complement of elements to five; the major elements are the carpometacarpus and phalanges (Howard 1929; Proctor and Lynch 1993). Essential adaptations for flight in birds are the enlarged sternum for the attachment of flight muscles and the placement of the coracoid and clavicle (furcula) between the scapula and the sternum to form a rigid framework for powered flight. Some bird bones are pneumatic (Higgins 1999). The pelvic girdle and the hindlimbs are also highly modified. Fusion of some thoracic, lumbar, sacral, and caudal vertebrae within the framework of the pelvis forms the synsacrum. Some elements of the pes (hindfoot) are fused to form the tarsometatarsus. The elements of the leg (femur, tibiotarsus, and tarsometatarsus) reflect the uses of these limbs. They are greatly elongated in wading and other long-legged birds such as the herons (Ardeidae) and cranes (Gruiformes). They are much shorter but massive in raptors (Falconiformes), penguins, and parrots (Psittacidae). Pelagic birds, such as albatrosses (Diomedeidae), combine large wings with small hindlimbs.

Adult humans no longer use their forelimbs for locomotion but for specialized tasks such as carrying and handling. The hand is very flexible and the opposable thumb allows for delicate manipulation of objects as well as grasping. This is one of the features to which we owe our success as a species. Other primates have dexterous hindfeet and forefeet.

Functional Morphology of Protection

Protective coverings come in the form of hard shells or armor. Among vertebrates, these are major portions of the vertebrate skull, scales, and bony scutes. Invertebrates associated with archaeological sites are preserved because of their hard protective shells or exoskeletons.

Most of the protective elements of vertebrates are derived from dermal or membrane bone (Kardong 1995:231, 325). Cranial elements of mammals, birds, reptiles, and amphibians, such as the frontal and parietal, are all dermal bone. Dermal bone grows outward along its margins and when one of these elements comes into contact with neighboring ones, continued growth in size ceases. The junctions between these elements, called sutures, continue to be remodeled and fuse in many older individuals.

Turtle and armadillo shell is covered by horny keratinized skin over bony plates of dermal origin. In armadillos the bony plates do not fuse together; they lie with their sides abutting each other to form a solid but flexible shell. Each plate has a distinctive morphology that includes holes in the bone through which hairs grow. Turtle shell includes: a carapace, which is the dorsal portion of the shell, the plastron or ventral portion, and a bridge on either side between the two (Figure A2.5). The keratinized scutes in turtle shells overlap bony plates beneath. The scutes are rarely preserved in archaeological deposits but their outlines are impressed on the bony plates. These plates are composed of dermal bone, which is fused with underlying skeletal structures such as the ribs and vertebrae. The sutures between the bony plates may be fused in older individuals of land dwelling turtles such as box turtles (*Terrapene carolina*) and tortoises (Testudinidae). The dermal bones of some animals, such as crocodiles, lie within the skin. Such osteoderms have a distinctive morphology with a central ridge or keel and are aligned along the body, forming the characteristic bumps along their backs.

Some fishes also have a bony armor. This takes the form of dermal scutes in sturgeons (Acipenseridae), plates in the boxfishes (Ostrachiidae), and spines of porcupinefishes. Sturgeons' scutes closely resemble those of the crocodiles although they are more sharply textured. The boxfishes, as the name implies, are encased in a box-like shell composed of hexagonal bony plates. The surface of these plates is textured and they lie side-by-side. The spines of porcupinefishes have three radiating arms that lie in the skin and a fourth that penetrates the skin. The spines are close together, giving the fish the appearance of a porcupine.

Teeth as derivatives of the dermis have a close relationship with tooth-like dermal denticles in the skin of cartilaginous fishes and with some kinds of scales. Scales of some fishes, such as the diamond-shaped ganoid scales of the gars (*Lepisosteus* spp.), are very hard and shiny. They resemble teeth in structure. Scales of birds, reptiles, and fishes and structures like hoofs, nails, and feathers are also derived from the skin and are composed of keratin.

Egg shells are occasionally recovered from archaeological sites (Keepax 1981; Sidell 1993). Egg shells are composed mainly of calcite microcrystals and organic material. The microcrystals are usually laid down in a thin layer over an inner membrane. Shells owe their strength to their shape. Once they are broken, they lose much of this advantage and become very fragile. High magnification aids in the identification of egg shells.

The soft body parts of sea urchins are protected within an egg-shaped test surrounded by calcite spines. The test is composed of fused calcite plates called ossicles. These are perforated by pores for tube feet. People, sea otters (*Enhydra lutris*), and triggerfishes (Balistidae) are among the few predators that can penetrate these spiny defenses.

Molluscan shells are composed of organic conchiolin and calcium carbonate layers that are dense and hard. These, and the periostricum on the outer surface of the shell, are secreted by the mantle. Calcium carbonate takes two common forms, one of which, calcite, is slightly denser and less soluble than the other form, aragonite (Vermeij 1993). Different shell microstructure imparts advantages to the organism living under various environmental conditions, but all shell structures are especially strong under compression. As with eggs, the shape of molluscan shell, sometimes approaching that of a sphere, augments this strength (Vermeij 1993).

Crustaceans and insects have chitinous exoskeletons. Chitin is a high-molecular-weight nitrogenous polysaccharide (Brusca and Brusca 1990:468). A portion of the chitinous cuticle, the endocuticle, is calcified in crustaceans (Brusca and Brusca 1990). Calcification is a process by which calcium salts are deposited as calcite, vaterite, and hydroxyapatite (Stevenson 1985). The thickness of the cuticle and its calcified portion

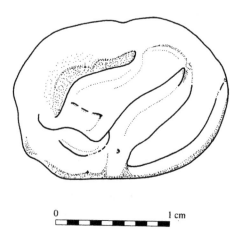

FIGURE 3.16. Gastroliths of a land crab (Gecarcinidae). Drawn by Virginia Carter Steadman.

0   1 cm

varies a great deal throughout the exoskeleton and between species. Parts of the exoskeleton are thin and flexible, but parts that are more heavily calcified, such as the chelipeds and the mandibles, are thick and rigid (Stevenson 1985; Vermeij 1977).

Crustaceans grow by periodic molt or ecdysis. During this process, the old exoskeleton is shed and, before the new exoskeleton hardens, the body swells by absorbing fluids. This results in a larger new exoskeleton in a stepwise growth pattern. During molt, calcium is absorbed from the old exoskeleton and deposited in a pair of sacs in the gut to form gastroliths (Figure 3.16). Gastrolith formation is a mechanism for conserving calcium. As the new chitinous exoskeleton hardens, gastroliths are shed into the gut where the stored calcium is reabsorbed and deposited into the new exoskeleton. They are typically produced by those species that live in calcium-poor environments. Gastroliths are only present in the "soft-shelled" stage in those animals that produce them. This is a vulnerable period in their lives.

Hermit crabs (infraorder Anomura, e.g., *Coenobita clypeatus*) gain protection for their soft body parts by taking shelter in empty mollusc shells. They modify the mollusc shells in which they live by thinning the wall of the shell and chipping the outer lip (Scudder and Quitmyer 1998). They scout out new, larger shells to occupy as they grow. For some, the scarcity of large snail shells is a limiting factor (Vermeij 1987).

Other Hard Tissue Structures

Some hard tissues are distinctive but do not fit in discussions of feeding, locomotion, or protection. They are important because they are durable and because they may provide information about age, sex, and season of death of the individual.

Among these other hard structures are the antlers and horns in the ungulate order, Artiodactyla. The antlers of deer grow annually from pedicels on the frontal bone.

As antlers grow, they are covered by a layer of vascularized skin, called velvet, which transports necessary minerals and protein. When they reach full size and the animal's hormone levels increase in response to the breeding season, the blood supply to the antlers is cut off, the velvet dries, and is rubbed off. The antler is shed once the mating season is over. Horns differ in many respects from antlers. Horns are bones (horn cores) projecting from the frontal bones of the skull that are covered by a keratinized sheath and are not branched. The horn core and sheath grow during much of an animal's life and neither is shed. Horns occur in buffalo, gazelle, ibex, and many other bovids. Some domesticated bovids, such as sheep and cattle, are polled and have no horns. Pronghorns (*Antilocapra americana*) differ from the bovids. They also have a bony horn core that grows from the frontal bone and is not shed; however, the keratinized sheath covering the horn core is shed annually.

Other important structures are otoliths. These are found in the inner ears of fishes and function in hearing and equilibrium in the animal. They are composed of calcium carbonate in the form of aragonite. During the formation of otoliths, an organic matrix (otolin) is deposited followed by the deposition of aragonite around the organic fibers. Both are deposited by the endolymphatic fluid in the sac-like pockets (sacculus, utriculus, and lagena) of the semicircular canal (Pannella 1980; Wheeler and Jones 1989:114). The shapes of otoliths conform to the contours of the sac in which they are deposited. Thus, otoliths are often distinctive and identifiable. The sagitta, which forms in the sacculus, is usually the largest of the three types of otoliths. Some fishes have distinctive otoliths that form in all three pockets. Otoliths increase in size by the addition of layers of aragonite as the animal grows in response to environmental conditions and feeding activity. As with other incremental growth structures, these layers generally correspond to seasonal growth and other factors (Cailliet, Love, and Ebeling 1986; Higham and Horn 2000).

A calcified tissue found in the medullary cavity of long bones of birds is called medullary bone. Medullary bone is a storage tissue for calcium and fat during the period when eggs are laid. It is found in the lumen of the long bones of many female birds (Driver 1982; Higgins 1999; Rick 1975; Simkiss 1967). The stored tissue provides calcium for egg shell production and fat for yolk production. Most birds lay eggs following a precisely scheduled time of the year, and medullary bone is present only during that time.

ANATOMICAL VARIATION

Variations within each species are related to ontogeny, sexual dimorphism, geographic or population-based differences, and individual or idiosyncratic differences. Ontogenetic changes, those that occur during growth and maturation, are manifested in the supporting tissue not only by increasing size resulting from growth but also in changes in proportion, the size of muscle attachments, wear on the dentition, and development of secondary sex structures such as antlers and tusks. Many animals exhibit profound differences between adult males and females. This is known as sexual dimorphism. These differences may be simply in the size and the robustness of the skeleton and dentition, but, often, they are accompanied by other morphological differences such as those related to courtship display or bearing young.

Size is linked to both age and sex. Some animals segregate in their environment according to size and age. For example, the young of some fishes are confined to nursery grounds close to shore, but older and larger individuals live and feed in open deep-water channels. Animals also may congregate along sexual lines into bachelor herds separate from the dominant male, females in his harem, and young of the year, as is seen among vicuñas (*Vicugna vicugna*). These two facets of animal life, age and sex, are addressed in more detail later in this chapter.

Individual variations are the result both of genetic variability in an animal population and of the environmental conditions under which an animal grows and develops. All animal populations exhibit some degree of individual variation, although variation tends to be greater among lower vertebrates, such as reptiles and fishes, than among the higher vertebrates such as mammals and birds. Animals, such as cheetahs (*Acinonyx jubatus*) in Africa and panthers (*Puma concolor*) in parts of North America, have experienced population contraction in recent evolutionary history and are genetically uniform. This uniformity poses a danger from the standpoint of species survival. Animal variation of all kinds has important implications for interpreting details of human use and environmental change in archaeological materials.

SIZE

The size of animals is an important biological concern. Individual size in different animal populations varies through time and in different locations. Animals on islands, whether they are actual islands, habitat islands, or isolation in captivity, tend to differ in size from their mainland or wild relatives (Foster 1964). Animals under intense predation show a decline in size as a result of overexploitation (Sutherland 1990). Such a decline also may reduce the age at which animals breed and the size of the progeny they produce. This effect is seen both with intensive predation of sea urchins by sea otters and overfishing of Atlantic cod (*Gadus morhua*) by people (Trippel 1995).

Overall body size, as well as the size and proportions of body parts, are important biological parameters in identifying species and assessing the stature and status of animal populations. Many fundamental relationships exist among body dimensions. For this reason, biologists routinely record the standard measurements of the animals they collect as part of the data that accompany reference specimens (Figures A3.1–A3.4). Such measurements show that there is a relationship between the size of parts of an animal and the whole animal. Parts of an animal might be the length or width of a skeletal element. The dimension for the whole animal might be the animal's length, height, or weight. Some general correlations are found between the size of various dimensions of weight-bearing elements and the weight of animals in related taxa. For some studies, separate correlations are made for males and females and for different breeds of domestic animals. Biological data from reference specimens are an essential resource for demonstrating such relationships. All such correlations are only as good as the size and the composition of the sample measured, and the accuracy of the measurements.

Modern biological data show a relationship between body weight, length, or height and other aspects of skeletons and exoskeletons. One of the approaches used to study this relationship is to establish an index or ratio between dimensions, such as body weight and element weight or the height of the shoulders (withers) and a measurement of some dimension of an element. Skeletal weight of many large artiodactyls, such as pigs, cattle, and sheep, is approximately 7.5 percent of the total body weight (Reed 1963). Other animals have different relationships between hard-tissue characteristics and body weight. For example, the shell weight of eastern oysters (*Crassostrea virginica*) is approximately 78 percent of their total body weight. However, small oysters have proportionally greater shell weight (86 percent) compared with large oysters (77 percent shell weight).

The height of a standing animal at its shoulders is a common way to describe the size of livestock. This relationship can be expressed as a percentage: for example, the metacarpal length among cows is 16.7 (range 15.5 to 17.8) percent of the height of the shoulders (Chaplin 1971:91). This can also be expressed as an index such as shoulder height divided by greatest length of the metacarpus, which happens to be 5.98. In Chaplin's study, fifty-five specimens were measured to establish the correlation between the metacarpal length and shoulder height. Such correlations between skeletal dimensions and body dimensions must be based on measurements taken of a large sample of individuals whose size, age, sex, and, where appropriate, breed are known. When several correlations between skeletal elements and shoulder height or body weight are established, reasonably accurate relationships result.

Linear Fit

The variables for such sets of data can be plotted in a scatter diagram to study the relationship between them. In Figure 3.17a, the relationship between skeletal weight of some terrestrial mammals is plotted on the X-axis against total weight on the Y-axis. An example is a plot of measurements of the metacarpal length against shoulder height (e.g., Wijngaarden-Bakker and Bergström 1988). A similar approach correlates dimensions of fish skeletal elements and total weight or length (Desse and Desse-Berset 1996; Leach et al. 1996). A regression line is fitted to these variables by the method of least squares. Regression is a method by which the changes in one variable relative to another are examined. As one dimension increases, such as metacarpal length, so does the length of the entire leg and, consequently, the shoulder height. If a good fit for these data is found, it can be used to predict the value of Y for a given value of X. This method uses the formula:

$$Y = a + bX, \tag{3.1}$$

where

$a =$ the Y-intercept
$b =$ the slope

Allometric Scaling

Allometric scaling is another approach relating the size of a whole animal to the dimensions of a part when the relationship is not linear (Figure 3.17b). This relationship is found among animals of such wide extremes in size as a shrew (Soricidae) and a buffalo (*Bison bison*). Allometric scaling "deals with the structural and functional consequences of changes in size or scale among otherwise similar organisms" (Schmidt-Nielsen 1984:7). "An amazing number of morphological and physiological variables are scaled, relative to body size, according to allometric equations" (Schmidt-Nielsen 1984:15). These formulae take the general form:

$$Y = aX^b. \tag{3.2}$$

The logarithmic form simplifies computation:

$$\log Y = \log a + b(\log X), \tag{3.3}$$

where

$a =$ the Y-intercept
$b =$ the slope

This equation describes the allometric growth curve of such familiar changes in proportion as the size of the human head relative to body weight. The equation also describes changes between two variables that are not related to growth but rather to two similar organisms of different sizes. The relationship between the skeletal structure

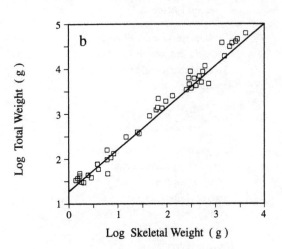

FIGURE 3.17. Scatter plots showing the relationship between the total weight (Y) and the skeletal weight (X) of some terrestrial mammals: (a)
is the linear relationship between total and skeletal weight following the formula: $Y = 108.07 +
16.601X$; $r^2 = 0.962$; $N = 51$; and (b) is the allo-
metric relation between total and skeletal weight
in these same data following the formula $\log Y =
1.2802 + 0.97573 (\log X)$; $r^2 = 0.985$; $N = 51$.

supporting the body weight of an elephant and the structure that supports a shrew is one
of allometry and can be described by the allometric equation (Schmidt-Nielsen 1984:45).
This equation describes the line that statistically best fits the data and is calculated by
the method of least squares. This function is a mathematical relationship that enables
us to predict what values of variable Y correspond to given values of variable X. The
regression formula describes the relationship between two variables without addressing
the cause or consequence of this relationship.

The values of the allometric constants (a and b) in such formulae are derived from
a set of reference specimens with known whole body weights and dimensions of the
skeletal or exoskeletal elements (Table 3.4). Several precautions must be observed when
deriving such a formula. Measurements are of fundamental importance and must be
accurate and repeatable. A number of guides are available and can be used to standardize
measurements (e.g., Driesch 1976; Morales and Rosenlund 1979). When other measurements are made, the parameters must be clearly defined and, if possible, accompanied

Table 3.4. *Some allometric regression formulae*

	N	Slope (b)	Y-intercept (a)	r²
(a) Constants for allometric regression lines describing the relationship between shell or skeletal measurements and total weight or standard length:				
Greatest Breadth (mm) of occipital condyles to Total Weight (g) in terrestrial mammals	59	3.37	−1.105	0.97
Depth (DC) of the femur head (mm) to Total Weight (g) in terrestrial mammals	59	2.78	0.696	0.97
Atlas Width (mm) to Total Weight (g) in Teleosts	50	2.05	1.162	0.72
Atlas Width (mm) to Standard Length (mm) in Sciaenidae	152	1.93	0.61	0.65
Atlas Width (mm) to Total Weight (kg) in Sciaenidae	146	−1.83	1.77	0.71
Aperture Height (mm) to Total Weight (g) in marine gastropods	59	1.93	−1.642	0.96
(b) Constants for the allometric regression lines describing the relationship between shell or skeletal weight and total or soft tissue weight:				
Skeletal Weight (kg) to Total Weight (kg) in:				
mammals	97	0.90	1.12	0.94
birds	307	0.91	1.04	0.97
turtles	26	0.67	0.51	0.55
snakes	26	1.01	1.17	0.97
sharks and rays (Chondrichthyes)	17	0.86	1.68	0.85
bony fishes (Actinopterygii)	393	0.81	0.90	0.80
non-Perciformes	119	0.79	0.85	0.88
catfishes (Siluriformes)	36	0.95	1.15	0.87
Perciformes	274	0.83	0.93	0.76
sea basses (Serranidae)	18	1.08	1.51	0.85
porgies (Sparidae)	22	0.92	0.96	0.98
drums (Sciaenidae)	99	0.74	0.81	0.73
flounders (Pleuronectiformes)	21	0.89	1.09	0.95
Shell Weight (g) to Soft Tissue Weight (g) in:				
marine gastropods	135	0.92	−0.16	0.89
marsh periwinkle (*Littorina irrorata*)	62	0.94	−0.34	0.97
shark eye (*Neverita duplicata*)	16	0.55	0.38	0.81
eastern mudsnail (*Nassarius obsoletus*)	50	1.06	−0.44	0.93
bivalves	80	0.68	0.018	0.83
eastern oyster (*Crassostrea virginica*)	100	0.97	−0.77	0.97
stout tagalus (*Tagelus plebeius*)	46	0.99	0.29	0.95
Shell Weight (g) to Total Weight (g) in:				
marine gastropods	59	1.01	0.164	0.99

Note: Key to abbreviations: Formula is $Y = aX^b$; where Y is total weight, standard length, or soft tissue weight; X is a dimension, skeletal weight, or shell weight; a is the Y-intercept; b is the slope; and N is the number of observations (Reitz and Cordier 1983; Reitz and Quitmyer 1988; Reitz et al. 1987; Wing and Brown 1979). See the text for an explanation of total and soft-tissue weight.

by an illustration. When an allometric equation for a regression line is calculated, it will be accompanied by statistical information about the significance of the regression and the confidence limits on either sides of the regression line (Simpson et al. 1960; Sokal and Rohlf 1969). These data indicate the reliability of a scaling relationship for predictive purposes. Allometry can be used in predicting one variable when a related one is known, but care must be taken to stay within the range of the data used for establishing the formula (Schmidt-Nielsen 1984:32). Allometry is used to understand extinct species better, but this must be done with caution.

Variables are related in different ways. An allometric regression may have a negative or positive slope. Regression curves with a negative slope are seldom seen in relationships between skeletal dimensions and body weight. One example of a negative relationship is the height of the molar crown of a bovid and the weight of that animal's body (Klein and Cruz-Uribe 1984:46). This is because the body increases in weight with age but, at the same time, teeth are worn down and, therefore, molar or cheek teeth crown height decreases. Scaling body weight with skeletal or exoskeletal dimensions usually results in a positive slope of an allometric regression line. The relationship between the height of the aperture of a whole array of marine snails and their total weight has a positive slope greater than 1. When two variables change at the same rate, the slope of this regression is 1, and the relationship is isometric. Isometric relationships are only found in geometrically similar bodies whose measurements are proportional. However, if measurements are taken to predict surface area or weight, these relationships are not isometric because the surface area or weight does not increase in a one-to-one ratio; instead, it is allometric.

SIZE AND AGE

Size and age are linked, but ontogenetic, sexual, geographic (population-based), and individual, or idiosyncratic, variations confound the relationship. Under favorable conditions, most animals grow faster and attain larger size at an earlier age than do animals growing under conditions of inadequate forage, harsh climatic conditions, overcrowding, and high incidence of disease. Under optimum nutritional conditions, mammalian tooth replacement is accelerated, but a diet of coarse forage will wear teeth down rapidly (Hillson 2005:214–15). The influence of environmental conditions also is seen among many invertebrates. For example, oysters that settle in shallow waters where they are exposed during low tide remain small and those that settle in deeper waters richer in nutrients may grow to their full genetic potential.

The relationship between size and age is more pronounced in animals with indeterminate growth than in ones with determinate growth. Mammals and birds have determinate growth, meaning that they reach an adult size and stop growing (with some latitude for individual variation) Indeterminate growth, typical of lower verte-brates and invertebrates, occurs by the addition of new bone or shell to the grow-ing surfaces or by periodic shedding and renewing exoskeletons throughout the life of the animal. Animals with indeterminate growth continue to grow throughout life, however, they do so at an ever slower rate. The rate of growth is an individ-ual response to environmental conditions and may produce some old individuals that are smaller than young ones in areas with optimum conditions (Quitmyer et al. 1985).

Size and Age in Animals with Determinate Growth

Two of the primary developments related to age among animals with determinate growth are reduction in bone porosity and remodeling to assume adult form and size as the individual matures (e.g., Prummel 1987a, 1987b, 1988, 1989). The skulls of adult mam-mals are usually elongated compared to those of juveniles. Elements of very old animals have more surface sculpturing, ossification of ligaments and tendons occurs, muscle attachments are more pronounced, and epiphyseal sutures are obliterated (Chaplin 1971:90). Although adult mammals and birds will be larger than young ones, once fusion takes place further growth in most body dimensions is no longer possible, even though remodeling continues through life.

The manner in which long bones of mammals and birds grow controls the size they reach at maturity. Growth in endochondral bone, typical of many mammalian vertebral and limb elements, takes place around the periphery of the center of ossification and between the shafts and the articulating ends of the element (Figure 3.18; Hildebrand 1982:169–70; Walker 1987:166–72; White and Folkens 2005:46–8). The cartilaginous pri-mary center of ossification for a long bone, called the diaphysis, is ossified around its periphery (i.e., between the developing element and the surrounding periosteum). Because of the involvement of the periosteum in the production of osteocytes that secrete bone, this type of bone is also called periosteal bone. During the process of remodeling, periosteal bone is deposited on the outside of the diaphysis. The marrow or medullary cavity inside the growing diaphysis also enlarges. Periosteal bone is compact and dense. The bone toward the ends of the shaft and near the epiphyses of each element retains the trabecular structure of cancellous bone.

Growth in length generally occurs at one or both ends of the diaphysis (Figure 3.18). Secondary centers of ossification, or epiphyses, form at these ends. Growth between the diaphysis and the epiphysis takes place primarily in a cartilage disk known as the epiphyseal plate, or metaphysis, as cartilage is replaced by bone. It is growth in this area that results in elongation of the developing element. Although cartilage is usually absent

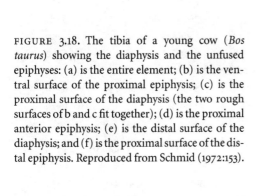
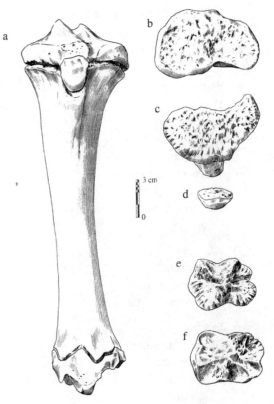

FIGURE 3.18. The tibia of a young cow (*Bos taurus*) showing the diaphysis and the unfused epiphyses: (a) is the entire element; (b) is the ventral surface of the proximal epiphysis; (c) is the proximal surface of the diaphysis (the two rough surfaces of b and c fit together); (d) is the proximal anterior epiphysis; (e) is the distal surface of the diaphysis; and (f) is the proximal surface of the distal epiphysis. Reproduced from Schmid (1972:153).

in zooarchaeological specimens, its presence may be surmised from the pitted, uneven surfaces of diaphyses and epiphyses of immature bone where the epiphyseal plate once existed.

When adult size is reached in mammals, the epiphyseal plate is replaced by bone and the epiphysis fuses to the diaphysis. In some elements, such as the proximal femur and humerus, several epiphyses must first fuse with each other before eventually fusing as a group with the diaphysis. As maturation continues, the epiphyseal line is slowly remodeled and is not visible in old individuals. In some elements (e.g., the astragalus) there is no epiphysis and growth occurs from a single primary center of ossification. As an example of the extent of this process, at approximately 6 months a developing human fetus has 800 centers of ossification, there are 450 at birth, and the adult skeleton has 206 elements (White and Folkens 2005:47). This process takes several years, but its completion often is associated with sexual maturity.

Birds also have centers of ossification. Epiphyses are cartilaginous in immature birds and are largely absent in adults (Higgins 1999; Hildebrand 1982; Silver 1970:300). Elements usually ossify early in birds. They may be completely ossified by 5–8 months of age in the domestic chicken (*Gallus gallus*). When the elements are completely ossified, growth ceases.

Table 3.5. *Age in months when epiphyseal fusion of different skeletal elements may be completed in some mammals*

	Pig	Deer	Cattle	Goat	Sheep
Early fusing:					
Humerus, distal	12–18	12–20	12–18	11–13	3–10
Scapula, distal	12		7–10	9–13	6–8
Radius, proximal	12	5–8	12–18	4–9	3–10
Acetabulum	12	8–11	6–10		6–10
Metapodium, proximal		(fused before birth for many taxa)			
Phalanx 1, proximal	24	17–20	18–24	11–15	6–16
Phalanx 2, proximal	12	11–17	18–24	9–13	6–16
Middle fusing:					
Tibia, distal	24	20–23	24–30	19–24	15–24
Fibula, distal	30				
Calcaneus, proximal	24–30	26–29	36–42	23–60	30–36
Metapodium, distal	24–27	26–29	24–36	23–36	18–28
Late fusing:					
Humerus, proximal	42	≥42	42–48	23–84	36–42
Radius, distal	42		42–48	33–84	36–42
Ulna, proximal	36–42	26–42	42–48	24–84	36–42
Ulna, distal	36–42	26–35	42–48		42
Femur, proximal	42	32–42	42	23–84	30–42
Femur, distal	42	26–42	42–48	23–60	36–42
Tibia, proximal	42	26–42	42–48	23–60	36–42
Fibula, proximal	42				
Vertebral centrum	48–84	35–42	84–108		48–60

Note: Data from Noddle (1974; goat), Purdue (1983; white-tailed deer), Schmid (1972:75; pig, cattle, and sheep), and Silver (1970; pig, cattle, and sheep).

Epiphyseal fusion and closure of cranial sutures, tooth growth, and replacement sequences are related to age (Tomé and Vigne 2003). The exact schedule these follow is influenced by individual variation, nutrition, health, sex, domestication, geographic location, climate, and other environmental factors. The age at which fusion occurs varies among elements and species, but some elements consistently fuse early in the maturation process and others fuse very late. Although the chronological age at which epiphyseal fusion occurs is variable, the sequence of fusion appears to be relatively constant among mammals and can be used to establish age classes (Table 3.5; Lewall and Cowan 1963; Moran and O'Connor 1994; Morris 1972; Noddle 1974; Purdue 1983; Schmid 1972; Silver 1970).

Teeth begin wearing down as soon as they emerge from the maxilla and mandible. Tooth wear in mammalian dentition is measured by the height of the crown of the tooth and by changes in the surface morphology related to exposure of dentine as the enamel is worn away (Davis 1987; Hillson 2005:215–22; Payne 1973; Silver 1970; Tomé and Vigne 2003). The crown heights of teeth with closed roots are reduced by attrition and can be used to estimate the relative age among herbivorous mammals (Klein 1981, 1982; Klein et al. 1983; Klein and Cruz-Uribe 1983, 1984:46–55; Morris 1972; Spinage 1973). However, the abrasiveness of the forage and its effect on the speed of tooth wear, which are critical environmental variables, can only be determined by comparison of tooth wear with chronological age (see incremental growth structures later in this chapter).

Antlers and horns also reflect age. Antlers increase in size, weight, and complexity with each year of growth, except in very old individuals (Banfield 1960; Brown 1983; Chaplin 1971:89; Goss 1983). Bovid horns increase in size, while porosity and roughness decrease (Armitage 1982; Armitage and Clutton-Brock 1976). The progress of maturation in these elements is influenced by the health of the animal. Deformities also occur as the result of mechanical damage or illness.

Interpretation of age-related sequences should always be based on biological data obtained from modern animals living in conditions similar to those that once prevailed near the archaeological site being studied. Published data on tooth eruption and epiphyseal fusion sequences are limited, and those that are available are not always applicable to zooarchaeological materials. Although the ages at which these events occur are relatively well-known for modern domestic animals, they are poorly known for most wild mammals and for ancient breeds of domestic ones. Epiphyseal fusion and tooth eruption sequences of domestic animals vary among breeds, as well as among male, female, and castrated animals. Castration alters the age at which the epiphyses fuse to the diaphyses (Chaplin 1971:81; though see Davis 1987; Moran and O'Connor 1994). It is likely that maturation sequences obtained for wild animals held in captivity do not reflect those of free animals (Morris 1972). However, Noddle (1974) found epiphyseal closure was earlier in domestic goats compared to feral ones. She attributed this to the lack of care given to the feral animals and to the selective breeding of domestic stock for rapid maturity. Intensive breeding that has resulted in today's domestic stock has doubtlessly changed the biological characteristics of these animals.

Size and Age in Animals with Indeterminate Growth

Bone growth in most other vertebrates and shell growth among molluscs does not cease at maturation. Indeterminate growth in such animals is accomplished by addition of bone or shell at the edge of the skeletal element or valve (Enlow and Brown 1956, 1957, 1958; Wheeler and Jones 1989:90). As a result of this manner of growth, it is possible to see regular bands of alternating widths in many elements of animals that have indeterminate growth (Figures 3.19a and 3.19b).

a

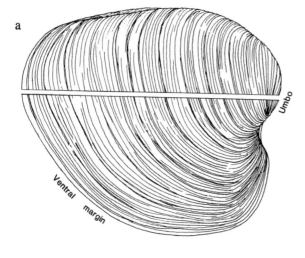

FIGURE 3.19. A southern quahog (*Mercenaria campechiensis*) showing the right valve, where it was sectioned (a), and a side view of the section (b). The section shows the narrow (translucent) growth increments associated with slow growth and broader (opaque) increments associated with more rapid growth. These represent an annual growth cycle as seen under transmitted light. Drawn by Merald Clark. Reproduced from Quitmyer and Jones (1992:248, 249); used with the kind permission of Irvy R. Quitmyer and William H. Marquardt.

b

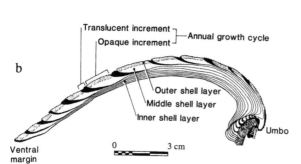

Many fishes have what are known as hyperostoses, which are sometimes called tilly bones (Figure 3.20; Driesch 1994; Meunier and Desse 1994; Smith-Vaniz et al. 1995; Wheeler and Jones 1989:112, 121). Although they appear swollen and pathological, they are normal and develop with age. These are expansive swellings of specific bones, often observed on the neural spines of the vertebrae, ribs, neural crest of the endocranium, pterygiophores, and cleithra. Hyperostoses are particularly common in several specific fish families (e.g., jacks [Carangidae], drums, and spadefishes [Ephippidae]). Some are distinctive in morphology. They are composed of cellular bone in contrast to the rest of the skeleton, which is acellular (Smith-Vaniz et al. 1995).

SEASONAL GROWTH

These tooth, skeletal, and shell changes all indicate relative age, although many environmental factors influence size and growth rates. Some of the variation in growth rates can be detected when actual chronological age can be determined through capture and

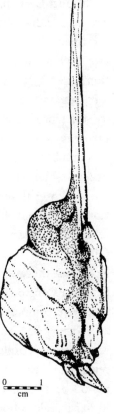

FIGURE 3.20. The first anal fin spine of a spadefish (*Platax* sp.) showing the hyperostosis of an interhaemal element. Drawn by Rosalind Wheeler. Reproduced from Wheeler and Jones (1989:113); used with the kind permission of Andrew K. G. Jones.

release research. Methods to examine this aspect of age rely on indicators of seasonal growth.

Some structures grow rapidly when food resources or other environmental conditions are favorable and grow more slowly when conditions are adverse. Variation in growth is seen in bands or increments in molluscan shells (Andrus and Crowe 2000; Deith 1983a; Milner 2001); fish scales, spines, otoliths, vertebrae, and opercula (Wheeler and Jones 1989); and mammalian teeth (Hillson 2005:159–68, 247–52; Klevezal and Shishlina 2001; Stutz 2002). Some of these correlate with seasonal cycles (Cailliet, Love, and Eberling 1986; Cailliet, Radtke, and Welden 1986). Thus, increments typically are examined for bands that might correlate with seasonal growth. Under polarized transmitted light, increments appear as alternating wide (opaque or dark) bands and thin (translucent or light) bands that represent periods of fast or slow growth. In many species, the number of annuli are closely correlated with the age of the animal at death and characteristics of the final band may provide information about the season of death. Incremental deposits are subject to a number of pre- and post-mortem processes.

Increments reflect the rate of growth during an annual cycle, with the most recent increment adjacent to its immediate predecessor. Incremental structures are defined as "distinct layers parallel with the formative surface of a hard tissue (dentine, bone, cement and their subtypes) which contrast with adjacent layers" (in Hillson 2005:247). Increments in other tissues are similarly described. They reflect changes in the growth rate responding to biomechanical stresses, metabolic rates, reproductive cycles, migration patterns, nutrition, and climatic cycles (Lieberman 1994; Stallibrass 1982). Most of these responses are to stimuli related to seasonal changes in food, temperature, humidity, and reproductive cycles. Growth may be slowed during the mating season, and is, therefore, sometimes not directly related to the availability of nutritious foods.

A number of terms are used to describe growth increments, such as translucent or opaque, white or black, wide or narrow, and dark or light rings, lines, zones, laminae, and layers (Coy et al. 1982; Deith 1983a; Gordon 1988; Morris 1972, 1978; Stallibrass 1982). Confusion about these terms reflects differences in study procedures that use either reflected or polarized transmitted light to examine stained or unstained specimens (Hillson 2005:201–206, 252–3; Lieberman 1994; Morris 1978:89–90; Pike-Tay 1991:35–6). Because the rate of increment formation is thought to vary in response to the seasonal periodicity of growth and reproductive cycles, increments are often discussed as though they were composed of seasonal bands (Higham and Horn 2000; Pike-Tay 1991:37–40). Narrow bands represent periods of slow deposition alternating with wider bands representing periods of rapid deposition. A pair of bands is called an annulus. In some regions, the broad increments are often equated with growth in a "summer" or "warm" period, and the narrow ones with growth in a "winter" or "cold" season. However, in warm regions hot summer temperatures and related environmental conditions are the limiting factor slowing growth and producing a narrow increment in some species. Although caution needs to be exercised when equating these bands with seasons, they do seem generally to reflect periodic nutritional and climatic variations that are rhythmic and roughly seasonal.

Although many animals respond to seasonal fluctuations by incremental growth, all increments are not controlled by the same periodic events. Critiques of incremental structures in mammals focus on the problems caused by fasting during mating and molting. Both of these temporarily halt cementum deposition around adult teeth, for example. Young of the same species may experience multiple periods of fasting and rapid growth that correspond to general metabolic changes. Decreased food intake during the winter influences the rate of cementum deposition. Some of these factors produce "false annuli" (Stutz 2002). True annuli correspond with the period of prolonged reduction in food intake, are continuous over extended portions of the cementum, and do not have fine, undulating lines. All of the environmental and physiological factors that influence annulus formation are unknown. Our current understanding is that they reflect changes in the strain from chewing different foods as well as in the nutritional quality of those foods (Lieberman 1993a, 1994). Growth, however, is primarily related to food availability and nutrition. False annuli, incomplete annuli, and annuli reabsorbed later in life complicate such studies.

In marine organisms, such as hard clams, oysters, and fishes, seasonal periods of fast and slow growth are responses to changes in the levels of dissolved oxygen, temperature, salinity, and nutrients reflecting daily tidal regimes and spawning. Growth rate is not constant, and careful biological study is needed to understand fully all of the factors that affect growth. Fishery biologists use scales to assess the age distributions of commercial fish stocks. Working with live fishes, undamaged scales are selected from specific places on the fish to analyze seasonal growth and age. Other structures, such as the operculum, vertebral centra, otoliths, and pectoral spines, are more durable and are successfully used for determining age and season of death in zooarchaeological materials (Brewer 1987; Colley 1990; Fowler 1995; Geffen and Nash 1995; Higham and Horn 2000; Morey 1983; Wheeler and Jones 1989). In biological studies undertaken to assess growth increments in these elements, tetracycline is injected into live fishes, which are returned to the water and recaptured after a given period of time. The tetracycline marks the growing element so that the exact chronology of the increments of growth between treatment and recapture is documented (Cailliet, Radtke, and Welden 1986).

New growth in molluscs and echinoderms is accomplished by deposition of new shell in layers at the edge of the shell or ossicle (Coutts 1970; Coutts and Higham 1971; Coutts and Jones 1974; Deith 1983a, 1983b; Jones 1980; Jones et al. 1978; Kennish and Olsson 1975; Koike 1973, 1975, 1979; Thompson et al. 1980). Growth in bivalves is along the entire circumference of the valve, whereas growth in gastropods is only around the aperture. Growth experiences daily and annual fluctuations. These fluctuations are seen in the cross section of the shell as successive wide and narrow bands of alternating mineral density (Figure 3.19; Jones 1983). Most age determinations are based on counts of annual cycles of wide and narrow bands in the cross-sectioned bivalve shell. Some hint of these is seen on the outer surface of some shells. These can be confused with shell sculpturing and, therefore, are not reliable unless verified by the cross-sectional view. The rate of growth can be studied in a living population by marking the shells with a notch at the margin and recapturing the marked animals after a known period of time to examine the amount of growth during the intervening period. Study of these shell changes is called sclerochronology. The subjects of this research are primarily bivalves such as Atlantic surfclams (*Spisula solidissima*), ocean quahogs (*Arctica islandica*), hard clams or quahogs (*Mercenaria* spp.), and Japanese clams (*Meretrix lamarkii*) (Chinzei et al. 1987; Jones 1983; Jones et al. 1990). Koike (1975) found daily growth increments as well as annual growth lines in the Japanese clam *Meretrix lusoria*. Some shell changes also are caused by environmental and life history changes. Growth responds to storms, attacks of predators, random events, seasonal temperature fluctuations (either high or low temperatures), tides, solar and lunar events, silt load in the water, and physiological stress related to spawning. Water temperature, dissolved oxygen, and food availability are the major factors.

Stable isotopes of oxygen (^{18}O and ^{16}O) do not undergo radioactive decay. However, in response to environmental variables, a change called fractionation depletes or enriches these isotopes. Measured as a ratio of the heavier isotope to the lighter one, fractionation in oxygen is temperature-dependent (Andrus and Crowe 2000; Deith 1983a; Mannino et al. 2003; Quitmyer et al. 2005; Schoeninger 1995; Shackleton 1973). The deviation from the standard is expressed in differential units (delta [δ]) relative to a standard and measured in parts per thousand (or per mil, ‰). The standard for oxygen is Standard Mean Ocean Water (SMOW). As temperature rises, the amount of ^{18}O declines relative to ^{16}O. The δ^{18}O value is reduced as water temperatures rise. Mollusc shells and fish otoliths contain a great deal of carbonate, and their growth reflects temperature and other ambient characteristics associated with carbonates. The carbonate fraction can, therefore, be used as a paleothermometer to characterize warmer and cooler conditions under which growth occurred (e.g., Quitmyer et al. 1997). Thus, oxygen isotopes can be studied for evidence of earlier environmental conditions. They may also indicate birth and death seasonality (e.g., Balasse et al. 2003).

Incremental growth and oxgyen isotopes are related in some cases (Andrus and Crowe 2000). Analysis of the ratio of ^{18}O to ^{16}O in the shell from the alternating wide and narrow bands shows that these bands correlate with water temperature in the quahog (Jones 1983; Jones and Quitmyer 1996). One interesting result of these investigations is that growth in quahogs is slowed, as shown by the narrow band in the shell cross section, during temperature extremes. These extremes are warm summer weather in the southeastern United States and cold winter waters in New England (Jones et al. 1989; Jones et al. 1990; Rhoads and Lutz 1980). Studies of oxygen isotopes show that banding is not necessarily always seasonal. Therefore, isotopic analysis should be conducted in conjunction with visual inspection of the increments (Andrus and Crowe 2000, 2002).

Related to investigation of seasonal changes are studies of the age of the individuals at death. To the extent that these increments represent annular growth, the number of paired increments reflects the number of annular growth cycles experienced by the individual. In molluscs, the size of the shell sometimes correlates with age, although individuals may grow at different rates under different environmental conditions (Jones et al. 1990). Age is an important parameter for understanding the intensity of exploitation, as was demonstrated in quahogs and Atlantic rangias (*Rangia cuneata*; Quitmyer and Jones 1997), and for the impact of prolonged and intensive exploitation on the adult size of individuals of Atlantic cod (Trippel 1995).

One must be aware that "different species vary greatly in the consistency with which they lay down growth lines and that extrapolation from one species to another is misleading and liable to result in erroneous interpretations" (Deith 1983a:425). It is, therefore, essential to have appropriate biological samples collected under known conditions that can be compared with the archaeological materials. Obtaining adequate reference material sometimes requires collecting or capturing species under controlled conditions at regular intervals throughout at least 1 year in the region of the zooarchaeological research (see Appendix 3 for information about managing such a comparative collection).

Some mammalian structures are temporary and occur during discrete seasons. Growth and shedding of antlers among deer follows a seasonal schedule. Antlers are grown normally only by male deer and are shed in the winter. Antlers grow as males approach the rutting season, and they are shed following breeding. The timing of antler growth varies according to the location. In Missouri, in the heart of the United States, antlers of white-tailed deer (*Odocoileus virginianus*) begin growth in the spring, velvet is shed by late August, and the antlers are shed at the end of the breeding season in late December or early January (Schwartz and Schwartz 1959:318). In the case of caribou or reindeer (*Rangifer tarandus*), both males and females have antlers but shed them at slightly different times, about 6 months out of phase, in the annual growth cycle. The timing of this sequence varies in different regions.

Other animal tissues respond to seasonal fluctuations but do not necessarily indicate a season of death or age. For example, medullary bone forms in the long bones of female birds during egg laying (Driver 1982; Rick 1975; Simkiss 1967). Most birds have a precisely scheduled time in the year when nest building starts and eggs are laid. Domestic chickens have a protracted egg-laying period. Therefore, medullary bone cannot provide seasonal information for chickens, but it does indicate that laying hens were butchered.

SEX

Body size and sex are closely related in many organisms. The size and robusticity of an animal and size of a specific structure often differ between males and females. Males are larger than females among many mammals and birds but not for all. In animals with indeterminate growth, such as reptiles and fishes, the female is sometimes larger than the male – occasionally much larger. Although very large softshell turtles (Trionycidae) are almost certainly females, small individuals can be either males or small females. One of the most extreme examples of size difference between males and females is found in anglerfishes (Lophiiformes). The male anglerfish is tiny and becomes parasitic on the female, to the point of mingling their blood supply. This is an adaptation for finding each other in the dark abyssal depths. The degree of size difference can be assessed by a series of measurements taken on known male and female specimens. When measurements are plotted, the curves may be bimodal if males and females differ in size in the dimension measured (Davis 1987; Rackham 1994:10).

Along with larger overall size, some specific skeletal and dental structures are relatively larger in many male animals. For example, the length and shape of bovid horn cores are associated with sex, although it is not always possible to distinguish clearly among oxen, cows, and bulls (Armitage 1982; Armitage and Clutton-Brock 1976; Grigson 1974, 1975, 1976, 1982a, 1982b; Stallibrass 1982). The size of canines reflects sex as well. In the case of suids, the canine in females is small compared to male suids; in female equids the canine may be either small or unerupted (Getty 1975:460, 1269). Males are distinguished by the epiplastron that projects forward from the plastron in male gopher tortoises (*Gopherus polyphemus*; Figure 3.21), as well as the large claws on the front feet of sea turtles and alligators (*Alligator mississippiensis*). Some turtles that live on land, such as the box turtle and gopher tortoise, have sexually dimorphic plastrons that are more concave in males to accommodate the female carapace during breeding. Differences in the shape of pelvic elements are useful in distinguishing between males and females in some mammals (Boessneck 1969; Edwards et al. 1982; Uerpmann 1973).

Some structures are exclusively found in only one sex. A baculum (penis bone) is present in male rodents, carnivores, and some primates. In deer, the presence of antlers and pedicles indicates male animals, except in the reindeer. Birds also have some sexually diagnostic features (Carey 1982; West 1982). Spurs develop on the tarsometatarsus of male gallinaceous birds (Galliformes), such as quail, pheasant, peafowl, turkeys, and chickens, but are absent among most, but not all, females. Among males, spurs increase in size with age, but females sometimes develop spurs (De Cupere et al. 2005; Silver 1970). Medullary bone indicates a female bird (Driver 1982; Rick 1975; West 1982).

GENETIC AND ISOTOPIC STUDIES

Two basic biological phenomena hold particular promise for zooarchaeological applications: genetics and isotopic studies. These require specialized knowledge about genetics and geochemistry as well as sophisticated analytical equipment. They are usually studied by specialists in these fields or under their guidance. This same observation applies to studies of blood proteins and lipids (e.g., Dudd and Evershed 1999). Applications to archaeological materials must be considered experimental in nature and the results viewed with appropriate caution.

Genetic Studies

The study of DNA in archaeology, termed "archaeogenetics" by Renfrew (2000), offers much important information about the histories and identities of the peoples, plants, and animals found in archaeological sites. Nuclear DNA (nDNA) contains the instructions on how to build and maintain living tissue that will be mediated through enzymes and other biochemicals (Sykes and Renfrew 2000). These instructions are communicated

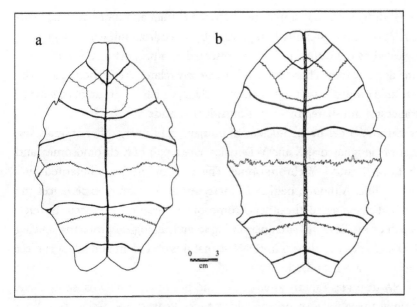

FIGURE 3.21. The projecting epiplastron of (a) a male gopher tortoise (*Gopherus polyphemus*) compared with (b) a female. Drawn by Virginia Carter Steadman.

through different combinations of four organic chemicals: adenine (A), cytosine (C), guanine (G), and thymine (T). These four chemicals are the nucleotide bases that, along with sugars and phosphates, join to form DNA. All of the DNA in an organism is referred to as the genome, organized into chromosomes contributed by both parents, and packed inside the cell nucleus. The arrangement of nDNA is similar within a species, although unique for each individual within a species. Because nDNA has contributions from both parents, the chromosomes are subject to recombination that results in the unique genetic make up of the progeny. In domestic animals, nDNA may reveal characteristics that were favored during the domestication process. Some DNA is also contained outside of the nucleus, in the mitochondria. This mitochondrial DNA (mtDNA) is inherited only from the mother and her female ancestors.

Extracting and sequencing DNA from ancient animals, such as those from archaeological sites, holds much promise (Fernández et al. 2005; Geigl 2005). Ancient DNA (aDNA) extracted from bone or other tissues from archaeological sites has accumulated contaminants. The DNA from microorganisms, scavengers, and people who handled the specimens during excavation all add to the DNA record in the specimen. However, through use of specialized techniques, the aDNA of animals can yield results that may be followed by subsequent studies or elaborate on knowledge obtained from other sources. For example, aDNA from extinct Pleistocene European cave bears (*Ursus spelaeus*) was sequenced and a bear family tree constructed (Noonan et al. 2005). The aDNA from the cave bear compared to the DNA of modern bears provides information about functional differences and similarities between extinct and modern bears. This phylogenetic relationship is presented graphically by a dendrogram, where degrees of relatedness revealed by the DNA study are represented by a proportional length of the branches of the dendrogram. Those animals least closely related are farthest apart. The more closely related groups cluster together into a clade, which is a group of organisms with a single ancestor not shared by species outside that clade.

Two of the chromosomes in the nucleus of humans, and many other animals, are sex chromosomes, designated as X and Y. Females have a pair of X chromosomes, and males have both an X and a Y chromosome. The Y chromosome is inherited only from the paternal line. Although neither of these sex chromosomes experiences the recombination that characterizes the other chromosomes, variation does occur through mutations. Much of the DNA research pertaining to archaeological problems is being done with mtDNA. The advantage of mtDNA is that it is abundant and is not subject to recombination or paternal inheritance.

Although DNA degrades rapidly after death, and has other problems, some DNA survives in animal tissue for a surprisingly long time (Pruvost and Geigl 2004; Yang et al. 2005). Thus, aDNA provides important information about the evolutionary and migratory history of people, the organisms associated with people, and trade routes (e.g., Arndt et al. 2003; Bonnichsen et al. 2001; Bradley 2000; Edwards et al. 2004; Geigl and Pruvost 2004; Haak et al. 2005; Haynes et al. 2002; Kozlov and Lisitsyn 2000; Savolainen et al. 2002; White and Folkens 2005:346–348; Zeder, Bradley, Emshwiller, and Smith 2006; Zeder, Emshwiller, Smith, and Bradley 2006). Archaeogenetics also may assist in distinguishing among species that are difficult to separate on the basis of morphology (Barnes and Young 2000; Newman et al. 2002; Yang et al. 2004), suggest former applications for tools (Shanks et al. 2001), and provide evidence for disease organisms (Bathurst and Barta 2004; Mays 2005). In this respect, archaeogenetics may serve purely zoological interests in the evolutionary trajectories of various taxa by providing historical samples from Pliocene and Pleistocene contexts. Ancient plant DNA can inform us about the domestication of crop plants and the development of agriculture that accompanied animal domestication.

Stable Carbon (C), Nitrogen (N), and Strontium (Sr) Isotopes

Biochemical analysis of some common chemical elements in human skeletal tissue, in the food items, or in the residue adhering to tools, offers another perspective on nutrition, diet, and other aspects of economic and social life (Ambrose 1993; Bocherens et al. 2000; Ezzo 1994; Katzenberg 2000; Larsen 1997: 270–301; Price et al. 1992; Richards et al. 2003; Sandford 1993; Schoeninger 1995; Sillen et al. 1989; White 2004; White et al. 2001). Biochemical analysis also may provide evidence for changes or stability in land use (Emery et al. 2000), herd management (Balasse and Tresset 2002; Copley et al. 2004), exchange networks (Schulting and Richards 2002), residential patterns (Balasse et al. 2002; Hoogewerff et al. 2001), social structure (Privat et al. 2002), feeding behavior and foddering (Makarewicz and Tuross 2006), differentiating among morphologically similar taxa (Balasse and Ambrose 2005; Noe-Nygaard et al. 2005), and ceremonial behavior (White et al. 2001). Biochemical analysis of dietary regimes typically focuses on the stable isotopes of ^{12}C, ^{13}C, ^{14}N, ^{15}N, ^{87}Sr, and ^{86}Sr. The stable isotopes ^{16}O and ^{18}O usually are studied for information about temperature and seasonal periodicity, but they also reflect the oxygen signature of the water an individual drinks over a life time, which may provide evidence for residential stability or migration (Dupras and Schwarcz 2001). This very same residential mobility, as well as trade in animals or their products, are facets of human behavior that confound interpretation of stable isotopes (Schulting and Richards 2002).

Stable isotopes of these elements differ in terms of the number of neutrons they possess and are distinguished from isotopes of these elements that are unstable and used for dating, such as ^{14}C (although see Yoneda et al. [2002]). Although referred to as "stable," in fact, even the stable isotopes are subject to some postmortem processes (diagenesis; Garvie-Lok et al. 2004; Trueman et al. 2004; White and Folkens 2005:413–14). They may not account for the diverse dietary sources of people and the animals associated with them (Müldner and Richards 2005), especially in aquatic and marine settings. Isotopic ratios also may vary among tissues (O'Connell et al. 2001).

Carbon and nitrogen stable isotopes show a trophic level effect in which the relative proportions of one isotope to another change in a systematic way as matter and energy are transferred from the consumer to its food source measured against a standard (Figure 3.22; Ambrose 1993; see Chapter 4 for a discussion of trophic levels). The standard for carbon is a marine fossil, *Belemnitella*, from the Pee Dee formation in South Carolina (USA). This is abbreviated as PDB. The standard for nitrogen is atmospheric nitrogen (Ambient Inhalable Reservoir [AIR]). Naturally occurring reduced organic carbon in plant and animal tissues is generally depleted in ^{13}C compared to PDB so δ^{13}C levels are negative compared to the standard (Herz 1990). The δ^{15}N values are generally positive because most resources have higher amounts of ^{15}N compared to AIR (Ambrose 1993). As ^{12}C and ^{13}C pass through the food chain from plants to consumers, δ^{13}C is strongly modified, making it possible to distinguish among the plant and animal food sources. δ^{15}N is only slightly enriched and so gives direct evidence of the plant foods consumed, specifically of legumes versus nonlegumes.

Carbon isotopes are the most common of the isotopes studied for dietary information and interpretations derived from diet (e.g., Bocherens et al. 2000; Buikstra and Milner 1991; May 1997; Noe-Nygaard 1988a). Plants convert carbon dioxide into more complex molecules by what are known as the C_3, C_4, and crassulacean acid metabolism (CAM) photosynthetic pathways. During this process, plants discriminate between two stable carbon isotopes, ^{13}C and ^{12}C, preferring ^{12}C over ^{13}C (Ambrose 1993; Herz 1990). The average $\delta^{13}C$ value of C_3 plants is $-27.1 \pm 2.0‰$, and the average $\delta^{13}C$ of C_4 plants is $-13.1 \pm 1.2‰$. Thus, the values of $\delta^{13}C$ of C_3 and C_4 plants do not overlap, although the average $\delta^{13}C$ range for CAM values falls between that for C_3 and C_4 plants. The ratio of ^{13}C to ^{12}C changes as these isotopes pass through the food chain, reflecting isotopic fractionation. Plants with these different photosynthetic pathways have distinctive ratios of ^{13}C to ^{12}C, as do the herbivores that consume them, and the carnivores feeding on the herbivores (Figure 3.22).

A population eating temperate and cold zone plants or animals feeding on these, including fishes, would have $\delta^{13}C$ approaching those of C_3 plants. The C_3 pathway is the most common route and C_3 plants have lower (more negative) $^{13}C/^{12}C$ ratios than do C_4 plants. C_3 plants include wheat (*Triticum aestivum*), rice (*Oryza sativa*), all root crops, legumes, vegetables, nuts, honey, and most fruits. These are often from plants that prefer areas with high winter rainfall, high latitude, or high altitude (Ambrose 1993). Algae and phytoplankton are also C_3 plants.

A human population eating mostly tropical grains and animals grazing on C_4 plants would have $\delta^{13}C$ levels approaching those of C_4 plants. Plants with C_4 metabolism take up more ^{13}C than do C_3 plants and have characteristically higher (less negative) $^{13}C/^{12}C$ ratios than C_3 plants (Figure 3.22). Plants with C_4 metabolism include mono-cotyledonous herbaceous plants such as millet (*Panicum miliaceum*), maize (*Zea mays*), sorghum (*Sorghum vulgare*), some amaranths (*Amaranthus* spp.), chenopods (*Chenopodium* spp.), sugarcane (*Saccharum* spp.), tropical pasture grasses, and salt-marsh grasses (Ambrose 1993; Benedict et al. 1980; Peters and Vogel 2005). These are generally found in sunny and dry habitats with high temperatures and strong sunlight during the growing season (Ambrose 1993).

CAM plants fix carbon dioxide by either C_3 or C_4 pathways depending on environmental conditions such as salinity, day length, night temperature, and water stress (Figure 3.22). Consequently, their ratios are intermediate (Boutton et al. 1984), but in hot, arid regions they have $\delta^{13}C$ values similar to C_4 plants. CAM plants include cacti (Cactaceae), euphorbs (Euphorbiaceae), agaves (Agavaceae), bromeliads (Bromeliaceae, e.g., pineapple [*Ananas comosus*]), and orchids (Orchidaceae, e.g., vanilla [*Vanilla* spp.]).

Applications of these principles to marine settings are more problematic than the above review suggests. Marine plants have a less negative $\delta^{13}C$, relatively closer to C_4 plant ratios. Thus, marine fishes and mammals have $\delta^{13}C$ values that are less negative than terrestrial animals feeding on C_3 foods and values that are more negative than terrestrial animals feeding on C_4 foods. In coastal areas where C_4 plants were not consumed, changes in $\delta^{13}C$ may indicate a shift in the relative importance of marine and terrestrial food sources (Larsen 1997:281–2).

Carbon isotopes are studied from both the organic (collagen) and inorganic (hydroxyapatite) portions of bone and teeth to interpret dietary combinations (Ambrose 1993;

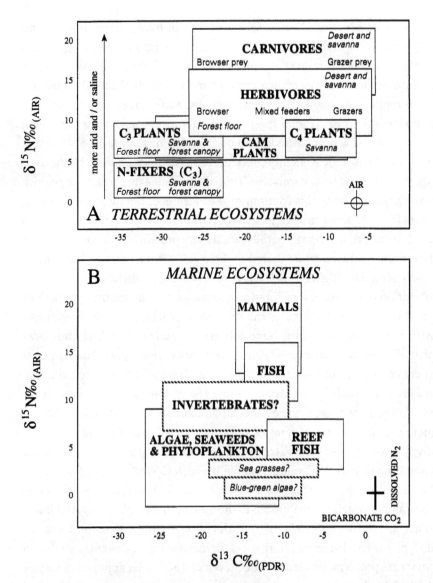

FIGURE 3.22. Isotopic variation in nature (Ambrose 1993:87). Used with the kind permission of Taylor and Francis and Stanley H. Ambrose.

Ambrose and Norr 1993; Copley et al. 2004). Collagen reflects the $\delta^{13}C$ of the protein sources in the diet. The carbonate component of bone and teeth, apatite, is produced from the carbohydrates, fats, and protein of the whole diet (Ambrose and Norr 1993). These are usually abbreviated as $\delta^{13}C_{col}$ and $\delta^{13}C_{ap}$. The difference between $\delta^{13}C_{col}$ and $\delta^{13}C_{ap}$ is an index of meat consumption and trophic level. Lipids (fatty acids and cholesterol) in bone are another source of isotopes, designated as $\delta^{13}C_{FA}$ (Copley et al. 2004).

The stable nitrogen isotopes ^{15}N and ^{14}N are present in most animal proteins and reflects the δ^{15}N values in plants, specifically legumes and nonlegumes (e.g., Figure 3.22; Larsen 1997:282–4; van der Merwe et al. 1993; White 2004). Legumes obtain nitrogen from both the atmosphere and soil; nonlegumes obtain it only from the soil. Because soil nitrates and ammonia have higher ^{15}N levels than AIR, nonlegumes have higher δ^{15}N values than do legumes (peas [*Pisum* spp.], peanuts [*Arachis* spp.], beans [*Phaseolus* spp.]). Thus, aridity, soil acidity, altitude, and other conditions influence δ^{15}N values. Unlike carbon, the ^{15}N isotope is slightly concentrated as it passes up through the food chain from plants to herbivores to carnivores. Thus, the ^{15}N values become more positive as nitrogen is transferred along this continuum. Nitrogen does not distinguish among protein sources from the same animal, such as meat, milk, or blood. Nitrogen isotopes in collagen reflect the isotopic signals of the main dietary protein sources over a decade or more of the individual's life rather than the whole diet or for a short period of time. Marine animals often have higher δ^{15}N levels than do terrestrial animals.

The combination of carbon and nitrogen may demonstrate the relative proportions of marine and terrestrial organisms in the diet. Most marine δ^{15}N are more positive than AIR, and, consequently, the bone collagen in marine animals is more positive than that of terrestrial vertebrates (Figure 3.22; Larsen et al. 1992). Marine plants have higher concentrations of ^{15}N than do terrestrial plants so that marine mammals have higher δ^{15}N values than do terrestrial mammals (Ambrose 1993; Sealy and van der Merwe 1988). At the same time, marine fishes and mammals have δ^{13}C values that are relatively more positive than those of terrestrial animals feeding on C_3 plants and δ^{13}C values relatively more negative than do terrestrial animals feeding on C_4 plants. In other words, marine animals have δ^{13}C values that fall between C_3-and C_4-based terrestrial plants (Schoeninger and Moore 1992). In areas where C_4 plants are rare, the δ^{13}C value reflects marine and terrestrial contributions to the human diet (Ambrose 1993). Unfortunately, similar δ^{13}C values are produced by distinct combinations of marine foods, C_3 plants, and C_4 plants (Ambrose and Norr 1993). In many instances, isotopic studies in marine contexts are problematic for a number of reasons and other approaches may be necessary (Yoneda et al. 2002). Combining isotopic studies with zooarchaeological and archaeobotanical data may resolve some of these issues.

Strontium is also related to dietary components, but is subject to complex biogenic and diagenetic processes (Ezzo 1994; Larsen 1997:288–9; Price 2000; Sillen and Sealy 1995). Strontium is an alkaline earth metal present in trace amounts and acquired through food from the local rocks and groundwater. Isotopic ratios of strontium are not fractionated and are associated with the geological substrate where the organisms lived. Concentrations of strontium, a ratio of strontium to minerals such as calcium(Ca) or barium(Ba), or a ratio of ^{87}Sr to ^{86}Sr are applied to dietary studies (e.g., Burton and Price 1990; Price et al. 1985; Sealy et al. 1991). Plants absorb strontium from the soil, along with calcium. Although plants absorb strontium roughly in equal proportions to its presence in the environment, the amount of strontium decreases in the food chain because animals preferentially excrete strontium and retain calcium. Animals cannot excrete most of the strontium they ingest, however, and what remains is deposited in bone and tooth enamel. Because of the trophic relationship, strontium ratios may provide information on the relative proportions of plants and animals in the diet as well as between terrestrial and marine food sources. Herbaceous vegetation (shrubs) accumulates higher strontium concentrations than do grasses, therefore, browsers have higher concentrations than do grazers. Carnivores have lower strontium-to-calcium ratios than do herbivores, and omnivores have intermediate ratios.

Because strontium ratios are sensitive to local geochemistry, changes in strontium ratios may indicate mobile residences during early growth and development, migration patterns, and external cultural influences (Bentley et al. 2004; Hodell et al. 2004). This type of study is done by taking advantage of the sequence for maturation in dental enamel and bone. By comparing the strontium ratio in enamel, which forms early in life, with ratios in bone, it is possible to see if individuals moved during their lives. Although such studies are more commonly done on human remains, they also may be conducted on other animal remains, particularly to test the foreign or local origins of livestock as a proxy for trade and migration (e.g., Poll et al. 2005).

CONCLUSIONS

The biological information summarized in this chapter is basic to zooarchaeological research. To develop the biological background needed for zooarchaeological research, students will be required to learn about these concepts and techniques through their own reading of the literature. Most of the information needed for an adequate background for a particular geographic area will be organized taxonomically in the biological literature for specific regions and organisms. In addition, it is important to have practical first-hand experience with faunal samples from archaeological sites. It is only through such experience that one learns which remains are identifiable, how to demonstrate their identity, and what taxonomy and anatomy mean for studies of human behavior and the environment.

4

Ecology

INTRODUCTION

Ecology is "the study of the natural environment, particularly the interrelationships between organisms and their surroundings" (Ricklefs 1973:11). Ecologists investigate where animals live, what they eat, when and where they find their food, when they breed, what groups they form, and what biotic and abiotic conditions are favorable for their successful existence. Hunters and fishermen have a wealth of such information obtained empirically and passed down to them from the accumulated knowledge of generations who applied this to procure the resources required for survival. The targeted species vary through time with changing technologies and consumption patterns. They also differ from place to place according to available fauna and regional cuisines. Reconstruction and analysis of past behavior relies on present-day knowledge of the ecology of the animals represented in archaeological contexts. Life history information about these animals may suggest where and when they were caught, and which capture methods were most successful.

Caution must be used in framing hypotheses about how hunting, trapping, collecting, and fishing was conducted. In the first place, archaeological concepts of time and space are different from ecological concepts (Grayson and Delpech 1998; Lyman 2003). Capture success must be measured in the context of the technology employed at a particular time and place. Given sufficient patience some fishes can be caught by hand, although we might think a net or spear would be required. Similarly, one would expect that capturing a large predator, such as a puma, would require a substantial weapon. However, the explanation given by a herder for how he killed a puma in the high Andes was that he ran the animal down on foot and killed it with a stick. Such fortuitous catches can occur. However, a stable subsistence system is founded on firmer ground, based on biological and ecological knowledge, allowing for repeated and reliable success in securing targeted species.

Ecologists focus on several different levels of organization, from organisms and their populations to the whole community of which they are a part. The ecology of organisms and their populations includes such topics as: habitat and food preferences, trophic levels, dietary requirements, social environment, and life history strategies. Community ecology is concerned with ecosystem structure, food webs, productivity, and species richness, diversity, and equitability. Ecological methods include an evaluation of the adequacy of sample size and measures of similarity between communities.

ORGANISMS AND THEIR POPULATIONS

Each organism has a unique niche and life history strategy. A niche is defined as "all interrelationships of an organism with its environment" (Ricklefs 1973:522). As such, a niche encompasses the food an animal consumes, where the animal lives throughout its life, and how the animal interacts with other competing species. A niche may be either "plastic" or "rigid" depending on the specialization of the organism. Life history strategies evolve in the context of the environment and involve such aspects of an animal's life as fecundity, growth and development, age at maturity, parental care of the young, and longevity. Some species are thoroughly studied, whereas the life histories of many others are poorly understood. Knowledge of the life history and niche of a prey animal is critical for a successful predator. Chief among this knowledge is where and when an animal can be found.

Habitat Preferences

Habitat preferences and the distribution of animal populations are fundamental concepts in ecology. Understanding habitat preferences is also of great importance for interpreting human economic strategies. Each animal represented in a faunal assemblage indicates procurement in the habitat where that animal is typically found. This focus may be very broad for animals that range over diverse and widespread habitats, such as white-tailed deer (*Odocoileus virginianus*) that graze and browse in meadows, dry scrub brushland, mixed forest edges, orchards, and salt marshes. The habitat preference of other animals may be very specific, such as the splash zones of rocky shores where nerites (Neritidae) cling to rocks or the intertidal sandy beaches where coquinas (Donacidae) burrow. The best bioindicators are those animals with narrow habitat and feeding preferences. Such animals are often small in size and have a sedentary or territorial phase in their life history. Therefore, different animals provide different degrees of precision about the habitats they and their human predators exploited in the past.

The occupation of a habitat may change or expand during the daily, annual, or life cycle of an animal. Both external environmental factors, such as the weather, and internal factors, such as growth and reproduction, influence changes in habitat choices. Harsh weather or reduced food supplies trigger hibernation or aestivation. Conditions that are harsh for one animal can be optimum for another. In the context used here, *harsh* implies limiting to a specific animal in some way.

Hibernation is a retreat from cold conditions and aestivation is a retreat from hot and/or dry conditions. In both cases, the retreat can be for extended periods of time and be accompanied by behavioral and physiological changes. True hibernation involves accumulation of body fat and withdrawal to a sheltered location, as well as physiological changes that reduce metabolism and lower body temperature and heart rate. These changes result in a state of torpor lasting for a period of weeks or even months. Such a change is well-known among American black bears (*Ursus americanus*), as well as some woodchucks (*Marmota monax*) and ground squirrels (*Spermophilus* spp.). Hibernation also occurs in reptiles. Some snakes congregate in rock crevices, alligators burrow into the mud, and gopher tortoises confine themselves to their burrows. Some species hibernate at higher latitudes but remain active throughout the year in more temperate regions of their range. In hot climates, many animals actively forage in the cooler parts of the day or avoid hot periods by aestivating. Box turtles (*Terrapene carolina*) retreat under leaves and close their shells to escape periods of both hot and dry weather.

Another way some animals avoid harsh weather or insufficient food resources is to leave altogether, migrating to other feeding grounds or breeding sites. Some animals ascend mountains during the spring and summer and descend during cold parts of the year. Such vertical migration is common among elk or red deer in much of the North American West where animals spend the summer on open mountain pastures and the winter on lower wooded slopes. A similar schedule is kept by some herders of domestic flocks in Alpine regions (Brush 1976; Netting 1976). Other migrations are vast journeys, such as those undertaken by many waterfowl (Anseriformes) from ranges in northern latitudes to others in southern latitudes following traditional flyways. The consummate long-distance migration is that of Arctic terns (*Sterna paradisaea*) that fly from Arctic breeding grounds to Antarctic pack ice and back each year, a journey of 16,000 km each way. Migrations often are predictable, although in many cases some members of a species remain as resident populations in the more temperate zones of their migration route and do not complete the migration.

Another pattern of changing habitat occupation occurs during the life histories of some animals. One of the best known and most dramatic is seen in salmon (Salmonidae), which are born in freshwater rivers, descend the rivers to the sea where they spend most of their lives, and reascend rivers in masses at the end of their lives to spawn and die. This migration style is called anadromous. The equally amazing migration from marine to freshwater, called catadromous, is exemplified in the life history of freshwater eels (Anguillidae). Eels are born in the Sargasso Sea, migrate as larvae in the Gulf Stream, and reach the eastern and western Atlantic coasts to ascend freshwater rivers as little fishes known as elvers. These grow and mature in freshwater until reproductive maturity triggers their return to the Sargasso Sea to spawn a new generation. In both cases, these life histories, with massive, precisely scheduled migrations, provide a reliable, rich source of protein for harvest by humans and other animals.

Some life history changes in habitat are less dramatic but also influence human exploitation. Many coastal marine fishes do not spend their entire lives in one habitat. Some fishes spawn near coastal inlets, and the larvae are swept into estuaries or shallow bays where the young grow and develop in shallow water, seagrass meadows, or along mangrove-lined embayments. As adults, they may return to deeper channels or to ocean waters. Examples of this life history pattern in the Gulf of Mexico and Caribbean are fishes such as the tarpons, snooks (*Centropomus* spp.), gray snappers (*Lutjanus griseus*), and red drums (*Sciaenops ocellatus*) (Odum and McIvor 1990; Seaman 1985:307 ff.). These coastal fishes were as important in the past as they are today (e.g., Newsom and Wing 2004).

Many of our most familiar animals actively disperse during the adult stage of their life history, but some animals have very widely dispersing larvae and territorial or stationary adults. Many reef fishes, and invertebrates such as sea urchins and land crabs (Gecarcinidae), have larval stages that develop in the pelagic plankton stream. Recruitment into coastal habitats is at the mercy of ocean currents. Particular ocean current and temperature conditions must be met before the larvae are swept back toward a suitable habitat, where they settle onto a coastal reef or into inshore waters. The plankton stream sometimes delivers the young to regions other than those occupied by the parent stock. A life history that includes a planktonic stage allows for wide dispersal; however, recruitment of new generations may not occur at uniform levels, particularly in areas of unidirectional current or where the conditions for settlement are small and remote, as on isolated islands (Sale 1991).

Food Preferences

As with habitat preferences, food preferences range from broad to specialized and may change seasonally or as the animal passes through different life stages. Some animals change their diets completely during their lives. For example, many frogs and toads consume plants and detritus in the larval or tadpole stage and shift to a carnivorous diet as adults.

Our species has one of the broadest food preferences among animals. As a consequence of this and other coping strategies, we are able to inhabit most of the dry land of the world. Many of the animals that people use also have broad food preferences and are widely distributed in many habitats throughout the world. Deer include many species, such as roe deer (*Capreolus* spp.), elk or red deer, Père David's deer (*Elaphurus davidianus*), huemal (*Hippocamelus* spp.), brocket deer (*Mazama* spp.), mule and white-tailed deer

(*Odocoileus* spp.), and caribou or reindeer, all of which are targeted by humans. These herbivores convert plant material that is largely in a form that cannot be used by humans into meat and raw materials that are more useful to our species.

However, most animals have more limited food preferences. Even animals with generalized food preferences have favorites among the range of foods that are acceptable. Animals with specialized food preferences include koalas (*Phascolarctos cinereus*), which eat eucalyptus leaves, and giant pandas (*Ailuropoda melanoleuca*), which eat bamboo. These animals have restricted ranges and clearly would not have widespread importance in human economies, although they might be important locally.

Food preferences are used to lure a prey species. Just as anglerfishes use their modified first fin-ray, which looks like a small fish, to attract prey animals, people use baits that rely on food preferences to attract targeted species. As every farmer knows, an agricultural plot attracts an array of animals that might be called garden pests. Linares (1976) has termed hunting the complex of animals that are lured to garden crops "garden hunting." Hunting such animals has the dual function of protecting the crops but securing animal protein for the diet. Linares, in fact, suggests that there is little use for domesticated animals as long as garden hunting is possible. Such systems break down if hunting is too intense, and animal populations are overexploited (see Chapters 8 and 10).

Classification by Food Category: Trophic Levels

Whether an animal is a specialized or generalized feeder, it can be classified by what it eats. These categories, called trophic levels, are constructed by the general overall diet of an animal, even though this diet varies seasonally with changing availability of resources. The most familiar trophic levels in most habitats are: (1) the primary producers, plants that convert sunlight and nutrients into plant tissue; (2) the primary consumers, herbivores that feed directly on plants; (3) secondary consumers, carnivores and omnivores that feed on both plants and animals; (4) tertiary consumers, top carnivores that feed exclusively on other animals; and (5) detritivores that consume dead plant and animal tissue and waste products, reducing them to more basic elements and allowing the cycle to begin again.

Although trophic levels often are described simplistically in terms of producers and primary, secondary, and tertiary consumers, feeding strategies are actually more complex than these categories imply. Categories used to characterize feeding strategies of primary consumers go beyond the familiar grazers and browsers. In addition to animals that eat primarily grass, shrubs, and herbs, some primary consumers feed on bark, fruit, seeds, nectar, gum, and combinations of these and in the process may ingest animals (Eisenberg 1981:247–63). Consuming these different plant parts and products requires different morphological, physiological, and behavioral adaptations. Among some organisms, feeding behaviors and the trophic levels change as the organism matures.

Dentition is linked to feeding strategies and, hence, to trophic level. For example, the dentition of herbivorous mammals that consume mostly plant leaves, stems, cambium, and woody structures is characterized by hypsodontic teeth. Extremes in hypsodonty are found in mammals that eat the coarsest vegetation, usually grasses, because of the greater numbers of abrasive silica bodies (phytoliths) in their tissues. Phylogeny also plays an important role in the degree of hypsodonty. Most horses have teeth with higher crowns than do artiodactyls. Within an ancestral line, grazers tend to have greater hypsodonty than browsers (Van Valkenburgh 1994).

Accompanying specialized morphology of the dentition are adaptations in the digestive system. Some herbivores have special compartments in the gastrointestinal tract where plant cellulose is fermented by symbiotic protozoa and bacteria, reducing it to a form that can be digested by the herbivore (Eisenberg 1981:247–63). A symbiotic relationship between two organisms is of mutual benefit to each and is often obligate, having developed through coevolution.

Other primary consumers are seed eaters (granivores) or nectar feeders (nectarivores), terms that more accurately reflect their diet. Many small mammals, such as rodents and rabbits, have diets based on fruits, seeds, and other plant parts. They too have many of the adaptations, such as hypsodont teeth and symbiotic organisms in a specialized digestive tract, seen in larger grazing and browsing mammals. In addition, many of these smaller herbivores have manual dexterity and cheek pouches, making food handling and storage possible. Nectar feeders have quite different adaptations. Typically, nectar feeders, such as hummingbirds (Trochilidae) and some bats, have long tongues to lap nectar from the corollas of flowers. Their hovering flight gives them the time needed to accomplish this.

Many secondary consumers regularly eat fruits and other plant material as well as vertebrate and invertebrate prey. Mammals such as raccoons, bears, pigs, and people eat fruits as part of a diverse diet that includes other plant and animal tissues. These secondary consumers generally do not have many of the morphological adaptations that characterize primary consumers. Instead, omnivores have more generalized dentition with low crowns (bunodont) adapted for crushing food from both plant and animal sources.

The top carnivores, or tertiary consumers, feed exclusively on flesh and have morphological, physiological, and behavioral adaptations that make such a diet possible. Dentition is a key carnivore feature. In mammals, the canines are well-developed and the molars and premolars are adapted for shearing. Among carnivorous reptiles and fishes, teeth are either pointed for piercing and holding prey, which is swallowed whole, or blade-like for shearing flesh to subdivide a prey animal into bite-sized pieces. Many animals with fairly undifferentiated pointed teeth also have one or more larger canine-like teeth at the corners of the mouth in the same approximate position as the canine in the mammalian jaw. Among animals without teeth, their beaks and claws are often the first line of attack on capturing and processing food. In birds, the shape of the bill (rostrum) and the horny epidermis (rhamphotheca) that covers it are correlated with foraging methods and food preferences (Zusi 1993). Among these shapes are the hooked beaks of many flesh-eating birds such as the hawks and owls (Strigiformes). Parrots also have hooked beaks, but these are used for climbing, cracking seeds, and stripping rind from fruits. Other toothless carnivores, such as snapping turtles (Chelydridae), have hooked jaws covered by horny sheaths, an adaptation for piercing and holding prey as well as a formidable means of defense.

Dietary Requirements for Energy and Nutrients

Regardless of the trophic level at which an animal feeds, its diet must fulfill its energy and nutritional needs in order for it to survive and reproduce. Food must be available in adequate quantity and quality. Some animals can fast for long periods of time. Animals break down food mechanically and chemically with the help of symbiotic organisms and specialized enzymes, store minerals that are essential for life but in short supply, such as calcium, store food in the form of caches or body fat, or have the ability to move to "greener pastures" when local sources are depleted. Water, oxygen, nitrogen, carbon, minerals, and vitamins are essential for animal life. Carbohydrates, fats, and proteins are formed from these nutrients, the basic building blocks from which an animal derives energy and nutrients for metabolic functions, maintenance, growth, and reproduction. Many nutrients are required and the diverse adaptations found among animals ensure these requirements are satisfied. Morphological and behavioral adaptations are the most obvious. Symbiotic relationships with other plants and animals are usually inconspicuous although these relationships are equally important.

Because this volume is focused ultimately on the ecological relationships of people, human dietary requirements will be reviewed briefly. Human nutritional requirements are usually summarized in terms of essential nutrients. Essential nutrients must be obtained from food because our bodies cannot make them, at least not in sufficient quantities. Essential nutrients are: proteins, carbohydrates, fats, minerals, water, and vitamins. Proteins, carbohydrates, fats, and vitamins are organic compounds containing oxygen, hydrogen, and carbon (Whitney and Rolfes 2008:7). Minerals and water are inorganic nutrients. Carbohydrates, fats, and proteins provide energy, but vitamins, minerals, and water do not.

Food energy is measured in kilocalories (kcal) or kilojoules (kJ) (Whitney and Rolfes 2008:7). The kilocalorie (1,000 calories) is the amount of heat required to raise the temperature of one kilogram (1,000 g) of water one degree centigrade. Kilocalories are abbreviated as kcalories or kcal, though they are sometimes referred to as Calories. A kilojoule is a measure of work energy; a joule is the amount of energy expended to move one kilogram one meter by a force of one newton. A kilocalorie equals 4.2 kJ.

The amount of kilocalories contained in energy nutrients is variable. Less energy is required to metabolize energy from fats and carbohydrates than from proteins. Proteins are used for energy only when carbohydrates and fats are limited. One gram of carbohydrate contains four kilocalories, as does one gram of protein, and one gram of fat contains nine kilocalories (Whitney and Rolfes 2008:9). Foods low in fat and high in water, such as vegetables and most fruits, are poor sources of energy (Wing and Brown 1979:46).

Carbohydrates provide about half of the energy that human diets require (Whitney and Rolfes 2008:101). They are found in virtually all plants, but milk, shellfish, and organ meats are among the few animal carbohydrate sources (Pike and Brown 1975:26–7; Whitney and Rolfes 2008:101). Starch, sugar, and cellulose are all carbohydrates. Most plant carbohydrates are stored as starch, which is a complex sugar. Grains are the richest source of starch, but legumes and tubers are also starch sources. Humans eventually convert most carbohydrates into glucose, a simple sugar known as blood sugar because it is the principal carbohydrate in blood. Glycogen is the storage form of carbohydrates in animals (Pike and Brown 1975:26–7; Whitney and Rolfes 2008:105). The human body maintains a steady blood glucose level by storing glucose as glycogen and fat until blood sugar levels drop, at which time glycogen is drawn out of storage and put to use (Whitney and Rolfes 2008:114). Cellulose is the primary constituent of plant cell walls, but it is more important as a source of fiber than of energy (Whitney and Rolfes 2008:106).

Lipids include triglycerides (fats and oils), phospholipids, and sterols, such as cholesterol (Whitney and Rolfes 2008:139). They provide energy, a means of transporting fat-soluble vitamins and hormones into and out of cells, insulation, and protection to the body. Because the amount of glycogen stored in the liver is limited, excess glucose may be converted into triglycerides for storage in fat cells (Whitney and Rolfes 2008:113, 114, 139, 142, 155). This is the primary energy supply rather than glycogen. Lipids can be obtained from both plants and animals (Whitney and Rolfes 2008:144–6, 157–9, 161–2). Most vegetable and fish oils are rich in polyunsaturated fats and usually have low melting points. Most saturated fats are from animals, although some tropical plant oils, such as coconut and palm oils, are also saturated. Saturated animal fats are solid in form and do not spoil as readily as unsaturated fats (Whitney and Rolfes 2008:142–3). This is an important factor in food preservation and in products such as candles and cooking oils. Fats are also important because they give foods the flavor, texture, and aroma that people find so agreeable (Whitney and Rolfes 2008:161).

Proteins are chemical compounds that combine carbon, hydrogen, and oxygen with nitrogen (Whitney and Rolfes 2008:181). Dietary protein is the primary source of the amino acids from which other proteins are made (Whitney and Rolfes 2008:185, 201). Proteins play a role in growing, maintaining, and repairing tissue; making enzymes, antibodies, hormones, and visual pigments; maintaining fluid and acid balance; transportation; and blood clotting (Whitney and Rolfes 2008:189–93). Enzymes are protein catalysts that play important roles in making and breaking chemical bonds. Antibodies, hormones, and collagen are also made of amino acids.

As many as 50,000 different proteins and about 20 amino acids combine into many different sequences, each with different properties and functions (Whitney and Rolfes 2008:182, 187). Not all amino acids are essential. The essential amino acids cannot be manufactured by the body and must be obtained from food. These are isoleucine, histidine, leucine, lysine, methionine, phenylalanine, threonine, tryptophan, and valine (Whitney and Rolfes 2008:182). Proteins are a critical source of the nitrogen needed to build the nonessential amino acids. A food that contains all of the essential amino acids is considered a complete protein source. The amount of amino acids absorbed from a protein source during digestion is another aspect of protein quality. A high-quality protein is one that supplies the essential amino acids in a form that humans can use.

Obtaining regular quantities of high-quality protein is an important subsistence goal because amino acids are not stored. Further, all of the essential amino acids and nitrogen must be ingested at the same time for protein synthesis to occur (Whitney and Rolfes 2008:195, 201). If one essential amino acid is missing, none will be used. Although both plants and animals provide proteins, animals are more likely to be complete, high-quality protein sources. Plants also have less protein per gram (Whitney and Rolfes 2008:195). To obtain essential amino acids from plants, it is necessary to combine plants whose low-quality proteins are complementary (Whitney and Rolfes 2008:195–6), such as the Mesoamerican combination of maize (*Zea mays*) and beans (*Phaseolus vulgaris*).

Vitamins are organic compounds. They do not provide usable energy; they support the processes by which other nutrients are digested, absorbed, metabolized, or excreted. Vitamins function in combination with each other so that a deficiency in one vitamin is often associated with deficiencies in one or more other vitamins. They are fragile and subject to destruction when exposed to acid, alkali, air, heat, or light during food processing or storage (Whitney and Rolfes 2008:10). Vitamins are divided into fat-soluble and water-soluble groups. Fat-soluble vitamins are primarily obtained from animals and water-soluble vitamins from plants. Fat-soluble vitamins (A, D, E, and K) are stored in the liver and adipose tissue for long periods of time, and some can be synthesized. People are unlikely to be deficient in fat-soluble vitamins if reasonable amounts are consumed over time (Whitney and Rolfes 2008:369, 379). Water-soluble

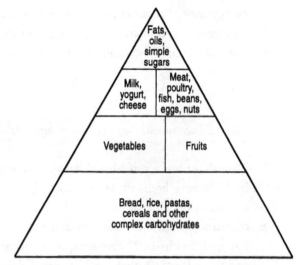

FIGURE 4.1. Diagrammatic relationship of nutritional requirements.

vitamins are the B vitamins (biotin, folate, niacin, pantothenic acid, riboflavin, thiamin, vitamin B_6, and vitamin B_{12}) and vitamin C. Vitamin B_{12} is unusual because it is obtained almost exclusively from animal sources (Whitney and Rolfes 2008:344). Water-soluble vitamins are excreted so they are needed in frequent, small doses to avoid deficiency diseases. Owing to these distinct vitamin sources, neither a strictly vegetarian nor a strictly carnivorous diet will ordinarily meet human vitamin requirements.

Minerals are inorganic elements. The major minerals are calcium, phosphorus, potassium, sulfur, sodium, chloride, and magnesium (Whitney and Rolfes 2008:408–9). These are present in the body in amounts larger than 5 g; calcium phosphate, for example, is a major mineral because it is a component of bone. Most minerals are present in smaller amounts. Some trace minerals are iron, zinc, manganese, copper, iodine, fluoride, chromium, selenium, and molybdenum (Whitney and Rolfes 2008:409, 464). Although only small amounts of most minerals are required, they are important because they maintain the body's fluid, electrolytic, and acidity levels. Many interact with other minerals, vitamins, and enzymes in complex exchanges. Diseases that impair growth, metabolism, reproduction, and the ability to perform normal activities may be due either to deficiencies of minerals or excess amounts. Minerals are not necessarily altered by food preparation, but they can become difficult to absorb. For example, phytic acid in legumes and grains binds calcium, iron, and zinc, and oxalic acid in spinach and other greens binds calcium and iron (Whitney and Rolfes 2008:409). Minerals may also be leached from foods during processing and storage.

Thus, food webs and trophic levels are basic concepts in human nutrition. People, just as all other animals, meet energy needs by feeding directly or indirectly on plants, as one version of the diagrammatic relationship of nutritional requirements highlights (Figure 4.1). By consuming at the lowest trophic level possible as often as possible the energy costs of subsistence are managed, while other important nutrients are obtained. Adequate nourishment for most humans depends on consuming a variety of foods from all trophic levels, with plants contributing a larger daily portion of the diet than animals.

Social Environment: Aggregations of Animals

Animals within a suitable habitat may be solitary and widely dispersed or aggregate in flocks or schools of densely packed individuals. These social habits may change seasonally or as the animal ages. Even though a school of fish, flock of birds, or herd of mammals appears randomly arranged, spacing is maintained among groups and among individuals. The advantages of aggregation are cooperative vigilance to detect and defend against predators, enhanced ability to find mates or coordinate breeding, and increased feeding efficiency. Some animals are solitary for most or only part of the year. Solitary and dispersed existence is common among top carnivores. Bears, weasels (Mustelidae), and some birds of prey are solitary for parts of their lives. Other carnivores, such as wolves (*Canis lupus*) and lions (*Panthera leo*), are social animals that live in packs or prides. Within these groups, they establish dominance hierarchies. Reproduction and rearing young brings many animals together in large congregations or breeding colonies. Dramatic examples of this are seen among the sea lions (*Zalophus californianus*), northern elephant seals (*Mirounga angustirostris*), and nesting colonies of birds like gannets (*Morus bassanus*) and terns (*Sterna* spp.). This distribution is a seasonal concentration and differs from animals living permanently in gregarious herds of mammals, flocks of birds, or schools of fishes.

Concentrations of animals and the promise of a protein bonanza attract human attention and in some cases systematic exploitation. Humans have different hunting and fishing strategies to capture widely dispersed, solitary animals; gregarious, densely packed animals; or breeding animals that are temporarily densely concentrated.

Social Environment: Territories and Social Hierarchies

Behavioral mechanisms ensure the distribution of each species in such a way that competition is reduced and adequate resources are available. This is achieved in two different but sometimes overlapping ways. Territories are marked by scent, advertised by song, or defended by overt or threatened aggression. They space individuals for purposes of feeding or breeding. Such territories may be maintained by individuals, breeding pairs, or even social family groups. Buffer zones sometimes surround neighboring territories. Buffer zones between wolf pack territories are refuges for prey species that prosper in the absence of intense hunting pressure (Mech 1979). When social groups share a territory, or are not territorial, organization is usually established along lines of hierarchy with dominant and subordinate relationships among individuals.

Life History Strategies: Population Growth and Regulation

One model of population growth describes increases at exponential rates until carrying capacity is reached and the rate of growth levels (Odum and Barrett 2005:127–31). The carrying capacity of the environment for a particular animal population is the point where the population is stable and the birth rate and death rate are equal (Wilson and Bossert 1971:104 ff.). A graphic representation of this model is a logistic curve with initial gradual increase in population, followed by accelerated increase, until equilibrium is met and the curve levels off or even declines.

Factors regulating population density and maintaining stability are called "density-dependent" factors (Ricklefs 1973:466). They include the availability of food, abundance of predators and disease, numbers of suitable nesting sites, intraspecific competition and cannibalism, and many others. In a simple model: population growth and resulting increased population density stresses the resources; resources become scarce; some animals may emigrate; physiological changes may affect survivorship of some members of the population; outright starvation and disease ensues; and the population's density is reduced, ultimately returning to equilibrium levels. If one considers interactions between several populations at three trophic levels, such as the abundance of plants, herbivores, and predators, a variety of complex behaviors are observed (Krebs et al. 1995). For example, the 10-year population cycle of snowshoe hares (*Lepus americanus*) results from the dynamic interaction between the hares, their food supply, and the mammals and birds that prey on them (Krebs et al. 1995).

Other factors, termed "density-independent," do not act to maintain stability of the population. A density-independent factor might be adverse weather conditions that would have an impact on all members of a population irrespective of their density.

An array of physiological and behavioral characteristics interact to form a species' response to maintaining population stability. Those traits that favor rapid population growth at low population densities are called *r* strategies. Land crabs are *r* strategists. Each individual female may produce as many as 1,200,000 eggs a year, which are deposited in the intertidal zone during high tide (Powers and Bliss 1983). From there, the developing eggs lead a precarious life in the plankton until environmental conditions are right for the young crab to settle out along the shore, scramble up on land, and find cover from a phalanx of eager predators. At the other end of the demographic spectrum are *K* strategists; animals with traits favoring competitive abilities at population levels near the carrying capacity. Humans, with a long period of high investment into small numbers of young, are *K* strategists.

A dramatic growth in human and nonhuman populations resulted from the expansion of Eurasian and African peoples into the Americas, Australia, and New Zealand after A.D. 1492 (Crosby 1994). Human colonists were accompanied by domestic stock and commensal animals that found large areas with few competitors or predators. Population growth among many of the animals introduced into "virgin" lands resulted in exponential rates of increase. Many of the introduced domestic stock established feral populations that are still abundant today. After being introduced in Australia, swine "were soon fending for themselves in the bush, where they reproduced into multitudes of thousands and tens of thousands, flowing across the coastal plain to and through the mountains" (Crosby 1994:68). The introduction of Old World rabbits (*Oryctolagus cuniculus*) into Australia resulted in a similar population rise with catastrophic consequences.

Predation pressure on a prey species is a density-dependent factor in which the individual birth rate of the predator depends on the amount of food available, which is related to the population density of its prey species. Predator–prey relationships are very complex and the subject of increasingly complicated ecological models. The first attempts to model this relationship were the Lotka–Volterra equations that describe the oscillating interaction between the population density of the prey species and its predator species. In this model, high prey densities stimulate higher birth rates of the predator, which in turn increases the death rates of the prey. In reality, these relationships are rarely so simple. A complicating factor is that few predators rely solely on a single prey species, and some predators may change their preferred prey as either the predator or the prey matures. Additionally, factors other than predation and food supply affect the density of a population. The whole set of interactions that have an impact on a population and its density are encompassed in the ecological system or ecosystem.

Life History Strategies: Age Structure and Survivorship Curves

The life cycles of plants and animal vary greatly. Some species live only a single year within which time they must mature and reproduce. Others develop slowly and continue to reproduce over a period of many years. To examine the patterns of birth, growth, and death in a population, the numbers of individuals at each age are plotted to construct an estimated life table and survivorship curve. Survivorship curves are

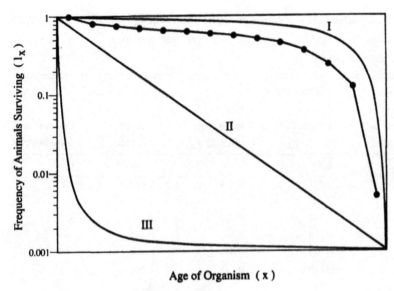

FIGURE 4.2. Survivorship curves: smooth lines are three theoretical curves, I, II, and III, following Deevey (1947). The dotted line is a curve based on female age distribution among nomadic cattle of east Africa (Dahl and Hjort 1976:48). See Table 4.1 for age in years for each data point on this curve. The vertical axis (Y) is a logarithmic scale.

used in assessing vulnerable periods in the population's life history. The frequency of individuals surviving is plotted on a logarithmic scale on the Y-axis against the age of the organism plotted on an arithmetic scale on the X-axis (Begon et al. 1986:139–40; Wilson and Bossert 1971:112–13). Three types of survivorship curves describe different life history patterns (Figure 4.2). Type I forms a convex curve reflecting survivorship of organisms that experience very low mortality until old age. Organisms with this type of survivorship curve are considered by ecologists to be K strategists. Type II is plotted as a straight line indicating that the probability of death remains constant at each age. Type III takes the form of a concave curve indicating a high level of mortality among larval and young individuals, but once the organisms have survived this vulnerable period, they have a good chance of reaching maturity. Most reef fishes have Type III survivorship curves. They produce more than a million eggs that develop into larvae in the pelagic plankton stream. This provides a rich food resource for a whole array of plankton feeders. The few survivors, approximately 1 percent, settle in a coral reef and are recruited into the reef population (Sale 1991). Animals with such a life history are r strategists.

A life table is an age-specific summary of the mortality rates and age distribution of a population. Life tables reflect intervals of ages in years (X) for the organism and the observed number of individuals alive (n_x) at the start of each age interval. From these data, the proportion of those surviving at the start of each age interval (1_x), the

Table 4.1. *Life table constructed for female age distribution among nomadic cattle of east Africa. These data are presented by Dahl and Hjort (1976:48) and form the basis for their simulations of herd productivity*

Age in years X	Observed number of individuals n_x	Proportion surviving at the start of age interval 1_x	Number dying within age interval d_x	Rate of mortality q_x	Percent distribution
1	185	1.000	0.205	0.205	13.6
2	147	0.795	0.054	0.068	
3	137	0.741	0.049	0.066	
4	128	0.692	0.038	0.055	30.3
5	121	0.654	0.027	0.041	
6	116	0.627	0.038	0.061	
7	109	0.589	0.032	0.054	
8	103	0.557	0.049	0.088	
9	94	0.508	0.054	0.106	39.9
10	84	0.454	0.092	0.203	
11	67	0.362	0.119	0.329	
12	45	0.243	0.119	0.490	
13	23	0.124	0.119	0.960	
14	1	0.005			16.2

Note: Key to abbreviations: X is age interval; n_x is the number of individuals of a cohort alive at the start of age interval X; 1_x is the proportion of individuals surviving at age interval X where the frequency range is from 1 to 0; d_x is the number of individuals of a cohort dying during the age interval X to $X + 1$; q_x is the finite rate of mortality during the age interval X to $X + 1$.

number of individuals dying during each age interval (d_x), and the rate of mortality (q_x) are calculated (Figure 4.2; Table 4.1). An age interval of 1 year is appropriate for the female age distribution of nomadic cattle in eastern Africa because they breed annually and animals can be aged accurately (Begon et al. 1986; Dahl and Hjort 1976:42–8). A sample size of at least 150 individuals is considered adequate for this type of analysis (Krebs 1989:420). The second column of Table 4.1 contains the observed numbers of individuals (n_x) at each age. These are standardized in the 1_x column, which is headed by a value of 1.000 and all subsequent values are brought in line (e.g., $1_x = 147 \times 1.000/185 = 0.795$). The number dying within the age interval is the difference between 1_x and 1_{x+1} (e.g., $d_x = 1.000 - 0.795 = 0.205$). The rate of mortality may be thought of as the probability of dying in a particular age interval and is calculated by dividing d_x by 1_x (e.g., $q_x = 0.054/0.795 = 0.068$). The resulting life table indicates vulnerable periods during an animal's life.

Life tables for domestic animals reveal a slaughtering schedule as well as stock losses to natural causes and husbandry failure. The data on the age distribution of a baseline nomadic cattle herd are derived from several sources by Dahl and Hjort (1976). They used these baseline data to simulate herd productivity as a result of life history changes among females. The life table can be subdivided into several categories according to stages in the life history and mortality rates accompanying these stages. The youngest animals, calves, are typically vulnerable. In this case, they have a 20-percent mortality rate. Calves constitute 13.6 percent of the herd. Heifers, in the age intervals from 2 to 4 years, make up 30.3 percent of the baseline herd and have a much lower death rate (6 percent). Mature breeding cows, in the age intervals from 5 to 9 years, make up the major category of the herd (39.9 percent) and have a low mortality rate. The lowest mortality rate, 4 percent, is among the newly mature cows in the 5-year age bracket. Once the cows are beyond breeding age, their mortality rate increases rapidly. These old animals make up only 16.2 percent of the herd. This herd life table was used to simulate herd productivity resulting from changes in calving rate (the percentage of cows producing calves on an annual basis), changes in calf mortality, and the length of the calving period (years that cows breed successfully) (Dahl and Hjort 1976).

This curve reflects a herding strategy that places value on the products of a herd of largely mature female cattle (Figure 4.2). Curves similar to the Type I curve reflect a livestock husbandry objective that enhances reproduction, services such as draft or burden bearing, and products such as wool, milk, and blood. Animal husbandry practices that maintain only a very few intact males and slaughter the majority for meat would have a survivorship curve similar to Type III for the male segment of the herd.

COMMUNITY ECOLOGY

Community ecology is concerned with the interactions between associated plants and animals. These relationships are infinitely complicated as they are directly or indirectly interwoven in a web of predator–prey, competitive, and mutualistic (commensal and symbiotic) relationships. All of the life histories of the members of a community interact with one another, challenging our ability to understand this fabric as a whole. Aspects of ecosystem structure, food webs, productivity, and diversity are reviewed here in terms of their bearing on human ecology.

Communities of organisms are groups of populations that typically occur together (Ricklefs 1973:590). These groups of "plants and animals occur as continua, some species becoming more abundant as others decrease in importance along environmental gradients" (Ewel 1990:8). Some communities are clearly demarcated whereas others are not. A pond usually has a clear edge, although this rises and falls with wet or dry weather. Scrub vegetation may gradually blend into mixed hardwoods where the soil retains more moisture. Each recognized community has a set of attributes that distinguishes it from others. A terrestrial community has similar soil, temperature, and water regimes that promote the growth of a characteristic association of plants, which, in turn, provide appropriate habitats and food for a particular array of animals. Marine and freshwater aquatic communities, governed by oceanographic or limnological factors, are also composed of particular assemblages of organisms.

A tropical estuary, as depicted in Figure 4.3, shows the close proximity of different communities. The intertidal rocky splash zone with chitons (Chitonidae), limpets (Fissurellidae), West Indian topsnails (*Cittarium pica*), and nerites all live very close together and have adaptations allowing them to cling to rocks washed by waves. Sea urchins and a small school of silversides (Atherinopsidae) live in the shallow inshore waters. The mangroves lining the shore are host to a whole community of organisms (Odum and McIvor 1990). The branches of mangroves provide nesting locations for wading birds like egrets (Ardeidae) and ibises (Threskiornithidae). Mangrove roots offer holdfasts for hooked mussels (*Ischadium recurvum*) and Caribbean oysters (*Crassostrea rhizophorae*). The waters around the mangroves are important nursery areas for tarpons, mullets (*Mugil cephalus*) snooks, snappers, and shrimps (*Penaeus* spp.). These reflect associations of animals in adjacent communities. Many of these interact with each other, for example, herons feed on the small fishes, which in turn are nourished by the breakdown of plant material from the mangroves. This is only one example of associations among plants and animals and the interrelations within and among communities. No organism lives in solitude outside a community.

Ecosystem Structure

An ecosystem is a "unit that includes all the organisms (the *biotic community*) in a given area interacting with the physical environment so that a flow of energy leads to clearly defined biotic strictures and cycling of materials between living and nonliving components" (Odum and Barrett 2005:18; see also Odum 1983:17). The term "ecosystem" is the contraction of ecological system and is synonymous with environmental system. The boundaries of an ecosystem are set by the viewer. An ecosystem can be as large as the ocean or as small as a coral head or the rumen of a cow. An ecological system usually is reduced to smaller, more manageable segments or subsystems (Odum and Barrett 2005:5, 75; Odum 1983; Ricklefs 1973). In making a subdivision, the flow of energy and cycling of products from outside the boundaries into the subsystem, as well as those within the system and leaving the system, must be considered. People have had a direct or indirect impact on the most remote ecosystems, an influence that should be taken into account in analyses of all systems. Likewise, the characteristics of the ecosystem within

FIGURE 4.3. Adjacent habitats in a tropical coastal setting with rocky splash zone, shallow inshore waters, fringing mangroves, and mountain headlands. Drawn by Molly Wing-Berman.

which a human population resides is vital for an understanding of human behavior and adaptations.

Critical abiotic aspects of an ecosystem are temperature, precipitation, and rates of evaporation. These three climatic parameters define terrestrial life zones (Holdridge 1967) or biomes (Whittaker 1975). They play a major role in determining the vegetation of a region, although knowledge of local climatic and biological effects must be known for a more precise definition of a biome's boundaries. If average temperatures alone were used to define life zones, one would see a succession of latitudinal regions and corresponding altitudinal belts; ranging from tropical at the equator to subtropical or low montane as one moved to higher latitudes or up mountain slopes. This would be followed by temperate or montane, boreal or subalpine, subpolar or alpine, and polar or nival zones (Figure 4.4; Begon et al. 1986:609). This describes only one aspect of the ecosystem, that controlled by temperature. In all latitudes and altitudes, a range of moisture zones also exists (Cox et al. 1976). In the tropical zone, the biomes range from rainforest through savanna grassland and thornscrub to desert. These are defined by moisture measured by evapotranspiration rates and precipitation, as well as temperature. Along the temperature gradient from temperate to subpolar, dry forests are replaced by steppes in the cool temperate latitudes, by dry scrub in the boreal latitudes, and by moist and dry tundra in the subpolar region. In temperate zones, the biomes include forests characterized by mixed conifers and evergreen or deciduous hardwoods, grasslands, and deserts. Coniferous forest composed of only one or two species is characteristic of the boreal zone. Vegetation in the subpolar or alpine zone typically includes low-growing plants such as lichens, mosses, sedges, and dwarfed trees growing on permafrost.

In addition to temperature and moisture, other environmental conditions influence terrestrial ecosystems. These include the porosity of the soil and its ability to retain water; the presence of prevailing winds and their influence on evaporation; topography, especially its role in intercepting moisture carried by the winds blowing from the ocean and in promoting drainage; the occurrence of fire; and biotic factors associated with primary consumers, including people and their domestic animals.

Marine and freshwater aquatic habitats are characterized by some of the same environmental parameters of temperature, in addition to light, salinity, nutrients, and water flow. Great water depths and turbidity reduce light and, thereby, the growth of the primary producers at the base of the food chain. The productivity of a body of water is augmented by nutrient run-off from the land and upwelling of deeper nutrient-rich water. Water depth, temperature, and the sources of nutrients differ among freshwater habitats, such as marshes, lakes, streams, and rivers, as they do among marine habitats such as estuaries, shallow continental shelves supporting coral reefs, algal beds, and sea-grass meadows, and the open ocean. Estuaries, algal beds, reefs, swamps, and marshes are among the most productive habitats, rivaling the productivity of tropical forests.

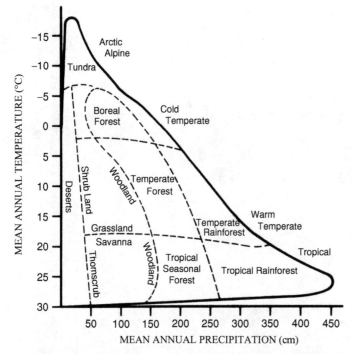

FIGURE 4.4. The distribution of major terrestrial biomes with respect to mean annual temperature and mean annual precipitation, following Whittaker (1975:167).

Food Webs

The interactions between organisms within a community include their position in food webs (Ricklefs 1973). Food webs are based on primary producers, the consumers they support, and reduction of organic material by detritivores (Yodzis 1993:26–38). Food webs can also be thought of as trophic pyramids, with the largest mass of organisms (biomass) in terrestrial ecosystems at the base of the pyramid or food chain and diminishing upward toward the top of the pyramid with the top carnivore (Wilson and Bossert 1971:152–3). The biomass of plant material in terrestrial communities far exceeds the biomass of herbivores feeding on it. Likewise, herbivore biomass is greater than biomass of its carnivore predators. This is not necessarily true in an aquatic community where many of the primary producers are single-cell plants or phytoplankton, which reproduce quickly but may not have a great biomass at any one time. Many plankton feeders are large; among the largest are baleen whales.

Connectance and the role of keystone species in a community are important facets of food webs. Connectance refers to the links of species consuming the same prey species. Linked species are potential competitors. Keystone species are members of a community that control the integrity and persistence of the community. The importance of keystone

Table 4.2. *Net annual primary productivity and standing crop biomass estimates for contrasting communities of the world, simplified from Whittaker (1975:224)*

Ecosystem type	Area[1]	Net primary productivity per unit area[2] normal range	mean	World net primary production[3]	Biomass per unit area[4] normal range	mean	Annual world biomass[5]
Tropical rain forest	17.0	1,000–3,500	2,200	37.4	6.0–80	45	765
Temperate deciduous forest	7.0	600–2,500	1,200	8.4	6.0–60	30	210
Boreal forest	12.0	400–2,000	800	9.6	6.0–40	20	240
Savanna	15.0	200–2,000	900	13.5	0.2–15	4	60
Temperate grassland	9.0	200–1,500	600	5.4	0.2–5	1.6	14
Cultivated land	14.0	100–3,500	650	9.1	0.4–12	1	14
Swamp and marsh	2.0	800–3,500	2,000	4.0	3.0–50	15	30
Lake and stream	2.0	100–1,500	250	0.5	0.0–0.1	0.02	0.05
Other[6]	71.0	0–2,500		27.27	0.0–200		503.5
TOTAL CONTINENTAL	149		773	115		12.3	1,837
Open ocean	332.0	2–400	125	41.5	0.0–0.005	0.003	1.0
Upwelling zones	0.4	400–1,000	500	0.2	0.005–0.1	0.02	0.008
Continental shelf	26.6	200–600	360	9.6	0.001–0.04	0.01	0.27
Algal beds and reefs	0.6	500–4,000	2,500	1.6	0.04–4	2	2.0
Estuaries	1.4	200–3,500	1,500	2.1	0.01–6	1	1.4
TOTAL MARINE	361		152	55		0.01	3.9
FULL TOTAL	510		333	170		3.6	1,841

Note: Key: 1 = 10^6 km²; 2 = dry gm/m²; 3 = 10^9 dry metric tons organic matter/yr; 4 = dry kg/m²; 5 = 10^9 dry metric tons of organic matter; 6 = other continental ecosystem types, for example, tropical seasonal forest, temperate evergreen forest, woodland, tundra, and desert.

species was demonstrated in an experiment by Paine (1966) in which he removed ochre starfishes (*Pisaster ochraceus*) from northwestern Pacific coastal tidepools and observed the resulting changes in species composition. Removing the predatory starfishes from the tidepools allowed mussels (Mytilidae) to proliferate, thereby crowding out other invertebrates. With observation of the controlling organisms in other communities, this concept has broadened to "functional groups" of organisms that together stabilize the community (Stone 1995). People hold the position of keystone species in many of the communities we inhabit and exploit. The ways in which food webs relate to productivity, diversity, and stability are complicated and best explored in other texts (e.g., Odum and Barrett 2005).

Productivity

The primary producers (usually measured in dry grams per square meter per year) at the base of the food web determine the productivity in an ecosystem. This productivity is, of course, affected by temperature, light, moisture, nutrients, and other environmental factors. Productivity decreases from the wet tropics to temperate regions; particularly in areas either too dry or too cold to support forests (Table 4.2; Begon et al. 1986:631). Swamps and marshes, located between terrestrial and aquatic communities, are especially productive. This is so because water is not a limiting factor, emergent plants are exposed to light for photosynthesis, and abundant minerals are available owing to decomposition of detritus. Aquatic productivity is highest in shallow inshore waters and estuaries. Coral reef productivity is among the highest of all natural communities (Ricklefs 1973:638 ff.).

Energy, ultimately coming from the sun, flows through a food chain with losses at each trophic level. The loss at each transfer is on the average about 90 percent, whereas at the same time the quality of the energy is enhanced by about 10 percent (Odum and Barrett 2005:108, 113; Odum 1983:16). This is why the top predators in any community are few and must range widely. By choosing energy as a currency within an ecosystem, simplified models of the energy flow through the system can be constructed (e.g., Odum and Barrett 2005:113; Odum 1983). Systems ecological models diagram the storage of water, minerals, and soil in the system as well as the work done by different components. Producers are one of the biological components and convert sunlight by photosynthesis into stored plant tissue. Consumers, in higher trophic levels, recycle water and minerals, respire, and perform all the biological functions required for growth and reproduction. Decomposers break down tissue to make the basic constituents for life available. Simulations of ecosystems allow computer manipulation of interacting components of the model to understand better the flow of energy through a system as it is conceived.

Richness, Diversity, and Equitability

"Understanding the origins and the maintenance of organic diversity are two of the most challenging intellectual problems in all science" (McGowan and Walker 1993:203). The richness of species is one of the fundamental characteristics of an ecosystem. Richness is the number of taxa in a community or region. As the sampling of any community is increased, the probability of adding rare species also increases. For this reason, comparative studies normalize the species count or richness of the sample with the sample size, which is the number of individuals in the sample (Schluter and Ricklefs 1993:4). The diversity of a region, sometimes called gamma diversity, can be "partitioned into two components: local (alpha) diversity and turnover of species between habitats or localities (beta diversity)" (Schluter and Ricklefs 1993:4). Diversity among faunal assemblages from archaeological sites must, by its nature, be gamma diversity – diversity on a regional scale.

General patterns of species richness exist between numbers of species and latitude, climate, productivity, habitat heterogeneity, habitat complexity, disturbance, and size of islands and their distance from the mainland source of species (Schluter and Ricklefs 1993:2 ff.). Species richness is related in a general way to climate. Conditions favoring high terrestrial productivity, such as warm temperatures and abundant moisture, are associated with high diversity. Notable exceptions to the correlation of high productivity to high diversity are salt marshes, which typically have high productivity but low diversity. A contributing factor to low species diversity may be the lower complexity of salt marsh vegetation. Habitat complexity, such as multiple layers in the vegetation of tropical forests, correlates with high species diversity (Begon et al. 1986:795). Disturbance in the environment, when it is intermediate in intensity, also promotes species diversity by providing a mosaic of patches at different stages of succession. The diversity of organisms on islands increases with island size and decreases with the distance of the island from the mainland source of species. The relationship between sample area and species richness within continents is not as strong as is seen in islands. As species richness within communities becomes the focus of investigation, the relationship between local and regional diversity will be better understood (Holt 1993:77–8). When all of these relationships are examined more closely, most are confounded by exceptions. Regional and historical processes and the interconnectedness of natural phenomena are all factors that have left their mark on local diversity (Ricklefs and Schluter 1993:350 ff.).

The latitudinal diversity gradient (LDG) is a large-scale pattern of diversity. It is illustrated by a curve showing greatest richness and diversity in tropical latitudes and diminished richness and diversity in higher latitudes, both north and south of the equator (Figure 4.5; Begon et al. 1986:801). The out of the tropics (OTT) model proposes that many lineages (genera and families) originated in the tropics, persisting there even as they expand out of the tropics. The OTT model applies to most groups

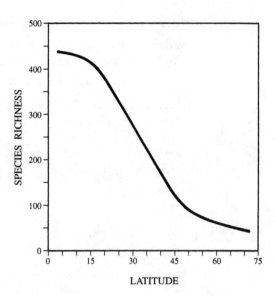

FIGURE 4.5. Decline in richness of mammalian species with increased degrees of latitude. © (1995) American Society of Mammalogists. Modified from *Journal of Mammalogy*, by Kaufman (1995:329) and used with their kind permission. Reprinted by permission of Alliance Communications Group, a division of Allen Press, Inc.

of organisms, for example, a study of marine bivalves over the past 11 million years supports this OTT model (Jablonski et al. 2006; Weir and Schluter 2007).

Ecologists frequently use a measure developed from information theory to describe the diversity of biological systems (Krebs 1989; MacArthur 1965; Pielou 1966; Shannon and Weaver 1949). These measures combine data on numbers of categories (taxa) and abundance within each category to describe the heterogeneity of a system. Diversity by this definition reflects the amount of uncertainty in predicting the identity of an individual picked at random from the community, that is, the heterogeneity of the sample.

One index of diversity is the Shannon–Weaver function, also referred to as the Shannon–Wiener function:

$$H' = -\sum_{i=1}^{s}(p_i)(\log\ p_i),\qquad\qquad (4.1)$$

where

H' = information content of the sample

p_i = the relative abundance of the ith taxon within the sample

Log p_i = the logarithm of p_i. This can be to the base 2, e, or 10; the examples in Table 4.3 use the natural log, e

s = the number of taxonomic categories

With this measure of diversity, samples with an even distribution of abundance between taxa have a higher diversity than samples with the same number of taxa but with disproportionately high abundance of a few taxa. More taxonomic categories

Table 4.3. *Example of the calculation of species diversity in (a) a sample in which four species are equally represented compared with (b) a sample in which one of the four species predominates*

(a) Taxon	p_i	$\mathrm{Log}_e\, p_i$	$p_i\, \mathrm{Log}_e\, p_i$
$i = 1$	0.25	-1.3863	-0.3466
$i = 2$	0.25	-1.3863	-0.3466
$i = 3$	0.25	-1.3863	-0.3466
$i = 4$	0.25	-1.3863	-0.3466
			-1.3863
			$H' = 1.3863$
			$V' = 1.0000$
(b) Taxon	p_i	$\mathrm{Log}_e\, p_i$	$p_i\, \mathrm{Log}_e\, p_i$
$i = 1$	0.95	-0.0513	-0.0487
$i = 2$	0.02	-3.9120	-0.0782
$i = 3$	0.02	-3.9120	-0.0782
$i = 4$	0.01	-4.6052	-0.0461
			-0.2512
			$H' = 0.2512$
			$V' = 0.1812$

Note: Key to abbreviations: Shannon–Weaver function is $H' = -\Sigma\, (p_i)$ $(\mathrm{Log}_e\, p_i)$ where H' is the information content of the sample; p_i is the relative abundance of the ith taxon within the sample; and $\mathrm{Log}_e\, p_i$ is the logarithm of p_i. Equitability is measured as $V' = H'/\mathrm{Log}_e\, S$ where H' is the Shannon–Weaver function; and S is the number of species in the community.

lead to greater diversity values when samples show the same degree of equitability in abundance.

Measures of heterogeneity combine two independent concepts, species richness (the number of species) and equitability (the degree to which species are equally abundant). Examination of equitability independent of richness is also of interest. Equitability is calculated by scaling the heterogeneity measure to the theoretical maximum (Hurlbert 1971; Peet 1974). Equitability (V') is measured as:

$$V' = H'/\mathrm{Log}_e\, S, \tag{4.2}$$

where

H' = the Shannon–Weaver function
S = the number of species in the community

In the two examples presented in Table 4.3, four taxa are represented in different relative abundances. In example 4.3a, the taxa are represented evenly, producing a diversity index $H' = 1.39$ and equitability $V' = 1$. In example 4.3b, the four taxa are unevenly represented, producing a diversity index $H' = 0.25$ and equitability $V' = 0.18$. Equitability values close to 1.0 indicate even distribution of taxa, whereas lower values suggest dominance of one taxon or a few taxa.

ECOLOGICAL METHODS

Sample Size

Sampling must be done in all scientific endeavors. The objective is to examine a sample that is large enough to reflect the composition or character of the population being studied. Unless a sampling protocol is established through a pilot study, most studies must determine what is an adequate sample size and how to reach it without excessive expenditure of time during the research project itself. The objectives of the research dictate the nature of the samples that are taken, though certain minimum data must always be recorded. To sample the species in a community, the objective is to include most if not all of the species. However, to sample the age or size structure of a population in the community, the objective would be to include the full range of ages large enough to construct a survivorship curve or sizes to reflect a normal distribution. Frequently, the size or number of replicate samples cannot be anticipated or predetermined because the density of the species is unknown. To overcome this obstacle, an empirical approach can be taken with replicate samples analyzed until a sample size that appears to describe adequately the composition and character of the population under study is reached.

The relationship between numbers of individuals and numbers of species is not a straight line when samples are large enough to include rare species. As sample size increases, new species are added at a decreasing frequency so that the resulting plot between individuals and species counts rises steeply and then levels off as increasingly rare species are added. A sample size closest to the asymptote of this curve would include common as well as rare taxa and would be considered an adequate representation of the population from which the sample was drawn. Theoretically, if a community with very few species is sampled, the asymptote is reached almost immediately. On the other theoretical extreme, if a large region composed of many communities is sampled, new species will be added continually and the asymptote will not be reached until the sample is huge. This is an approach for testing adequacy in sampling used in ecological and paleontological research (Krebs 1989; Vermeij 1987:57). To test this relationship, data for numbers of individuals and species can be plotted on a graph and a linear

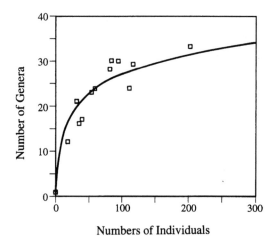

FIGURE 4.6. Rarefaction curve of sample size (numbers of individuals) and species richness (number of genera) based on faunal samples from the West Indies. The formula for this particular curve is: $\log Y = -2.0848 + 14.52(\log X)$; $r^2 = 0.87$.

regression constructed (Figure 4.6). The strength of the relationship is demonstrated by the variance (r^2). A similar test for the adequacy of sample size of material culture is proposed by Kirch and his colleagues (1987).

In any sort of comparison between faunas, application of analytical tests must only be made with adequate samples. All diversity measures are particularly sensitive to sample size. Under some circumstances, adequate samples cannot be made and then analysis must be descriptive.

Similarity Measures

Ecologists frequently compare communities of plants or animals from different locations or at one location after the passage of time. A number of different indices of similarity are available (Krebs 1989:293–309). The percentage similarity measure is both easy to calculate and one of the best quantitative similarity coefficients available (Krebs 1989:304–5; Renkonen 1938). It is little affected by sample sizes in the range of 100 to 5,000 or by species diversity (Krebs 1989:305). The index is calculated using the formula:

$$P = \sum \text{minimum}\,(p_{1i}, p_{2i}), \qquad (4.3)$$

where

   P = percentage similarity between samples 1 and 2,
   p_{1i} = percentage of species i in community 1, and
   p_{2i} = percentage of species i in community 2.

Table 4.4. *Calculation of the percentage similarity among the average number of domestic animals kept by peasants with small, medium, and large herds in the Laguna Blanca Reserve, Argentina*

Animals	Small herds		Medium herds		Large herds	
	Number	%	Number	%	Number	%
Donkeys	–	0	–	0	50	3.7
Horses	1	0.8	4	1.0	10	0.7
Llamas	15	11.5	90	23.0	600	44.9
Cattle	2	1.5	8	2.0	25	1.9
Goats	50	38.5	90	23.0	200	15.0
Sheep	62	47.7	200	51.0	450	33.7
Total	130		392		1,335	

percentage similarity between small and medium herds: $PS = 0 + 0.8 + 11.5 + 1.5 + 23.0 + 47.7 = 85$ percent

percentage similarity between medium and large herds: $PS = 0 + 0.7 + 23.0 + 1.9 + 15.0 + 33.7 = 74$ percent

percentage similarity between small and large herds: $PS = 0 + 0.7 + 11.5 + 1.5 + 15.0 + 33.7 = 62$ percent

Note: Data from Rabinovich et al. (1991:337–58).

The example in Table 4.4 shows how this is calculated (Krebs 1989:307). The data in this example are the average numbers of domestic animals kept by peasants with small, medium, and large holdings in the Laguna Blanca Reserve, Argentina (Rabinovich et al. 1991:337–58). Percentage similarity is used to compare the distribution of livestock kept. The first step is to tabulate the average abundance of each domestic animal, donkeys (*Equus asinus*), horses (*E. caballus*), llamas, cattle, goats, and sheep kept by each peasant class. Second, their relative abundance (or percentage) is calculated; this must add up to 100 percent. In a comparison between any two of these, the lowest percentage for each animal is added, which results in the percentage similarity. As can be seen in this example, the small and medium herd sizes are more similar in composition than either is to the large herd composition.

CONCLUSIONS

Knowledge of ecosystems and the biology of plants and animals in them is essential for any attempt to understand the nature of human existence in an environment, human use of biological resources, and paleoenvionments. The accumulated influence of human behavior throughout history has modified ecosystems. Plants and animals have become extinct, extirpated from a region, or introduced to a region throughout the course of human existence. We must use our knowledge about the biology of organisms and the ecology of a system to interpret the impact of these processes on our species. Biological and ecological studies are fundamental. Without them, interpretation of archaeological faunal samples cannot be made.

5

Disposal of Faunal Remains
and Sample Recovery

INTRODUCTION

Forces that form an archaeological deposit occur throughout the history of the site. This sequence of events includes the initial disturbance to the location as it became a locus of human affairs, the activities that occurred at the site while it was the scene of purposeful human activity, and what happened there once people "abandoned" it (Andrews 1995; Davis 1987; Huntley and Stallibrass 2000; Klein and Cruz-Uribe 1984; Koch 1989; Lyman 1994c; O'Connor 2005; Sandweiss 1996; Schiffer 1983). The study of the changes that influence a deposit is called taphonomy. This word was coined by the Russian paleontologist Efremov (1940) and means literally the laws of burial. In its strictest interpretation, this concept applies only to the processes resulting in burial and what happens subsequently, but, for archaeological contexts, it is necessary to consider the human processes preceding discard and burial at the same time. The steps involved in sample recovery and study also alter what we learn from archaeological sites.

Stimulated by the important ways in which these processes alter deposits, zooarchaeologists are keenly interested in the nature of these changes and how they modify the cultural record by superimposing other patterns. Some taphonomic studies are directed toward the processes of change themselves. Other researchers study the processes by which the original deposit was formed and analyze excavated data in terms of how the deposit changed through time. Some remains of human occupations lie almost undisturbed for millennia. In other cases, the deposited remains are so altered that the only trace of them is higher phosphate values at the site compared to the surrounding area (Scudder et al. 1996). The magnitude of the changes in the archaeological record varies from site to site and from the initial deposit to laboratory analysis. Studies of these processes in the archaeological record are greatly improved by combining zooarchaeological evidence with data from other sources, such as soils, plants, and arthropods (e.g., Huntley and Stallibrass 2000).

These modifications fall into two categories: (1) first-order processes over which archaeologists have no control, and (2) second-order changes for which archaeologists and zooarchaeologists are responsible. First-order processes are themselves foci of research because they yield information about human decision-making processes, the history of the deposit, and former environmental conditions. Second-order changes encompass decisions made during excavation, identification, and analysis. We tend to view all of these changes as losses, but materials also are added to deposits. Most of these processes also affect collagen, apatite, isotopes, ancient DNA, and other biological and geochemical evidence (e.g., Andrus and Crowe 2002; Banerjee and Brown 2004; Geigl 2005; Haynes et al. 2002; Stutz 2002; Trueman et al. 2004; White 2004; White and Folkens 2005:347).

MODEL

The taphonomic history of a faunal assemblage is modeled in various ways (Clark and Keitze 1967; Davis 1987; O'Connor 2000b; Noe-Nygaard 1988b). All of these models emphasize decline in the integrity of the original information: first, through alteration of evidence before, during, and after burial; second, during the recovery of a sample of the buried remains; and finally, through presentation of the analyzed results. Our model (Figure 5.1) illustrates these successive losses by decreased sizes of the boxes representing ever-diminished assemblages. The life assemblage of the region at the bottom of the model is large and diverse compared with the portion of the native fauna used by people, which becomes the death assemblage. The choices of which animals to use or avoid differ from one culture and region to another. However, all people are selective in the animals they use and the purposes for which they use them. The discarded remains of the animals from these uses constitute the deposited assemblage.

The remains of all the animals used by people living at the site will not be recovered from the site, because either their remains were discarded beyond the excavated portion of the site or their remains did not survive deposition. The deposited assemblage contains the durable remains of animals either intentionally buried, thrown on a refuse heap, or lost at the site. The initial refuse (deposited assemblage) is subject to change even when the site is inhabited. While the site is occupied, active areas of the site are cleaned, and activities move from one place to another within the site. Foot traffic across the site crushes some of the refuse. The plant and animal refuse attracts scavengers and commensal animals. Animals, such as mice and land snails, find food and shelter at the site and their bodies become part of the assemblage if they die there, along with insects and botanical materials. Other animals living at the site, such as the owl roosting in the overhanging tree, regurgitate pellets of inedible animal remains that mingle with debris related to human economic and social life. These processes change the composition and condition of the deposited assemblage. Both losses and additions must be recognized in order to distinguish them from refuse disposal by people and, by extension, the animals that were a part of their daily lives.

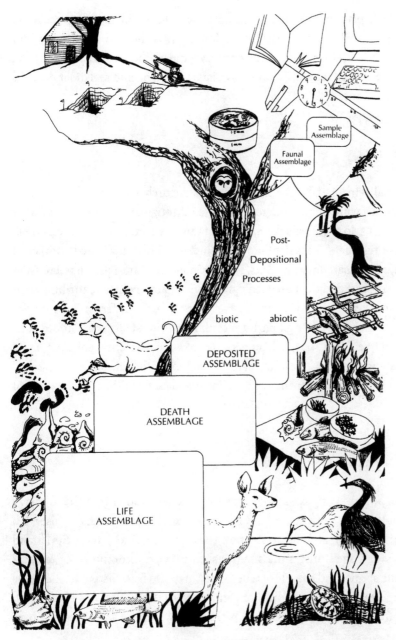

FIGURE 5.1. The possible pathway from a life assemblage to the archaeological assemblage with some of the major changes that can alter the assemblage. Drawn by Molly Wing-Berman.

Through time, both biotic and abiotic postdepositional processes further change the deposited assemblage. Plant roots and burrowing animals alter deposits. Landfills, dam construction, and land clearances alter the integrity of archaeological deposits. Although the scope and the frequency of these activities have changed in recent centuries, humans have engaged in earth-moving activities for millennia wherever they lived. Abiotic processes include displacement by wind and water flowing across the site, percolation of water through the sediments, climatic conditions such as alternating periods of dry and wet, cold and hot weather. Sediments borne by wind and water add to the deposit as do volcanic ashes, called tephra. Tephra may blanket a region and seal older deposits beneath more recent ones.

TYPES OF DEPOSITS

Disposal of animal remains is at the heart of much zooarchaeological research. Past uses and associations with animals are reconstructed through an examination of what survives in a deposit. Most deposits fall into one of three generalized categories: (1) kill or processing site residue, (2) residential refuse, including that associated with small camps, hamlets, and urban environments, (3) and intentional burials. Characteristics of the faunal assemblage and their archaeological context are important attributes that distinguish among these types of deposits. Each represents a different facet on the continuum of human behavior (e.g., Bartram et al. 1991; Bird et al. 2002; Gifford et al. 1981; McNiven and Feldman 2003; Milner 2002; Monks 2005; Savanti et al. 2005; Stahl 1999). To understand the full range of human interactions with their natural and social environments, it is important for the study to include data from the full spectrum of deposit types.

Kill, Collection, or Processing-Site Residue

A kill, collection, or processing site represents a single activity rather than the full array of behaviors that might be present at multifunctional sites. Kill sites, such as a bison kill site (Speth 1983; Wheat 1972), a fishing station (Bassett 2004; Butler 1993; Butler and O'Connor 2004), or a shell-processing site (Meehan 1982), are composed of remains dominated by one species and a few tool types. They may also have distinctive elements or taxa reflecting processing, transportation, and disposal decisions (Bird et al. 2002). These sites are often occupied very briefly or perhaps only during a specific season over several years.

Residential Refuse

A more common focus of excavation is the accumulated refuse associated with a residential site. These may be short-term camps or long-term stable occupations where members of the entire family group or several families reside and at which many different activities occur. At the more complex end of this spectrum, a small portion of a large, urban center such as Paris or London may be excavated, although some of these urban sites may not be residential (e.g., Reitz et al. 2006). Village or urban refuse usually has a relatively high species diversity and includes an array of material culture. Residential debris may be only a thin scatter accumulated over time to form a midden or pile of refuse. Refuse that is not moved out of the way is likely scattered and damaged by foot traffic, scavengers, wind, and water. With careful examination, it is sometimes possible to detect episodes of disposal either underfoot or elsewhere. Sometimes refuse is moved to trash deposits or dumped into ravines or abandoned structures. It may be possible to detect discarded episodes in redeposited trash. For example, when a basket of bivalves is discarded in this way, the valves may be cupped within one another, and the mass may retain the form of the overturned container. Refuse often is concentrated in particular areas within a structure, such as around a hearth or along a barrier such as a wall (Friesen and Betts 2006). Sweepings may represent cleaning that results in the remains being sorted by size (Schiffer 1983). Refuse deposited in pits, wells, and latrines is partially protected from such damage and, therefore, might be a more complete representation of what was discarded. Wells used for refuse disposal often retain some water, and plant and animal remains discarded in such anaerobic conditions would be particularly well-preserved.

Intentional Burial

Animal burials are typified by skeletal completeness (e.g., Alhaique and Cerilli 2003). They are often associated with human burials or important architectural features at the site. Intentionally buried animals or animal parts are usually less subject to exposure and foot traffic. Frequently dogs are intentionally buried, and their completeness attests to the protection this offers (e.g., Morey 2006). In the Andes, both colonial documents and archaeological evidence point to the ritual sacrifice of llamas, alpacas (*Vicugna pacos*), and guinea pigs (*Cavia porcellus*) (Morales 1995; Murra 1965). Several young camelids, probably llamas, were found as offerings under a central pyramid in a coastal Peruvian site (Shimada and Shimada 1985) and mummified guinea pigs were placed in ritual contexts at other coastal sites (Rofes 2004; Sandweiss and Wing 1997). A site on the coast of Ecuador occupied between 7,000 and 10,000 years ago had several primary human burials and two large secondary burials that included the remains of several individuals. Associated with one skull in each of the two groups of secondary burials was a cache of South American fox teeth (*Pseudalopex* [= *Dusicyon*] *sechurae*) from at least seventeen individuals (Wing 1988). This find is a remarkable record of purposeful behavior in burial practice and survived at least 7,000 years with little alteration. Generally, burials and their offerings are particularly vulnerable to human disturbance from looting.

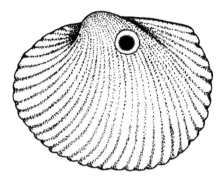

FIGURE 5.2. Kill hole in the umbo of an ark (Arcidae) made by a carnivorous marine snail (superfamily Muricacea), dorsal view. Drawn by Tina Mulka.

FIRST-ORDER CHANGES: TAPHONOMY

First-order changes occur as animals are captured, killed, and used, as materials are deposited (biostratinomy), and after deposition (diagenesis). These changes end when excavation begins. They have an impact on not only the physical animal remains, but also the chemical and genetic components of bone, shell, and teeth. Thus, the evidence for animal use in the past is altered, resulting in an incomplete and distorted view of earlier relationships between humans and their environments. Knowing the types of changes that can occur and how to assess the degree of disturbance is important for interpretations of archaeological faunal assemblages. The paleoecological and taphonomic literature details the many causes of changes in the archaeological record, how these changes are manifested in fossils and subfossils, and the character of physical and chemical changes in animal tissue (Behrensmeyer and Hill 1980; Hedges and van Klinken 1995; Lyman 1994c; Schiffer 1983; Weigelt 1989).

It is often difficult to attribute first-order changes to specific causes, especially to distinguish features that do not represent human activities from those that do (Borella 2003; Light 2005; Mondini 2002; Steadman et al. 2002; Zohar et al. 2001). Patterned marks may provide evidence of human activity (Guilday et al. 1962); however, as will be reviewed below, other biostratinomic and diagenetic forces also modify faunal remains in a patterned manner (Lyman 1994c). Attribution of many of the marks on specimens caused by butchering, handling, gnawing, and abrasion is possible when they are carefully prepared and examined under high magnification (Fisher 1995; Minniti and Peyronel 2005; Shipman 1981).

Both the biology of animals and the technology of people must be considered before a cause can be attributed to a modification. For example, predation by molluscs that drill holes in the shell of prey species to gain access to their soft body tissue is quite common, particularly in tropical marine waters. Not all molluses drill holes, however. The most common groups of marine snails that drill holes in the shells of their prey are the moonsnails (Naticidae) and the murexes (Muricidae) (Vermeij 1987:167–73). The holes are drilled in the shell near the umbo or occasionally at the edge (Figure 5.2). The holes

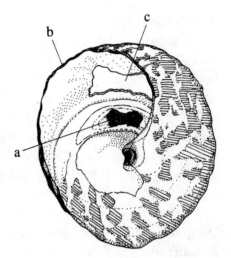

FIGURE 5.3. West Indian topsnail (*Cittarium pica*) showing modification of the shell by the resident land hermit crab (*Coenobita clypeatus*): (a) Thinning of the body whorl and (b) chipping of the aperture lip. Later, a heron (Ardeidae) broke the thinned body whorl to extract the crab (c). The drawing views the topsnail from the anterior end. Drawn by Virginia Carter Steadman.

themselves are round and some have beveled edges. Such holes could easily be mistaken for ones drilled by people to hang the shell as a pendant. Other alterations are made by hermit crabs, which modify mollusc shells to serve as residences to protect their soft bodies (Vermeij 1987:240–55). For example, a land hermit crab (*Coenobita clypeatus*) modified a West Indian topsnail by thinning the wall of the body whorl and chipping the lip of the aperture (Figure 5.3). Superimposed on these modifications is a fracture through the thinned outer whorl made by a heron (Ardeidae) that took the shell by the edge of the aperture and hit it on a rock to expose the hermit crab's soft body (Scudder and Quitmyer 1998).

FIRST-ORDER CHANGES: CULTURAL TRANSFORMATION PROCESSES

Although the concept of taphonomy as defined by Efremov is very important, it needs to be expanded to include the human element to be relevant to archaeological sites. This human element is, of course, one of the central processes that defines archaeological sites. Many of the zooarchaeological lists of taphonomic processes include these in their series of processes, distinguishing between biotic (the living animal) and thanatic (killing through discard) processes, for example. These distinctions are helpful on a conceptual level, but distinguish among behaviors that are neither mutually exclusive nor unidirectional.

Michael B. Schiffer (1976:28–30) offers a useful way to consider human behavior and archaeological site formation by defining two broadly different contexts and four general processes by which items move from one context to the other. The two contexts are the Systemic context (S) and the Archaeological context (A). The Systemic context may be viewed as the living community of humans and other organisms and the

Archaeological context is the one into which these materials are deposited to become the archaeological site. Materials in an archaeological site pass through these two contexts, sometimes more than once, through C-transforms, the laws that govern the regularities in cultural transformation processes. N-transforms are nonhuman processes. Patterned alternations may result from both C-transforms and N-transforms.

Schiffer identifies four broad processes as materials move between Systemic and Archaeological contexts depending on the direction of the transformation. S–A Processes are those associated with cultural deposition by which materials are transformed from the Systemic context to the Archaeological context through discard, abandonment, or loss. A–S Processes are those in which materials are transformed from the Archaeological context back into Systemic context, through the actions of scavengers, looters, erosion, construction activities, and excavation as items return to the cultural context; perhaps to loop back into the Archaeological context at a later time. A–A Processes are those associated with the movement of materials from one context to another within the Archaeological context. This may happen through clearing land, plowing, channelization, or bioturbation as the soil that forms the archaeological site is relocated but the items remain buried. S–S Processes are those in which items remain in the Systemic context because they continue to be valued, perhaps as tools, heirlooms, or sacred objects. Such animal remains may survive many years before being discarded, lost, or destroyed. We can never know the full history of a faunal specimen, but it is safe to assume that very few were used or deposited exactly where they are recovered during subsequent excavation.

Building on the concept that animal remains are mobile within archaeological sites, we may also distinguish between de facto refuse, primary refuse, and secondary refuse. Refuse that is abandoned in an activity area probably because it was dropped or lost is de facto refuse. For example, small items left behind when the floor is swept or the hearth is cleaned is de facto refuse. Primary refuse is trash discarded at the location of use. Animal remains discarded at a kill site would be primary refuse. Secondary refuse is trash deposited at some location other than where it was used. This includes kitchen middens and the fill in most pits.

In addition to location and context, other first-order changes with a cultural origin are modifications made by people during the capture and use of animals and their parts. Modifications are an important source of information about an assemblage's history as well as a reminder of how different the life assemblage is from the sample assemblage. It is likely that a specimen will bear evidence of several modifications. A single specimen may be fragmented during butchering; burned during cooking or tossed into the hot coals of a hearth; gnawed by carnivores and rodents attracted to freshly discarded refuse; trampled after even the most undiscriminating scavenger no longer finds it attractive; exposed to chemical changes from water percolation, penetration of roots, and burrowing animals; and/or broken during excavation. Pathologies also are modifications to the normal appearance of hard tissue, though not the result of

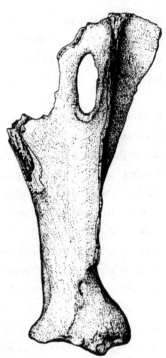

FIGURE 5.4. The right scapula of a red deer (*Cervus elaphus*) with a healed fracture that pierced the blade. This example of a perforation fracture is one of many found in Ertbølle culture sites in Denmark. The hole is partially healed, indicating that the animal survived the first attack (Noe-Nygaard 1975:158). Used with the kind permission of Nanna Noe-Nygaard.

taphonomic processes (see Chapters 6 and 7). To sort these modifications sequentially requires close attention to the details of their characteristics, and is not possible in some cases (e.g., Costamagno et al. 2005). Cultural interpretations of the ritual value of animals or parts of animals alter the archaeological record, resulting in the discard or heirlooming of skeletal remains in ways that differ from the discard of food refuse and alter, or remove, evidence for their use (McNiven and Feldman 2003).

The following five sections follow the progression of modifications that might be expected as the result of killing; skinning and butchering; cooking and preservation; burning; and use as a raw material. Many of the same behaviors produce similar changes and these changes are not unidirectional. For example, many treatments result in fragmented specimens; it is seldom possible to conclude that fragmentation is due exclusively to human or nonhuman agency or exactly when it occurred (Alen and Ervynck 2005; Mateos 2005; Outram 2005). Each of these modifications has serious implications for the formation of the archaeological record.

Killing

Repeated patterns of healed fractures support a reconstruction of a hunting practice. The injuries to the scapula of red deer are interpreted by Noe-Nygaard (1989) as injuries inflicted by Mesolithic hunters (Figure 5.4). Some animals had escaped earlier wounds, as their healed injuries indicate. Holes in the scapula need not be the result of injuries inflicted by hunters, however. Holes in cattle scapulas from Roman sites resemble those reported by Noe-Nygaard, but are believed to be the result of hanging shoulder joints for smoke curing (IJzereef 1981:134–5; Schmid 1972:42).

Evidence for the way an animal was slaughtered may be observed. Slaughter of domestic animals in the Eurasian tradition begins with cutting across the animal's throat (e.g., Cope 2004). The traditional way of slaughtering herd animals in the Andes is by cutting across the back of the neck, severing the spinal cord. Death is swift by both methods. Tracing the antiquity of these two traditions depends on finding specimens with cut marks on the dorsal or ventral sides of the atlas and on the occipital region. Other cuts may be attributed to killing the animal, but could also be the result of dismembering the carcass. Just as holes are bored in shells by predatory molluscs to reach the soft body parts (Figure 5.2), kill holes are made by people with the same intent. The flesh of large conches and whelks (Melonginidae and Buccinidae), such as lightning whelks (*Busycon sinistrum*), is extracted by first cutting across the whorl near the apex to force the animal to release its hold on the shell (Figure 5.5). The cause of death is more obvious for pit vipers recovered from some middens located in southern Florida where skull elements of pit vipers are absent and those of nonpoisonous water snakes (Colubridae) are present. Killing a dangerous pit viper by removing its head is a prudent precaution and an effective way to kill such animals.

Skinning and Butchering

Skinning and subdividing the carcass into primary, secondary, and tertiary units sometimes leaves marks on specimens. Disarticulation marks reflect a number of complex behaviors designed to dismember the carcass (primary butchery) and subdivide it into smaller units of meat (secondary butchery). Such marks indicate cultural definitions of units of meat and may be highly patterned within an assemblage (Guilday et al. 1962). They also indicate the way meat was transported, distributed, and prepared. Dismembering the carcass may also reflect the size of the cooking vessel and the type of food, as well as the status or ethnicity of the producers and consumers. Cutting and breaking can be accomplished with different tools, each of which leaves distinctive marks on the resulting fragments (Fisher 1995; Johnson 1985; Noe-Nygaard 1989; O'Connor 2000b; White and Folkens 2005:60–2). Characteristics of each mark reflect the type of tool used, the angle of the cutting edge, the pressure exerted, whether the meat was cooked or not, and the condition of the specimen (Shipman and Rose 1983a; Walker and Long 1977). Some of these processes may leave no marks (Shipman and Rose 1983a) and others are difficult to attribute to human or nonhuman agents. As a general rule, repetition of marks at the same location and an anatomical reason for the marks are

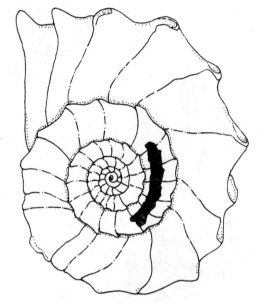

FIGURE 5.5. Kill hole in a lightning whelk (*Busycon sinistrum*) made by human foragers. Drawn by Virginia Carter Steadman.

two broad criteria that indicate the cause of the mark (Guilday et al. 1962; Higgins 1999), but attribution based on such characteristics should be verified by other evidence. The pattern of fragmentation and the types of elements represented may provide additional evidence of butchering decisions.

Skinning marks are often similar to those made by killing the animal and dismembering the carcass. However, the location of skinning marks can be diagnostic. They usually are found on the skull near the snout and around the mandible, at the base of the antlers and ears, and around the metapodia and phalanges. In these locations, the skin is tightly attached to the underlying element and is difficult to remove without damaging the hide or cutting the underlying bone. In most cases, of course, the skin can be removed without marking the underlying elements. In skinning some animals, such as fur-bearing animals, phalanges and metapodia may be left with the skin. This practice may be suspected when the collection is dominated by such elements or where they are missing (Baxter and Hamilton-Dyer 2003).

Noe-Nygaard (1989) defines five distinctive skinning and butchery marks made by humans: blows, chop or hack marks, cut marks, scrape marks, and saw marks. Impact marks caused by blows are produced by hitting elements with a semiblunt, pointed instrument, as during marrow fracturing and tool fabrication (Figure 5.6; Noe-Nygaard 1989). Blows result in minute fragments around the rim of the fracture on the impact side, a radial striation at the impact point, and a flake scar on the opposite side. This might produce spiral fractures with a roughened, stepped surface (Shipman 1981).

Chop or hack marks have a deep, nonsymmetrical "V" shape and lack striations (Figure 5.7; Noe-Nygaard 1989; Shipman 1981). Hacks tend to cluster around the large

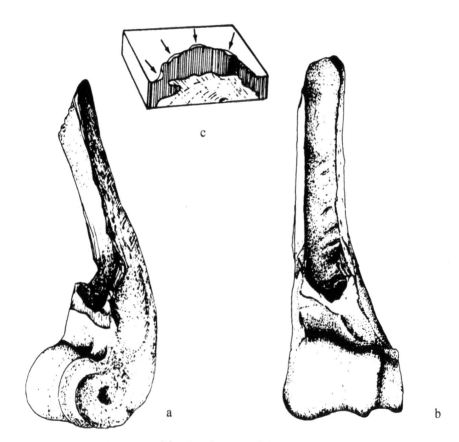

FIGURE 5.6. Bone modifications from Mesolithic sites in Denmark: Impact marks caused from a blow to the distal end of a red deer (*Cervus elaphus*) humerus seen from two perspectives (a and b); diagrammed in (c). Drawings courtesy of Nanna Noe-Nygaard and used with her kind permission (see Noe-Nygaard 1989:479).

joints formed by long bones, but also are found on the shafts. They are evidence that some large instrument, such as a cleaver, was used. Presumably a cleaver, hatchet, or ax would be employed as the carcass was dismembered during primary butchery rather than after the meat was cooked.

Cuts (called slices by Shipman [1981]) and scrapes are characterized by small incisions. They may have a "V" shape that sometimes grades into a "U" shape and the walls of the groove have fine striations parallel to the long axis of the cut (Shipman 1981). Cut marks are probably made by knives during skinning, when disjointing the carcass, or when removing meat before or after cooking (Figure 5.8). Scrape marks are small, shallow cuts running down the surface of the element and often are the result of filleting (Figure 5.9). Cuts and scrapes are more likely to occur during secondary butchery. They are distinguished from trampling abrasion and carnivore gnawing by the context of the specimen, as well as by the location, frequency, and repetitiveness of the mark on the specimen. The outline of the channel and the presence of fine striations found

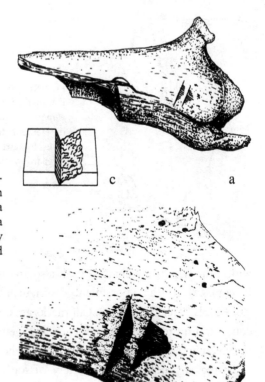

FIGURE 5.7. Bone modifications from Mesolithic sites in Denmark: Chop or hack marks on
the distal end of a red deer (*Cervus elaphus*) tibia
(a). A detail of such marks is seen in (b) and a
diagram is presented in (c). Drawings courtesy
of Nanna Noe-Nygaard and used with her kind
permission (see Noe-Nygaard 1989:478).

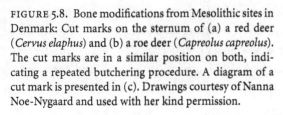

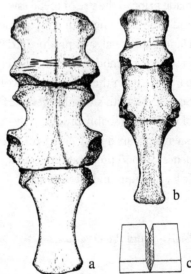

FIGURE 5.8. Bone modifications from Mesolithic sites in
Denmark: Cut marks on the sternum of (a) a red deer
(*Cervus elaphus*) and (b) a roe deer (*Capreolus capreolus*).
The cut marks are in a similar position on both, indi-
cating a repeated butchering procedure. A diagram of a
cut mark is presented in (c). Drawings courtesy of Nanna
Noe-Nygaard and used with her kind permission.

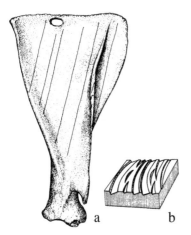

FIGURE 5.9. Bone modifications from Mesolithic sites in Denmark: Scrape marks on the blade of a red deer (*Cervus elaphus*) scapula (a), resulting from the removal of meat from the element; diagrammed in (b). Drawings courtesy of Nanna Noe-Nygaard and used with her kind permission (see Noe-Nygaard 1989:464, 472).

within the wall of the channel itself also are diagnostic (Shipman 1981; Shipman and Rose 1983a). It is also possible to distinguish between cut marks made by metal and stone tools (Greenfield 1999). Cut marks are distinguishable from gnaw marks by their concentration in particular spots on the element. Rodent gnawing produces closely parallel marks that are distinctive from the more randomly aligned cut marks.

Sawing is produced by a variety of tools including metal-toothed instruments (Figure 5.10; Noe-Nygaard 1989; Schmid 1972:42–3, 47–8). Sawing marks on compact bone surfaces appear as serrations that cross each other at acute angles. An element may be repeatedly scored down its length or around the circumference in preparation for breaking it and to separate the ends from the shaft of long bones. Such modifications made prior to the use of metal saws are often called grooved and snapped (Figure 5.10a and 5.10b). Sawing with a metal-toothed tool is indicated by small parallel serrations. Hand-held metal saws produce striations that are more coarse (Figure 5.10d) than those produced by modern bandsaws (Figure 5.10c). Sometimes the striations are missing, particularly on the articular ends of elements with little compact bone. Thin compact bone layers with smooth, even-surfaced modifications that would not be produced by blows were probably produced by saws. These often are called clean-cut or smooth-cut. Sawing occurs during either primary or secondary butchering. Sawing may not be evidence of food preparation, as this method also is used to make tools and ornaments (e.g., Alhaique and Cerilli 2003).

Cooking and Preservation

Cooking removes organic constituents and alters some aspects of isotopic and elemental composition (e.g., Andrus and Crowe 2002). Length of cooking and the size and shape of the element all affect how completely organic material is removed and, consequently,

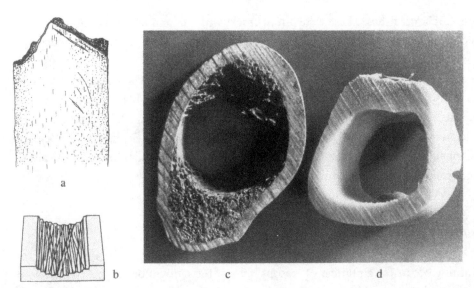

FIGURE 5.10. Bone modification as a result of sawing: (a) Saw mark on a red deer (*Cervus elaphus*) rib from a Mesolithic site in Denmark produced by a cutting implement; (b) diagram of sawing on red deer rib; (c) a specimen sawed with a modern bandsaw; and (d) an archaeological specimen from Hannon's Saloon, Old Sacramento, California modified with a handsaw. Figures 5.10a and 5.10b are used with the kind permission of Nanna Noe-Nygaard (see Noe-Nygaard 1989:478); 5.10c and 5.10d are used with the kind permission of Sherri Gust (see Gust 1983) and the Center for Anthropological Studies, Albuquerque, New Mexico. Photograph by Jeanette Schulz.

how brittle the cooked specimens become (Chaplin 1971). Bone may be reduced so much that it will not survive in an archaeological deposit. Cooked meat is usually boiled, baked, or roasted. When meat is roasted, those parts of the joint most thinly covered by flesh are exposed to the flame and burn.

Meat and fish also are cured by salting, sometimes followed by smoking. Preserved meats and fish may have elements removed, thereby leaving evidence for cured meats only at the site where it was prepared. Shoulders that are smoked after curing sometimes have characteristic holes in the scapula and evidence that the meat-bearing bone was trimmed (Bartosiewicz 1995 b; IJzereef 1981:134–5; O'Connor 2000b:77; Schmid 1972:42).

Many sites yield the remains of very small fishes. These usually are represented by vertebrae, many of which are essentially complete, with accessory spines intact. There are few methods of preparing these fishes without damaging the skeleton. They were probably included in either a soup or a fish sauce that would allow elements to go to the bottom of the container and be discarded after the sauce or soup was consumed (Van Neer and Lentacker 1994), but fish sauce is posited for many other types of deposits as well (Van Neer et al. 2005). Roman cuisine included fish sauces, a concept that originated in the Mediterranean and spread throughout the Roman Empire. They typically were made from small fishes like herrings (Clupeidae) as well as the butchered waste of larger fishes. These were put in crocks with salt and left in the sun for several months; the mixture was stirred frequently. Spices and oil were sometimes added and the liquid sauce, called garum, decanted. The residue, called allec, included the fish elements and was discarded or left at the bottom of the container. These sauces were prized so highly that sometimes even the residue was used to flavor a bland meal (Toussaint-Samat 1992:373–4), and they also were used in medicinal recipes (Prowse et al. 2004). A wide range of other animals were also used, including squids (Cephalopoda), octopus (Cephalopoda), lobsters, sea urchins, cuttlefishes (Cephalopoda), mussels (Bivalvia), and scallops (Pectinidae; Prowse et al. 2004).

Burned Specimens

Burning occurs for a number of reasons. One of these might be that part of the bone is exposed to flames during roasting. Presumably this was a rare event unless people wanted to eat "burned" meat or prepared a burnt offering. Otherwise burning may be the result of an accident or trash disposal. The accident could either happen during cooking or when the structure burned. Burning may also occur if bone is used as fuel (Théry-Parisot 2002; Théry-Parisot et al. 2005).

An excellent demonstration of the changes caused by burning is the comparison between two halves of an element, half of which was burned and half of which was not (Coy 1975). The burned half is 5 percent smaller in diameter than the unburned portion and is black whereas the unburned portion is chalky white. Whenever bone is burned, but particularly under the hottest conditions, it shrinks. Specimens burned under different intensities of heat may have different colors (Lyman 1994c:384–92; Shipman et al. 1984; Stiner et al. 1995). Bone burned under relatively low temperatures is black because the organic components are carbonized. Bones exposed to greater heat, which oxidizes carbon, become brittle and appear white or light blue in color. Complete oxidation of the organic component of bone that contributes to its flexibility leaves only the brittle mineral component. Complete oxidation of the organic component produces calcined bone.

Experiments attempt to correlate color changes with temperatures, but variables, such as size and density of the element and the intensity of the fire, make such correlations difficult. The conditions of the fire, the length of time bone is exposed to heat, and the fire's intensity influence the transformation of specimens. Most normal roasting chars specimens, but they might survive, whereas their disposal in a fire pit might further reduce their organic constituents to the point that they would disappear from the archaeological record. Some of the colors routinely considered evidence of burning may be evidence of other postmortem processes instead (White and Folkens 2005:54).

Bone, Teeth, Horn, and Shell as Raw Materials

Vertebrate and invertebrate hard tissues have qualities that make them valuable as raw materials. Bone is tough and resilient, teeth are hard and sharp, horn sheaths are translucent and pliable, and shell is hard and nacreous. Horn, mollusc shells, and some turtle shells may serve as cups, bowls, or other containers. These innate characteristics of different raw materials make them suitable for particular uses as tools, toys, ornaments, and other uses. Constituents of vertebrate skeletons, such as grease and fat, also have nonfood uses, such as lamp oil, candles, waterproofing, and lubrication. Small fragments of cattle long-bone shafts and the absence of cancellous bone at the ends of the elements in a Roman site led Schmid (1972) to conclude that this deposit was residue from glue production.

Bone's combined characteristics of toughness and resilience make it a useful component of tools that absorb shock, such as antler punches and handles used in flaking flint, or to pierce material, such as bone awls and needles. Certain elements are repeatedly used when long straight tools are needed, such as bone pins made from the metapodia of artiodactyls. These are either sharpened at one end or the metapodia are split lengthwise and then sharpened at the end. The proximal end of the artiodactyl ulna makes an excellent awl or punch. Many of these pins or awls are so modified that little of the original shape remains, thereby making attribution of the taxon and element difficult. However, when a series of specimens in different stages of production are found this procedure can be recreated (Wing 1972). Antler is a particularly popular raw material (e.g., Alhaique and Cerilli 2003).

Many teeth are, by their nature, sharp. They were used by their original owners for cutting flesh and by humans for cutting everything from fibers to wood. Many of the wood carvings in the southeastern United States have fine striations on their surface that correspond to the serrations along the blades of shark's teeth. Shark teeth are found in these contexts, with abraded blades signifying wear from use. Notches cut in the edges of the blades and holes drilled in the roots of teeth indicate hafting to a tool handle (Kozuch 1993).

Teeth with holes drilled through their roots, presumably to hang them as pendants, are common artifacts. Dog canines modified in this way are frequently found. The importance of carnivore teeth is shown by a bone that was carved into the shape of a bear tooth (Schallmayer 1994:80). This artifact even includes a hole drilled through the simulated root.

The keratinized epidermal horn sheath is rarely preserved, yet it has useful qualities. Horn lends itself to production of powder horns, goblets, combs, knife handles, and other decorative objects. Because these are rarely preserved, inferences that such an industry existed are based on finding the bony horn cores, such as those found at

Roman sites (e.g., Schmid 1972:47) and some urban European sites of the Middle Ages (e.g., Bartosiewicz 1995b:74–5; IJzereef 1981:135; Morales 1988; O'Connor 1988:137).

Shell has many qualities that lend it to the manufacture of tools and ornaments, and shells were widely used. Some species of the gastropod *Murex* yield a highly-valued purple dye (Minniti 2005), which distinguishes it from use as food, tools, or ornaments. Marine shells were traded over great distances inland in many areas. For example, marine shells were traded from the Gulf of Mexico and the Gulf of Cortez into the southwestern United States (Brand 1938). Shells were also traded from both the Pacific and the Caribbean to ceremonial centers in central Mexico (Kolb 1987). Shells, particularly thorny-oysters (Spondylidae) with their beautiful colored spines, were traded into the high Andes from the Pacific Ocean. Spondylids were traded as ornaments in the Mediterranean as well (Chilardi et al. 2005; Ruscillo 2005). In all these locations, shells were made into ornaments displaying their attractive colors and shiny surfaces.

Where stone suitable for tool-making was unavailable, shell may have been used instead (e.g., Serrand and Bonnissent 2005). One such area is southern Florida where stone is predominantly soft limestone and many of the marine shells are large and thick. Several members of the whelk or conch family have a thick lip and central column and large body whorl. These were used to make cups, weights possibly used for net sinkers, cutting tools, hammers, celts, and adzes (Marquardt 1992). In some cases, dead and even fossilized, shells were used as tools (Serrand et al. 2005).

FIRST-ORDER CHANGES: ADDITIONAL BIOTIC PROCESSES

When the remains of animals leave the Systemic context and enter the Archaeological context, another group of biotic and abiotic processes continue altering the materials. Biotic processes are associated with plants and animals. The biotic disturbances for which they are responsible change faunal remains from the time refuse is first discarded and continue until the material is excavated. Both plants and animals move soil, a process called bioturbation (e.g., Peacock et al. 2005). Scavengers are attracted to any edible remnants adhering to refuse, whether discarded on the ground or buried. Some loss will occur from such scavengers though the magnitude of these losses varies according to the animals incorporated in the refuse, the condition of the discarded material, and the presence of house and yard animals, particularly dogs, cats (*Felis catus*), pigs, rats, and chickens. These animals not only destroy some materials, they move them from one place to another, and they add additional materials to the site.

Dogs are well-known for chewing bones. Walters (1984, 1985) monitored refuse composed of animal carcasses that he threw out from a camp site in Central Australia. After 6 months he recovered only 2 percent of this refuse. He attributed the loss to scavenging packs of dogs. Others have conducted similar experiments documenting major losses caused by both domestic dogs and pigs or have observed major losses in ethnographic settings (e.g., Munson 2000; Wheeler and Jones 1989:69–74).

To determine whether losses of this magnitude occur where no domestic animals were kept as well as to determine whether differential survival of vertebrate and invertebrate remains can be demonstrated, a similar experiment was designed to compare the numbers of fish and molluscan remains 6 months after they were discarded on an island free of domestic animals (Wing and Quitmyer 1992). The losses were not as great as those reported by Walters (1985). All of the molluscs and about three-quarters of the fishes deposited were subsequently recovered. The loss of fishes depended a great deal on how the carcass was prepared. If it was whole and uncooked it disappeared. However, filleted carcasses and cooked refuse were likely to be undisturbed. Birds and crabs were among the organisms that scavenged the refuse, although a complete inventory of all the animals that visited the site was not made.

Gnawing

An array of animals gnaw bones, including humans. Chief among them are nonhuman primates; rabbits and hares, squirrels (Sciuridae), beavers, mice and rats (Muridae), porcupines (Hystricidae and Erethizontidae), canids, raccoons, weasels (Mustelidae), hyenas (Hyaenidae), felids, and artiodactyls (Haynes 1980; Miller 1975; Noe-Nygaard 1989; Payne and Munson 1985; Selvaggio and Wilder 2001; Sobolik 1993; White and Folkens 2005:55–7; Yohe et al. 1991). Artiodactyls sometimes produce "forked" specimens and antler fragments with zigzagged margins or multiple, parallel, grooved marks on proximal and distal ends (Brothwell 1976; Sutcliffe 1973). Reptiles such as desert tortoises (*Gopherus agassizii*) and varanid lizards (Varanidae) also gnaw bone (Miller 1975; Walters 1985).

Rodents are among the most common animals that gnaw archaeological specimens (Figure 5.11a). Rodents, whose incisors grow throughout life, must use their incisors to keep them aligned. They leave characteristic parallel grooves that are closely spaced and flat bottomed, corresponding to their dentition (Lyman 1994c:figure 6.15). These parallel grooves are often along the specimen's edge but sometimes cover the entire surface.

Carnivores use carnassials, canines, and incisors when they gnaw bone, leaving irregular, broad grooves and pit-like fractures (Figure 5.11b; Lyman 1994c:figures 6.20 and 6.21). The cancellous ends of long bones are the first to be gnawed by most carnivores and this leaves a shaft with ragged ends (Haynes 1980; Klippel et al. 1987; Sutcliffe 1970). They also produce splinters, furrows, punctures, and short nicks (Miller 1975; Haynes 1980; Sutcliffe 1970), although dogs can remove meat without leaving marks (Haynes 1980; Kent 1993). Some chewed bone is swallowed and further modified or destroyed.

Experiments indicate that diaphyses are more likely to survive predation by spotted hyena (*Crocuta crocuta*) than are the distal or proximal ends, perhaps because of their higher bulk density (Lyman 1984; Marean and Spencer 1991; Miller 1975). This pattern of gnawing is the same for dogs and other carnivores. Shipman (1981) found that carnivores leave elongate grooves that vary from "V" to "U" in cross section with the bottom of the groove smooth (Miller 1975). Spiral fractures are occasionally produced by carnivores (Haynes 1980).

Gnawing provides information about several different processes. One of these is evidence for whether humans or nonhumans were the primary agents responsible for the recovered assemblage. Another is evidence for human activities, because specimens that were gnawed by nonhumans probably were not buried promptly after use. Although burial would not preclude gnawing, exposure of specimens for any length of time might result in gnawing. Gnawed materials also indicate the presence of scavengers and predators that may have introduced faunal materials to the site, moved them, or destroyed them. Gnawing results in the loss of material, which can be extensive (Lyon 1970; Walters 1984). As with negative evidence in archaeofaunal samples, in general the absence of gnawing does not mean there were no scavengers at the site (Haynes 1980; Hill 1989).

Digestion

Specimens that travel through a digestive tract are exposed to acids and enzymes during digestion. Such specimens may simply be chunks of cancellous or compact bone with sharp edges between thin, eroded faces; scalloped surfaces; circular holes; and sometimes a high degree of polish (Behrensmeyer 1978; Klippel et al. 1987; Shipman 1981; Sutcliffe 1970). Pitting on the surface of bone indicates where digestion began (Lyman 1994c:figure 6.24). In an experiment to document the impact of digestion on fish elements, Wheeler and Jones (1989:69–75) fed fish to a dog, a pig, and a rat, as well as eating some themselves. They then collected the feces, sieved out the fish remains, and examined them for damage from chewing and digestion. The kinds of damage observed were then compared with those seen in an archaeological deposit of a latrine pit from Coppergate, York. This study of the survival rate of bone first fragmented by chewing and then exposed to digestive juices demonstrates that as much as 80 percent is lost. Despite the serious bias that this causes, some identifiable traces of digested specimens can be recovered with fine-gauge sieves (Payne and Munson 1985), as well as in coprolites.

Another aspect of digestion is troublesome in archaeological contexts: the presence of stomach and intestinal contents that enter the archaeological record as regurgitated pellets, scat, or in discarded butchering waste (e.g., Lyman 1994c: 204–5; Nicholson 2000).

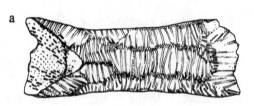

FIGURE 5.11. Gnaw marks made by (a) a rodent
and (b) a dog. Drawn by Virginia Carter Steadman.

The stomach contents of butchered animals may include the remains of other animals
that might plausibly have been eaten by people, such as fishes and small mammals.
Bassett (2004) identifies lines of evidence that might distinguish between assemblages
produced by fishing and those produced by discarded stomach contents. These characteristics include the presence of fishing technology and tools used to make nets, evidence
of mastication and digestion by humans, presence of human paleofeces, soil chemistry,
evidence for seasonal periodicity, the presence of fishes at sites where primary butchery did not take place, the presence of the presumed nonhuman predators where the
possible stomach contents are recovered, and the size, habits, and habitats of both the
fishes and the presumed nonhuman predators. Some of the same remains that might
be of human origin might also be deposited by other organisms, for example, both
cormorants (*Phalacrocorax* spp.) and people eat anchovies along the Peruvian Pacific
coast. The presence of a problematic find, such as small fishes, in human coprolites is
solid evidence that they were eaten by people in at least some cases (e.g., Rhode 2003).

Commensal Animals

Some of the animals found in archaeological assemblages are commensal animals that
literally "eat at the same table" as humans. Some commensal animals are scavengers and
others are symbionts. Some animals are attracted to the built environment because it

offers easy food, safer hiding or nesting places, a more open canopy, or fewer competitors (O'Connor 2000a). Commensals can be pests that cause a great deal of damage to crops and stored goods. If they have no economic importance, commensals may live in quiet spots away from the major activity areas. They and/or their food may come to a refuse heap attracted to the moist, rich, organic deposits, die in the refuse, and their bodies become incorporated in the faunal assemblage (Alhaique 2003; Nogueira de Queiroz 2004; Sampson 2000). Animal remains may also enter the archaeological record as regurgitated pellets or droppings from other animals (Nicholson 2000; Saavedra and Simonetti 1998; Weissbrod et al. 2005). Scavengers are typically small rodents, lizards, toads, and land snails, but they may include mammals, birds, and reptiles. As with most site-formation processes, multiple activities may produce similar results, and it is difficult to distinguish among the processes and the outcomes. They may actually not be separate activities.

Symbiotic commensals may be encrusting organisms such as barnacles and bryozoans living on and with shellfish, sea turtles, and whales (e.g., Piana 2005). These symbionts do not enter the midden under their own power, but come to the site attached to other organisms. Some species of barnacles attach to specific marine animals, such as sea turtles or whales, and when these barnacles are found in an assemblage they provide indirect evidence for the presence of their host animals.

As the culinary behavior of the past is not well-known, decisions about what is edible must be made cautiously. To decide what was commensal and what was consumed in the past is often difficult because size and flavor are not good criteria. Some organisms that might be commensal, such as grubs, anchovies, escargots, limpets, goose barnacles, dogs, or agoutis (*Dasyprocta leporina*), also may have been eaten by people (e.g., Murphy 2001). Squirrels (Sciuridae) and guinea pigs are features of some diets, but not of others (e.g., deFrance 2006). Small animals played an important role in the diet of prehispanic farmers in the southwestern United States (Szuter 1994). Several characteristics taken together help distinguish between commensals and discarded food refuse. Many commensals are small; some land snails are less than 5 mm long. Commensals, as well as intentionally-buried animals, may be characterized by skeletal completeness. Some small vertebrates are almost complete or even mummified. Specimens that are unmodified by burning or cutting may be the remains of commensal animals (Simonetti and Cornejo 1991).

Trampling

Damage from trampling is important to recognize because it reflects the depositional history of the site and because the modifications it leaves may be confused with butchering marks and intentional fragmentation. Trampling may be due to human or to animal traffic. Trampling might be typical of a house floor, a barnyard, or a stable. Traffic may be light, hardly disturbing a carcass, and leaving few if any marks on surviving elements. Under heavy traffic, a carcass may be widely dispersed and the individual specimens scratched and broken.

Trampling moves specimens from their depositional context, fragments them, and produces marks on the surviving specimens (Shipman and Rose 1983b). Trampling may produce a characteristic fragmentation pattern such as "wishbone" breaks at the mandibular symphysis and "snaps" of scapula and pelvis (Gifford 1981; Noe-Nygaard 1989), as well as grooves and scratches (Behrensmeyer et al. 1986). Marks produced by trampling usually are randomly oriented, relatively shallow scratches (Fiorillo 1989). When the soil matrix is coarse and has large sand grains, such scratches are easily visible without magnification. However, if the matrix is soft material, such as dried leaves and pine needles, the specimen's surface may be so polished that it is similar in appearance to worked bone. Attributing such abrasions to trampling may be incorrect because similar marks also are caused by sedimentary particles, aeolian processes, or aquatic transport (Gifford 1981; Shipman and Rose 1983a). Abrasions may remove diagnostic features of other marks (Shipman 1981; Shipman and Rose 1983a, 1983b). Observations of the natural disintegration of carcasses track some of these changes (Behrensmeyer and Hill 1980).

Other Processes

Long after the deposit has lost any attraction to scavengers, plants and other animals continue to modify the deposit. Plant roots sometimes leave characteristic dendritic patterns or lightly etched grooves on specimens (Lyman 1994c:376; White and Folkens 2005:59). Burrowing animals, such as earthworms, snails, and pocket gophers, mix the sediments, disturbing the stratigraphic position of materials. Such bioturbation may significantly alter the association of materials within a deposit. Microorganisms, such as bacteria and fungi, also degrade the deposit (Jans et al. 2004; O'Connor 2000b:24; Smith et al. 2005).

FIRST-ORDER CHANGES: ABIOTIC PROCESSES

Abiotic processes are associated with inanimate forces such as wind, rain, floods, earthquakes, and other phenomena. Organic material, whether it is wood, bone, or shell, deteriorates with exposure to wind, water, and sun, as well as to alternate freezing/thawing or wet/dry conditions. Wind blowing across organic material will dry it and ultimately break it down by scouring the surface with windblown sediments. Flowing water moves organic materials, realigns them, and abrades them both with the force of the water and with water-borne sediments. Materials also are buried by sediments blown or washed into the deposit, an important aspect of preservation. Organic materials preserve best when depositional conditions are stable.

Climate, Temperature, and Moisture

Temperature and moisture are climatic conditions that influence preservation. Organic materials protected from harsh weather conditions are more likely to survive than are materials exposed to alternate cycles of drying and wetting or freezing and thawing. Changes in depositional environment promote shrinkage and expansion of organic material, causing it to lose integrity. This provides access to the interior of the tissue for microorganisms and enhances decomposition. The amount of rainfall also encourages or discourages microorganisms responsible for decomposition. Limited water at arid sites retards microbial activity. Materials deposited in calm waters or bogs, in permanently dry deserts, caves, or crypts, or ones immediately covered by soil escape some of the damage of exposure to fluctuating climatic elements. In permanently dry or frozen conditions, or where temperatures are very high or very cold, such as high altitude caves, desert sites, and glaciers, decomposing organisms also are discouraged.

Aerobic and Anaerobic Environments

The amount of oxygen in the deposit is also important. Many decomposing organisms require oxygen to sustain them. Such aerobic organisms, including bacteria, are often responsible for rapid decomposition. Anaerobic decomposers operate in environments with little oxygen. They are more lethargic and perform the work of decomposition very slowly. Preservation of organic tissue is particularly good in permanently wet conditions because these are anaerobic contexts where the decomposers are slow. This is one reason why bogs, wells, latrines, and similar damp conditions yield such surprisingly rich organic deposits. However, such contexts must remain wet. If the deposit dries out, the tissue will crack as it dries, and aerobic decomposers will have access to these organic contents.

Soil pH

The soil constituents themselves alter skeletal tissue. Fluctuations in the water table and dissolved minerals in the soil replace organic constituents of bone with minerals. A characteristic of soil critical for preservation is its acidity or alkalinity, as measured by pH. The ideal pH for the preservation of the bone mineral hydroxyapatite is 7.8–7.9. Under alkaline conditions, pH values higher than 8, bone mineral dissolves at an increased rate as the alkalinity rises (Linse 1992). At the other end of the pH scale, increasingly greater bone destruction takes place for every degree below neutral (Gordon and Buikstra 1981). Hydrogen ions, from organic acids such as humic and fulvic acid from plant decay in the soil, combine with the minerals in bone and shell. This puts them in solution, thereby leaching these tissues of their critical mineral constituents. The calcium ions that are put into solution by this process may be reprecipitated as bone salts lower in the soil column (Scudder 1993; Scudder et al. 1996). Animal tissues are destroyed differentially. The least-calcified elements, such as those of infant and juvenile animals, are the first to go into solution. The enamel crowns of adult teeth are the most resistant.

Mollusc shell forming the matrix of a shell midden deposit neutralizes the relatively small amount of hydrogen ions in soil. pH from sixty different points in an Archaic shell mound in southwestern Florida ranges from 6.7–8.8. The median value of this range is a pH of 7.8, which is ideal for bone preservation (Scudder 1993). The shell matrix of at least some shell mounds also protects small delicate bones by sheltering them under a shell "umbrella" that sheds water (Scudder et al. 1993). In this way, shell buffers the pH of the deposit and protects vertebrate remains from mechanical damage, thereby providing better conditions for bone survival. Such data are necessary for all archaeological sites and their surroundings to evaluate the effect of soil pH on deposited remains. Additional systematic studies of soil pH and other characteristics need to be conducted.

Fragmentation

Fragmentation occurs at all stages from the initial procurement and use, throughout deposition, and during excavation and study. The type of fracture and the extent of breakage offer important clues about the history of the specimen (Lyman 1994c). It is necessary to distinguish between modifications that occurred during recent excavation or transport and those caused earlier (Outram 2005). Light-colored breaks or scars that are clearly a different color from the rest of the specimen should be carefully examined as they may be evidence of excavation or other recent damage. Breaks or scars that are the same color as the rest of the specimen are more likely to have occurred either before or during deposition. As we have discussed in this chapter, fragmentation results from butchering, food preparation, and trampling. Weathering also results in breakage. Because widely different activities can result in fragmentation, the context of the fragmented specimens and the elements and species represented by them (if that can be determined) must be carefully evaluated in determining the cause(s) of the breakage.

Sometimes the sequence of modifications also may indicate which are recent and which are not (Shipman and Rose 1983b).

Weathering and Other Processes

Weathering is one of several natural processes by which nutrients are recycled. The severity of the weathering conditions, the length of the exposure to them, and the size and density of the element influence the speed of this process. Experiments and observations establish a scale of degrees of weathering and history of exposure.

A strong environmental force is the flow of water. Through time, streams may cut at the edges of archaeological sites, or flood them entirely. Tides during high or rising water levels may undercut a site and wash remains down the beach slope. Laboratory experiments designed to replicate water flow over skeletal remains map changes in the orientation of elements. When this information is applied to the orientation of skeletal elements at archaeological sites subject to flooding, it provides clues to such phases in the history of the site.

Weathering often combines with root-etching, microbial action, and insects to alter the deposit. Surviving specimens showing the effect of such forces may help distinguish between assemblages produced by humans and nonhumans (Behrensmeyer 1978; Gifford 1980, 1981). Weathering reflects climatic variables in specific habitats, body size, and age (Behrensmeyer 1978). Weathered specimens are usually demineralized, with a mosaic pattern of cracked and flaking compact bone (Miller 1975; Tappen 1969, 1976; Tappen and Peske 1970). Behrensmeyer (1978) proposes six weathering stages. Bones in each stage, one through five, show progressively greater damage; the last of these stages may not survive in many archaeological settings (Miller 1975). Small, compact elements, such as phalanges, carpals, and tarsals, weather more slowly than do other elements (Behrensmeyer et al. 1979). Some weathered specimens bear a dendritic pattern of shallow grooves similar to that produced by roots or fungi (Lyman 1994c:375–7; Shipman 1981).

Weathering and other taphonomic processes may also produce longitudinal fractures extending from the proximal end of the element to the distal one. These may bend around the shaft and be confused with fractures made by humans to extract marrow that often are referred to as "spiral fractures" (Lyman 1994c:318). Shipman (1981) suggests that Type I spiral fractures have fracture planes between adjacent bundles of collagen fibers and are produced by torque in the direction of the predominant collagen fibers or by breaking the bonds between adjacent bundles of fibers. Type II fractures run perpendicular to the predominant direction of the collagen fibers and would require considerable torsional stress to produce. Type II fractures are unlikely to be caused by weathering and trampling (Shipman 1981).

Conditions Promoting Preservation

Organic materials protected from biotic and abiotic processes tend to preserve best. Material deposited under still water, in the permanently dry conditions of a desert, cave, or crypt, or immediately covered by soil escapes some of the damage of first-order changes. Organic remains excavated from permanently wet sites, such as the Swiss lake dwellings and the Somerset Levels in England, as well as at Ozette Village and Hoko River in coastal Washington, are astoundingly well-preserved (Purdy 1988; Schibler 2004). The wood, seed, and plant fiber preservation in water-saturated sites paradoxically can only be equaled at desiccated sites in deserts or caves. What these two apparently opposite conditions share is that damage from trampling tends to be low, bacterial activity is low, and environmental conditions are relatively stable. The location of the site may be a guide to the destructive processes that might be expected. For example, a deposit in the lowland tropics should not experience freezing and thawing cycles, but it may be subjected to alternating wet and dry periods and leaching from water percolating through the sediments. Even under these conditions, the hardest, densest bones, teeth, and shell are more likely to survive. These are less damaged by chemical disturbance and tend to be more able to resist mechanical fracturing and fragmentation.

TAPHONOMIC RESEARCH

Our understanding of conditions in the past is guided by what we know about the present. This is based on the theory of uniformitarianism. Experiments and observations provide insights into disposal patterns and suggest methods by which the degree of disturbance of a deposit and the amount of bias expected in the faunal sample can be assessed. They also permit us to assess factors that might impinge on comparisons of modern phenomena and archaeological ones, as might be done to reconstruct environments (e.g., Kenward 2006). Through such observations, we know that several different taphonomic processes act on archaeological material, superimposing multiple patterns of modifications, loss, and additions on the deposit. Interpretation of archaeological remains based on modern observations must be tempered by the possibility that some characteristics of animal remains and of human behavior in the past do not have modern analogues (Symmons 2004; Weinstock 2002).

Actualistic Studies

Modern observations and experiments of taphonomic processes and applied by analogy to conditions in the past are called actualistic or ecological studies. Taphonomic processes not only effect the types of species recovered and the types of elements represented but also have an impact on constituents, such as DNA, isotopes, and trace minerals, that are subject to diagenetic changes. Interpreting the results from studies of bone and shell constituents requires knowing the animal's diet and the region in which it lived, as well as changes that occur to tissues during burial. Experimental replication of taphonomic processes and observations of natural events demonstrate what type of alteration might be expected and which agent or process might be responsible. These experiments can be repeated with modified parameters.

Taphonomic research is designed to understand the consequences of first-order changes that destroy, augment, or modify a deposit. Many of these experiments are simulations designed to replicate different taphonomic conditions that alter the constituents and morphology of bone and shell and change the species composition of a faunal assemblage. Specimens burned at various temperatures, gnawed by rodents or carnivores, passed through a digestive tract, exposed to alternate freezing and thawing, and trampled bear diagnostic scars reflecting these experiences (Noe-Nygaard 1989). Recognizing the causal agents of such modifications allows reconstruction of some of the environmental forces that shape the species composition of the archaeofaunal samples, the elements represented, and the condition of the specimens.

Other investigations rely on observations of how animal carcasses decompose and disassemble, either before burial or afterward (Wijngaarden-Bakker 2000). Experimental exposure of carcasses and their skeletal components to different types of damage and comparison of the surviving debris with archaeological specimens allows interpretations of the burial history of the collection. The fortuitous death of an animal provides the opportunity to observe and document the position of the limbs; the deterioration of soft tissue and resulting dispersal of elements; the appearance of materials fragmented or gnawed by scavengers, trampled, or weathered; and the successive stages in the natural process of burial. For example, Haynes (1988a, 1988b) conducted long-term observations of skeletal changes, element loss, and dispersal of large animal carcasses in North America and Africa. Such observations help us to more accurately interpret environmental and human alterations of archaeological specimens. Other studies examine modern living and death assemblages for information about age and sex composition of herds and other biological parameters (e.g., Lubinski and O'Brien 2001; Marelli and Arnold 2001; Munson and Garniewicz 2003; Nicholson 2000; O'Connell et al. 2001; Outram 2001).

Ethnoarchaeology

Archaeological materials are largely human refuse, and, therefore, the ways animals and their carcasses are obtained, used, and discarded also contribute to the character of the deposit. Ethnographic information about animal procurement, husbandry strategies, food handling, storage, and refuse disposal obtained through ethnographic observation is as important as data about the many environmental forces that shape a deposit (e.g., Hayden 2001; Forbes 2002; Kent 1989; Lupo and O'Connell 2002; Moreno-García 2004; Mutundu 2005; O'Day 2004; Politis and Saunders 2002; Ryan 2005; Tveskov and Erlandson 2003). Such studies are sometimes referred to as ethnoarchaeology. Ethnographic observations form a link between contemporary material cultures and archaeological materials. Exploring the relationship between material culture and human behavior in modern societies strives to develop a theory of the relationships between people and the materials recovered from archaeological sites. Ethnographic observations and anatomical studies can augment reconstructions based on archaeological remains alone, although we must remember that peoples living today are not directly analogous to those members of our family who lived in the past.

Ethnographic information yields important details of human relationships with animals including how people butcher carcasses; the marks left by this process; how they open molluscs; which tools they use and when; how they subdivide catches from cooperative fishing or carcasses of large animals; how food is traditionally cooked; and how refuse is discarded. Ethnographic observations also provide information about herd management practices, food prohibitions, avoidances, and ritual associations. The Garbage Project in Tucson, Arizona, was an innovative ethnographic project that tested perceptions of the foods families consume and discard by studying trash in North American city dumps (Rathje 1979). The modifications these choices make to the foods originally purchased provide a better understanding of the degree to which remains excavated from archaeological sites are altered by similar decisions. Information about animal use is also obtained from such sources as probate inventories, travel accounts, bills of lading, tax and sales records, frescos, letters, figurines, and ceramic motifs (e.g., Henrikson 2004). Such evidence may not be accurate, and insights need to be verified in other sources (e.g., Piana 2005).

Isaac (1978:100) argues that "somewhere along the line in the evolution of human behavior two patterns became established: food-sharing and a division of labor." Food sharing is an almost universal human trait (Bicchieri 1972; Dwyer and Minnegal 1991; Marks 1976; Nietschmann 1973). Although sharing food beyond the nuclear family is widely practiced, the form that this takes varies among cultures. One extreme is reported among the Guayaki of Paraguay who have formalized distribution based on the rule that hunters may not consume the meat of game they have taken (Clastres 1972). More commonly, food is shared through kinship lines and to satisfy other social obligations (Nietschmann 1973). In many cases, when groups hunt or fish, the catch is divided among the participants, and the owner of the equipment, such as the boat or nets, is given an extra portion (O'Day 2004; Wing 1980). This bestows an economic advantage on those who provide equipment. Food sharing may also lessen the selective pressure on unsuccessful hunters and fishermen and provide an economic advantage to group living (Hames 1983:401; Hill and Hawkes 1983:187).

SECOND-ORDER CHANGES

One might think that once a specimen has survived the gauntlet of first-order changes, excavation and study would pose little danger. This is not the case. Second-order changes are those that occur during the recovery and identification stages of archaeological research. Although students often have difficulty perceiving excavation and study as sources of bias, second-order changes, in fact, play an important role in interpretations of the archaeological record because they compromise the integrity of the faunal assemblage. All archaeological excavation projects should include a zooarchaeologist, as well as an archaeobotanist and soils scientist, if recovery from the site is to be maximized. Advice from people trained in the recovery and study of geological and biological remains allows for better understanding of the excavation strategies by the entire archaeological team and permits assistance by the specialists on recovery methods during the field season.

Second-order changes include choices made about where to excavate, how to recover samples, and the degree of detail achieved during identification, analysis, and publication. Sampling the archaeological site and resulting materials is almost always required by practical considerations of time and resources (O'Connor 2000b:28–31). However, archaeological deposits are not uniformly distributed across a site, so the choice of where to excavate has an impact on the types of activities and associated faunal remains available for study. The size of the sample must be large enough to accurately reflect the types of animal remains in the deposit from which the sample was taken. The method of recovery has profound consequences. The skill of the person sorting materials prior to transferring them to the zooarchaeologist is a major source of bias, as is the level and thoroughness of identification. Identification of each class of animal must be integrated to understand as many aspects of the former environmental setting, economy, and social role of animals as the faunal assemblage allows. Choices regarding the information to include in a publication or report and arrangements for curation of the samples and data also are second-order changes (see Appendix 3). These postexcavation changes are the subjects of Chapters 6 and 7.

Excavation Location

Preventable losses of faunal data occur during several stages in an archaeological project, starting with the placement of the excavation units. Sample context should be selected with care because distinct refuse patterns are associated with different activity areas (Meadow 1978b; Stallibrass 2000; Uerpmann 1973). The types of deposits also reflect different interactions with animals, which would not be the same at kill and residential sites or for burials.

It is important to be sure that materials from appropriate contexts are studied. Comparison of funerary offerings with garbage is not appropriate unless the study is designed to compare animals in ritual settings with those from secular ones (Styles and Purdue 1991). If the research question pertains to subsistence, midden samples will provide more information about routine use of animals than will samples from temple mounds or burials. It is likely that the behaviors resulting in the disposal of materials in wells, hearths, houses, and middens compared to general sheet disposal are different (Armitage and West 1985; Reitz 1994a). The types of animal-related activities represented by materials from a house floor could also be expected to be different from those represented by discarded material in a footing trench for a large public building or along a river bank. Animal remains found in burials and storage pits probably provide only limited information about the full seasonal round and procurement technologies. Differences in behaviors associated with activity areas have an impact on all aspects of a zooarchaeological study.

This concern extends to decisions about whether only faunal materials from features, storage pits, hearths, and house floors are studied or if the sheet refuse also will be examined. The activities that produce features, and the types of animal remains contained in them, are quite different from those associated with general sheet refuse. The materials in features often represent very discrete periods of time and may be suitable for studying the specific seasonal activity or a ritual activity associated with the deposit. However, features may not be the best contexts to examine if the research questions are related to routine butchering habits, disposal activities, or annual cycles. Sometimes only faunal remains from column samples and features are recovered, and this also will influence the results of the study. Another aspect of excavation location is the proximity of excavation units to each other. Blocks of contiguous units generally sample discrete activity areas, but units scattered widely over the site sample a variety of activities. Examination of a single sample cannot hope to reveal the full range of activities at the site.

An inappropriate match between excavation location and research questions is a controllable bias. When at all possible, materials from all types of activity areas should be examined. Only in this way will it be possible to determine which deposits represent routine, daily interactions with animals and which deposits represent unusual events such as ritual display.

Screen Size

We have known for more than 50 years that inadequate screening or sieving of the deposit and inexplicable decisions about what to keep result in major losses. The appropriate size of the screen gauge that should be used has been exhaustively discussed (e.g., Emery 2004b; Payne 1972b, 1975, 1992). Animal remains in many sites are very small and fragile, a characteristic that dictates the recovery strategy. Small organisms yield important information about site-formation processes, subsistence decisions, technology, and paleoecological settings. Although some faunal assemblages do not have small specimens, each assemblage should be tested during the preliminary field work to determine the appropriate recovery technique. Sieving with a fine-gauge screen requires extra time and effort but recovers a more complete sample of the nonrenewable archaeological context that is destroyed by excavation.

Quantitative studies require a sampling approach that enables each of the species used at a site to have an equal opportunity to be recovered, with no skewing that will increase one taxonomic unit over another (Shaffer and Sanchez 1994). One might envision that there are some animals (or elements) that 6-mm (1/4-inch) meshed screens are likely to recover in large numbers; we might think of these as 6-mm animals. There is another group of animals (or elements) that are likely to pass through a 6-mm mesh but will be caught in the 3-mm (1/8-inch) mesh, we might think of these as 3-mm animals. It is important to ensure that both 6-mm animals and 3-mm animals have an equal opportunity to be represented in the samples studied if any quantification is anticipated.

Consistency and uniformity in an informed recovery strategy is the key. Under no circumstances should all of the 6-mm animal remains recovered and a fraction of the 3-mm animals be combined in a study. In a case where subsampling is required and 20 percent of the 6-mm fraction and 1 percent of the 3-mm fraction are selected for study, it is clear that the animals represented in the 6-mm fraction will have a greater opportunity to influence the studied assemblage and resulting interpretation. However, it would be false to argue that 80 percent of the subsistence effort was directed toward large animals characteristic of 6-mm fractions and very little effort directed towards smaller animals characteristic of fine-screen fractions unless both groups of animals had an equal opportunity to be represented in the list of taxa being considered. In fact, the two fractions in this example should not be combined at all because of sampling bias.

"Fine gauge" is a subjective term; to some people it means 6-mm but, for optimal recovery at many sites, flotation is necessary. The impact of flotation on interpretations of fishing strategies is demonstrated by plotting the size of fish vertebrae recovered from the Kings Bay site in southeastern Georgia in the United States (Figure 5.12). Fishes in this coastal collection are generally small, vertebral widths averaging 2.5 mm; very few fish vertebrae were captured in the 6.35-mm mesh. The Kings Bay data are interesting not only for the evidence they provide that very small fishes were exploited at this site but also because they indicate that fine-mesh netting or scoops were used to capture them. Some of these fishes may be juvenile individuals caught in their nursery grounds (Russo 1991b). The recovery of fishes in this size range is the rule rather than the exception when recovery strategies include a fine-gauge screen or flotation.

Other animals of economic importance or environmental significance can only be recovered with fine-gauge screens. Among these are shrimps, identified thus far by

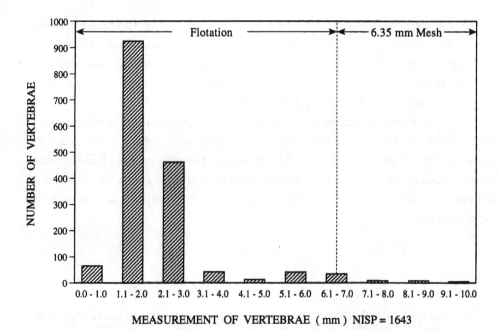

FIGURE 5.12. The size distribution of fish vertebral centra from the Kings Bay site on the Atlantic coast of Georgia, United States. This illustration shows those vertebrae that would be recovered with a 6.35-mm-screen gauge. NISP refers to the number of identified specimens used to compose this figure. Used with the kind permission of Irvy R. Quitmyer.

their mandibles (Figure 3.9). Shrimps are typically caught with fine-mesh nets, so their identification signals both a resource and a former technology (Quitmyer 1985). The impressed odostome (*Boonia impressa*) is a small gastropod that is an ectoparasite of oysters and lives for slightly over 1 year. The size of the odostomes associated with the host can be used as an indicator of the season when oysters were harvested. However, to establish the season of oyster harvest, the full size-range of this ectoparasite must be recovered, and this can only be done with consistent use of fine-gauge recovery methods (Russo 1991a). Fine-screening is also important to the recovery of small animals that might otherwise be missed, or are unexpected, in burial assemblages and other ritual contexts (e.g., Weissbrod and Bar-Oz 2004). Small organisms, such as terrestrial snails, insects, and parasites, may require even finer techniques, such as soil samples, to be recovered (e.g., Bathurst 2005).

Although the appropriate size of the screen gauge that should be used has been exhaustively discussed for many decades, many archaeologists appear not to understand the importance of this as a source of bias. It is true that some faunal assemblages do not have small specimens, but their absence should not be presumed. Sieving with a fine-gauge screen requires extra time and money, but the screen recovers a more complete sample of the nonrenewable archaeological deposit and is critical to adequately testing many biological and anthropological hypotheses. Many examples of this relationship could be offered. To cite one example, prey-choice models argue that humans rank large-bodied animals as high-ranked resources and preferentially target such animals, perhaps shifting to lower-ranked, smaller-bodied animals as populations of large-bodied animals decline. However, if the subsistence strategy targets large numbers of small-bodied organisms, such as small schooling fishes collected with a net, the return rate of these small-bodied animals could be much higher and substantially alter the interpretation (e.g., Butler and Campbell 2004). Such an alternative cannot be assessed unless the recovery method employed in the field was designed to recover small fishes or other small-bodied organisms. Much of the discussion pertaining to the use of large-bodied prey in optimal foraging theory is likely incorrect if it is based on samples that were not fine-screened.

Skimming

Selective recovery of only those animals that somehow strike the archaeologist's fancy results in a biased sample that does not reflect the range and relative abundance of species in the faunal assemblage. In the early days of faunal studies, samples were made with the intent of obtaining at least one representative of each species, usually mammalian, pertinent to the study. These were qualitative collections; there was no concern for relative frequencies or more-sophisticated quantification approaches (Simpson et al. 1960:109). Sometimes this was done to reduce transport or identification costs. This approach still exists among archaeologists who select what they think is a "representative sample" from their screen or from the soil and ask the zooarchaeologist to examine the material. They may ask the analyst to "look over" their unscreened fraction or they may select only whole elements to send for study. The result of such "skimming" (Simpson et al. 1960:109) cannot be accommodated in a quantified study (Chaplin 1965, 1971:24; Lawrence 1973; Parmalee 1985; Reed 1963; Schmid 1972:18; Shotwell 1955; Uerpmann 1973).

   Excavation of a shell mound can result in samples that are huge and costly to transport, examine, and store. Some contexts from such sites are more appropriate for faunal studies than others and this governs the priorities that are set. The appropriate way to prioritize field samples is to consider the relevance each has to the research design rather than to randomly discard specimens the field crew thinks are unidentifiable or simply does not recognize. All faunal specimens from high-priority faunal contexts should be saved. Sometimes the research schedule or budget do not permit studying all of the materials in high-priority contexts immediately. In such cases, the ideal must yield to the practical. The compromise is to subsample in the laboratory rather than discard in the field. Subsampling should be done with the overall research objectives in mind and the subsample must be large enough to be representative of the sample as a whole. The method for subsampling must be agreed on by the archaeologist and the zooarchaeologist. All specimens contained in high-priority samples, not just a few interesting ones, should be studied and curated. The unstudied portion should be saved for future research.

Sample Size

Sample or subsample size is another important factor in obtaining a representative faunal assemblage (see pages 113–114 and Figure 4.6). Chance alone will play a larger part in the composition of the faunal assemblage if a sample is too small. Archaeological deposits are finite and some are too small to provide an adequate sample. Others, where preservation is poor, also do not yield sufficiently large samples, and they may be biased toward remains that are most resistant to destruction. In comparisons between sites or between parts of a site, the sample sizes in both components should be adequate and comparable. It should be noted that the species richness in an archaeological sample does not necessarily reflect the richness or diversity in the region but only those animals that were used by the occupants of the site or were incidentally incorporated in the site and whose remains were preserved, recovered, and identified. In those collections where few species are represented, richness may not adequately indicate an adequate sample and another measure of adequacy must be devised, perhaps representation of all skeletal elements of the few species that are present or a full spectrum of age classes. Further confirmation of the adequacy of a sample is obtained by ensuring that sample size and statistical tests based on the sample are independent (Grayson 1981).

DOCUMENTING THE MAGNITUDE OF CHANGE

Some bias exists in every faunal sample excavated from an archaeological site. Judging the magnitude and nature of such biases is important for the study of these samples. Clearly, if small animals are missing from the collection, an appropriate screen may not have been used in the field to recover the remains. Most other biases accumulate throughout the history of the deposit. However, the zooarchaeologist can sometimes assess the magnitude of the disturbance to the deposit. Those deposits that show little evidence of postdepositional disturbance may be closer in composition to the refuse originally deposited at the site.

The presence and condition of commensal animals is one way to assess the degree to which the deposit may have altered over time. Commensal animals are attracted to human refuse by the food and moisture it offers. Among these are land snails. The presence and abundance of a land snail, such as the liptooth (*Polygyra* spp.), in a deposit may be a measure of how long refuse was exposed for their dining pleasure. When they are abundant in a deposit, it is likely that refuse was exposed for long enough for land snails to come to the deposit and die there; suggesting that other postdepositional additions may also be present. The house mouse (*Mus musculus*) is another common commensal animal. Mice may become part of the archaeological deposit after becoming trapped in a refuse pit from which they could not escape. Other commensals, such as small snakes and toads, add to the refuse by also falling into such pits and dying there. When the remains of such animals are absent from a deposit this may indicate that the pit was filled rapidly, covering and protecting the refuse from disturbance and destruction by exposure to environmental forces (Armitage and West 1985; Reitz 1994a).

Pairing the two shells of a bivalve, such as a clam, and documenting the distance between all pairs of valves can be a measure of the disturbance of a shell midden deposit (Koike 1979). Valve pairing is possible with the clam (*Meretrix lusoria*) because the hinge of each individual is distinctive and only the two valves of the same individual will close. Another trait that allows pairing is the shell pattern, which is distinctive for each individual. Relying on these characteristics, Koike (1979) was able to match pairs and measure the distance the valves of each pair were from each other in the site. If the deposit was exposed to little disturbance, one would expect pairs of valves to lie close together as they were dropped after the body of the clam was extracted.

CONCLUSIONS

Extensive alterations of the living community occur as it transitions into the study assemblage, but these should not discourage students from pursuing zooarchaeological studies. The faunal assemblage is the only hard evidence for animals that were used in the past. Although this record of animal use was doubtlessly altered in many ways, it remains possible to learn much about human interaction with the environment. That the animals recovered were not the only animals used at the site should be acknowledged and the degree to which the recovered remains accurately reflect the assemblage of animals originally used by people or present at the site should be considered. The first step toward such a consideration is gathering primary data (Chapter 6). The importance of first- and second-order changes is further examined as secondary data are derived (Chapter 7) and interpreted (Chapters 8, 9, and 10).

6

Gathering Primary Data

INTRODUCTION

Archaeofaunal specimens offer unique opportunities for biological and anthropological inquiry, providing insights into the relationship between humans and their environments obtainable in no other way. However, first- and second-order changes alter the image of former lives available from faunal remains. Because some second-order changes develop during the process of gathering and analyzing data, thoughtful application of appropriate methods is important. A zooarchaeological study consists of three parts: (1) identification, (2) analysis, and (3) interpretation. Some of the methods used for identification are introduced in this chapter and are followed by analysis (Chapter 7), and interpretation (Chapters 8, 9, and 10). Important aspects of collection management, publication, and curation follow these chapters (see Appendix 3).

Clason's (1972) definitions of primary and secondary data distinguish between identification and analysis. The identification stage can be equated with collecting primary data and the analytical stage with deriving secondary data. Primary data are observations that can be replicated by subsequent investigators, such as element representation and taxonomic identification (e.g., Daly 1969; Lawrence 1973; Schmid 1972). Secondary data include age classes, sex ratios, relative frequencies of taxa, butchering patterns, dietary contributions, and procurement strategies. They are derived from primary data by means of indices and other quantification techniques. Primary data may be viewed as more descriptive and objective than secondary data and subject to less interpretive latitude. Using Lyman's (1994a) terminology, primary data are based on observational units or empirical manifestations and secondary data are analytical products.

No absolute distinction can be made between primary and secondary data, but the general concept serves as a useful organizing principle for this chapter and the following one. As much primary data as possible should be clearly recorded during the initial study (Grigson 1978). One reason for this is that legal and ethical standards may lead to the reburial of animal remains or their curation in remote facilities. Often unexpected, new questions arise during or after the investigation and future researchers should be able to extrapolate secondary data from primary data even if the assemblage is inaccessible. The choice of secondary data is guided by the nature of the collection and the research design that is the focus of subsequent reports and publications.

All of the methods developed by zooarchaeologists cannot be surveyed here. However, some methods of identification and analysis are basic to all zooarchaeological work, and it is these that are reviewed here. The perfect method does not exist and no single technique is appropriate, or even necessary, for every study. Analysts should familiarize themselves with the strengths and weaknesses of these methods before applying them to their own research. They should select applications suited to the specific assemblage being studied and the project's research goals without exceeding the interpretive capacities of the materials and methods (Lawrence 1973). The choice should also anticipate that data summarized in publications must be adequate to support the conclusions.

Much zooarchaeological research is guided by the scientific method, which requires that concepts be testable, that hypotheses can be disproved, and that the results be independently verified. For results to be accepted as valid, independent researchers should be able to obtain the same results if they apply the same methods. It is important that the methods be thoroughly described, scientifically sound, appropriate to the materials, and applied in such a way as to avoid introducing further bias. The researcher must demonstrate that these conditions prevailed during the study and that known, unavoidable biases were controlled. Issues related to materials and methods must be resolved before results can be interpreted, theories tested, and conclusions drawn.

THE HYPOTHETICAL COLLECTION

A Hypothetical Collection is used in this chapter and in Chapter 7 to demonstrate identification and analytical methods. This has two advantages. One is that many methods are interrelated – referring to a single collection shows the chain of evidence from the initial rough sort through analysis. For example, to demonstrate the relationship between fragmentation and estimates of body size or age classes, it is useful to observe both in the same collection. The other reason is that few collections contain all the primary data required for the wide range of procedures surveyed in this chapter and in Chapter 7. To follow the steps of identification and analysis throughout the same collection, it is necessary to create a collection that offers a wide variety of research opportunities.

The Hypothetical Collection is based on data from St. Augustine, Florida, in the southeastern United States (Figure 6.1). The Hypothetical Site is a residential lot occupied by a prestigious Spanish household in Spanish Florida between A.D. 1700 and 1765, just before the colony was ceded to England. The Hypothetical Collection contains both

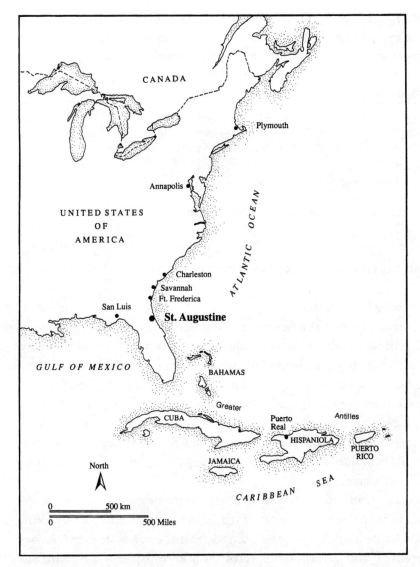

FIGURE 6.1. Map of Spanish Florida showing the location of St. Augustine.

domestic and wild species identified from all vertebrate classes, as well as molluscs and crustaceans (Table A4.1). It was recovered using a stack of 6-mm (1/4-inch) and 3-mm (1/8-inch) mesh screens, producing both a 6-mm and a 3-mm fraction. Five distinct behavioral contexts are represented: nonfeature sheet refuse, a large trash pit (Feature 8), two small trash pits (Features 9 and 10), and a well (Feature 11). The stratigraphy and material culture indicate these were distinct activity areas. Although this collection is modified to meet the needs of an instructional aid, these "hypothetical" data typify animal use in Spanish Florida (Quitmyer 1990; Reitz 2004a; Reitz and Cumbaa 1983; Reitz and Scarry 1985).

Table 6.1. *Hypothetical Collection: Vertebrate summary showing the impact of screen size on the Number of Identified Specimens (NISP)*

Taxonomic group	NISP, 3 mm		NISP, 6 mm	
	N	%	N	%
Mammals	20	1.0	13,947	87.1
Birds	31	1.6	233	1.5
Reptiles	3	0.2	190	1.2
Amphibians	10	0.5	38	0.2
Sharks, rays, and fishes	1,896	96.7	1,596	10.0
Total	1,960		16,004	

QUANTIFYING RELATIVE ABUNDANCE OF DIFFERENT TAXA

This volume is not a statistical text, but quantification is necessary to compare animal use through time and space. Quantification involves statistical analysis that ranges from expressing abundance in relative terms to calculating diversity indices or computing hypothetical economic models. The goal of quantification is to define characteristics that clearly differentiate among groups. Care must be taken to collect primary data in such a way that this can be done. Quantitative sampling requires that each of the species used at a site has an equal opportunity to be recovered, with no skewing to increase one taxon over another. This requires consistency in both field and laboratory methods. Skimming should be avoided and the activity areas being compared or combined should be appropriate (see Chapter 5).

Consistent use of a standard recovery technique is very important for zooarchaeological quantification. When the vertebrate data in the Hypothetical Collection are separated into 3-mm and 6-mm fractions (Table 6.1), considerable differences are found. Recovery technique has a particularly strong impact on the relative frequency of mammals to fishes. Not only are there differences in the relative proportions of taxonomic groups, but the 3-mm fraction has several taxa (e.g., herrings, killifishes [Cyprinodontidae], and silver perches [*Bairdiella chrysoura*]) that are not present in the 6-mm fraction. Furthermore, very small mullet individuals are present only in the 3-mm fraction and recovery technique also influences the relative proportions of large and small molluscs. It appears that there were major cultural differences between these two components, even though we know the sole difference between them is screen size. It is possible to combine these fractions during analysis only because both 3-mm and 6-mm fractions were collected consistently during excavation. The remains of both large and small animals had an equal opportunity to be recovered.

Most statistical tests require independence of the units being compared and many quantification procedures assume the observations are independent. Ideally, it would be possible to demonstrate that all of the specimens in a faunal collection are from different individuals or from the same individual. Unfortunately, it is impossible to control specimen independence for most archaeological materials; in fact, the assumption that specimens are related is intrinsic to many secondary data. Although it is possible to evaluate sample context, recovery techniques, and sample size, independence is a criterion for an adequate sample that cannot normally be assessed and is unlikely to be met. It is important to recognize this when developing research designs and arguing in support of an interpretation.

All primary data are influenced by sample size (e.g., Grayson 1984; Kintigh 1984; Simpson et al. 1960:193–201). This caution cannot be repeated too often as generations of researchers overlook its significance. Small samples generate a short species list with undue emphasis on one species in relation to others. For example, one sample from the Hypothetical Site contains only seven taxa, but when all of the samples are combined there are eighty-seven taxonomic categories (Table A4.1). Sample size also influences the range because the observed range is dependent on the number of observations made (Simpson et al. 1960:80). This has a significant impact on the secondary data.

Quantitative comparison among samples may be done with more confidence when the samples are similar in context, recovery method, and sample size. Some might argue identification and analysis should be conducted only if these conditions are met. Certainly if these conditions are not met, it would be unwise to conduct complex statistical applications and a more descriptive analysis is justified. However, some sites, contexts, or samples simply do not have as much faunal material as one would wish. Small collections may provide important insights, nevertheless, but they may need to be approached in a more descriptive way. In deciding how to approach quantification, the zooarchaeologist should be guided primarily by the questions being addressed and the need to execute the research design using techniques that are consistent, clear, and appropriately conservative.

LITERATURE REVIEW AND REFERENCE COLLECTION

Prior to beginning the study, the investigator should review the archaeological, zooarchaeological, and biological literature for the time period, cultural system, locality, and biome being studied (Reed 1963). The analyst should review previous work at the site, at contemporaneous sites, at sites in a similar environment, and at sites with similar cultural systems. For example, are there broad patterns of animal use found at sites along rivers that are distinctive from those found at sites located near seasonally dry lakes? The review should also include natural histories from the region so that species that may have been locally common when the site was occupied and those that were probably not present can be anticipated. For example, all zooarchaeologists should be

familiar with the temporal significance of chickens when working on materials from
Europe, Africa, and the Americas (Carter 1971; Hernández 1992; MacDonald 1995;
Storey et al. 2007; West and Zhou 1988). From this preparation, a list of the taxa that
may be identified, the questions addressed previously, and the methods applied to similar collections can be prepared. Preliminary work should include a visit to the site if
the zooarchaeologist is not part of the field crew.

An equally important preliminary step is to obtain access to a reference collection
with specimens for the region being studied (see Appendix 3). It cannot be stressed too
emphatically that identification and subsequent analysis is only as good as the reference
collection. Archaeological specimens should be used as reference materials only when
the animal is extinct and no modern reference specimens can be obtained.

Access to a good reference collection was critical to the study of the Hypothetical Collection. The collection required familiarity with 10 classes and 300 species encompassing
approximately 60,000 distinctive elements. Not all of these species or elements are in the
archaeological collection, but these species are found in the region now, occurred there
in the past, or might have been there. For example, evidence for exchange of animals
between Mexico and Spanish Florida is documented only because the reference collection contains skeletons of the double-striped thick-knee (*Burhinus bistriatus*). This bird
is native to Central and South America (Meyer de Schauensee 1970:82), and its presence
in the Hypothetical Collection probably is related to the movement of people between
Mexico and Spanish Florida. With a less-extensive reference collection, this important
aspect of interregional trade and political affiliations would not be known. Clearly, this
large, complex archaeofaunal collection could not be identified from memory, but all
collections, no matter how small, should be examined using reference materials.

PRIMARY DATA

Primary data are recorded during the identification phase (Table A3.1). They include elements represented, taxonomic identification, specimen count, modifications, pathologies, anatomical features of age and sex, measurements, and specimen weight. Primary
data should always be recorded. Although primary data should be replicable, this does
not mean they are free of biases related to taphonomic processes, excavation strategies,
and identification procedures. Some of these biases will be discussed in this chapter.

In our laboratories, archival and primary data are recorded on file cards (Figure 6.2).
The name of the site, the collection's accession number, and provenience information are
recorded at the top of the card. The accession number contains four digits designating
the site. This is followed by the serial number, four digits that designate the taxon. For
each archaeological sample there will be one card for each taxon, with the same accession
number and a unique serial number. The accession number and the serial number form

SPECIES CARD	Card _1_ of _1_

Taxon _Odocoileus virginianus_   Site # _SA36 - 4_   Access # _0242_   Serial # _0482_

Provenience _Sq 109N 112E Zone 3_   Level _1_   FS# _245_   Screen Size _3 mm_

#	DESCRIPTION
1	mandible, horizontal ramus with P_2 thru M_3, rt
	P_4 is permanent ⌈⌈ ⌈⌈ ⌈⌈ ⌈⌈-
1	femur, rt, distal, unfused epiphysis
1	femur, rt, distal, fused, in 5 pieces, old break
1	femur, rt, shaft below lesser trochanter, fusion
	indeterminate. Multiple small cuts on anterior shaft
1	astragalus, rt, measured
1	calcaneus, rt, fused, complete

Wt. _57.8_ (g) MNI _2_   Element _6_

SPECIES CARD	Card _1_ of _1_

Taxon _Odocoileus virginianus_   Site # _SA36 - 4_   Access # _0242_   Serial # _0812_

Provenience _Sq 109N 112E Zone 3_   Level _2_   FS# _340_   Screen Size _3 mm_

#	DESCRIPTION
1	P_4, lt, partial, deciduous
1	antler tine fragment
1	cervical vertebra, centrum unfused
1	scapula, lt, at glenoid fossa, unfused
2	humerus, lt, distal, fused, cut
1	radius, lt, diaphysis - proximal fused, distal unfused
2	radius, lt, proximal, fused
1	tibia, lt, proximal, unfused epiphysis
1	astragalus, rt, cut, measured

Wt. _62.0_ (g) MNI _3_   Element _11_

FIGURE 6.2. Hypothetical Collection: Examples of data cards for white-tailed deer (_Odocoileus virginianus_).

a catalogue number, a unique, sequential number for each taxon in an archaeological sample. In Figure 6.2, the first four digits (0242) are the site's accession number, followed by the serial number assigned to each taxon in each separate sample. The data card for white-tailed deer from Square 109N112E, Zone 3, Level 1 in the Hypothetical Collection has the catalogue number 02420482, while deer remains recovered from Level 2 of this same unit and zone has the catalogue number 02420812 (Figure 6.2). These are two separate cards. As part of the field procedure, a sequential number called a Field Sample number (FS#) was assigned to each sample bag in the field and this number is used to organize records of the primary data. The FS# is the primary link with all field notes and other records from the Hypothetical Site. It is an essential organizing tool that appears on all archaeofaunal notes related to the collection. The recovery technique is also recorded on each card.

The description field is filled with primary data (Table A3.1). The open format of the card permits as much primary data to be recorded about each specimen as necessary without limiting the notes to a few spaces or predetermined categories. This is particularly helpful when working on assemblages containing many classes with widely different elements. Clearly, all of the information listed in Table A3.1 will not be available for all of the specimens in a sample and the open-ended design also permits economizing on space and card stock when possible. Data from these cards are easily used in collection management and have been entered into several generations of computerized data files. Because the data are not reduced to abstract codes, they are more clearly and accurately understood by subsequent scholars.

Identification of Human Remains

Human remains may be sent to the zooarchaeologist for any number of reasons, but often this is because taphonomic processes destroyed evidence of their original context or because they were found in contexts other than those where burials or inhumations were expected. People lose teeth, toes, and fingers in the course of their daily activities. In some cases, the human material is more extensive. They may be finds associated with ritual bundles or caches whose behavioral context is now lost. More likely, they were waste and discarded as such. This may even apply to fetuses and infants, who might not have been accorded the status of "human" until they reached a particular age and were incorporated into the community through the appropriate rite of passage. It may also be the case that the individual was an outcast or a stranger and was not eligible for the burial rites reserved for members of the community. It is particularly difficult to recognize fetal or infant remains in the field, perhaps because these small skeletons have such a different appearance compared to adult skeletons (Humphrey 2000; Scheuer and Black 2004).

Thus, zooarchaeologists should anticipate finding human remains and be able to recognize them when they are encountered, particularly in a fragmentary state and from young people. Although the comparative collection should contain human remains to aid in identification, excellent references are available to assist in the identification and handling of human materials (e.g., Cox and Mays 2000; Hillson 2005; Katzenberg and

Saunders 2000; Steele and Bramblett 1988; Roskams 2001:199–208; White and Folkens 2005). Copies of these manuals should be present in any zooarchaeological laboratory and should be consulted even though it is likely that the project coordinator will request later that these materials be sent to a specialist in human osteology. Many of the names for elements are different in human osteology than in nonhuman osteology, so if the zooarchaeology laboratory is to do a preliminary identification, these manuals should be consulted for the appropriate terminology.

If the specimens are indeed human, in many cases they will require special handling to conform to applicable cultural patrimony agreements (although see Outram et al. [2005] for an argument in favor of having a zooarchaeologist study these materials). Arrangements should be made in advance with the project director regarding how such human remains should be handled. The project director should be informed at once when the identity of such remains is confirmed.

ELEMENTS REPRESENTED

Identification is a multistep process that usually involves deciding what element is represented by the specimen as well as attributing it to a taxonomic category (Driver 1992; Lawrence 1973; O'Connor 2000b; Parmalee 1985; Schmid 1972:21, 30–49). Identifying the elements represented in the sample and the taxonomic attribution are part of the same process. It is difficult to argue that one of these should happen first, because the sequence varies with each specimen. The exact procedures followed depend on the analyst's skill, work habits, and the established protocol of the laboratory (see Hesse and Wapnish [1985:70] for an example of the sorting process).

Element identification refers to the types of elements represented by the specimens in the sample. As we discussed in Chapter 5, many cultural and noncultural processes fracture specimens; seldom will specimens be complete elements. Determining which elements are represented is also a preliminary step toward examining fragmentation as a form of modification. When describing specimens in a sample, it is important to do so with particular emphasis on characteristics that may be needed to interpret fracture patterns (see the discussion of modifications in this chapter and in Chapter 7).

For vertebrate specimens, the element represented and the side (i.e., left, right, or axial) should be recorded (Figure 6.2; Table A3.1). Anatomical terminology should be used to note that the specimen is from the lateral, medial, anterior, posterior, proximal, distal, or shaft portion of the element (see Appendix 2; White and Folkens 2005:67–74). Driver (1985) refers to these as breakage units to avoid suggesting that all fragmentation is the result of butchering. Both articular ends and shaft portions must be identified because shaft portions provide important information about first- and second-order changes as well as exchange networks (Bunn and Kroll 1986; Marean and Spencer 1991;

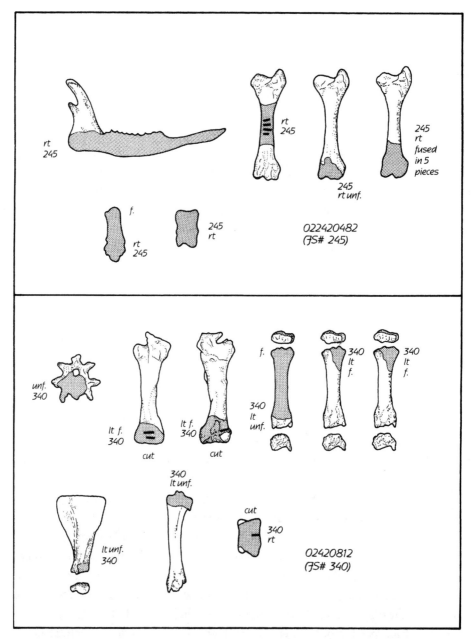

FIGURE 6.3. Hypothetical Collection: Drawing of white-tailed deer (*Odocoileus virginianus*) specimens recorded in the two samples presented in Figure 6.2. Key: rt, right; lt, left; f, fused; unf, unfused; FS#, Field Sample number.

Outram 2001, 2002; Todd and Rapson 1988). If the specimen is a tooth, notes should be made about which specific tooth it is, whether it is mandibular or maxillary, and its side (see Figure 3.6).

These same general characteristics apply to molluscs and crustaceans (e.g, Claassen 1998). Echinoderm test, spines, and parts of the Aristotle's lantern can be identified. In

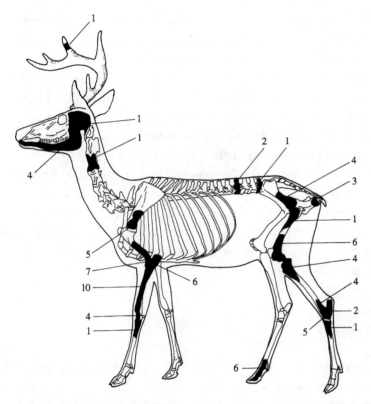

FIGURE 6.4. Hypothetical Collection: White-tailed deer (*Odocoileus virginianus*) skeleton summarizing specimens identified in the collection. Not illustrated: 1 tooth.

the case of chitons, it may be possible to determine which of the eight dorsal shell plates is present, particularly the anterior and posterior plate. Symmetry is not applicable for gastropods, but descriptions of the columella, apex, and aperture should be recorded. Bivalves have left and right valves, and particular attention should be paid to the symmetry of the hinge portion. The calcareous plates within which adult barnacles (Cirripedia) live are also identifiable. The exoskeleton of crabs, lobsters, and other decapods may be represented by many fragments that are difficult to record, but symmetry for the mandibles and cheliped can sometimes be determined (see Appendix 2).

Many devices may be used to describe specimens in greater detail. Anatomical terms, such as deltoid tuberosity or lesser trochanter, may be used to indicate which portion of the element is represented (e.g., Morlan 1994). Schematic drawings (e.g., Figure 6.3) are helpful during analysis and easily converted into a summary for publication (e.g., Figure 6.4; Brinkhuizen 1994; Gifford et al. 1981; Lauwerier 1993b; Lyman 1977). If greater detail is needed, data may be summarized using diagnostic or fragmentation zones (Dobney and Rielly 1988; Garcia and Rackham 2000; Knüsel and Outram 2004; Marean et al. 2001; Morales 1988; Münzel 1988). In Figure 6.5, radius specimens from the Hypothetical Site are enumerated in eight diagnostic zones, and each specimen is counted in every zone in which the specimen has been found. The counts of each zone are totaled. Alternatively, specimens may be recorded under one of two columns depending on whether the zone is more or less than 50 percent present. Others classify specimens as complete, three-quarters, half, one-quarter, or less than one-quarter of their original size without use of diagnostic zones (Klein and Cruz-Uribe 1984:108). Some measure the length or width of the fragment to document such attributes (e.g., Enloe 1993). These techniques are used more often for mammals (e.g., Morales 1988; Sadek-Kooros 1975:142) than for other tetrapods, fishes, or invertebrates, but they could be applied to such organisms (e.g., Sampson 2000; Wheeler and Jones 1989:133).

Other morphological features should also be recorded, such as the shape of bovid horn cores and oyster valves (e.g., Armitage 1982; Crook 1992). These features usually are reflected in measurements (see elsewhere in this chapter and in Chapter 7), but sometimes important characteristics do not lend themselves to objective recording procedures and more lengthy descriptions may be necessary. Illustrations can be invaluable aids in recording such attributes.

TAXONOMIC ATTRIBUTION

O'Connor (2000b:39) makes the excellent point that when we assign archaeological specimens to a taxonomic category, we are not so much identifying them with absolute certainty as we are attributing them to a taxonomic category based on morphological characteristics found in both the archaeological specimen and in several comparative specimens of known identity. It is important to be conservative in interpreting the resulting list of identified taxa. Conceivably, one might identify the taxa present in a sample without identifying elements represented. This is all that would be required to produce "laundry lists," and it is apparent that attributions of species reported in many early faunal studies were based on informal familiarity with some key elements, rather than on formal identification of specimens. In most cases, however, the objective is to identify the animals represented and assign them to a taxonomic group following verifiable and distinctive morphology. This requires identifying both elements and taxa represented in the sample as a single step.

Final taxonomic attribution is based on morphological features, age, and sex, as well as geographical and individual variation (Chaplin 1971:39; Lawrence 1973). This requires comparing each archaeological specimen with reference specimens. Contrary to the notion that there are no unidentifiable bones (Binford and Bertram 1977), specimens should be identified to a particular taxon only if they can be unquestionably assigned to it on the basis of morphological features found through comparison with reference specimens after all other possible attributions are excluded by the same procedure. For example, it should not be assumed that all Indeterminate Mollusc specimens in a collection are eastern oysters (*Crassostrea virginica*) just because most mollusc specimens identified below the phylum Mollusca are eastern oysters. It takes experience to know

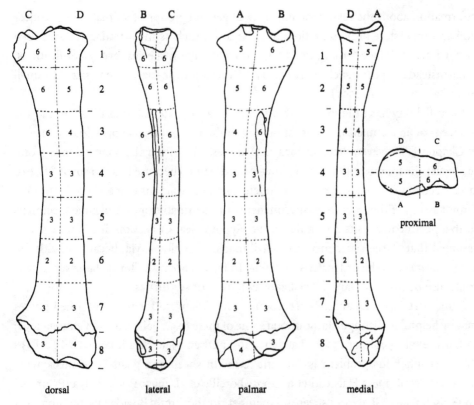

FIGURE 6.5. Hypothetical Collection: An example of diagnostic zones for white-tailed deer (*Odocoileus virginianus*) radius specimens, following Münzel (1988). A grid is created by combining four proximal-distal columns with eight medial-lateral rows. The numbers refer to zones created by this grid and the letters to the lines that delineate the zones. The numbers within each zone are the total number of specimens that include the zone either in whole or in part.

which taxonomic attributions can be made reliably to which taxonomic level and which attributions, regrettably, are not possible (e.g., Driver 1992; Morales 1993a). Relatively few specimens are identifiable to the species level and none is identifiable to the subspecies level. At the same time, the more specific the taxonomic attribution, the more detailed the study can be, and the more useful the primary data for studies of human behavior and biological phenomena.

So, what does "identifiable" mean? In the Hypothetical Collection, all of the specimens are considered identified, but some are identified to lower taxonomic levels than others. A large number of specimens could only be classified as Indeterminate Vertebrate or Indeterminate Mollusc. These higher-level attributions should be recorded and reported, just as are those to species; they may be helpful in evaluating site-formation processes and cultural activities (Parmalee 1985). The higher categories may be further broken down into "large," "medium," and "small" classifications (Uerpmann 1973). If this is done, the criteria should be noted in the report so it is clear whether "small" means "small specimen" or "specimen from a small animal." These classifications provide information about the relative significance of general groups of animals in the collection and their state of preservation. Some indices, such as the artiodactyl index used in portions of the western United States, do not rely on species-level identifications, using instead categories such as artiodactyl-size, lagomorph-size, rodent-size, and small mammal (Byers et al. 2005).

Identifiability has little to do with size. The atlas of a killifish is as distinctive as the humerus of an elephant if one is familiar with the morphological principles reviewed in Chapter 3. However, Watson (1972:224) argues, "the bigger the bone it comes from, the bigger the fragment that can no longer be identified because it is too small." Use of large-sized animals at a site results in indeterminate specimens that are also large. One cannot assume either that small specimens are unidentifiable or that all large specimens from a postmedieval site are cattle. In the Hypothetical Collection, it cannot even be assumed that "large" specimens are attributable to Artiodactyla, because equids are large mammals in the order Perissodactyla. In fact, in Spanish Florida large specimens could also be from humans, black bears, dolphins, or sea turtles.

Some parts of some animals are notoriously difficult to identify. Published guides may be helpful in distinguishing among some of these (e.g., Balkwell and Cumbaa 1992; Colburn et al. 1991; Ford 1990; Lawrence 1951; Olsen 1960; Steadman 1980). Perhaps the most infamous problem is encountered with sheep and goats (Boessneck 1969; Boessneck et al. 1964; Halstead et al. 2002; Loreille et al. 1997; Payne 1985a; Prummel and Frisch 1986). Goats and sheep are members of the family Bovidae in the subfamily Caprinae. They are sometimes called small bovids or caprines or combined into that interesting zooarchaeological creation: the "sheep/goat." Some distinctions depend on measurements rather than morphological features (see Chapter 7). In the end, however, most specimens in troublesome groups will be referred to taxonomic levels other than genus or species. The criteria for problematic attributions should be recorded.

Although every effort should be made to study all specimens as thoroughly as possible, sometimes a highly focused research question, limited time, or financial constraints impose restrictions on which specimens warrant an extensive expenditure of time and which do not. The first criterion should be maintaining comparability within the assemblage and addressing the project's research design. Some specimens are not as relevant to the research and may, regrettably, receive less attention than ones more germane to the project's goals. Specimens that provide diagnostic information about taphonomic processes, age, sex, seasonality, butchering habits, technology, and biogeography may receive special attention (e.g., Morales 1993a). For example, determining the species for a kingfish (*Menticirrhus* sp.) otolith that has growth increments and can be measured might be worth more effort than identifying other elements. Such choices should never be made in the field, and the unidentified fractions should not be discarded.

Some researchers advocate limiting identifications to predetermined elements (Davis 1987:35; Wheeler and Jones 1989:58–9); others do not identify shaft fragments or incomplete articular ends. Limiting identification to a predetermined list may be necessary in some circumstances, but it precludes many studies. It may not be possible to use skeletal frequency to study butchering techniques and exchange systems or to compare specimen counts of one taxon to another if all specimens do not have an equal opportunity to be included in the primary data. Restricted identification lists also preclude intersite comparisons unless all researchers use the same list. Further, elements on an abbreviated priority list may not be identifiable in every taxon found in the collection. For example, many first dorsal spines cannot be identified beyond Indeterminate Fish and would probably not be included on most high-priority element lists; but the first dorsal spines of catfishes (Siluriformes) and triggerfishes are very distinctive, at least to the level of family. Although most pterygiophores are not identifiable, the first pterygiophore of surgeonfishes (Acanthuridae) is highly distinctive.

SPECIMEN COUNT

Specimen count refers simply to the number of specimens in a sample. Counting specimens is one of the original quantification procedures and is extensively reviewed (e.g., Brain 1969; Chaplin 1971:64–7; Daly 1969; Gilbert and Singer 1982; Grayson 1984; Klein and Cruz-Uribe 1984:24–32; Lyman 1982; Mengoni 1988; Noe-Nygaard 1977; O'Connor 2000b; Payne 1972a; Perkins 1973; Reed 1963; Uerpmann 1973; Watson 1972, 1979). Specimen count is sometimes abbreviated into a useful acronym, NISP (Payne 1975), referring to the number of identified specimens, but fragment count and bone count are used with the same meaning. A number of other abbreviations may be used, such as NR for number of remains (Morales et al. 1994) and TNF for total number of fragments (Gilbert and Steinfeld 1977). At one time faunal studies commonly included only taxonomic attribution and specimen count. Although we do not recommend doing so, specimen count can be obtained without identifying specimens to either taxon or element. Sometimes specimens are counted just like any other artifact to demonstrate spatial patterns (e.g., South 1977:179–82).

Although specimen counts seem subject to few procedural biases, counting does require some decisions (Chaplin 1971:64–5; Ringrose 1993; Watson 1972, 1979). The most routine instance occurs when counting specimens that crossmend. Chaplin (1971:65) advocates counting these as separate pieces and others recommend counting them as one piece if the specimens clearly go together (Clason 1972). Crossmendable specimens found in the same sample usually are produced by breakage during deposition, excavation, or subsequent handling. Some researchers recommend that at least 50 percent of a given portion should be present for the specimen to be counted, and they count most metapodial condyles and the two central pig metapodia as half numbers rather than whole numbers (e.g., Albarella and Davis 1996:3). A similar problem arises in counting burials or teeth still in the mandible. These alternatives to counting each and every spec-imen are intended to avoid counting fragments from the same element more than once. Some advocate only identifying proximal and distal ends in order to avoid duplication when counting, but this introduces other problems, as discussed earlier.

Anticipating some of the secondary data derived from specimen count, Clason's approach appears to be the more generally useful one. Counting crossmending spec-imens as one specimen, as is done with the femur in Figure 6.2, does not preclude counting the specimens individually whether they crossmend or not, if appropriate notations are made. Counting only those specimens that represent at least 50 percent of the dimension, as advocated by Albarella and Davis, might be useful whenever it appears entire elements had formerly been present but are now highly fragmented. It might also be necessary when budgets or schedules do not permit a thorough study. Whatever decision is made, the criteria should be included in the methods and everyone working on the project should conform to the protocol.

In the case of the Hypothetical Collection, all specimens that crossmend are counted as one specimen regardless of what percentage of the element they represent, even though they are not actually glued together. This applies to preexcavation and modern breaks, as well as to epiphyses and diaphyses that are separate but go together. For example, the five crossmendable specimens of the distal femur in FS# 245 are counted as one specimen, with a note of how many specimens actually are present in case this may be needed in the future (Figures 6.2 and 6.3). The dark color of the broken surfaces suggests this is an old break. The mandible and its associated teeth in this same sample also count as one specimen. Both of these cases are recorded in such a manner that future researchers can count them in a different way should their research designs require it.

In the interest of time, specimens identified only as Indeterminate Vertebrate, Inde-terminate Mollusc, and Indeterminate Invertebrate are not counted (see Table A4.1). In these cases, the variety of organisms that probably are included in these categories is so great that counting would confer an exaggerated sense of accuracy on the attribution. Additionally, some of the indeterminate specimens are so small it is unlikely that they can be counted with any degree of accuracy.

MODIFICATIONS AND PATHOLOGIES

Modification refers both to marks on specimens and to breakage patterns. Both ver-tebrate and invertebrate specimens should be examined for modifications. Analysis of food processing and distribution as well as other site-formation processes combines information about the types of elements represented in the assemblage, their frag-mentation characteristics, and marks on the specimens (e.g., Bunn and Kroll 1986; Gifford-Gonzalez 1989; Luff 1994; Marean 1992; F. Marshall 1986; L. Marshall 1989;

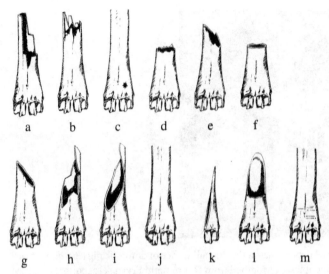

FIGURE 6.6. Some typical modification characteristics: (a) stepped or columnar (b) sawtoothed
or splintered, (c) punctured, (d) transverse, irregular, (e) oblique, irregular, (f) transverse,
regular, (g) oblique, regular, (h) spiral, irregular, (i) spiral, regular, (j) irregular break, (k) tool,
(l) grooved, and (m) cut. Modified from Sadek-Kooros (1975) and drawn by Daniel C. Weinand.

Serrand and Bonnissent 2005; Weissbrod et al. 2005). Fragmentation is difficult to separate from other modifications because often the same behavior causes both and for
many research questions they must be evaluated together. Ideally, modifications associated with first- and second-order changes are noted as primary data without ascribing a
causal agent to them, although usually some causal association cannot be avoided even at
this preliminary stage. High-powered magnification greatly improves the descriptions
and subsequent interpretations of modifications (e.g., Rose 1983; Shipman 1981).

In the case of modifications that might be the result of tool manufacture or use, careful
consideration must be given to distinguishing between those patterns that are the result
of intentional modification and use-wear and those that are the result of the animal's
normal activities or of natural damage (e.g., Light 2005; Olsen 1989; Rabett 2004). Tools
and ornaments made of bone and teeth are important modifications that may provide
insights into both economic and social life (e.g., d'Errico and Vanhaeren 2002).

Many characteristics of fracture patterning, such as the amount of shaft recovered,
are recorded when the element portions represented are noted; but attributes of marks
on the specimens also need to be described. Fragmentation characteristics, such as the
location of the fracture, characteristics of the fracture surface, the presence of primary
and secondary fractures, and the orientation of the fracture as transverse, oblique,
or spiral to the long axis should be recorded (Mateos 2005; Morales 1988; Outram
2002; Sadek-Kooros 1975; Shipman et al. 1981). Fractures can be described as stepped,
splintered, punctured, transverse and irregular, and oblique and irregular (Figure 6.6).
Characterizing spiral fractures as marrow fracturing should be avoided at this stage

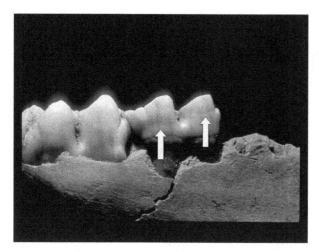

FIGURE 6.7. Linear enamel hypoplasia on the lingual surface of domestic pig (*Sus domesticus*) molars. Arrows indicate hypoplasias. Modified from Dobney and Ervynck (2000:598) and used with the kind permission of Elsevier and Keith Dobney.

(Haynes 1983; Miller 1975). Evidence of the way the animal was killed, as well as marks associated with extracting soft tissue, skinning, and butchering, should be recorded in descriptive terms. These include cuts, scrapes, chops or hacks, blows, and saw marks (Figures 5.6–5.10; Fisher 1995; Johnson 1985; Noe-Nygaard 1989; Shipman and Rose 1983a). The color of burned specimens and the portion of the specimen burned should be noted (McCutcheon 1992; Nicholson 1995; Shipman et al. 1984). Gnaw marks (Figure 5.11), evidence of digestion, use of the specimen as raw material, and trampling abrasions are also important (e.g., Behrensmeyer et al. 1989). Behrensmeyer's (1978) weathering stages are useful for recording weathering characteristics. Recent modifications should be recorded as such. Munsell soil color charts provide a standard for recording colors associated with burning, burial, and weathering.

Congenital anomalies and pathological specimens should be described in detail (Baker and Brothwell 1980; Davies et al. 2005; O'Connor 2000b:98–110). Pathologies may range from supernumerary and malformed teeth, to bone diseases, to healed or unhealed fractures, or unusual wear patterns. Often the pathology is irregular in appearance. These irregularities are the result of stress during growth and development, exposure to pathogens, inherited anomalies and diseases, intentional or unintentional injury, and activity patterns. Invertebrates may also have evidence of predation or other stresses (Figures 5.2 and 5.3).

Dental or enamel hypoplasias, essentially growth arrest lines in mammalian teeth, are particularly interesting pathologies because they indicate periods of stress experienced by animals when they were young (Figure 6.7; Dobney and Ervynck 2000; Teegen 2005). They appear as transverse lines, pits, and grooves in the enamel. As in humans, hypoplasias denote periods when growth stopped and then resumed. Growth may have stopped for a number of reasons, but often it is a response to poor nutrition or disease.

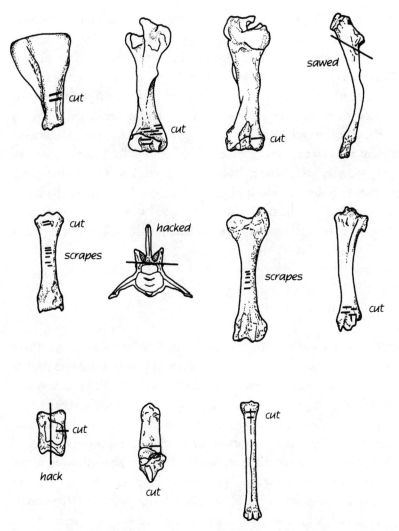

FIGURE 6.8. Hypothetical Collection: Location of butchering marks on white-tailed deer (*Odocoileus virginianus*) specimens in the collection.

Because enamel does not remodel, and tooth development follows a regular chronological sequence, these dental pathologies not only provide indirect evidence of a severe stress, but may also indicate the age when the stress occurred and the frequency of such stresses. The literature for human hypoplasias provides a good tool for recording dental abnormalities (Larsen 1997:43–7; White and Folken 2005:329).

These features are difficult to record and it is often unclear what caused the modification or pathology. However, as primary data, the location of irregularities in the specimen should be described and drawn. These descriptions can be guided by the literature in human osteology (e.g., Larsen 1997; White and Folkens 2005). For the Hypothetical Collection, the element drawings are used to note modifications (Figures 6.3 and 6.8). These observations are quantified in a table listing the number of specimens with

modifications (Table A4.2). This summarizes the number of specimens on which modifications are observed rather than the number of modifications themselves. Instead
of counting the dozens of scrapes down the anterior surface of these specimens, it is
noted that a radius and a femur are modified in this way. In the case of specimens with
multiple modifications of different causes, such as a cut mark, sawing, and rodent-
gnawing, each of these modification types is counted separately. The diagnostic zones
used to indicate which portions of elements are present (Figure 6.5) can also be used
to record the location and extent of modifications (Dobney and Rielly 1988; Quintana
2005; Helmer 1987; Morales 1988; Münzel 1988; Sadek-Kooros 1975). Because many
terms are abbreviated in published illustrations showing the locations of modifications, it is recommended "hack" be used instead of "chop" so as to avoid confusion
between "c" (cuts) and "c" (chops). Languages other than English will require different
choices.

ANATOMICAL FEATURES OF AGE AND SEX

Many physiological events respond to seasonal periodicity and age (Chapter 3). These
provide the basis for interpretations of season of death and human behaviors such as
sedentism, mobility, storage, and husbandry strategies (see Chapter 8). Because sexual
maturation is part of the ageing process, evidence for one of these also pertains to the
other (e.g., Davis 2000; d'Errico and Vanhaeren 2002; Ruscillo 2006). Anatomical features reflecting age include form and porosity of the specimen; epiphyseal fusion and
closure of cranial sutures; tooth growth and replacement sequences; tooth wear; incremental structures associated with growth; and antler and horn development and size
(e.g., Chaplin 1971:76–90; Deith 1983a, 1983b; Ioannidou 2003a; Tomé and Vigne 2003;
Turner 1977; Wilson et al. 1982). Those reflecting sex include unique morphological
features, secondary sexual characteristics, and size (Chaplin 1971:100–7; Clutton-Brock
et al. 1990; Wilson et al. 1982). Allowances must be made for individual as well as
regional variation, particularly among domestic animals (e.g., Moran and O'Connor
1994). The timing of the physiological processes underlying these anatomical features
is variable and should be recorded in such a way that will permit their evaluation
within a range rather than as points. As primary data, these observations are restricted
to recording morphological features from which age and sex may be estimated and
do not extend to deriving absolute or relative age, age classes, and sex ratios (see
Chapter 7).

　　Many of the characteristics associated with age are difficult to quantify but can be
described in qualitative terms. These include characteristics associated with maturation
in animals with determinate growth, such as reduction in porosity, development of
muscle attachments, thin compact bone layers, a relatively wide marrow cavity with

little cancellous bone, and adult shape. Notes about the size, texture, and shape found in animals with indeterminate growth also may be recorded in general terms. For example, ten of the Indeterminate Bird specimens in the Hypothetical Collection are very porous, as are one chicken specimen and one turkey specimen. These observations indicate some juvenile birds are represented in the collection. In some cases, measurements may be developed to document these relative characteristics.

Epiphyseal Fusion

Degree of epiphyseal fusion and closure of cranial sutures in animals with determinate growth are important anatomical features (Chaplin 1971:80–1; O'Connor 2000b:92–6; Schmid 1972:74–5; Silver 1970; Tomé and Vigne 2030). The status of cranial sutures should be described whenever possible. However, epiphyseal characteristics are usually more commonly observed in archaeological materials.

Epiphyseal fusion occurs in stages (Noodle 1974; Purdue 1983; Wilson 1978). Epiphyses may be open, with the epiphysis separate from the diaphysis, semifused, with the epiphysis and diaphysis partly united but the trabeculae interrupted, or fused (Lewall and Cowan 1963). In fused specimens, the epiphyseal line may still be visible or it may be completely obscured. All of these indicate different stages of maturation and probably different ages at death. Rather than indicate the condition of fusion only for unfused specimens, the degree of fusion should be recorded every time or it should be noted that degree of fusion could not be determined (see Figure 6.2). It is important to record that the specimen is from the proximal or distal end of the element because these fuse at different developmental stages (Table 3.5). In the Hypothetical Collection, degree of fusion is noted on the data cards (Figure 6.2), on the element drawings (Figure 6.3), and on the specimen distribution work sheet (Table A4.3). All of the fusion data for deer are then summarized on fusion work sheets (Table A4.4).

Payne (1985b) suggests using either complete or nearly complete unfused diaphyses or unfused epiphyses, but not both, when recording fusion data, in order to avoid counting specimens from the same element more than once. However, Crabtree (1989:109) recommends counting both epiphyses and diaphyses after attempting to match unfused epiphyses and their associated diaphyses. When a match exists, the specimens fit together convincingly. Crabtree's approach is used with the Hypothetical Collection. Where matches could be achieved, the specimens are counted as a single, unfused specimen. Unfused epiphyses and diaphyses that could not be matched are counted as separate specimens. In the Hypothetical Collection, there are no examples of mends across the epiphyseal line for white-tailed deer. However, if these observations were restricted just to epiphyses, the number of observations for deer in the Hypothetical Collection would be reduced from nine unfused specimens to five unfused epiphyses (Table A4.4). The three unfused diaphyses and the unfused ilium would be ignored and the sample size, already small, would be reduced further.

Tooth Eruption Sequences

Notes about mammalian tooth growth and replacement are more useful if they are based on a series of teeth still in the mandible or maxilla rather than on loose, individual teeth, although data for loose unassociated teeth should be recorded if possible. As with epiphyseal fusion, the replacement of deciduous dentition generally follows an established sequence, although the exact age when teeth are fully erupted is variable (Chaplin 1971:78; Noodle 1974; O'Connor 2000b; Payne 1973; Silver 1970; Tomé and Vigne 2030; Wilson et al. 1982).

When recording data for teeth, it is important to note if the tooth is deciduous or permanent and to what extent the crown and roots are developed (Hillson 2005:223–45). Even after the tooth has emerged from the mandible or maxilla, secondary dentine continues to form in the pulp cavity (Morris 1978; Spinage 1973) so the developmental characteristics of the root should be noted along with those of the crown. The deciduous P_4 of artiodactyls is particularly important. (In some academic traditions, deciduous premolars may be designated by lower case "m"; see, e.g., A. Grant 1982 and Figure 6.9.) This is also one of the most useful teeth if age profiles from crown heights will be estimated (Klein and Cruz-Uribe 1984:53). The mandible in FS# 245 has a slightly worn M_3 and a permanent P_4, indicating this individual was at least a subadult when it died, and the single P_4 in FS# 340 is deciduous, indicating a juvenile (Figure 6.2; Severinghaus 1949).

Tooth Wear

Tooth wear continues the range of observations that can be made beyond the age when epiphyseal fusion and tooth eruption is completed (Carter 1975; Chaplin 1971:85–8; Grant 1978; Hillson 2005:214–23; O'Connor 2000b; Payne 1973, 1985a). It is one of the few sources of information about age after sexual maturity is reached in animals with determinate growth. The chief disadvantage is that wear reflects the nature of the food eaten, especially the amount of grit consumed when eating, as well as the general nutritional well-being of the animal in question, and these variables may not correlate with age.

Several standardized recording systems are available. These reduce the need to describe wear qualitatively, though some degree of subjectivity continues to exist. For example, the mandibular teeth can be recorded in terms of one of the tooth wear stages (TWS) recommended by Grant (Figure 6.9; A. Grant 1982). Payne (1973) proposes a

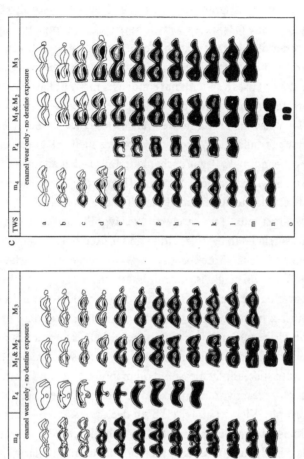

FIGURE 6.9. Mandibular tooth wear stages for (a) pig (*Sus domesticus*), (b) cattle (*Bos taurus*), and (c) sheep/goat (Caprinae); TWS refers to tooth wear stage and m_4 is used instead of deciduous P_4. Modified from Annie Grant (1982:92–4); used with her kind permission.

system for caprines using diagrammatic symbols (Figure 6.10; see also Deniz and Payne 1982; Levitan 1982; Payne 1985a, 1987). Payne's system is accompanied by a code that can be used in computer files, but the system can be used for other artiodactyls and without the code (Albarella et al. 2005; Legge and Rowley-Conwy 1988:33–4; Stiner 1994:290). Zeder (1991:92, 2006b) uses a system that condenses many of Payne's stages. Using such systems, unworn teeth can be recorded as well as teeth so severely worn that only the roots remain. Thus far, such systems are available only for domestic bovids and some cervids, but not white-tailed deer. Eventually systems such as Figures 6.9 and 6.10 should be available for other animals. Payne's schematic approach is adapted to record the teeth in the Hypothetical Collection deer mandible (Figure 6.2). Tooth-wear systems such as this can be converted into quantitative data for use in tables and histograms when sample sizes are larger than is the case with the Hypothetical Collection.

Crown height is related to tooth attrition and is used to estimate age at death (Klein 1981, 1982; Klein and Cruz-Uribe 1983, 1984:46–55; Legge and Rowley-Conwy 1987:34; O'Connor 2000b). Crown height is "the minimum distance between the occlusal surface and the line separating the enamel of the crown from the dentine on the roots, measured on the buccal surface of mandibular teeth and on the lingual surface of maxillary ones" (Klein and Cruz-Uribe 1984:46). For consistency, Klein recommends measuring crown height on the anterior lobe of teeth with lobes, such as those of artiodactyls, and suggests that it may be more successfully measured on mandibular teeth (Klein et al. 1983). The measurement is more readily accommodated on loose teeth because the enamel/dentine juncture is accessible (Klein et al. 1983). Both deciduous and permanent teeth should be measured. Incisors may be less suitable than cheek teeth in many species (Spinage 1973) and are less likely to be recovered than premolars and molars.

Incremental Structures

Although increments provide important age and environmental information, they normally are not examined as part of the basic collection of primary data at the earliest stage of a study. Studies of archaeological teeth focus on increments in cementum and enamel (e.g., Burke and Castanet 1995; Coy et al. 1982; Hillson 2005:159–68, 245–53; Koike and Ohtaishi 1987; Landon 1993; Lieberman et al. 1990; O'Connor 2000b; Pike-Tay 1995; Sathe 2000; Pike-Tay 2001; see Chapter 3). Increment formation may not be uniform on all teeth even in the same individual, so it is important to study the same tooth consistently. Premolars and molars are more likely to be useful for archaeological purposes than incisors and canines. Increments in otoliths, mollusc valves, and other tissues in animals with indeterminate growth are also studied (e.g., Brewer 1987; Coutts and Jones 1974; Jones et al. 1990; Luff and Bailey 2000; Morey 1983).

Experience and skill are needed to prepare increments. The thin-sectioning procedures used to study modern materials must be modified for fragile archaeological

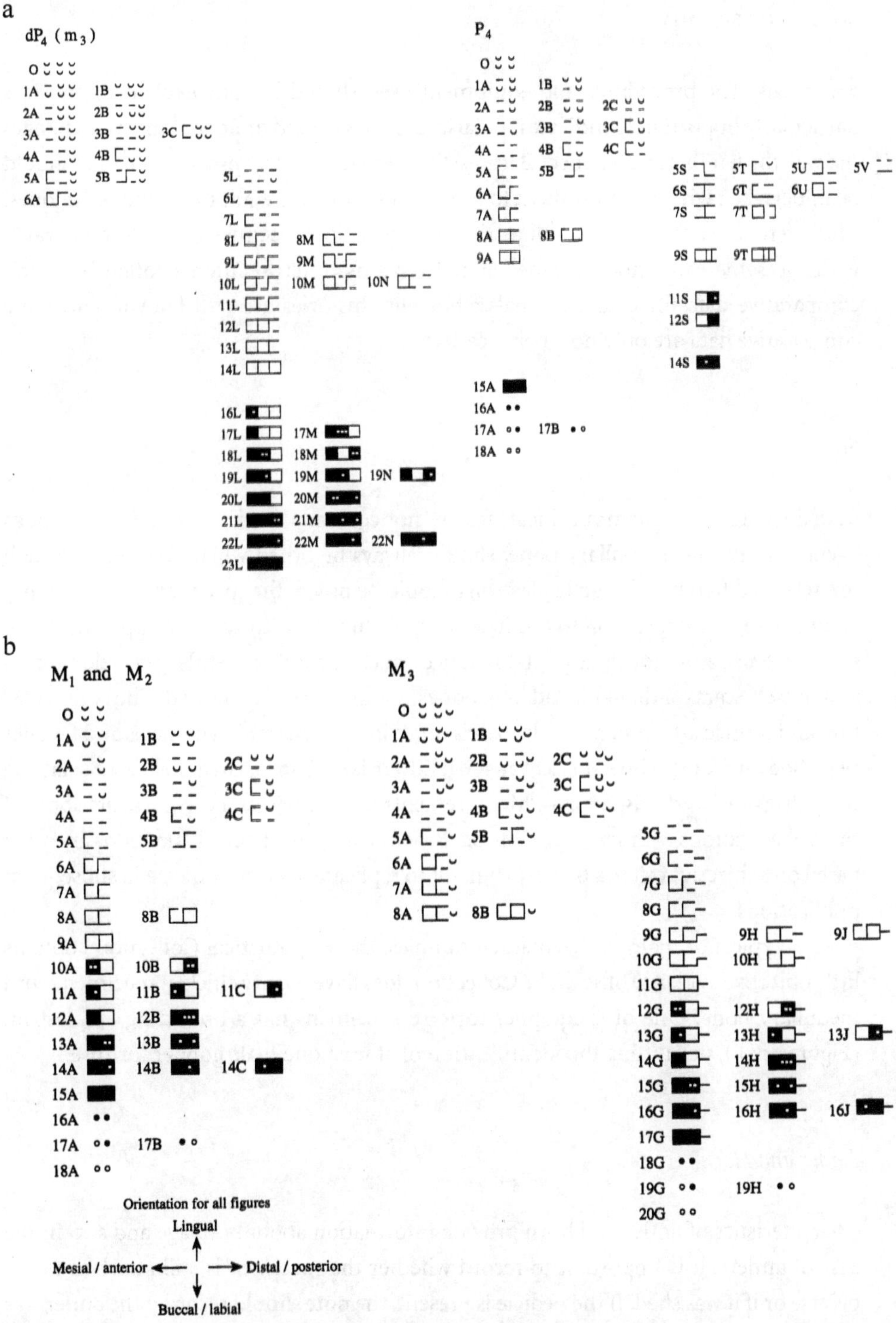

FIGURE 6.10. Codes for caprine mandibular tooth wear stages. The numbers are based on the sequence of steps by which wear progresses: 0 is unworn and 23 is extremely worn. The letters distinguish variants of the same numerical stage; for example, 1 A and 1 B are variations of the wear typically found at stage 1 (Payne 1987). (a) presents the deciduous P_4 (or m_3) and adult P_4 and (b) is the wear stages for M_1, M_2, and M_3. Modified from Payne (1987:610–11) and used with the kind permission of Elsevier and Sebastian Payne.

specimens. The procedures and equipment used should be fully explained, and it is particularly important to indicate if polarized light was used or not because this changes the way the bands are described. Because these are destructive procedures, they should be undertaken with a commitment to use the best available equipment and techniques. The reference specimens, as well as the archaeological specimens, should be curated with the same care afforded other faunal remains. Interpretation is often based on comparative data for extant animals whose life histories are well-known, and these comparative data are only now being collected.

Sex

Sexually diagnostic anatomical features are not common, and characteristics, such as bacula, spurs, and medullary bone, should always be noted when present. Although sex-related differences in turtle plastrons should be noted, the specimens must be fairly complete for the depression found in some male turtle plastrons to be apparent. More subjective size and morphological differences, such as the relatively larger male canines and muscle scars on the skull and long bones, should also be described. The conformation and muscle attachments of the pelvis differ in most mammalian males and females (e.g., Boessneck 1969; Boessneck et al. 1964; Edwards et al. 1982; Greenfield 2006; Hatting 1995; Prummel and Frisch 1986). Measurements may be necessary to correlate some of these observations with sex (e.g., Clutton-Brock et al. 1990). These distinctions are often based on subjective criteria that are difficult to replicate or communicate in subsequent publications.

As is typical of many archaeofaunal samples, the Hypothetical Collection contains little objective evidence of sex. The Collection does have twenty chicken specimens with medullary bone. One of the gopher tortoise specimens has a projecting epiplastron (Figure 3.21 a), permitting the identification of at least one male gopher tortoise.

Antler and Horn

Characteristics of antler and horn provide information about both age and sex. In the case of antlers, it is important to record whether the specimen is still attached to the pedicle or if it was shed. If the pedicle is present, the note should record if the antler was attached when the animal died. If antlers are represented only by tine fragments, this should be made clear (see Figure 6.2). An antler still attached to the pedicle provides important seasonal information, while a shed antler or an antler tine could be a piece collected for use as a tool at some other time of the year (e.g., Alhaique and Cerilli 2003; Schibler 2004).

Table 6.2. *Hypothetical Collection: Horn core attributes for cattle* (Bos taurus)

Dimension	Measurement	Age class	Interpretation and description
46	30.7	3	short horn ox; pathology
46	41.1	4	short horn female
46	43.7	4	short horn ox or medium horn female
46	53.9	3–4	medium horn female or ox
46	56.1	3–4	medium horn female or ox
46	57.9	4–5	medium horn female
46	64.4	2	medium horn ox
47	125.0	3	short horn ox; pathology
47	190.0	4	short horn female
47	330.0	4–5	medium horn female

Note: Dimensions follow Driesch (1976); measurements are in mm; age class follows Armitage (1982).

Horn core characteristics that should be recorded include surface texture and appearance of the horn core as well as measurements related to size (e.g., Armitage 1982; Armitage and Clutton-Brock 1976; Clutton-Brock et al. 1990). Males tend to have larger horns than females, but breed must also be considered when describing the attributes of horn cores (Armitage 1982). The interrelatedness of breed, sex, and age in recording horn core attributes is shown in Table 6.2 for the Hypothetical Collection.

MEASUREMENTS

Measurements are important primary data. Conforming to the exact definition and orientation of standards already in the published literature, when it is at all possible, increases opportunities for comparative studies (e.g., Desse and Desse-Berset 1987–1996; Driesch 1976; Haag 1948; Morales and Rosenlund 1979; Sternberg 1992). If other dimensions more suitable to the specific research problem are defined these should be illustrated or fully described (e.g., Plug 2005). To record the size and shape of elements accurately, measurements are taken from several different points because two different specimens of the same element can be the same length but differ in width. To describe the degree to which the specimens are robust or gracile, for example, a ratio can be made between several measurements that compare length and width of the distal end of an element (e.g., Bartosiewicz 1995b:53). Such applications will be addressed more fully in Chapter 7.

Most specimens are fragmentary and, consequently, most measurements must be of single dimensions or between recognizable features found on only a small portion of an element. When burned specimens are measured, this should be noted. Elements exposed to heat are altered in size (Buikstra and Swegle 1989; Coy 1975; Driesch 1976:3; Pearce and Luff 1994; Shipman et al. 1984). Measurements of such specimens are primarily useful only in research related to the impact of heat. Specimens boiled, or otherwise exposed indirectly to heat, may not show evidence of this experience. Measurements are generally recorded in millimeters, although centimeters are sometimes used for very large dimensions.

Measurements are usually of fully adult dimensions as determined by epiphyseal fusion. If the measurement is of an unfused specimen or a deciduous tooth this should be recorded (e.g., Albarella et al. 2005; Driesch 1976:4; Gilbert and Steinfeld 1977; Zeder 2001). When an unfused specimen is measured, the notes should include whether it is the epiphysis or diaphysis (e.g., Table A4.5). In some cases, it is difficult to determine whether the measured specimen is from an adult or a subadult, especially if the element is an astragalus, which becomes well-ossified relatively early in the maturation process. In such cases, a conservative assignment should be made.

Measurements of some specimens in the Hypothetical Collection are included, along with data from other sites, in Table A4.5. Very little of the Collection is measurable. Because measurements often are used to compare multiple observations of one dimension (such as the distal breadth of the metacarpus) against those of another dimension (such as the greatest length of the metacarpus), such sample size biases are a problem. Sometimes sufficient data for metrical analysis will be obtained only after working on many collections from a region. To develop a pool of measurements, it is important not to let opportunities to obtain them pass.

SPECIMEN WEIGHT

Additional primary data are provided by specimen weight. Specimen weight is not used extensively by zooarchaeologists because so many factors are known to influence it (Chaplin 1971:67–9; O'Connor 2000b; Uerpmann 1973). Chief among these biases are changes in weight that occur when elements are heated and during deposition (see Chapter 5). Nevertheless, specimen weight is used in many interesting ways (e.g., Erlandson 1994; Stahl 1995), and it should be recorded for each taxon in each sample along with other primary data (see Figure 6.2).

CONCLUSIONS

Clearly, even primary data involve interpretations. Accuracy at this step comes with experience and it is important analysts recognize their own limitations. When in doubt, either consult someone who has expertise in these areas or choose the conservative procedure. Many times, the importance of these early steps in a faunal study is discounted; they may even be left to junior members of the laboratory staff. All secondary data and subsequent analyses are suspect if primary data are not recorded accurately by skilled individuals. It may cost more or take longer to have a well-trained professional record primary data for archaeofaunal samples, but it is false economy to ask an untrained member of the field crew to assume this responsibility. It is also a disservice to future scholars who will presume, or at least hope, that primary data were recorded clearly, accurately, and consistently.

Secondary Data

INTRODUCTION

Although the importance of accuracy in describing primary data cannot be overemphasized, this is only one of the steps in gathering data that are needed to interpret an assemblage. The ultimate goal is to relate animal remains to the other materials from the specific site and to other sites so that larger cultural and biological inferences can be made (Schmid 1972:7; Smith 1976). To make these larger inferences, it is often necessary to derive secondary data by estimating relative proportions or specific indices from the primary data. Secondary data, by their nature, are less descriptive and more subjective than primary data. Secondary data, often derived from primary data mathematically, summarize many primary observations and require explanation and interpretation. Disagreements about all aspects of secondary data are numerous.

The secondary data reviewed in this chapter are: estimates of body dimensions, construction of age classes and sex ratios, relative frequencies of taxa, skeletal frequencies, estimates of dietary contributions; modifications, and niche breadth. These are clearly interrelated and can be interpreted in terms of many different research questions either together or alone. Methods for deriving secondary data often are developed to pursue a specific research problem and may not be widely applied. Regional zooarchaeological traditions and the frequency with which specific methods appear in the literature are strongly correlated. The methods for deriving secondary data surveyed in this chapter are widely used and have broad applications. To place secondary data in their research context, brief summaries of interpretive applications are included with each type of data.

Many of these interpretations are based on studies of recent materials that test, under modern, observable conditions, aspects of stable isotopes (e.g., Andrus and Crowe 2000), ancient DNA (e.g., Kimura et al. 2001), growth and development (e.g., Lubinski and O'Brien 2001; Milner 2001; Zeder 2001), and other components of secondary data (e.g., Bochenski and Tomek 2000; Dirrigl 2001; Hoffman et al. 2000; Wijngaarden-Bakker 2000). Modern control samples demonstrate that the relationships on which interpretation of secondary data depend are not simple, unidirectional, or independent. Even within a relatively small geographical range, or over a relatively short time span, variability is found among the modern biological, chemical, and physical responses on which secondary data are based. Therefore, modern studies should be used cautiously as analogues of the past, and interpretations of zooarchaeological applications should be equally cautious.

Where direct measurement is not possible, as is the case with the archaeological record, zooarchaeologists cope with ambiguity through careful application of ethnographic observation and analytical tools (Yellen 1977a:12). It may not be possible to pursue enquiries that require the "fossil" or "sample" assemblage to be a precise mirror of "life," "death," or "deposited" assemblages or that observations be demonstrably independent of each other. The basic assumption of all archaeological research must be that the recovered assemblage is, in some way, representative of the "life" assemblage. However, caution is called for in the face of many intangible and intractable biases.

Because we cannot go back in time to check our conclusions through direct observation or precisely replicate our "experiments," interpretations should be conservative and tested through further research. Secondary data are interpretations of primary data, not direct measurements. Rather than avoid deriving secondary data, it is better to test them repeatedly with multiple observations from well-excavated, large samples using several analytical tools to verify or refute conclusions drawn previously. Peer review is a valuable procedure and is only one of the many reasons publishing zooarchaeological results is important. However, for some questions and for some samples, the much-maligned laundry list may be the best choice.

ESTIMATES OF BODY DIMENSIONS

An important aspect of most studies is the size and conformation of animals in the past and variation within populations. Estimates of body dimensions support a number of further interpretations. A change in dimensions may suggest that an animal population responded to changes in human or nonhuman predation, to food availability, or to climatic changes (Klein and Cruz-Uribe 1984:94–8; Marelli and Arnold 2001). Body size reflects human choices about which species to capture, or avoid capturing, and which habitats to exploit. Body dimensions may indicate whether intense exploitation had an impact on the size and life histories of surviving individuals in the population (Cabral and da Silva 2003; Sutherland 1990), and they also are used to assess the nutritional contribution of animals to the diet.

Many aspects of faunal data must be considered when estimating and interpreting body dimensions. Body dimensions are related to age, sex, geographical range, nutrition, and individual variation, and it is necessary to consider all of these variables when evaluating body dimension data (Armitage 1982; Badenhorst and Plug 2003; Davis 2000; Steadman 1980; Weinstock 2000). Body dimensions, age, and sex are all important, related aspects of domestication (e.g., Storå and Lõugas 2005; Zeder 2001). Sample size is important because the range is dependent on the number of observations made (Simpson et al. 1960:80). The indices used to interpret morphometric data must be based on modern data, although the exact relationship between modern and archaeological data cannot be established. Free-ranging modern animals are probably more similar to wild or early domestic proportions than are carefully tended modern domesticates, but this is not inevitably the case (e.g., Albarella et al. 2005). Archaeological recovery technique is important because screens that are too large will not recover remains of small individuals.

Once specimens are fused or, in the case of the astragalus, are no longer porous, it is not possible to determine if it is from a young animal or an adult. The likelihood that specimens from subadults will be measured as adults is increased by the observation that some early-fusing elements are more dense than later-fusing ones (e.g., the proximal and distal humerus; Driesch 1976:5, 7; Lyman 1994c:246–8; compare Table 3.5 to Lyman 1984). Because the proximal and distal ends of many elements fuse at different developmental stages (Davis 2000; Silver 1970), the fused end of an otherwise subadult animal will be measured as adult without the researcher knowing whether the missing portion is unfused or fused (Driesch 1976:4). Consequently, early-fusing elements, whether from maturing subadults or mature adults, have a better opportunity of surviving site-formation processes and of being included in estimates of body dimensions than do late-fusing specimens from mature animals. However, early-fusing elements from subadults have essentially reached their mature size once they fuse, and the probability that measurements of elements from subadults are undetected may not be a major

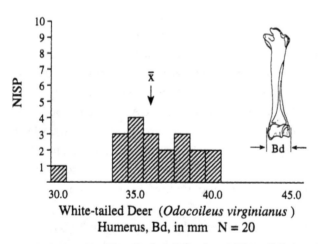

FIGURE 7.1. Hypothetical Collection: White-tailed deer (*Odocoileus virginianus*) measurements. Dimension is the distal breadth (Bd) of the humerus as defined by Driesch (1976:76).

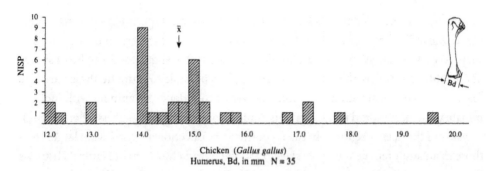

FIGURE 7.2. Hypothetical Collection: Chicken (*Gallus gallus*) measurements. Dimension is the distal breadth (Bd) of the humerus as defined by Driesch (1976:116).

bias. At the same time, well-ossified, fused elements are ideal for making tools and may not be included in the refuse commonly studied by zooarchaeologists (Payne 1972a). This is a strong reason why zooarchaeologists should examine worked specimens (see Appendix 3).

Metrical data are presented and applied in a number of ways. At the very least, one may find a simple list of descriptive statistics reporting the range, mean, standard deviation, and number of measurements for each dimension. Such descriptions are often the prelude to additional analysis. Direct measurements may also be presented graphically either as a comparison between one or more dimensions or as a histogram showing measurements of a single dimension. Metric data can be used without directly estimating body size (e.g., Ballbè 2005; Davis et al. 2005; Fraser 2001; Legge 2005; Lentacker 1994; Maltby 1979:77; Zeder 2001, 2006a, 2006b). In the Hypothetical Collection, measurements of the distal humerus (Bd) are plotted for white-tailed deer (Figure 7.1) and chickens (Figure 7.2). In both cases additional data from other St. Augustine collections are included because few specimens in the Hypothetical Collection could be measured. There appear to be two distinct groups of deer measurements: one represented by the very small humerus and the other including measurements clustering around the mean. Chicken measurements span a wide range but most fall in the smaller end of the range. Without any further analysis, these data could be interpreted as evidence that there was some variation in body size in these species. This approach, however, does not tell us how large these animals were or whether they are relatively larger or smaller than animals elsewhere or at other times. For further interpretation, however, it is often necessary to make additional comparisons and quantification.

Comparisons with Reference Skeletons and Ratios

The most direct approach to learning more about size or conformation is to compare archaeological specimens with reference skeletons (e.g., Roselló Izquierdo and Morales

Muñiz 1994). If the reference skeleton and the archaeological specimen share, for example, a similar distal humerus width, they might be similar in other aspects of body size and shape as well. Where standard measurements, such as total length, total weight, or shoulder height, accompany the reference skeleton, it is possible to estimate these variables for the archaeological animal with some degree of confidence. In animals with indeterminate growth, standard measurements could also reflect age (e.g., Desse-Berset 1994).

Many of the deer specimens in the Hypothetical Collection are somewhat larger than those in an adult female reference skeleton in the Florida Museum of Natural History's Environmental Archaeology Laboratory. This individual (FLMNH Z4567) lived on a coastal island 100 km north of St. Augustine and weighed 42 kg when it died. Although there were undoubtedly fluctuations in weight during the lives of both the reference and the archaeological animals that are not reflected in this approach, we can assume that some of the archaeological adults weighed at least 42 kg and that most weighed more than this.

In addition to direct comparisons, indices or ratios based on modern data are used to estimate body dimensions. As we described in Chapter 3, a common way to estimate the size of livestock is shoulder height, which is estimated for archaeological specimens using several different formulae (e.g., Audoin-Rouzeau 1991; Badenhorst and Plug 2003). These different shoulder height formulae can produce dissimilar results when applied to archaeological materials (Bartosiewicz 1995b:45). Ratios used to estimate body size of archaeological animals from element dimensions must be based on reference measurements taken from a large sample of individuals whose size, breed, age, and sex are known. These ratios may require estimating the age and sex for each specimen used in the index as a companion step. Estimates of shoulder height are usually derived from metapodial length, but whole metapodia are often rare in faunal samples. Some formulae estimate live weight of cattle based on known skeletal weight and archaeological specimen weight for selected elements (e.g., IJzereef 1981:56–8, 66). When several such correlations are applied to the measurements of different skeletal elements, reasonably accurate estimates of body size from archaeological specimens are achieved.

Allometric Regressions

The allometric relationship between whole body dimensions and skeletal or shell dimensions also is used to estimate body size or conformation (e.g., Bartosiewicz 1988, 1995b:45; Béarez 2000; Casteel 1974; Enghoff 1983; Morales and Rodríguez 1997; O'Connor 2000b:116–177; Purdue 1987; Reitz et al. 1987; Wheeler and Reitz 1987; see Chapter 3). The relationship is applied to estimates of original dimensions, such as total weight, length, or height from measurements of archaeological dimensions, such as femur head depth, valve length, centrum width, or otolith length.

Formula:

$$Y = aX^b \text{ or } \log_{10} Y = \log_{10} a + b (\log_{10} X)$$

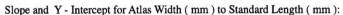

Y = Standard Length
X = Atlas Width
a = Y - Intercept
b = Slope

Slope and Y - Intercept for Atlas Width (mm) to Standard Length (mm):

Taxon	Slope (b)	Y - Intercept ($\log_{10} a$)
Sciaenidae	1.93	0.61

Archaeological Data:

Atlas Widths: 4.3, 9.1, 17.6 mm

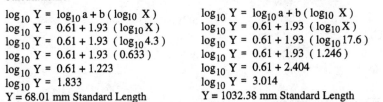

Calculations:

$\log_{10} Y = \log_{10} a + b (\log_{10} X)$
$\log_{10} Y = 0.61 + 1.93 (\log_{10} X)$
$\log_{10} Y = 0.61 + 1.93 (\log_{10} 4.3)$
$\log_{10} Y = 0.61 + 1.93 (0.633)$
$\log_{10} Y = 0.61 + 1.223$
$\log_{10} Y = 1.833$
Y = 68.01 mm Standard Length

$\log_{10} Y = \log_{10} a + b (\log_{10} X)$
$\log_{10} Y = 0.61 + 1.93 (\log_{10} X)$
$\log_{10} Y = 0.61 + 1.93 (\log_{10} 17.6)$
$\log_{10} Y = 0.61 + 1.93 (1.246)$
$\log_{10} Y = 0.61 + 2.404$
$\log_{10} Y = 3.014$
Y = 1032.38 mm Standard Length

The estimated range for red drum Standard Length is 68.0 - 1032.4 mm

FIGURE 7.3. Hypothetical Collection: Steps to estimate Standard Length (SL) of red drum (*Sciaenops ocellatus*) from atlas width.

Allometric formulae are particularly useful for estimating dimensions of animals with indeterminate growth such as fishes and molluscs. For example, it is possible to estimate the Standard Length of red drums in the Hypothetical Collection (Figure 7.3). To make this estimate, constants obtained from reference skeletons (Table 3.4) are used in a regression formula to predict the Standard Length (*Y*) of red drums from the anterior centrum width (*X*) of the smallest and largest red drum atlas in the archaeological collection. This application suggests that the Standard Length of red drums in the Hypothetical Collection ranged from 68 mm to 1,032 mm. With only three measurements (Table A4.5), however, analysis of the sample mean is not practical, and these results probably do not reflect the range or the average size of red drums used at the site.

Ratio Diagrams

When reference materials are limited, it may not be possible to estimate absolute body dimensions. A ratio diagram may be used to compare the dimensions of archaeological specimens relative to those of a single reference specimen that serves as a standard (e.g.,

Table 7.1. *Hypothetical Collection: White-tailed deer* (Odocoileus virginianus) *measurements, range, mean, standard deviation (SD), and sample size (N); measurements in mm*

Element, dimension	Range	Mean	SD	N
Humerus, Bp	41.0–46.9	44.2	3.0	3
Humerus, Bd	30.0–40.3	36.3	2.5	20
Radius, Bp	30.5–36.5	33.3	1.9	15
Radius, Bd	27.3–40.0	31.2	3.7	15
Metacarpus, Bp	23.5–26.1	24.4	1.0	7
Metacarpus, Bd	24.0–30.7	27.7	3.4	4
Femur, Bp	47.2–52.8	49.3	2.5	4
Femur, Bd	46.7–51.5	49.2	2.0	5
Tibia, Bp	48.9–54.3	52.6	2.2	5
Tibia, Bd	27.8–34.7	31.1	2.0	21
Astragalus, GLl	31.7–37.6	35.0	2.4	8
Astragalus, GLm	31.4–35.5	33.6	1.6	7
Astragalus, Bd	19.3–23.5	21.9	1.5	9
Calcaneus, GL	69.2–89.0	76.8	7.6	6

Note: Dimensions follow Driesch (1976). Data are from Table A4.5.

Albarella et al. 2005; Albarella et al. 2006; Cossette and Horard-Herbin 2003; Haber and Dayan 2004; Lyman 2004; Mengoni Goñalons and Yacobaccio 2006; Payne and Bull 1988; Peters et al. 2005). The standard does not represent a "normal" or average animal; it is simply a known reference against which trends are observed.

This method is applied to deer measurements in the Hypothetical Collection. The archaeological data are summarized in Table 7.1 and the steps followed to obtain the logged ratio of the archaeological observation to the standard (d) are presented in Table 7.2. In Figure 7.4, d is plotted against the standard, which is the 42 kg adult female reference specimen (FLMNH Z4567) used earlier. To construct the ratio diagram, one solves for d; X is the mean of the archaeological measurements for a specific dimension in an archaeological sample, and Y is the same dimension in the standard (Simpson 1941; Simpson et al. 1960:357–8). The mean is used in this example rather than the individual points, although individual points or the minimum and maximum values provide greater detail (e.g., Arbuckle and Bowen 2004; Payne and Bull 1988). It does not matter to what base the measurements are converted, although one should be consistent in order to maintain comparability. The impact of sample size on this estimate is clear because very few Hypothetical Collection specimens could be measured and the Hypothetical Collection data are augmented with data from other sites.

Positive values indicate dimensions that are relatively larger than the standard, and negative values indicate dimensions that are relatively smaller than the standard. When

Table 7.2. *Hypothetical Collection: Data used to construct a ratio diagram for white-tailed deer* (Odocoileus virginianus); *measurements in mm*

Element and dimension	Archaeological material (X)			Standard (Y)		
	N	Mean	$\log_e X$	Meas	$\log_e Y$	d
Humerus, Bp	3	44.2	3.789	41.4	3.723	0.066
Humerus, Bd	20	36.3	3.592	32.2	3.472	0.120
Radius, Bp	15	33.3	3.506	31.3	3.444	0.062
Radius, Bd	15	31.2	3.440	27.4	3.311	0.129
Metacarpus, Bp	7	24.4	3.195	23.4	3.153	0.042
Metacarpus, Bd	4	27.7	3.321	24.2	3.186	0.135
Femur, Bp	4	49.3	3.898	47.5	3.861	0.037
Femur, Bd	5	49.2	3.896	43.3	3.768	0.128
Tibia, Bp	5	52.6	3.963	45.2	3.811	0.152
Tibia, Bd	21	31.1	3.437	26.8	3.288	0.149
Astragalus, GL1	8	35.0	3.555	31.5	3.450	0.105
Astragalus, GLm	7	33.6	3.515	30.0	3.401	0.114
Astragalus, Bd	9	21.9	3.086	19.6	2.976	0.110
Calcaneus, GL	6	76.8	4.341	72.8	4.288	0.053

Note: Dimensions follow Driesch (1976). Meas = measurement. For archaeological materials, the mean of all measurements for the specified dimension is used, whereas for the reference specimen that serves as the standard, a single measurement is used. Formula: $d = \log_e X \log_e Y$.

trying to distinguish wild from domestic animals, or males from females, both groups may fall above or below the standard. However, domestic or female dimensions usually cluster at the smaller end of the range, and wild or male dimensions usually cluster at the larger end. The archaeological deer specimens in the Hypothetical Collection consistently have dimensions that are larger than those of the reference specimen (Figure 7.4). This appears to be part of a historical trend for decreasing body size in this region (Purdue and Reitz 1993). There also appears to be some variation in the archaeological deer dimensions that might reflect conformation. Neither relationship is clear when these same archaeological specimens are simply compared to the reference skeleton.

Attribution of Closely Related Species and Domestic Taxa

One of the primary applications of measurements is to distinguish between closely related taxa with similar morphologies but dissimilar body dimensions (e.g., Bocheński and Tomek 2000; Plug 2005; Shigehara 1994; Stahl 2005). Body dimensions also distinguish wild from domestic taxa and among different breeds (e.g., Albarella et al. 2006;

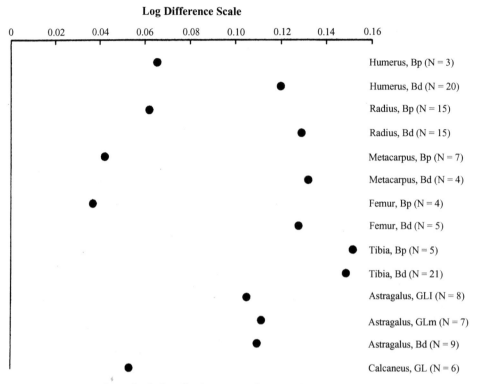

Log Difference Scale

FIGURE 7.4. Hypothetical Collection: Ratio diagram showing the size of white-tailed deer (*Odocoileus virginianus*) compared to the size of a modern standard. Based on the formula: $d = \log_e X - \log_e Y$; where d is the logged ratio; X is the mean of a specific dimension in the archaeological sample; and Y is the same dimension in a known standard. The vertical line is the standard. Positive values are larger than the standard and negative values are smaller than the standard. See Table 7.2 for data.

Mengoni Goñalons 2006; Zeder 2001). Sexual dimorphism has an impact on the use of osteometry to distinguish between domestic and wild animals, and among breeds because males, females, and castrates of the same breed achieve different sizes and have different body proportions. For example, Figure 7.1 could indicate that both female and male deer were hunted, and Figure 7.2 may be evidence that two or more chicken breeds were present at the Hypothetical Site.

Distinguishing between closely related species, hybrids, or domestic and wild animals, usually is done by calculating indices that have diagnostic value in order to establish a relative comparison of body dimensions. Most commonly this involves establishing a ratio between two dimensions and plotting them against a third. This approach is used by Armitage and his colleagues (1984) to distinguish between the Norway rat and the black rat. By applying their formula to the Hypothetical Collection (Figure 7.5), it appears that both Norway (*Rattus norvegicus*) and black (*R. rattus*) rats are present at the Hypothetical Site.

Formula: Diastema Index = (Dh / Dl) (100)

Dh = Diastema Height
Dl = Diastema Length
H   = Height of Mandible at M_1

Archaeological Data:

	Dh, mm	Dl, mm	H, mm
Mandible #1	4.3	7.0	6.5
Mandible #2	5.3	8.5	7.9
Mandible #3	3.8	5.3	5.1
Mandible #4	3.9	5.8	5.7

Calculations:

Mandible #1   Mandible #3
(4.3 / 7.0)(100)   (3.8 / 5.3)(100)
(0.6143)(100)   (0.717)(100)
61.43 (*Rattus norvegicus*)   71.7 (*Rattus rattus*)

Mandible #2   Mandible #4
(5.3 / 8.5)(100)   (3.9 / 5.8)(100)
(0.6235)(100)   (0.6724)(100)
62.35 (*Rattus norvegicus*)   67.24 (*Rattus rattus*)

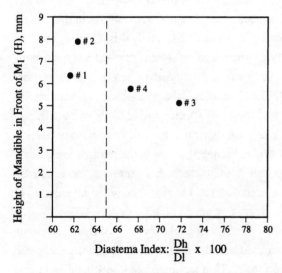

FIGURE 7.5. Hypothetical Collection: Using measurements to distinguish between Norway rats (*Rattus norvegicus*) and black rats (*R. rattus*) following Armitage et al. (1984).

CONSTRUCTION OF AGE CLASSES

Age classes, based on age at death, indicate the frequency with which a specific cohort of animals was used and therefore provide information about production, exchange, and other economic activities, especially seasonal ones. When data cluster in a single age class, this could indicate targeted hunting or culling strategies. Alterations in a long-established age class pattern may indicate environmental change, the presence of domesticated animals, or changes in other cultural systems. Age at death provides information on herd management practices, such as the use of younger animals for food, selective seasonal slaughter patterns, or slaughter of old animals after their ability to provide by-products or labor is diminished (e.g., Table 4.1). Age classes of domestic animals may demonstrate that the species was produced and consumed at the site (wide range of ages present), imported (restricted age range), or largely raised for slaughter and consumption elsewhere (prime-aged animals missing). It is not necessary to kill animals if blood, milk products, or wool and hair are used. This increases the likelihood that animals used for these products will survive into old age. Age classes of molluscs and fishes may indicate habitats exploited, season of capture, or capture technology.

An exact chronological determination of age for an archaeological specimen is unlikely because it would be necessary to know almost precisely when the animal was born (e.g., Lauwerier 1983). Although we can assume reproductive cycles in the present are generally similar to those of the past, it is impossible to verify this. Further, modern studies of some wild species indicate that the breeding season may extend over many months. For example, deer on coastal islands near St. Augustine breed from September to December (Osborne et al. 1992:46). The chronological age at which events related to growth occur varies among members of the same species and is likely to be different between wild species and their feral, free-ranging, transhumant, or sedentary descendants. This means the date of birth and all subsequent stages in the maturation process must be viewed as ranges rather than points (see Chapter 3; A. Grant 1978; Watson 1978). This precludes estimating age in terms of calendrical months, but, when interpreted in a broader sense, estimates of age at death are important secondary data.

Except when the specimens are from a burial, it is generally not possible to evaluate age from the perspective of actual individuals because the relationship among recovered specimens is usually unknown (Watson 1978). That is, we do not know if a distal fused humerus is from the same actual individual as a distal fused tibia. For this reason, age may be estimated for the same individual from different specimens many times.

To interpret anatomical data for age, one should use large comparative data sets obtained from an environmental setting as similar to that formerly prevailing at the archaeological site as possible for the species in question (e.g., Rolett and Chiu 1994; Tomé and Vigne 2003). If it is necessary to augment local age data, additional information should be obtained from ecologically and biologically similar organisms. For example, it would be inappropriate to use cementum increments from boreal forest wild caribou as reference materials for the evaluation of cattle from a tropical savannah. This caution presumes other members of the research team agree that the environmental factors influencing growth today are similar to those at the site in the past, which may not be the case (e.g., Bailey et al. 2000). The environment has changed at some sites so much that modern maturation sequences are probably dissimilar from those in the past.

Silver (1970) cautions that accurate estimates of a domestic animal's age can be made only when it belongs to a species or breed for which age characteristics are well-documented and the nutritional level is known, it is represented by most of its skeleton, and it is not yet fully adult. Data for modern free-ranging, feral, or wild relatives of domestic animals may provide better models of maturation in early domestic animals than do data for modern domestic animals of the same species (Zeder 1991:93). A similar observation could be made for nondomestic animals. The relationship between modern animals and those in the past is, itself, an interesting field of research.

Animals with Determinate Growth

Growth curves can be used to construct mortality profiles in animals with determinate growth. Epiphyseal fusion, tooth eruption, tooth wear, and growth increments are primary data used to estimate age at death and to construct age classes (Ruscillo 2006). Many of the biases that influence estimates of body dimensions also have an impact on the use of epiphyseal fusion as a way to construct age classes. Especially important is the observation that unfused and incompletely ossified specimens are less likely to survive archaeologically than are specimens that are fused (Klein and Cruz-Uribe 1984:43; Munson 2000; Payne 1972a; Watson 1978). This skews the evidence toward age classes represented by elements that fuse early in the maturation process and were fused when the animal died. Early-fusing elements that were unfused when the animal died are likely to be underrepresented, as are less dense late-fusing ones. In some cases, such as in Africa where it is difficult to distinguish among the many bovid species, epiphyses are identified only to family and therefore offer limited interpretive value (Klein and Cruz-Uribe 1984:43).

Although the timing of fusion is highly variable, the sequence of fusion appears to be generally consistent among mammals (Table 3.5), and it is this that can be used to establish relative age classes (Chaplin 1971:80–1; Davis 2000; Fandén 2005; Moran and O'Connor 1994; Silver 1970; Tomé and Vigne 2003; Zeder 2006b). Because each age class is usually represented by only a few specimens and fusion ranges overlap, Chaplin (1971:129–33) recommends dividing the material into three groups based on the age at which fusion generally occurs: (1) animals aged 10 months or less, (2) those between 18 and 24 months, and (3) those older than 36 months. The use of months gives a false sense of accuracy that can be avoided by grouping specimens into general chronological ranges such as early, middle, and late (Gilbert and Steinfeld 1977). A more conservative approach also accommodates ranges of skeletal maturation that may extend beyond 36 months (e.g., Fandén 2005). The ambiguity inherent in age grouping is somewhat reduced by recording each specimen under the oldest group possible whenever there is uncertainty about semifused specimens. It should now be clear why it is necessary to note whether the portion of the element represented in the collection is a proximal or distal epiphysis or diaphysis, and to describe the degree of fusion as advocated in Chapter 6.

Fusion is much more informative for unfused specimens of elements that fuse early in life and for fused elements that complete growth at the end of the maturation process. A dimension that fuses early, such as the distal humerus, and is represented by a fused archaeological specimen, could be from an animal that died soon after the dimension fused or many years later. Unfused specimens from middle and late categories may be from animals that were actually juveniles at death. Highly porous compact bone is indicative of juvenile or subadult elements, but porosity is a relative observation compared to fusion sequences and is not readily accommodated in quantified analyses. Metapodia are particularly useful for identifying subadult animals because the medial line of the diaphysis fuses at a very young age, while the distal epiphysis fuses to the diaphysis much later. Both stages of this process are observable when the distal diaphysis is present. Ideally sex would be factored into this evaluation, but it is usually difficult to determine sex from the same specimens that provide evidence of fusion. These observations provide additional reasons for exercising caution if correlating the sequence of fusion with an exact calendrical age.

The age structure of deer in the Hypothetical Collection is estimated following Chaplin (1971:129). First the specimens identified are combined into a specimen distribution worksheet (Table A4.3). On this list, unfused, fused, and indeterminate specimens are noted. In the case of unfused specimens, it is necessary to distinguish between epiphyses and diaphyses, and the code for this is included at the bottom of the table. Then, the fused and unfused specimens are further summarized in a fusion worksheet (Table A4.4). Based on these data, the percentages of fused and unfused specimens in each age class are calculated (Table 7.3).

Although the ranges of many elements in these groups overlap, a general trend can be established by this procedure. In this case, unfused specimens in the early-fusing category are equated with juveniles, and fused specimens in the late-fusing category are equated with adults. Unfused specimens in the middle- and late-fusing groups are equated with subadults in the absence of any notes indicating the presence of the porous bone characteristic of juveniles. Although fused early- and middle-fusing specimens

Table 7.3. *Hypothetical Collection: White-tailed deer* (Odocoileus virginianus) *NISP subdivided into age categories following Chaplin (1971:129)*

Early-fusing specimens:
  Number unfused 2; Number fused 19; Total NISP 21
    percent unfused = $(2)(100/21)$ = 9.5 percent
    percent fused = $(19)(100/21)$ = 90.5 percent

Middle-fusing specimens:
  Number unfused 1; Number fused 7; Total NISP 8
    percent unfused = $(1)(100/8)$ = 12.5 percent
    percent fused = $(7)(100/8)$ = 87.5 percent

Late-fusing specimens:
  Number unfused 6; Number fused 10; Total NISP 16
    percent unfused = $(6)(100/16)$ = 37.5 percent
    percent fused = $(10)(100/16)$ = 62.5 percent

Note: Data are from Table A4.4.

could be from adults, the conservative interpretation is that they offer only indeterminate evidence for age at death. Although juvenile specimens are present in the Hypothetical Collection, subadult and adult specimens are more common.

Such data can be presented in tabular form (e.g., Crabtree 1989:70; Payne 1972a), as histograms showing the percentage killed in an age range and before a given age (Chaplin 1971:131), or as ternary (3-pole) graphs (e.g., Greenfield 2005). If bar diagrams are used, the sample size should be included in the figure. These calculations may be made for each element (e.g., Crabtree 1989:71) rather than for groups of elements, as is done in Table 7.3 and Figure 7.6. Such data can be used to derive survivorship curves, cumulative frequency graphs, or fusion scores (e.g., Magnell 2005; Munson 2000; Zeder 1991:90–1; 2001).

Tooth eruption sequences provide an estimate of age at death. If the animal was killed before all permanent teeth erupted, it is possible to obtain a relative age at death based on a sequence of tooth eruption similar to the sequence for fusion (e.g., Greenfield 2005; Haber and Dayan 2004; Lowe 1967; Lubinski and O'Brien 2001; Maltby 1979:56; Munson 2000; Severinghaus 1949; Zeder 1991:143, 2006b). This approach is often used to age living game or domestic mammals. Tooth eruption sequences are considered to be more reliable indicators of relative age than fusion because enamel is more durable than bone. For this reason, teeth of both young and adult animals may have equal survival potential, which is not the case with bones of young animals. However, tooth eruption is subject to individual and environmental variations based on nutrition and health, especially as this relates to pathologies and diseases of the jaw (Grant 1978). As with fusion sequences, tooth eruption should be used to indicate a sequence of relative ages rather than an absolute age and should be based on comparative data from the region (e.g., Rolett and Chiu 1994).

Once the epiphyses are fused and permanent teeth are present, evidence for adult age is more difficult to obtain. Distinguishing between young adults and older ones is usually done using subjective evaluations of cranial sutures, horn or antler development, pathologies, and other characteristics associated with age (Armitage 1982; Silver 1970). One common approach is to estimate the degree of tooth wear (d'Errico and Vanhaeren 2002; Grant 1978; Greenfield 2005; Haber and Dayan 2004; Klein et al. 1983; Klein and Cruz-Uribe 1983; Klein et al. 1981; Lubinski and O'Brien 2001; Payne 1973; Rowley-Conwy 2000). Tooth wear begins when the tooth erupts, and continues throughout the life of the animal. Consequently it provides a relative indicator of age for animals that survive past the age when fusion and tooth eruption is completed. Individual variation among populations of the same species confounds comparative studies as do pathological conditions (Chaplin and White 1969; Klein and Cruz-Uribe 1984:52–5). Grant (1978) reports that teeth may not even be worn uniformly on both the left and right mandible of the same individual. Analysis of tooth wear is more effective if a complete tooth row is present. These data may also be presented as cumulative frequency graphs, survivorship curves, harvest profiles, or ternary graphs (e.g., Arnold and Greenfield 2004; Greenfield 2005).

Eruption sequences and tooth wear can be combined. As is often the case, dental sequences are quite rare in the Hypothetical Collection. Only one deer mandible is present. It contains teeth from P_2 through M_3. The P_4 is a permanent tooth and the M_3 is fully emerged and somewhat worn. Teeth in this mandible are recorded in Figure 6.2 following Payne (1973) and Grant (1978; see also Figures 6.9 and 6.10; Levitan 1982). This pattern of tooth wear is similar to that of a reference specimen that also lived in a sandy coastal environment and was $3\frac{1}{2}$ years old when it died. The significance of a single observation is difficult to evaluate, but this mandible does confirm the conclusion drawn from the fusion data that at least one adult is present in the collection.

Another approach to estimating age at death is to examine growth increments. In animals with determinate growth, few adult tissues have growth increments, however, some success has been achieved with annuli in tooth cementum (e.g., Burke 2000; Burke and Castanet 1995; Landon 2007). These annuli are usually examined to obtain information about season of death rather than age at death, however, theoretically age at death and season of death are closely related in many regions. Using this type of evidence to estimate age at death, for example, Pike-Tay (1991:106–7) reports that many more red deer in the Upper Paleolithic samples she studied are from juvenile classes rather than from older groups. This interpretation is supported by tooth eruption and wear evidence.

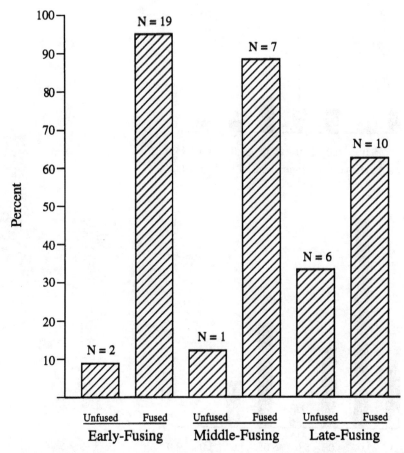

FIGURE 7.6. Hypothetical Collection: Histogram of white-tailed deer (*Odocoileus virginianus*) age groups.

Animals with Indeterminate Growth

Age at death and age classes are most commonly based on estimates of body size and growth increments in animals with indeterminate growth. Small individuals often represent young age classes, perhaps even young of the year, while large individuals should represent older animals. In Figure 7.7, the measured dimensions of sea catfish (Ariidae) otoliths and mullet atlases in the Hypothetical Collection are plotted. This approach is sensitive to sample size, however, and the mullet measurements indicate there are at least two age classes in the collection, probably more. One of these age classes is very young and the other is older. These age classes would occupy distinct habitats, and each was probably captured with different techniques. The sea catfish data do not appear to cluster into distinct age classes, which may indicate a more continuous breeding season. If the archaeologist had used only a 6-mm mesh, these possibilities would not have been

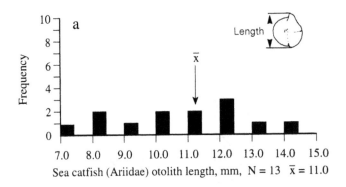

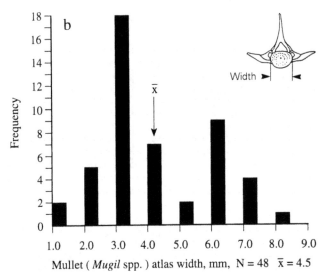

FIGURE 7.7. Hypothetical Collection: (a) Sea catfish (Ariidae) otolith length and (b) mullet (*Mugil* spp.) atlas width measurements.

considered, because individuals from the young age classes (small individuals) would not have been recovered (see Figure 5.12).

Increments are used to estimate age at death in molluscs and fishes (Luff and Bailey 2000; Mannino and Thomas 2001). By counting pairs of increments representing annuli in hard clams (*Mercenaria mercenaria*), Quitmyer and his associates (1985) found that the mean age of modern clams is older than that of clams recovered from the archaeological site (Figure 7.8a) and that shell length in modern clams does not always correlate with age (Figure 7.8b). A similar approach can also be applied to fish otoliths. Figure 7.9 shows the frequency of annuli in Atlantic croaker (*Micropogonias undulatus*) otoliths from sixteenth-century deposits near St. Augustine. Interpreting each annulus as a year's growth, the figure shows that a wide range of age classes is present, although the younger age groups dominate the collection (Hales and Reitz 1992).

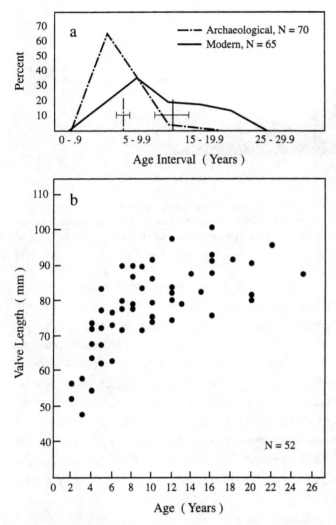

FIGURE 7.8. Characteristics of hard clams (*Mercenaria mercenaria*) based on increment counts and measurements of modern and archaeological (A.D. 1000–1500) clams from Kings Bay, Georgia: (a) age intervals based on increment counts of modern clams compared to archaeological ones (vertical bar indicates mean and horizontal bar indicates one standard deviation); and (b) scatter diagram showing the relationship between valve length and age. Modified from Quitmyer et al. (1985:34); © (1985) by the Southeastern Archaeological Conference and reprinted by permission from *Southeastern Archaeology*, Volume 3, Number 1. and Irvy R. Quitmyer.

SEX

Sex is basic to many interpretations, especially those related to husbandry strategies, predator–prey relationships, and food preferences. It is derived from morphological characteristics, as well as the size of the many processes and muscle attachments that vary with sex as well as age (Ruscillo 2006). The more rugged nature of specimens from

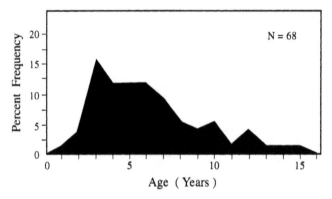

FIGURE 7.9. Age at death of Atlantic croaker (*Micropogonias undulatus*) from a sixteenth-century Contact Period deposit at the Fountain of Youth site near St. Augustine based on annuli in otoliths. Modified from Hales and Reitz (1992:84) and used with the kind permission of Elsevier.

males may bias sex ratios in favor of males. In those species where females have horns or antlers, adult male antlers and horns are more likely to survive deposition than the lighter, smaller antlers and horns of young individuals or females. More commonly, sex ratios are derived from relative differences in body size reflected in measurements. Large sample sizes and modern comparative data are essential to interpretations of archaeological data. Interpretations of morphometric data are usually based on variations in modern populations, which are probably not identical to those in the past, for both domestic species and wild ones. It is possible that demographic information in the faunal assemblage reflects postmortem choice of body parts to remove from the kill site rather than selective killing patterns (Weinstock 2000). Body size, age, and sex are closely related in life, as primary data and as secondary data. Whenever possible, evidence for all three parameters should be examined together.

In those species where males and females are sexually dimorphic, this is often reflected in measurements. One way to extrapolate sex from measurements is to plot the dimensions of an element against other dimensions from the same specimen (e.g., Crabtree 1989:38–40; Howard 1963; Magnell 2005; Rowley-Conwy 2000; Weinstock 2000, 2002). This is usually done with fused dimensions to avoid confusing size differences due to sex with those due to age, but it has even been applied to teeth by combining morphological and metrical variables (d'Errico and Vanhaeren 2002). Ideally, the elements selected for this application should be ones most directly related to sex, such as the pelvis (e.g., Wilson 1994). Many indices calculate the relationship between the width of either the distal or proximal end of an element, the diameter of the shaft, and the greatest length of the metapodia (e.g., Figure 7.10; Higham 1969a, 1969b; IJzereef 1981:46). Unfortunately, this considerably reduces the sample size because metapodia may be absent in the collection if they were left at the kill site, redistributed with the cut of meat, or used to make tools and ornaments. Metapodial elements also fuse relatively early in an animal's life. The

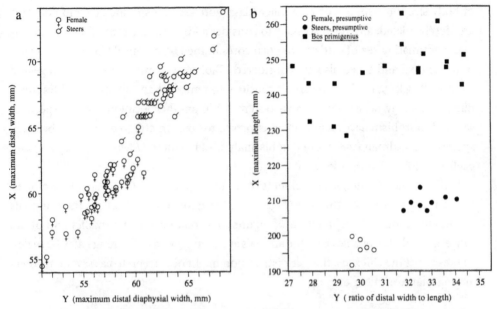

FIGURE 7.10. Scatter diagrams of (a) modern Aberdeen Angus metacarpal bones and (b) bovine metacarpal bones from Troldebjerg, a Danish prehistoric settlement. Modified from Higham (1969b:140, 142); used with the kind permission of *Current Anthropology*, University of Chicago Press, and Charles F. W. Higham.

astragalus is commonly used, but, because this element does not grow by epiphyseal fusion, it is difficult to distinguish between young animals and adults except by degree of porosity (although see Davis [2000]). Usually, complete elements are lacking, so indices showing a ratio of distal width and distal length to total length or of other dimensions are often developed (Figure 6.10; e.g., IJzereef 1981:46; Maltby 1994:97). Modern reference measurements are sometimes included in these figures for additional comparisons.

The normal distribution for sexually dimorphic mammals is a bimodal curve. If castrated domestic animals are present in the collection, there may be a trimodal curve, with castrate measurements falling between females and intact males. This curve is influenced by the age of the animal when it was castrated and other factors (Chaplin 1971:101; Clutton-Brock et al. 1990). The relative proportions of castrated animals are different, perhaps because growth continues for a longer period of time in castrated animals. For example, the metacarpus tends to be relatively short and slender in cows, short and broad in bulls, but long and slender in steers (Davis 1987:Figure 1.24; IJzereef 1981:46). The absence of separate groups may mean that the faunal assemblage contains the remains of only one sex (see Chaplin 1971:102), or it could indicate there is no sexual dimorphism in that species (Klein and Cruz-Uribe 1984:41).

The relationships among intact males, castrated males, females, individual and regional variations, and breed is a complex one (Albarella et al. 2005; Badenhorst and Plug 2003; Davis 2000; Zeder and Hesse 2000). Conformation and the normal range of body size for a species or breed, age class, and sex in a specific geographical area are closely related, and it is necessary to consider all three at the same time. For example, in estimating sex of cattle from horn cores in the Hypothetical Collection, the age of the animal and breed also are considered (Table 6.2; Armitage 1982; Armitage and Clutton-Brock 1976). Because size is sensitive to temporal and spatial variables, male dimensions may be similar to those of females in another location. These aspects of sexual dimorphism have an impact on efforts to use osteometry to distinguish between species, as Steadman (1980) found in his analysis of northern (*Meleagris gallopavo*) and ocellated (*M. ocellata*) turkeys.

Earlier in this chapter, measurements from the Hypothetical Collection were plotted for deer (Figure 7.1) and chickens (Figure 7.2) to explore the size range of these animals at the site. Another interpretation of Figure 7.1 is that deer at the smaller end of the range are probably females, and the animals at the larger end of the range may be males. In the case of the chickens, the size distribution might be interpreted as several roosters among a large number of hens.

RELATIVE FREQUENCIES OF TAXA

The number of identified specimens (NISP), the minimum number of individuals (MNI), and the specimen weight are used to estimate relative frequencies of taxa in faunal assemblages. Relative frequencies permit synchronic and diachronic exploration of environmental fluctuations, successions, taphonomic, recovery and sampling biases, and cultural differences. Relative frequencies of taxa are most commonly used to augment age and sex ratios, to identify specialized sites or activity areas, and to compare animal use by distinctive social groups through time and space. They also are used to evaluate the relative importance of animals in diets obtained through various subsistence strategies. Relative frequencies form a particularly important line of evidence in studies of markets and exchanges between producers and consumers. A shift in taxa may also indicate domestication (e.g., Davis 2005). This section will review NISP and MNI and then consider relative frequencies generally. Rarely is specimen weight used directly to document relative frequency, although there are exceptions (e.g., Stahl 1995; Teeter and Chase 2004; M. Uerpmann 1993).

Number of Identified Specimens (NISP)

Specimen count, or the NISP, is primary data. However, it is commonly used to estimate the relative frequency of taxa, which is an analytical product. In such applications, NISP is criticized by some and championed by others (Bobrowsky 1982a; Chaplin 1971:67; Grayson 1973, 1984:20–4; O'Connor 2000b; Perkins 1973; Ringrose 1993; Watson 1972; White 1953a). Although future analysts should be able to duplicate NISP reliably, applying specimen count to estimates of relative frequencies of taxa is more problematic. By using it as a measure of abundance, the analyst assumes that cultural and noncultural fragmentation is uniform, recovery rates are constant for each taxon, and all taxa have an equal opportunity to be counted. It is usually difficult to know whether the specimens are independent of one another (Grayson 1973, 1979), and, therefore, the relationship between the number of specimens and diet is unclear (White 1953a). NISP is related to the number of identifiable elements in each animal, site-formation processes, recovery techniques, and laboratory procedures.

Differences in numbers of elements and identifiability are particularly significant issues in assemblages containing crustaceans, molluscs, fishes, reptiles, birds, and mammals. These animals have widely different kinds and numbers of hard tissue; the same elements are not present in all species. Even in animals with similar elements, these are not equally identifiable. Identifiability is a function of both the number of anatomically similar, and, therefore, potentially misleading species in an assemblage and the degree of breakage or erosion suffered by each specimen. Some elements are much more likely to be identified in large numbers and others may not be identified at all. For example, a pig has forty-four teeth, while a marsh periwinkle (*Littorina irrorata*) has only one apex. Not only does the periwinkle have fewer parts to identify, the parts must be relatively complete to be identified, whereas pig teeth can be identified readily from very small fragments. These simple differences have considerable relevance for interpreting the role of these animals at the Hypothetical Site (Table A4.1).

Another important bias is that some elements are more likely to survive than others. As reviewed in Chapter 5, specimens from molluscs, fishes, amphibians, reptiles, birds, and mammals do not survive the hazards of deposition equally (Chaplin 1971:64–5). One reason so many middens are dominated by molluscs is that their shells survive much better than do the bones and teeth of vertebrates, although often as thousands of indeterminate invertebrate specimens. Likewise, because enamel preserves better than bone, animals with teeth, primarily mammals, have a better chance of being recovered and identified than do vertebrates without teeth or invertebrates, such as crustaceans. NISP of some tissues and some animals may slowly increase during deposition, while other specimens are lost through chemical and physical processes. Such attritional factors are not uniform between sites, between temporal components within the same site, or even among excavation units.

Cultural practices related to transportation, butchering, distribution of meat, cooking, disposal, and nonsubsistence uses of elements have an impact on NISP as these activities destroy or disperse material (e.g., Bunn et al. 1988; Kent 1993). For example, if most elements of a large-bodied animal or elements that were easy to process were routinely left at the kill site, but small animals or elements that required more time to process were brought back to the consumption site intact, NISP will reflect these decisions. People may also have reduced elements into small, indeterminate fragments to extract oil, grease, gelatin, and glue (e.g., Mateos 2005; Alen and Ervynck 2005), or they may have removed them from the excavated area as tools, ornaments, and through exchange networks.

Recovery techniques and laboratory procedures also bias NISP. If a 6-mm screen is used, most specimens smaller than 6 mm will be lost, reducing NISP for taxa with small elements (Figure 5.12). Compensations can be made for differential recovery rates by deriving "recovery constants" for the recovery rate of taxa of various body weights in each screen size (Thomas 1969). However, it is much better to use a smaller screen in the first place. We have already reviewed the importance of recovery technique in the Hypothetical Collection (Table 6.1). Decisions not to identify some specimens (e.g., ribs, shaft fragments, or fish vertebrae) or to restrict identification to a short priority list (e.g., mollusc apex, columella, and hinge; chiton plates; fish otoliths) considerably skew NISP and limit opportunities to compare NISP among collections, sites, or research groups (e.g., Todd and Rapson 1988).

These considerations are all represented in the Hypothetical Collection. The impact of identifiability on NISP in the Hypothetical Collection is very clear. Mullet vertebrae are readily identified to genus and are common in the collection (NISP = 761), but identifying vertebrae as hardhead catfish (*Ariopsis felis*) rather than to the order (Siluriformes) or family (Ariidae) is difficult (Table 7.4). Hence, mullet NISP is often higher than hardhead catfish NISP. Fragments of pig teeth are readily identified to species although it is sometimes difficult to distinguish among fragmentary deer, cattle, and caprine teeth. One could easily interpret the species list as evidence that NISP is high for pigs because of their teeth and for cattle because of their carpal and tarsal elements, but deer and caprines are undercounted because their elements are difficult to distinguish and, in the Hypothetical Collection, they are not represented by high numbers of these diagnostic elements.

The relative frequency of taxa is explored in many ways using NISP (e.g., Cannon 2000; Gilbert and Singer 1982; Maltby 1985:137; Tchernov 1993; Thomas 1971); although perhaps the most common use is to examine estimates of skeletal frequency that are reviewed later in this chapter. To correct for differential ease of identification, some suggest dividing NISP either by the number of elements per taxon the analyst is able to identify or by the number of identifiable elements per taxon actually recovered and identified in the assemblage under study (Perkins 1973; Perkins and Daly 1968). The latter alternative may correct for cultural bias in the kinds of elements recovered when a primary processing locality is excavated instead of the consumption site. Another application is to calculate an index of fragmentation by dividing the number of identified

Table 7.4. *Hypothetical Collection: Skeletal groups for fishes, NISP*

Taxa	Otolith	Other cranial	Atlas	Other vertebra
Ariidae Sea catfish family	13	37		167
Ariopsis felis Hardhead catfish		249		
Bagre marinus Gafftopsail catfish		11		
Mugil spp. Mullets	1	171	48	761
Sciaenidae Drum family		16		379
Bairdiella chrysoura Silver perch	5		2	
Cynoscion spp. Seatrouts		2	2	2
Leiostomus xanthurus Spot		1		
Menticirrhus spp. Kingfishes		7	4	70
Micropogonias undulatus Atlantic croaker		3	1	
Pogonias cromis Black drum	1	24		1
Sciaenops ocellatus Red drum	1	35	3	1
Total	21	556	60	1,381

Note: Data are from Table A4.1.

specimens by the number of indeterminate ones or to develop indices such as the artiodactyl index (e.g., Byers et al. 2005). In some cases, a simple index of fragments per square meter may indicate changes in animal use (e.g., Schibler 2004).

Minimum Number of Individuals (MNI)

Estimates of the MNI are another widely used category of secondary data (Stock 1929; White 1952, 1953a). Shotwell (1955:330; 1958:272) defines MNI as the smallest number of individuals that is necessary to account for all of the skeletal elements (specimens) of a particular species found in the site. Although MNI is the most common abbreviation,

MIND and NMI also are found in the literature. Critiquing MNI might be considered a growth industry among zooarchaeologists (e.g., Bobrowsky 1982a; Bökönyi 1970; Casteel 1977; Chaplin 1971:69–75; Clason 1972; Fieller and Turner 1982; Grayson 1973, 1978, 1979, 1984; Klein and Cruz-Uribe 1984:24–38; Krantz 1968; Lyman 1994c:100–2; Nichol and Wild 1984; O'Connor 2000b; Payne 1972a; Perkins 1973; Plug and Plug 1990; Ringrose 1993; Steele and Parama 1981; Uerpmann 1973; Watson 1979; Ziegler 1973:25). Although this intense review is very helpful, it has produced terminological confusion about the meaning of the concept (Casteel and Grayson 1977; Lyman 1994a).

As with NISP, MNI is related to the number and identifiability of elements in each animal, site-formation processes, recovery techniques, and laboratory procedures. Unlike NISP, which describes the actual number of specimens present in the samples studied, MNI is solely an analytical product. MNI estimates should not be interpreted as actual individuals; more actual individuals may have been used at the site, or only portions may have been used. The white shark in the Hypothetical Collection (Table A4.1) is represented by a fossil tooth and is probably a curio for which the concept of MNI is irrelevant. To estimate MNI, it is necessary to consider not only identifications and elements represented, but also age, sex, size, and archaeological context. This is a much more complex measure than NISP.

Before considering the biases of MNI, it is necessary to review some of the methods used to derive it. MNI is based on the observation that vertebrates, as well as many crustaceans and molluscs, are symmetrical; elements from either side or the midline are distinctive. White (1953a:397) proposes that this can be used to estimate MNI, for which one should "separate the most abundant element of the species found (usually the distal end of the tibia) into right and left components and use the greater number as the unit of calculation." For example, the deer specimens in FS# 340 include three left radius specimens with the proximal end fused (Figure 6.3). The specimen drawings confirm that these must be from three individuals. At the most basic level, this means some parts of at least three deer skeletons are represented in this sample, although more deer may have been used at the site, or only portions may have been used. Although the assumption behind the use of symmetry to estimate MNI is that a left and right element may actually form a pair of elements from the same individual animal, in practice, actually pairing elements is a very difficult process and rarely is attempted (for an exception, see Zeder and Arter 2007). When we refer to paired specimens, it is on the basis of symmetry rather than of matched pairs of elements that actually are from the same biological individual.

Bökönyi (1970) and Chaplin (1971:69–75) recommend considering evidence for age, sex, and size in addition to symmetry when estimating MNI, a process Klein and Cruz-Uribe (1984:26) refer to as "matching" (e.g., Flannery 1967:157; Smith 1975a:34; Zeder and Arter 2007). Using FS# 340 as an example again, the proximal radius fuses very early (Table 3.5). Therefore, all of the three individuals estimated from symmetry were probably at least subadults when they died. However, the distal end of one diaphysis is unfused, indicating this individual was not an adult when it died. Such an evaluation is not possible for the other two individuals. This same sample also has a partially worn deciduous P[4] and an unfused scapula. Both are evidence for a juvenile deer not represented by the radius fragments. Therefore, there may be the remains of four individuals in this sample rather than three. However, because it is possible the deciduous P[4], the unfused distal radius, and the unfused scapula are from a single individual that died just at the end of 18 or so months, only three individuals are estimated for this sample: one juvenile and two older than 18 months. In practice MNI is usually estimated with some consideration of such observations, although publication constraints may prohibit making these procedures clear.

Klein and Cruz-Uribe (1984:26–9) suggest a procedure in which fragments of elements are recorded numerically on the basis of the percentage of the skeletal part present in the sample, as fractions of complete elements (i.e., 0.50, 0.33, 0.25). These fractions are then summed. Referring to Figure 6.3, the distal humeri in FS# 340 may be tabulated as 1.0 and 0.75, summed to 1.75. This suggests an MNI for this element of two. The approach advocated by Davis (Albarella and Davis 1996:3–4), in which at least 50 percent of a dimension must be present for it to be counted, with exceptions made for metapodia and some other elements, is similar. A procedure such as this is particularly important if MNI is estimated by a computer program.

Another common way to estimate MNI divides the number of specimens identified for each element by the number of such elements present in a skeleton (Binford 1978:70). In the case of symmetrical elements, there would be two in each skeleton; axial elements would be divided by one and phalanges of artiodactyls by eight. Binford abbreviates the results of this calculation as "MNI" (Binford 1978:69–70; Thomas and Mayer 1983:355), although evidence for symmetry need not be recorded, and it is a procedure that White (1953a:397; Shotwell 1955) specifically counsels against. The use of the term "MNI" by Binford creates confusion with White's definition of MNI as the minimum number of individual animals necessary to account for the identified specimens based on symmetry (Lyman 1994a:50). Although some argue that each specimen actually does represent a separate individual (Perkins 1973), this concept is not in keeping with the traditional meaning of MNI. Whenever MNI is used in this volume, it is with the meaning of White's MNI modified to include age, sex, and size as recommended by Bökönyi and Chaplin, but it is not based on actual matched pairs (sensu White). Except where specifically noted, Binford's approach to MNI (sensu Binford) is not used in this volume.

MNI is related to the number and identifiability of elements in each animal. High MNI estimates are related to the number of identifiable symmetrical or singular axial elements. Animals such as bivalves, gars, snakes, and turtles usually are represented primarily by nonsymmetrical elements, such as valve fragments, ganoid scales, vertebrae, and carapace fragments. In such cases, MNI estimates will always be lower than seems reasonable given the number of identified specimens. For example, there are no symmetrical pit viper elements in the Hypothetical Collection – all fifty specimens are vertebrae. The MNI for this snake is estimated to be one. In such cases, MNI could be estimated by counting the vertebrae present in the analytical unit and dividing by the number of vertebrae in a reference skeleton. If this step is followed, it is important to realize that nonmammalian vertebrate species may have a range of vertebrae rather than a fixed number and that it is likely that most caudal vertebrae are not recovered or identified.

Many first- and second-order changes have an impact on MNI. Transportation, processing, storage, distribution, consumption, and discarded mean skeletal portions of carcasses are gradually dispersed over a wide area and a long period of time, only a portion of which is included in the excavated area (e.g., Bartram et al. 1991:142; Bunn et al. 1988; Gilbert and Singer 1982). Food exchange and preservation are particularly important. Prior to refrigeration, large quantities of meat had to be quickly distributed, or preserved, so the meat did not spoil. For this reason, as well as to maintain social cohesion, food exchange is a hallmark of human life. However these actions rapidly disperse the skeleton of an animal. This is particularly likely for large-bodied animals, as small animals might be consumed by an individual household (e.g., Kent 1993:352). This also is an issue with urban samples where marketing meat products was probably a substantial factor in their formation (e.g., Bartosiewicz 1995b; Maltby 1994; Reitz and Zierden 1991; Reitz et al. 2006; Zeder 1991:36–7). It is for these reasons that the relationship between MNI and the actual number of individuals used in the excavated activity area or at the site as a whole is unclear.

Recovery techniques and laboratory procedures also are important, particularly sample size. MNI often correlates with the number of specimens in the collection and the number of taxa (Bobrowsky 1982a; Casteel 1977; Gejvall 1969:4; Grayson 1984; Shotwell 1958; Uerpmann 1973). The number of individuals is often plotted against the number of taxa to visualize the extent to which sample size is a bias in the collection (Figure 4.6). It is particularly likely that the NISP of gastropods and some other molluscs will match the MNI because of the nature of their identifiable hard tissue (i.e., columella and apex).

MNI is influenced by the manner in which data from archaeological proveniences are aggregated during analysis. The aggregation of separate samples into one analytical unit ("minimum distinction") allows for a conservative estimate of MNI, while the "maximum distinction method," in which MNI is estimated for each archaeological sample, yields a much larger estimate (Grayson 1973, 1984:31; O'Connor 2000b). The number of subdivisions may depend on the research problem, the degree of temporal control, and the number of discrete excavation units. Two particularly important components of aggregation are the field decisions about where to place units and whether to use arbitrary metric levels or follow natural stratigraphy during excavation. The zooarchaeologist should know how excavation units and strata relate to cultural activity at

Table 7.5. *Hypothetical Collection: NISP of white-tailed deer* (Odocoileus
virginianus), *diamondback terrapin* (Malaclemys terrapin), *gopher tortoise*
(Gopherus polyphemus), *and pit viper* (Viperidae) *in five archaeological contexts*

Taxa	Deer	Terrapin	Gopher tortoise	Pit viper
Nonfeature contexts	20	1	30	
Feature 8	46		1	
Feature 9				50
Feature 10	3	1	4	
Feature 11	11		12	
Total	80	2	47	50

Note: Data are from Table A4.1.

the site before attempting to estimate MNI, and use cultural units for estimating MNI
rather than arbitrary ones related to excavation logistics. The basis for aggregation
should always be described in the report.

The results of such aggregation decisions are seen in the Hypothetical Collection,
which has five archaeological contexts thought to be distinct cultural units (Table 7.5).
MNI is estimated for each of these five analytical units. Single specimens of diamondback
terrapin (*Malaclemys terrapin*) are identified in two deposits and are interpreted as the
remains of two individuals, one of which is in the nonfeature contexts and the other
in Feature 10. Because all pit viper specimens are in Feature 9, only one individual is
estimated; but if one vertebra had been in Feature 9 and forty-nine vertebrae in Feature
11, two individuals would be estimated. The gopher tortoise is represented by unpaired
elements in each context except Feature 11, which contains two right hypoplastron
specimens. This suggests the remains of single individuals in all of the analytical units
except Feature 11, which has the remains of two individuals. However, combining the
deer data in FS# 245 and FS# 340 does not increase the number of estimated individuals
and reinforces the interpretation that one of the three individuals estimated for the
nonfeature context is a juvenile and the others are at least subadults (Table 7.6).

In most cases, MNI is estimated for the lowest taxonomic level within a systematic
hierarchy. Under these criteria, preference is given to taxonomic attributions that include
both genus and species over ones that include only genus; to genus over family; to family
over order, etc. MNI is not normally estimated for a higher taxonomic category when
specimens in that category could relate to lower taxa. For example, MNI is not estimated
for the possible cat (cf. *Felis catus*) because the single specimen could be from one of
the verified cat individuals (*Felis catus*; Table A4.1). In another example, MNI is not
estimated for the specimen identified for the sandpiper family (Scolopacidae) because
that specimen could be from the common snipe (*Gallinago gallinago*), which is a member
of the scolopacid family.

Table 7.6. *Hypothetical Collection: White-tailed deer* (Odocoileus virginianus) *MNI estimates subdivided into age categories and archaeological contexts*

Context	Juvenile	Subadult	Adult	Indeterminate
Nonfeature contexts	1	1	1	
Feature 8	1	1	2	
Feature 9				
Feature 10				1
Feature 11		2	1	
Total	2	4	4	1

Sometimes a higher MNI is estimated at the family or subfamily level than at the species level. Following the research protocol for the Hypothetical Site, the higher number would be used rather than the smaller one. This quandary arises in a few specific cases. One of these is caprines. In the Hypothetical Collection, eighteen specimens are identified as goat or sheep (Caprinae), and three are identified as goat (*Capra hircus*). For which taxonomic level should MNI be estimated: for the species or for the subfamily? In this case, MNI is estimated for both, and the higher number is used in subsequent calculations. Three caprine individuals are included in the total MNI for the collection and used to calculate relative percentages even though it is for the subfamily rather than the species. One of the caprines could be a goat, which is presented in the species list as a parenthetical note (Table A4.1). The same problem sometimes occurs for two species (*Ariopsis felis, Bagre marinus*) of the sea catfish family because the most common elements for estimating MNI often are otoliths, which are difficult to distinguish between the two species (Table 7.4).

MNI estimates are probably the most common type of secondary data, quite independent of White's objective of estimating edible meat. It is one of the only ways to compare mammals, birds, reptiles, amphibians, fishes, and molluscs. Many of the problems with MNI are overcome by careful excavation and evaluation of the archaeological data, combined with cautious zooarchaeological analysis. When estimating MNI, it is important to remember that it is the *minimum* number of individuals necessary to account for the identified elements of a particular taxon, and there are some research questions for which MNI is not the appropriate analytical tool.

Specimen Weight

Specimen weight is infrequently used to evaluate relative frequencies of taxa. It is particularly helpful in quantifying degree of fragmentation for various taxa, spatial and temporal attributes of specimens, relative size of specimens, and distinctions between primary

Table 7.7. *Hypothetical Collection: Summary of NISP, MNI, specimen weight, and sample biomass data*

Taxonomic categories	NISP		MNI		Weight		Biomass	
	N	%	N	%	g	%	kg	%
Wild terrestrial mammals	104	2.6	19	2.3	1,157.7	4.4	15.65	11.9
Domestic mammals	416	10.4	30	3.6	9,079.4	34.6	102.2	78.0
Wild birds	51	1.3	26	3.1	70.84	0.3	1.108	0.8
Domestic birds	62	1.6	10	1.2	76.5	0.3	1.06	0.8
Turtles	50	1.3	8	1.0	121.0	0.5	0.91	0.7
Sharks, rays, and fishes	1,528	38.2	130	15.7	315.14	1.2	6.72	5.1
Commensal vertebrates	120	3.0	12	1.4	51.5	0.2	1.086	0.8
Edible molluscs	1,199	30.0	394	47.5	15,280.09	58.2	2.315	1.8
Commensal invertebrates	465	11.6	200	24.1	116.96	0.4		
Total	3,995		829		26,269.13		131.049	

Note: Only those taxa for which MNI is estimated are summarized in this table. Data are from Table A4.1.

and secondary refuse (Erlandson 1994:151, 154; Peacock et al. 2005; Zeder 1991:107, 219). Dividing the specimen weight for a taxon by NISP yields an average weight per fragment that is useful for interpreting taphonomic history for different taxa. For example, the average weight of deer specimens in the Hypothetical Collection is 13.4 g, while the average weight of the cattle specimens is 36.2 g. Cattle specimens are, therefore, usually larger than those of deer and may be less fragmented. Specimen weights make categories such as Indeterminate Mammal, which have few other applications, more useful. For example, 13,079 Indeterminate Mammal specimens weighing 7,945 g (0.6 g/fragment) is quite different from 202 cattle specimens weighing 7,310 g (36 g/fragment) and helps the reader visualize the differences between these two taxonomic levels.

Specimen weight is sometimes used to establish relative frequencies among animals (e.g., Driesch 1993; Stahl 1995:158). Anderson (1983) uses specimen weight to estimate MNI and examine anatomical distribution. M. Uerpmann (1993) uses specimen weight (abbreviated WIF) to compare vertebrates in a collection comprised primarily of cattle, caprines, and fishes. She finds that fishes are dominant using either NISP or specimen weight, but cattle constitute 3 percent of the collection based on NISP and 17 percent based on specimen weight. The same phenomenon is present in the Hypothetical Collection (Table 7.7).

In some cases, specimen weight is used as a proxy for the amount of meat contributed by a species (e.g., Uerpmann 1973; Zeder 1991:90). For example, if specimen weight for deer is 1,076.4 g, it may have contributed 4.1 percent of the meat in the Hypothetical Collection (1,076.4 g/26,269.13 g; Table 7.7). This application will be discussed in greater detail with other methods for estimating dietary contributions.

Relative Frequencies of Taxa and Their Interpretation

All of these quantification devices are subject to a number of biases. Difficulty translating NISP into diet was one of the motivations for using MNI (White 1953a). Grayson (1979) argues field procedures, taphonomic analysis, and statistical manipulation can overcome the weakness of specimen count for establishing relative frequencies. Perhaps the most intractable bias is the lack of comparability among researchers that makes it difficult, perhaps even impossible, to conduct intersite comparisons. For the sake of comparability, highly individualistic treatments should be avoided whenever possible.

Analysts working with collections containing animals other than mammals continue to find that comparisons of relative frequency based on NISP are fraught with interpretative problems because of the variability in numbers of identifiable elements between taxa and differences in preservation. It is for this reason that many argue NISP should be used only when comparing similar species and not across broad taxonomic boundaries. Uerpmann (1973:309) suggests that comparisons using NISP can be made within size categories, such as cattle compared to horses (*Equus caballus*) or caprines compared to pigs or large dogs. Within a class, such as mammals or birds, the number of skeletal elements also is more uniform, so that NISP may be a good measure of relative abundance within an order, such as artiodactyls; a family, such as bovids; or a single species, such as deer.

MNI or NISP should not be used exclusively to address every research question. Each provides information that cannot be derived from the other; their use should be based on the characteristics of the collection being studied and the questions being addressed. If either of these measures were used alone to quantify the Hypothetical Collection much information would be lost. Based on NISP, eastern oysters would dominate the analysis (Table A4.1). Based only on MNI, much information would be lost for taxonomic levels such as goat or drum family (Sciaenidae). MNI is not usually estimated for these taxonomic levels following the protocol established for the research project at the Hypothetical Site. In evaluating human behavior at the Hypothetical Site it is important to know there are 379 drum vertebrae in the collection, even though they could not be identified to a lower category and are not used to estimate MNI. Their presence may indicate that whole fish, rather than fillets, were brought to the site, for example.

It is often suggested that MNI and NISP measure two different aspects of a collection. Payne (1985b) argues that NISP minimizes the importance of species represented by only a few specimens and exaggerates the importance of species whose elements are more readily identified, especially when fragmented or poorly recovered. However, he suggests that MNI emphasizes the importance of rare animals in small, well-recovered samples; a single specimen always represents at least one individual whereas some taxa may be represented by many unpaired specimens and also count as a single individual. Klein and Cruz-Uribe (1984:30) suggest that MNI is a minimum estimate of the number of individuals in a collection, and NISP is the maximum number. The actual number of individuals is somewhere in between and cannot be determined.

Many interesting studies are based on relative frequencies of taxa. Taxa may be combined, using MNI, NISP, or specimen weight, so that interpretations can focus on relative frequencies of animals representing different catchment areas (estuarine versus flood plain) or captured by different technologies (trapping versus netting), for example. In the case of the Hypothetical Collection (Table 7.7), such a summary suggests fishing was a very important subsistence activity. Estuarine resources comprise the vast majority of the collection regardless of whether the conclusion is based on NISP, MNI, or specimen weight. To keep the sample universes of various taxonomic groups uniform, only those taxa for which MNI is estimated are included in Table 7.7, MNI being the measure that is obtained for the fewest number of entries in the species list. Other options include graphing the percentage of one taxon against that of another (e.g., Randsborg 1985) or developing an index of two taxa against one of those taxa or some other variable (e.g., Byers et al. 2005; Szuter and Bayham 1989; Ugan and Bright 2001). Such indices may be termed "prey indices" (see Darwent 2004).

"Similarity measures" (Table 4.4) compare relative frequencies of taxonomic groups. This technique is used here to compare some of the taxonomic groups in the Hypothetical Collection with a sixteenth-century Spanish collection from St. Augustine. The comparison shows that the Spanish collections are similar to one another, indicating a relatively homogeneous use of resources within the town (Table 7.8). A sharper contrast is found between the hispanic Hypothetical Collection and contemporaneous data from a site occupied by free Africans (Fort Mose) near St. Augustine (Reitz 1994b).

SKELETAL FREQUENCY

The frequency of specimens from different parts of the skeleton is important in studies of taphonomy; butchering, transport, food preparation, and disposal habits; nutritional analysis; activity areas; site function; economic institutions; and social organization. It is particularly important in studies focusing on exchange of animals and portions of animals in complex societies via markets, as well as ethnic and status differences. Skeletal frequencies may distinguish among commensal animals, animals used for food, and those used as beasts of burden, in rituals, or for other nonfood purposes. Skeletal

Table 7.8. *Hypothetical Collection: Calculation of percentage similarity among some vertebrates from a sixteenth-century Spanish site in St. Augustine; an eighteenth-century African site, Fort Mose; and the Hypothetical Collection, using MNI*

	SA 26-1 sixteenth century		Hypothetical eighteenth century		Fort Mose eighteenth century	
	MNI	%	MNI	%	MNI	%
Wild, noncommensal mammals	24	6.1	19	9.0	6	2.7
Domestic animals	38	9.6	45	21.2	6	2.7
Wild birds	28	7.1	26	12.3	6	2.7
Gopher tortoises	12	3.0	5	2.4		
Sharks and rays	15	3.8	8	3.8	4	1.8
Sea catfishes	44	11.1	24	11.3	34	15.5
Mullets	168	42.4	53	25.0	10	4.5
Drums	67	16.9	32	15.1	154	70.0
Total	396		212		220	

Percentage similarity between SA 26-1 (sixteenth-century) and Hypothetical Collection (eighteenth-century): $PS = 6.1 + 9.6 + 7.1 + 2.4 + 3.8 + 11.1 + 15.1 + 25.0 = 80$ percent
Percentage similarity between Hypothetical Collection and Fort Mose: $PS = 2.7 + 2.7 + 2.7 + 0 + 1.8 + 11.3 + 15.1 + 4.5 = 41$ percent

Note: Sixteenth-century data from Reitz and Scarry (1985: Table 24); Hypothetical eighteenth-century data from Table A4.1; Fort Mose data from Reitz (1994b).

frequencies are commonly used to research the evolution of early hominid behavior, especially to identify the point in our family's history when we became hunters.

Analysis of skeletal frequency is based on the concept of postmortem disturbance (Shotwell 1955; Voorhies 1969). Skeletons of species dying of natural causes and buried immediately are expected to be relatively complete because they were subject to little postmortem disturbance prior to burial. Carcasses that experience postmortem disturbance are expected to be less skeletally complete when excavated. The degree of completeness is important to environmental reconstruction because it may distinguish between animals that were part of the proximal community and those that were from more distant ones. In theory, animals that lived near the site might be more skeletally complete because they were transported over a shorter distance prior to deposition and, therefore, were subjected to fewer opportunities for loss during transportation.

This natural process is similar to that associated with humans. In general, the skeletons of nonfood animals should be less disturbed than those of food animals. For example, commensal animals may be more skeletally complete than animals used for food because the commensal's carcass may be casually discarded intact. Skeletons of animals with economic value to humans may be less complete because they steadily disintegrate as a result of human food processing and other activities from the time the animal dies until the surviving specimens reach the zooarchaeologist. This is a useful concept for distinguishing between animals that may have been used by people as food, in rituals, commensal to the site, or brought to the site by other animals (e.g., Lentacker et al. 2004; Sampson 2000; Szuter 1988; Thomas 1971).

Skeletal frequencies may also distinguish between animals killed some distance from a village and those killed nearby if heavier, less desirable portions of a carcass are left behind at the kill site, and more valued portions of a carcass brought back to camp. This concept is referred to as the "schlepp effect" (Perkins and Daly 1968). Frequencies may not only distinguish between animals killed some distance from the site and those killed nearby, they may also distinguish between domestic animals and wild ones. A domestic animal, if killed in or near the village, should be more skeletally complete than a wild animal killed further away, because heavy elements with little economic value would not be transported any great distance. This principle extends to the association of skeletal frequencies with trade, urban markets, status, ethnicity, and ritual (e.g., Bowen 1992; Crabtree 1990; McNiven and Feldman 2003). Similarly, collections that contain primarily specimens from the foot and tail may be the residue of fur and hide trade (e.g., Baxter and Hamilton-Dyer 2003).

The problem is determining which elements are "valuable" or "prestigious," to whom, and under what circumstances (e.g., O'Connell et al. 1990). Elements that are not valued for food may be taken back to camp because they offer convenient handles or because they are important raw material for bone meal, tools, glue, ornaments, or gaming pieces. This is particularly true for elements of the lower legs, including carpi, tarsi, metapodia, and phalanges. Pickled pigs feet continue to be an important ritual food in New Year celebrations in the United States today. The head is usually thought to have little value because it has little meat, however, brains are often used to dress leather (Spier 1970:117) and the cranium provides a useful container for this soft tissue. The cranium, therefore, may be transported at great energetic expense because the brain is an important by-product. The brain and other organs also are desirable food, not just to earlier hominids (e.g., Stiner 1994:229) but to wealthy housewives in Atlantic coast colonies in North America (e.g., Hess 1981). Distinguishing whether crania or other less "valuable" elements were broken to extract the brain for curing hides, to eat, or for other purposes might be very difficult. We should avoid extending our own concepts of usefulness to other cultures without considering alternative explanations (e.g., Alen and Ervynck 2005).

Skeletal frequency may indicate several important aspects of a site's history. A high degree of skeletal completeness may indicate that the animal was killed nearby, that the species' habitat was near the site, that the animal was relatively intact when discarded or was not disturbed substantially once buried, or that the deposit was a burial of a pet, a ritual offering, or a sacrifice. Animals with few elements represented may indicate transport, extensive butchering activity, sharing, or a great deal of postmortem disturbance for other reasons. These are just a few of the potential interpretations that are based on skeletal frequency. To determine which were responsible for the specific observation, it is important to combine skeletal frequency with other lines of evidence, such as size and shape of elements, modifications, collecting bias, the activities of scavengers, and context (deFrance et al. 2001; Voorhies 1969; Wolff 1973).

Most studies of skeletal frequencies distinguish between taxa in the archaeological collection that are relatively complete skeletally and taxa represented by few specimens. A common approach is to classify fragmentary specimens or elements into skeletal portions. Other approaches quantify ratios of observed to expected specimens or classify specimens on the basis of their predicted utility or food value. None of these actually estimates nutritional contribution, although dietary value is the premise on which some rankings are based. Although these are often considered methods by which to examine use of mammals, these same approaches may be applied to other classes of animals (e.g., Morales 1993b).

Skeletal Portions

Skeletal portions are usually based on skeletal elements, anatomical regions, or butchering units. Skeletal elements refer to specimens that can be attributed to a specific element, such as the humerus or cleithrum (e.g., Mena et al. 2004; Morales et al. 1994). Anatomical regions or carcass units are groups of adjacent elements such as axial, forelimb, or feet (e.g., Miracle 2002; Wilson 1989). These are distinguished from butchering units, which may include portions from adjacent skeletal elements, adjacent anatomical regions, only part of an element, or only one anatomical region (Lyman 1977; Schulz and Gust 1983). The problem is to get from archaeological specimens to anatomical regions, breakage units, and butchering units in such a way that ultimately taphonomic processes and human decisions about animal use can be studied.

This effort is confounded by the relationship between fragmentary specimens and elements and by methods used to estimate what is often referred to as the number of individuals. Lyman (1994b) points out that usually studies of skeletal portions are based not on the number of elements, but on the number of identified specimens (NISP) that represent an unknown number of elements. Until we reach the section in this chapter on utility indices, NISP is treated as though each fragment is independent in most of the following examples. As we will see later in this chapter, an estimate of the number of reconstructed elements may also be used.

Some techniques report specimens as skeletal elements. A very simple approach is to list the number of identified specimens according to the elements they represent, such

Table 7.9. *Hypothetical Collection: Summary of some mammalian specimens by anatomical regions, NISP*

Skeletal group	Mole	Rabbit	Rat	Raccoon	Cat	Pig	Deer	Cattle	Caprine
Head	2	4	4	1	8	111	7	24	4
Axial				2	4	2	4	65	
Forequarter	4	2		2	2	34	28	27	4
Hindquarter		3			1	23	22	61	6
Forefoot						3	5	4	3
Hindfoot		1				7	8	10	3
Foot		5		3	6	13	6	11	1
Total	6	15	4	8	21	193	80	202	21

as on the specimen distribution worksheet (Table A4.3). Because these follow natural anatomical organization they require little explanation other than descriptions of how specimens are counted (e.g., Bartosiewicz 1995b:31; Crabtree 1989:22). The data may also be presented using diagnostic zones for each element (e.g., Dobney and Rielly 1988; Knüsel and Outram 2004; Münzel 1988).

If NISP is summarized as anatomical regions, it is important to be clear about the elements assigned to a region (e.g., Landon 1996:47; Lev-Tov 2004; Stiner 1994:242). In the Hypothetical Collection (Table 7.9), the Head category includes only skull and mandible fragments and teeth; vertebrae and ribs form a separate Axial category; the Forequarter category includes the scapula, humerus, ulna, and radius; the Hindquarter category includes the innominate, sacrum, femur, patella, and tibia; the Forefoot category includes carpal and metacarpal elements; the Hindfoot category includes tarsal and metatarsal elements; and the Foot category contains elements identified only as metapodial elements and phalanges. In cases where data are further summarized into categories such as Head, Axial, and Limb (e.g., Zeder 1991:226) it is particularly important to be clear about which elements are assigned to each category.

Another common technique is to present the anatomical distribution of NISP graphically. In many cases, specimen counts are presented on a skeleton such as Figure 6.4 (e.g., Hesse and Wapnish 1985:94–5; Sampson 2003). It is possible to summarize all NISP for a particular element (e.g., seven humerus fragments) or present portions of each element separately (e.g., four proximal tibia and four distal tibia fragments). Both styles are used in Figure 6.4. In a more synthetic illustration, the data are presented as percentages (e.g., Morales et al. 1994). In Figure 7.11, in addition to an anatomical bar chart, specimens in four percentiles are coded so that the most abundant ones are more readily apparent on the accompanying skeleton. The data may also be presented in graphs by element (e.g., Enloe 1993; Tchernov 1993) or anatomical region (e.g., Figure 7.12; Emery 2004a). NISP should always be incorporated into such figures, or

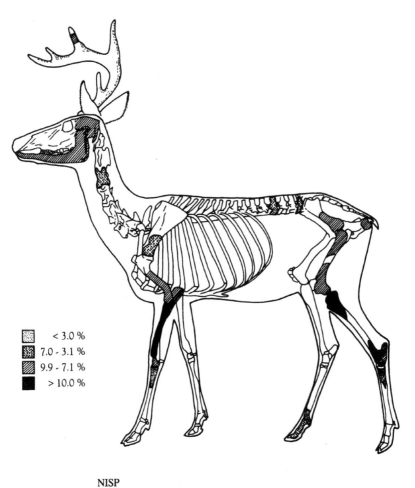

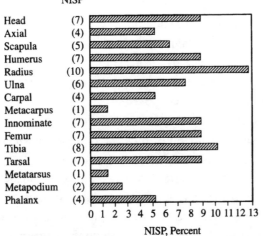

FIGURE 7.11. Hypothetical Collection: Specimens identified as white-tailed deer (*Odocoileus virginianus*) shown anatomically using the Number of Identified Specimens (NISP) (after Morales et al. 1994:47).

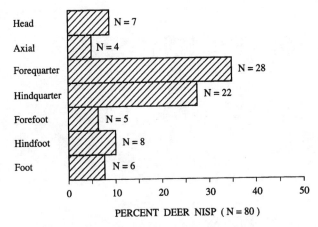

FIGURE 7.12. Hypothetical Collection: Histogram of white-tailed deer (*Odocoileus virginianus*) specimens.

provided in a companion table, so that sample size can be evaluated with the other evidence. It should be clear whether NISP is being depicted, as is the case in all of the Hypothetical examples, or the number of elements that may be represented by those fragments.

Alternatively, the specimens may be grouped as high-value, medium-value, and low-value meats based on the presumed or demonstrated quantity and quality of the meat associated with different elements (e.g., Uerpmann 1973). Frequently, skeletal portions in these cases are derived from modern cuts of meat such as round, loin, or brisket as defined by the meat industry or government agencies (e.g., Lyman 1979). Such classifications are common when postmedieval materials are studied (e.g., Bartosiewicz 1995b:37–42; Szuter 1991) but also are used with much earlier deposits (e.g., Thomas and Mayer 1983:373). When a value is assigned to such butchering units, it is often based on current market prices or presumed meat value.

Ratios of Observed to Expected Specimens

Ratios of observed specimens to expected ones are constructed in many different ways. Usually the ratio of each element represented in the collection is calculated against an expected number of those elements to ascertain the degree of skeletal completeness (e.g., Cerón-Carrasco 1994; O'Connor 2000b; Thomas and Locock 2000). The primary difference among these approaches is that in some cases the expected value, which serves as the norm, is derived from the archaeological collection itself and in other cases the expected value is based on anatomical relationships.

In the preceding examples of skeletal frequencies, all of the specimens from an element are combined (Figures 7.11, 7.12; Table 7.9). Therefore, shaft fragments, as well

Hypothetical Collection: Radius

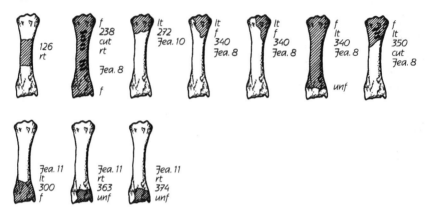

Hypothetical Collection: Ulna

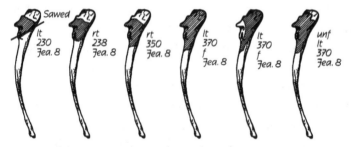

FIGURE 7.13. Hypothetical Collection: Illustrations of white-tailed deer (*Odocoileus virgini-anus*) radii and ulnae identified. Key: rt, right; lt, left; Fea., Feature; f, fused; unf, unfused; the number is the Field Sample number (FS#).

as both distal and proximal aspects of whole elements could be used. However, when analysis distinguishes between proximal and distal ends, as is often the case with ratios of observed to expected specimens, shaft portions and whole elements pose a problem. For example, in Figure 7.13, the ulnae fragments from FS# 230, 238, 350, and the unfused left ulna in FS# 370 are shaft fragments rather than proximal ends. These were so recorded in Table A4.3, however, in Tables 7.10 and 7.11, they are treated as proximal. The radius is a more difficult situation: there are one shaft, six proximal ends, and four distal ends in the collection, for an apparent total of eleven specimens. Yet, there are actually only ten specimens. This can complicate analysis based on distinctions between proximal and distal aspects of elements (e.g., Crabtree 1989:8; Maltby 1985).

Decisions about how to handle this problem should be based on the research question involved. The primary purpose of using observed to expected ratios is to determine whether there is differential representation of skeletal portions that correlates with habitual treatment of carcasses. In St. Augustine, with a few exceptions, most groups of

Table 7.10. *Hypothetical Collection: Observed/expected ratio for white-tailed deer* (Odocoileus virginianus); *expected based on NISP*

Element	Observed	Expected	O/E ratio
Radius, proximal	6	6	1.00
Ulna, proximal	6	6	1.00
Scapula	5	6	0.83
Humerus, distal	5	6	0.83
Mandible	4	6	0.67
Radius, distal	4	6	0.67
Femur, distal	4	6	0.67
Tibia, proximal	4	6	0.67
Tibia, distal	4	6	0.67
Astragalus	4	6	0.67
Ilium	3	6	0.50
Ischium	3	6	0.50
Intermediate carpal	2	6	0.33
Calcaneus	2	6	0.33
Metapodium, distal	2	6	0.33
Radial carpal	1	6	0.17
Ulnar carpal	1	6	0.17
Metacarpus, proximal	1	6	0.17
Acetabulum	1	6	0.17
Femur, proximal	1	6	0.17
Os malleolare	1	6	0.17
Metatarsus, proximal	1	6	0.17

specimens appear to include adjacent portions of different elements forming butchery units that are "joints" of meat. The primary question is whether joints containing the proximal radius and distal humerus are more common than those associated with the distal radius and carpals. For this reason, the observed value used for the distal radius is four rather than three, and the radius shaft fragment is not included in this calculation.

If shaft fragments are not routinely identified, it would be impossible to argue that most deer specimens are from distal and proximal ends, because the alternative hypothesis, that most specimens are shaft fragments, is untested and untestable. Furthermore, the complete radius and the radius shaft fragment indicate that some units of meat were not "joints." This must be considered when evaluating skeletal portions in terms of butchering units and other processes. If observed-to-expected ratios were to be applied in other interpretive settings, another decision might be required, and the one made here must continually be reevaluated.

Table 7.11. *Hypothetical Collection: Percentage survival for white-tailed deer* (Odocoileus virginianus) *based on the number of each element expected for eleven individuals*

Element	Observed	Expected	Percentage survival
Radius, proximal	6	22	27.3
Ulna, proximal	6	22	27.3
Scapula	5	22	22.7
Humerus, distal	5	22	22.7
Mandible	4	22	18.2
Radius, distal	4	22	18.2
Femur, distal	4	22	18.2
Tibia, proximal	4	22	18.2
Tibia, distal	4	22	18.2
Astragalus	4	22	18.2
Ilium	3	22	13.6
Ischium	3	22	13.6
Intermediate carpal	2	22	9.1
Calcaneus	2	22	9.1
Metapodium, distal	2	44	4.5
Radial carpal	1	22	4.5
Ulnar carpal	1	22	4.5
Metacarpus, proximal	1	22	4.5
Acetabulum	1	22	4.5
Femur, proximal	1	22	4.5
Os malleolare	1	22	4.5
Metatarsus, proximal	1	22	4.5

Expected Value Derived from NISP:

In this approach, the element with the highest number of specimens in the archaeological collection becomes the expected value (Table 7.10). In many cases, the number in the observed column is the number of identified specimens (NISP) for each element rather than the number of reconstructed elements (Klenck 1995; Lyman 1988, 1994b; Voorhies 1969). Values in the expected column are based on the frequency of the most common element (the highest NISP), which in Table 7.10 is the proximal radius. The other observed values are divided by six, the expected value. For consistency, the expected value is reduced from six to three for nonsymmetrical elements, such as the atlas, and increased for elements such as first phalanges. It also is possible to distinguish between left and right elements, or between hindquarters and forequarters, using this method.

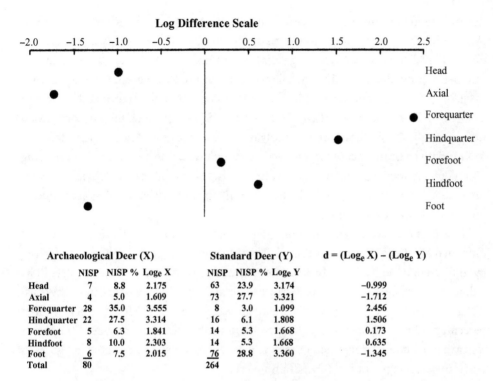

Log Difference Scale

−2.0	−1.5	−1.0	−0.5	0	0.5	1.0	1.5	2.0	2.5

Head
Axial
Forequarter
Hindquarter
Forefoot
Hindfoot
Foot

	Archaeological Deer (X)			Standard Deer (Y)			$d = (\text{Log}_e\ X) - (\text{Log}_e\ Y)$
	NISP	NISP %	Log_e X	NISP	NISP %	Log_e Y	
Head	7	8.8	2.175	63	23.9	3.174	−0.999
Axial	4	5.0	1.609	73	27.7	3.321	−1.712
Forequarter	28	35.0	3.555	8	3.0	1.099	2.456
Hindquarter	22	27.5	3.314	16	6.1	1.808	1.506
Forefoot	5	6.3	1.841	14	5.3	1.668	0.173
Hindfoot	8	10.0	2.303	14	5.3	1.668	0.635
Foot	6	7.5	2.015	76	28.8	3.360	−1.345
Total	80			264			

FIGURE 7.14. Hypothetical Collection: Ratio diagram of white-tailed deer (*Odocoileus virginianus*) skeletal portions using NISP. Based on the formula: $d = \log_e X - \log_e Y$; d is the logged ratio; X is the percentage of each skeletal portion identified as deer in the archaeological collection; and Y is the percentage of this same portion in a complete skeleton. Positive values indicate that the skeletal portion is more abundant compared to the standard and negative values indicate that the skeletal portion is underrepresented.

Expected Value Derived from Anatomical Relationships:

Another way to examine skeletal completeness is to compare the observed number of archaeological specimens to the number expected if the skeleton was complete. Often, the expected number of elements is the number in a single complete skeleton (e.g., Korth 1979). For example, in Figure 7.14, the number of identifiable elements in a complete, undisturbed deer skeleton is a standard against which the number of archaeological specimens referable to each element type is compared as a ratio (e.g., Reitz and Zierden 1991; see Stiner 1994:264 for a variation on this approach). This is the same method used earlier to analyze body size of deer (see Figure 7.4; Simpson 1941), except that NISP is used instead of measurements.

In some cases, the expected number of elements is derived by estimating what is termed the expected number of individuals (Table 7.11; e.g., Dodson and Wexlar 1979; Shipman and Walker 1980). In applications of this method to modern data, the number of individual skeletons is actually known because it was observed during fieldwork or determined in the course of an experiment (e.g., Brain 1981:23, 277; Klippel et al. 1987). When applied to archaeological materials, the number of individuals is not directly observed and must be derived (e.g., Binford 1978:69–72; White 1953a). Usually the number of individuals is estimated following Binford (e.g., Legge and Rowley-Conwy 1988:69) rather than following White (e.g., Wolff 1973); though there are other ways to estimate MNI (e.g., Klein and Cruz-Uribe 1984:27; Stiner 1994:244, 390). In some cases, unfortunately, the methods are so poorly explained that it is not possible to tell how MNI is derived or in what sense it is used. Although we do not recommend estimating "MNI" in any way other than sensu White, if it is, this should be made clear. It seems preferable, however, not to apply the term "MNI" to any derivative unless estimated in the sense advocated by White.

These data are used in a number of different ways. In Table 7.11, the MNI for deer is estimated following White (Table A4.1). The values in the expected column are derived by multiplying deer MNI (11) by two; the assumption being that eleven complete individual skeletons should be represented by two of each paired element, i.e., by twenty-two distal humeri. The percentage survival, sometimes referred to as percent preservation or percentage representation, is calculated by dividing the observed number of fragments for each portion by the expected number. Such data may also be presented in figures in terms of percentage survival (e.g., Brain 1981:23).

Corrected Frequency and Other Ranking Systems

Corrected frequency is another way to consider specimens represented. Hesse and Perkins (1974) propose dividing the number of specimens for each element by the expected number of times that element occurs in one individual of that species based on symmetry. This procedures yields a corrected frequency (Figure 7.15; Gilbert and Steinfeld 1977). The expected number of specimens would be two for symmetrical appendicular elements; one for single axial elements, such as the atlas; six for the innominate; eight for first phalanges; or a higher number for teeth. This is essentially the same procedure Binford (1978) later used to estimate what he called MNI, though Hesse and Perkins (1974) suggest it as an intermediate step toward estimating a relative frequency (RF) that could be used instead of MNI, by which they mean MNI sensu White.

Relative frequency (RF) is the mean corrected frequency for each species (Figure 7.15; Hesse and Perkins 1974). Relative frequency may be adjusted by omitting the first (*F*) and last (*L*) corrected frequencies in the ranked list to compensate for overly abundant or underrepresented specimens, permitting analysis to focus on the middle range of ranked specimens. This is an abstract number that can be used for a number of additional comparisons (Hesse and Perkins 1974:151).

Element	NISP	Expected	Corrected Frequency (CF)	
Radius, p	6	+ 2 =	3.0 (F)	
Ulna, p	6	+ 2 =	3.0	
Scapula	5	+ 2 =	2.5	
Humerus, d	5	+ 2 =	2.5	
Mandible	4	+ 2 =	2.0	
Radius, d	4	+ 2 =	2.0	
Femur, d	4	+ 2 =	2.0	
Tibia, p	4	+ 2 =	2.0	
Tibia, d	4	+ 2 =	2.0	
Astragalus	4	+ 2 =	2.0	
Innominate	7	+ 6 =	1.2	
Calcaneus	2	+ 2 =	1.0	
Metapodium, d	2	+ 2 =	1.0	
Metacarpus, p	1	+ 2 =	0.5	
Metatarsus, p	1	+ 2 =	0.5	
Femur, p	1	+ 2 =	0.5	
1st phalanx	2	+ 8 =	0.25	
2nd phalanx	1	+ 8 =	0.12	
3rd phalanx	1	+ 8 =	0.12 (L)	
N = 19	64		28.19	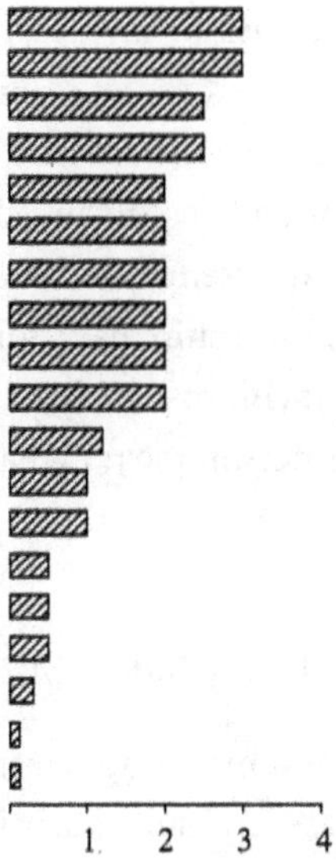 1 2 3 4

Relative Frequency (RF) = 28.19 + 19 = 1.484
Adjusted RF   = CF - F + L + N
                        28.19 - 3.12 + 17 = 1.475

FIGURE 7.15. Hypothetical Collection: Corrected frequencies for white-tailed deer (*Odocoileus virginianus*) using NISP (after Hesse and Perkins 1974). Corrected frequency estimated by dividing the number of specimens for each element type (e.g., scapula) by the number of times the whole element occurs in the skeleton for white-tailed deer.

Utility Indices

Some indices rank animal body parts according to their utility (e.g., Binford 1978; Jones and Metcalfe 1988; Lyman et al. 1992; Metcalfe and Jones 1988). Utility may guide decisions made by a hunter about which portions of a carcass to transport from a kill site to a consumption one and which portions to leave behind (Figure 2.5). The same concept may also be used as evidence of commercial or social contexts. The definition of utility varies considerably because a carcass, or a portion of a carcass, may have a number of uses in addition to food. However, utility usually refers to food value, often specifically to meat and fat. Utility indices also are used to distinguish between assemblages that represent scavenging behavior and those that may be the result of human use of carcasses.

Binford's (1978) utility indices relate utility to elements incorporating Nunamiut decisions about the use of caribou and sheep in their northern Alaskan economy. The indices (Binford 1978:15) are based on data from a bull caribou that was between 3 and 5 years old and two domestic sheep. One of the sheep was a 90-month-old female in poor health and the other a 6-month-old lamb in good health. Binford does not include differences in age, sex, size, health, or latitude in his indices. His indices are widely used to study early hominid behavior in many parts of the world, especially in Africa. It remains to be seen whether the amount or distribution of fatty tissues in a single arctic cervid or in two Nearctic domestic sheep has any relationship to that in subtropical or tropical wild ungulates during the Pleistocene. Ecological research demonstrates that considerable differences in body size and composition exist among most arctic, temperate, and tropical animals. Efforts to develop more biologically appropriate indices are very important (Blumenschine and Caro 1986; Brink 1997; De Nigris and Mengoni Goñalons 2005; Emerson 1993; Lyman et al. 1992; O'Connell and Marshall 1989; Monks 2005).

Modified General Utility Index (MGUI):

Binford's (1978:72–5) most popular index is the modified general utility index (MGUI), which is based on several subsidiary indices incorporating components of utility: meat, marrow, and bone grease utility, and general utility. The difference between the modified general utility index (MGUI) and the general utility index (GUI) reflects Binford's concern about "riders" (1978:74). Riders are elements that have little utility by themselves but are firmly attached to elements with higher values, such as the ulnar carpal. He argues it is necessary to extrapolate from the GUI to the MGUI because low-ranked riders may be transported from the kill site while attached to high-utility elements.

MNI, MAU, and MNE:

Binford (1978:67–72) originally used what he called MNI, which is sometimes referred to as fractional MNI. As we described earlier in this chapter, he calculates MNI by dividing the specimen count (NISP) for each element by the number of such elements present in a skeleton as Hesse and Perkins suggest (1974) for calculating corrected frequency. Side is not determined as a preliminary step. Later Binford (1984:50) changed "MNI" to "MAU," defining "MAU" as the minimum number of animal units. He obtains MAU by dividing "the minimum number of different specimens referable to a given anatomical part used in classification," also known as the minimum number of elements (MNE), by the number of such elements present in a skeleton as before (Binford 1984:50–1). MNE is derived by determining how many elements are represented by the fragmentary remains, based on the presence of overlapping landmark features, and, hence, is not the same as NISP.

These indices have many permutations (e.g., Bunn 1993; Bunn and Kroll 1986; De Nigris 2004; Klein et al. 1999; Landon 1996:141; Loponte and Acosta 2004; Lyman 1994a; Marean 1992; Muñoz 2004; Pickering et al. 2003; Ringrose 1993; Savanti et al. 2005; Stiner 1991, 1994, 2002). One of the chief variations occurs in the way MNE is estimated. Lyman

(1994b:290) defines MNE as the "minimum number of complete skeletal elements necessary to account for all observed specimens" and recommends basing the estimate on the number of whole elements that can be reconstructed from the identified specimens (e.g., Bunn 1986; Morlan 1994). This step defines butchering units. However, Marean and Spencer (1991:650) obtained MNE by estimating a percentage circumference for shaft fragments in a procedure similar to that used by Klein and Cruz-Uribe (1984:27) to estimate MNI (see also Marean et al. 2001). In some cases, shaft fragments are excluded from the study (e.g., Stiner 1994:237–8), although others argue that including shaft fragments is essential (e.g., Bartram 1993; Bunn and Kroll 1988; Marean and Spencer 1991; Pickering et al. 2003). If only articular ends are included, it is important to make this quite clear. However, it is more appropriate to estimate MNE from all available specimens. It seems particularly unwise to base interpretations of marrow use on analytical units that exclude those portions of adult mammalian elements that contain the marrow cavity and most of the white marrow (Emerson 1993; Stiner 1994:291; Vehik 1977).

Often it appears that MAU is obtained by dividing the NISP recovered for each element by the number of such elements present in a complete skeleton instead of estimating MNE first (Binford 1978:72, 1984:80–1; Thomas and Mayer 1983:366). After deriving MAU, the largest MAU value is used as a standard. All of the other MAUs in the assemblage are divided by the standard and multiplied by 100 to establish a normed scale designated as %MAU (e.g., Binford 1984:80–1; Bunn and Kroll 1986; Morlan 1994; Thomas and Mayer 1983:366). Another way to characterize this is that %MAU is the ratio of each element's MAU standardized as a percentage of the highest MAU value in the collection. In addition to examining these derivatives themselves, MAU or %MAU for each element portion can be plotted against the MGUI and compared to those associated with various economic strategies (e.g., Grayson 1989a; Lyman 1992; Messineo 2003; Metcalfe and Jones 1988; Thomas and Mayer 1983:367–8).

Unfortunately, some researchers continue to use "MNI" in Binford's 1978 sense, and to estimate MNE and MAU in a variety of ways, some of which appear mutually contradictory. In the interest of collegiality, we will not identify offenders in this section, but we note that the practice contributes to the confusion among the use of all three applications. It also is common for publications to omit any discussion at all as to how MNI, MNE, or MAU are estimated, presuming that these terms are more clear than they are in practice. Because of this confusion, it is recommended that these abbreviations not be used unless the author is prepared to provide at least a minimal explanation with reference to the literature (e.g., sensu Binford [MAU], Lyman [MNE], or White [MNI]), so it is possible for the reader to know what is meant by these abbreviations. The use of a short definition, such as "minimum number of elements," is inadequate because there have been at least five different approaches, published since 2000, that produce a number called "MNE." There are probably more but this cannot be judged because most authors do not describe how they derive their estimates.

Table 7.12. *Hypothetical Collection: Meat utility indices and bone mineral densities for white-tailed deer* (Odocoileus virginianus)

Element	NISP	MNE	MAU	%MAU	FUI	VD
Radius, proximal	6	6	3.0	100.0	1323	0.52
Ulna, proximal	6	6	3.0	100.0	1323	0.37
Humerus, distal	5	5	2.5	83.3	1891	0.51
Scapula	5	4	2.0	66.7	2295	0.35
Radius, distal	4	4	2.0	66.7	1039	0.40
Tibia, proximal	4	4	2.0	66.7	3225	0.31
Tibia, distal	4	4	2.0	66.7	2267	0.50
Astragalus	4	4	2.0	66.7	1424	0.56
Innominate	6	3	1.5	50.0	2531	0.33
Femur, distal	4	3	1.5	50.0	5139	0.32
Mandible	4	2	1.0	33.3	590	0.51
Calcaneus	2	2	1.0	33.3	1424	0.49
Metacarpus, proximal	1	1	0.5	16.7	461	0.66
Femur, proximal	1	1	0.5	16.7	5139	0.37
Metatarsus, proximal	1	1	0.5	16.7	1003	0.65
Metapodium, distal	2	2	0.5	16.7	578	0.50
Lumbar vertebra	2	2	0.3	10.0	1706	0.29
1st phalanx	2	2	0.25	8.3	443	0.45
Cervical vertebra	1	1	0.2	6.7	1905	0.17
2nd phalanx	1	1	0.12	4.0	443	0.29
3rd phalanx	1	1	0.12	4.0	443	0.25
Humerus, shaft	2					0.53
Radius, shaft	1					0.68
Femur, shaft	2					0.57

Note: NISP is the number of identified specimens. MNE is the minimum number of different specimens referable to a given anatomical part. MAU is the minimum number of animal units. %MAU is the normed MAU. FUI (food utility index) values from Metcalfe and Jones (1988); FUI for distal metapodia was obtained by averaging the FUI for the distal metacarpus and metatarsus. Volume density (*VD*) is the average bone mineral density (g/cm^3) of Lyman (1994c, table 7.6). In most cases MNE encompasses more than one *VD* scan site and the average *VD* of the relevant area is presented here.

Clarity in describing methods will do a great deal to eliminate much of the confusion that surrounds these applications and subsequent interpretations. On the basis of priority, "MNI" should be restricted to the sense proposed by White. "MNE" as defined by Lyman, and estimated on the basis of diagnostic or fragmentation zones, especially if it is impractical to attempt an actual physical refit of the archaeological specimens, also appears to be a useful concept for many applications. If scholars are careful to define their methods in estimating "MNE," it is possible that this term can be salvaged. For example, Stiner (1994:236–47) clearly defines MNE and subsequently uses it to develop

Table 7.13. *Hypothetical Collection: Rank of white-tailed deer* (Odocoileus virginianus) *elements based on NISP percentage, corrected frequency, MNE percentage, and %MAU*

NISP Figure 7.11		Corrected frequency Figure 7.15		MNE Table 7.12		%MAU Table 7.12	
Element (NISP)	%	Element	CF	Element	%	Element	%MAU
Radius (10)	12.5	Radius, p	3.0	Radius, p	10.2	Radius, p	100.0
Tibia (8)	10.0	Ulna, p	3.0	Ulna, p	10.2	Ulna, p	100.0
Head (7)	8.8	Scapula	2.5	Humerus, d	8.5	Humerus, d	83.3
Humerus (7)	8.8	Humerus, d	2.5	Scapula	6.8	Scapula	66.7
Innominate (7)	8.8	Mandible	2.0	Radius, d	6.8	Radius, d	66.7
Femur (7)	8.8	Radius, d	2.0	Tibia, p	6.8	Tibia, p	66.7
Tarsal (7)	8.8	Femur, d	2.0	Tibia, d	6.8	Tibia, d	66.7
Ulna (6)	7.5	Tibia, p	2.0	Astragalus	6.8	Astragalus	66.7
Scapula (5)	6.3	Tibia, d	2.0	Innominate	5.1	Innominate	50.0
Vertebra (4)	5.0	Astragalus	2.0	Femur, d	5.1	Femur, d	50.0
Carpal (4)	5.0	Innominate	1.2	Mandible	3.4	Mandible	33.3
Phalanx (4)	5.0	Calcaneus	1.0	Lumbar	3.4	Calcaneus	33.3
Metapodium (2)	2.5	Metapodium, d	1.0	Calcaneus	3.4	Metacarpus, p	16.7
Metacarpus (1)	1.3	Metacarpus, p	0.5	Metapodium, d	3.4	Femur, p	16.7
Metatarsus (1)	1.3	Metatarsus, p	0.5	1st phalanx	3.4	Metatarsus, p	16.7
		Femur, p	0.5	Cervical	1.7	Metapodium, d	16.7
		1st phalanx	0.25	Metacarpus, p	1.7	Lumbar	10.0
		2nd phalanx	0.12	Femur, p	1.7	1st phalanx	8.3
		3rd phalanx	0.12	Metatarsus, p	1.7	Cervical	6.7
				2nd phalanx	1.7	2nd phalanx	4.0
				3rd phalanx	1.7	3rd phalanx	4.0

Note: d = distal; p = proximal.

an anatomical completeness index. "MAU" is used in so many different ways that the concept may require a new nomenclature. The concepts behind "MNE" and "MAU" are clearly useful in many settings even if their present application is muddled.

MNE, MAU, and %MAU are estimated for the Hypothetical Collection using drawings such as those in Figure 7.13. For example, the six proximal radii fragments appear to represent a minimum number of six elements, producing an MNE of six in Lyman's terminology (Table 7.12). The MNE (6) is divided by the number of radii in an undisturbed skeleton (2), yielding an MAU of 3.0. %MAU is obtained by dividing the radius MAU by the largest MAU in the collection (which is the proximal radius) and multiplying by 100. The %MAU for the radius is 100. This is very similar to the procedure for establishing an observed/expected ratio or corrected frequency index where the expected value for each element is based on anatomical frequency (Table 7.13).

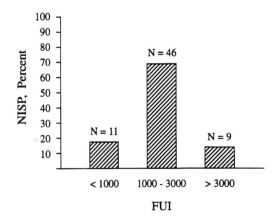

FIGURE 7.16. Hypothetical Collection: Food Utility Index (FUI) plotted against NISP percent for white-tailed deer (*Odocoileus virginianus*), following Purdue et al. (1989).

Food Utility Index (FUI):

Metcalfe and Jones (1988) propose a food utility index (FUI) to replace Binford's MGUI. FUI is derived from a caribou meat utility index (MUI). This is defined as the gross weight of a part minus the dry bone weight of that part, where gross weight is the weight of bone, meat, marrow, and bone grease of each body part (Metcalfe and Jones 1988:489). Like Binford, they modify the meat utility index to account for riders, producing a numerical FUI for each element. Because they are justifiably concerned about using an index based on a single arctic caribou, Purdue and his colleagues (1989) recommend grouping elements into three categories based on their respective FUI number: those with a low FUI (<1,000), those with a medium FUI (1,000–3,000), and those with a high FUI (>3,000) (see Figure 7.16).

   Commonly %MAU is plotted against one of the utility indices (e.g., Bartram 1993). For the Hypothetical Collection, the plots of NISP to FUI (Figure 7.16) and of %MAU to FUI (Figure 7.17) are virtually identical, probably because %MAU is a derivative of NISP. In both cases, we see that some specimens with low utility are rare in the collection, as are some with high utility.

Summary of Skeletal Frequencies

Skeletal frequencies are studied in many other ways (e.g., Gifford et al. 1981:80; Klein 1989; Marshall and Pilgram 1991), and there are innumerable critiques of many aspects of skeletal frequency (e.g., Morlan 1994; Ringrose 1993). None of these methods eliminates the need to evaluate data in terms of biological, taphonomic, archaeological, and ethnographic evidence. It is advisable to examine animal remains, including skeletal frequencies, from a number of perspectives using several techniques because similar patterns are caused by many different agents (e.g., Castamagno et al. 2005;

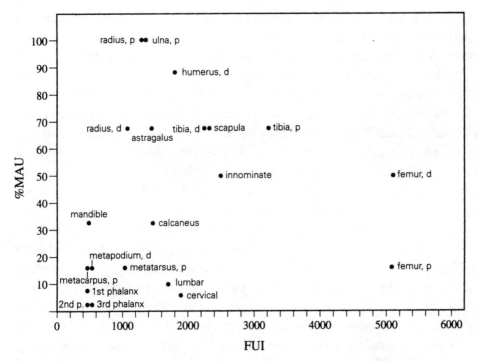

FIGURE 7.17. Hypothetical Collection: Food Utility Index (FUI) plotted against %MAU for white-tailed deer (*Odocoileus virginianus*).

Mengoni-Goñalons 1986; Todd and Rapson 1988). These indices are not the answer to the question but are merely steps toward the answer.

One of the most important criticisms directed toward some of these procedures is that the descriptions of them are inadequate, making it difficult to replicate the research or to evaluate the results. It is particularly difficult in many cases to determine how MNI, MAU, or MNE are defined and what the relationship between NISP, MNE, and MNI might be (Lyman 1994a, 1994c:510; Morlan 1994). Thomas and Mayer (1983:366) are among the few scholars who make the distinction clear, although they use the same abbreviation (MNI) in both senses; their 1983 publication preceded Binford's 1984 definition of MAU. It is not easy to explain some of these procedures in the limited space provided by most publications, which could be reason enough for not using them. The terminological problem reinforces the importance of reviewing the literature before defining new concepts and of defining new terms clearly (Lyman 1994a).

Probably the most important difficulty with body part frequencies is that specimens in many, but not all, samples appear to be those most likely to survive a wide range of site-formation processes (Brink 1997; Cruz and Elkin 2003; Grayson 1989a; Hoffecker et al. 1991; Kreutzer 1992; Lyman 1984, 1985, 1992). To show this relationship in the Hypothetical Collection, Lyman's volume density (VD; [1984, 1994c:Table 7.6]) is used (see Lam et al. 2003; Marean 1992:91; Munro and Bar-Oz 2005; Symmons 2005; Wapnish and Hesse 1991 among others). His values are averaged because in most cases the portion of each element represented in the Hypothetical Collection includes more than one scan site (Table 7.12). When volume density is plotted against NISP, we see that elements with low density are often, though not always, underrepresented in the Hypothetical Collection (Figure 7.18). Further, many specimens with high food utility, such as the proximal and distal femur, have relatively low density and may be underrepresented in the Hypothetical Collection for this reason. However, some specimens with high density also are rare. Brain (1981:21) observes that this also is related to the order in which fusion occurs (see Table 3.5). Symmons (2005) finds that density for specific elements is highly variable and is best considered as a range rather than as a point (see also Izeta 2005). Many utility curves could be the result of such relationships (Grayson 1989a).

The similarities among the element rankings provided by these various approaches are striking (Table 7.13). Given the multitude of first- and second-order changes to which the Hypothetical Collection has been subjected, the results presented in Figure 7.11 seem as helpful in understanding the collection as any of those presented in Table 7.13. Figure 7.11 is conservative, requires the least amount of manipulation, and is subject to less misunderstanding in terms of procedures. The chief advantage of Figure 7.11 is that it does not require estimates of MNI or MNE in all their various permutations and presents primary data that are often lost in these calculations.

The choice of how to explore skeletal frequency, or whether to do so at all, will depend on the specific research problem. Much of this discussion is based on the assumption that meat, fat, and marrow are the critical components in transport decisions. Ethnographic observations suggest decisions about what to transport and how far, as well as how to butcher and redistribute carcasses, are actually made on the basis of many variables, some of which are not directly related to food value (e.g., Bartram et al. 1991; Gifford-Gonzalez 1993; O'Connell et al. 1990; O'Connell and Marshall 1989; Yellen 1977b). Many of the assumptions about economic value reflect our own biases about the merits of elements and their associated meat. Although meat and fat were, and are, important, humans transport animal products over very great distances for many other reasons.

It also is likely different human groups, using different animals in different latitudes and cultural contexts, did not conduct themselves as foragers do today. This appears to be the conclusion to be drawn from the various, often contradictory, ethnographic observations of extant human behavior. Given the diverse ways modern humans use animal carcasses, it seems particularly unlikely that early hominids living in a tropical bushland and modern arctic hunters, for whom *domestic* sheep were second only to caribou in importance, made similar decisions about carcass value. This does not mean that ethnographic analogies should be avoided, but there should be sound biological and cultural reasons for using them.

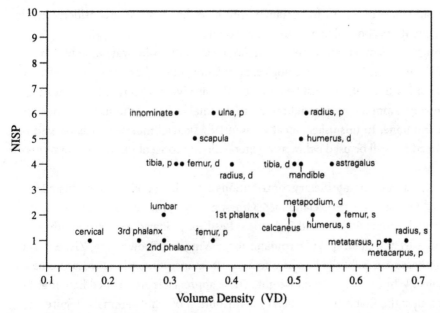

FIGURE 7.18. Hypothetical Collection: Plot of volume density (VD) against NISP for white-tailed deer (*Odocoileus virginianus*).

ESTIMATES OF DIETARY CONTRIBUTION

Estimates of dietary contribution are closely related to skeletal frequencies (e.g., Kreutzer 1992; Stiner 1994). Many methods explore skeletal frequency by ranking materials in terms of dietary value without actually estimating the nutritional yield of each portion. Most zooarchaeologists base their studies primarily on bones, teeth, and valves and, therefore, often discuss dietary contributions in terms of elements or anatomical regions instead of kilograms of meat, calories, or vitamins (for exceptions, see Munson et al. 1971; Shawcross 1967). Strictly speaking, a humerus is not the same thing as meat and a mandible is not tongue, although the soft and hard tissues with which each is associated are related. Just as NISP and MNI should not be confused with the actual number of animals used at or near a site, estimates of meat weight and dietary contributions among animals identified in the collection should not be confused with the total amount of meat consumed at the site.

Estimates of dietary contribution generally refer to the amount of edible or usable meat an animal, or group of animals, might contribute. Usually bone, hide, and visceral weights are subtracted from total live weight to obtain the usable or edible meat weight. "Edible" and "usable" are culturally defined classifications and there is considerable variation in which tissues are considered edible (e.g., Bowen 1992). For example, edible tissues may include marrow, tongue, brains, visceral organs, antlers, bone, skin; portions of some of these; or none of these. Usable tissue might be either edible or inedible; for example, hide and antlers are important by-products that may not be considered edible. In other situations, both skin and antlers are eaten.

Although the elements represented and modifications may indicate what was considered edible or usable by the archaeological population, often the classification of tissues as edible or inedible either must be based on the surviving hard tissue or assumed. In the following examples, meat weight refers to the total weight of the animal minus skin, viscera, and bone. In this usage, meat is essentially skeletal muscle and associated fat. The term edible will be used below as a general dietary concept rather than in terms of specific tissues.

Techniques that estimate dietary contributions are widely applied and evaluated (e.g., Casteel 1978; Chaplin 1971; Cleland 1966; Grayson 1973, 1979; Kubasiewicz 1956; Lyman 1979; Parmalee 1965; Perkins and Daly 1968; Reed 1963; Shawcross 1967; Smith 1975a, 1975b; Stewart and Stahl 1977; Uerpmann 1973; Wing and Brown 1979; Ziegler 1973). Most are based on published data, reference skeletons, dimensional measurements, MNI (sensu White), or specimen weight. These approaches are divided here into two broad groups: the first estimates dietary contribution of whole animals (Figure 7.19), and the second estimates dietary contribution from archaeological specimen weight (Figure 7.20).

Estimates of Dietary Contribution of Whole Animals

The most common way to study dietary contribution is to estimate the amount of meat an individual animal might contribute by directly comparing the archaeological specimen with a reference skeleton (Figure 7.19, Method 1). If the dimensions are similar, the weights of the two animals are probably similar. This is the same approach used to estimate other body dimensions earlier in this chapter and depends upon having information about total weight, visceral weight, and skin weight available for reference specimens. This is just one of many reasons for collecting such information when assembling a reference collection (see Appendix 3). This method provides an estimate for a single individual.

Method 2 (Figure 7.19) predicts total weight from a measured archaeological dimension for a single individual using allometry (e.g., Shawcross 1975; Zohar et al. 1994). As we discussed in Chapter 3, the relationship between body mass and skeletal dimensions is generally nonlinear, or allometric (e.g., Shawcross 1975). As weight increases, there is a disproportionate increase in the mass and dimensions of skeletal elements due to allometric growth. This relationship is found within a species (Wheeler and Reitz 1987), among vertebrates (Prange et al. 1979), in molluscs (Reitz et al. 1987), and between sexes (Bartosiewicz 1987). Allometry is often used to predict original body dimensions, such as total length from a measured dimension of an archaeological specimen (e.g.,

Method 1: Estimate of meat weight for individuals of a given taxon by comparison with a reference skeleton:

Data from reference specimen: FLMNH Z4567, female

> Total weight = 44 kg
> Two fetuses = 2 kg
> Total weight minus the fetuses = 42 kg or 42,000 g
> Skin weight = 4 kg
> Viscera = 8.25 kg
> Skeletal weight = 2.33 kg
> Meat weight = 27.42 kg or 27,420 g (Total weight minus skin, viscera and skeleton)
> Percentage of total weight that is meat weight = 65.3 percent

Application:

> Match femur from site with femur from FLMNH Z4657.
> Estimate of total weight: 42 kg
> Estimate of meat weight: 27.42 kg

Method 2: Total weight predicted using dimensional allometry:

> Formula: $Y = aX^b$ or $\log_{10} Y = \log_{10} a + b \,(\log_{10} X)$
> Y = the estimated total weight (g) of the archaeological animal
> X = the measured dimension, in this example, the greatest depth of the femur head (DC) for the archaeological specimen
> a = the Y-intercept of the linear regression line
> b = slope of the regression line

Data: X = 23.3 mm depth of femur head (DC)

Application using the form $\log_{10} Y = \log_{10} a + b \,(\log_{10} X)$:

$$\log_{10} Y = 0.696 + 2.783 \,(\log_{10} 23.3)$$
$$\log_{10} Y = 0.696 + 2.783 \,(1.367)$$
$$\log_{10} Y = 4.501$$
$$Y = 31{,}721 \text{ g or } 31.72 \text{ kg}$$

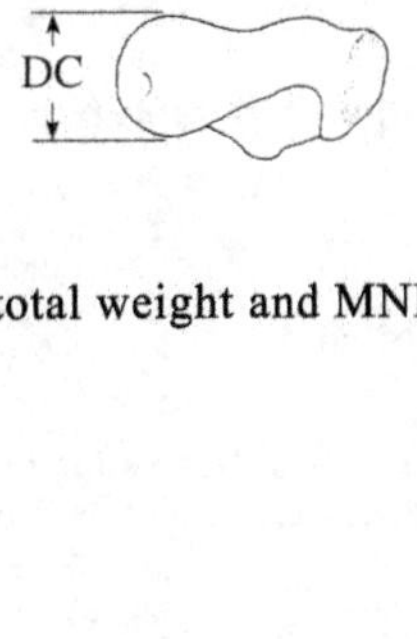

DC

Method 3: Meat weight derived from a percentage of total weight and MNI (White 1953a):

Application:

> Deer total weight = 32 kg (Osborne *et al.* 1992: 38)
> 32 kg x 50 percent = 16 kg
> Deer MNI = 11 (from Table A 4.1)
> 16 kg x 11 = 176 kg of meat

FIGURE 7.19. Hypothetical Collection: Estimates of white-tailed deer (*Odocoileus virginianus*) dietary contribution based on concepts of individuals using total weight or measured dimensions. The illustration shows the greatest depth of the femur head (DC) as viewed from above. See Table A4.5 for archaeological deer measurements.

Figure 7.3). In Figure 7.19 it is used to estimate total weight of a deer individual from the depth of the femur head (DC) from Table A4.5. This application of allometry might be termed "dimensional allometry" and provides an estimate of total weight for a single individual from a measurement.

Method 3 provides an estimate of the dietary contribution for all of the estimated deer individuals in the collection using a percentage of total weight and MNI to estimate meat weight (Figure 7.19). This approach, often identified with White (1953a), is based on

Method 1: **The weight method (Reed 1963), where meat weight is estimated from archaeological specimen weight assuming that the skeletal weight of large mammals is approximately 7.5 percent of total weight and that edible meat is 50 percent of total weight:**

Formula: $\dfrac{\text{skeletal weight, kg}}{\text{total weight}} = \dfrac{\text{archaeological specimen weight, kg}}{X}$

Data: Archaeological specimen weight for deer = 1.0764 kg (from Table A 4.1)

Application: $0.075 = \dfrac{1.0764}{X}$

Total weight = 14.352 kg
edible meat weight = 14.352 kg x .50 or 7.176 kg

Method 2: Ziegler's estimate of meat weight (1973):

Formula: $\dfrac{\text{known edible meat weight}}{\text{known skeletal weight}} = \dfrac{\text{archaeological meat weight (X)}}{\text{archaeological specimen weight (Table A 4.1)}}$

Data from reference specimen FLMNH Z4567:
Known meat weight = 27.42 kg or 27,420 g (Total weight minus skin, viscera, and skeleton)
Known skeletal weight = 2.33 kg

Application:

$\dfrac{27.42 \text{ kg}}{2.33 \text{ kg}} = \dfrac{\text{meat weight (X)}}{1.0764}$

$11.8 = \dfrac{\text{meat weight (X)}}{1.0764}$

meat weight = 12.7 kg

Method 3: Sample biomass predicted using specimen weight in an allometric formula:

Formula: $Y = aX^b$ or $\log_{10} Y = \log_{10} a + b \ (\log_{10} X)$
Y = the estimated sample biomass (kg) contributed by the archaeological specimens for a taxon
X = specimen weight of the archaeological specimens for a taxon
a = the Y-intercept of the linear regression line
b = slope of the regression line

Data: X = 1.0764 kg (deer specimen weight from Table A 4.1)
Application using the form $\log_{10} Y = \log_{10} a + b \ (\log_{10} X)$:
$\log_{10}Y = 1.12 + 0.90 \ (\log_{10} 1.0764)$
$\log_{10}Y = 1.12 + 0.90 \ (0.032)$
$\log_{10}Y = 1.149$
$Y = 14.1$ kg

FIGURE 7.20. Hypothetical Collection: Estimates of white-tailed deer (*Odocoileus virginianus*) dietary contribution based on archaeological specimen weight. See Figure 7.19 for reference specimen data and Table A4.1 for deer specimen weight from the Hypothetical Collection.

known relationships among total weight, skeletal weight, visceral weight, skin weight, and meat weight derived from the literature. White estimates the amount of meat contributed by a species in several steps. First, the amount of meat in a single carcass is obtained by multiplying the total weight of a species by a percentage of that total weight that could be used. Total weight is obtained from the literature. The value used in this example is the mean weight of yearling male deer on one of the sea islands north of St. Augustine in 1981, 32 kg (Osborne et al. 1992:38). In reality there is a great deal of variation in individual body weight during the year. The percentages of total weight that White estimates to be usable are 70 percent for birds and short-legged mammals and 50 percent for long-legged mammals. Second, the MNI of the species, in this case deer, is estimated. Finally, the amount of meat that one individual of that species might yield (16 kg) is multiplied by the estimated number of individuals (11). The estimated meat weight should not be taken literally, but put in the context of similar estimates of other species in the collection. Estimates of meat using a percentage that is edible, regardless of what that percentage may be, assume the relationship between hard tissue and meat is linear. Modifications on this approach are numerous (e.g., Anderson 1988, 1989; Cleland 1966:85–6; IJzereef 1981:184–7; Munson et al. 1971; Smith 1975a:33–6, 1975b; Stewart and Stahl 1977).

Estimates of Dietary Contribution from Specimen Weight

The preceding methods estimate meat weight for whole animals or for all of the estimated individuals in the archaeological collection. However, estimating meat weight for entire animals makes no allowance for disposal of portions of the animal beyond the excavated area or such behaviors as exchange. Archaeological specimen weight is often used to estimate only that amount of meat related to the archaeological materials, eliminating the need to consider whole animals or carcasses (e.g., Chaplin 1971:68; Cook and Treganza 1950; Kubasiewicz 1956). The chief disadvantage of using specimen weight is that it is altered by first-order changes such as leaching and mineralization (e.g., Chaplin 1971:68).

One use of specimen weight is what Chaplin (1971:67–8) calls the weight method (Figure 7.20, Methods 1 and 2; see Casteel 1978). In Reed's (1963) version of the weight method (Method 1), meat weight contributed by domestic artiodactyls is estimated from archaeological specimen weight by assuming that the skeletal weight is approximately 7.0 to 7.7 percent of the total weight of the domestic artiodactyl following research by Kubasiewicz (1956). This is often rounded to 7.5 percent and used to estimate the total weight of a number of birds and mammals from archaeological specimen weight. The estimated total weight is multiplied by 50 percent (White's estimated percentage of usable meat for long-legged animals) to estimate meat weight. Method 1 should not be applied to animals other than artiodactyls unless the relationship between skeletal weight and total weight is established for the animal in question.

Ziegler (1973:30–1) uses White's 50 and 70 percent values of total weight to estimate meat weight from published average total weights of carcasses when such information is not available for reference materials. However, he shows that the proportion of total weight that is comprised of skeletal weight varies widely when this relationship is calculated directly from reference collections, a procedure that he considers to be preferable. Ziegler (Figure 7.20, Method 2; 1973:29–31) advocates modifying Reed's method by dividing known meat weight by known skeletal weight to obtain a conversion factor relating skeletal weight to meat weight for each species. This conversion factor is then multiplied by archaeological specimen weight to estimate the meat weight contributed by that species (e.g., Erlandson 1994:59; Rick et al. 2002). Method 2 is used to estimate weight for amphibians in the species list (Table A4.1) because no allometric formula is available. In the case of the frog or toad (*Rana/Bufo* spp., *Bufo* spp.), a known skeletal weight (4.4 g) is divided by a known total weight (28.5 g).

One of the problems common to the procedures advocated by White, Reed, and Ziegler is that it is necessary to extend the relationships between total weight, skeletal weight, and meat weight found in animals with determinate growth today to those in the past because direct observation is not possible (Chaplin 1971:67–9; Stewart and Stahl 1977). We need to be aware of size change through time and space. The total weight of species with determinate growth varies because of geographical range, age, sex, season, and nutritional condition (e.g., Albarella et al. 2005; Purdue 1987). Adult white-tailed deer may weigh between 34 and 181 kg (Burt and Grossenheider 1964:230) because of such factors. Yet, often White's (1953a) average total weight of 90 kg (200 lb) for deer is used as the average total weight for this species, regardless of where the archaeological site is located. White's choice may have been appropriate for his geographical area, but it is not applicable in other portions of the deer's range, and it should not be extended to other cervids, other artiodactyls, or other ungulates. Great care must be exercised to obtain weights that are similar to those of animals from the region being studied. Even when modern weights are obtained from the appropriate locality, we know that the body size of some wild animals has changed even in relatively recent times (Purdue 1980; Purdue and Reitz 1993; Smith et al. 1995).

Of equal importance, the concept of an "average" total weight does not apply to animals with indeterminate growth. For example, black drums (*Pogonias cromis*) today weigh between 500 g and 45 kg (McClane 1978:119) depending on age and environmental conditions. It is clearly unsatisfactory to use 22 kg as an average total weight of black drums in the Hypothetical Collection, especially in light of evidence that the size range of some fishes has changed in relatively recent times in this area (e.g., Hales and Reitz 1992). Thus the first assumption made by estimates of meat weight from modern total weights is that modern weights are accurate for earlier time periods and that the use of an average total weight is valid.

Using allometry and archaeological specimen weight to estimate body mass or sample biomass avoids the problems of estimating an average total weight and of assuming a linear relationship between total weight, skeletal weight, and meat weight (Figure 7.19, Method 3 and Figure 7.20, Method 1). The relationship between specimen weight and meat or total weight is described by the allometric formula in Chapter 3 and referred to by Casteel (1978) as the power function (see also Casteel 1974, 1976). This allometrically estimated total weight is termed "sample biomass" to distinguish it from the estimates derived using other methods. Sample biomass as used here is an estimate of the total weight that the archaeological specimen weight may represent. Estimates in Figure 7.20, Method 3 as well as the biomass column in Table A4.1 are predicted from specimen weight using this approach. The regression formulae are presented in Table 3.4. In the case of many of these formulae, the allometric relationships are between skeletal weight and total weight rather than meat weight, but they can just as readily be established between meat weight and skeletal weight.

Because allometric predictions of sample biomass are based on a biological relation-ship, estimates of dietary contributions using allometric formulae have a lower inherent error than other approaches (Casteel 1978; Wing and Brown 1979:131). Such estimates can provide information about the quantity of sample biomass from the materials recov-ered and are not based on assumptions about which tissues are edible or how many individuals are present in the sample. Other advantages of allometric predictions are that the relationship exists for all living organisms and holds true through time as well. It is, therefore, possible to integrate all of the vertebrate and invertebrate classes into a dietary regime using modern data (e.g., Table 7.7).

Just as with MNI, the manner in which the data from the excavation units are aggre-gated influences the estimates of sample biomass obtained from archaeological specimen weight. This is so because of the aggregation of several individuals and the nature of the allometric relationship in which weight increases in a nonlinear fashion. If, for example, sample biomass for an oyster is estimated allometrically for two separate features, the resulting estimate will be greater than if the combined oyster valve weight is used. The difference in the two estimates is a difference between what would be predicted for two small animals and for one larger one.

This leads to another difficulty with this approach: the allometric constants (a and b) are derived from observations of living individuals. When measurements are used to estimate total weight or some other dimension, the concept of the individual is maintained (Figure 7.19, Method 2). However, when archaeological specimen weight is used to predict sample biomass, as in Figure 7.20, Method 3, the concept of the individual is, of necessity, lost (Barrett 1993; Jackson 1989). But, the constants used in Figure 7.20, Method 3 were obtained from a calculation where X was skeletal weight and Y was total weight, data obtained from large samples of reference specimens. For this reason, these particular formulae predict the relationship between X and Y using archaeological specimen weight as though X is the weight of an entire animal's skeleton; the amount of total weight predicted (Y) is that which would be found on a single whole carcass with that amount of skeletal weight. This results in an estimate that intuitively seems low (see Barrett 1993).

Summary of Estimates of Dietary Contribution

As with all other methods, none of these ways to estimate dietary contribution from animal remains is entirely satisfactory. Each has inherent problems largely associated with site-formation processes and with the fact that we do not know what the relationship of the studied sample is to the original assemblage of animals. It is nevertheless important to evaluate dietary contribution because subsistence is one of the most fundamental aspects of human interaction with the environment. Given the degree of uncertainty, conservative interpretations of dietary data should be tested against data drawn from other lines of evidence.

The methods illustrated in Figures 7.19 and 7.20 fall into two groups based on very different philosophical points of view. The methods described under group one (Figure 7.19) estimate the total weight or meat weight of one individual in the faunal sample by comparing its skeletal dimensions with a similar-sized reference specimen (Method 1); using an allometric formula that establishes a relationship between a skeletal measurement and total weight derived from an array of reference specimens (Method 2); and using published values of the average total and usable meat weight of the species (Method 3).

For both Method 1 and Method 2, further steps are necessary to derive an estimate of meat weight for all of the individuals in the collection comparable to the result produced by Method 3. Because Method 1 provides an estimate of meat weight for a single individual (27.42 kg), this estimate must be multiplied by MNI (11) to obtain an estimate of meat weight contributed by all deer individuals in the Hypothetical Collection (301.62 kg). For Method 2, the estimated total weight for the individual would be multiplied by 50 percent to obtain meat weight, as well as by MNI, to obtain an estimate of the meat weight that might be contributed by eleven deer individuals (Figure 7.21 a). One might use 65 percent, derived from the percentage of total weight that is meat weight in the reference specimen, instead of White's 50 percent. In that case, the amount of meat contributed by eleven individuals would be estimated as 227 kg. Methods 1 and 2 suggest a range of 32–42 kg total weight per individual, although the three methods suggest a meat weight range of 175–302 kg for all individuals. The assumption of estimates of dietary contribution of whole animals is that all of the edible meat from all of the individuals of that species was consumed by the people disposing of the materials under study. Incompleteness of the skeletal elements represented would be explained primarily by taphonomic processes.

The methods described in group two (Figure 7.20) do not attempt to estimate the amount of meat provided by complete carcasses of a taxon in the sample but instead estimate the amount of meat adhering to the specimens actually recovered. The three methods described in Figure 7.20 use an approximate percentage of skeletal weight to total weight (Method 1); the relationship between skeletal weight and edible meat weight

a   Estimate for deer using Method 2 from Group One
(Figure 7.19)

Step 1: estimate total weight for individual deer

Log_{10} Y = 0.696 + 2.783 (Log_{10} X)
where: Y = total weight, g
X = depth of femur head, 23.3 mm in average individual
Y = 31,721 g or 31.72 kg total weight

Step 2: estimate meat weight using 50 percent
(White 1953a)
31.72 kg × .50 = 15.86 kg meat weight

Step 3: extrapolate to deer MNI in the Hypothetical Collection to obtain cumulative individual meat weight
15.86 kg × 11 MNI = 174.46 kg

b   Estimate for deer using Method 3 from Group Two
(Figure 7.20)

Step 1: estimate sample biomass

Log_{10} Y = 1.12 + 0.90 (Log_{10} X)
where: Y = estimated sample biomass, kg
X = specimen weight, 1.0764 kg
Y = 14.1 kg sample biomass

Step 2: estimate meat weight using 50 percent
(White 1953a)
14.1 kg × .50 = 7.1 kg meat weight

Step 3: unnecessary; this method takes into account all of the individuals because it is based on the total specimen weight of all deer in the Hypothetical Collection

c   Estimate for bony fishes using Method 2 in Group One
(Figure 7.19)

Step 1: estimate total weight for individual fish

Log_{10} Y = 1.162 + 2.05 (Log_{10} X)
where: Y = total weight, g
X = atlas width, 4.7 mm
Y = 346.6 g or 0.35 kg total weight

Step 2: estimate meat weight using 84 percent
(Wing and Brown 1979:132)
0.35 kg × 0.84 = 0.294 kg meat weight

Step 3: extrapolate to 122 bony fish individuals in the Hypothetical Collection to obtain cumulative individual meat weight
0.294 kg × 122 MNI = 35.9 kg

d   Estimate for bony fishes using Method 3 in Group Two
(Figure 7.20)

Step 1: estimate sample biomass

Log_{10} Y = 0.90 + 0.91 (Log_{10} X)
where: Y = sample biomass, kg
X = bony fish specimen weight, 0.808 kg
(specimen weight of all Indeterminate and other bony fishes in Table A 4.1)
Y = 6.68 kg sample biomass

Step 2: estimate meat weight using 84 percent
(Wing and Brown 1979:132)
6.68 kg × 0.84 = 5.61 kg meat weight

Step 3: unnecessary; this method takes into account all of the individuals because it is based on the total specimen weight of all bony fishes in the Hypothetical Collection

FIGURE 7.21. Hypothetical Collection: Comparing the results of methods that estimate individual weights and sample biomass for (a) white-tailed deer (*Odocoileus virginianus*) and (b) bony fishes using allometric formulae in Table 3.4, Figure 7.19, and Figure 7.20. Bony fish specimen weight is the total specimen weight of all bony fishes, including Indeterminate Fish from Table A4.1; cartilaginous fishes are excluded. Bony fish atlas width is an average of all atlas widths from Table A4.5.

of a reference specimen to estimate meat weight from archaeological specimen weight (Method 2); and an allometric formula derived from data associated with reference specimens to estimate sample biomass when skeletal weight is known (Method 3). Methods 1 and 3, which estimate total weight, can be further extrapolated to estimates of meat weight using the percentage proposed by White (50 percent) or others. In the case of deer, 14.1 kg of sample biomass may represent 7.1 kg of meat weight when sample biomass is multiplied by 50 percent (Figure 7.21 b). The methods in group two predict deer meat weights of between 7 and 13 kg for the Hypothetical Collection.

The results of these two distinct approaches to estimating potential amounts of meat that deer contributed to the diet can be applied to other animals in the sample. For comparative purposes, we perform the same estimates of cumulative individual total weight and sample biomass applying allometric formulae to bony fishes in the Hypothetical Collection (Figure 7.21 c and 7.21 d). When the results of the two approaches are compared, they differ substantially. The cumulative individual meat weight for deer is twenty-four times more than the sample biomass estimate, and the cumulative individual meat weight for bony fishes is six times greater than the sample biomass estimate.

These differences need explanation. Some of the differences are the product of tapho-nomic losses. If taphonomic loss explained all of these observed differences one would expect greater loss of the more fragile fish remains compared with the sturdier deer remains. However, the disparity between the two estimates of deer meat weight is much greater than that found for fishes. Another explanation is that some of the difference in meat weights estimated for individuals (Figure 7.21 a and 7.21 c) and from specimen weight (Figure 7.21 b and 7.21 d) is the result of shared carcasses. Although eleven deer individuals are estimated, only small portions of each animal were used within the excavated part of the site. Bony fishes, on the other hand, are very small: the average individual may have weighed 345 g. These small fishes were not shared and, therefore, estimates of dietary contribution based on individuals and from specimen weight are more similar.

MODIFICATIONS AND PATHOLOGIES

Skeletal parts represented, fragmentation, and marks on specimens are closely related and provide information on a number of site-formation processes (Muñoz 2004; Murphy 2001). In terms of human activities, butchering and cooking techniques are of particular interest (e.g., Olsen 1994). Modifications attributable to intentional human behavior are helpful in distinguishing between commensal animals and food animals (e.g., Crabtree 1989:98; Nicholson 2000; Simonetti and Cornejo 1991).

The location and types of marks may indicate how the animal was used. For exam-ple, Crabtree (1989:104–5) interprets modifications on cat specimens from West Stow as evidence of skinning and marks on horse specimens as evidence that that horses were consumed (Crabtree 1989:109). Olsen (1994) reports marks on dog specimens as evi-dence that they were consumed, which is supported by the types of elements represented and their location in the site. Modifications related to butchery may indicate the ethnic identity of the butcher, the social standing of the consumers, whether butchery was for household consumption, feasting, or trade, and whether the butcher was a specialist producing standard cuts for a discriminating market or a local householder intent on maximizing the amount of food and other products obtained from the carcass (e.g., Albarella and Serjeantson 2002; Alen and Ervynck 2005; Cope 2004; Murphy 2001). Holes and other modifications on cattle scapula may be evidence that the shoulder was suspended (O'Connor 2000b:76–77). Characteristics associated with burning may pro-vide evidence of cooking techniques, waste disposal, sacred offerings, or other uses of fire (e.g., Peters 1993; Spiess and Lewis 1995; Théry-Parisot et al. 2005). Some modifica-tions are caused by hanging trophies for display (Bartosiewicz 1995b:55), others indicate tools and ornaments (e.g., Bourque 1995; Middleton et al. 2002; Serrand et al. 2005) or taphonomic history (e.g., Bar-Oz et al. 2004).

Fragmentation was discussed earlier (see Chapter 5 and earlier in this chapter) but some approaches assess fragmentation as a form of modification (e.g., Boyle 2005; Marshall 1990:240–1; Outram 2001, 2002; Sadek-Kooros 1975). Maltby (1985:45) suggests calculating fragmentation in two ways. In the first, the number of proximal articulations (excluding unfused epiphyses) is calculated as a percentage of the total number of proximal and distal articulations (e.g., 6 proximal radii divided by 7 distal articulations equals 86 percent). In the second, the number of shaft fragments is expressed as a percentage of the total number of articulations plus shaft fragments (e.g., 3 radii shafts divided by 10 articulations equals 30 percent). In the case of the Hypothetical Collection, this procedure indicates that the proximal ends of radii are much more common than the distal ones or the shafts. The loss of the distal radius may be the result of its relatively lower density and the loss of the shaft may reflect butchering techniques or difficulty identifying shaft fragments (Table 7.12). These two percentages may be plotted against one another along with data from other elements or other collections.

The marks themselves should also be considered (e.g., Boyle 2005; Luff 1994). Usually the types of butchery and other modifications are presented as figures (Figures 6.8, 7.22) or tables (Table A4.2). Where sample sizes are large enough, it is possible to consider modifications in terms of their location (i.e., anterior, posterior, medial, or lateral aspect of the element), as well as the orientation and direction of the cut or blow (e.g., Crabtree 1989:101; O'Connor 1984:37). Cuts and hacks on deer specimens in the Hypothetical Collection are at locations related to food preparation (Figures 6.8 and 7.22). Hacks and saw marks on specimens of other species also are at locations usually associated with primary butchery. Sawing was accomplished with a metal tool and was used to butcher both wild and domestic mammals. The midshaft cuts are shallow scrapes associated with filleting. The atlas/occipital regions and the scapula blade, which could suggest the cause of death, are missing, so there is no evidence for how the animals died. The mandible fragments do not have marks typical of skinning, but some of the cut marks on the proximal metatarsus may be caused by skinning. None of the deer specimens show signs of gnawing, trampling, or digestion.

Pathologies provide information about a number of aspects of animal life (Bartosiewicz and Bartosiewicz 2002; Bathurst and Barta 2004; Davies et al. 2005; Gautier 2005; Levine et al. 2000; Niven et al. 2004; O'Connor 2000b: 98–110; Thomas and Mainland 2005). Diet and health are related to how animals were used, husbandry methods, and cultural attitudes associated with them. Pathological conditions provide information about the health of animals in the past, about breeding populations, and the conditions under which the animals lived. Health and diet are related to the wider economic and social structures within which animals lived, and died. Evidence may be found of the stresses related to traction, weight-bearing, transhumance, stalling, penning, and crowding. The presence of wild animals with healed injuries is evidence that animals associated with deities might be given special care (Gautier 2005). Pathologies

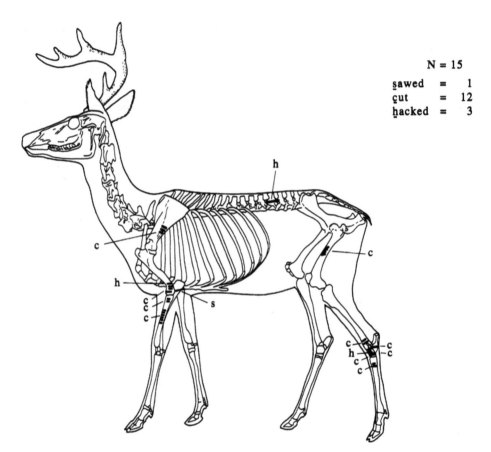

N = 15
sawed   =   1
cut   =   12
hacked =   3

FIGURE 7.22. Hypothetical Collection: Butchering marks for white-tailed deer (*Odocoileus virginianus*) shown on a skeleton.

can be particularly informative where domestication is suspected or verified. As with human skeletons, it is often difficult to associate the evidence of a pathology with the cause, and, therefore, interpretations are often limited. Molecular techniques may provide additional information (e.g., Bathurst and Barta 2004).

The most common modification in the Hypothetical Collection is burning (Table A4.2). None of the deer specimens is burned, but large numbers of turtle specimens are burned. To present this graphically, the number of burned specimens for mammals, birds, turtles, and fishes is divided by the number of specimens in each category (Figure 7.23). More than a third of the turtle specimens are burned. Most of these burned turtle specimens could not clearly be identified as fragments of either carapace or plastron (carapace/plastron) or of a specific species, which highlights the relationship between burning and fragility. It also suggests that turtles were roasted in their shells. None of the specimens showed evidence of pathological conditions.

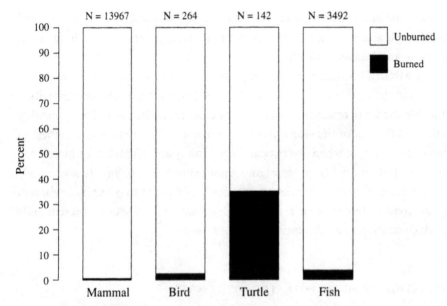

FIGURE 7.23. Hypothetical Collection: Histogram comparing burned and unburned specimens for mammals, birds, turtles, and fishes. Burned specimens are divided by the total number of specimens for each class.

NICHE BREADTH

Niche breadth facilitates discussing food habits in terms of the variety of animals used in the site (diversity) and the evenness (equitability) with which those species were used. As we discussed in Chapter 4, "richness" is the number of species used at the site; "diversity" is the relative importance of species present; and "equitability" is the evenness with which these resources are used. These concepts make it possible to discuss human subsistence in terms of generalist and specialist strategies. Generalists use a wide variety of animals in roughly equal numbers, but specialists use many individuals of only a few species. Cleland (1976) refers to these as diffuse and focal strategies. Differences in animal use characterized by diversity and equitability may distinguish ethnic groups, social strata, or urban settings compared to rural ones (e.g., Leonard and Jones 1989; Rothschild 1989). Niche breadth may also indicate a subsistence strategy's relationship to carrying capacity and concepts such as optimal foraging theory and prey choice (e.g., Jones 2004; Loponte and Acosta 2004). Changes in niche breadth may indicate either a cultural or an environmental change (e.g., Darwent 2004).

NISP, MNI, specimen weight, and sample biomass can all be used in formulae that explore strategies of resource use in terms of niche breadth. Owing to the cultural filter, diversity in an archaeological sample does not reflect diversity in the region but only in those animals that were used by the occupants of the site or were incidentally incorporated into the collection and whose remains were preserved, recovered, and identified. Sample size is a component of these indices (e.g., Emery 2004b; Kintigh 1984, 1989; Shannon and Weaver 1949:13).

Based on MNI, the diversity of molluscs in the Hypothetical Collection is low ($H' = 1.213$) but the equitability ($V' = 0.623$) is high (Figure 7.24). The low diversity is due to the dominance of oyster individuals in the collection. The moderate equitability reflects the fact that six of the seven taxa are represented by very similar numbers of individuals. Interestingly, when diversity and equitability are calculated for biomass in the sample, both diversity ($H' = 0.738$) and equitability ($V' = 0.379$) are low, largely owing to the dominance of oysters as a meat source compared to other invertebrates. This is a common pattern for coastal sites, where a wide range of taxa are present, only a few of which contribute a substantial amount of meat.

INTERPRETATION OF THE HYPOTHETICAL COLLECTION

The purpose of the Hypothetical Collection is to show the interrelatedness of primary and secondary data and to follow the chain of evidence from the initial rough-sort up to analysis. Recovery technique and sample size both have an impact on this collection and influence all levels of data collection from taxonomic attribution through diversity estimates. For example, the absence of a normal curve in the sea catfish otolith measurements (Figure 7.7) and the distribution of deer body part frequency (Figure 7.11) may be consequences of sample size.

Some analysis is precluded by attribution problems. It continues to be impossible to determine the identity of the equids at St. Augustine. Being unable to take some attributions to the species level means that MNI is estimated for a variety of taxonomic levels, and complicates analysis at several points. Access to a good reference collection was very important, but it did not resolve all identification problems. Identification also required being aware of regional and individual variations in conformation, size, maturation sequences, and distribution.

Many of the ways to derive secondary data build on each other. This is particularly evident in the relationships among body dimensions, age, sex, and skeletal frequencies. Although many prefer estimating age from teeth rather than from degree of fusion, teeth are rare in the Hypothetical Collection, perhaps because primary butchery of some animals removed the cranium and mandible elsewhere. Fusion could be recorded for only half of the deer specimens. The skeletal portions represented reflect the potential of specimens to survive site-formation processes. The elements of young animals may be underrepresented and their use may appear low for this reason. Due to site-formation processes, fusion for both the proximal and distal ends of a deer element was observed in only four specimens and it is possible that specimens from the same living animal were placed

Diversity formula: $H' = -\sum_{i=1}^{s} (p_i)(\log_e p_i)$

where H' is the information content of the sample and p_i is the relative abundance of individuals for each taxon in the collection.

Step 1. Divide the MNI for each taxon by the total MNI for the collection to obtain the relative abundance of individuals for each taxon (p_i)
Step 2. Obtain the natural $\log_e$ of p_i
Step 3. Multiply p_i times the natural $\log_e$ of p_i and sum the products
Step 4. Change the sign

		Step 1	Step 2	Step 3	Step 4
Taxon	MNI	p_i	$\log_e p_i$	$(p_i)(\log_e p_i)$	H'
Littorina sp.	36	0.097	- 2.333	- 0.226	
Crepidula sp.	9	0.024	- 3.730	- 0.090	
Neverita sp.	9	0.024	- 3.730	- 0.090	
Ilyanassa sp.	27	0.073	- 2.617	- 0.191	
Crassostrea sp.	240	0.649	- 0.432	- 0.281	
Tagelus sp.	39	0.105	- 2.254	- 0.237	
Mercenaria spp.	10	0.027	- 3.612	- 0.098	
Total	370			- 1.213	1.213

Equitability formula: $V' = H' / \log_e S$
where H' is the Shannon–Weaver function and S is the number of taxa for which MNI was estimated.

Step 1. Count the number of observations (S); in this example there are 7.
Step 2. Obtain the natural log of S
Step 3. Obtain H'
Step 4. Divide H' by $\log_e$ of S to obtain V'

Step 1	Step 2	Step 3	Step 4
S	$\log_e S$	H'	V'
7	1.946	1.213	0.623

FIGURE 7.24. Calculating diversity and equitability using the Shannon–Weaver (Shannon and Weaver 1949) and Sheldon (Sheldon 1969) formulae.

in two separate age groups. Some evidence for age and sex may be lacking because of the way carcasses of older or younger animals were butchered, processed, or distributed.

Measurements that might assist in taxonomic attributions, age and sex estimates, and breed attributions are missing for many reasons. Rarely could two dimensions of the same specimen be measured. For example, only seven proximal and four distal metapodia were measurable and none of these measurements was from the same specimen. This may be due to factors such as butchery and disposal off-site, the lower leg being left in the hide or metapodial elements being used to make tools or destroyed when tendons were removed. Horn cores are very rare, perhaps for similar reasons. However, the artiodactyl astragalus survives well, but because there is no epiphyseal plate it is not as useful for estimating age at death.

All of the approaches demonstrated in Chapters 6 and 7 suggest that units of meat from the forelimb and hindlimb are common in the collection, although other elements are represented as well. The presence of mandible and cranial elements may indicate that some butchery took place on the site, that the head was considered a unit of meat, or that hides were cured on the site. All of the excavation units were located close to the primary residential structure on the site; most primary butchery refuse was probably discarded further from the main house. The proximal humerus is missing altogether. This is probably due to its low density or because carnivores destroyed it. The blade of the scapula, and the shafts of the femur, tibia, and metapodia, could have been removed to make buttons and other tools and ornaments, or they may have been destroyed during removal of the marrow or making glue.

The deer data in the Hypothetical Collection do not conform closely to any of the proposed utility curve models for kill/butchery sites or consumption sites (Figure 2.5; Lyman 1985; Metcalfe and Jones 1988; Thomas and Mayer 1983:368). They are most similar to the reverse utility curve anticipated for a kill site at which elements from low-utility cuts of meat are abundant and those from high-utility ones rare because they were removed to the consumption site (Metcalfe and Jones 1988:figure 5 d). Before interpreting these data as evidence for a kill site, however, we must recall that the Hypothetical Site was in the heart of one of the largest urban centers in eighteenth-century North America; that it was occupied by a wealthy, influential member of the community; and that the wild animal being examined was unquestionably killed elsewhere. We might expect to find the gourmet utility strategy at sites such as this. Perhaps deer carcasses were butchered on the property rather than field-dressed; the meat associated with the femur may have been shared with other households, the associated skeletal elements may have been used as raw material, or the bones may have been destroyed by other processes. The missing skeletal elements are ones with relatively low density.

Food preparation probably was the primary cause of the modifications, although it is not possible to evaluate negative evidence. Rodent and carnivore gnawing on some specimens indicates that some trash was not buried immediately. Food preparation involved filleting meat from elements, as well as hacking the tightly articulated joints at the elbow and ankle, sawing, and cutting. Many of the cuts are associated with these joints as well. Some of the cut marks may be associated with skinning. All of the filleting marks are on shaft fragments, which demonstrates the importance of studying shafts as well as articular ends of long bones. Roasting over a flame may have been a common way to cook turtles. Had only an abbreviated list of elements been identified, the high incidence of burned turtle specimens would not have been observed because this was primarily on carapace/plastron fragments.

Summaries of NISP, MNI, weight, and sample biomass are all related to site-formation processes, sample size, and analytical decisions. However, NISP probably does not adequately characterize the relationship among the taxonomic groups identified because of the uneven number of elements in organisms as diverse as deer, gopher tortoises, slippersnails (*Crepidula* spp.), and crabs (*Callinectes* spp.). MNI places these diverse organisms on a more uniform basis. Sample biomass indicates that domestic mammals provided most of the meat, which is reflected in low diversity and equitability ($H' = 1.485$; $V' = 0.378$; $N = 51$). This raises the interesting question as to why species richness is high (richness $= 52$), diversity is moderate ($H' = 2.639$), and equitability is high ($V' = 0.668$) when MNI is used as the basis for quantification, and the reverse is the case for sample biomass.

CONCLUSIONS

Many of the primary and secondary data reviewed in Chapters 6 and 7 were also discussed by Chaplin in 1971. There are very few new methods. However, today we have a much better understanding of the strengths and weaknesses inherent in such data. In many respects, the technical criticisms that dismay students reflect the fact that zooarchaeologists now ask complex questions that require precision in the supporting evidence. No longer is it sufficient to document that animals were domesticated, that clams were collected, or that large fish were caught. We now want to know why or how people did this and what impact such activities had on human history and on the world in which we live. Zooarchaeologists attempt to extrapolate important principles about human behavior and the relationship between human society and the environment from what continues to be a limited number of primary observations. It is difficult to derive the rich complexity of human behavior from shell, teeth, and bone fragments, but we should not stop trying.

The diverse methods and criticisms of them also reflect the research perspectives of zooarchaeologists working in many different settings. We are intrigued, for example, by the distinction made by Klein and Cruz-Uribe (1984:3) between the death assemblage and the deposited assemblage. This distinction is necessary for research into scavenging or foraging behaviors of australopithecines, but it seems remote to studies of economic systems at residential urban sites in complex societies. Champions of NISP rather than MNI and dietary contributions rarely attempt to integrate multiple classes of animals into subsistence strategies. Often, their own research focuses on differential survival of specific skeletal portions of large mammals, for which MNI is not useful. Methods designed to study single, whole animals often are inadequate for examining relative portions of a shared resource, and vice versa. When considering how to derive secondary data, it is extremely important to think about the materials being examined and the research question to which the data will be applied.

As Reed (1963:215) observes, "there is no single magical formula, but judgement must still enter the calculations." Familiarity with biological principles, thorough recovery techniques, large sample sizes, and conservative application of identification and quantification procedures are fundamental to good zooarchaeology. It is important to test hypotheses using more than one line of evidence and samples from more than one site. It also is important to persevere. The relationship between humans and animals is one of the most basic aspects of human life. In the remaining chapters, we evaluate some of what we have learned about the human condition and the world in which we live from the study of animal remains from archaeological sites.

8

Humans as Predators: Subsistence Strategies and Other Uses of Animals

INTRODUCTION

Reed (1963:209) refers to interpretation in zooarchaeology as a "fascinating maze of intermixed science and art." Primary and secondary data form the basis for these interpretations, which often focus on the relationship between humans and animals in subsistence strategies, with humans in the role of predator. From the perspective of ecology, people balance the amount of time and energy required to obtain resources against the energy, nutrients, and other benefits these resources provide. The consequences of these choices are fundamental to the human condition. Subsistence strategies are ways by which people obtain a variety of nutrients regularly, while ensuring that the costs required to find, catch, transport, process, distribute, and use them do not exceed the benefits they yield. In addition to this basic use, animals are interwoven into almost all other aspects of human life.

It is important to distinguish among nutrition, menus, diet, and cuisine. Nutrition is a measure of the physiological adequacy of a diet in terms of basic biological requirements for growth, repair, and reproduction. Although there is a basic need for nutrients, this need can be met by a variety of foods that people may ignore or value. Menus are the lists of food items available, whether or not they are eaten (Armelagos 1994). Diets are the food and drink actually consumed from among those available. The composition and quantity of a diet varies annually depending on nutritional value of each food, as well as the age, sex, and status of the consumer (Dennell 1979). Many different choices are made about how foods are procured, distributed, prepared, and served. The results of these choices constitute culturally distinctive foodways or cuisines. Cuisines define the combinations of foods; the manner of preparation; the style of cooking; the social rules governing when, how, and by whom they are prepared and eaten; and the circumstances under which they are eaten (Farb and Armelagos 1980:190; Miracle 2002). Each of these defines a culture and serves important biological and social functions, although they may not be readily observed in archaeological data.

Thus, subsistence strategies are the product of dynamic interactions between people and their environments and involve diverse biological, cultural, and ecological factors (e.g., Loponte and Acosta 2004; Miracle and Milner 2002; Styles and Klippel 1996). Zooarchaeologists study them from the perspective of animals, generally using ecological and economic models of energy management. Much of the research into humans as predators focuses on the identification of specific foods, as does this volume, but this requires interpreting combinations of primary and secondary data rather than analysis of a single data set (see Brewer 1992). The natural resource base, energetics, nutrition, diet, demography, and human health are intertwined with the structure and function of the social environment, including settlement, resource management, technology, cultural history, as well as economic, political, kinship, and belief systems (Bogucki 1988; Ellen 1982:277–9; Hardesty 1977). These form that highly complex pattern of learned, shared behaviors called culture.

Owing to this complexity, many give priority to one or the other of these topics and subdivide them endlessly into smaller and smaller theoretical units that represent disciplinary boundaries and funding opportunities. We cannot stress more strongly that these topics should be viewed as an integrated whole because that is the way our primary subject animal, *Homo sapiens*, uses them. It is for this reason that interdisciplinary collaboration improves studies of human behavior – it is the only realistic perspective on that behavior. Such collaborations link biological and ecological parameters with archaeological context, material culture, plant and animal data, human biology, archival information, and ethnographic observations.

People are broadly classified as hunter-gatherers, horticulturists, agriculturists, or pastoralists on the basis of strategies associated with characteristic settlement patterns, technologies, population structures, and social institutions (e.g., Bates and Lees 1996:13, 153, 233). Such classifications are admittedly too broad and overlook significant cultural diversity within each category and among the categories. At a very broad level, many of the criteria used to define each of these categories reflect the way plant and animal resources are acquired. In that sense, these classifications represent points along a continuum from dependence on wild foods to reliance on domesticated ones (e.g., Gragson 1992b; Kent and Vierich 1989). Many people whose primary subsistence activity is farming also may gather and tend wild plants, set traps in their gardens, and fish. Wild plants and animals continued to be used in many parts of the world after farming and herding began (e.g., Boyle 2005; Legge and Rowley-Conwy 1987; Plug and Voight 1985; Szuter and Bayham 1989; Zvelebil and Dolukhanov 1991). Even today many urban dwellers include wild resources, such as seafood or venison, in their diets, sometimes going to great expense to obtain these for themselves.

Some distinguish between hunter-gatherers who forage opportunistically and those who collect following a planned, logistic strategy (e.g., Binford 1980; Lieberman 1993b). Others use "forager" or "gatherer" in a general sense rather than "hunter-gatherer" to emphasize that food acquisition is highly variable and cannot be characterized by a simple dichotomy of man the hunter of large mammals and woman the gatherer of plants (e.g., Bates and Lees 1996:13; Cane 1996). The term "forager" also permits a primarily fishing strategy to be recognized (Grier et al. 2006). Even a superficial review of the zooarchaeological literature suggests that such distinctions fail to capture the variety of ways people obtain and use nutrients and are only useful as abbreviations for much larger, more complex, relationships (e.g., Kim and Grier 2006).

The interpretation of animal remains as evidence of humans as predators is reviewed here in terms of nutritional requirements, spatial and temporal organization, technologies, and social institutions. The interaction between humans and domestic animals is a particularly important part of human behavior and is more fully explored in Chapter 9. The relationships between humans and animals are studied from many other, equally fruitful, perspectives.

Various models are proposed to study humans as predators. Among the most popular are variations of optimal foraging theory, which classify taxa into high-ranking and low-ranking resources based on the size of the animal. High ranking animals would be targeted preferentially because of their large body size. The use of low-ranked, small-bodied animals might be considered, therefore, evidence of long-term food stress. This perspective is widely tested and critiqued (e.g., Ballbè 2005; Darwent 2004; Grayson and Delpech 1998; Henrikson 2004; Jones 2004; Outram 2004; Schmitt et al. 2004). The model as usually presented is too focused on hunting large-bodied vertebrates, particularly terrestrial vertebrates, to interpret the rich array of criteria, processes, and outcomes involved as humans meet nutritional and social needs. This is especially true for aquatic settings where the vast amount of fishes, shellfishes, and birds present in such assemblages clearly overwhelms the occasional artiodactyl's dietary potential (e.g., Butler and Campbell 2004; Luff and Bailey 2000; Mitchell and Charles 2000). However, this concern also applies to other settings (e.g., Madsen and Schmitt 1998). Instead, we summarize a model that permits the continuum of nutritional and social needs to be considered and explains why, even today, city-dwellers glorify the hunt though it is likely the only wild foods they eat are fish and shellfish.

JOCHIM'S MODEL

Models of energy conservation, procurement adequacy, or nutritional acquisition based on energetic laws presume humans balance the merits of a resource against the costs of acquiring it (e.g., Ellen 1982; Jochim 1979). A model proposed by Jochim (1976, 1981) is particularly useful for evaluating human economic behavior from an ecological perspective using zooarchaeological data. The model assumes people make rational decisions to reconcile competing objectives, but ultimately to ensure regular and sufficient intake of energy and nutrients (Jochim 1976:4–5; 1981:64). To do this, decisions are made about which resources to use, in what quantity, when, from where, and by whom. These are based on three interrelated variables: (1) resource use schedules, (2) site placement, and (3) demographic arrangements (Jochim 1976:11). Although developed for the study of hunter-gatherer economies, this model also applies to agricultural, pastoral, and urban systems.

Two goals guide resource use decisions (Jochim 1976:19). One of these is to achieve secure levels of food and other resources. Diversity helps to achieve a reliable subsistence base. The other is maintaining energy expenditures (costs) within a predetermined range given the settlement pattern and population size. Costs include time, effort, distance, the expense of the technology, personal risk, and risk of failure. Satisfying desires is also an important consideration (Jochim 1976:19–21). Desirable secondary goals may include good taste (largely based on the fat content), variety (rare things), prestige, and maintaining the division of labor. From the perspective of zooarchaeology, the amount of fat in meat is related to flavor, juiciness, and tenderness. Anyone on a fat-free diet can appreciate the value placed on these characteristics. Animal tissues are also either the sole or the most metabolically-efficient source of complete proteins, fat-soluble vitamins, and some minerals.

Balanced against these needs and desires are characteristics of the resources themselves. Resource variables include weight, density, aggregation size, mobility, fat content, and nonfood yields such as prestige (Jochim 1976:23). Prestige items are typically luxuries that are risky to acquire and large. Obtaining foods that confer prestige fosters dietary diversity. The normal diet will be based on low-risk resources that have moderate yields: foods such as plants and molluscs that are normally reliable and can routinely be acquired by women, children, and older members of the community. Hunting is an activity involving high risk and low return, while gathering offers high returns for low risk. Usually a generalized strategy will be followed because it reduces risk; but a few adventurous hunters enhance their prestige by obtaining unusual, high-risk foods that are tasty because of their high fat content. These strategies are modified to reduce costs by managing geographical variables, settlement patterns, exchange systems, and technology. Energetic extravagances, such as feasts, are supported by meeting basic nutritional requirements through more efficient and less costly mechanisms. High cost to obtain and process an animal can be correlated with higher social status.

Settlement size, location, and spacing are ways to control costs by minimizing distance (Jochim 1976:50). In this context, access to raw materials, potable water, fuel, security, and shelter are considered in residential decisions and must be balanced against proximity to a valued food resource (e.g., Meehan 1982:26, 34, 66). Jochim (1976:60) argues settlements will normally be close to less mobile, more dense, and less clustered resources. Density refers to the amount of time required to find a resource; dense resources require less search time. Clustering refers to the amount of a resource acquired per trip; unclustered resources require more pursuit time. These same resources may be the most dependable, but least prestigious, and probably will be plants or invertebrates rather than vertebrates. These factors have an impact on the degree of sedentism, the scheduling of resource use, and relationships between base and extraction camps (Jochim 1976:61). Extending this model to other economic systems, settlement patterns also may be related to the location of other communities, trade routes, raw materials, fields, and herds.

The number of people supported by the resource base is an important ingredient of a subsistence strategy and is related to demographic characteristics of the community. Yield, costs, and risks are defined by the demographic characteristics of a community, such as group size, population structure, fertility, length of life, and the density of the residential pattern (Buikstra and Mielke 1985; Jochim 1976:70). It is necessary to ensure reproductive viability and maintain social interaction while staying below the region's carrying capacity. Group fissioning, warfare, delayed marriage, postpartum taboos, and prolonged lactation are some devices by which human population size is controlled.

NUTRITION AND DIET

Most cultural systems meet the normal demands of adequate nutrition with such success that we tend to ignore this fundamental requirement except during disasters. Nevertheless, meeting nutritional needs on a daily basis is fundamental to human survival. For this reason, the concept of nutritional adequacy is central to theoretical models. It is difficult to conclude, from a list of resources identified in an archaeological assemblage, that the nutritional level was adequate because this depends not only on the quantity and quality of the diet but also on the demography and health status of the people supported by the resources. Evaluating nutritional adequacy from a list of identified resources depends on the relationship between the samples being studied and the original deposit.

No single food provides all of the necessary nutrients summarized in Chapter 3, which means that people must obtain nutrients from a wide variety of foods to be adequately nourished (Farb and Armelagos 1980:27–39). Thus, dietary flexibility and variety are necessary to meet nutritional requirements. In addition, there must be physiological and cultural ways to avoid frequent nutritional stress by ensuring that essential nutrients are continually available. These two constraints form the basis of subsistence strategies.

There are no absolute standards for nutritional adequacy. Individual nutritional needs are based on factors such as genetics, basal metabolism, body size, age, sex, activity level, overall health, the amount of other nutrients consumed, as well as on environmental variables, such as altitude, humidity, and temperature (Dufour 1994; Pike and Brown 1975:815–19, 876; Whitney and Rolfes 2008:16–19, 254). Nutritional requirements are greater when new tissue is being formed. Children, pregnant or nursing women, and people recovering from illness or trauma require more of some nutrients than do adults in good health. Some human populations have adapted physiologically to what might otherwise be considered an unbalanced diet (e.g., Moran 1979:131). For these reasons modern recommended dietary allowances may not be appropriate for archaeological populations (Pike and Brown 1975:817).

Assessing nutrition for an archaeological population relies heavily on human skeletal evidence of nutritional status. This is obtained from growth and development patterns, skeletal morphology, and demographic profiles (Buikstra et al. 1986; Huss-Ashmore et al. 1982; Larsen 1997; Larsen et al. 2007; Steinbock 1976:322; White and Folkens 2005). It is difficult to attribute skeletal characteristics to specific nutritional causes because skeletal evidence often is generalized and reflects interrelated physiological, genetic, health, and environmental factors. Growth rate, size, shape, and other features in human tissue also provide evidence for activity levels and work habits associated with food acquisition (e.g., Benfer 1990; Kennedy 1986; Larsen 1997; Larsen et al. 2007; Molleson and Hodgson 1993).

In only a few cases do nutritional diseases leave characteristic osteological signatures (Huss-Ashmore et al. 1982; Steinbock 1976:322; White and Folkens 2005). These diseases include rickets, scurvy, dental decay, and some anemias. General evidence of stress, some of which may be of nutritional origin, is found when growth is so disrupted that it has an impact on the size and shape of bone and teeth (Huss-Ashmore et al. 1982; Larsen 1997). Arrested growth may produce transverse or Harris lines in bone and enamel hypoplasias in teeth. For either of these to form, the individual must survive the stress and growth must resume. Although it is not possible to identify the stress that caused growth to be interrupted, these lines provide evidence the individual experienced stress of some nature during childhood, which might be related to nutrition.

Human skeletons provide some evidence about nutritional status, but because this evidence is ambiguous, it must be augmented with information about the resources that were actually consumed. Stomach contents and coprolites (paleofeces) provide direct evidence of such foods (e.g., Fry 1985; Reinhard 2007; Sobolik 2007). Fecal steroids also provide information about the sex of the consumer (Sobolik et al. 1996). Such evidence has a poor survival rate except in excellent preservation contexts. However, the wealth of information contained in these remains expands our definition of what people ate and who ate it, beyond our own concepts of what is edible and what is not (Rhode 2003).

Even when we are able to obtain remains of plants, animals, human skeletons, stomach contents, and coprolites, differences in site-formation processes and data collection often make the analytical results incomplete or incompatible (e.g., Munson et al. 1971). Stable isotopes and trace elements augment our limited knowledge. Although this evidence does not enable us to reconstruct diets, it does identify a profile of foods consumed and suggest a relative percentage of various food sources. These sources are typically broadly divided into categories such as leafy plants, nuts, seeds and grasses, sea mammals, fishes, shellfishes, or terrestrial meats (e.g., Newsome et al. 2004; Yoneda et al. 2004). Another approach is to explore the protein sources of the diet compared to the total diet and trophic levels (e.g., Prowse et al. 2004; White 2004). Stable isotopes in animals that share the human diet also may augment or be proxies for direct measurement of isotopes and trace elements in human remains (e.g., Pechenkina et al. 2005; White 2004). The combination of stable isotopes, trace elements, and human skeletal evidence with plant and animal identifications is a particularly powerful approach to the study of humans as predators.

SPATIAL DIMENSIONS

Subsistence studies not only examine basic nutritional needs and diets, but they also explore the strategies people use to procure nutrients and whether such activities are sustainable (Siracusano 2006). Resources are not used in direct proportion to their natural abundance and humans do not wander aimlessly about the landscape looking hungrily for food each day. People manage where they live, when they live there, and the tools they use to acquire, control, and process resources based on the energy and other nutrients these activities require. These choices are balanced against the return offered by the available resources. The spatial and temporal characteristics of subsistence activities and resources must be considered to manage the costs and risks of subsistence while obtaining adequate nutrition in the form of an acceptable diet. This requires varying the habitats exploited and the methods used on the basis of familiarity with spatial and temporal aspects of animal behavior to obtain resources when they are most abundant, in top condition, or do not conflict with other resources (e.g., Gragson 1992a).

Site-catchment analysis focuses on the spatial component of procurement (Munson et al. 1971; Styles 1981:11). The premise is that the time and energy required to search for food, capture it, and transport it can be controlled by means of settlement patterns. This does not exclude exchange with more distant locations but focuses on resources needed on a daily basis by a community (Figure 2.6; Higgs 1975:ix; Higgs and Vita-Finzi 1972; Higgs et al. 1967; Roper 1979; Vita-Finzi and Higgs 1970:7). Zooarchaeologists infer catchment area from the characteristics of the resources identified from the site, for example, large numbers of pelagic fishes may indicate that off-shore areas were included in the catchment area (e.g., Van Neer and Gautier 1993). Such spatial attributes of resources in a catchment area can be managed through settlement patterns (Gifford et al. 1981; Lieberman 1993b; Wapnish and Hesse 1991).

People vary their residence from highly mobile to exclusively sedentary, often combining the extremes of mobility and sedentism in complex ways (e.g., Anderson 1988; Kent 1989). Some foragers are sedentary, and many farmers and pastoralists are residentially

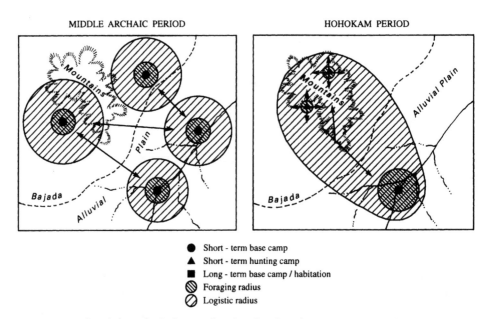

MIDDLE ARCHAIC PERIOD   HOHOKAM PERIOD

- ● Short - term base camp
- ▲ Short - term hunting camp
- ■ Long - term base camp / habitation
- ⊗ Foraging radius
- ⊘ Logistic radius

FIGURE 8.1. A hypothetical example of regional settlement patterns and socioeconomic changes from the Middle Archaic to the Hohokam Period in the southwestern United States (Szuter and Bayham 1989:88). Used with the kind permission of Cambridge University Press, Christine R. Szuter, and Frank E. Bayham.

mobile. For example, many farmers travel long distances to reach their fields each day and occasionally move their residences along with their fields. Residential mobility of portions (transhumance) or all (long-range pastoral nomads) of a pastoral population is characteristic of herders moving their flocks to meet the animals' forage requirements (Bates and Lees 1996:154). Others practice sedentary pastoralism in a mixed plant and animal husbandry system. Portions of largely sedentary populations may travel great distances and be absent from home for long periods of time, especially traders. Although the primary reason for mobility is economic, people also move for ritual, social, or political reasons (e.g., Kent and Vierich 1989; Meehan 1982:32), although these moves are usually for shorter time periods and may be part of an annual ritual calendar that also has an ecological component. In some cases, men and women may follow different residential patterns, with men being more mobile than women (Larsen et al. 2007; Rhode 2003).

Residence patterns are related to the subsistence and other activities that take place at each location. Manipulating the degree of sedentism or mobility is a way to respond to spatial and temporal periodicity in area resources. Opportunistic foraging, or use of small animals, may be energetically feasible only if the resource will be transported over a short distance (Figure 8.1; Szuter and Bayham 1989). A planned, logistic strategy takes place over a greater distance and usually involves larger yields (Figure 8.1). Some camps are occupied repeatedly throughout the year or even continuously and the subsistence activities that take place at each vary accordingly. Other camps are moved in response

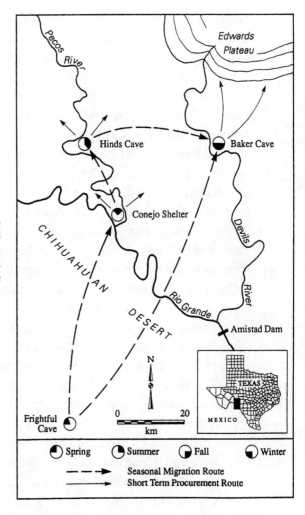

FIGURE 8.2. Map of the Lower Pecos Region, the Chihuahuan Desert, United States and Mexico, illustrating the seasonal round hypothesized by Shafer (1986; from Sobolik 2007). Used with the kind permission of Springer Science and Business Media and Kristen D. Sobolik.

to seasonal patterns of resource availability (Figure 8.2; Sobolik 2007). Such residential mobility was not uncommon in the past. Locations may be occupied because both food and raw materials are available at a location (e.g., Minniti 2005; Legge 2000; Serrand and Bonnissent 2005).

Dense concentrations of people may occur if the population is sedentary. This has an impact on trash disposal, sanitation, and public health. Trash may be discarded differently depending on the length of time the site is occupied. A processing or mealtime camp occupied only briefly will probably produce smaller deposits containing a limited array of animal remains, compared to a home base occupied for a long period of time by more people (e.g., Meehan 1982:112). Life in crowded situations, especially those with poor sanitation, increases exposure to communicable diseases (e.g., Reinhard 2007).

Sedentism carries the risk of overexploiting local resources or altering the environment so that they have an impact on local resources in other ways (e.g., Szuter and Bayham 1989). To avoid exceeding the local carrying capacity, people may target a large range of animals to spread the impact of exploitation widely enough that it is sustainable, move to areas that have not experienced exploitation pressures, or change their technology. Randomizing where resources are sought is another way to limit the risk of overexploitation (e.g., Moore 1969). The relatively high richness and diversity of plant and animal remains at archaeological sites suggest that people generally avoid targeting a limited range of resources, which is one way to avoid overexploiting resources in the catchment area. Sedentary populations may use a wider variety of animals, depend on smaller animals, or rely more on mass-capture techniques (e.g., Kent 1989). If the carrying capacity of the catchment area is exceeded people may change their subsistence strategy by targeting different resources, acquiring new social ties, such as trade partners, controlling their own population size; or developing domestic food sources. Portions of the human population may become seasonally migratory or transhumant. A single human population may respond to exploitation pressure by combining all of these responses into a new subsistence strategy.

Caution must be exercised when interpreting faunal data as evidence of overexploitation because other events could produce changes in the types of resources used or in the population characteristics of resources. A new procurement technology may select small, young individuals concentrated in nursery areas. This may indicate a cultural change unrelated to a change in resources in the catchment area itself, such as a change in trade or purchasing habits (e.g., Coy 1996). A change in body size also may reflect a climatic change unrelated to human predation but to which both predator and prey must adapt.

Catchment analysis is also the basis for reconstructing habitats near a site from the plant and animal remains. The concept of distal and proximal habitats and the animals associated with each are used to define catchment areas. This is one of the purposes of techniques that use skeletal completeness, such as the corrected number of specimens (CSI; Shotwell 1955; Thomas 1971), to distinguish between animal remains transported from a distal community and those transported from nearby ones. For example, when the composition of a faunal assemblage is predominantly marine animals where only freshwater ones now live, this evidence is used to hypothesize environmental change. Underlying this hypothesis is the logic of catchment areas: people meet many of their most basic needs by using resources located close to where they live (e.g., Cooke 1992).

TEMPORAL DIMENSIONS

Temporal aspects of the resource base are affiliated with spatial dimensions in subsistence strategies. Temporal availability refers to tidal, daily, seasonal, or annual cycles that reflect variations in photoperiod, temperature, moisture, and metabolism (Monks 1981; Wright et al. 1989). These have an impact on the reproductive cycles of animals; their distribution; the costs and risks of acquiring them; and the quality of their nutrients and by-products. It is only in modern industrial societies with cold storage and global markets that people enjoy fresh food throughout the year. In the absence of these facilities people cope with seasonal rhythms, fluctuating abundances of edible resources, and conflicts that arise if more than one resource is available at the same time (Coe and Flannery 1964; McGovern 1994). Plants provide food for animals that migrate to this seasonal source or go through cycles of lean and fat conditions as plants grow, flower, fruit, and die. People adjust to periods of scarcity and plenty by storing food, moving to more favorable locations, sequentially choosing different sets of resources, and developing exchange networks.

The accessibility of animals varies during parts of each day or season. Although the catchment area may contain a habitat in which a species is found, that animal may only be there occasionally. For example, sea turtles change habitat during the day; they may be taken from sea grass flats or from nesting beaches depending on the time of day or season. Some animals are diurnal, nocturnal, or crepuscular in response to their own food sources and as a way to avoid predators. Others are migratory. In coastal locations, tidal ebb and flow has an impact on the distribution of animals more than the time of day. Seasonal floods and droughts, temperature, solar insolation, humidity, dissolved oxygen, and evaporation also have an impact on the distribution, nutritional quality, accessibility, and abundance of resources. Other animals are essentially immobile, with little variation in daily or seasonal cycles. Some animals are relatively harmless or quite dangerous depending on the season. Such changes often make animals either inaccessible or particularly vulnerable to specific capture techniques at a particular time and place.

Subsistence strategies encompass responses to such temporal changes. Daily and seasonal cycles in resources influence where sites are located, when they are occupied, the number of people that live there, and the activities that occur at them. The capture strategy also may be altered to take advantage of daily or seasonal changes in habits and habitats. Temporal periodicity also has an impact on the organization of the social institutions through which people obtain and distribute resources. The coordination of labor among men and women of different age groups, as well as among communities, may vary during the day or year (e.g., Gragson 1993; McGovern 1994).

Managing temporal periodicity is an important part of subsistence strategies (Flannery 1967, 1968). Periodic cycles require people to coordinate their own activities with those of resources available at specific places or times of the year. Some preferred species are targeted only during portions of the year and others are acquired whenever the opportunity occurs (e.g., Meehan 1982:80). Not only may the timing of specific animal-use activities conflict, but in many cultures animal use must harmonize with farming schedules. Resolving scheduling conflicts may require using the resource during only a portion of the day or year even though it is available at other times. Highly periodic resources, even though abundant and nutritious, may be ignored. Personal and social activities such as ritual cycles, resting, playing, and visiting are also important activities that need to be scheduled (Gragson 1993; Winterhalder 1981).

Seasonal periodicity is explored using many forms of archaeological evidence, such as elemental isotopes, trace elements, increments, soil chemistry, coprolites, human mortality patterns, mortuary habits, and artifact types (Dincauze 1976:96–7; Hoogewerff et al. 2001; Monks 1981; White 1993). Zooarchaeologists are particularly interested in the seasonal aspects of scheduling found in animal remains. A number of primary and secondary data are collected specifically for the purpose of estimating when an animal died and associating this with the season in which it was procured.

Zooarchaeologists emphasize seasonal periodicity in animals, but plant resources may be even more important both in subsistence strategies and as a source of evidence for seasonal patterns in human behavior. It is important to correlate seasonal data from animals with the reproductive parts of plants, such as fruits, nuts, and seeds, because these edible parts tend to be available during relatively brief periods of each year. Preservation and storage of edible plant and animal parts may complicate seasonal interpretations, but the combination of seasonal data from both plants and animals may independently support seasonal interpretations. Figure 8.2 shows one model for associating residential mobility with seasonal availability through a combination of plant and animal evidence.

Many inferences about seasonal activity at a site are based on the identity of specific animals in a collection (Monks 1981). The premise is that most resources are present, abundant, or in prime condition at specific times and that they are most likely to be used during those periods rather than at other times. Perhaps the most classic example of this relationship is the pattern found among some human populations on the northwest Pacific coast of North America, where fishing anadromous salmon in the summer during their spawning runs up freshwater rivers was, and is, an important subsistence activity. By inference, the presence of such seasonal resources is interpreted as evidence for a subsistence activity that took place when these animals were most abundant in area waters. Inferences based on seasonal presence or abundance also can be made using latitudinal and altitudinal differences. The presence of commensal and parasitic animals also provides evidence of seasonal behavior by virtue of their association with their hosts.

The season in which animals are present, accessible, in good condition, rapidly growing, and reproducing is associated with warm or wet seasons. However, for some animals high temperatures or heavy rainfall may cause them to migrate, retreat to areas where they are inaccessible, or slow their growth rate (e.g., Quitmyer et al. 1997). Although migratory animals may indicate winter activity in parts of their range, they provide evidence of other seasons elsewhere. Where turtles hibernate during the winter, their presence in an archaeofaunal assemblage probably does indicate a warm weather extractive activity. However, in areas where these same species are active throughout the year,

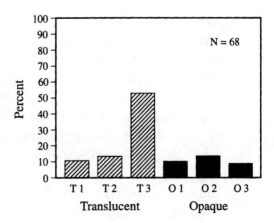

FIGURE 8.3. Seasons of collecting for hard clams (*Mercenaria mercenaria*) based on characteristics of narrow translucent (*T*) growth increments and broader opaque (*O*) increments; viewed under transmitted light. The numbers refer to three shorter growth phases (1–3) within each growth increment (*T* or *O*). These shorter phases are derived from the relative width of each increment. Modified from Quitmyer et al. (1985:34); © (1985) by the Southeastern Archaeological Conference and reprinted by permission from *Southeastern Archaeology* Volume 4, Number 1, and Irvy R. Quitmyer.

their presence in a faunal collection provides no seasonal information at all. In some cases, our assumptions about seasonal habits of animals are flawed (e.g., Felger et al. 1976).

Physiological events associated with growth and reproduction are often strongly seasonal (Monks 1981). These include epiphyseal fusion, tooth eruption, antler development, medullary bone deposition, and incremental growth. One of the most common lines of evidence is the cycle of growth in cervid antlers, although shed antlers are not useful for inferring seasonal activity at the site because they may be stored or used for many years. Incremental growth structures in mammalian teeth and in animals with indeterminate growth also provide seasonal information, with the final growth increment indicating the season in which the animal died (e.g., Burke 2000; Lieberman 1994). For example in Figure 8.3, the presence of translucent and opaque increments in various stages of growth indicates that hard clams were used essentially throughout their growth cycle and, therefore, throughout the year (Quitmyer et al. 1985; Russo and Quitmyer 2007). Use peaks, however, in the fall of the year. The $\delta^{18}O$ values in the terminal growth band in sea catfish (*Galeichthys peruvianus*) otoliths and cockle (*Trachycardium procerum*) valves from two coastal Peruvian sites indicate that fishing occurred during both warm and cool parts of the year, but particularly during the cool season. By extension, this suggests multiseasonal occupations, if not year-round residence (Reitz et al. 2008).

If the death assemblage is sufficiently large, the relationship between age and sex in animal populations, known as population structure, provides information on the age at death and the season at death (Monks 1981). The age and sex composition of a living population varies seasonally, with variations within each population reflecting differences in sex and individual variation. If hunters or herdsmen target a specific age or sex following a seasonal schedule, this will be reflected in the archaeological materials as a cluster of animals into a specific sex or age group (e.g., Plug 1989). In cases of catastrophic death assemblages, such as those that may result from driving animals over a cliff, the age and sex profile will be more inclusive. Size of fish also may indicate targeted age classes and be associated with seasonal fishing, although capture technology and the choice of which fish habitat to exploit also play a role in the selection of fish size.

The archaeological context excavated is an important variable to consider when studying seasonal periodicity (Spiess and Lewis 1995). Settlement and refuse disposal patterns are sometimes associated with seasonal cycles in which human populations aggregate or disperse along with their chosen resources (Figure 8.2). Small summer, or winter, extractive camps are usually irregularly arranged and larger settlements occupied by more people during other seasons may be very formally organized. Some of these larger camps or villages are associated with community ceremonies, such as rites of passage (e.g., Meehan 1982:31–2). Some kinds of structures are associated with specific seasons, for example, heavy plank houses with winter and light-framed, informal structures with summer; internal versus external hearths; or the presence of storage pits (e.g., Monks 1981:219; Wagner 2007). A large midden may accumulate if the site is occupied by many people over several years. Large sites may be occupied only during that part of the year when resources are abundant in the area, but reoccupied over several generations. Seasonal, extractive camps occupied briefly by only a few people would not be expected to have large accumulations of refuse. Trash deposits at extractive sites may contain the remains of only a few species whose physiological processes indicate they all died during the same season.

For these reasons, some resources used by a community will not be deposited or recovered within the excavated area. If the human community had separate summer and winter houses at the same site, and only refuse from the summer house is studied, this will bias the interpretation (e.g., Wagner 2007; Zeder and Arter 2007). Extractive camps and small features are more likely to yield precise seasonal information than are larger contexts, such as sheet refuse or zones, but small deposits may be difficult to locate or uninteresting to excavators. Even in a large faunal assemblage, only a few specimens offer evidence for seasonal periodicity, reducing the number of observations to a few cases. Although closed contexts, such as features, are more likely to contain seasonally discrete deposits, the likelihood of recovering enough specimens to obtain a relevant sample from such contexts is much lower than if the excavation is in a midden, the contents of which are less likely to be seasonally discrete. The smaller the analytical unit, the more specific the seasonal estimate can be, but the more likely the sample will be too small to be reliable.

A particularly difficult situation arises in the case of contemporaneous sites occupied by the same human population during different segments of the year. For example, one of two sites may be a fall camp at which animals were initially captured and processed. The other site could be a large winter village to which a portion of the dressed carcass was transported and where the carcass was eventually consumed and the remaining part of the skeleton discarded. In such cases, the same animal might be present at two sites occupied at different times of the year. This is particularly likely to be the case with fish, which often are captured and processed at briefly-occupied fish camps during annual fish migrations. Much of the skeleton, if not all of it, may be discarded at the fish camp. In this case, there may be very little evidence of fish use at the base camp. In other cases entire carcasses are removed from extractive sites to be processed and consumed elsewhere at other times. The extractive camp may not be correctly interpreted as a fishing station, and it may be assumed that the base camp was occupied during the fishing season and that fishing took place from the base camp, even though that may not have been the case. Transportation, preservation, and storage decisions clearly have an impact on the amount and types of materials recovered.

In most cases, seasonal characteristics provide evidence for when the resource died, not for when or how long a site was occupied. It cannot be assumed that a site with a seasonally diagnostic resource was necessarily occupied when this resource was abundant because capture technology, transportation decisions, exchange systems, preservation techniques, and storage devices all are designed to obscure such a relationship (e.g., Anderson 1988). If you dig gopher tortoises out of their dens, it does not matter that they voluntarily emerge only during warm weather. Storage may mean that a resource killed in one season, or at one site, is used at some other time or in some other place.

Likewise, although a resource is seasonally abundant, it does not follow that the site was abandoned when the resource was unavailable. For example, the absence of molluscs that died in cold months cannot be interpreted as evidence the site was unoccupied during those months. Food taboos or scheduling conflicts may mean that an abundant resource is not used at all. Some people never eat sturgeons, eels, sea urchins, barnacles, and limpets regardless of seasonal availability, even though these may be relished by people who do value them as food (Walsh 1996). Another response to seasonal shifts in migratory animals is to change the hunting strategy to focus on other animals during other seasons. Such seasonal shifts in hunting strategy address temporal variation while avoiding residential mobility (Burke 2000). A wide spectrum of data and procurement activities associated with resource acquisition and avoidance must be considered to determine when a site was unoccupied. The absence of a resource cannot be interpreted as evidence that the site was unoccupied when that resource was abundant.

Many other factors have an impact on seasonal indicators. Because elements of juvenile animals do not preserve well, evidence of warm or wet season activities, such as young mammals and birds, may be underrepresented in faunal collections. The movement of items within a site may mix materials from different seasons together. Archaeological stratification usually represents the compression of many years of activity. This is called time averaging by paleontologists (e.g., Lyman 2003). Sample size and indicators of seasonal periodicity are directly related. Analysis based on the presence of seasonal markers is particularly subject to sample size biases because a single specimen may carry more importance than it would in a large sample.

Associating biological periodicity with temporal, and spatial, aspects of human subsistence requires collapsing annual variation into an average that ignores unpredictable variability, annual extremes, and subtle long-term environmental changes. Inferring seasonal periodicity from the presence of animals and from physiological data is based on the assumption that modern climatic and biological cycles are similar to those in the past, which may not be the case (Quitmyer et al. 2005; Sandweiss et al. 2004). Seasons vary in timing, intensity, and length both annually and over longer climatic cycles. Plants and animals modify their reproductive patterns accordingly. Associating age at death with season is particularly difficult because it combines estimates of the rate of growth and development with assumptions about the birth date of the animal in question. Physiological events rarely can be precisely assigned to an absolute chronological date. They occur within and among populations of the same species within a range and should be interpreted in general terms, such as warm versus cold, or wet versus dry.

The same data that provide the basis for seasonal inferences also are used as evidence for other aspects of subsistence strategies and for environmental reconstruction. In particular, the assumption that the presence of an animal indicates a specific season should be tested against the possibility that the animal's presence may indicate selectivity associated with habitat choice, technology, exchange systems, or an altered environment. Differences between noncontemporaneous sites may indicate a change in animal procurement through time due to changes in either the cultural or the natural environment. Literature that describes biological conditions from the specific environmental context of the site under study should be consulted. However, if the environment has changed considerably since the site was occupied, or the animal was obtained through exchange, analogies using modern biogeographical data may be inappropriate.

TECHNOLOGY

Technology is another way to manage nutritional, spatial, and temporal return for effort. Tools capture or tend animals by taking advantage of their preferred habits and habitats. Different tools and methods are used during the year to take advantage of changes in the environment and animal behavior during annual cycles such as those between wet and dry seasons (e.g., Gragson 1992b). Some species are emphasized because they are easy to acquire with little personal risk; they provide a good balance between the costs involved in obtaining them and yield; the techniques to catch them are reliable; they store well; and their by-products can be used to make other objects. However, time and energy must be expended to make, maintain, and deploy the tools as well as to prepare, distribute, and store their products. Some resources require elaborate processing before they can be used and many food preparation implements are difficult to make, use, and maintain.

When complex tools are used in subsistence activities, often an extra portion is given to the owner of the equipment (e.g., Nietschmann 1973:186; O'Day 2004). Many aspects of technology might also require specific or general ritual or magical accompaniments or have social meaning beyond the simple act of acquiring the raw materials, making the device, and using it (e.g., Choyke et al. 2004; Johnson 2005).

Many materials are used to make tools. Often tools are made from plant materials, further emphasizing the relationship between plant and animal resources in human economies. The fibers used must be able to tolerate the different stresses each tool encounters (e.g., Salls 1989; Wendrich and Van Neer 1994). For example, the cordage in a basketry scoop will experience different stress than materials used in a harpoon, a fence, or a carrying bag. Animal parts are also used as raw materials for tools. Some of these applications take advantage of natural forms of the element with or without further modifications (e.g., Rabett 2004). Acquiring the raw materials to make tools and the manufacturing process are important ingredients in spatial and temporal patterns, as well as of exchange systems, political networks, and other aspects of social behavior.

The acquisition of raw materials, the production of tools, and the use of the tools is often associated with a specific age, sex, residential unit, and social status (e.g., Gragson 1993). These distinctions may vary in response to seasonal changes and the number of people needed to accomplish the task (e.g., Cane 1996). Decisions are also made about how many people should be involved in the activity and the amount of preparation and coordination required. Group size and composition may vary seasonally from an individual effort to a communal one involving most of the community (e.g., Driver 1990; Gragson 1992b).

Although evidence for some techniques may survive in the faunal record (e.g., Noe-Nygaard 1975; Serrand and Bonnissent 2005), many tools are perishable, and those that do survive may be incorrectly identified. For example, stone or shell net weights may not be recognized after the binding that holds them to the net decomposes, and net gauges are rarely identified even when the animal remains indicate that these must be present (Leech 2006:105; Walker 1992a). It is unlikely that the diversity of technologies found ethnographically or represented in graphic arts will ever be seen in the archaeological record (e.g., Altuna 1983; Gifford 1978; Rau 1884; Rostlund 1952; Roth 1970; Shaffer et al. 1995; Stewart 1977). Analogies from ethnographic studies are invaluable if only because they remind us of the wide range of animals that are taken using methods and tools that leave no archaeological evidence. Serjeantson's (1988) description of capturing thousands of seabirds by simply seizing them by hand from ledges and burrows is a case where the capture technology is archaeologically invisible. Other examples are not difficult to find. The Twana of the Pacific northwest coast place branches in tidal water to encourage herring to lay eggs on these roe-collection devices (Oswalt 1976:145). The Owens Valley Paiute of the southwestern United States dig a trench around trees to trap caterpillars driven from trees by smoke (Oswalt 1976:132). Although such ethnographic accounts aid interpretations of subsistence efforts from archaeological remains, they must be used with caution because we cannot know if our analogies are appropriate.

Capture Tools and Methods

Oswalt's (1973, 1976) classification of procurement technologies is a useful way to summarize the array of tools and methods used to capture and manage animals. He classifies food-getting technologies as instruments, weapons, and facilities based on the amount of time and personal attention required to use the devices. In Oswalt's (1976:43) terminology, simple and complex refer to the number of different parts or units combined to make the tool. Some tools require little effort to manufacture and have few parts. For example, porcupine quills, stingray spines, and rodent teeth require little modification before they are used to mark, pierce, or incise objects. Other instruments require several steps, for example, when sinew is used as a cord to attach a stone to a wooden handle or animal teeth are imbedded with resin along the edge of a club. Although we often associate tool types with specific classes of animals (i.e., fish with hand-held lines; large mammals with spears or arrows), actually a variety of animals can be captured by similar tools when these are modified to take advantage of the characteristics of the targeted animal. For example, nets are used to capture dicrodon lizards (*Dicrodon* spp.) in a miniature version of a cattle drive; the lizards are driven along fences leading into a small corral where they are trapped (Holmberg 1957). The lizards commonly found in archaeological sites in Ecuador and Peru (e.g., Chauchat 1992; Reitz and Masucci 2004) might have been taken by such devices.

Instruments (Figure 8.4) are hand-manipulated tools used primarily on resources capable of little movement and offering minimal personal hazard (Oswalt 1976:64). These are active techniques that are costly in terms of energy because they require people to focus their attention on the task and may conflict with other activities. Instruments include sticks and stones used to club sleeping birds or sea lions, to dislodge clams, to dig or pull burrowing animals out of holes, or to dispatch animals captured or cornered through other means. When used to drive animals from dens, fire and water become instruments. Herring rakes, crabbing sticks, knives, and tools used to bleed, poll, or castrate livestock are also instruments.

Weapons (Figure 8.5) are hand-held devices thrown at or placed in the paths of animals capable of significant motion so as to kill or wound them (Oswalt 1976:79). Weapons work best for mobile animals that do not follow set paths and may, therefore, avoid traps or ambushes. They also control the personal risk that comes from getting too close to dangerous animals. Simple weapons may be stones, lances, boomerangs, or other throwing sticks. Gaffs, bows and arrows, harpoons, blowguns, bolas, and slings are more complex. These may be enhanced with poison. Some have toggles, drag anchors,

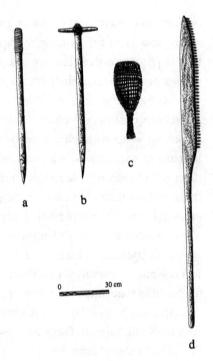

FIGURE 8.4. Instruments: (a) Surprise Valley Paiute digging stick, southwestern United States; (b) Klamath digging stick, Northwest coast; (c) Owens Valley Paiute seed beater, southwestern United States; and (d) Twana herring rake, Northwest coast (Oswalt 1976:70). Used with the kind permission of Wendell H. Oswalt.

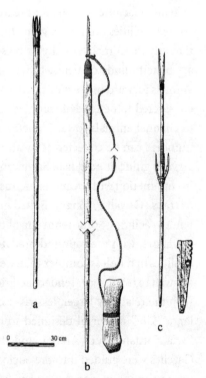

FIGURE 8.5. Simple and complex weapons: (a) simple weapon, a Tanala leister, Madagascar; (b) complex weapon, an Ingura dugong harpoon dart, northern Australia; and (c) complex weapon, an Iglulik bird dart and throwing-board, northern Canada (Oswalt 1976:93, 98). Used with the kind permission of Wendell H. Oswalt.

or floats to exacerbate the wound, increase bleeding, slow the animal down, or mark its progress as it flees. Although weapons are important devices for acquiring animals, they require the active presence of a person, usually capture only one animal at a time, require people to focus their attention on the activity, and limit the other activities that can occur at the same time (Oswalt 1976:103).

Facilities control or protect animals (Oswalt 1976:105). They make animals less risky targets for weapons or eliminate the need for weapons. Facilities are efficient ways for humans to acquire food while controlling the energy expended, minimizing physical danger, and avoiding the risk of failure (Oswalt 1976:105). Many facilities are costly to make and maintain, but they can be used repeatedly and often capture more than one animal at a time. They are particularly useful in obtaining a large amount of food during a season when it is either plentiful or in prime condition. The resulting surplus can be stored for later use or exchanged. Game fences, weirs, fish nets, fish traps, rabbit nets, fish poisons, torches used to hold deer spellbound, hunting blinds, disguises, and lures are facilities that control the movement of animals rather than kill them. The ultimate objective may be to kill the animal, but holding it still also may be the intent, as it often is with domestic animals. Facilities are sometimes owned by a community or a kin group (e.g., Builth 2006; Nishimura 1975). Facilities are considered to be tended or untended depending on the number of people required to be present for the device to serve its purpose (Oswalt 1976:107).

Tended facilities (Figure 8.6) require the presence of at least one person. Examples of tended facilities are lassos, game blinds, hunting disguises, seines, and dip nets. Lures that attract animals visually or by sound are also considered to be tended facilities as are baited blinds or fields. Drives in which fire, sounds, or objects are used to force animals forward into a natural or artificial enclosure, over a cliff, or into a pitfall are also considered to be tended facilities (Oswalt 1976:112). Sometimes guide fences are used to channel animals toward a net, a pitfall, a deadfall, or a poisoned pond where large numbers can be collected (Oswalt 1976:112). Fish weirs are obstructions in water that serve to guide or hold fish. Sometimes these alone take the fish but often weirs are used in conjunction with weapons such as leisters, or with other facilities such as nets, poison, or traps (Oswalt 1976:120). Baited hooks, lures, and gorges attached to lines are usually tended facilities. Some tended facilities are designed to protect crops and livestock from predators, with the captured predator also being consumed (Oswalt 1976:116). Tended facilities may be less complex than weapons but often require more cooperation to deploy (Oswalt 1976:129–30). Tended facilities compensate for the expense of constructing them with the relatively larger, less risky capture rate. An example of a tended facility is the large "kite" or corral designed to capture Persian gazelles (*Gazella subgutturosa*) in Syria, Jordan, Saudi Arabia, and the Sinai Desert (Legge and Rowley-Conwy 1987). Gazelles were guided into the enclosures by large fences. In some places the fences for one enclosure overlap those of an adjacent enclosure.

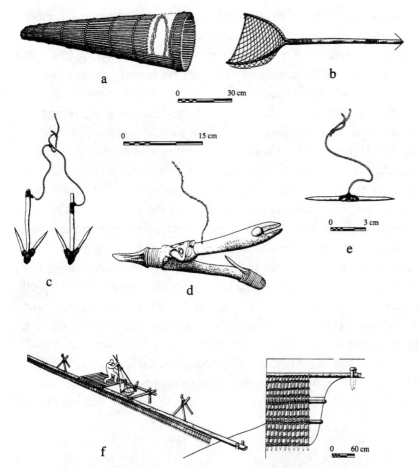

FIGURE 8.6. Tended facilities: (a) Tanala cone-shaped fish scoop, Madagascar; (b) Tanala dip (scoop) net, Madagascar; (c) Klamath composite fish hook, Northwest coast; (d) Tlingit halibut hook, Northwest coast; (e) Klamath fish gorge, Northwest coast; and (f) Twana salmon weir and dip net platform, with profile of weir, Northwest coast (Oswalt 1976:119, 125, 127). Used with the kind permission of Wendell H. Oswalt.

Tended facilities, such as snares, deadfalls, and other traps, also may be converted to untended ones. Untended facilities (Figure 8.7) do not require people to be present (Oswalt 1976:131). Most take advantage of the routine habits of targeted species. They also fit into busy schedules because they can be tended at times when other activities are less pressing. Animals that are nocturnal or cryptic are more readily captured with untended facilities rather than weapons or tended facilities.

Methods and tools conform to the behavior of the animals they are intended to capture or control (e.g., Akazawa 1988; Piana 2005; Steadman and Jones 2006; Stewart 1994). If a specific species is targeted, the tool must match the animal's characteristics closely. In such cases, a weapon, which is more selective than poisons and weirs, may be used. However, if a general range of animals is satisfactory, a facility may be preferred.

Among the characteristics that need to be considered are whether the animal is mobile or immobile, harmless or dangerous, nocturnal or diurnal, solitary or communal, terrestrial or aquatic, and wild or domestic. Solitary, nocturnal animals are best taken with untended facilities, whereas diurnal, schooling or herd animals may be taken with surround drives or cast nets. The degree to which the habits of the animal are dependable must also be considered. If an animal regularly moves from a low-tide resting spot into shallow waters to feed during high tide, or follows a predictable path, facilities will take advantage of this habit. Animals such as parrotfishes, that live in net-damaging coral reefs or rocky outcrops and do not readily take hooks, may seek the apparent, but mistaken, safety of a trap. Animals that congregate in rookeries or schools (such as nesting birds or sea lions, anchovies, and mullets) are more efficiently taken with nets than solitary animals. In quiet waters, fish poisons capture large numbers of fish, particularly small ones or ones susceptible to the chemical used.

Capture devices also take advantage of the animal's size and morphology (e.g., Steadman and Jones 2006; Wendrich and Van Neer 1994). The size of the trap's mouth, the net gauge, the hook or gorge, or the strength of the line will attract and capture some animals while letting others escape (e.g., Cooke and Rodríguez 1994; Coutts 1975). Basketry scoops are more useful in capturing small fishes in shallow waters. It is possible to select from the net animals considered edible and throw back, or use as bait, those that will not be eaten. Some fishes eagerly take hooks or gorges, but such devices will capture few fishes that are herbivores with small mouths that do not take hooks, such as mullets.

Food Processing and Preservation

Traditions in processing foods, what parts of a carcass are brought back to the home site, the ways animal carcasses are butchered, and how the food is cooked all leave distinctive patterns of skeletal distribution and modifications. Food processing and storage may require special technologies. Carrying devices, such as mesh bags, cords, or hollowed gourds, are basic but essential tools. One of the earliest domesticated plants (Erickson et al. 2005; Heiser 1989), the bottle gourd (*Lagenaria siceraria*) is an important utility species. Transportation of large animals may require careful planning. Part of the carcass may be left behind at the kill site, or some members of the human community may go to the kill site to process it. Processing techniques reflect ethnic or economic preferences and the social complexity of the community (e.g., Belcher 1994; Cope 2004; Daróczi-Szabó 2004; Heinrich 1994; Van Neer and Ervynck 1994, 2004). In some cases, they also may indicate that the meat is destined to be dog food (e.g., Thomas and Locock 2000).

The process of killing and butchering carcasses into primary, secondary, and tertiary units is culturally patterned but also conforms to the morphology of the animal (e.g.,

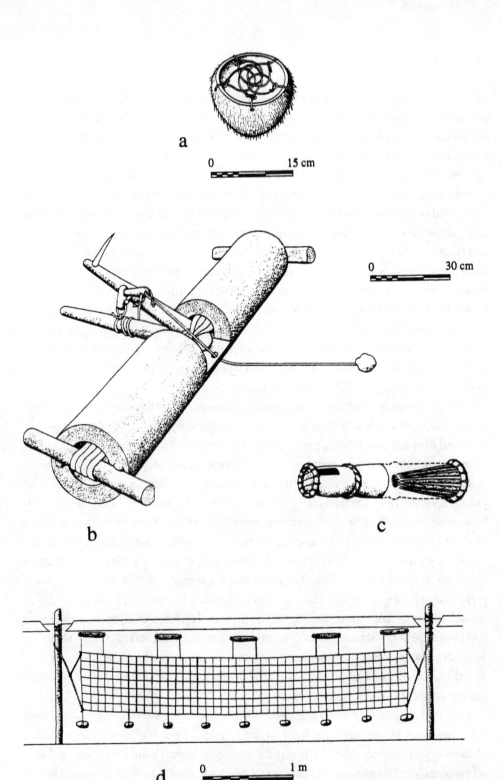

a

0   15 cm

b

0   30 cm

c

d   0   1 m

FIGURE 8.7. Untended facilities: (a) Simple snare, Pukapukan baited coconut shell bird snare, Cook Islands; (b) complex trap, Tanaina torque trap, Alaska; (c) Tanala baited eel trap, Madagascar; and (d) Ingalik whitefish net set beneath river ice, Alaska (Oswalt 1976:136, 141, 146). Used with the kind permission of Wendell H. Oswalt.

Luff 1994). Ethnographic examples demonstrate considerable variability in ways to kill, transport, skin, and eviscerate animals (Kent 1993; Yellen 1977b). This is primarily based on energetics: people do not carry home parts of a kill that provide little food or few useful by-products, but the definition of what is useful or valuable is not the same in every cultural or environmental setting. Many nutrients are lost when the carcass is trimmed and tissues considered inedible are discarded. Secondary and tertiary butchery are related to the number of people to be fed; whether the food will be roasted, boiled, fried, or prepared in another fashion; the size of the cooking vessel; and how the meat will be served. For example, larger units of meat roasted over a fire or boiled in a very large pot will serve a large number of people, and smaller portions, prepared in smaller vessels, serve fewer people (e.g., Bunn et al. 1988; Gifford-Gonzalez 1989; Kent 1993; O'Connell et al. 1988, 1990; O'Connell and Marshall 1989; Yellen 1977b). Modifications are closely associated with the tools and skills butchers bring to this task (e.g., Luff 1994). Processing techniques are quite different for animals of different sizes and morphologies and vary depending on whether the meat will be used fresh or preserved. Similar issues pertain to molluscs (e.g., Milner 2002; Prummel 2005).

Food preservation is an important aspect of subsistence influencing both the nutritional quality of foods and their availability through the year (e.g., Bowen 1988; Van Neer and Ervynck 2004). Some processes, such as fermentation, enhance nutrition, but vitamins are subject to loss, particularly if the process requires prolonged exposure to heat. Techniques such as drying, salting, smoking, and pickling require skill, time, and usually a variety of specialized containers and other tools. Some processes are particularly costly, especially those that render fat and oil from muscle and other tissues. Many of these involve extracting oils, grease, jellies, and marrow in ways that highlight the simplistic nature of utility indices (e.g., Alen and Ervynck 2005; De Nigris and Mengoni Goñalons 2005; Munro and Bar-Oz 2005; Serjeantson et al. 1986; Stokes 2000b). Food preservation is often recognized by the types of elements represented in, or absent from, an archaeological collection (e.g., Brinkhuizen 1994; Hoffman et al. 2000; Serjeantson 1988; Wijngaarden-Bakker 1984; Wijngaarden-Bakker and Pals 1981; Zohar et al. 2001). Some of these elements are associated with the container in which the food was processed or stored (e.g., Lauwerier 1993b; Studer 1994). First- and second-order changes destroy much of this evidence, however.

Study of the lipids, proteins, sugars, and stable isotopes in the residue on ceramics and other tools may elaborate on the information obtained from traditional identification of elements represented, the identity of the animals present in the collection, and kill-off patterns (e.g., Brown and Heron 2005; Craig et al. 2005; Dudd et al. 1999; Morton and Schwarcz 2004; Mukherjee et al. 2005; Shanks et al. 2001). Such studies clarify the functions of containers, the use of these containers to process foods, the identity of the species of animal from which the residue derived, husbandry strategies, and the role of processed foods in the overall diet. DNA and blood protein from stone tools and animal remains from the same location may tell us which tools were used for which task, although as Shanks and his collegues (Shanks et al. 2005) found, the results may be more complex than anticipated. In their study, DNA from canids was common on the stone tools they studied, and the DNA of the prey species found in the archaeological assemblage was absent on these tools. This could be evidence that canids were butchered using these tools, or that canids licked the stone tools, replacing the DNA of bison (*Bison bison*) and bighorn sheep (*Ovis canadensis*) with their own DNA.

Most preservation techniques enhance storage potential but may change the quality of the food item (e.g., Van Neer and Ervynck 2004). Storage is important where resources are marked by distinct seasonal periodicity (e.g., Perlman 1980). More effort may be spent on obtaining foods that preserve well or store for a long period of time than on those that must be consumed at once. Storage has costs of its own because stored foods must be protected from decomposition, vermin, fungi, and theft. Storage facilities, such as root cellars and ice houses, may be difficult to construct and maintain. To distinguish storage in an archaeological assemblage, it may be necessary to consider a wide range of primary and secondary data such as taxonomic attribution; distribution and identity of elements represented; bone density and survival potential; fragmentation and other modifications; size range; diversity; and the habits and habitats of the species represented, in addition to archaeological context (e.g., Zohar et al. 2001).

Raw Materials, Ornaments, Tools, and Toys

Obtaining raw materials such as lithics; minerals and spices, especially salt; and other products is an important element in human subsistence (e.g., Bogucki 1988:190). The quantity, quality, and accessibility of raw materials may dictate when or where an animal is used. Some animals usually interpreted as food may actually have been used for other purposes in addition to, or instead of, food (e.g., Serrand et al. 2005). For example, tabby is a combination of oyster shell, lime, and sand that was a common building material along the North American Atlantic coast prior to the twentieth century A.D. Tabby tends to decompose over time, and the shell fragments become part of the archaeological matrix, which complicates deciding which shell fragments represent food.

Many animal parts are used as raw materials (e.g., Bowen 1992; Thomas and Locock 2000). Mammals, including cats and dogs, provide furs and skins (e.g., Baxter and Hamilton-Dyer 2003; Gidney 2000; Lapham 2004; McCormick 1991; Murphy 2001). Birds provide down, feathers, and skins (e.g., Avery 1985). Molluscs are well-known as raw material for ornaments and tools (e.g., Reese 1980; Chilardi et al. 2005; Minniti 2005; Ruscillo 2005; Serrand et al. 2005). Antlers and horn cores are widely used for purposes such as drainage conduits and building materials (e.g., Armitage 1989a, 1989b; Olsen 1994). Bone is a source of glue and grease used in such products as candles, body oils, neatsfoot oil, pomades, shampoo, lubricants, and pigments, and to cap containers of preserved food. Bones and teeth often are used as ornaments and tools (e.g., Choyke and Bartosiewicz 1994; d'Errico and Vanhaeren 2002; Middleton et al. 2002; Vanhaeren et al. 2004). Animal products are used for scarification or to engrave ceramic, stone, bone, and wooden objects. Gaming pieces and toys also are made of bone (e.g., Minniti and Peyronel 2005; Schallmayer 1994:73). Manufacture of these objects may be associated with social status (Gidney 2000) and may be located in a specific area within the community (Serjeantson 2000). Tanners and butchers, for example, may be excluded from the core of an urban area and may be people of a lower status in the community. In some cases, it may be possible to reconstruct stages in the manufacture of some items (e.g., Mayo and Cooke 2005). Many of the objects made from these raw materials are everyday implements, toys, musical devices, and ornaments; but some were destined for use as amulets, rituals, and hunting magic (e.g., McNiven and Feldman 2003; Prummel 2001).

EXCHANGE SYSTEMS

Many components of a subsistence strategy extend beyond the production of food. Producing, distributing, and consuming goods and services, such as fuel, perishable commodities, durable raw materials, fertile lands, good fishing grounds, and safe trade routes, are also related to subsistence. Additionally, social institutions must be maintained. Economies manage and mobilize procurement, production, exchange, and consumption toward these ends (Barker and Gamble 1985:5; Earle 1980, 1982; Jochim 2006). Productivity, surplus, storage, exchange, specialization, wealth, social complexity, and political institutions are important aspects of economic systems (Brumfiel and Earle 1987). An increase in exchanged goods may be associated with diminished mobility. Many aspects of social organization facilitate or restrict access to resources (e.g., Cachel 2000; Choyke 2004). Among these are residential patterns, group size, nonkin partnerships and alliance mechanisms, political organizations, food-sharing norms, food processing technologies such as storage, kinship organizations, and marriage. Managing exchange systems is a way to resolve variability in resource availability and scarcity (e.g., Cannon 2000).

Animal products must be consumed or preserved relatively soon after the animal dies or they will spoil. One of the important roles of exchange is to avoid wasting animal products by giving them to others. This keeps resources circulating within the community, lessens waste, and solidifies social relationships. Exchanges may take place casually on a daily basis among people who know one another well, occur between trading partners who are fictive kin, or involve a series of intermediaries who are unknown to each other and whose actions are regulated by government officials. They may involve various degrees of residential mobility or sedentism by all or portions of the community. Two ends of this complex acquisition continuum can be described as direct procurement and trade, but mechanisms along this continuum include direct procurement within seasonal rounds, sporadic direct procurement, sporadic exchange, informal exchange among real or fictive kin, reciprocity, redistribution, and trade by specialists that may or may not involve markets (e.g., Maltby 1985; Polanyi 1957; Zvelebil 1985). Such exchanges enable communities to enjoy access to distant resources without residential mobility. They are neither limited to urban centers or state-level political units nor are they mutually exclusive (e.g., Deshpande-Mukherjee 2005; Reitz and Masucci 2004). Each of these different modes of acquisition vary in terms of mechanisms and regularity of movement of nonlocal goods and each is commonly associated with a general form of social organization.

In reciprocity goods and services are given with no immediate expectation of return and no overt attempt to assess the value (Hardesty 1977:83–9). Much reciprocity is balanced, with both sides of the exchange reciprocating more or less equally, however, some is unbalanced, with one party attempting to get a good deal, perhaps by theft or raiding. Balanced reciprocity is particularly common within kin groups and egalitarian communities where it solidifies social bonds (e.g., Kent 1993; Yellen 1977b). Foods or animals are routinely exchanged at weddings, funerals, and other important ritual occasions (e.g., Flannery et al. 1989).

Redistribution is an exchange system found in societies with social inequality where elites accumulate resources, store them, and later redistribute them (e.g., Barker and Gamble 1985). In some cases, the obligation is to redistribute all of these goods, but, often, some or most are retained as personal wealth or for the benefit of the kin group, religious hierarchy, or state. Communal feasts in chiefdoms, such as the potlatch of the American northwest coast or the pig feasts of New Guinea, are ceremonial forms of redistribution. Redistribution often appears to manage extremes in resource availability (Brumfiel and Earle 1987; McCormick 2002).

Markets are trade mechanisms in which the transactions are impersonal and produce a profit. They are associated with increased social stratification, unequal access to goods such as meats, and interactions between coastal and inland sites or rural and urban locations as centers of production and consumption (e.g., Crabtree 1990; Hall and Kenward 1994; Heinrich 1994; Redding 1991; Reitz and Masucci 2004; Reitz and Zierden 1991; Wapnish and Hesse 1991; Zeder 1991; Zvelebil 1985). Such strategies reflect both market demands and the potential of the natural environment, which may be changing in response to modifications in the agricultural landscape or climatic cycles (e.g., Bowen 1996; Randsborg 1985). Evidence for lack of specialization may indicate an early stage in the development of state control over production and distribution between rural and urban sectors of a regional economic system (e.g., Serjeantson et al. 1986; Stein 1987). Reduced use of wild animals sometimes is associated with urbanization and market economies, although wild game traded from rural areas can be an important urban status marker (e.g., Reitz 1987; Van Neer and Ervynck 2004). Urban and rural trade, the types of animals used, the types of elements represented, butchering marks, and the tools used are interrelated (e.g., Luff 1994; Maltby 1989; Perdikaris 1996). Differences are found between animals butchered in commercial contexts and those butchered by individual householders (e.g., Crabtree 1991; Luff 1994; McCormick 1991; Redding 1991). There also may be differences in the sex and age mortality patterns of livestock slaughtered in rural locations for local consumption or urban markets compared to livestock raised and slaughtered in urban settings (e.g., Wilson 1994). Livestock on the hoof may figure prominently among the trade goods (e.g., Poll et al. 2005), as might fish (Van Neer and Ervynck 2004).

The ubiquity of exchange systems in human life is one of the primary reasons zooarchaeologists are uneasy about using MNI as a quantification device and also must be considered when estimating dietary contributions. Reciprocity, in particular, is so fundamental that all archaeological sites bear the evidence of it. The zooarchaeological implication of exchange is that the presence of elements from an animal does not mean that the whole animal was consumed by the inhabitants of the excavated portion of the site. Different criteria may apply to sharing meat from large and small animals. Large animals may be shared widely within a kin group or widely throughout the community (e.g., Zeder and Arter 2007), whereas a smaller animal may be shared only around the hearth where it was cooked (e.g., Gifford-Gonzalez 1989; Kent 1993; Walters 1984). Prime cuts of meat may be given to honor reciprocal or other obligations. However, when every household has a mother-in-law, the preferential distribution of prime cuts of meat to the hunter's mother-in-law will mean every house, hearth, or midden has access to prime cuts. This is, of course, the purpose of reciprocity and some forms of redistribution, to ensure that all members of the community share in food and other resources, although perhaps not equally or simultaneously.

ANIMALS AS SOCIAL MARKERS

Animals, nutrition, menus, diets, and cuisine are interwoven with many cultural institutions; attempts to separate them are artificial (e.g., Bowen 1992; Clark 1987; Crabtree 1990; Goody 1982; Grant 2002; IJzereef 1988; O'Connor 1996; O'Day et al. 2004; Subías 2002). The role of animals as social markers is the distinction between nutrition and cuisine. Components of cuisine, such as when foods are consumed, who eats together, the spices used, food combinations, and other aspects of food consumption, are rarely accessible archaeologically but are the basis of cultural identity. Cuisine also involves concepts of social order, propriety, role expectations, and belief systems. It may even be codified into sumptuary laws. Interpreting the social meaning of animal remains, however, is impeded by our own assumptions about the merits of specific types of foods and the attributes of animals (e.g., Bassett 2004; Stokes 2000b; Van Neer and Ervynck 2004) and misplaced faith in the veracity of literary traditions (e.g., Murray et al. 2004).

Animals and animal parts play roles in social life independent of their use as food. When interpreting these roles, distinctions are made between sacred or divine religious activities in special precincts and the secular or profane activities that are part of daily, domestic life (e.g., O'Day 2004). As with most dichotomies, these distinctions fail to capture the full range of behaviors from the casual, normal, secular rituals of daily life to a very sacred ritual performed occasionally by a holy person following a precise format in a monumental context from which the public is excluded. This continuum includes the small magic that many of us perform each day without thought to the grand mysteries and occult knowledge of an inherited or ascribed priestly class. Both small rituals of daily life and grand ceremonies may be private or public, performed by everyone or by only a special few, or conducted any place or only in a special place.

Sacred behavior or rituals are not readily distinguished from domestic or secular behavior by the nonutilitarian objectives of the former. The ability to make offerings or sacrifices of a particular kind is both an act of faith and a symbol of wealth, power, and status. Wealthy members of modern communities are expected to support local religious institutions and charities handsomely and rarely do so without a ceremony promising them some form of everlasting recognition complimented by catered food service. Such donor ceremonies challenge other wealthy people to make a similar or larger gift. For institutions of higher education, among others, such rituals are absolutely essential and are very utilitarian. They are preceded, accompanied, and followed by very formal, proscribed behaviors that are performed with the same adherence to correct procedures as any contagious or imitative magic performance or meeting with a god might be. Practitioners of the art (development officers) are highly trained and greatly resent, or fear, the meddling of amateurs. Animals or food are present at most, if not every, stage.

All archaeological deposits formed by human agency involved ritual. However, much of the symbolic content of animals leaves no distinctive evidence. We need only think of academic receptions, conference banquets, coffee breaks, family reunions, office parties, and similar rituals of unification and solidarity. In these cases, animals and foods are sacred not so much because of their own intrinsic characteristics but because of the time, place, and participants in the event. In fact, some of the foods featured on such occasions are ones that are normally disdained but have the advantage of being available in large quantities for little cost. Through the lens of archaeology, the structure and function of these occasions is lost. Alterations in the social role of animals also may produce shifts in faunal composition that are very similar to those associated with changes in seasonal and temporal patterns, technology, exchange systems, and the environment (e.g., Milner 2002; Muir and Driver 2004). In some cases, the social or ritual use of animals will also alter what is discarded in the archaeological record or where it is discarded (McNiven and Feldman 2003).

Status and Ethnicity

Animals and their by-products distinguish between the social elite, commoners, and slaves, as well as signify ethnic affiliation in complex societies (e.g., Lev-Tov 2004; Reitz and Scarry 1985; Scott 2001, 2007). Status is a person's relative standing in a community and is based on such attributes as ability, kinship, residence, occupation, amount of income, and source of income (Warner and Lunt 1941). Social status is often equated with economic status, although it is possible to be wealthy but be held in low esteem, or to be a poor member of the elite. In multiethnic communities, ethnicity is also a component of status. To validate status, it is necessary to behave appropriately and to display the proper markers of the status, that is, eat the proper foods at the proper time in the proper way in the proper place. It is difficult to know which foods or animals are prestigious and which ones are not if you are unfamiliar with the symbolic lexicon (e.g., Bowen 1992). Often, foods that offer high amounts of energy and fat, or which are exotic, large, and costly in terms of time and effort, are more highly valued or preferred foods and delineate rank. Meat from young animals and foods associated with a dominant ethnic group for other reasons are also status markers. Variety is also a valuable attribute of food.

The relationship between social organization and food is a complex one. At a fundamental level, women and children often eat different foods than do men – even today. Foods distinguish clans, lineages, moieties, and ethnic and other social groups from each other (e.g., Groenman-van Waateringe 1994; IJzereef 1988; Marti-Grädel et al. 2004). In a stratified community, food may signal conformity to prevailing norms of food consumption, particularly by individuals who fear being too different or who want to validate a higher status in the community (e.g., Scott 2007). Food also may be used as a marker of social identity to distinguish a colonizing group from an indigenous one, by either or both sides (e.g., deFrance 2006). Changes in foodways, especially the appearance of exotic animals, are often associated with migrations, colonization, and acculturation (e.g., Hongo 1993; MacDonald et al. 1993; Mondini et al. 2004; Nyerges 2004; Wickler 2004). It is not necessarily the case that the foods associated with a conquering ethnic group will become the dominant foods in the new multiethnic colony (e.g., Reitz and Scarry 1985). In such communities, the foods used by one social group to define itself or affirm its cultural origin may be misinterpreted by neighboring social groups.

Animals symbolize these economic, political, and social relationships (e.g., Bartosiewicz 1995a; Cooke 1993, 2004; Stokes 2000a). The use or avoidance of specific animals or types of animals reflected in dietary laws defines social boundaries (e.g., Lernau et al. 1996). Such expressions reflect fundamental concepts about animals, their place in the world, and their relationships to us (e.g., Bowen 1992). Who manufactures, or uses, particular animals or animal parts and how they are displayed is a way to signal social status, conformity to social expectations, and affiliation with a specific social group (e.g., Janetski 2005; Serjeantson 2000). Changes in the ways animals and animal parts are displayed may be evidence of a change in norms regarding private and public displays and the overt accumulation of prestige or elite goods. Social distinctions also may be reflected in the tools (stone or metal) used to butcher animals (e.g., Greenfield 1999). Folk taxonomy and Linnaean taxonomy reflect concepts about the proper organization of the world and our place in it (Serjeantson 2000).

Some animals serve recreational or other purposes, such as hunting and hawking (e.g., Murphy et al. 2000). Many are simply pets, which nevertheless keep the modern pet food industry flourishing and provide emotional comfort to those of us who care for them. Our attachment to these animals should not blind us to the fact that the choice of which pet to keep, and how we care for it, is a significant modern social symbol.

Belief Systems and Rituals

The attributes of animals and the products they provide are closely linked with cognition and belief systems (e.g., Bartosiewicz 1995a:61–3; Eastham 1988; Gautier 2005; MacDonald 1995; Miracle and Milner 2002; Noddle 1994; Plug 1987a; Prummel 2001; Ryan and Crabtree 1995). Animals symbolize the relationship between humans and the spiritual, cultural, and natural world. Today, we find many examples of this association, such as the symbolism of young, virginal animals or white ones with purity (e.g., Flannery et al. 1989). Particularly common are symbols of fertility or a season, such as associations between migrating birds and spring (e.g., Eastham 1988). Rituals involving animals play out multiple layers of cosmological, social, and gender relationships (e.g., Morales and Morales 1995). Although difficult to isolate in faunal assemblages, such concepts are an important component of their formation.

Food and health are linked in many ways. Such concepts are reflected in classifications of foods as hot or cold, hard or soft, and dry or wet (e.g., Farb and Armelagos 1980:99; Lindenbaum 1987). These concepts are related to larger symbols of social life such as: male and female, pure and impure, sacred and profane, and the distinction between life and death. Routine food avoidances, as well as taboos imposed after a birth, before engaging in battle, and at important moments in the ritual calendar, are based on such concepts. Food and maternal care are virtually synonymous in many belief systems.

Some animals are so important in the community that ensuring their fertility, or success in their capture or management, is critical to the community and must be secured by the proper ritual. A group may avoid killing a specific species to encourage the animal's spirit to protect the rest of the community from harm and to flourish so that other members may enjoy its bounty. Such avoidance behavior may be ritually violated to reinforce the structural relationship of the community, to enhance the fertility of the animal in question, or for other reasons (e.g., Moreno-García 2004). The remains of some prey species may be displayed in a sacred place or in a sacred way to honor the animal's spirit (e.g., Tanner 1979:75, 92, 172).

In twenty-first century North America animal totems are associated with team sports, and ritual regalia displaying these animals are proudly worn. At the University of Georgia, the remains of deceased totemic animals (bulldogs) are ritually buried on the grounds of the sacred sports arena, and their tombs are honored, even photographed, by thousands of visitors each year. The honor paid the Georgia bulldogs is unfathomable in those societies that consider dogs unclean or vermin. Animal totems are not confined to this century, although evidence for an animal's symbolic meaning may not survive or may survive in a way that leaves its role unrecognized. Such associations directly influence the zooarchaeological record (Politis and Saunders 2002).

Many large and small rituals use animals to invoke blessing, healing, and protection for the community and its members while ensuring success in life or death. These are particularly likely to occur at rites of passage during which the use of the animal symbolizes the change in status and role being announced, conferred, and validated by the ritual. A particular species, age, sex, or color may be considered to be an appropriate sacrifice or commemorative offering. Animals, or portions of animals, also may be used in divination (e.g., MacDonald 1995; Moore 1969). The ability to offer a particularly expensive animal, or object representing the animal, reflects on the social standing and wealth of the individual or group making the sacrifice or offering (Bartosiewicz 1995a; Wapnish and Hesse 1991). Animals also may be used to invoke or dispel a curse. In some cases, animals destined for sacrifice may be fed special foods in preparation for the ritual (e.g., White 2004). Information about the age at death, season of death, and elements represented may provide information about the season of sacrifice, suggest why a particular offering was made, and demonstrate the combination of ritual and economic objectives (e.g., Legge et al. 2000).

Normal uses of animals and sacred ones often are distinguished by archaeological context (e.g., Minniti and Peyronel 2005; Styles and Purdue 1991; Wapnish and Hesse 1991). Burials characterize the most obviously sacred animal remains, although not in the case of a butcher's yard. When animal burials are recovered from ritual contexts, such as inside temples or with human burials, their ritual purpose is readily ascertained (e.g., Crabtree 1995; Gautier 2005; Guzmán and Polaco 2003; Sandweiss and Wing 1997). Although these sacred uses of animals may occur only in sacred places, many rituals involving animals occur in normal, secular areas as routines of daily life where the sacred use of animals is indistinct from the profane use. The differences between profane and

FIGURE 8.8. Crocodilian image from an "Alligator Ware" vessel, Chiriqui province, Panama, painted between A.D. 1100 and 1520 (Cooke 1993:189). Used with the kind permission of Richard Cooke.

ritual uses of animals may be reflected in the identity of the animal, its age or sex, season of death, butchering patterns, and evidence for cremation or burial (e.g., Noe-Nygaard and Richter 1990; Prummel 2001).

Animals form much of the iconography, oral traditions, and literature of many cultures, symbolizing spiritual and human communities and social relationships among them (Levy 1995). Often, these images are highly stylized, and it may be difficult to determine what specific animal, if any, is actually intended. In other cases, distinctive attributes facilitate an attribution but often in the context of anthropomorphic and other stylized features (Figure 8.8; Cooke 1993). The prominence of animals in texts, paintings, carvings, and myths may or may not be duplicated in faunal assemblages (e.g., Altuna 1983; Guzmán and Polaco 2003; Levy 1995). For example, cattle were highly valued as a sign of status in Anglo-Norman settlements in Ireland and the faunal record is dominated by beef rather than pork (McCormick 1991). However pork, rather than beef, is prominent in Irish literature of the time. Such examples illustrate that text-derived evidence for animal use is often different from that found in the faunal record. It should not be assumed that the documentary source is "correct" and the archaeological one "flawed" (e.g., Coy 1996; Murray et al. 2004). In many cases, these differences reflect efforts to avoid taxes, fines, or social penalties; contrasts between real and ideal human behavior; perceptual distinctions between the literate elite and the illiterate poor; or differences in the knowledge of men and women (e.g., Bowen 1988; Hoffmann 1994; Lauwerier 1993a).

Feasting and Fasting

Animals and food are ubiquitous ingredients of sacred behavior as well as highly symbolic ingredients of secular life. This is particularly obvious in the context of feasting and fasting (e.g., Albarella and Serjeantson 2002; Crabtree 2004; Knight 2001; McGuire and Hildebrandt 2005; Müldner and Richards 2005; Jochim 2006; van Gennep 1960; Warner and Lunt 1941; Welch and Scarry 1995). The meaning of animals and food extends well-beyond their nutritional and energetic merits.

The type of food and the way it is presented signals many aspects of both secular or profane functions (e.g., Douglas 1975; Goody 1982; Grantham 1995; Jameson 1987). Some foods are viewed as the basis of a meal, whereas others are merely snacks or beverages (Farb and Armelagos 1980:102–3). These categories often have little relationship to actual nutritional content. Sweet, caffeine drinks and alcoholic beverages, consumption of which is vital to many daily private and public rituals, have very high caloric value, but they are seldom classified as food by the people who use them. In some cases, it is not so much what the specific food is, but what is served with it, whether it is hot or cold, and when it is served that is important. The display and exchange of food and meals signifies the importance of social occasions. Reciprocal food exchanges mark all rites of passage and most other ritual occasions, including those in the ritual calendars of industrialized nations. Persistent failure to reciprocate a food gift with a similar one will, at the very least, result in social ostracism even in the most urbanized, complex societies.

Hayden (2001:26) defines a feast as "*any sharing between two or more people of special foods* (i.e., foods not generally served at daily meals) *in a meal for a special purpose or occasion*" (italics are Hayden's; see also Dietler and Hayden 2001). Such occasions might be a postharvest feast, a potlatch, a wedding feast, a liturgical meal, or a feast held to honor or install a leader. Looked at from another perspective, large groups of people might take advantage of a windfall, such as a whale beaching, to conduct outstanding social business (Piana 2005).

How would we distinguish between debris deposited as the result of feasting or other ritual and ceremonial behaviors and those produced by the smaller rituals of daily life? The usual contextual features that distinguish ritual from secular animal use, such as material culture, living surfaces, and depositional sequences, may not be sufficient (e.g., Emery 2004a). When one of the traditional sources of evidence for a ritual precinct is not obvious, the animal remains themselves may distinguish among these two broadly different forms of animal use. Table 8.1 lists some criteria that generally appear to distinguish deposits that are the result of ceremonial animal use from routine use. Although the criteria are not mutually exclusive, the combination of several of these could distinguish between routine and special contexts. If feasting or some other ritual behavior produced the animal remains, we should be able to distinguish these in the faunal record because they differ from secular animal remains using such predetermined criteria as a standard. Many of these criteria require that ritual contexts be compared to secular ones. Unfortunately, such a comparison is not possible if excavation strategies have failed to sample both ritual and secular contexts using appropriate screen size to capture both large and small offerings (Kansa and Campbell 2004; Weissbrod and Bar-Oz 2004; see Chapter 5).

Table 8.1. *Characteristics of ritual animal use, broadly defined*

The individual taxa deposited as a result of ritual behavior might:
exhibit anomalous or atypical behavior;
be unpredictable;
be large-bodied;
be available infrequently or for short periods of time;
be found in only a few locations;
be present in low numbers;
be highly mobile;
be from habitats otherwise seldom utilized;
be rare or exotic;
involve risk of personal injury or failure;
require considerable time to find, pursue, or capture;
require a high degree of skill to acquire;
be costly to acquire in terms of time, energy, or technology;
be satisfying in terms of fat, taste, tenderness, calories, or nutrients;
exhibit behaviors inspiring fear or respect, or embodying admirable attributes;
exhibit unusual features such as bright colors or soft fur; and
reinforce social norms, such as the divisions of labor, kinship, political structure, or group
   identity.

Deposits containing ritually-significant animals might:
exhibit an unusual distribution among animal classes;
contain high quantities of food residue that cannot be explained by preservation;
exhibit an unusual taxonomic ubiquity, richness, diversity, and/or equitability;
contain animals from a higher or lower mean trophic level;
contain an unusual quantity or type of butchering debris;
contain a large percentage of high-quality body parts, often measured as food utility;
be skeletally complete;
exhibit an age and sex distribution weighted in favor of a specific age class or sex;
show signs of roasting, ritual sacrifice, or other modifications; and
contain human remains.

Note: Compiled from Anderson and Boyle (1996), Ballbè (2005), Hayden (2001), Jackson and Scott (2003), Jochim (1976), Kansa and Campbell (2004), Kelly (2001), Kent (1989), Lentacker et al. (2004), McCormick (2002), Pauketat et al. (2002), Potter (2000), Purdue et al. (1989), Saunders et al. (2005), Scott and Jackson (1995), Styles and Purdue (1991), and Yerkes (2005).

CONCLUSIONS

Ecological and economic concepts, such as energy management, settlement patterns, demography, and technology, are often placed theoretically in opposition to explanations based on social complexity, belief systems, and cultural maintenance (Bettinger 1991; Tchernov 1992b; Zvelebil 1985). Although it is sometimes necessary for conceptual purposes (or for the purpose of organizing a book) to consider these aspects separately, it is important not to lose sight of the anthropological reality that these concepts are part of cultural systems that are whole cloth. Academic dichotomies such as mobile versus sedentary, forager versus collector, or fishing versus trapping had and have no reality in the actual behavior of the people we study, which is probably why it is so difficult to find definitive evidence for them in animal remains.

The acquisition of energy and other nutrients must be the primary concern of any population for the continued existence of themselves, their progeny, or their culture. If the archaeological record tells us nothing else, it is that humans have by and large addressed the mechanics of the problem. The other lesson the record teaches us is that people embellish their lives with a wealth of distinctions in which animals are important. Animals are both food and symbol. Although this volume emphasizes animals as food, we personally would find it difficult to live only on nutritional supplements. We surround ourselves with animals that communicate a great deal about the way we view the world and our place in it. We have no intention of eating any of them even though we know keeping them has financial (energetic) consequences, and someone else might find these pets meaningless, revolting, or tasty.

9

Control of Animals Through Domestication

INTRODUCTION

The association between humans and domestic animals is one of the closest relationships existing among species. This relationship is considered to be mutualistic because both members benefit. Domestic animals owe their distinctive physical and behavioral characteristics, care, and feeding to the humans who control them. People, in turn, modify their own behavior and technology to manage the breed and provide for the biological needs of their domesticates. If success is measured by the numbers of offspring produced and consequent population increase, clearly the mutualistic relationship between humans and their major domesticated animals is a success (Rindos 1984).

The change from a hunting way of life to one incorporating animal husbandry was a profound one. Davis (1987:126) states that animal domestication "ranks in importance alongside the discovery of fire and tools." Animal husbandry and plant cultivation are the foundations of modern civilization. The effect of domestication on animal and plant populations and on the environment has been, and continues to be, profound. It is not surprising that the origins of domestic animals, their wild progenitors, the region(s) where domestication took place, and the spread of animal husbandry, as well as cultural conditions that promoted these economic changes, are the focus of so much study (e.g., Davis 2005; Vigne et al. 2005).

Domestic animals have many characteristics by which we recognize them and that distinguish them from wild animals. The distinctive characteristics of domestic animals include conformation and variability, social behavior, and the contexts within which they occur. The most dramatic examples of variability are seen in dogs. A dog may be a fluffy little shih-tzu (the Chinese lion dog), a miniature poodle living a pampered life in a house or apartment, a large doberman guarding property, a maremma guarding livestock, or a hound seeking foxes, lost people, or illicit substances. These are all clearly dogs, but selective breeding for different roles in human society accounts for their varied appearances. Dogs, as well as most other domestic animals, have coat colors and textures quite different from wild animals. Many are white or are randomly spotted, neither of which is a good adaptation for eluding detection by predators, except in snow-covered land. Domestic animals are also distinctive for their well-developed social behavior. They tolerate close confinement in a setting dominated by people. Many of these characteristics are present in other domestic animals and distinguish them from their wild progenitors. People rely on these behavioral and physical characteristics to recognize and control domestic animals.

The domestication of the major domestic animals occurred far back in time, and no conscious memory of this process persists. Initially, domestic animals were indistinguishable from the wild forebears from which they evolved in response to human selection. Zooarchaeological research relies on fragmentary skeletal remains and archaeological context to detect changes in the skeletons and contexts that accompanied domestication and finally produced distinctive domestic breeds. This research cannot use most of the characteristics that we now use to recognize an animal as domestic or wild because most of these are not preserved in the archaeological record. Archaeological remains of animals are generally stripped of their distinctive fur or fleece, coat colors, and ear shapes. Only fragmentary remains of their skeletons and teeth persist and equally tenuous vestiges of the conditions of their lives remain. Therefore, morphological characteristics augmented by ancient DNA, lipids, stable isotopes, and indirect evidence provide important insights into the ancestry of domesticates (Copley et al. 2005; Craig et al. 2005; Vigne et al. 2005). It is on these slender threads that our knowledge of this development in human history hangs.

ARCHAEOGENETICS

Genetic studies examine the phylogenetic relationships among domestic animals to identify the wild progenitor(s), the number of domestication events, the geographic location where domestication occurred, and when. Phylogeography traces the geographic expansion of human populations accompanying their domesticates (e.g., Geigl and Pruvost 2004; Kozlov and Lisitsyn 2000; Renfrew 2000). The data from genetic studies, combined with more precise dating of archaeological contexts and animal specimens, provide a fuller picture of human manipulation of other species and the consequences for both (e.g., Troy et al. 2001; Vilà et al. 2001; Zeder, Bradley, Emshwiller, and Smith 2006; Zeder, Emshwiller, Smith, and Bradley 2006).

Documenting genetic changes wrought by domestication is based on an examination of haplotypes, that is, units of genetic material extracted from tissues of modern domestic animals on the assumption that they retain features of early domestic animals from the same geographic area (Bradley 2006; Sykes and Renfrew 2000). These haplotypes are extracted by sequencing primarily from mitochondrial DNA (mtDNA). The use of mtDNA has many advantages: (1) each cell has many copies of mitochondria making them easier to sample particularly from ancient DNA (aDNA) extracted from degraded cells; (2) mitochondrial DNA has a higher mutation rate than nuclear DNA (nDNA) and, therefore, exhibits changes that accumulated during the relatively short span of time during which people domesticated plants and animals; and (3) mitochondrial DNA reflects the maternal contribution to inheritance and, therefore, is not subject to recombination with paternal genetics expressed in the Y chromosome. Because mtDNA provides only one side of the inheritance story it may be augmented by haplotypes sequenced from the Y chromosome. For example, the sequencing and analysis of both mtDNA and Y chromosomes of African cattle demonstrate their hybrid nature with *Bos taurus* and *B. indicus* ancestry (Bradley 2000; Bradley et al. 1996). Although the Y chromosome is complementary to mtDNA, it is less polymorphic and provides less information about domestication events. Microsatellites are another form of genetic material; these are repetitions of short segments of the nDNA genome (Luikart et al. 2006). Microsatellites are contributed to the genome by both parents; their high variable makes them useful in comparing levels of diversity and relationships among populations.

Genetic studies of extant animals have clarified the sequence of events leading to domestication (Bradley 2000; Zeder, Bradley, Emshwiller, and Smith 2006). The results of these studies are presented graphically as phylogenetic trees that depict the degrees of similarity or differences between individuals or among groups of individuals. Groups of animals with similar haplotypes indicating relatedness form a clade and are on separate branches of the tree from the clades of more distantly related animals. When populations with dissimilar haplotypes (in separate clades) are found in more than one geographic location, this suggests different lineages produced by two or more domestication events. These events may represent the domestication of two different subspecies of a wild progenitor or the breeding (introgression) of an introduced domesticate with a wild ancestor.

Studies of mtDNA, Y chromosomes, and microsatellites provide information on genealogy. However, they generally do not point to those characteristics that were selected during the process of domestication. Nuclear DNA may reveal the emergence of particular genes that controlled the morphological changes seen in modern domestic animals (Bradley 2006). Studies of the living animals record endpoints of domestication and analysis of modern animal haplotypes do not reveal the genetic makeup of the early domesticates. Ancient DNA extracted from well-dated archaeological animal remains and haplotypes extracted from mtDNA provides details about the history of domestication otherwise lacking. Studies of aDNA could distinguish diversity in the earliest domesticates from the variation accumulated among modern animals (Bradley 2006). Genetic study of plants also indicate multiple domestication events and, in some cases, domestication of different subspecies (Zeder, Bradley, Emshwiller, and Smith 2006).

THE TAXONOMY OF DOMESTIC ANIMALS

Domestic animals owe their morphology and behavior to selective breeding controlled by people. Furthermore, they can interbreed with the wild descendants of their common ancestors and produce fertile offspring. Where domestic breeds and their wild relatives occur together, they are only kept from interbreeding by human control. In these respects, domesticates differ from wild animals living under conditions of natural selection. For these reasons, some taxonomists advocate treating the nomenclature of domestic animals differently from the traditional binomen (genus and species) governed by the International Code of Zoological Nomenclature (Gentry et al. 1996, 2004).

A number of systems propose to describe differences between domestic and wild animals (Corbet and Clutton-Brock 1984; Clutton-Brock 1999:220; Gautier 1993; Groves 1995). These proposals range from eliminating scientific names for domestic animals to adding a designation such as the prefix "f.d." (for forma domestica; e.g., *Bos primigenius* forma *taurus*) or quotation marks around the specific name (*Bos primigenius* "familiaris") to indicate a domesticated animal. In *Mammal Species of the World* (Wilson and Reeder 2005), wild and domestic taxa are synonymized usually, but not always, following the laws of priority. For example, the name for domestic dogs is placed as a synonym of the wild ancestor, the wolf (*Canis lupus*), even though *C. familiaris* has priority by its description on a preceding page of the *Systema Naturae* (Linnaeus 1758). Even though dogs and wolves do interbreed, they usually can be distinguished and have been called by separate names for a very long time. Zoological nomenclature has important and overriding value despite the inherent problems with using binomial nomenclature for domestic animals. Recognizing this, Gentry and her colleagues (Gentry et al. 2004) proposed retaining the Linnaean system of nomenclature for domestic animals. This proposal was approved by the International Commission on Zoological Nomenclature (Opinion 2027, March 2003). We follow this ruling and retain the names of certain wild species, such as *Capra aegagrus* and *Ovis orientalis*, in addition to the names for their domestic derivatives: goats (*Capra hircus*) and sheep (*Ovis aries*) respectively (Table 9.1).

NATURE OF DOMESTIC ANIMALS

Archaeogenetics, stable isotopes, and trace elements provide information about the steps leading to domestication, changes in other aspects of the diet that occurred as a consequence of animal domestication, herding practices, ritual use of animals, exchange patterns, and environmental change (Bocherens et al. 2000; Chilardi et al. 2005; Schulting and Richards 2002; Schulting et al. 2004; White 2004). The most familiar of our domestic

Table 9.1. *Major domestic animals, their presumed wild ancestors, region(s) of domestication, and approximate date of first domestication. The taxonomy follows Gentry et al. (1996, 2004).*

Domesticate	Presumed wild ancestor	Region of domestication	Approximate date B.P.
rabbit, *Oryctolagus cuniculus* (L., 1758)	wild rabbit, *Oryctolagus cuniculus* (L., 1758)	Europe	500
guinea pig, *Cavia porcellus* (L., 1758)	wild guinea pig, *Cavia aperea* Erxleben, 1777	Andes	7000
dog, dingo, New Guinea singing dog, etc., *Canis familiaris* L., 1758	gray wolf, *Canis lupus* L., 1758; multiple domestication events (Vilà et al. 1997)	Eurasia: east Asia	13000–15000
cat, *Felis catus* L., 1758	wild cat, *Felis silvestris* Schreber, 1777	Eurasia	8000
donkey, *Equus asinus* L., 1758	wild African ass, *Equus africanus* Heuglin and Fitzinger, 1866; two clades from Nubian and Somali subspecies (Beja-Pereira et al. 2004)	northeast Africa	2000
horse, *Equus caballus* L., 1758	wild horse, *Equus ferus* Boddaert, 1795; multiple domestication events	Kazakhstan	6000
pig, *Sus domesticus* Erxleben, 1777*	wild boar, *Sus scrofa* L., 1758 and southeast Asian subspecies *S. s. vittatus*; at least 6 domestication events (Larson et al. 2005)	Eurasia: east Asia, Europe; north Africa	9000
bactrian camel, *Camelus bactrianus* L., 1758	wild camel, *Camelus ferus* Przewalski, 1873	central Asia	4500
dromedary, *Camelus dromedarius* L., 1758	extinct wild camel, *Camelus* sp.	western Asia, southern Arabia, north Africa	6000
llama, *Lama glama* (L., 1758)	guanaco, *Lama guanicoe* (Müller, 1776)	Andes	6000
alpaca, *Vicugna pacos* (L., 1758)	vicuña, *Vicugna vicugna* (Molina, 1782)	Andes	6000
water buffalo, *Bubalus bubalis* (L., 1758); river and swamp breeds	wild water buffalo, *Bubalus arnee* (Kerr, 1792); at least two lineages	Asia: India and China	4500
cattle, *Bos taurus* L., 1758, zebu cattle, *Bos indicus* L., 1758, and hybrids	aurochs, *Bos primigenius* Bojanus, 1827, Indian aurochs, *Bos namadicus* Falconer, 1859	Europe, western Asia, north Africa	9000

(continued)

Table 9.1 *(continued)*

Domesticate	Presumed wild ancestor	Region of domestication	Approximate date B.P.
goat, *Capra hircus* L., 1758	bezoar goat, *Capra aegagrus* Erxlaben, 1777; multiple domestication events, at least three centers	Eurasia: Fertile Crescent, Asia, Europe, Mongolia	10000
sheep, *Ovis aries* L., 1758	Asiatic mouflon, *Ovis orientalis* Gmelin, 1774; multiple domestication events, at least three centers	Eurasia: Near East and India	9000
chicken, *Gallus gallus* (L., 1758)	red jungle fowl, *Gallus gallus* (L., 1758) (West and Zhou 1988)	southeast Asia	8000
turkey, *Meleagris gallopavo* (L., 1758)	wild turkey, *Meleagris gallopavo* (L., 1758)	Mexico	2000
domestic duck, *Anas platyrhynchos* L., 1758	mallard, *Anas platyrhynchos* L., 1758	southeast Asia	5000
domestic goose, *Anser anser* (L., 1758)	graylag goose, *Anser anser* (L., 1758)	Europe	5000
muscovy duck, *Cairina moschata* (L., 1758)	muscovy, *Cairina moschata* (L., 1758)	northern South America	700
pigeon, *Columba livia* Gmelin, 1789	rock dove, *Columba livia* Gmelin, 1789	southwestern Asia	3500
goldfish, *Carassius auratus* (L., 1758)	wild goldfish, *Carassius auratus* (L., 1758)	eastern Asia	1000
honey bee, *Apis mellifera* L., 1758	wild honey bee, *Apis mellifera* L., 1758	Europe	1500
domestic silk moth, *Bombyx mori* (L., 1758)	Chinese wild silk moth, *Bombyx mandarina* (Moore, 1872)	China	3000

Note: The abbreviation B.P. indicates an approximate date before the present. This indicates the times when the domestication of different animals can be demonstrated morphologically. The abbreviation L. stands for Linnaeus. This table is modified from Clutton-Brock (1999:221–3) and Davis (1987:127).

*A tradition in American zooarchaeology is to identify both the pigs introduced during European colonization of the Americas as well as the pigs that went feral after introduction as *Sus scrofa*. Following Gentry et al. (2004), the name of the domesticate should be *Sus domesticus*, however, this name has not been used in the Americas. Instead domestic pigs, feral pigs, and wild hogs introduced specifically for hunting are all called *Sus scrofa* in the Americas. This tradition is maintained here because of the importance of understanding that all members of the genus *Sus* are introduced to the Americas, the vast majority in the domestic state. Use of the term *Sus domesticus* at this point would make earlier identifications unclear.

animals arose from multiple domestication events. Some of these domestication events may have been independent, such as cattle and pigs, or an early primary event followed by one or more secondary events, such as probably occurred in goats with a primary center and at least four other more restricted lineages in Asia (Albarella et al. 2006; Bradley 2000; Bradley 2006; Bradley and Magee 2006; Zeder 2006a).

Much of this research focuses on the vast Eurasian land mass that spreads east and west of the Fertile Crescent. This region of temperate latitudes shares similar environmental conditions of day length, temperature, and rainfall. Diamond (1994a) postulates that the spread of crops and domestic animals along this broad latitudinal belt was unimpeded by biological constraints. One important center of domestication in this region, though not the only one, was the Fertile Crescent, a broad arc bounded on the west by the Mediterranean coast and to the north and east by eastern Turkey and the Zagros Mountains (Figure 1.1). The key suite of plants and animals first domesticated in this region are barley (*Hordeum vulgare*), wheat, pigs, cattle, goats, and sheep (Table 9.1). The Fertile Crescent suite of domestic plants and animals extends from Ireland to the Indus Valley and enriched agricultural development to the east in China and Japan (Diamond 1994a). Because of their importance, these animals are intensively studied, producing widely varying views on the driving forces behind domestication (Armitage 1986; Bellwood 2005; Benecke 1994; Clutton-Brock 1999; Davis 1987; Hemmer 1990; Herre and Röhrs 1973; Mason 1984; Zeuner 1963).

Although the precise timing of domestication cannot be determined, this process peaked for many of the more important domestic animals between 6,000 and 9,000 years ago (Table 9.1). This is a relatively short time span in the grand scheme of human history. The domestication of animals goes hand-in-hand with or slightly follows the domestication of plants. This was clearly a time when people began to exert control over many resources, and the control of one may have stimulated the management of others.

Domesticates of the Americas, such as llamas, alpacas, guinea pigs, muscovy ducks (*Cairina moschata*), and turkeys (see Table 9.1), are generally not widespread, and the origins of their domestication are less well-known. Therefore, examples from the Americas are used in the following discussion to illustrate the process of domestication in addition to evidence from better-known centers of animal domestication such as southwestern Asia. Parallels are drawn between animal domestication in Eurasia and Africa with other parts of the world.

Domestic animals can be grouped according to the ways that they are used. Dogs are distinctive both for their early domestication date and for the many roles they play in human society. Other domesticates are either herd animals maintained on pastures or animals kept close to the house or barnyard. These differ in the ways they are managed, butchered, and their meat is distributed.

Dogs

The most outstanding exception to all other domesticates is the dog, which is also the earliest domestic animal. Based on morphological and contextual characteristics, domestic dogs are first distinguished from their wild ancestors, wolves, about 12,000 years ago (Clutton-Brock 1995). MtDNA evidence supports the conclusion that dogs descended from gray wolves (*C. lupus*) alone and that dogs and wolves continued to exchange genes through backcrossing events (Vilà et al. 1997; Savolainen et al. 2002; Wayne et al. 2006). Based on rates of mutations, these studies suggest that the initial domestication began long before morphological changes are recognized in archaeological materials. Perhaps "the change around 13,000 to 15,000 years ago from nomadic hunter-gatherer societies to more sedentary agricultural population centers may have imposed new selective regimes on dogs that resulted in marked phenotypic divergence from wild wolves" (Vilà et al. 1997:1,689). Several lineages of dogs accompanied people across the Bering Straits during the Late Pleistocene (Leonard et al. 2002). No evidence exists that these dogs interbreed with wolves in the Western Hemisphere. European colonizers brought their own dogs with them to the Americas in recent centuries, apparently discouraging breeding with native dogs based on the absence of a clade unique to pre-Columbian dogs among modern dogs in the Americas (Leonard et al. 2002).

The great alliance between people and dogs may have arisen from rearing wolf pups (Clutton-Brock 1984). The wolf, as a social animal, may have been grafted into the social structure of the people with whom it was associated. Dogs eat whatever humans eat, either first-hand or second-hand as camp scavengers. Dogs were raised for food in some areas such as southwest Asia and prehispanic Mexico (Wing 1978). Dogs became indispensable to human existence and accompanied humans throughout the world. In addition to companionship, the early dogs may have provided assistance in hunting and protection for the home site. As a life with herd animals developed, dogs assumed expanded roles as protectors and herders of other domestic animals.

Dog burials are often associated with human burials. In the Caribbean, dogs are found only in burial sites and were not viewed as food (Newsom and Wing 2004:210). An early archaeological find demonstrating this close relationship is the burial of a wolf pup or early dog pup lying under the left hand of a human in a tomb from Ein Mallaha, in northern Israel, dating to 11600 B.P. (Davis and Valla 1978). Burial of an animal connotes the special role the animal plays in the social life of the people and suggests a belief in an afterlife (Morey 2006). Occasionally, other animals assumed some of these roles. Raccoons are associated with human burials in Mexico. The remains of a South American fox associated with human burials dating from 7500–5500 B.C. in coastal Ecuador gives time depth to the management of if not the domestication of a canid other than dogs (Wing 1988).

Other Domestic Animals

Other domestic animals are either herd animals or house or barnyard animals. Each of these groups has certain characteristics in common. Herd animals include donkeys, horses, camels (*Camelus* spp.), llamas, alpacas, reindeer, cattle, water buffaloes (*Bubalus bubalis*), goats, and sheep. House or barnyard animals include cats, guinea pigs, rabbits (*Oryctolagus cuniculus*), pigs, chickens, turkeys, mallards (*Anas platyrhynchos*), and pigeons (*Columba livia*). All of these animals were occasionally used for food or their meat was their primary value. None of these animals was kept only for meat; they provided other products or services. It is these products and services, as well as the care that each group requires, that set herd animals and house animals apart.

Herd Animals:

Herd animals convert grasses and shrubs, inedible to humans, into animal biomass. In many cases, this requires a transhumant migration with livestock herded from low-elevation, winter pastures to summer pastures at higher elevations or to pastures in different areas at the same elevation. This movement is necessary to avoid overgrazing one area and to keep the herd or flock close enough together to allow protection of the animals and prevent straying. To accomplish this, one or more people, often accompanied by one or more dogs, must stay with the flock or herd.

Herd animals provided numerous products and services once their domestication was well-established (e.g., Mulville and Outram 2005). In addition to providing meat, most, although not all, Eurasian herd animals are milked. Some herders in Africa use milk and blood in preference to meat. Bone, hides, and horn are widely used for tools and ornaments. Elements, such as metapodia and astragali, were used in some medieval European cities as building materials (Armitage 1989a, 1989b). In the past, camelid scapulas were used for weaving tools, and bovid horn sheaths were used as containers such as powder horns. Another product is wool, obtained by selective breeding among both New and Old World camelids, angora goats, and sheep. A whole industry of spinning and weaving arose around the production of wool. This provides a renewable supply of material for warm clothing, replacing hides and furs so necessary for life in the cold grasslands where many herd animals were kept. Dung is widely used for plaster and fertilizer, but is particularly important as fuel where wood is scarce.

Services provided by herd animals take advantage of their strength, such as traction and bearing burdens. Donkeys, horses, camels, and llamas are, of course, consummate burden bearers and, with the exception of llamas, they will carry a human rider. Donkeys, horses, cattle (particularly oxen), and water buffaloes are widely used for traction. This has had a far-reaching and important impact on trade and commerce; the spread of customs, language, and disease; agricultural tasks including clearing land, tilling soil, grinding grain, and irrigation. These animals are incorporated into every facet of human life and their importance cannot be overemphasized.

The most widespread herd animals are horses, cattle, goats, and sheep. Their ecological flexibility and the wide range of services and products they supply accounts for their long history of dominance among domestic stock. This livestock suite has spread throughout most of the temperate world. They also have a history of use in the tropics, although in the most extreme environments they are replaced by specialized herd animals.

Specialized herd animals fill many of the same roles in extreme environments such as deserts, tundra, and marshes. Elephants (*Elephas maximus*) are used in the humid tropics of India and Burma for traction, but they are not considered domesticated because they rarely reproduce in captivity. Dromedaries (*Camelus dromedarius*) are used for traction, burden bearing, fiber, and milk in the tropical deserts of north Africa. Reindeer are used for traction and meat by the Lapps in the northern tundra of Scandinavia. Yaks (*Bos grunniens*) provide transport, milk, and fiber to people living at high elevations in the Himalayas. Ecologically, such high elevations are equivalent to the tundra zones. Perhaps the most adaptable and widespread of these specialized herd animals is the water buffalo, which is used throughout tropical Asia and America for traction, meat, and milk. Although we consider these to be specialized herd animals, their importance in the places where they occur should not be underestimated.

House or Barnyard Animals:

House or barnyard animals differ in many ways from herd animals. These animals are smaller and consume many of the same foods eaten by humans. Although they may be obliged to scavenge on their own, most are also fed to keep them tame and near the house. All provide meat. In addition, fowl produce eggs. For example, chicken eggs are widely eaten, although they are taboo in southeast Asia and sub-Saharan Africa). Pig bristles and poultry feathers are important, but specialized, commodities.

Early animal husbandry in China centered around dogs, pigs, and chickens (Chow 1984; West and Zhou 1988). Dogs and pigs were domesticated independently in eastern and western Asia (Clutton-Brock 1999:58, 92–3; Olsen 1985:12). This same group of three domesticates accompanied early colonists to the Pacific Islands. In some areas, according to historic accounts, dogs were more highly esteemed for food than pigs although archaeological finds of pig are more frequent (Titcomb 1969). Both dogs and pigs were cherished and occasionally breastfed by women who apparently saw no inconsistency in later eating these animals. Dogs were buried with humans, and both dog and pig teeth were used for ornaments (Titcomb 1969). Ethnographic studies describe the important ritual that grew up around the keeping and eating of pigs in New Guinea (Rappaport 1967).

Several barnyard animals are believed to be sacred animals in many places and are used for sacrifice and divination, most notably guinea pigs, cats, and chickens. Guinea pigs are widely used for ritual and healing in the Andean region (deFrance 2006; Morales 1995). Such practices are ancient. Cats were considered sacred animals in ancient Egypt. They were revered in life and mummified in death during the first millennium B.C. Many were excavated from tombs during the early years of this century, but, regrettably, most were used for fertilizer (Clutton-Brock 1999:138). Had these large samples been saved for study, they would provide information about the demography, disease, conformation, and genetic variability of the population. Study of the coat pattern and conformation of cats today provides insights into the sources of these populations (Lloyd 1986).

PROCESS OF ANIMAL DOMESTICATION AND METHODS OF STUDY

We see in our domestic animals the end-product of a long process of domestication. Animals such as camels, cats, and chickens fill roles in human society as different as burden bearer and mouse catcher, as well as egg layer and greeter of the morning (with its inherent symbolism). Consequently, each animal presented unique challenges for domestication. Understanding this process relies on the study of the remains of animals undergoing changes from wild to domestic, augmented by what we know about animal biology and human uses of animals. The presumed steps in this process of domestication are outlined in the remainder of this chapter. This is accompanied by a description of the methods used to study this process. In outlining the process of domestication every case cannot be discussed, only some of the most salient points presented.

The study of animal domestication is a major focus of much zooarchaeological research. Much of this research uses osteological evidence for domestication and the context of the animal remains augmented by genetic studies. This may never identify an animal in the initial stages of domestication, when control of its breeding begins, but it can document changes in size, proportion, morphology, and demography that accompany human control of a segment of an animal population during the shift from hunting to animal husbandry. Cases made for the development and spread of domestication must be based on large samples and multiple lines of evidence all pointing to the same conclusions. When conclusions do not agree, as they do not for the dates for the initiation of domestication of the earliest osteological remains of the domestic animal in question, the sources of the different results need to be examined.

The vast majority of human existence, more than 99 percent of the history of our species, was fueled by hunting, fishing, and gathering ways of life (Davis 1987:126). During this long period, people made observations and accumulated knowledge about the ecology and behavior of the animals around them that were critical for survival. Such observations of the social behavior of animals, including the timing of mating and the birth of young, choices of foods, and periods of activity were important to hunters but were also essential to the first people who tamed and subsequently domesticated these animals.

Capture and Control of Animals

One hunting and fishing strategy is to lure an animal into close range by use of bait so it can be captured. Such a bait may be food secured inside a trap or grain scattered on the ground. An unintentional bait is produce in an agricultural plot. Hunting animals attracted to agricultural plots is described as garden hunting; agricultural products are protected by hunting herbivorous competitors, such as collared peccaries (*Pecari tajacu*), deer (*Odocoileus virginianus*), agoutis (*Dasyprocta punctata*), and pacas (*Agouti paca*), attracted to the garden (Linares 1976). Linares maintains that because garden hunting provides both the plant and animal portions of a balanced diet, there is little need for domesticated animals.

Neusius (2007) uses faunal data from a series of sites of Anasazi horticulturists in southwestern Colorado to establish objective criteria to recognize a garden hunting strategy. Crucial among these is the behavior of the species represented in the site. Only animals attracted to the produce of the garden plot would be subject to garden hunting. Animals attracted to gardens might include a diverse array of species or only a few; thus diversity by itself is not a good measure of this hunting strategy. However, if the majority of species represented in the site frequent gardens and fields, garden hunting can be inferred.

Animals that venture near human habitation to eat refuse from meals, to rob crops, or to raid food stores expose themselves to people and the domesticated environment (Hemmer 1990; Zeuner 1963). In addition to being caught, the outcome of this exposure can be a commensal association. Commensal relationships are usually associations of species that live together to the serious detriment of neither. The house mouse (*Mus musculus*), Norway rats, and black rats are commensal animals. They prefer to share human shelter and stored food and have accompanied people around the world. The role of these rodents in a commensal relationship may not be benign as they consume lots of stored food and carry diseases, such as the plague, which are dangerous to human health. The guinea pig was domesticated following what is believed to be a commensal association with people (Gade 1967). As commensal animals, guinea pigs were probably attracted to food refuse and sought out the relative warmth of human shelters. Following this period of commensal association, closer management and control of breeding resulted in a fully domestic animal during the early cultural history in the Andes. In the past few hundred years, mice and rats have also been domesticated. All three are important laboratory animals; the name "guinea pig" is synonymous with experimental testing.

One of the disadvantages of living without a domestic food source is the need to cope with periods of scarcity and depletion of prey resources within the catchment area of the site. One solution is storage of foods by drying or preserving. Another is keeping wild animals corralled close to the home site until they are needed. Evidence for maintaining animals alive in captivity until they were needed for food is found in both archaeological and ethnographic examples. During early seafaring days, tortoises were taken from islands such as the Seychelles and kept on shipboard as a supply of fresh meat. They were taken at such a rate that the island tortoise populations became seriously endangered or exterminated. In his accounts of aboriginal fishing in the Greater Antilles, the early chronicler Bartolomé de las Casas describes corrals in which 500 to 1,000 sea turtles were confined at a time, readily accessible to shore (Sauer 1966:183).

Taming

Control of the movement of a captured animal is a step toward the control of other aspects of the animal's life. This degree of control is best achieved when the captive animal is caught as a young individual and imprints on its human captor. An appealing scenario proposed by Reed (1977) depicts the live young of animals orphaned by a hunt brought back to the home base where they were adopted and nurtured, particularly by little girls. This is based on the observation that children's play is preparatory to their roles as adults. Caring for small and helpless animals conforms to a young girl's future role as caregiver. Rearing such pets and the adjustments of these animals to human controls may have, at least sometimes, led to domestication (Serpell 1989).

Keeping tame animals has been widely practiced among people of many different cultures, not only today but in the past. One way we document the history of keeping tame animals is by studying representations such as murals. One must be cautious in interpreting such illustrations, even though some are so clearly represented they leave little doubt about the details of the picture. One such illustration is a scene from an Egyptian tomb (c. 2500 B.C.) in which gazelle, addax, ibex, and oryx (all Bovidae) are clearly shown with collars and leads, and some are eating out of troughs. Another part of the same illustration shows hyenas (Hyaenidae) tied and forcibly fed (Zeuner 1963:434). Cheetahs (*Acinonyx jubatus*) were caught and kept in great numbers by the royalty of Egypt and India where they were used in hunting. They do not breed successfully in captivity and the stock had to be replenished with animals caught in the wild.

Detecting tame animals from their remains in archaeological contexts must be based on the distribution of the animal and the nature of the archaeological find. A tame animal would not be morphologically different from other members of its species because the control of its breeding would still be subject to natural selection. A tame animal might, however, be removed to a place outside its natural range. Most reports of faunal samples interpret finds of species outside their present known ranges as change in the former range of the species rather than transport of captive animals. Both possibilities should be considered. To recognize human transport of an animal, the previous range of the species, which may have been quite different from its present known range, must be accurately determined. Most easily recognized is the transport of tame captive animals to islands whose borders are clearly defined. The absence of a species from the paleontological record and its sudden appearance in archaeological contexts may point to human introduction of an animal or an animal part.

A distinction must be made between trade in animal parts, such as sea shells to inland locations, and the transport of live captive animals. A good example interpreted as each of these comes from an archaeological site on Bonaire, Netherlands Antilles (Newsom and Wing 2004:72). One specimen is the major part of a skeleton of a young capuchin monkey (*Cebus* sp.) and the other is a worked ulna of an ocelot (*Leopardus pardalis*). Neither of these species is known from Bonaire but they do occur on the adjacent Venezuelan mainland. The partial monkey skeleton represents a young animal, which probably did not survive the rigors of captivity. The single ocelot specimen was modified by a human hand and was probably brought or exchanged in trade to the island from the mainland. In contemporary times, many wild animals illicitly captured for the pet trade die compared to the few that adjust to captivity. These odds may not have changed much through time.

Many examples of the introduction of animals to islands by humans are known. Presumably, these were captive and tame. The earliest documented translocation took place between 10,000 and 19,000 years ago. This is the introduction of the cuscus (*Phalanger orientalis*) to New Ireland in Melanesia (Flannery and White 1991). The source of this animal was probably the island of New Britain. A number of other introductions followed this one. Another marsupial, the dusky pademelon (*Thylogale brunii*), was probably introduced to New Ireland about 7000 B.P. and also originated in New Britain (Flannery and White 1991). The introduction of domestic dog and pig accompanied by the presumably unintentional introduction of two species of rats (*Rattus exulans* and *R. praetor*) to New Ireland occurred between 3000 and 2000 B.P. (Flannery and White 1991). A third of the species encountered in archaeological contexts from New Ireland are species introduced by people at least two millennia ago.

A great variety of animals were introduced in other parts of the world. Captive foxes (*Urocyon littoralis*) were introduced to the California Channel Islands by colonists (Collins 1991). The prehispanic inhabitants of the West Indian archipelago also transported a number of plants and animals in their colonizing effort. Some of those brought from the South American mainland and carried up through the Lesser Antillean island chain were opossum (*Didelphis marsupialis*) and agouti (*Dasyprocta leporina*) (Newsom and Wing 2004:107–8; Wing 1989). The direction of introductions was not one way; the Greater Antilles rivaled the South American mainland as a source of animals kept in captivity and transported to smaller islands with fewer native land animals. The extinct hutia (*Isolobodon portoricensis*), formerly endemic to Hispaniola, was introduced to Puerto Rico and the Virgin Islands. It was intensively used, particularly at inland sites on Puerto Rico. The animals in some of these populations differ in size, which is believed to be the result of human selection (Reynolds et al. 1953).

Could this practice of managing animals in captivity and moving them around be confined to islands? This does not seem likely, simply on the grounds that in order to transport a mainland animal it would first have to be caught and maintained in captivity. A convincing case is made for a well-organized trade in macaws between Mexico and the American Southwest (Hargrave 1970; Minnis et al. 1993). Feathers of the scarlet macaw (*Ara macao*) originated in tropical Mexico and were traded throughout the North American Southwest during prehispanic times. The site of Casas Grandes in Chihuahua has extensive macaw breeding facilities with nesting boxes and pens and is believed to be the center of this trade. A similar trade continues today.

The "Walking Larder"

Even more control over breeding, selection, and management is achieved by the domestication of animals referred to as the walking larder (Clutton-Brock 1989). Relatively few captive animals were fully domesticated. Only seven domestic animals are of major worldwide importance. They are dog, donkey, horse, pig, cattle, goat, and sheep (Table 9.1). Nine domestic animals are important regionally but are not of worldwide significance. These are Bactrian or two-humped camel (*Camelus bactrianus*), dromedary or one-humped camel (*Camelus dromedarius*), llama, alpaca, reindeer, gaur (*Bos gaurus*), yak (*Bos grunniens*), banteng (*Bos javanicus*), and water buffalo. Eleven small domestic animals are kept for various purposes and many are also of worldwide importance. Included in this group are the rabbit, guinea pig, cat, chicken, turkey, mallard, goose, pigeon, goldfish (*Carassius auratus*), honey bee (*Apis mellifera*), and silk moth (*Bombyx mori*). Some of these animals were domesticated repeatedly from wild progenitors. This list does not include animals domesticated within the last few hundred years, such as mice and rats for laboratory experimentation or fancy birds and fishes for the pet trade. Even when these are added to the list, the number of domestic animals is small.

An animal must possess a suite of physiological and behavioral features to be successfully domesticated (Diamond 1994b). First, they must be at the bottom of the food pyramid and efficiently convert plant food to meat. Dogs might be thought of as an exception to this requirement because they are in the order Carnivora. However, they are omnivores in their eating habits. They consume a lot of human waste in the form of refuse and feces and, by doing so, keep the home site clean. They generally do not compete with people for food (to do so would jeopardize their existence). Second, the growth rate must be quick, plant food must be converted efficiently, and sexual maturity reached early. Third, breeding must be achieved without complex courtship ritual. Fourth, the animal must not be programmed for instantaneous flight. Fifth, they must have a well-organized social structure with overlapping home ranges and a dominance hierarchy in which people assume the dominant role. Some animals become aggressive and hard to manage as they mature, and such animals are not good candidates for domestication. All of these characteristics are necessary in an animal for its successful domestication (Diamond 1994b).

Control of Breeding

The necessary conditions for domestication include not only management in captivity but also control over breeding in the captive stock. This controlled breeding was not initially based on a sophisticated understanding of genetics or necessarily oriented toward a particular phenotypic outcome. Instead, selection was both intentional for a desired trait and unintentional as a result of the conditions of confinement in the human environment. Only animals that could tolerate close contact with other members of their species and with people and were flexible enough to adjust to the quantity and quality of food that was provided would survive to reproduce progeny with some of their characteristics. (Full domestication of horses may have been protracted because domestic mares continued to breed with wild stallions [Olsen 2006].) Intentional selection for particularly desirable traits may have focused on characteristics of behavior as well as the physical appearance and many of these traits are linked. Selection for endearing and playful behavior is accompanied by physical traits usually associated with young animals (Gould 1986). Thus, early selection was subject to constraints of the human environment and choices of behavioral and physical traits that were important for cultural conditions of the time.

What we know about selection during the early stages of animal domestication is based on the skeletal morphology, size, and biological characteristics of domestic animals and their wild ancestors. When small groups of animals, for example, a few captives, are isolated from the larger population and breed only among themselves they are subject to the "founder" effect (Mayr 1942). Each individual has a limited range of the genetic variability of the parent population as a whole and, therefore, can only transmit some of this limited variation to its progeny. Thus, by controlled breeding of a small core of individuals, their inherited characteristics can, by chance, depart in a trajectory from wild populations with large gene pools whose breeding is subject to the constraints of mating under natural selection. Some changes in size and morphology of individuals in a captive breeding population may unwittingly be the result of such genetic drift.

Confinement and life in an environment modified by human activity increases some pressures on an animal while diminishing others. An animal finding itself confined experiences greater intraspecific conflict but diminished interspecific competition and predation. For example, smaller horns of sheep, goats, and cattle may have resulted from a release from male combat during breeding. Such an animal is dependent on humans for the amount and composition of food provided and experiences a limited choice of mates. These changed circumstances have an impact on a captive breeding population.

A reduction in over all size is widespread during early domestication of the larger animals such as pigs, cattle, goats, and sheep. Change in proportions also occurs with domestication such as shorter snouts in pigs and dogs. An explanation for this decrease in size is that when animals were first confined in limited enclosures, they did not receive high-quality foods in adequate quantities. Smaller size confers an advantage to animals when food is limited. The size reduction associated with early domestication followed or coincided with a size reduction that occurred in many species as a result of environmental changes at the end of the Pleistocene (Davis 1987:118).

Smaller domesticates, such as guinea pigs and chickens, do not show an initial decrease in size in the early stages of domestication. In fact, they tend to increase in size. It is likely that supplying adequate food to these small animals was not difficult. Protection from predators may have been sufficient to allow them to realize their full genetic potential for size and provided no adaptive advantage to small size.

Adaptations to confinement dominated by humans may have some similarities with adaptation to the constraints posed by life on small islands. Large mainland animals are often represented by smaller species on islands and, conversely, many small mainland species are represented by larger island relatives (Foster 1964; Heaney 1978). Limited food is believed to be the most important factor affecting body size changes in island populations. Other factors, such as diminished predation pressure and interspecific competition, also come into play in the relationship between island area and body size of mammals (Heaney 1978; Tchernov and Horwitz 1991).

Size decline over a period of time as an indicator of domestication is reported for all of the major Eurasian domesticates. Measurements of teeth and skeletal elements in series of occupations extending over the period from one representing a hunting economy to one representing a herding economy can show this decrease in size. This may be confounded by demographic changes accompanying herd management where females were maintained throughout their reproductive life and males were slaughtered as young individuals. Such changes are shown in size reduction of goats between 8,000 and 9,000 years ago in sites in the Fertile Crescent, in cattle between 7,000 and 8,000 years ago in sites in the western half of the Fertile Crescent, and, in pigs, early domestic forms occurred at about 8,500 years ago in the northern portion of the central Fertile Crescent and extending to the Mediterranean Sea (Smith 1995:53–67). As more material is studied, these dates will be revised. As with all such studies, finding adequate sample sizes of measurable specimens from comparable contexts is difficult. Data on size changes in animal remains and their correlation with early stages of domestication are documented from sites in the Fertile Crescent and from its eastern margin in what is now Afghanistan,

Pakistan, and Iran (Clutton-Brock 1999; Crabtree et al. 1989; Davis 1987:135–40; Meadow 1984; Smith 1995:53–67).

Several measurements of different dimensions must be taken to detect any change in size between the animal remains from two separate strata. Although a particular species is abundantly represented, it may not always be possible to take sufficiently large numbers of measurements of any one dimension. Ideally, sample sizes should be large enough to establish the mean, range, and standard deviation for each skeletal or tooth dimension of the populations from successive deposits. Included in such measurement from a site would be females and males, and possibly also castrated individuals, all of which can have different but overlapping size ranges (Figure 7.10). The significance of such comparisons is diminished by samples that are too small.

In addition to changes in the size of most domesticates, changes in proportions are common (Figure 9.1). These proportional changes involve the shape of the head and reduction in the size of the brain. Relatively short snouts and high foreheads of domestic pigs contrast markedly with the long snouts and straight profiles of wild boars (Figure 9.1 a). Some breeds of cattle, such as the Niatu of Argentina, have a similarly shortened snout (Figure 9.1 b). Even more familiar are the many toy breeds of dogs with short broad muzzles, big eyes, high foreheads, and rounded heads (Figure 9.1 c). These skull proportions are characteristic of juvenile individuals. Many also have fluffy fur similar to the coats of puppies rather than a coat of a mature animal with stiff guard hairs and woolly undercoat. Yet, these juvenile characteristics are found expressed in skeletal remains of individuals that are adults based on their fully erupted dentition and fused elements. This condition, the retention of juvenile characteristics in a sexually mature individual, is known as neoteny.

Our domestic animals have undergone millennia of both conscious and unconscious selection, but the juvenile traits are manifest among the earliest characteristics of domestication and reveal the practical choices made (Gould 1986). Selection for individuals that were most submissive in a relationship in which the humans dominated would be important. Clearly, within animal social structure, juvenile individuals are the least dominant. Selection of the most submissive individuals would be accompanied by fewer or less-developed physical characteristics by which they could communicate dominance. Dominance in wolves is signaled by adult head proportions, ears that stand up, a ruff of hair around the shoulders that can be raised, and a straight tail that can also be raised. Many breeds of dogs have long ears and curly tails that cannot be raised, and lack massive or even distinguishable manes. These characteristics may be physical vestiges of early selection for submissive animals that were physically unable to signal dominance and, thus, could be controlled and dominated by humans.

Studies of proportion are based on measurements. Measurements of two dimensions, such as length and width, are needed to distinguish between an element that is robust or gracile or a snout that is narrow or broad. Whole skulls are rarely found in archaeological

FIGURE 9.1. Shortened snout and high forehead traits found in many domestic animals: (a) skull of a pig of the Middle White breed, length *c.* 37 cm; (b) skull of an ox of the Niatu breed, length *c.* 36 cm; and (c) skull of a pekingese, length *c.* 8 cm. Reproduced from Clutton-Brock (1999:figures 2.5, and 2.10). Used with the kind permission of the Natural History Museum and Juliet Clutton-Brock.

context, except in burials. However, domestic animals, particularly dogs, are more likely to be buried and have complete or relatively complete skulls and associated postcranial elements. Even when complete skulls are not preserved, an indication of the shortened face can be seen in crowded teeth. Shortened mandible and maxilla do not necessarily occur in conjunction with a decrease in the size of the teeth they must accommodate. More typically, teeth become crowded and overlap each other in the shortened muzzle. One of the characteristics of early domestic dogs is crowded teeth, particularly premolars, and a reduction in the sizes of the canine and the carnassial (Hillson 2005:270).

Morphological characteristics are often, but not always, related to size and proportion. A morphological characteristic seen in many domestic animals that have horns is a change in the cross-sectional shape of the horns. This change affects the way the horn twists. Early domestic goats from Jericho had straight scimitar-shaped horn cores. By the Early Bronze Age goats with horn cores that twisted and had concave medial surfaces predominated (Clutton-Brock 1999:79). Large horns are energetically costly and less adaptive when an animal is released from male combat during breeding (Zeder 2006a). Ultimately, some breeds of livestock are hornless, the polled condition. The earliest evidence for polled sheep is from the 7500–6750 B.C. phase at the site of Ali Kosh in southwestern Iran (Armitage 1986). Depictions of polled cattle first appear on Egyptian tombs dating about 3500 B.C. Polled sheep are easier to handle and are favored by farmers to this day. Cattle, likewise, occur in the polled condition. At the other end of the spectrum some cattle have enormous horns, such as the long-horned breeds of Europe and some of the African breeds such as the Kuri from around Lake Chad (Epstein 1971; Rouse 1973).

Coat color is rarely documented in archaeological remains, even though it has broad implications for the process of domestication. The expression of a particular coat color can be achieved by overt selection of those animals that progressively exhibit the desired phenotype. Although the genetic basis for coat color was not known, the parental input of this characteristic was understood. White color is rarely seen in temperate or tropical regions, except among shorebirds, and, yet, white, because of its purity, was often an aim of human selection. Llama coat color was of great importance to the Inca because animals of particular colors were required for different ritual sacrifices. Every October 100 spotless white llamas were sacrificed to the sun. "Viracocha [the creator] preferred brown; each August and September, 100 brown animals were sacrificed to protect the newly planted maize against frost. Particolored llamas were sacrificed to Thunder . . . Pure black was also prized for sacrifice because the animal was black 'all over', even to the snout" (Flannery et al. 1989:112).

Coat color, either white or black, is associated with behavior patterns amenable to domestication (Hemmer 1990:130). Animals that are either black or white tolerate greater stress, are less shy, more trusting, and have looser social bonds. The link between behavior and coat color is believed to be a shared biochemical synthetic pathway between the precursors of coat color pigments and neurotransmitters (Hemmer 1990:189). An important characteristic of the coat other than color is the fineness of wool. Both of these features continue to be goals of animal breeding.

Sometime during the course of domestication an animal develops characteristics by which it can be recognized as domestic. However, these characteristics may be coat coloration but not the skeletal change necessary for recognition in an archaeological context. Once osteological change associated with domestication can be documented one must assume the species had been domesticated for generations. It is, nevertheless, useful to make a distinction between an animal that is demonstrably domestic and the process of domestication by which it transformed into this mutualistic relationship with humans. By recognizing this process, we acknowledge the many different relationships between our species and others, not all of which result in a morphologically domestic form.

Demographic Changes

Demographic changes, such as evidence of planned harvest of particular age and sex segments of stock, and castration of some of the males, are also part of the process of animal domestication. One of the main distinctions between wild and domestic animals is that domesticates can be maintained for the products they provide such as blood, milk, wool, and progeny. If the value of the stock lies in their function as beasts of burden or for traction, the most useful segment of the population will be castrated males, and mature females as a source for stock renewal. Similarly, if wool is the primary product, both males and females can provide this resource. However, if conflicts are to be avoided and mate selection controlled, the majority of the males will be castrated. However, if milk or meat is the primary product, then mature females will be the focus of the animal husbandry practices in order to grow the herd and freshen milk production. Males will be slaughtered when or before they obtain optimum weight gain. To examine these different animal husbandry practices, and the carefully planned harvest of livestock associated with them, both the sex and age at death must be known (Payne 1973). Different management practices are often confounded by accidental deaths, disease, abnormal environmental conditions, or market forces.

Present-day practices of llama herding in the Puna of Ayacucho, Peru, follow carefully timed traditional schedules (Flannery et al. 1989). An important time in the ceremonial calendar is the annual ritual blessing of the herd, when the animals' ears are notched for identification, and decorated with colorful tassels sewn in their ears (Figure 9.2). During this ritual, usually held in August, offerings are made and some of the livestock is redistributed (Flannery et al. 1989). Females in the herd are kept exclusively for breeding, which begins when they are 3 years of age. The gestation period is $11\frac{1}{2}$ months, with births occurring between January and March. Usually only one male in a herd is kept intact, and the rest are castrated to reduce conflict generated by females in estrus. Pack trains are composed of castrated animals more than 3 or 4 years of age.

Occasionally younger animals in training accompany the pack train but do not carry a burden. Great care is given to the size of the cargo animals carry. Usually it is evenly divided and the total weight does not exceed 11 kg. Llamas will not carry excess weight and if overburdened they will lie down and cannot be persuaded to move. Despite carrying relatively light loads, many animals used for transport develop stress-related diseases, such as arthritis and bone spurs, after 10 or more years of service. When they are no longer useful for breeding, fiber production, or work, they are slaughtered, and the meat is dried for later use and exchange. Pack trains move commodities between life-zones found at different altitudes. Dried meat, freeze-dried potatoes, and wool are brought from the high altitudes in exchange for maize and other commodities from the foothills, a process that strengthens ties within extended families and distributes products. The antiquity of some of the present-day practices may be seen in a Mochica vessel (200 B.C.–A.D. 600) portraying a pack llama (Figure 9.3).

Evidence for Demographic Change

To recognize demographic changes, the age and, if possible, the sex of the animals represented by the skeletal remains must be determined (Wilson et al. 1982). This relies on the changes that occur during the growth of animals as they mature from juveniles to adults and in the expression of unique characteristics that distinguish adult females from adult males (see Chapter 3). These developmental changes and sex differences are expressed more clearly in the skeletal remains of some animals than others. In all cases,

FIGURE 9.2. Llama pack train in the Andean highlands. Drawn by Molly Wing-Berman.

FIGURE 9.3. Pottery model of a llama sitting down but loaded with a woven bag on its back and identification notches in its ear. From Donnan (1976:94). Photograph by S. Einstein; reproduced with the kind permission of The Regents of the University of California.

stages of epiphyseal fusion within the skeleton and tooth eruption and wear occur within a range of time and may differ between early domestic stock, modern domestic breeds, and wild or feral animals living in different ecological zones. Choice of appropriate sequence of characteristics for determining age at death of animals is important. Once age criteria are established and the age distribution of a sample estimated, demographic changes can be analyzed and illustrated by survivorship curves.

As any farmer knows, losses of livestock occur despite the best-laid plans and do not always conform to planned management practices. Protection against predators is never complete, and crowding in corrals facilitates the spread of diseases. A particularly virulent disease among newborn llamas and alpacas, called enterotoxemia, is caused by the *Clostridium* bacteria (Wheeler 1984). An average of 50 percent mortality from this cause occurs in the first 40 days of life in these animals today. A steady, major loss of this magnitude would leave its mark in the archaeological record. The faunal samples from several Andean sites, such as Junin and Telarmachay, have relatively sudden and significant increases of the remains of newly-born camelids. At Telarmachay the presence of neonatal animals goes from 35 percent to 57 percent to 68 percent within three excavation levels of one occupation phase deposited between 6800 and 5000 B.P. (Wheeler 1985:65). This is interpreted as evidence for maintaining domestic camelids in corrals.

Introduction and Spread of Domestic Stock

The introduction of animals to regions where they did not formerly exist is another line of evidence for domestication. It has a long history and profound ecological consequences. Animals were introduced to new areas from early times in many areas (e.g., Wing 2007). For example, the islands in the Mediterranean were at the crossroads of early travel and commerce, and animals were among the traded items (Groves 1989). Many of the animals found on these islands were probably brought there by people because they are absent in the Pleistocene record and are unlikely to have reached these islands without human intervention. Goats and sheep appear to be very primitive domestic stock that escaped human control and became feral. Cats and pigs have characteristics of wild animals and were probably introduced as such. A number of other wild animals, such as shrews, weasels, deer, mice, and hares, were also early introductions. The other wild animals introduced into the islands demonstrate that a cultural value was placed on them. The taxonomic affinities of these animals suggest their origins and the direction of the trade.

Domestic animals expanded their range as people expanded theirs. Dogs were the earliest domesticated animal. Genetic studies identify at least four separate domestic lineages that accompanied people throughout the world. Among the large domesticates are beasts of burden such as donkey, horse, camel, and dromadary. These animals promoted trade and human interaction across the great region from China to Europe and into Africa. Other large domesticates, such as water buffalo and cattle, are used for traction and, thus, are associated with soil cultivation necessary for the production of some domestic crops. Among their other benefits, these animals both produce milk, which requires human physiological adjustments to produce the enzyme lactase as an adult in order to digest the lactose in milk (Hollox et al. 2006).

In the Andes, camelids were domesticated between 5500 and 2500 B.C. in the high altitude grasslands known as the Puna. From there, domestic stock are found in the highland valleys after 1750 B.C. and in the central Peruvian coast after 450 B.C. (Wing 1986). In South America, the spread of domesticates is north–south along the Andean mountain chain and west to the Pacific coast. The spread of Andean domesticates could not extend into the humid tropics to either the north or the east because of environmental limitations (Diamond 1994a).

The spread of domestic animals did far more than introduce livestock into cultures that subsisted on wild resources. Horses, first ridden around 4000 B.C., revolutionized land transport. The subsequent invention of wheeled vehicles further facilitated the transport of goods. With this enhanced mobility came the spread of ideas and lan-guages (Diamond 1991). Human population growth powered by agriculture and animal husbandry led to the spread of crops and domestic animals, the expansion of people with these technologies, and intermarriage with native populations and the diffusion of genes (Jones 1991; Sokal et al. 1991).

Changes in Faunal Composition

Domestic animals were not immediately and universally embraced but rather were incorporated as they fit into an established economic system. Acceptance of domestic stock in the Americas after A.D. 1492 followed different paths. Horses were so readily accepted by Native Americans that they preceded European explorers into the North American West (Anthony 1990; Diamond 1991). Pigs were initially important in many pioneering communities. These are ideal animals for colonists moving into new areas as they mature early, produce large litters, and require relatively less care and fodder than other domestic animals (Crabtree 1990; Zeder 1994). Goats and sheep, however, were not immediately incorporated into the Americas during the earliest phases of European colonization (Reitz 1992).

To document these changes in faunal assemblages, a series of faunal samples of ade-quate size must be quantified. Changes in the faunal composition would accompany demographic and morphological changes in the remains of the domestic animals (e.g., Davis 2005). It is also necessary to have faunal data from time periods prior to the pre-sumed introduction in order to verify the historical absence of these animals, remember-ing that absence in the faunal record may not signify absence of a local wild population.

Pathologies

Certain pathologies may indicate care and protection by humans or what might be thought of as occupational accidents or illnesses resulting from animal husbandry prac-tices (Baker and Brothwell 1980; Davies et al. 2005). Evidences of care and protection are seen in the healed fractures that occur among the skeletons of dogs and farm animals. That these fractures healed indicates that care was given to the animal for the period of time the animal was incapacitated by its injury. Healed injuries are observed in wild animals also but perhaps more commonly among social animals. Crowding in unsanitary corrals can result in an epidemic sweep of disease. Intense inbreeding also has inherent negative effects by increasing the chances of inheriting deleterious recessive genes. Often animals with such a genetic load do not survive infancy.

Pathologies that result directly from some animal husbandry practices are stresses manifest as arthritic conditions on legs that have been shackled and vertebrae that have borne the weight of riders. Tethered animals often exhibit injuries to the lower leg. Tethering was practiced in Anglo-Saxon times in England to restrain pigs (Crabtree 1990). Those individuals that strained at their tether often injured the distal tibia. These injuries may be breaks that subsequently healed or infections and massive deformities (Crabtree 1990:28). Teeth show signs of wear from bits (Anthony and Brown 1989; Diamond 1991). Thus, domestication is associated with an array of pathologies. On the other hand, injured animals receive shelter from predators and a supply of food while they recover. Some of these features are not necessarily pathological but are related to functional adaptations of bone to work-related activities (e.g., Johannsen 2006).

Deliberate alterations of domestic animals are common husbandry practices continuing today. Among these are: castration; removing horns, not by selective breeding but by the knife; changing the shape of horns by tension; docking tails, particularly of sheep and dogs; and notching ears to change their shape, as is done for some breeds of dogs, or to mark the animal, as can be seen in the Moche pottery model of a llama (Figure 9.3). Some of these alterations cannot be seen in the normal osteological remains, so we must rely on representations illustrating docked tails and trimmed or notched ears.

Castration is a particularly common practice among herdsmen who typically retain only a few intact males to service females and use castrated individuals for draft or burden-bearing work. Castration can sometimes be seen by the effect this has on stature and horn development. The age at which the animal is castrated influences these effects (Hatting 1975). Castration may alter the age at which skeletal elements fuse. Growth in stature is prolonged, and the resulting elements of a castrated animal may be longer than in intact males or females (Davis 1987:44–5). Although castration results in taller stature, the range of measurements of females and intact and castrated males may overlap, confusing the signature for this practice. Such changes in the conformation of the domestic animal are not limited to results of selected breeding but may be the result of other forms of manipulation.

Another modification visible in archaeological remains is alteration of teeth. An example of this is the removal of the lower fourth premolar of dogs (30 percent of 26 mandibles) excavated from West Indian sites (Wing 1991). This appears to be a deliberate practice. The crowns of these teeth are broken off, and, usually, some vestige of the root remains in the alveolus when it is healed over. We can only speculate why this was done, but perhaps it was intended to help secure a restraint.

Artifacts

Artifacts related to animal husbandry take the form of animal restraints, corrals, tools used in spinning and weaving wool, presence of the fabric itself, and illustrations or models of animals under domestication (e.g., Arbogast et al. 2003). Much of this evidence survives only under special conditions. Fabrics are fragile and are not preserved under normal conditions, but, in the coastal deserts of Peru and in rock shelters in the Andes, remarkably good conditions for preservation exist. Spinning and weaving kits are found intact, and many examples of woven fabric are recovered. The Moche period on the north coast of Peru is distinguished by its magnificent representational pottery that allows unambiguous interpretation. A view into the past is clearly portrayed by the drawing of a llama with a spotted coat restrained by a rope around its neck or by the pottery model of a llama sitting down but loaded with a woven bag on its back and identification notches in its ear (Figure 9.3; Donnan 1976). This model, made more than 1,000 years ago, could be modern in the details of the stripes on the bags carried by the llama. The method of marking an animal by ear notches is still occasionally used for identification. Moche is a coastal art form, and, presumably, the pack animal so accurately portrayed was used to exchange goods with the highlands. Other illustrations are not so clear and caution must be exercised in their interpretation.

Associated Landscape Changes and Material Culture

To maintain herds or flocks and to obtain work or products from them involves landscape changes (e.g., Karg et al. 2006). Stone walls were built by early New England farmers to clear and delineate their fields. Now many of these New England stone walls run through second-growth forest. Large areas of the rocky high elevation plateaus in the Andes were cleared centuries ago, and the rocks used to build the walls around corrals for llamas and alpacas. In the Andes, terraces and walls above the tree line are still clearly visible. Vestiges of such walls can be seen in the background in Figure 9.2. The road system connecting the far-flung parts of the Inca empire is also visible (Hyslop 1984). Many of these roads were paved and bordered by stone walls. Much of this cultural development was made possible by the labor of llamas.

Grazing and browsing changes the landscape in many ways. Simply by walking along accustomed paths the foot traffic packs the earth. This can be clearly seen on hillsides, where small terraces are produced by animals grazing back and forth across the slope. Wallows made by water buffalo, dusting areas made by llamas and alpaca, and the rooting behavior of pigs locally change the soil and vegetation. Selective feeding on choice plants can change the composition of a pasture by allowing the less-choice plants to become dominant. Overgrazing is a well-known outcome when too many animals are maintained in an area that cannot sustain them (e.g., Mainland 2006). This often results in erosion, loss of topsoil, and the degradation of the land.

Animal husbandry and agriculture usually go hand-in-hand. In the Andes, not only do llamas transport commodities, among them agricultural goods, but the corrals are also used alternately for enclosing livestock and planting potatoes in the enriched soils. Dung is used for fuel as well as fertilizer. Fuel is of particular importance in a region that is above the tree line and where frost can occur any night in the year.

These animals bear another valuable product, fiber. Both llamas and alpacas bear fine warm wool, and alpacas are particularly well-known for their wool. One consequence of the Spanish conquest was disruption of the Inca herding system and loss of some of the breeds that produced particularly fine fiber (Wheeler et al. 1995). At the present time, most of the llama wool is coarser than alpaca wool and used for utilitarian purposes such as woven cloth for bags and braided ropes. The bags are usually striped as they are made by alternating the natural colors of the wool from these multicolored animals. Ropes used to tie the bags on to the llamas or for other purposes are braided from different colored wool. Slings used to hurl pebbles at lagging or wayward animals are made in the same way. A whole way of life at high altitudes revolves around these domestic animals, which also play an important role throughout the region. The importance of native domestic herds declined after the introduction of Eurasian horses, pigs, cattle, goats, and sheep.

The complementary functions of llamas and alpacas is similar to that of goats and sheep in Eurasia. Goats and sheep are often kept in mixed flocks. Typically, goats browse and produce milk and sheep graze and provide wool. However, some of the finest wools, angora and cashmere, are produced by goats, and the rich milk of sheep is particularly valued for making yogurt and cheese.

Return to the Wild

In the absence of human care, control of breeding, and food supplies, formerly domestic animals become feral. Feral animals are domestic animals that live in the wild under natural selection, usually, but not necessarily, outside of habitats modified by people. Some feral dogs, for example, live on the periphery of human habitations, feeding at garbage dumps and occasionally on livestock. Feral dogs share a remarkably similar form, being slender, medium-sized animals that are social. Many of their characteristics, once again selected by natural processes, revert to forms that more closely resemble their wild ancestors. Feral pigs become tall, slab-sided animals with long snouts. Feral piglets often have spotted sides similar to the wild condition. The loss of domesticates to a human society would have a profound effect on an agricultural way of life and subsistence. In most cases, feral animals are only those few that escape confinement and are not a complete loss of whole herds or flocks of animals except perhaps in crisis situations.

CONCLUSIONS

Domestic animals are truly man-made but subject to all of the forces governing the survival of other organisms. The mutual dependence established between humans and their domesticates has profound effects on human societies and the environments within which they live. Much remains to be learned about this relationship and its role in human history.

10

Evidence for Past Environmental Conditions

The ecology of humans in respect to interactions with other species and the landscape, and the consequences to both humans and animals, are major themes in zooarchaeology. Human beings are both players promoting environmental change and spectators adjusting to changing environmental conditions. Habitats and specific animal populations thought to be pristine today, unmodified by human activities at any time in the past, may actually have had a substantial impact from human activities (e.g., Branch et al. 2005; Broughton 2004; Builth 2006; Mainland 2008; Mannino and Thomas 2001; Peacock 1998; Uchiyama 2006). Humans are not the only agents of environmental change. Environments may be altered by climate change, tectonic activity, tsunamis, plant and wildlife diseases, insects, storms, fires, and landslides, among the host of natural disasters that have an impact on ecosystems with or without human initiative.

Landscape changes initiated either by people (anthropogenic) or by so-called natural processes (nonanthropogenic) can be small or large, local or worldwide. Small changes, such as a storm or a path through the woods, may be elusive and hard to trace. However, the path may become a traditional trade route and ultimately a paved highway. Some human activities have an impact on huge areas or are global. For example, the Greenland ice sheet and Swedish lake sediments contain elevated levels of copper and lead that correlate with mining and smelting of these metals in the Roman Empire 2,000 years ago (Hong et al. 1994, 1996; Renberg et al. 1994). In many cases, both anthropogenic and nonanthropogenic variables have an impact on human and nonhuman habits and habitats (e.g., Amorosi et al. 1994; Edwards et al. 2005). For example, storms can be severe enough to cause landslides that alter local ecosystems and bury whole communities (e.g., Daugherty 1988). Such changes cause stress to which organisms, including people, respond in many ways.

To study environmental stasis or the sequences of landscape changes requires integrating the whole spectrum of archaeological evidence using a sequence of deposits from which adequate samples are available (Albarella 2001; Evans 2003; Evans and

O'Connor 2001; Leech 2006; Nicholson and O'Connor 2000; Quitmyer and Reitz 2006; Shackley 1981; Steadman and Jones 2006; Wilkinson and Stevens 2003). Any changes that are found in a single species, or at a site, must be verified by multiple lines of evidence to determine their causes on a regional scale (e.g., Butler and Campbell 2004). The accumulation of evidence from large samples and multiple sources pointing to the same conclusion strengthens characterizations of former conditions, the timing and sequence of any changes, and whether the changes are a cause or a consequence of human agency.

ENVIRONMENTAL CHANGES AND THEIR CAUSES

At one time, it was generally agreed that the Holocene environment was relatively stable. Many ecologists and geologists continue to perceive the predomestication Holocene environment as a primeval, pristine, baseline against which to measure environmental changes of the past century. This perspective presumes that early peoples were either so much a part of nature that they lived in harmony with it or that they were technologically incapable of causing much harm. The major exception to this perspective is the question of megafaunal extinctions at the end of the Pleistocene for which humans have been at least coincidentally implicated (e.g., Miller et al. 2005).

Many anthropologists either agreed with this perspective or they interpreted their data under other paradigms. Some explanations prior to the 1960s were strongly coached in the perspective of environmental determinism, with environmental change identified as the primary motivator of human history. Much of this research focused on what was called the "Neolithic Revolution." Ironically, many of the studies designed to prove these hypotheses contributed to the growth of more sophisticated environmental studies demonstrating that early concepts of the development of social complexity and domestication were inaccurate. In part due to reaction to these excesses, environmental archaeologists, including zooarchaeologists, were reluctant to pursue data that linked human history with the environment beyond subsistence studies. The biological research of the late twentieth century, however, slowly, perhaps inevitably, generated an ever larger body of data that could only be explained as evidence for environmental change in the Holocene. In some cases, the change was not of human agency and in others it was.

Studies of former environmental conditions have several goals. One of these is to reconstruct earlier environments by demonstrating stasis or change in that environment compared to present-day attributes. Due to the cultural filter, it is theoretically possible that stasis in the archaeological record may mask a change in the resource base itself, and vice versa. If evidence for a change in the archaeological record is found, then the next step is to determine if it is from first and second order processes (Chapters 5–7) or cultural choices related to settlement patterns, technology, exchange systems, or social distinctions (Chapters 8–9). One has to query whether major changes would occur in cultural institutions without some environmental component, but that is a hypothesis that can be tested if a change is demonstrated in the archaeological record. If the change observed in the archaeological record cannot be attributed to nonenvironmental factors, the next goal is to explore the extent to which humans were responsible for the change or reacted to it (e.g., Luff and Bailey 2000; Mannino and Thomas 2001).

Such changes may be viewed as stresses with two broad sources of that stress: environmental change and human behavior. Environmental change can result in changes in community composition independent of human predation. This is particularly the case for climate change, which until recently was more likely caused by agencies other than humans. In aquatic settings, changes may result from the removal of top predators or from a reduction in nutrients available. Responses may include a reduction in body size, reproduction at an earlier and/or smaller body size, and other changes in growth and reproductive habits. Stresses that are the result of human action are also environmental changes to which both human and nonhuman populations and communities must respond. Should the stress become too great, particularly in the case of climate change, individual animals or entire populations and communities may shift their range to a more favorable setting, essentially following their preferred habitat by shifting their distribution patterns.

An important source of evidence, therefore, is the presence (or absence) of indicator species based on present-day biogeography (phytogeography and zoogeography), (e.g., Peters and Pöllath 2004; Teta et al. 2005). Most biological communities do not have precise spatial boundaries. They are collections of populations with similar, but not identical, requirements. Plant distributions correspond to climate, soils, topography, latitude, and altitude. Evidence for this association is found in macrobotanical remains, wood charcoal, pollen, and phytoliths. Contractions and expansions of plant communities will likely be mirrored by changes in the distribution of animals. As a generalization, small animals have smaller home ranges, tend to have more specific ecological requirements, and are better environmental indicators than are larger animals, which often feed and reproduce over a wider area. Animals with specialized niches are also more vulnerable to environmental change.

If we interpret the data as evidence that the animal was locally present, then we must extrapolate from relative abundance in the archaeofaunal record to abundance in the former environment using quantitative approaches that are fraught with hazards. Variability in abundance, body proportions, body size, population structure, and other characteristics is very common in modern populations and in archaeological assemblages. Variation in the archaeozoological record over time could be highly significant for resource management, but at what point do we impute significance to that variation?

Finally, we have to make a causal attribution. Reduced to its simplest form, the most likely causes for variation are that the environment changed or that human behavior changed. It is necessary to distinguish between environmental change per se to which humans responded and human-induced change. Environmental change could be traced to people altering the environment, including the animals, or it could be that the climate changed without human intervention. The change in resource use may also be an entirely cultural consequence of economic or political developments, such as a new cultural group emigrating into the area or the independent, serendipitous invention of a new technology.

Such associations provide a basis for reconstructing past environments and populations. Reconstructions based on biogeographic evidence are strengthened by the addition of data from environmentally-sensitive isotopes and incremental growth structures in trees, vertebrates, and invertebrates, as well as long-term trends in body size, age-class frequencies, reproduction, and recruitment (e.g., Avery 2004; Mannino and Thomas 2001; Marelli and Arnold 2001; Miller et al. 2005). Geology and soil science document the impact of events such as altered water courses, volcanic ash falls, sea level fluctuations, and tectonic events.

Caveats

The absence of a specific organism in the archaeological record may not mean that the organism was absent from the environment (e.g., Lyman 1995). For a variety of reasons, people may have avoided that particular animal, or, due to first and second order processes, its remains were not identified in the studied assemblage. It is particularly important to avoid the assumption that resources that are highly valued today were equally valued in the past. Absence could indicate that people did not view the animal as a resource at that specific time or that they considered the animal taboo and avoided it. It could also mean that the animal was present and used but is not represented in the samples studied for environmental, cultural, and methodological reasons. Of course, absence in the archaeological record could mean that the animal was truly absent within the catchment area of the site.

Positive evidence is more easily evaluated; but before using this evidence to reconstruct former environments or to argue for environmental change, environmental studies must consider the possibility that an apparent range expansion is primarily evidence of human introductions that might result in environmental change rather than a natural range expansion responding to nonhuman factors. Humans are particularly prone to introduce animals into new locations (e.g., Royle 2004). This might be done within the context of domestication but is also found to occur among otherwise "wild" animals (e.g., Langemann 2004; Lauwerier and Zeiler 2001; Newsom and Wing 2004;

Phoca-Cosmetatou 2004; Sykes 2004). It is possible that some animals or their parts
were traded or brought to the site from a distance (e.g., Sykes 2004). Such an animal
is the Pacific thorny-oyster (*Spondylus calcifer*), which was traded from its source in
tropical waters north of Peru to Andean sites high in central Peru as well as Teotihuacan
in the interior of Mexico (Kolb 1987). Care must be taken to distinguish such trade
goods from local products and to distinguish between trade and major environmental
changes as explanations for the presence of these organisms at the site. Environmental
studies based on zoogeography are particularly sensitive to this caveat. If the animal is
present today because it was introduced by humans centuries ago, its presence cannot
be used as the basis of a management plan and may even support plans to remove the
animal from its artificially expanded range.

Because so much of the evidence for climate is the same evidence used for seasonal
periodicity in resource use, the critical task when using archaeological data is to distinguish between evidence of former environments and the consequences of seasonally
sensitive aspects of human behavior. Most of the biological and geochemical characteristics that signal environmental change are related to temperature and humidity, therefore,
evidence for long-term spatial distributions reflecting environmental change may also
be evidence for seasonal rounds. Seasonal periodicity and environmental change can
be distinguished by combining biogeographic, geochemical, and growth habit data for
environmentally-sensitive animals. For example, oxygen isotope measurements in fish
otoliths and mollusc valves also can define season of capture of individual organisms,
and, by extension, seasonal fishing schedules in addition to marking changes in water
temperature that might be related to environmental change.

Reconstruction of the Past Environment

Analysis of archaeological faunal assemblages provides many clues about former environments (e.g., Armitage and West 1985; Deith and Shackleton 1988). The basic assumptions of such analyses are that the ecological requirements of modern taxa have not
changed during the Holocene, although their distribution might have done so, and
that people concentrated their subsistence efforts within a nearby catchment area, with
allowances for exchange systems. In North American sites, the presence of gopher tortoises suggests the proximity of sand ridges with pine, oak, and wire grass vegetation;
coquina (*Donax denticulatus*) indicates sandy marine beaches; and eastern oysters signal
exploitation of brackish, inshore water. Environmental reconstruction is rooted in our
understanding of such phenomena in the present, of processes that promote change,
and of the scope of the human impact on the environment.

Some of the most specific ecological information is obtained from insects, spi-
ders, mites, internal and external parasites, terrestrial gastropods, and freshwater snails

(Kenward and Carrott 2006; Smith and Howard 2004). Many of these organisms are recovered only in soil samples, coprolites, and stomach contents (Evans 1972; Kenward 1978; Reinhard 2007; Shackley 1981:137–53; Sutton 1995). Some are pathogens that afflict wildlife, domestic plants and animals, and people. They provide a great deal of information about past environments, although many factors other than environmental change may be responsible for their distribution (Bathurst 2005; Horrocks et al. 2003; Kenward 2004, 2006; Panagiotakopula 2004; Schelvis et al. 2005). Some of these are adapted now to the human environment (Brothwell 2000; Kenward and Carrott 2006).

Each class of small organism provides different types of information. Terrestrial gastropods of the British Isles are described and categorized according to the habitats in which they are usually found, for example, freshwater marsh, terrestrial shade-loving, terrestrial open-country, wild undisturbed habitats, and man-made habitats (Evans 1972:194–203). On the basis of these habitat associations and the abundance of each in soil horizons at Avebury on Salisbury Plain, England, it is possible to document the sequence of landscape changes from forested woodland, to an episode of land clearing, followed by open grassland, and ultimately construction of stone henge (Evans 1972:168–74). Unfortunately, in many parts of the world, the habitat requirements of terrestrial gastropods are not known. Many are attracted to the moist refuse of a midden. They vary in abundance throughout a site, which may indicate the relative length of time that the refuse was exposed.

Parasites provide information about crowding, ventilation, and hygiene in addition to information about the environmental setting beyond the site (e.g., Bain 2001; Bathurst 2005; Panagiotakopula 2004). Parasite species and numbers differ substantially at Antelope House and Salmon Ruin, in the North American southwest (Reinhard 2007). Both sites were probably occupied year round by populations of similar size. However, these populations differed in their hygiene and the focus of their foraging activities. At Antelope House, where parasite loads were high, living space was crowded into a poorly ventilated cave and feces were deposited indiscriminately around the site. Foraging by these people focused on wetland plants, which promoted infection with some facultative parasites from the moist soils. In contrast, the people from Salmon Pueblo lived under less crowded conditions with well-defined, isolated latrines. Their foraging preferences focused on drier habitats. The difference in the parasite loads and its influence on the inhabitants of the two sites was further corroborated by a higher incidence of skeletal pathology among the human remains from Antelope House.

Environmental interpretation can be quite detailed when based on a complex of species with specific ecological requirements. An excellent example comes from the study of the environment created in the urbanization of Roman York (Hall and Kenward 1990; Kenward and Carrott 2006). The presence of a suite of grasses and herbs associated with meadows, and the different life stages of the insects, form an assemblage that indicates the presence of spoiled hay or dung. The larvae of a species of stable fly (*Stomoxys calcitrans*) affiliated with horse dung points to the stabling of horses and the urban landscape. One of the grasses found in the stables is a calcareous grassland turf that does not grow on the soils found near York today (Hall and Kenward 1990). All of the other forage species, many of which are typically found in the modern riverside meadows, could grow near the town. This evidence could mean that horses occasionally grazed in distant pastures on calcareous soils, with the remains of the distant forage plants deposited as dung in the stalls. Alternatively, hay made of these grasses may have been brought to the stable. A similar association between fly puparia, animal dung, and human behavior is reported from Germany (Schmidt 2006).

Distant habitats may be represented in archaeological sites because products from distant sources were brought to the site through trade network. Llamas in the Andean highlands facilitated the distribution of goods between different ecological zones so that herders living in the highlands could exchange potatoes (*Solanum* spp.) and other indigenous tubers, such as oca (*Oxalis tuberosa*), grown at high elevations for maize (*Zea mays*) and squash (*Cucurbita* spp.) grown on the lower slopes of the Andes and coca (*Erythroxylon coca*) leaves from the humid Amazonian lowland slopes (Flannery et al. 1989). In addition to bearing commodities into habitats in which they did not grow, llamas themselves were driven to regions where neither they nor their wild ancestors lived before their range was expanded through human mediation.

A characteristic of animal products brought from beyond the immediate catchment area is that their remains are more fragmentary and relatively less abundant than remnants of plants and animals from within the catchment area. These features are the basis of Shotwell's (1958) method for distinguishing animals from proximal and distant communities. The method is sample-size dependent and, of course, does not assign a cause to the taxa that are well-represented and those that are not (Grayson 1984:75–81). Two different interpretations of taxa that are well-represented and come from a proximal community can be proposed: (1) they were staples in the diet; or (2) they are the remains of animals that lived and died at the site and had little to do with the human subsistence economy. Only through careful comparison of multiple data sets and consideration of the archaeological context can one distinguish between these different interpretations.

Information about the ecological characteristics of animals is gleaned from a variety of sources. Species that have economic importance today are particularly well-known. Modern fisheries data accumulated from years of surveys allow predictions about where specific age and size classes of coastal fishes occur. When applied to the remains of marine organisms excavated from an archaeological site, this information may indicate local conditions near the site that made the acquisition of a particular complex of fishes possible. For example, an assemblage composed entirely of marine species suggests fishing in coastal waters, whereas a combination of marine and estuarine species suggests that some fishing took place near a river mouth. These interpretations are based on such parameters as the temperature, salinity, turbidity, and dissolved oxygen tolerances of the identified marine species. Some species used in the past are extinct and their habits and habitats are not known, such as the rice rats (Sigmodontinae) found in archaeological sites in the Lesser Antilles (Newsom and Wing 2004:95).

Further information about former habitats is derived from species composition and individual size or age profiles (e.g., Lyman 2004; Marelli and Arnold 2001). Presuming that a fine-gauge sieve was used to recover the full range of body sizes, the size of fishes and the types of fishes may suggest the presence of a nursery ground close to the site. To speculate whether the archaeological fishes were caught in nursery grounds, their size must be estimated and compared with the sizes of juvenile fishes today. If comparably small individuals are found in the archaeological collection, this could indicate that nursery grounds once existed near the site, even if they do not occur there today. In the case of oysters, their shape and size reflects the environmental conditions in which they live (Crook 1992; Kent 1988). Those that settle in large colonies where individuals are tightly packed together have relatively long, narrow shells, and those living less tightly clustered have relatively broader shells. Oysters in subtidal waters rich in nutrients grow larger than those living in intertidal waters where they are exposed during low tide.

Use of Faunal Data to Understand Change

In the absence of more parsimonious first-order, second-order, and cultural explanations, changes in the composition of faunal assemblages associated with a sequence of occupations point to environmental change. Human choice of resources, changes in technology or the spatial and temporal aspects of subsistence, or differences in archaeological recovery and analysis could produce evidence for change as well. These need to be eliminated as causes before environmental change can be inferred, whether or not that change might be anthropogenic or nonanthropogenic (e.g., Glasgow 2005). With these precautions observed, some sequences of faunal assemblages reflect environmental changes caused by climatic, geological, or human factors.

The scale of past events is much finer in archaeological sites, where 100-year intervals can be detected, compared with geological time scales that are usually much longer. With this finer time scale, smaller environmental fluctuations during the Holocene, such as slow sea or lake level rise and variations in water conditions, can be detected (e.g., Teta et al. 2005; Van de Noort and Fletcher 2000). For example, successive changes in the vertebrate and invertebrate species composition were observed in archaeological sites along Florida's southwestern coast (Walker 1992b). Changes in the species composition of fishes and molluscs with different salinity tolerances suggest estuarine conditions fluctuated from a more marine to a more freshwater regime, perhaps due to sea level change. At a low sea level, the salt water wedge would not extend as far into the embayment as it would at higher sea levels. At low sea levels, waters near the site might be less saline but become more so as higher-salinity marine conditions moved further into the embayment as sea levels rose. These hypothesized sea level fluctuations are corroborated by geological studies of beach ridge progression and surface sea temperature based on the constituents of oceanic cores, thus bringing independent evidence to bear on the interpretation (Keigwin 1996; Walker 1992b; Walker et al. 1995). Such small fluctuations in the sea level would have a profound impact on the people living along the coast and determine what part of a region or site was habitable by people.

Oxygen isotopes offer a way to analyze changes in sea surface temperatures (Andrus et al. 2002a, 2002b). Oxygen isotope ratios measured in a Japanese clam (*Meretrix lamarckii*) are correlated with relative water temperatures during the Holocene of central Japan (Chinzei et al. 1987). Comparable evidence for temperature changes is seen in other organisms from the coast and in deep-sea cores during this same time period. These data correspond to fluctuations in the sea level around Japan.

The environmental changes that initiated changes in animal populations influenced people as well as their prey species. Annual variation in temperature, sea level changes, and shifts in humid and dry vegetational regimes altered the sizes, shapes, and distribution of animals exploited by people. Faunal remains from archaeological sites occupied over long periods of time document that people were able to adapt to dynamic environments. By adapting to these changes and manipulating the animal populations with which they shared fluctuating conditions, people were, themselves, a force in the environment.

HUMANS AS A FORCE IN THE ENVIRONMENT

Human disturbance has complex and far-reaching consequences for plant and animal populations. This is not just a phenomenon limited to the industrial world and its burgeoning human population. The loss, change, and displacement of plant and animal species is associated with humans throughout the Holocene and with all organisms since life began. To survive, all species must adjust to environmental changes and to other organisms with which they share the environment, move to ecological zones that meet their requirements, or survive as relict populations of a once widespread species. Plant and animal populations today are the result of long and sustained direct and indirect interaction with people. People burn the landscape, coppice trees, introduce pathogens and other organisms, and consume local plants and animals. These activities, and others, have an impact on many organisms indirectly if not directly.

Island Ecosystems

Both introductions and extirpations alter island landscapes (e.g., Royle 2004). The rise and fall of the sea level may be small but significant, particularly if it breaks or creates a land bridge between the mainland and islands. Animals isolated from a mainland population evolve under the constraints of the island resources and diverge from the mainland population. The combination of introduced animals, agriculture, deforestation, and hunting has produced major changes in the vulnerable faunas of islands (Flannery 1990; Serjeantson 1990; Steadman 1995; Vigne 1992). Many island animals evolved in the absence of predators. Also, the size of animals on islands differs from the size of their mainland ancestors. Many large animals become smaller, such as the dwarf mammoth from Wrangel Island in the Siberian Arctic (Vartanyan et al. 1993). However, moas (*Dinornis maximus*) and elephant birds (*Aepyornis maximus*) were large-bodied island descendants of much smaller birds (Trotter and MacCulloch 1989). Many birds that evolved in the absence of predators lost the ability to fly, as is seen in some rails (Rallidae) and pigeons (Columbidae). Animals with such evolutionary changes were easier for colonists on islands to catch. Being easier to catch jeopardized many of these evolved island species.

The extinction of one species often has a domino effect on associated species. Some animals have evolved unique symbiotic relationships with other plant and animal species such that the loss of one threatens the health and even the survival of the other. For example, the extinction of the dodo (*Raphus cucullatus*), a large, flightless relative of the pigeons endemic to Mauritius in the Indian Ocean, endangers the plants that relied on these birds for dispersal and germination.

Many extinct and extirpated island species were replaced by introduced species, including domestic animals. Colonization of Pacific islands by people and their dogs, pigs, and chickens decimated many island-adapted species. Steadman (1995) reveals that the sweep of people into the tropical Pacific over the last 2,000 years resulted in a loss of bird life that perhaps exceeded 2,000 species, a 20 percent reduction of the bird species of the world, and 85 percent loss of the native species of birds on the Pacific islands. This loss has obvious implications for the insects these birds consumed and the plant seeds they dispersed.

Similar changes also take place on the mainland although the fauna is, on the whole, less sensitive to rapid extinctions because most mainland populations are more extensive and have a population reservoir from which to repopulate locally extirpated populations. Additionally, mainland faunas have the full complement of prey and predator species and, therefore, retain some defenses against human predation (Diamond 1990a, 1990b).

Harvesting Effort

Humans act as agents concentrating animals as a harvesting technique. People concentrated wild animals through drives and roundups. A dramatic account of such an organized roundup is found in Garcilaso de la Vega's (1961:194) description of the annual royal hunt of the Incas. These hunts were highly organized and involved tens of thousands of people who made a huge circle chasing all wildlife to the center of a constricting noose of people. The animals concentrated by this roundup included various species of carnivores considered harmful pests and killed immediately. A census was made of the animals captured. Game animals, both camelids (guanaco [*Lama guanicoe*] and vicuña) and deer (huemal [*Hippocamelus antisensis*] and white-tailed) were sorted into categories. Some were slaughtered for their meat, and individuals judged to be the best for reproduction were released to insure a population of game for subsequent hunts. Some guanaco and vicuña were shorn before being released. The meat from these hunts was redistributed and dried for consumption throughout the year. Roundups were strictly controlled and spaced out to occur only every 4 years in any one district, and hunting between roundups was prohibited, punishable by death. Such drastic culling doubtless changed dynamics of animal populations.

Overexploitation

People living in a fixed location and targeting the local plants or animals run the risk of overexploiting those resources. Solutions to this problem are: (1) to target a large range of organisms to spread the consequences of exploitation widely enough so that it is sustainable; (2) to change from one targeted organism to another when overexploitation reduces the population density of the first; (3) to move to a new area that has not come under exploitation pressures; or (4) to exchange goods with other areas, thereby reducing pressure on local resources.

Overexploitation reveals the limitations of environmental resources whether it is through excessive grazing by domestic stock, land clearing and resulting soil erosion, or overfishing and overhunting resulting in population declines. Resource depression, a decline in prey population abundance caused by harvesting pressure, is the outcome most frequently attributed to human behavior. Relentless exploitation influences the composition of animal populations short of extinction. Intensive exploitation of a particular size class of a wild species alters the life history characteristics of the species (Sutherland 1990; Mannino and Thomas 2001). Intensive selective harvest of large individuals favors species that mature early and grow slowly. Under the premise of the foraging theory, it is argued that high-valued prey will be depressed relative to low-valued prey, thus becoming less abundant in the landscape and less common in archaeological deposits (Butler and Campbell 2004).

One of the debates in conservation literature focuses on the question of top-down or bottom-up environmental impacts on marine settings (e.g, Pauly et al. 1998; Ware and Thomson 2005). As predators feeding relatively high on the food chain, human impact on the organisms they feed on may influence predator–prey relations at high tropic

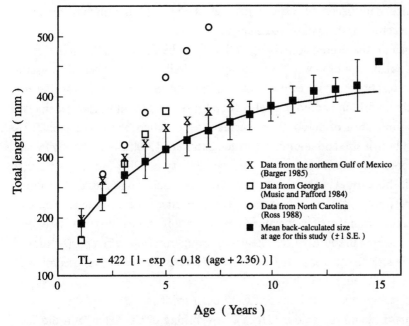

FIGURE 10.1. Von Bertalanffy growth curve fit to back-calculated size at age for Atlantic croaker (*Micropogonias undulatus*). Modified from Hales and Reitz (1992:86) and used with the kind permission of Elsevier.

levels (top-down impact), thereby affecting all organisms in an ecosystem as well as ecosystem processes. However, to the extent that nutrients become limited, humans are also constrained by the primary production rate (bottom-up processes) of the resource base and vulnerable to adverse impacts on that base.

Evidence for these responses are found in archaeological materials. Changes in faunal composition as a result of human activity are widely reported (Crosby 1986; Martin and Klein 1984; Steadman 1995). A decrease in the size of the targeted species resulting from intense exploitation at a level beyond which the population could not sustain itself can be measured (e.g., Mannino and Thomas 2001). A change in the demographic profile and life history of a species also can be documented (Quitmyer and Jones 1997). In such a case, intense exploitation would result in a relatively greater number of young individuals. In a study of Atlantic rangia clams (*Rangia cuneata*) and hard clams (*Mercenaria* spp.), Quitmyer and Jones (1997) found that the age composition of some clams was depressed. Intentional selection of smaller and younger clams was considered an unlikely explanation. Instead, they interpreted this as evidence of prolonged intensive exploitation. Changing fishing strategies during the 3,000 years prior to the seventeenth century A.D. and comparison of these archaeological data with modern catches demonstrate that the growth rate of the Atlantic croaker is now more rapid and the life span is shorter than it was in the past (Figure 10.1; Barger 1985; Hales and Reitz 1992). If the resource base continues to be degraded, the archaeological site may be abandoned, which in itself may be evidence of unsustainable exploitation habits. Overexploitation may, of course, not be the sole cause for these observed changes.

Actual change in the overexploited population must be documented for that to be the primary explanation of any of these changes. Dalzell (1998), for example, examines archaeological literature for evidence of change induced by subsistence fishing and reports traditional fishing had no impact on coral reef fish communities over the last 1,000 years in some areas of the southern Pacific Ocean. Butler (2001), however, attributes declines in fish size and abundance in the Southern Cook Islands in the Pacific to human overexploitation between cal A.D. 1000 and 1700. Allen (2002) found that large-bodied inshore fishes became more abundant over time at one site and less abundant at another; both sites are on Aitutaki Island, Southern Cook Islands. Nagaoka (2002) reports the mean size of barracouta (*Thyrsites atun*) populations may have been affected by overfishing in southern New Zealand. Broughton (1999:48) reports a similar decline in body size for sturgeon (*Acipenser* sp.) as a response to human predation at the Emeryville Shellmound in California.

Within the archipelago of the eastern Caribbean evidence for overfishing is also variable. Grouard (2001) finds no evidence of overfishing in Guadeloupe in the later part of the Early Ceramic Age (ca. 500 B.C.–A.D. 600) and in the Late Ceramic Age (ca. A.D. 600/800–1500) on the basis of changes in fish size and composition. Wing and Wing (2001) report that the mean trophic level of catches and the size of reef fishes declined in the Virgin Islands during the Early Ceramic Age (see Froese and Pauly [1998]; Pauly and Christensen [1995]; Pauly et al. [1998, 2000] for discussion of fish trophic levels). Newsom and Wing (2004:197) suggest overfishing during the Late Ceramic Age caused declines in fish size and changes in fish community composition due to increased exploitation by a growing human population (see also Wing [2001]).

Extinctions: Sitzkrieg versus Blitzkrieg

It is clear that people had an impact on the plants and animals with which they shared the land. In some cases, human migration and animal extinctions appear to be correlated (Martin and Klein 1984; Martin and Stuart 1995; Roberts 1998:81). Most of Australia's large mammals became extinct shortly after humans arrived on that island continent (Miller et al. 2005). Large mammals vanished over Eurasia in a sequential fashion about 50,000 years ago. The die-off of megafauna such as sloths (Megalonychidae), mammoths (Elephantidae), mastodons (Mammutidae), horses, and others in North America appears to have taken place during one moment of time about 11,000 years ago (Martin and Stuart 1995). However, a close examination of the radiocarbon dates of these North American extinctions suggests that they occurred over an extended time and that humans may have been part of the North American landscape for a longer time than previously understood (e.g., Grayson 1989b; Grayson and Meltzer 2003). Whether these extinctions were caused solely by hunters, environmental changes, such as climatic fluctuations, or a combination of these factors is hotly debated (e.g., Patton 2000; Shapiro et al. 2004). The two sides of the debate frame their arguments in the context of a Blitzkrieg, a lightning-fast war, as opposed to a Sitzkrieg, a war of attrition conducted by sitting and allowing other factors to weaken adversaries (Diamond 1989).

Domesticating the Landscape

Enhancing the habitat of preferred species may be considered to be domestication of the environment (Yen 1989). Certain beneficial nondomestic plants were promoted in the past as they still are today. This may take the form of simply clearing around valuable trees in the forest, whether this was hazelnut (*Corylus* spp.) trees in the European forests or sago palms (*Metroxylon sagu*) in New Guinea, to remove or discourage competing plants, thereby benefitting the plants most useful to human economies (e.g., Alcorn 1981; Dimbleby 1967; Fowler 2007; Groube 1989). The Guayaki of Paraguay and the Warrau of Venezuela practice a form of management by felling palm trees to provide optimal conditions for beetle larvae that are later harvested as a succulent, rich food item (Clastres 1972:160; Roth 1970:211). On an even broader scale, Australian aboriginal foragers burn vegetation to encourage the growth of useful grasses and replant the growing stems of harvested wild yams (*Dioscorea* sp.) to ensure their continued production (Smith 1995:17). Such activity modifies the plant composition of the forest and has an impact on the animal species that depend on forest products. The practice of domesticating the environment doubtless has considerable time depth.

The disturbed and enriched soils around human habitations promote the growth of specific suites of plants. Accumulations of shell in middens and mounds change the soils and this in turn provides the suitable conditions for the growth of certain plants. In the southeastern United States, these plants include red cedar (*Juniperus silicicola*) and zamia (*Zamia integrifolia*). It may not be incidental that cedar bark is widely used for basketry, and the tubers of zamia were grated to produce the flour used as a dietary staple (De Boyrie Moya et al. 1957; Swanton 1979). The association of the bottle gourd with people in Peru may have been facilitated by similar activities.

Clearing land and cultivating crops changes characteristics of the soil and vegetation, which influences the distributions of nondomestic animals. The edge effect produced by clearing and cultivation and the concentration of crops attracted many of the wild herbivores prized by people for food (Linares 1976). Even urban areas have a suite of plants and animals that flourish in such disturbed environments (e.g., O'Connor 2000a). In North America, such animals include gray squirrels (*Sciurus carolinensis*), coyotes (*Canis latrans*), raccoons, and many native birds; introduced commensal animals such as mice, rats, pigeons, starlings (*Sturnus vulgaris*), and English sparrows (*Passer domesticus*); and feral dogs and cats. All of these are attracted to human habitation for food and shelter.

Effects of Plant and Animal Husbandry

One of the most profound changes to the environment wrought by human culture was the domestication of plants and animals and the shift from foraging to farming and from hunting to animal husbandry (see Chapter 9). Domestic animals and food crops were taken along with other cultural innovations to new areas, where neither the domesticated forms nor their wild ancestors had lived previously. This shift did not occur suddenly or simultaneously throughout the world. In much of the Western Hemisphere cultivation of plants and agriculture developed in the absence of a major domestic animal other than the dog (Smith 1995). Animal husbandry was practiced in the absence of plant cultivation in a few places such as Lapland. In other parts of the world, plant cultivation and animal husbandry evolved in tandem. The earliest domestication and cultivation of plants probably preceded the domestication of livestock such as pigs, cattle, sheep, and goats. With the control of animals and food plants, these economies became increasingly dependent on the products of farming. Such control of plants and animals had a profound impact on the organisms subject to this control and on the environment within which they lived.

The introduction of domestic animals into new areas where they came in contact with indigenous domesticates or into virgin territories devoid of competitors or pathogens had a major impact on many ecosystems. In particular, Australia, the oceanic islands, and the Americas were subjected to the introduction of animals originally domesticated in Eurasia and northern Africa. As human colonists spread into Australia and Oceania, they brought with them dogs, pigs, and fowl. Introduction of these animals had disastrous consequences for the native faunas of the islands (Steadman 1995), a process that continues today. Plant, animal, and pathogen introductions also had an impact on native organisms (Crosby 1986, 1994).

Animal domestication transformed species as much as farming and herding practices modified the environment in which they lived (Karg et al. 2006). Shelters, corrals, and enclosures built to contain herds and store grain are some of the accommodations made to maintain domestic animals that also influence the surrounding area. Animals driven between pastures, to water, or to market wear deep paths along traditional routes. Grazing across steep hillsides cuts small terraces across the land. Intensive grazing induces vegetational changes, and overgrazing results in erosion and degradation of the soil. Several domestic animals assisted in changing the landscape by clearing forests to create conditions for tilling the soil. When cultivation is accompanied by canals, irrigation, or terracing, environmental modifications are amplified.

Spanish colonization of the Americas provides an example of the environmental influence on domestic stock and the importance of the perception of the American indigenous populations about the relative value of the introduced animals (Crosby 1986; Reitz and McEwan 1995). When Spaniards expanded into the Americas their complex of herd animals included primarily cattle, goats, and sheep. It might be expected that the colonists would attempt to transfer this complex in their pioneering effort. Goats and sheep did not prosper in the southeastern United States and the Caribbean, where this transfer was first attempted. Pigs and cattle, however, flourished. Cattle in Hispaniola grew to very large size and very quickly became the basis for an active trade in hides from the Caribbean to Europe (Reitz and Ruff 1994). Pigs did so well that they almost immediately went feral, and licenses to hunt them were issued as early as A.D. 1508 on the Caribbean island of Hispaniola. Pigs also thrived in the forests of the North American Atlantic coastal plain. By rooting through the forest floor, they changed the undergrowth vegetation in zones where deer and turkeys used to exist without competition. Horses, and to a lesser extent chickens (Carter 1971), spread among Native Americans ahead of Eurasian and African colonists.

Not only do population numbers increase, but the size and conformation of some animals change in new environments. Cattle introduced into the Caribbean realized their genetic potential and attained the size of the wild progenitor. This was demonstrated through measurements taken on the cattle specimens excavated from the early historic site of Puerto Real in Hispaniola (Reitz and Ruff 1994). Pigs that went feral in North America became tall, slab-sided animals with long noses through natural selection in the new wild environment. These examples illustrate the consequences of diminished competition, disease, and predation on population growth, as well as physical changes under renewed natural selection in feral conditions.

Another consequence of keeping domestic animals and introducing them to new regions is the spread of diseases associated with them (Brothwell 2000). Through the close association of humans and their domesticated animals, there is a relationship between the length of years in the domesticated state and the numbers of parasites shared with humans. For example, dogs, with a long history of association with humans, share many diseases with people whereas poultry, which were domesticated relatively recently, share the fewest (Southwood 1987). When people with domestic animals and their diseases moved into areas already populated, such as Australia and the Americas, diseases spread rapidly among people without antibody defenses (Crosby 1994).

APPLIED ZOOARCHAEOLOGY

As an outgrowth of the research we have reviewed, zooarchaeologists are in a unique position to apply their knowledge to conservation biology and resource management.

For many years, the biological evidence accumulated regarding topics such as biogeography, environmental change, and preindustrial traditions in animal use was largely used to address anthropological, biological, and ecological topics ranging from the evolution of species to optimal foraging decisions to ritualism. Zooarchaeologists might observe, in the course of such research, that present-day management decisions used flawed assumptions about the past, but rarely did they become involved in the public debate about environmental change and sustainable harvest of wild resources. However, as evidence accumulates to support conclusions regarding the human role in environment change, fewer zooarchaeologists can ignore the implications of the historical trends they find.

At the same time, resource managers are learning that they need data from time periods before the twentieth century to guide their decisions. This is particularly the case as resource managers come to realize that their benchmarks for natural or original conditions, which they hope to restore, are not being met. One reason for this is that their benchmarks are, themselves, based on an inaccurate assessment of the impact that people had on the environment throughout the Holocene or on concepts about former ecosystems that are not supported by the archaeological evidence (e.g., Frazier 2004; Langemann 2004; Phoca-Cosmetatou 2004; Whitehouse and Smith 2004). Hence, zooarchaeology is increasingly involved in environmental research with applied objectives.

Zooarchaeological data have significant applications in conservation management due to the time depth of the archaeological record and the regional nature of many analyses (Butler and O'Connor 2004; Danzell 1998; Lauwerier and Plug 2004; Lyman 1996; Mulville 2005). The zooarchaeological record yields historical trends in population and community composition that are rarely available from other disciplines for the late Pleistocene and the Holocene. In particular, the archaeological record clearly demonstrates that the Holocene was not as stable as once thought (e.g., Kenward 2004; Sandweiss et al. 2004; Teta et al. 2005). Zooarchaeologists are consulted about many aspects of conservation and resource management because of their knowledge about the recent past (geologically-speaking) and a long-term perspective (ecologically-speaking) associated with the human presence. Zooarchaeologists may be asked to document former climate regimes, explain the history of present-day animal distributions, contribute materials for conservation genetics, describe ancient breeds and their histories, and offer advice about the reintroduction of animals. They may become involved in civic and political actions, economic development initiatives, and the legislative process by providing information to community advocates as well as policy makers regarding conservation problems and sustainable levels of hunting and fishing. Zooarchaeologists may collaborate with law enforcement agencies and forensic scientists in the enforcement of laws and treaties pertaining to the protection of species and trade in live animals or their products (Badenhorst and Plug 2004). Zooarchaeologists may even find themselves engaged as expert witnesses in lawsuits or offering testimony before governmental panels regarding highly-emotional topics (e.g., Mulville 2005). The implications of our contribution to the public debate and decision-making process underscores the importance of sound scientific methods during identification and analysis to ensure that the information contributed is as accurate as current knowledge permits.

Modern resource managers need to examine their assumptions carefully in light of the archaeological information about human/environmental interactions. For example, ancient fishing was not a simple, inflexible strategy (Andrus et al. 2002b; Reitz 2001, 2004b; Sandweiss et al. 2004). In Peru, some of the changes in fishing strategy were probably responses to nonanthropogenic changes in the resource base associated with changes in El Nino/Southern Oscillation (ENSO), as well as other geological, atmospheric, and oceanic phenomena. The primary role ascribed to nonanthropogenic factors for changes in the ancient Peruvian fishery may or may not be supported by additional research. However, the important point is that the fishing strategy, and probably the structure of the fishery itself, changed markedly in the twentieth century and that the consequences of those changes have had a severe impact on an ecosystem that, otherwise, appears extremely resilient.

Some cautions need to be repeated for the new audience of resource managers unfamiliar with the strengths and weaknesses of this unique record. We have all been asked to tell a wildlife manager whether a specific animal was or was not present in the past, usually to decide whether it should be reintroduced or eliminated to a management area such as a national park or a biological preserve. Answering this important question is not simple (Lyman 1996).

Responding to management questions requires us to teach first. Resource managers appear to labor under the mistaken impression that "primitive man" ate anything that could be caught using simple, inefficient tools. The archaeozoological record does not support an image of random scavengers living in perfect harmony with their pristine, unaltered environment. People in the past were highly selective. They did not use whatever they could catch, and they controlled what they acquired by managing when, where, and how they acquired it. The explanations for these choices reflect responses that balanced environmental and cultural imperatives. People also altered their environment in the past, either intentionally or unintentionally (e.g., Fowler 2007; Jackson et al. 2001; Redman 1999). Essentially, the entire post-Pleistocene global history is a record of human interaction with the environment, and it is unlikely that many aspects of today's environment do not reflect that history. The outcome of this interaction was not necessarily benign. Responses to a management question, therefore, will often be more nuanced and cautious than the field biologist anticipates.

Each of these possibilities needs rigorous testing, which is, in itself, problematic for archaeozoological data (e.g., Amorosi et al. 1996). Nevertheless, the need for a historical perspective in conservation biology and resource management is painfully obvious.

Zooarchaeologists may not be able to answer questions about a species' presence or abundance easily or be able to conclusively document environmental change in each case, but we do know that the last century does not represent the previous 10,000 years (e.g., Redman 1999). Change through time is the very fabric of the archaeological record. For whatever reasons, the twentieth century is not typical of preceding centuries, which are themselves not unbiased examples of a stable relationship with an unmodified Nature. Managers need to examine the greatest time spectrum they can in order to determine which variables are necessary to sustain a species in today's environment and which are not. They also need to understand that the environment has been dynamic as has human use of and impact on their surroundings. Some changes may be a consequence of overexploitation or other human actions, and some may not be from human interference.

CONCLUSIONS

We can see from these examples that people are an important force in the environment, causing changes in other species and the landscape. The magnitude of these changes has accelerated with human population growth and increased density. It is unlikely that there was no anthropogenic impact on the environment during our species history or that people lived in perfect harmony with nature; they have always favored some species at the expense of others (Alvard 1993; Redford and Robinson 1991). Zoological and botanical data from archaeological sites are the primary evidence used to understand how people adjusted to environmental fluctuations and to what extent they themselves caused environmental change.

If resource managers and conservation biologists use archaeological data to manage modern resources, they must recognize that the answers will not be simple dichotomies of human versus nonhuman causality and anthropogenic resource depletion. The historical record presented by archaeological data should be viewed as a complex web in which environmental and cultural variables are woven together into a fabric rich with variety and surprises. The Holocene environment itself was not a uniform, stable stage on which people could depend. Flexibility is evident in both the cultural and the noncultural record. It remains to be seen if the need to be flexible was entirely due to nonanthropogenic environmental changes, or if people share some responsibility for changes in the resource base. Not only are many recent historical baselines derived from depleted or collapsed ecosystems (e.g., Jackson et al. 2001), their use in management plans presumes static ecological conditions, which the archaeological record demonstrates were not characteristic of many areas around the world.

11

Conclusions

INTRODUCTION

Developments in zooarchaeology over the past 50 years have transformed our knowledge of the associations between animals and people, and between them and other aspects of the environment. The field has grown from one in which a few biologists provided occasional identification services to one with full-time zooarchaeologists participating as regular members of interdisciplinary archaeological projects. Just as the number of professional zooarchaeologists has increased, so too has the number of laboratories with good reference collections. Progress is being made on all levels, from improved comprehension of site-formation processes to increased sophistication in research questions. We have a much better understanding of the diverse ways in which humans respond to the challenges and opportunities of their environments; the variety of roles that animals fill; the breadth of the animals' social meaning; the importance of cuisines in sustaining our biological and social lives; and the magnitude of our species' impact on the environment.

RELATIONSHIPS AMONG DATA AND INTERPRETATIONS

From the perspective of major anthropological and biological research questions, each of the seven types of primary data can be used to derive many interrelated types of secondary data (Table 11.1). For example, animal use is an important aspect of an economy, and animals fill other social roles. To study this, it is necessary to know which animals were used; how and where they were obtained; how individual animals or their products were distributed; how each animal contributed to the diet; whether skins and wool provided protection and warmth; how sinew, bone, teeth, and shell were fashioned into tools and ornaments; if animals provided traction, transport, or dung; and what was used and what was not used. The suitability of particular animals for these roles should not be based on our own concepts of how animals ought to be used. To address the

Table 11.1. *Some correlations between primary and secondary data and related concepts*

First- and second-order changes
  Additional primary data
    characteristics of organisms identified and their populations
    climate and soil data
    characteristics of archaeological deposits
    characteristics of hard tissue related to function and structure
  Secondary zooarchaeological data
    identification of closely related species and domestic taxa
    age and sex
    relative frequency of taxa
    skeletal frequency
    modifications
    niche breadth
  Related concepts
    proximal and distal communities
      commensal taxa
      biogeography
    nonfood uses
    subsistence strategies
      human demography, health, and activity level
      settlement size, location, and density
        disposal habits
        storage systems
      catchment area
      carrying capacity
      technology
      butchering and food preparation techniques
        transportation decisions
        food processing techniques
        raw materials, tools, and ornaments
        exchange and storage systems
      status, ethnicity, and belief systems
    archaeological methods
    zooarchaeological methods
Nutrition and diet
  Additional primary data
    environmental inventory
    taxonomic attribution of plant remains
    modifications of human skeletal remains
    coprolite and digestive tract contents
  Secondary data
    plants used as food, medicine, fuel, tools, ornaments, clothing, and construction
      material

Table 11.1 *(cont.)*

human skeletal evidence of disease and activity levels
stable isotopes and trace elements
estimates of body dimensions
identification of domestic taxa
relative frequencies of taxa
skeletal frequency
estimates of dietary contribution
modifications on nonhuman specimens
niche breadth
Related concepts
community ecology
human demography
subsistence strategies: paleonutrition, paleodiets, nutritional status
temporal dimensions
status, ethnicity, and belief systems
site-formation processes
archaeological methods
zooarchaeological methods
environmental impact
Spatial and temporal dimensions of animal use
Additional primary data
characteristics of organisms identified and their populations
environmental inventory
Secondary zooarchaeological data
estimates of body dimensions
identification of closely related species and domestic taxa
age and sex
relative frequency of taxa
skeletal frequency
estimates of dietary contribution
modifications
niche breadth
Related concepts
community ecology
human demography
choices in terms of which species, age, or sex to use
settlement size, location, and density
temporal dimensions
technology
exchange and storage systems

(cont.)

Table 11.1 *(cont.)*

status, ethnicity, and belief systems
site-formation processes
archaeological methods
zooarchaeological methods
environmental change

Technology: capture techniques, food processing, raw materials, tools, and ornaments
Additional primary data
identity and source of raw materials and tools
methods used to make tools
Secondary zooarchaeological data
estimates of body dimensions
age and sex
skeletal frequency
modifications
Related concepts
community ecology
spatial dimensions
settlement size, location, and density
catchment area
human demography
temporal dimensions
domestication
exchange and storage systems
status, ethnicity, and belief systems
site-formation processes
archaeological methods
zooarchaeological methods
environmental impact

Exchange systems
Additional primary data
identification of exotic raw materials
identification of exotic material culture objects such as ceramics and tools
identification of exotic iconography and architecture
Secondary zooarchaeological data
estimates of body dimensions
age and sex
relative frequencies of taxa
skeletal frequency
estimates of dietary contribution
paleonutrition and paleodiets
nutritional status
modifications
niche breadth

Table 11.1 *(cont.)*

Related concepts
  human demography
  settlement size, location, and density
  temporal dimensions
  technology
    food processing
    storage
  status, ethnicity, and belief systems
  social obligations
  rural and urban relationships
  long-distance exchange
  markets
  site-formation processes
  archaeological methods
  zooarchaeological methods
  environmental change

Animals as social markers
Additional primary data
  characteristics of habits and habitats of animals identified
  evidence of social boundaries in settlement patterns and material culture
Secondary zooarchaeological data
  estimates of body dimensions
  identification of closely related species and domestic taxa
  age and sex
  relative frequencies of taxa
  skeletal frequency
  modifications
  niche breadth
Related concepts
  human demography
  settlement size, location, and density
  temporal dimensions
  technology
  different breeds, ages, or sex used in different contexts
  exchange systems
  exotic animals
    status and ethnicity
    ritual behavior
    exchange networks
  value of meat
  animals as symbols of social relationships
    food taboos

(cont.)

Table 11.1 *(cont.)*

---

        totemic animals

        concepts of sacred and profane

     site-formation processes

     archaeological methods

     zooarchaeological methods

Domestication

   Additional primary data

     characteristics of habits and habitats of animals identified

     cultural chronology

        culture contact and frontiers

        presence of other horticultural, agricultural, or pastoral components

     environmental inventory

   Secondary zooarchaeological data

     estimates of body dimensions

     identification of domestic taxa

     age and sex

     relative frequencies of taxa

     skeletal frequency

     modifications and pathologies

   Related concepts

     human demography

     exotic animals

     settlement size, location, and density

     temporal dimensions

     animal husbandry

        population characteristics and animal behavior

        use of animal by-products, such as milk, cheese, eggs, blood

        use of animals for labor

        use of animal products as raw materials

     health status of animals

        husbandry techniques

        demographic information

        genetic relationships

        livestock diseases

     exchange systems

     evolution of animal husbandry and history of domestic breeds

     status, ethnicity, and belief systems

     site-formation processes

     archaeological methods

     zooarchaeological methods

     environmental impact

Table 11.1 *(cont.)*

Paleoenvironments
  Additional primary data
    characteristics of habits and habitats of animals identified
    biogeographical and other biological relationships
    environmental inventory
  Secondary zooarchaeological data
    estimates of body dimensions
    identification of closely related species
    age and sex
    relative frequency of taxa
    skeletal frequency
    niche breadth
  Related concepts
    site-formation processes
    faunal successions
      climatic indicators
      population characteristics
    exotic animals
    human demography
    catchment areas
    carrying capacity
    temporal dimensions
    technology
    exchange systems
    status, ethnicity, and belief systems
    site-formation processes
    archaeological methods
    zooarchaeological methods
    cultural chronology

many facets of the relationships between humans and animals requires us to approach the research from several perspectives. No single method will produce all of the data necessary to address these questions. Instead, primary data and related secondary data should be combined to study cultural and biological phenomena.

THE NATURE OF ZOOARCHAEOLOGICAL MATERIAL: COPING WITH AN INCOMPLETE AND ALTERED RECORD

The ultimate goal of much zooarchaeological research is to explore the causes, processes, organization, and consequences of human behavior through time and space from the perspective of animal remains. This is an elusive target. By its very nature, the archaeological record is not a faithful record of the site's history. Underlying the physical remnants of animals that are recovered are cultural practices concerning the procurement, care, and meaning of animals that can be glimpsed only occasionally. Organic remains are particularly vulnerable to alteration by site-formation processes. Consequently, our knowledge of animal use and the environments in which people lived is based on fragmentary, incomplete, and altered evidence.

These difficulties are challenges rather than barriers. When prudently and cautiously studied in well-reasoned steps, animal remains, incomplete as they are, do provide insights into the past. Based on the premise that zooarchaeological remains *are* the product of past phenomena, a cautious approach to their study is recommended, but there is no reason to ignore them altogether. What follows are some procedures that assist in meeting the challenge.

Take a Conservative Approach

In view of the fragmentary nature of the animal remains, it is important to take a conservative approach when collecting and interpreting data. Basic primary data should be gathered for all samples as unambiguously as possible. Cultural deposits must be recovered using fine-gauge screens for the maximum potential of each site to be realized. When decisions must be made in describing animal remains, the simpler, more conservative approach should be selected. Another aspect of a conservative approach is to provide clear and complete descriptions of the methods used so that others can compare their procedures and evaluate their results with yours (and you can be reminded about what you did when your memory lapses). In addition, all of the intermediate steps by which secondary data are derived, and that ultimately lead to interpretations of the data, should be clear, reasonable, and part of the written record. Notes should be curated as carefully as the specimens themselves.

Match Methods to Research Objectives

Methods should match research objectives. Each research objective requires specific observations and the development of special techniques and methods to probe them. Despite the wide range of techniques and methods available to zooarchaeologists, not all of these are suited to every collection, assemblage, site, region, or question. The choice of methods should be based on characteristics of the materials and the research objectives. Almost all of the methods reviewed in this volume can be unnecessary, overly complex, or produce false results in some research situations, but can be critical to developing and testing new theories in others.

It is particularly important to recognize the limitations imposed on faunal data by incomplete or inconsistent recovery techniques and small samples. The context with which the remains are associated is also important and must relate to the research questions. For example, kitchen middens, rather than burials, should be studied for evidence of routine food habits; however, food remains from sacred contexts provide interesting contrasts to those from secular ones. To study regional exchange systems, settlement patterns, and temporal periodicity, data from as many parts of the system as possible should be examined, not just one part.

Verify Through Observation, Experimentation, and Replication

The processes by which animals are included in archaeological deposits, how these deposits change, and the role of each animal at an archaeological site, rarely can be directly verified. Occasionally, intact remains are found under the good preservation conditions afforded by extremely dry, permanently wet, or extremely cold conditions. When well-preserved deposits are found, they remind us of the magnitude of our loss. Deposits with extraordinary preservation can be used to evaluate animal remains from more typical archaeological situations.

Interpretations should be substantiated through additional research. As much as we would like to step back in time to verify our interpretations directly, it is only possible to achieve indirect verification. Support for the hypothesis that the patterns observed in archaeological remains are the product of human behavior can be sought by drawing on ethnographic parallels and modern replication of archaeological patterns. These lend support to the premise that animal remains at archaeological sites are not random deposits. At the same time, ethnographic studies and experimental archaeology alert us to aspects of animal remains that are not the consequence of human behavior and inform us of the diverse ways in which humans interact with their environments. Textual and graphic evidence pertaining to the location and time period of the assemblage also helps verify interpretations based on animal remains. Such studies expand our interpretive horizons. At the same time, a rational basis for ethnographic, as well as biological, analogies must exist.

Through ethnographic observation, we know that food and nonfood resources are selected for use not just because they are available but on the basis of the time and energy needed to acquire the resource and its value in terms of other needs and desires. Only through studies of modern people following traditional subsistence patterns can the time-energy expenditures of activities be measured. The energetic cost of subsistence includes the manufacture of the tools and equipment used, the distance that must be traveled to the resource, and the cost of processing the food. These must all be considered in evaluating the net value of subsistence activities (Dufour 1983; Passmore and Durnin 1955). Animals that are more costly to catch than the energy they provide, however, may possess cultural values beyond nutrition. For example, eagles are important trophies in the social life of many peoples, although they offer relatively few calories in terms of the effort required to capture them. Such extravagances must be balanced against savings in other areas. Ethnographic observations inform us both of uses of animals and of resource management.

Because every deposit, site, and field season is slightly different, archaeologists rarely can precisely replicate the "experiment" that each excavation represents. It is, however, possible to verify results from one study by testing them against additional results from other sites, other regions, and other laboratories. Data and interpretations can be tested through further research with additional archaeological samples, especially ones representing different behavioral contexts. Verification comes from the consistency with which a pattern endures in the archaeological sequence. Food choices tend to be conservative and the technology that succeeds in repeatedly catching the same complex of animals also changes slowly. Consequently patterns of animal use change gradually. When a change is seen in an assemblage, the zooarchaeologist is alerted to broader changes in the natural and/or cultural environment.

Support also comes from internal consistency within each faunal collection. Most of the major research questions in zooarchaeology can be explored using several different types of primary data (Table 11.1). Verification of a hypothesis by more than one primary observation lends greater strength to arguments supporting or disproving it. For example, if one argues that the remains of very small fish species are stomach contents of larger fishes, or bait to catch them, then measurements demonstrating the presence in the faunal collection of large fishes would be necessary to verify this hypothesis.

Associated finds also verify or expand the interpretations that can be made. For example, fish hooks, net weights, and net gauges from a site should correspond with the sizes, morphology, and behavior of the fishes represented in the faunal samples. Food preparation techniques inferred from animal remains may be supported by grinding implements, the size and shape of vessels and other tools, and food residue burned onto pottery sherds. The use of wool is indicated by spinning and weaving implements associated with the remains of wool-bearing animals. Remains of animals from ecological zones beyond the catchment area may indicate trade, environmental change, or both. When there are remains of beasts of burden, domestication and transport systems are likely. For a fuller assessment of an economy, it is necessary to include information about plants used as food staples, condiments, medicines, tools, clothing, and building materials. Archaeogenetics, trace element analysis, and stable isotope studies further elaborate and test conclusions.

For these reasons, it is important to share data with colleagues working on the same or similar sites. Zooarchaeology is blessed by a general willingness to share data freely and this greatly enhances our ability to test interpretations against the findings of other researchers. This, in turn, obliges us to acknowledge and attribute such shared data, as well as the other contributions that colleagues, especially junior ones, make to our research.

Use an Interdisciplinary Approach

To achieve the goals of zooarchaeology, faunal data must be combined with other biological, inorganic, archaeological, and documentary evidence (e.g., Maltby 2006). Paleoenvironmental, paleoeconomic, and paleonutritional studies require the close coordination of data from multiple sources, such as plant remains, animal and human skeletal tissues, coprolites, bone constituents (isotopes and trace minerals), and material culture. If we find crowded, unventilated living conditions where there was no regard to sanitation, plant remains that were collected from wet locations that promote parasite spread, and evidence of a heavy parasite load in human coprolites, we have much more interesting and important insights into human behavior than a single line of evidence could provide (Reinhard 2007).

Synthesis of archaeological data sharpens our view of past human ecology. One excellent example is from a cave site on Mangaia, one of the Cook Islands (Kirch et al. 1992). The sequence begins with a diverse assemblage of endemic birds. This is followed by an increase in non-indigenous pigs and chickens, which had been domesticated elsewhere, and a decline in endemic birds and forest tree species. Ultimately, famine foods (e.g., pandanus kernels [*Pandanus* sp.]) are more prevalent; certain marine molluscs and reef fishes are smaller in size than previously; and changes in soils indicating erosion increase toward the top of the deposit. These observations are accompanied by other cultural and environmental changes. The combination of these many lines of evidence presents a stronger case for stress to an island ecosystem caused by human colonists (Kirch et al. 1992). This example illustrates the benefits of collaborative efforts that combine evidence from an array of specialized investigations.

Interdisciplinary collaboration is important in zooarchaeology because many of these other data types are beyond the skills and resources of a single zooarchaeologist to collect and analyze. They are usually studied by specialists whose data and interpretations must be integrated. Integrating different types of data is not easy for many reasons. One of the primary reasons is differential deposition, preservation, and recovery of each type of organic and inorganic residue. Achieving an integrated study within even the organic remains is hampered by the intrinsic lack of comparability among the many classes of tissues represented, such as nut shells, teeth, wood, mollusc valves, maize cobs, and bone. The first-order and second-order changes that modify these distinct biological tissues are themselves very different.

The other reason is that communication among specialists is often hampered by the press of other duties, lack of time, limited funds, or a weak commitment to synthesis within the project team. The necessary integration of data is promoted by the closest possible collaboration among all members of the archaeological team, including specialists focusing on particular aspects of the site and its remains. Integrated studies provide much more information than does the study of one aspect alone. Researchers should make every effort to overcome the hurdles that hinder interdisciplinary studies. Such collaboration provides additional support to original expectations, suggests alterations to those expectations, and expands interpretations in unexpected ways.

ADVANCES AND INSIGHTS IN MODERN ZOOARCHAEOLOGY

Surprisingly diverse and abundant animal remains are preserved at many archaeological sites. In many collections, we can tell that the remains of animals used by people are mingled with the remains of animals that lived and died in the same place without human intent. Together they represent the residue of food, jewelry, pets, animals used for labor, vermin, and insignificant animals that lived around the home but of whom people may have been largely unaware. All of them contribute to the fabric of human life and we learn a great deal about the human past through their study. Zooarchaeologists have made great strides toward understanding the processes and relationships among these materials. Enhanced understanding of human ecology and environmental change rests on the accumulation of data and methodological advances in zooarchaeology.

Methodological Advances

Zooarchaeologists now have a much greater appreciation that studies of the many ways people use animal resources rely on the comparability of faunal data. To achieve comparability among various components of a site or among sites, site-formation processes must be considered, recovery of organic remains must be optimal, and analysis must consistently be the best possible. First-order changes work against comparability, and there is little we can do about this. At the same time, improved knowledge of taphonomic processes, as well as a better understanding of ways to study their impact on animal remains, is an important advance.

We also have a much better understanding of the importance of sampling techniques and sample size than earlier zooarchaeologists enjoyed. The full range of activities at a site, and within a region, should be sampled if causes for variation in animal use are to be explored. It is not always possible, or even desirable, to excavate on a large scale. However, the limited salvage excavations prevalent today make it particularly important to extract animal as well as plant remains productively from the restricted portion of each site that is excavated. By this we mean that appropriately fine-gauge screens should be used to sieve the soil in the field and that bulk samples should be taken to recover as full a range of plant and animal remains as possible. Studying adequate samples is profoundly important to achieve representation of the majority of animals formerly present at a site. Only with recovery of an inventory that is as complete as possible, accompanied by inorganic and human biological evidence, can research integrate different lines of evidence to achieve a detailed understanding of the history of human experience. Many second-order changes can be controlled in the field, in the laboratory, and through the process of publishing.

Diverse Responses to the Challenges and Opportunities of the Environment

One of the most important zooarchaeological contributions to the study of human behavior is the insight that humans made use of a much wider array of animals than originally assumed and, at the same time, were highly selective in their food choices. Species lists developed using the full array of zooarchaeological methods combined with improved field techniques show that a much wider array of animals were used in the past. It is clear that a broad range of resources were included in human diets, extending well beyond large mammals. Even at sites occupied during the Pleistocene humans consumed a host of small mammals, birds, reptiles, amphibians, fishes, and invertebrates. For example, evidence from Middle Stone Age sites in Africa shows that molluscs and fishes were important components of very early human subsistence strategies (Brooks et al. 1995; Voigt 1975). At the same time, not all edible resources in the catchment area were consumed. At no point in the history of our species did humans eat whatever was available to them. The faunal record clearly shows that humans are selective broad-spectrum omnivores.

As faunal data from a growing variety of sites are studied and the results published, we gain a better understanding of variation in human ecology. For example, the economies of people who built monumental architecture were once thought to be based on domes-ticated herd animals and plant foods. However, the preceramic monumental site of El Paraiso (1800–1500 B.C.), on the desert coast of Peru, was supported by animals from the sea rather than the land, as well as wild, and some cultivated, plants (Quilter et al. 1991). Most of the animals from the site were fishes, chiefly anchovies. Another vital constituent of this economy was cultivated cotton, which was used to manufacture cordage, net-ting, and woven fabric. The sea along this part of the Pacific coast is characterized by upwellings that support abundant marine life. The products of the netting industry allowed access to this rich resource. Textile manufacture produced cloth for everyday use as well as prestige items. Together, these resources permitted social developments similar to those supported by domestic animals and food crops elsewhere.

Variety of Animal Roles and the Breadth of Their Social Meaning

Animals play a wide range of roles in human life. They provide food, shelter, clothing, status, symbols, and companionship. These roles and the social meaning of animals extend beyond their nutritional and economic value. Zooarchaeological research contributes substantially to our understanding of these roles.

One of the most important animal roles is associated with domestication. Controlling animals through domestication is a major step toward accumulating wealth, managing fluctuations in abundance and accessibility of resources, and acquiring animal products and services. Domestic animals provide meat, services, and products, such as hides, glue, grease, bone, feathers, milk, and eggs. They also represent accumulated wealth, which is used to create or to satisfy social obligations. The animals that form a farming system are carefully selected and complement each other within the system.

When one component of an economic system changes, the role of animals in that economy also changes. The sixteenth-century Spanish colonization of Florida and the Antilles required adaptation to new conditions by both Spaniards and their domestic stock. All did not flourish equally well in the American setting, and, as a result, people modified their traditional animal husbandry practices (Reitz and Scarry 1985). Similar human flexibility is demonstrated in the frontier setting of Fort Michilimackinac, Michigan, where the food taboo governing the consumption of pork was secondary to achieving social status for a Jewish household. Once the household attained sufficiently high status in the community, its members practiced their ethnic food taboos without jeopardizing their social standing in the community (Scott 2007).

Such adaptability is required whether people attempt to transplant their traditional economy to a new land or maintain ethnic foodways in life under frontier conditions. Zooarchaeological data show that people cope in multiethnic settings and under the changed circumstances caused by colonization by manipulating their animal resources to maintain ethnic identity, social status, and traditional economic strategies within the context of new environmental opportunities and constraints.

Increasingly, zooarchaeologists contribute to studies of social complexity and social organization. After many years of being largely ignored, human beliefs about animals are once again being examined. Such beliefs are so deeply instilled that animals symbolize clans, political parties, sports teams, and personal traits. Hypotheses about such beliefs are more commonly derived from and tested against material culture rather than from the animal remains alone, but finding animals in appropriate contexts provides important support to such hypotheses.

Importance of Cuisines in Our Biological and Social Lives

Another insight offered by zooarchaeologists highlights the use of animals for food and the development of traditional cuisines. Animal remains provide evidence that regional cuisines developed very early in human history. Once regional cuisines developed, they changed very little, but within broadly defined regional cuisines, humans make a variety of food choices. These often reflect social criteria rather than biological ones. The choices of foods in cultural settings are flexible and are modified in the face of changing population dynamics, subsistence pressures, seasonal and spatial periodicity, and social and cultural influences.

Plants are usually the staples in most cuisines, supplemented by meat from a chosen complex of animals. Beans, maize, and squash supplemented by meat form a basic food group that characterizes the traditional Mexican cuisine. This combination of staples supplies all of the nutrients required for a healthy diet. This is particularly true when the maize is processed with lime, which enhances the amino acid balance for human nutrition (Katz et al. 1974). Such complex processing must have taken a considerable amount of experimentation to develop, but once it was established, it became widely accepted among people for whom maize was a staple. This complex endures into the present century.

Differences in access to foods within a family or community have proved as difficult to document as steps in the development of cuisines. Methods that examine blood residue, stable isotopes, trace minerals, paleofecal steroid levels, fatty acid residues, and parasites hold promise for unraveling the details of past diets (e.g., Reinhard 2007; Sobolik et al. 1996). Some of these techniques have already demonstrated their value, although methods for applying them to archaeological materials and interpreting them are still developing. Many of these approaches have major issues of their own to resolve, but already they enhance the interpretive potential of animal remains and the integration of animal data with other classes of archaeological information.

Magnitude of Human Impact on the Environment

Clearly, the world in which we live is continually changing. Some of these changes are ones in which humans played no causal role. Others were caused by people directly or indirectly exploiting resources and manipulating other aspects of the environment. Domestication of both plants and animals had profound consequences for the environment and for the species that were manipulated – some of which eventually became domestic. Ecologists should not view current ecosystems as stable and should look for evidence of human impact on the history of these systems. The time perspective that archaeology offers is important for prudent management of resources today (e.g., Yalden and Carthy 2004).

Documenting the ages and sizes of fish caught under different fishing pressures and technologies is one way to investigate the human impact on resources. For example, Atlantic cod caught during medieval times around Iceland provide a contrast with those caught by the modern cod industry (Amorosi et al. 1996). The estimated lengths (based on dimensions of dentaries and premaxillas) of fish from four medieval sites are all larger than 40 cm and many are more than 100 cm. Such large individuals are rarely recorded in the modern trawl data from Iceland. This demonstrable decline in the size of cod is similar to that described for the Atlantic croaker caught off St. Augustine (Hales and Reitz 1992).

In the quest for food and other resources, environments are modified by clearing and burning, with the ensuing consequences for plant and animal species. Through zooarchaeological data, we can track these changes and gauge the magnitude of the human impact on the environment. Zooarchaeological data show that the human impact on marine environments is not always the same, and the impact does not always result in demonstrable changes in the exploited populations or communities.

FUTURE DIRECTIONS IN ZOOARCHAEOLOGY

When we wrote the first edition of this volume, we anticipated that many new zooarchaeological techniques, methods, and interpretations would be developed. In updating this volume, we found that over the past decade there are few new techniques, but there are many new applications and interpretations. In particular, applications of stable isotopes, trace elements, and archaeogenetics are making significant contributions to our understanding of the relationship between people and their environments. Increasingly, zooarchaeologists are pushing the boundaries of these studies, and some are developing the ability to conduct these studies on their own. This is an extremely promising trend, although we worry that it may tend to fragment once again the study of animal remains into specialized studies of single attributes of a deposit.

However, the fact that interesting results are produced when such data are combined warns us to avoid this fate. The integration of all types of archaeological and environmental evidence allows a more expansive study of human ecology. One of the most promising trends in zooarchaeology is the effort by many to bridge the barriers that separate zooarchaeology from other studies of the natural and social systems, and to break down the barriers that separate classes of data. These are mutually interacting systems, and we trust that the future of zooarchaeology is to focus on interactions between and among the various parts.

The topics reviewed in this volume, and many more, are all worthy of exploration. They require innovative approaches to solve them. Investigating them requires asking questions amenable to solutions; applying appropriate methods; developing strategies for integrating data; and replicating results through additional studies. The challenge is to gain a better understanding of human ecology within an environment that is continually changing, in part through the actions of humans. Our improved understanding of the nature of zooarchaeological material, human uses of animals, and the growing evidence for past environmental conditions has reached the point where worldwide coverage of this field is not possible in one book, or even several. As more methodological uniformity and greater theoretical development are achieved, we predict an enhanced global perspective will emerge. These will demonstrate that zooarchaeologists lead us to a better understanding of the human condition by asking not only what the finds are, but what they mean.

Appendix 1

Taxonomic List

Table A1.1. *Taxonomic list that includes all animals mentioned in the text*

Order	Family	Genus and species	Common name
PHYLUM CHORDATA: SUBPHYLUM VERTEBRATA			
Class Mammalia			
Marsupialia	Didelphidae	*Didelphis marsupialis*	common opossum
		Didelphis virginiana	Virginia opossum
	Phascolarctidae	*Phascolarctos cinereus*	koala
	Phalangeridae	*Phalanger orientalis*	cuscus
	Macropodidae	various	kangaroos
		Thylogale brunii	dusky pademelon
Insectivora	Soricidae	various	shrews
	Talpidae	various	moles
		Scalopus aquaticus	eastern mole
Chiroptera	various	various	bats
Primates	Cebidae	*Cebus* sp.	capuchin
	Cercopithecidae	*Papio* sp.	baboons
	Hominidae	*Homo sapiens*	humans
Xenarthra	Megalonychidae	various	giant ground sloth*
	Dasypodidae	*Dasypus novemcinctus*	nine-banded armadillo
Lagomorpha	Leporidae	*Lepus americanus*	snowshoe hare
		Oryctolagus cuniculus	domestic rabbit, European rabbit
		Sylvilagus spp.	rabbits
		Sylvilagus floridanus	cottontail rabbits
		Sylvilagus palustris	marsh rabbit
Rodentia (suborder Sciurognathi)	Sciuridae	*Marmota monax*	woodchuck

(cont.)

Table A1.1 *(cont.)*

Order	Family	Genus and species	Common name
		Sciurus carolinensis	gray squirrel
		Spermophilus spp.	ground squirrels
	Castoridae	*Castor canadensis*	beaver
	Geomyidae	*Geomys pinetus*	pocket gopher
	Heteromyidae	*Microdipodops* spp.	kangaroo mice
	Muridae (subfamily Arvicolinae)	tribe Microtini	microtine rodents
	Muridae (subfamily Murinae)	*Mus musculus*	house mouse
		Rattus exulans	Polynesian rat
		Rattus norvegicus	Norway rat
		Rattus praetor	New Guinea rat
		Rattus rattus	black rat
	Muridae (subfamily Sigmodontinae)	*Oryzomys* spp.	rice rats
Rodentia (suborder Hystricognathi)	Hystricidae	various	Old World porcupines
	Erethizontidae	various	New World porcupines
	Caviidae	*Cavia aperea*	wild guinea pig
		Cavia porcellus	domestic guinea pig
	Dasyproctidae	*Dasyprocta leporina*	agouti
		Dasyprocta punctata	agouti
	Agoutidae	*Agouti paca*	paca
	Capromyidae	*Isolobodon portoricensis*	hutia*
Cetacea (suborder Mysticeti)	various	various	baleen whales
Cetacea (suborder Odontoceti)	various	various	toothed whales
	Delphinidae	various	porpoises
	Monodontidae	*Monodon monocerus*	narwhal
Carnivora	Canidae	*Canis familiaris*	domestic dog, dingo
		Canis latrans	coyote
		Canis lupus	gray wolf
		Pseudalopex sechurae	South American fox
		Urocyon littoralis	Channel Island fox
	Ursidae	*Ailuropoda melanoleuca*	giant panda

Table A1.1 *(cont.)*

Order	Family	Genus and species	Common name
		Ursus americanus	American black bear
		Ursus spelaeus	cave bear*
	Procyonidae	*Procyon lotor*	raccoon
	Mustelidae	*Lontra canadensis*	otter
		Enhydra lutris	sea otter
		Mustela spp.	weasels
	Hyaenidae	*Crocuta crocuta*	spotted hyena
	Felidae	*Acinonyx jubatus*	cheetah
		Felis catus	domestic cat
		Puma concolor	cougar, panther, puma
		Felis silvestris	wild cat
		Leopardus pardalis	ocelot
		Panthera leo	lion
Pinnipedia	Odobenidae	*Odobenus rosmarus*	walrus
	Otariidae	*Zalophus californianus*	sea lion
	Phocidae	*Mirounga angustirostris*	northern elephant seal
Proboscidia	Elephantidae	*Elephas maximus*	Asiatic elephant
		Mammuthus primigenius	woolly mammoth*
	Mammutidae	*Mammut americanum*	mastodon*
Sirenia	Trichechidae	*Trichechus manatus*	manatee
Perissodactyla	Equidae	*Equus africanus*	African wild ass
		Equus asinus	domestic ass, donkey, burro
		Equus caballus	domestic horse
		Equus ferus	wild horse
Artiodactyla	Suidae	*Sus domesticus*	domestic pig
		Sus celebensis	Celebese wild boar
		Sus scrofa	wild boar
		Sus scrofa vittatus	Southeast Asian wild boar
	Tayassuidae	*Tayassu pecari*	white-lipped peccary
		Pecari tajacu	collared peccary
	Camelidae	*Camelus bactrianus*	domestic Bactrian camel, two-humped camel

(cont.)

Table A1.1 *(cont.)*

Order	Family	Genus and species	Common name
		Camelus dromedarius	domestic dromedary, one-humped camel
		Camelus ferus	wild camel
		Lama glama	llama
		Lama guanicoe	guanaco
		Vicugna pacos	alpaca
		Vicugna vicugna	vicuña
	Cervidae	*Alces alces*	elk, moose
		Capreolus spp.	roe deer
		Cervus elaphus	red deer, wapiti
		Elaphurus davidianus	Père David's deer
		Hippocamelus antisensis	huemal deer
		Mazama spp.	brocket deer
		Odocoileus hemionus	mule deer
		Odocoileus virginianus	white-tailed deer
		Rangifer tarandus	domestic reindeer, caribou
	Antilocapridae	*Antilocapra americana*	pronghorn
	Bovidae (subfamily Antilopinae)	*Gazella subgutturosa*	Persian gazelle
	Bovidae (subfamily Bovinae)	*Bison bison*	American bison
		Bos frontalis	mithan, gayal
		Bos gaurus	gaur
		Bos grunniens	yak
		Bos indicus	zebu cattle (syn. of *B. taurus*)
		Bos javanicus	banteng
		Bos nomadicus	Indian aurochs*
		Bos primigenius	aurochs (syn. of *B. taurus*)*
		Bos taurus	domestic cattle
		Bubalus arnee	wild Asian water buffalo
		Bubalus bubalis	domestic water buffalo
	Bovidae (subfamily Caprinae)	*Capra aegagrus*	bezoar goat
		Capra hircus	domestic goat
		Ovis aries	domestic sheep

Table A1.1 *(cont.)*

Order	Family	Genus and species	Common name
		Ovis canadensis	bighorn sheep
		Ovis orientalis	Asiatic mouflon (syn. of *O. aries*)
Class Aves			
Dinornithiformes	Dinornithidae	*Dinornis maximus*	great moa*
Aepyornithiformes	Aepyornithidae	*Aepyornis maximus*	elephant bird*
Galliformes	Odontophoridae	*Colinus virginianus*	bobwhite quail
	Phasianidae	*Gallus gallus*	domestic chicken, red jungle fowl
		Meleagris gallopavo	domestic turkey, wild northern turkey
		Meleagris ocellata	ocellated turkey
Anseriformes	Anatidae	*Anas platyrhynchos*	domestic duck, mallard
		Anser anser	domestic goose, graylag goose
		Cairina moschata	muscovy duck
Sphenisciformes	Spheniscidae	various	penguins
Procellariiformes	Diomedeidae	various	albatrosses, petrels
Phoenicopteriformes	Phoenicopteridae	*Phoenicopterus* sp.	flamingo
Ciconiiformes	Ardeidae	*Nycticorax nycticorax*	black-crowned night-heron
	Threskiornithidae	*Eudocimus albus*	white ibis
Pelecaniformes	Phalacrocoracidae	*Phalacrocorax* spp.	cormorant
	Sulidae	*Morus bassanus*	gannet
Falconiformes	Accipitridae	various	hawks
Gruiformes	Gruidae	various	cranes
	Rallidae	various	rails
Charadriiformes	Scolopacidae	*Gallinago gallinago*	common snipe
	Charadriidae	*Himantopus mexicanus*	black-necked stilt
	Burhinidae	*Burhinus bistriatus*	double-striped thick-knee
	Laridae	*Larus* spp.	gulls
		Sterna spp.	terns
		Sterna paradisaea	Arctic tern
	Alcidae	*Pinguinus impennis*	great auk*
Columbiformes	Columbidae	*Columba livia*	domestic pigeon, rock dove
	Raphidae	*Raphus cucullatus*	dodo*

(cont.)

Table A1.1   *(cont.)*

Order	Family	Genus and species	Common name
Psittaciformes	Psittacidae	*Ara macao*	scarlet macaw
Strigiformes	Tytonidae and Strigidae	various	owls
Apodiformes	Trochilidae	various	hummingbirds
Passeriformes	Corvidae	*Corvus ossifragus*	fish crow
	Turdidae	various	thrushes
	Sturnidae	*Sturnus vulgaris*	starling
	Icteridae	*Quiscalus quiscula*	common grackle
	Ploceidae	*Passer domesticus*	house sparrow
Class Reptilia			
Testudines	various	various	turtles
	Chelydridae	various	snapping turtles
		Chelydra serpentina	snapping turtle
	Cheloniidae	*Chelonia mydas*	green sea turtle
	Emydidae	*Malaclemys terrapin*	diamondback terrapin
		Terrapene carolina	eastern box turtle
	Testudinidae	*Gopherus agassizii*	desert tortoise
		Gopherus polyphemus	gopher tortoise
	Trionychidae	various	softshell turtles
Squamata (suborder Lacertilia)	Iguanidae	*Ctenosaura pectinata*	iguana
		Iguana spp.	iguanas
	Teiidae	*Dicrodon* sp.	dicrodon lizard
	Varanidae	*Varanus komodoensis*	Komodo dragon
Squamata (suborder Serpentes)	Boidae	*Python* spp.	pythons
	Viperidae	various	pit vipers
	Elapidae	*Naja nigricollis*	African spitting cobra
	Colubridae	various	colubrid snakes
Crocodylia	Alligatoridae	*Alligator mississippiensis*	alligator
	Crocodylidae	*Osteolaemus tetraspis*	broad-fronted crocodile
Class Amphibia			
Caudata	various	various	salamanders
Anura	Bufonidae	*Bufo* spp.	toads
	Ranidae	*Rana* spp.	frogs

Table A1.1 *(cont.)*

Order	Family	Genus and species	Common name
Class Chondrichthyes			
Lamniformes	Lamnidae	*Carcharodon carcharias*	white shark
Carcharhiniformes	Carcharhinidae	*Carcharhinus* sp.	requiem shark
		Galeocerdo cuvier	tiger shark
	Sphyrnidae	*Sphyrna* spp.	hammerhead sharks
Rajiformes	Myliobatidae	various	eagle rays
Class Actinopterygii			
Acipenseriformes	Acipenseridae	*Acipenser* sp.	sturgeon
Lepisosteiformes	Lepisosteidae	*Lepisosteus* spp.	gars
Amiiformes	Amiidae	*Amia calva*	bowfin
Elopiformes	Elopidae	*Elops saurus*	ladyfish
	Megalopidae	*Megalops atlanticus*	tarpon
Albuliformes	Albulidae	*Albula vulpes*	bonefish
Anguilliformes	Anguillidae	*Anguilla rostrata*	freshwater eel
Clupeiformes	Engraulidae	various	anchovies
	Clupeidae	various	herrings
Cypriniformes	Cyprinidae	*Carassius auratus*	goldfish
Characiformes	Characidae	*Serrasalmus* spp.	piranhas
Siluriformes	various	various	catfishes
	Ariidae	*Ariopsis felis*	hardhead catfish
		Bagre marinus	gafftopsail catfish
		Galeichthys peruvianus	sea catfish
Salmoniformes	Salmonidae	various	trout, salmon
Gadiformes	Gadidae	*Gadus morhua*	Atlantic cod
Lophiiformes	various	various	anglerfishes
Mugiliformes	Mugilidae	*Mugil* spp.	mullets
		Mugil cephalus	stripped mullet
Atheriniformes	Atherinopsidae	various	silversides
Cyprinodontiformes	Cyprinodontidae	various	killifishes
Perciformes	Centropomidae	*Centropomus* sp.	snook
	Moronidae	*Morone saxatilis*	striped bass
	Serranidae	various	sea basses
		Epinephelus sp.	grouper
		Centropristis sp.	sea bass
	Carangidae	various	jacks
	Lutjanidae	*Lutjanus* sp.	snapper
		Lutjanus griseus	gray snapper
	Sparidae	various	porgies
		Archosargus probatocephalus	sheepshead

(cont.)

Table A1.1 *(cont.)*

Order	Family	Genus and species	Common name
	Sciaenidae	various	drums
		Bairdiella chrysoura	silver perch
		Cynoscion spp.	seatrout
		Leiostomus xanthurus	spot
		Menticirrhus spp.	kingfishes
		Micropogonias undulatus	Atlantic croaker
		Pogonias cromis	black drum
		Sciaenops ocellatus	red drum
	Scaridae	*Sparisoma rubripinne*	yellowtail parrotfish
		Sparisoma viride	stoplight parrotfish
	Ephippidae	*Platax* sp.	spadefish
	Acanthuridae	various	surgeonfishes
	Sphyraenidae	various	barracudas
		Thyrsites atun	barracouta
	Scombridae	various	mackerels
Pleuronectiformes	Paralichthyidae	*Paralichthys* spp.	flounders
Tetraodontiformes	Balistidae	various	triggerfishes
	Ostrachiidae	various	boxfishes
	Diodontidae	various	porcupinefishes

PHYLUM ARTHROPODA: SUBPHYLUM UNIRAMIA
Class Insecta

Order	Family	Genus and species	Common name
Coleoptera	Dermestidae	various	carpet beetles
Hymenoptera	Apidae	*Apis mellifera*	honey bee
Diptera	Muscidae	*Stomoxys calcitrans*	stable fly
Lepidoptera	Saterniidae	*Bombyx mori*	silk moth
		Bombyx mandarina	wild silk moth

PHYLUM ARTHROPODA: SUBPHYLUM CRUSTACEA
Class Maxillopoda: subclass Cirripedia

Order	Family	Genus and species	Common name
Thoracica	Lepadidae	various	goose barnacles
	Balanidae	*Balanus* sp.	barnacle

Class Malacostraca: subclass Eumalacostraca

Order	Family	Genus and species	Common name
Decapoda	Penaeidae	*Penaeus* sp.	shrimp
	Nephropoidae	*Homerus americanus*	lobster
	Cambaridae	*Cambarus* spp.	crayfishes
	Coenobitidae	*Coenobita clypeatus*	land hermit crab
	Portunidae	*Callinectes* sp.	swimming crab, blue crab
	Xanthidae	*Menippe mercenaria*	Florida stone crab
	Gecarcinidae	various	land crabs

Table A1.1 *(cont.)*

Order	Family	Genus and species	Common name
PHYLUM MOLLUSCA			
Class Polyplacophora			
Neoloricata	Chitonidae	*Acanthopleura granulata*	West Indian fuzzy chiton
Class Bivalvia			
Mytiloida	Mytilidae	*Ischadium recurvum*	hooked mussel
Arcoida	Arcidae	various	ark
Ostreoida	Pectinidae	various	scallops
	Spondylidae	*Spondylus calcifer*	Pacific thorny-oyster
	Ostreidae	*Crassostrea rhizophorae*	Caribbean oyster
		Crassostrea virginica	eastern oyster
Veneroida	Cardiidae	*Trachycardium procerum*	cockle
	Mactridae	*Rangia cuneata*	Atlantic rangia
		Spisula solidissima	Atlantic surfclam
	Donacidae	*Donax denticulatus*	coquina
	Solecurtidae	*Tagelus plebeius*	stout tagelus
	Arcticidae	*Arctica islandica*	ocean quahog
	Veneridae	*Mercenaria campechiensis*	southern quahog
		Mercenaria mercenaria	hard clam, northern quahog
		Meretrix lamarkii	Japanese clam
		Meretrix lucoria	Japanese clam
Class Scaphopoda	various	various	tuskshells
Class Gastropoda			
Archaeogastropoda	Fissurellidae	various	limpets
	Trochidae	*Cittarium pica*	West Indian topsnail
	Neritidae	various	nerites
Mesogastropoda	Littorinidae	*Littorina irrorata*	marsh periwinkle
	Calyptraeidae	*Crepidula* sp.	slippersnail
	Naticidae	*Neverita duplicata*	shark eye
		Polinices sp.	moonsnail
Neogastropoda	Muricidae	various	murex
	Melonginidae	*Busycon carica*	knobbed whelk
		Busycon sinistrum	lightning whelk
	Buccinidae	various	conches, whelks
	Nassariidae	*Nassarius obsoletus*	eastern mudsnail
Heterostropha	Pyramidellidae	*Boonia impressa*	impressed odostome
Stylomatophora	Polygyridae	*Polygyra* sp.	liptooth, land snail

(cont.)

Table A1.1 *(cont.)*

Order	Family	Genus and species	Common name
Class Cephalopoda	various	various	squid, octopus, cuttlefish
PHYLUM ECHINODERMATA			
Class Asteroidea			
Forcipulatida	Asteriidae	*Pisaster ochraceus*	ochre starfish
Class Echinoidea			
Superorder Echinacea	Echinidae	*Tripneustes ventricosus*	sea egg

Note: Organization generally follows Brusca and Brusca (1990), Clutton-Brock (2002), Dickinson (2003), Nelson et al. (2004), Pough et al. (2004), Turgeon et al. (1998), and Williams (1989). For an alternative organization of mammals, see McKenna and Bell (1997).
*Indicates animals that are extinct.

Appendix 2

Anatomical Drawings

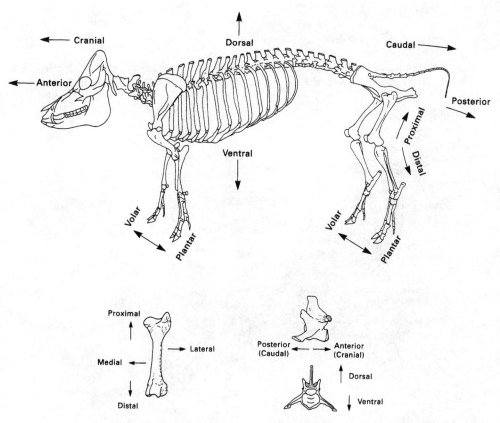

FIGURE A2.1. Directional terms for vertebrates using a pig (*Sus domesticus*). Modified from Davis (1987:54). Used with the kind permission of Simon J. M. Davis. Drawn by Evelyn Davis.

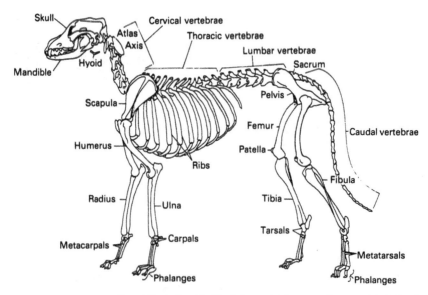

FIGURE A2.2. Dog (*Canis familiaris*) skeleton with some elements labeled. Modified from Davis (1987:54). Used with the kind permission of Simon J. M. Davis. Drawn by Evelyn Davis.

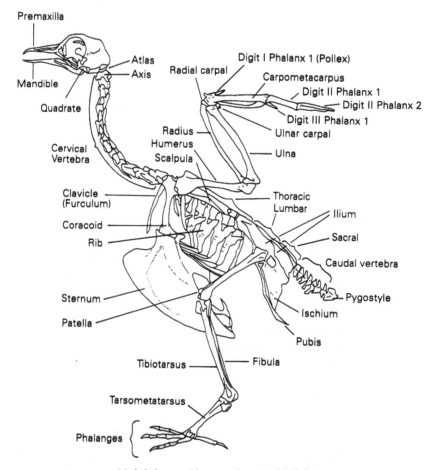

FIGURE A2.3. Bird skeleton with some elements labeled.

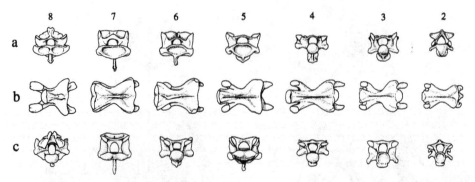

FIGURE A2.4. The cervical vertebrae of the snapping turtle (*Chelydra serpentina*): (a) anterior view; (b) ventral view; and (c) posterior view. Numbers refer to the position along the column; that is, 2 is the second cervical and 8 is the last cervical. Illustration modified from Hoffstetter and Gasc (1969:216).

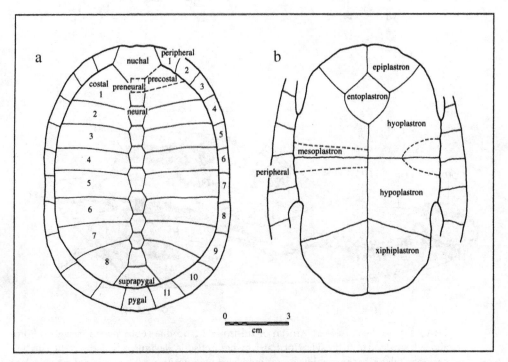

FIGURE A2.5. Turtle (a) carapace and (b) plastron with some elements labeled. Illustration modified from Zangerl (1969:320).

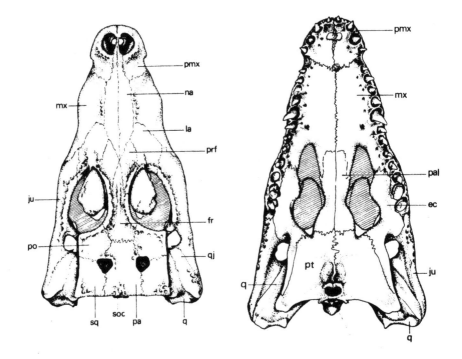

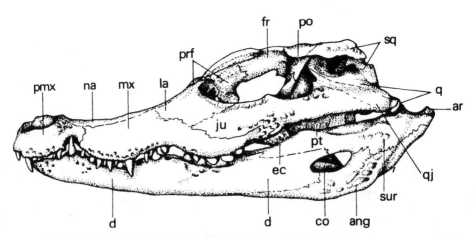

FIGURE A2.6. Skull of West African broad-fronted crocodile (*Osteolaemus tetraspis*), from above, below, and from the side. Not drawn to the same scale. Key: **ang**, angular; **ar**, articular; **bo**, basioccipital; **bs**, basisphenoid; **co**, coronoid; **com**, composite bone consisting of prearticular, articular, etc., fused; **con**, occipital condyle; **d**, dentary; **ec**, ectopterygoid (transpalatine); **ep**, epipterygoid (columella cranii); **ex**, exoccipital; **fa**, fang; **fm**, foramen magnum; **fr**, frontal; **ju**, jugal; **la**, lacrimal; **mx**, maxilla; **na**, nasal; **op**, opisthotic; **pa**, parietal; **pal**, palatine; **palt**, palatine teeth; **pmx**, premaxilla; **po**, postorbital; **pop**, paraoccipital process; **prf**, prefrontal; **pro**, prootic; **ps**, parasphenoid; **pt**, pterygoid; **ptf**, postfrontal; **ptt**, pterygoid teeth; **q**, quadrate; **qj**, quadratojugal; **smx**, septomaxilla; **soc**, supraoccipital; **sp**, splenial; **sq**, squamosal; **sta**, stapes (columella auris); **su**, supratemporal; **sur**, surangular; and **vo**, vomer (prevomer). Modified from Bellairs (1970:149).

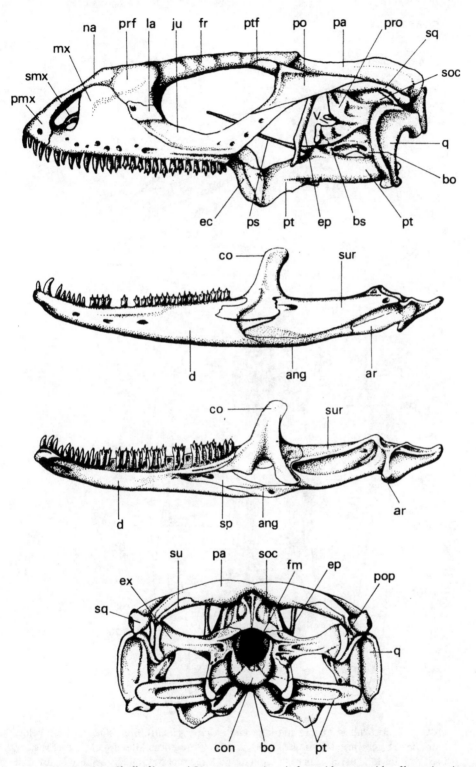

FIGURE A2.7. Skull of iguana (*Ctenosaura pectinata*), from side; outer side of lower jaw; inner side of lower jaw; from behind (in order from top to bottom). From Oelrich (1956: figures 5, 6, 28, 29); see also Bellairs (1970:134). Used with the kind permission of the University of Michigan Museum of Zoology. See Figure A2.6 for the key.

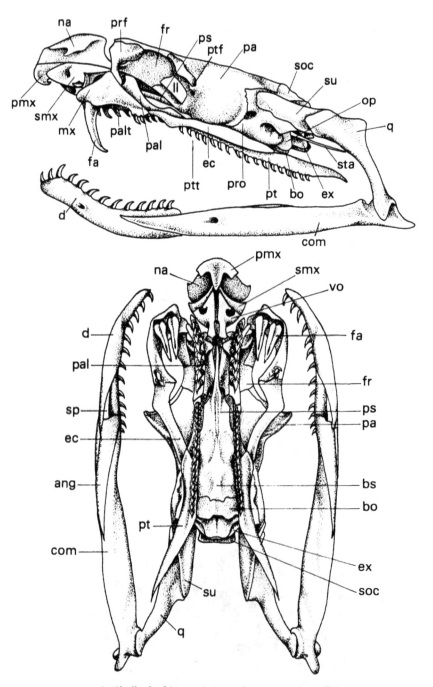

FIGURE A2.8. Skull of African spitting cobra (*Naja nigricollis*), from side and from below. From Bogert (1943:305); see also Bellairs (1970:160); © American Museum of Natural History. Used with the kind permission of the American Museum of Natural History. See Figure A2.6 for the key.

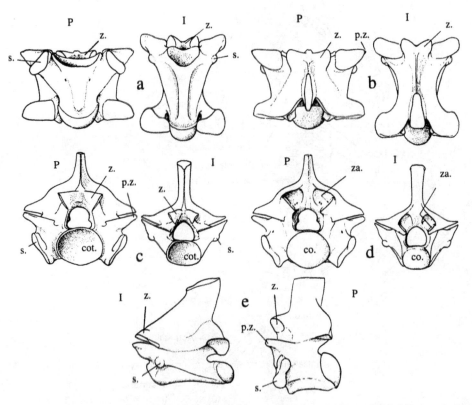

FIGURE A2.9. Python (P; *Python* sp.) and iguana (I; *Iguana* sp.) vertebrae: (a) ventral view; (b) dorsal view; (c) anterior view; (d) posterior view; (e) left lateral view. Key: **co.**, condyle; **cot.**, cotyle; **p.z.**, prezygapophysial process; **s**, synapophysis; **z.**, zygosphene; and **za.**, zygantrum. Illustration modified from Hoffstetter and Gasc (1969:250).

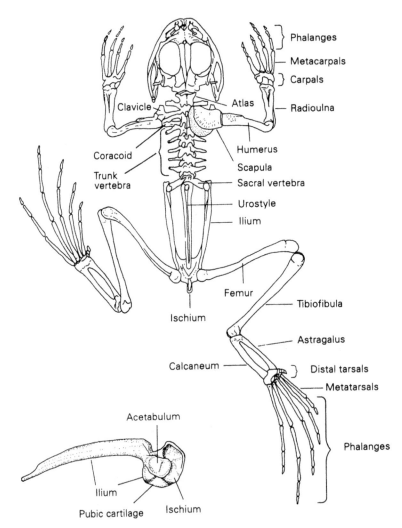

FIGURE A2.10. Frog (Ranidae) skeleton with some elements labeled. Illustration modified from Walker (1987:243). From *Functional anatomy of the vertebrates: An evolutionary perspective* (3rd ed.) by Liem et al. (2001). Reprinted with permission of Brooks/Cole, a division of Thomson Learning.

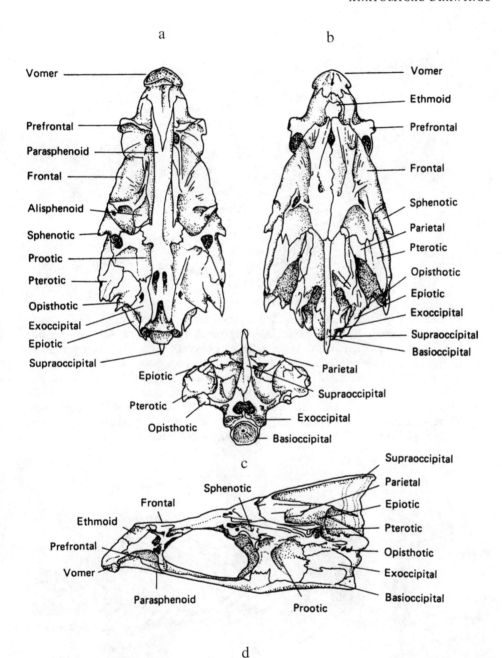

FIGURE A2.11. The cranium of a striped bass (*Morone* [=*Roccus*] *saxatilis*) with some elements labeled. Views are (a) ventral, (b) dorsal, (c) posterior, and (d) left lateral. Reproduced from Cannon (1987:17). Used with the kind permission of A. Cannon and Archaeology Press, Simon Fraser University.

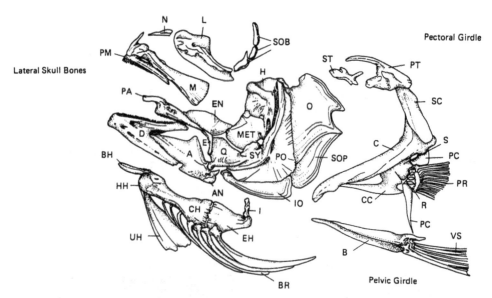

FIGURE A2.12. Lateral facial elements and appendicular skeleton of a striped bass (*Morone* [=*Roccus*] *saxatilis*). Key: **A**, articular; **AN**, angular; **B**, basipterigium; **BH**, basihyal; **BR**, branchiostegals; **C**, cleithrum; **CC**, coracoid; **CH**, ceratohyal; **D**, dentary; **E**, ectopterygoid; **EH**, epihyal; **EN**, entopterygoid; **H**, hyomandibular; **HH**, hypohyal; **I**, interhyal; **IO**, interopercular; **L**, lachrymal; **M**, maxilla; **MET**, metapterygoid; **N**, nasal; **O**, opercular; **PA**, palatine; **PC**, postcleithrum; **PM**, premaxilla; **PO**, preopercular; **PR**, pectoral fin; **PT**, posttemporal; **Q**, quadrate; **R**, radial; **S**, scapula; **SC**, supracleithrum; **SOB**, suborbital; **SOP**, subopercular; **ST**, supratemporal; **SY**, symplectic; **UH**, urohyal; **VS**, ventral fin. Reproduced from Cannon (1987:18–19). Used with the kind permission of A. Cannon and Archaeology Press, Simon Fraser University.

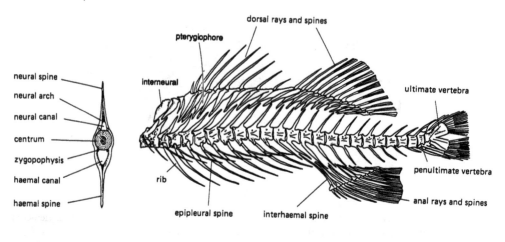

FIGURE A2.13. The axial skeleton of a striped bass (*Morone* [=*Roccus*] *saxatilis*). Reproduced from Cannon (1987:21). Used with the kind permission of A. Cannon and Archaeology Press, Simon Fraser University.

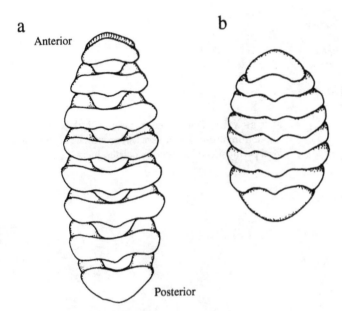

FIGURE A2.14. A West Indian fuzzy chiton (*Acanthopleura granulata*) (a) with its plates expanded so that the shape of each is visible and (b) as it is in life. Drawn by Virginia Carter Steadman.

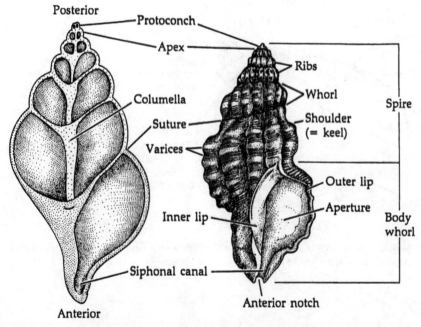

FIGURE A2.15. Internal and external features of a spiral gastropod shell (Gastropoda). Reproduced from Brusca and Brusca (1990:717G). Used with the kind permission of Sinauer Associates, Inc.

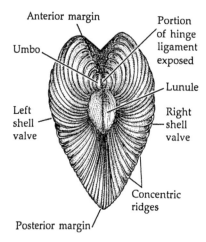

FIGURE A2.16. Dorsal view of a clam (Bivalvia). Reproduced from Brusca and Brusca (1990:717L). Used with the kind permission of Sinauer Associates, Inc.

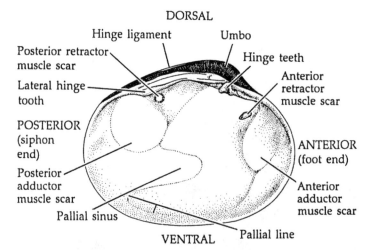

FIGURE A2.17. Inside view of the left valve of a clam (Bivalvia). Reproduced from Brusca and Brusca (1990:717K). Used with the kind permission of Sinauer Associates, Inc.

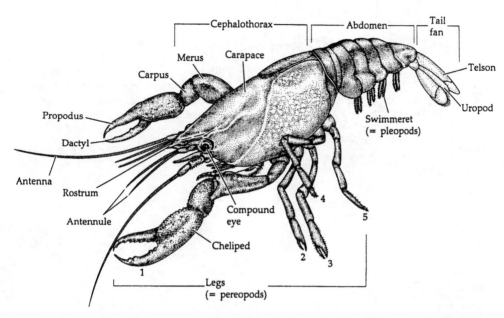

FIGURE A2.18. Crustacean external morphology of a crayfish (class Malacostraca, infraorder Astacidae). Reproduced from Brusca and Brusca (1990:601A). Used with the kind permission of Sinauer Associates, Inc.

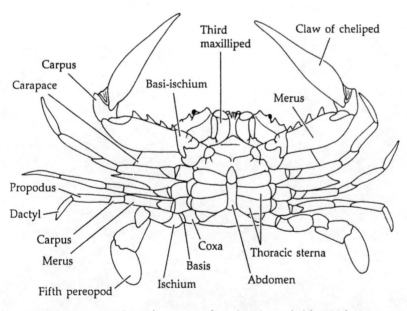

FIGURE A2.19. General anatomy of a swimming crab (class Malacostraca, order Decapoda, Portunidae), ventral view. Reproduced from Brusca and Brusca (1990:623B). Used with the kind permission of Sinauer Associates, Inc.

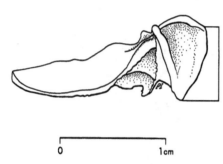

MH

FIGURE A2.20. Left mandible of a land crab (Gecarcinidae), interior view; MH is mandible height. Drawn by Paloma Ibarra. Used with the kind permission of Susan D. deFrance.

0   1cm

Appendix 3

Reference Collections, Management of Archaeofaunal Collections, Publication, and Curation

INTRODUCTION

Many aspects of zooarchaeology are associated with establishing a reference collection and with professional responsibilities regarding animal remains and data. Although the following comments are placed in an appendix, this does not mean they are minor aspects of zooarchaeology. Errors in handling animal remains create many of the second-order changes discussed in Chapter 5. These are avoidable biases, and steps should be taken to limit their occurrence. Many of the procedures associated with primary (Chapter 6) and secondary (Chapter 7) data are controversial and subsequent publications may not provide the details necessary for reanalysis. To clarify biases or resolve differences in interpretation, it may be necessary to review the original notes as well as both the studied and the unstudied portions of archaeofaunal assemblages.

An important development in archaeology is the growing awareness of the fragility of archaeological sites. No one should undertake excavation without a commitment to studying and curating all of the materials encountered. Excavation is destructive regardless of whether it is motivated by personal pleasure, economic profit, or a better understanding of the past. Although many of the following considerations are based largely on professional and ethical treatment of our natural and cultural heritage, increasingly they are governed by legal requirements as well. Most countries have laws governing the excavation of antiquities as well as their removal from the country of origin and importation into a second country. Within a country, many levels of administrative responsibility may exist. Clearly, both the letter and the spirit of rules, regulations, and laws pertaining to antiquities should be obeyed. Local, state, and national authorities, as well as appropriate educational institutions, should receive copies of reports and publications.

For these reasons, care of both reference and archaeofaunal collections is a major concern to zooarchaeologists. Responsible zooarchaeology includes: (1) care of reference collections, (2) management of archaeofaunal collections during study, (3) disseminating the results, and (4) long-term curation. These concerns should be anticipated by all researchers, and procedures for addressing these topics must be established before excavation begins.

REFERENCE COLLECTIONS

All zooarchaeological research is based ultimately on studies of contemporary animals. Therefore, access to a good reference collection is vital (Chaplin 1965; Driver 1992; Parmalee 1985; Rea 1986; Reed 1963). Identification and subsequent analysis is only as good as the reference collection. Use of actual skeletal elements permits direct comparison of archaeological remains with modern specimens of known identity from all angles, which is critical for an accurate attribution. Although attribution is assisted by keys and illustrated aids (e.g., Barone 1976; Cornwall 1956; Courtemanche and Legendre 1985; Desse and Desse-Berset 1987–1996; Getty 1975; Gilbert 1980; Gilbert et al. 1981; Gregory 1933; Helmer and Rocheteau 1994; Holman 1995; Koch 1973; Lawrence 1951; Libois and Hallet-Libois 1988; Libois et al. 1987; Lowe 1967; Miller 1968; Olsen 1964, 1968, 1972; Roselló 1986; Schmid 1972; Smuts and Bezuidenhout 1987; Sobolik and Steele 1996; Sternberg 1992; Walker 1985), these are not substitutes for a large reference collection. The reference collection constitutes the voucher for all identifications and should be referenced in reports and publications, just as the level of magnification used to examine incremental structures is noted.

The reference collection must be more extensive than one skeleton each of the most common extant animals in the study region. It should contain a series of skeletons for each animal endemic to the archaeological site, as well as for species that are not part of the modern fauna (Rea 1986). The reference collection should have multiple specimens of relevant species, reflecting size, sex, age, geographical, seasonal, and individual variations within and among taxa. It should include animals that may be present in the archaeological collection due to taphonomic processes, exchange, domestication, or range extensions. If some of the necessary specimens are unavailable, museums will usually arrange loans between institutions for a specified period of time. Archaeological specimens should not be used as reference materials unless no modern reference specimens are available.

Older museum reference collections are valuable resources, within limits. Traditionally, postcranial vertebrate skeletons were not saved. Usually, mammalogy collections hold primarily skins and skulls; ornithology collections consist of skins and, sometimes, skull, wing, and leg elements; and many herpetology and ichthyology specimens are preserved in alcohol. Most mollusc reference collections contain valves that retain their distinctive colors, whereas the archaeological materials are often devoid of color. However, most of these traditional reference collections do have good specimen-related information that is valuable for zooarchaeological research even if they do not have complete skeletons.

It may be necessary to develop a new reference collection (Chaplin 1971:41–8; 50–4; Davis and Payne 2003; Parmalee 1985). A reference collection is a rare and valuable tool that is not assembled indiscriminately or casually. The process of collecting, identifying, and preparing reference specimens is time-consuming and costly. Further, animal populations are threatened by habitat changes, pollution, and overexploitation. Scientists should collect only what is legal, ethical, and necessary, ensuring that no animal is wasted through careless handling. It is often possible to obtain specimens from other research projects so that it is not necessary to kill animals for the purpose of developing a reference collection. Regulations concerning transportation of animals or their parts across political jurisdictions must be considered. Usually, permits are required even to scavenge animal carcasses. To make wise use of stressed animal populations, arrangements should be made to place reference specimens and their associated data in a public repository even if prevailing laws do not require this. Care should be taken in handling carcasses to avoid infection with pathogens, such as rabies or those associated with decay (Doetschman 1947; Henry 1991; Irvinn et al. 1972; Schnurrenberger and Hubbert 1981). Preparing skeletal specimens is one of the best ways to become familiar with the functional morphology of different organisms.

Certain biological data should be recorded for each specimen. The identification must be accurate and accompanied by data on location, sex, reproductive condition, age, date of death, date of collection, name of collector, total weight, and visceral weight. Standard measurements should be recorded for all reference materials, although there is enough variation among "standard" measurements that these dimensions should always be defined (Figures A3.1–A3.4). Some of these measurements are not commonly used by biologists or veterinarians, but they are useful for archaeological applications. Sometimes soft tissues are preserved for future studies. For example, the reproductive tract may be saved to assess reproductive status or stomach contents to document food selection and parasite load. Each reference specimen should be assigned a unique number and the associated data should be recorded in a catalogue so that relevant data are associated with a specific specimen. The identity of the specimen must be maintained throughout this process by means of a tracking system. Embossed plastic labels with the processing number are indestructible during most methods of preparation and ensure that the specimen's association with its data is maintained.

Specimens are prepared in a number of ways (e.g., Anderson 1965; Bolin 1935; Colley and Spennemann 1987; Coy 1978; Davis and Payne 2003; de Wet et al. 1990; Grayson and Maser 1978; Hill 1975; Jannett and Davies 1989; Mori 1970; Parmalee 1985; Schmid 1972:26–7; Sommer and Anderson 1974; Wheeler and Jones 1989:177–85). Procedures must be developed for the specific climatic, social, and legal conditions encountered. Some experimentation will be necessary to determine what works best in a particular setting.

As a preliminary step, the skin, viscera, and major muscle masses are removed. Very large carcasses may be buried after preliminary defleshing and later exhumed; the length

Standard Measurements in Birds

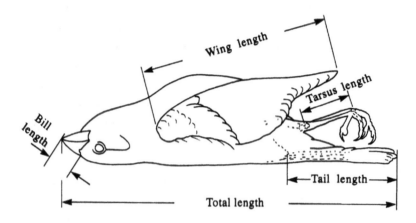

Standard Measurements in Mammals

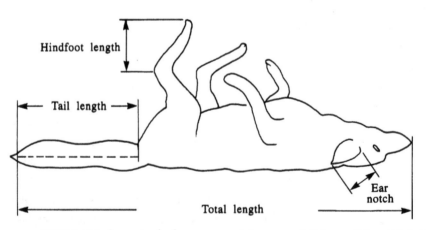

FIGURE A3.1. Some standard measurements in mammals (Mammalia) and birds (Aves).

of time required depends on the climate of the specific location and the condition of the carcass. Maceration in water makes use of bacterial action to remove soft tissue. Adding detergents that contain enzymes will enhance this process. Frequently changing the water will reduce the odor. Cooking, sometimes with a final cleaning by macerating, results in good specimens but requires more attention. Cooking at high temperatures or for a prolonged time will damage the elements. The third common way of preparing specimens is to allow carpet beetle larvae (Dermestidae) to consume the soft tissue. Dermestids reproduce only in warm temperatures with high humidity. Fleshed carcasses must be dried to leather hard before they are given to the dermestids, otherwise fly maggots will be problems. Once the specimen is cleaned by dermestids, it may still need

Standard Measurements in Turtles

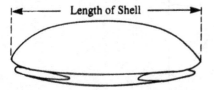

Length of Shell

Straight-line distance

Standard Measurements in Lizards

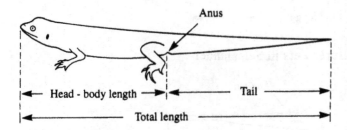

Anus

Head - body length   Tail

Total length

Standard Measurements in Snakes

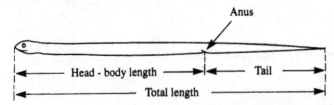

Anus

Head - body length   Tail

Total length

FIGURE A3.2. Some standard measurements in turtles (Testudines), lizards (Lacertilia), and snakes (Serpentes).

to be macerated or rinsed. Tight control over the dermestid colony must be maintained because they eat museum study skins and other organic material such as book paper and leather bindings, feathers, fur, wool, suede, and other fabrics. Molluscs are prepared by removing the soft tissue and cleaning and drying the shell. Soft tissue is removed from gastropods by heating the gastropods for a moment in a microwave oven. Crabs may simply be dried in an oven or in the sun. (Remember to clean the oven afterward.)

Once the reference specimen is clean, it should be curated. The inventory number associating the specimen with its data in the catalogue should be written on every element with indelible ink. The specimens should be stored in a sturdy, labeled container and arranged in some logical order. Some laboratories maintain reference specimens in taxonomic order. Others maintain reference materials as anatomical or synoptic collections in which like elements are stored together regardless of taxonomic affinity (e.g., all fish articulars are stored together). The primary goal should be to maintain the

Standard Measurements in Fish

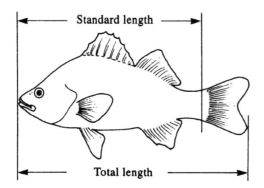

Standard Measurements in Salamander

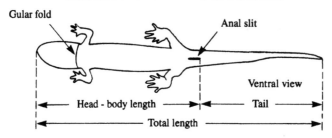

Standard Measurements in Toads and Frogs

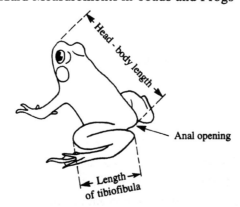

FIGURE A3.3. Some standard measurements in salamanders (Caudata), toads and frogs (Anura), and fish (Actinopterygii).

integrity of the specimens and to minimize the risk of poor handling and poor storage conditions.

Great care should be used when handling reference specimens. Reference materials should not be inadvertently mixed by having many species out at one time. If elements are not numbered (which may be the case if the element is too small to number legibly),

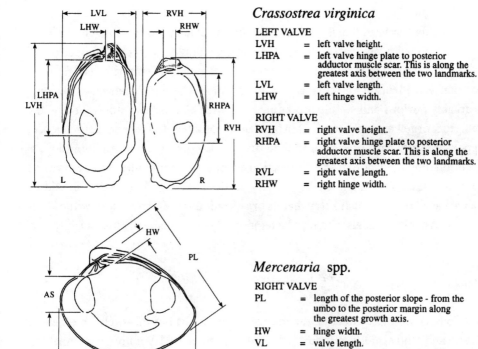

Crassostrea virginica

LEFT VALVE

LVH	=	left valve height.
LHPA	=	left valve hinge plate to posterior adductor muscle scar. This is along the greatest axis between the two landmarks.
LVL	=	left valve length.
LHW	=	left hinge width.

RIGHT VALVE

RVH	=	right valve height.
RHPA	=	right valve hinge plate to posterior adductor muscle scar. This is along the greatest axis between the two landmarks.
RVL	=	right valve length.
RHW	=	right hinge width.

Mercenaria spp.

RIGHT VALVE

PL	=	length of the posterior slope - from the umbo to the posterior margin along the greatest growth axis.
HW	=	hinge width.
VL	=	valve length.
AS	=	anterior adductor muscle scar. This is taken from the greatest growth axis.

Busycon carica

SH	=	shell height.
AL	=	apex to lip.
HS	=	height of spire.
AH	=	aperture height.
AW	=	aperture width.

FIGURE A3.4. Some standard measurements for eastern oysters (*Crassostrea virginica*), hard clams (*Mercenaria* spp.), and knobbed whelk (*Busycon carica*). Used with the kind permission of Irvy R. Quitmyer.

extra care should be exercised. Although vertebrate and mollusc hard tissues appear to be indestructible, rough handling and poor storage environments will damage them. Many reference specimens have spiral fractures because they were damaged by people who were in a hurry.

MANAGEMENT OF ARCHAEOFAUNAL COLLECTIONS DURING STUDY

Management of archaeofaunal collections begins in the field and continues in the laboratory. Personnel involved at all stages of the process should give thoughtful, early, and constant consideration to collection management. Many problems arise as a result of poor management of animal remains during excavation. These could be avoided by some remarkably obvious and simple procedures. We write this section, not to belittle the intelligence of archaeological crews, but because we routinely deal with the consequences of poor, probably hasty, decisions in these areas. The urgency of these admonitions is underscored by the fact that these collections, curated in perpetuity, will be revisited by future researchers long after the primary parties are gone. A collection should be arranged at all times in such a way that its organization is self-explanatory without the need to consult individuals who may be temporarily or permanently unavailable.

In the Field and Archaeological Laboratory

Some zooarchaeologists excavate the materials they study; but most rely on others to excavate and send samples to them. Field and archaeological laboratory personnel can help the zooarchaeologist in several ways. Although these may seem obvious to some readers, in our experience, they are not obvious to many, especially as people hasten to leave the field at the end of a long, difficult season. These steps should begin with the first sample bag so that the procedures are habitual by the time the last bags flood in from the field at the end of the season. Faunal remains should be given at least the same care as lithics and ceramics (Chaplin 1965, 1971:24; Daly 1969; Lawrence 1973; Rea 1986; Schmid 1972:2, 18). Field personnel should never decide what is identifiable and what is not (Lawrence 1973); all faunal remains should be sent for study in a well-lit laboratory with a reference collection.

Animal remains are fragile, and they break even when handled gently. They should be carefully cleaned and dried; if they are from a damp context, they should remain damp until conserved. The condition of excavated faunal remains should be carefully monitored, and they should never be exposed to quick or extreme changes, such as drying wet bone under high heat and light or exposing dry bone to water. Many of the spiral fractures attributed to marrow extraction are actually the result of "weathering" processes that occur after excavation.

Specimens should be placed in sturdy containers that are firmly sealed and labeled with an indelible pen (Rea 1986). Computer-generated labels should be checked for durability; many are not waterproof. Labels should also be placed inside the container. When the outside of a plastic bag becomes damp, labels made with "permanent" magic markers smudge and the interior label is the only way to identify the bag. If the materials are not dried before the container is sealed, mold will render the interior label illegible. When both "accidents" happen, as they do more times than seems credible, the provenience information for the sample is almost always irretrievable. If boxes are used, they should be taped closed even if the lid appears to fit tightly.

Each container should be numbered sequentially and a packing list with these numbers should be kept with the materials at all times; but especially when the materials are transferred to the zooarchaeologist. These numbers have a variety of names, such as inventory number, catalogue number, field number, lot number, sample number, accession number, and bag number. By whatever name, these numbers are important organizing tools. Some researchers assign multiple numbers with various meanings to artifacts; each such number increases the likelihood that errors and misunderstandings will occur. All specialists who will work with the samples would appreciate a single, simple, nonrepeated, sequential reference number that is used by everyone and is unambiguously linked to excavation context.

Usually faunal remains are transferred from the field to another location. The distance may be very short, but sometimes the materials will be shipped several times over long distances. Such moves, however, are essential for proper study. Rough handling during shipping damages biological remains. Shipping containers should not weigh more than a normal individual can carry comfortably. Specimens on the bottom of the box bear the weight of the ones on top. It should not be assumed that labels such as "This end up" or "Fragile" serve any purpose at all; often they appear to designate the shipping container as a special target for mishandling. Boxes receive a great deal of rough handling; well-padded samples should be sent in well-taped, sturdy boxes. Aluminum foil is not padding and, however appropriate it may be for radiometric dating such as carbon 14 dating, it should not be used for botanical or faunal specimens that will not be dated. If it is anticipated that these supplies will be difficult to acquire in the field, they should be taken into the field along with other necessary materials.

Records for the site should be sent with the samples. A list of the proveniences; their catalogue, accession, or field number; and a summary of the artifacts found in each context should be sent with the faunal materials. Site maps showing where the site is and the site's relationship to physiographic features, such as lakes and mountains, are essential. Records should include maps of the excavated areas and profile records. Zooarchaeologists do not care if these preliminary records have coffee stains on them; much of what we would like to accomplish cannot be done without maps, no matter how dirty. Field methods should be described in detail, especially screen-size and other recovery methods. This includes: (1) whether arbitrary (metric) or natural levels were used or a combination of the two; (2) definitions for zones, features, areas, and so forth; and (3) whether the depths were measured below surface or below datum. Volumetric information for the excavated units is important. This includes the volume of the site sampled, the volume of each level and the volume of the other contexts sampled.

Although the analyst should endeavor to become familiar with the excavation and recording technique used (and should consult with the field personnel whenever there is a doubt), field personnel can help by ensuring that records, such as maps and catalogues, are self-explanatory. A copy of the grant proposal or a preliminary field report will help the zooarchaeologist understand the site and the research objectives. The names and addresses of the archaeobotanist, soil scientist, and biological anthropologist should be provided. Obtaining this information is just one of many reasons zooarchaeologists should be involved in the planning and excavation stages.

Sometimes worked specimens are removed from samples sent to the zooarchaeological laboratory. This limits exploration of the full range of human uses of animals and hampers the study of modifications and element distributions. Arrangements should be made for the zooarchaeologist to examine tools and ornaments so these can be integrated into the faunal study. With the end-product of the production sequence in hand, the zooarchaeologist may see evidence of on-site manufacturing that would not be recognized if the final product were unknown to the zooarchaeologist (e.g., Wing 1972). This also provides an opportunity to diplomatically remove, from the "worked" category, specimens that appear worked to the untrained eye, but that actually are not (see Miller 1975 and Figure 2.3).

It is increasingly common that animal remains will be subjected to molecular and isotopic tests. Although most archaeologists anticipate the need for radiometric dating, they are less careful about handling specimens they do not expect to date. In anticipation of elemental, genetic, and similar studies, they should plan to collect animal remains and tools without touching them (White and Folkens 2005:345–7). This would include having disposable latex gloves, hair nets, masks, as well as sterile metal tools and clean containers available in order to avoid adding their own DNA and modern environmental chemicals to ancient samples. An associated soil sample should be collected at the same time and with the same care.

In the Zooarchaeology Laboratory

Remains from different archaeological contexts should never be mixed. One of the primary goals of field work is to find artifacts in situ (e.g., Roskams 2001). This means that artifacts are removed from the site in such a way that their relationship with each other, as well as with the strata in which they are found, is maintained. Materials from different temporal, spatial, and behavioral contexts must be kept separate. In the field, the significance of a slight change in soil often is unclear, and the field crew should segregate artifacts into separate samples whenever they are unsure about contextual relationships. This conservative field procedure produces a large number of very small samples that must not be mixed during subsequent handling without the explicit authorization and instruction of the project director.

At one time, it was common for animal remains to be separated into subgroups along phylogenetic lines (Parmalee 1985). An avian paleontologist would receive the bird specimens; a herpetologist the reptile and amphibian specimens; a malacologist the molluscs, and so forth. This approach is now much less common. Every effort should be made to see the relationship between humans and other animals as a living system rather than a phylogenetic tree. Only when faunal assemblages are evaluated as a whole can data be integrated and a unified pattern of environmental and cultural processes be considered. However, it is not possible to be equally skilled in identifying all classes of animals, and it is important to consult people with expertise in particularly difficult attributions whenever necessary. Ecologists and statisticians should also be consulted.

Zooarchaeologists should begin their work by establishing procedures to keep samples physically separate. Numbering specimens is a common way to do this, but it is not prudent to rely on this procedure. Numbering specimens in the 3 mm fraction may be impractical and is impossible for specimens in the 1.5 mm fraction. If the specimens are not numbered, it is important to work with only one sample at a time. For some procedures, it is necessary to have materials from more than one sample on the lab bench at the same time. In these cases, the specimens should be numbered if at all possible. If colored paint is used, the code for the color scheme should be kept with the materials at all times. Gummed colored dots are not acceptable substitutes except as the most temporary marker. Ink, paint, and gums are all contaminants and should be used only if deemed absolutely essential to the work or required by the curation facility. Because they are contaminants, it may be possible to convince the curation facility to waive this requirement.

Study involves curation (Chaplin 1965; Rea 1986). As the specimens are sorted, they should be placed into vials, bags, or boxes depending on arrangements for final curation. Each of these containers should be labeled with the sample's provenience information. By the end of the study, these labels also will contain the attribution for the taxon whose remains are contained therein and whatever additional information the curating facility requires. Table A3.1 lists the information routinely included on labels curated in our laboratories. The curating facility may stipulate the type of container and the information that should be on the label. Groups of containers from a single sample should be segregated from similar groups of containers in other samples. Under no circumstances should studied materials be discarded or returned to a common container as was once advocated (e.g., compare Reed [1963] to White [1956]). Invariably archaeological samples contain nonfaunal objects, as well as some mystery items. Arrangements should be made to reunite these with other nonfaunal materials.

Most specimens are fragments of elements and in some cases these crossmend. In general, it is preferable not to re-glue these fragments. Doing so creates a weak joint that will probably break again, causing further damage. Glue is a contaminant that precludes some future studies. Some research questions, however, require reassembly

Table A3.1. *Curatorial information and primary data included on labels and data cards*

Labels
Site name
Site number
Provenience and level
Field sample number (accession number, lot number, etc.)
Catalogue number from the data card
Taxonomic attribution from the data card

Data cards
Taxon
Site number
Accession number
Serial number
Site name
Provenience and level
Field sample number (or accession number, lot number, etc.)
Screen size
Number of specimens (not necessary for indeterminate vertebrate or invertebrate)
Element represented
Symmetry (left, right, axial, indeterminate)
Portion (proximal, distal, shaft)
Modifications (weathered, carnivore-gnawed, rodent-gnawed, burned, hacked, cut, sawed, worked, pathologies, etc.)
Degree of fusion (diaphysis/epiphysis is used only for unfused specimens)
Deciduous/permanent dentition
Tooth wear (see Payne 1973)
Other evidence of age (this will primarily be condition of deciduous P_4)
Sex
Measurements, in mm, may be recorded on a separate form (see Driesch 1976)
Other notes
Weight, in g
Estimate of Minimum Number of Individuals (MNI)
For mammals, prepare the element drawings. This will be primarily for taxa identified below Artiodactyla, but others also may require this step. The element drawings should have the catalogue number, fusion, and side noted beside each specimen drawn so it can be correlated with the data cards.

of specimens; in these cases, the type of glue used should be recorded on the specimen tag so that future conservators will know which chemicals were used.

The materials may require conservation treatments. This is particularly the case for specimens recovered from wet sites, but specimens from other settings sometimes require stabilization as well. Many products are available; the choice of which one to use will depend on the type of tissue involved and its condition. Bone, shell, enamel, and ivory all have different conservation requirements; as do wet, leached, burned, and worked specimens. Ideally, it should be possible to remove the chemical if future studies require it; it may be necessary to decide to save the specimen although it may preclude future studies. The curational facility should be consulted beforehand and a record of the treatment should be kept with the materials at all times.

Attribution is so important that the methods employed should be part of the permanent record (Driver 1992; Lawrence 1973; Rea 1986). Some argue that all identifications should be accompanied by notes specifying the basis for the attribution (Rea 1986). Although it may not be necessary, or even possible, to publish these criteria, the basis for each attribution should be clearly articulated, somewhere, and consistently applied. It is a good practice for laboratories to have specific, written procedures that everyone in the lab follows.

Primary data are recorded in many ways (Table A3.1; Clason 1972; Driver 1992; Grigson 1978; Lawrence 1973), but it is most important that the results be clear. Only procedures that are simple and replicable should be used, and none of these should be left to memory. Arcane codes or personal abbreviations should be avoided. If codes are used, the key should be kept with the notes at all times. It is not a good practice to alter established protocols casually because this makes it difficult to duplicate results later. In some cases, the project or the laboratory may have established procedures and the curational facility may have additional guidelines. These should all be followed closely.

It is commonly the case that materials and records will be restudied at a time and place when the original researcher may be unable to assist in the reanalysis for any number of reasons (deceased, location unknown, retired). Thus, it is important that the original records be understandable on their own merits, without the need to find the original researcher. (This assumes that reasonable efforts are made to contact the original scholar out of courtesy.) It is often impossible to publish the details needed for reanalysis. Thus, all abbreviations, codes, and notations should be either fully explained in the text or referenced to a readily available, reliable source. All records should be made in full. Links should be established in the publication that will give some clue about what was studied. Data should be recorded on high quality media, preferably archival quality. If archival quality media are not available, the materials and the records should be stored in a form that will minimize damage by environmental hazards and human error; perhaps with additional copies in more than one facility. The acknowledgment section of all publications should identify the facility where the materials and associated records are deposited. Records of primary data should be curated in a public repository with the same care as the faunal specimens themselves.

Many differences in recording techniques reflect whether the data will be computerized or not. Although computers are common in zooarchaeological labs, they are not universal and, unfortunately, advances in computer technology mean data entered on one system are accessible by another only with difficulty, if at all. At one time, computer programs were designed specifically for zooarchaeological data (e.g., Gifford and Crader 1977; Klein and Cruz-Uribe 1984; Meadow 1978a; Redding et al. 1975; Redding et al. 1978; Uerpmann 1978); but many find it satisfactory to use commercial products instead. Electronic files are mortal; back-ups should be maintained, and at least one hard copy should be kept on archival-quality paper.

Special Concerns Regarding Human Remains

It is important to anticipate the ethical and legal issues associated with human remains. Even the definition of what is a "human remain" is subject to legal definitions that vary from one jurisdiction to another. It is very likely that some human remains will be found among the other materials sent for study. Usually these are small finds whose recovery is unanticipated, but that does not mean they are exempt from the constraints that apply to formal inhumations and cremations. In many cases, even small finds are covered by international treaties, national laws, permit restrictions, and local protocols (Larsen 1997: 341–2; Roskams 2001: 199–200; Ubelaker 2000; Walker 2000; White and Folkens 2005:21–30, 352–3). This issue is most closely identified with the Native American Graves Protection and Repatriation Act (NAGPRA) passed in 1970 in the United States, but similar legislation exists in many countries. Even where the treatment of human remains is not codified, local sensitivities should be determined and respected. The issue of human remains and cultural patrimony is too complex to review here, but zooarchaeologists are not immune from its effects. The project director should inform the zooarchaeology laboratory in advance about how to handle human remains, even fragmentary ones. If the field personnel does not tell the laboratory how to handle these materials, it is prudent for the zooarchaeological laboratory to be sensitive to this issue and to verify the protocol before work begins. It may be necessary to return the remains to the project director for special handling, study by a human osteologist, or for reburial.

DISSEMINATING THE RESULTS

Dissemination of the results as well as long-term curation of the archaeofaunal materials and data are important aspects of our research (e.g., Chaplin 1965; Clason 1972; Grigson 1978; Lawrence 1973; Schmid 1972:23). With the increase in zooarchaeological research, concerns about access to zooarchaeological collections and data have grown. Zooarchaeologists should publish their research within a reasonable time after the initial study, and data should be recorded in such a way that the data will be intelligible to future scholars.

Table A3.2. *Checklist for zooarchaeology reports*

Section	Comments
Title page	Title of paper, author, author's address, and date
Abstract	No more than 100 words (see Landes 1966)
Introduction	Purpose of paper, literature review, set up for presentation of data from specific assemblage being reported
Materials	Description of archaeological site
Methods	Field recovery methods and zooarchaeological methods
Results	Description of what was found; no interpretation
Discussion	Interpret results and tie them to purpose as outlined in the Introduction
Conclusions	Summarize what was concluded as a result of the research
Acknowledgments	Acknowledge the funding source, owner of the site, and field personnel
Bibliography	Follow the *Chicago Manual of Style* or some other widely used style guide
Figures	
Tables	
Species list	
Summary table	
Elements represented	
Modifications	
Age	
Measurements, in mm	
Others as appropriate to the research goals	
Appendices	
List of proveniences	
Others as appropriate to the research goals	

The primary means by which zooarchaeological data are communicated is through reports. These usually, although not always, follow a standard outline (Table A3.2). The research objective of the work, the materials, and the methods should be carefully described. The remainder of the text may include discussions of topics such as seasonal rounds, butchering patterns, ceremonial uses of animals, or manufacture of tools – though seldom are all of these addressed in the same report. The tables should be quantified and provide the basic data on which the interpretation is based. It takes a great deal of skill to include a thorough description of the materials examined within a problem-oriented report; sometimes it is necessary to be very creative. These reports are generally printed in very limited numbers and distribution is problematical in many cases. This "gray" literature is growing daily, but it is rarely available to the general professional community let alone the public (Lauwerier and de Vries 2004).

Descriptive reports and synthetic publications are not the same thing. Reports do not absolve a scholar from formally presenting the data to as wide an audience as possible. Two ways zooarchaeologists communicate their results are through professional meetings and publications. The primary mission of professional associations is to foster this communication (Chaplin 1971; Davis 1987). Organizations, such as the Association for Environmental Archaeology, the Society of Ethnobiology, the Society of Archaeological Science, and the International Council of Archaeozoology, sponsor conferences. Many participate in these professional gatherings, where research results are presented as posters or papers. Much important information is exchanged informally at these meetings.

Results should be published in journals with wide circulation. This is particularly important now because so much research is funded through cultural resource management, mitigation, and rescue operations. Many societies and museums support journals such as *Archaeofauna, Environmental Archaeology, Journal of Archaeological Science, Journal of Ethnobiology*, and *International Journal of Osteoarchaeology*. The International Council of Archaeozoology Web site, and publications such as *Canadian Zooarchaeology* and *Ancient Monuments Laboratory Reports*, aid zooarchaeologists in their search for unpublished or limited-circulation reports. Bibliographies and surveys that list major works in zooarchaeology are helpful (e.g., Angress and Reed 1962; Bogan and Robison 1987; Driver 1993; Müller 1982, 1990, 1991; Stampfli and Schibler 1991). Many journals and newsletters carry book reviews and notes. Some laboratories and individuals post bibliographies on their Web sites.

When preparing an article for publication, authors need to squeeze methods, results, and interpretation into limited, costly space. Many of the problems associated with secondary data derive from inadequate descriptions of methods in publications caused by page or word limits imposed by publishers, or imposed by the average length of an article in the field of study. Complex, multistaged, or idiosyncratic procedures that are difficult to describe succinctly may be inappropriate because these cannot be clearly explained under publication constraints. In such cases, the results may not be replicable because subsequent researchers cannot duplicate the procedures. In other cases, the results and interpretations are rejected by colleagues at the peer-review stage simply because they cannot understand how they were obtained. For clarity, zooarchaeologists should anticipate publication when selecting methods for deriving secondary data. If the procedure is essential, but requires a lengthy description, some publishers may waive their page limits, or suggest including the description in a smaller font as notes. Tables and figures should be fully explained and legible. When drafting figures and tables, anticipate that these will be substantially reduced during publication. When presented at meetings, the numbers and letters on the figures and tables should be large. If color is used, remember that some readers are colorblind.

Results should be disseminated to public audiences (e.g., Marquardt 1994). The archaeological heritage of many nations is being destroyed rapidly by vandalism, commercial mining, the impact of modern activities on archaeological sites, and the simple passage of time. The public should be aware of the importance of archaeological sites for understanding both our past and our present. Professional archaeologists must involve the public and policy makers in the preservation of our heritage. Because much of our research is supported by public funds, we have an obligation to share our excitement and significant discoveries with the people who support our work. Youth organizations and adult clubs are eager to have professionals address their organizations. Tours of laboratories and excavations are important ways to keep the public informed of scientific research and the importance of protecting archaeological sites.

LONG-TERM CURATION

Zooarchaeologists are strong advocates for long-term, professional curation of modern reference collections, archaeofaunal samples, and the associated data (Cram 2004). The biases associated with collection management and curation decisions are particularly distressing as these materials represent the primary archive for the original study as well as for future research (e.g., Albarella and Serjeantson 2002; Brain 1981:10; Butler 1993; Shipman 1981; see Peters [1986] for a description of the way incomplete curation hampers restudies of important collections). Archaeofaunal collections are vouchers for the original research and should receive the same high quality care provided to all research vouchers. They should be housed in public repositories or similar facilities that have as their mission the care of collections and dissemination of knowledge derived from collections-based research.

Prior to excavation, the project director should enter into a formal agreement with an official repository whose mission is to care for materials and associated records. This might be either a public or a private institution, but the institution should have formal, written collection-management policies regarding acquisition, loans, deaccession, claims for return, storage, conservation, display, educational use, and research that encourage long-term curation and access to the specimens and associated data in a location with appropriate security and environmental controls. Such institutions should assume procedural and ethical responsibility for the materials, with the legal and financial support necessary for long-term care.

Zooarchaeological data can address many more questions than the initial researcher may have the time, funding, expertise, or interest to explore (e.g., Crabtree 2004). Although it is desirable for the published report to be sufficiently complete to encourage further analysis using data in the publication itself, restrictions on space may preclude this. Papers, posters, and published articles cover only a limited amount of the primary data. Refereed journals tend to publish papers devoted to method and theory rather than to the presentation and interpretation of primary or secondary data. For these and other reasons, many data remain unpublished. At the same time, future researchers will have new questions or want to compare data from several sites. It is the convention in most research to collect data directly rather than rely on other studies. Future scholars will almost always need access to both the studied and the unstudied animal remains, as well as access to the unpublished data, in order to pursue their research objectives. As archaeology grows in sophistication and new techniques are applied to faunal samples, many of the remains once thought to have been thoroughly studied, or able to provide little information, become more interesting. The repeated restudy of the Star Carr materials is but one example of the value curated collections may have many years after the original study (Clark 1954; Dark 2003; Legge and Rowley-Conwy 1988; Schulting and Richards 2002).

Museums and libraries are repositories where the samples and data receive permanent care. Notes should be curated for future reference in the same facility as the samples. If they are not in the same facility, their location should be clearly recorded. Some publications now require that authors include the location of notes and materials in the article. Storage should be in areas where environmental conditions, such as temperature, light, humidity, and insects, are controlled. In many parts of the world it is difficult to obtain acid-free containers, airconditioning, and secure storage cases; but every effort should be made to place the materials in as secure a condition as possible (e.g., Marquardt et al. 1982).

In some cases an institution will deaccession materials either by giving the materials to another institution or by destroying the materials. Although discarding parts of the assemblage may preclude new studies in the future, keeping an entire excavated assemblage has logistical and economic implications. If the decision is made to deaccession materials, great care should be exercised to anticipate, as best as possible, new studies and to ensure that thorough records are made of what was discarded and why.

Access to Data

In most cases, zooarchaeologists do not own the materials or the data temporarily in their care. The principle should be that data circulate freely, although this must be modified in local applications to reflect governmental regulations, agreements with funding agencies and indigenous communities, or similar restrictions. The access policies of the final repository will often stipulate the conditions of access, thereby removing some of the emotion from this issue.

In almost every case, faunal data are developed with public funds. Thus, as a general rule, data should be shared freely. However, scholars wishing to study the same samples should recognize the personal association that exists between researchers and the materials they study. Care should be taken to maintain a professional, collegial, and courteous association. Free access does not mean that the original researcher or the repository should be expected to generate reports, special tables, or files, or otherwise prepare data for subsequent scholars. The burden of the costs of access should be supported by the requestor: which may mean that the requestor must travel to the data and use them in situ.

Unpublished data are more problematic because the original researcher may have plans to publish them eventually. The problem arises with regards to what "eventually" means. Researchers should prepare a basic report for every faunal collection that could be provided on request within 1–2 years of completing the project. After some period of time, conventionally considered to be about 10 years, if the primary publication remains unpublished, the original researcher should consider turning the materials over to someone who will publish them.

CONCLUSION

Each faunal collection is different, as is each archaeological project. It will be necessary to modify the procedures suggested here to accommodate these settings. However, every effort should be made to ensure that the materials are subjected to as little additional loss as possible and to facilitate their survival in the years to come. Every zooarchaeologist must be an advocate for the responsible management of collections and the dissemination of data as widely as possible.

Appendix 4

Hypothetical Collection Data

Table A4.1. *Hypothetical Collection: Species list*

Taxa	NISP	MNI #	MNI %	Wt, g	Biomass, kg
Indeterminate mammal	13,079			7,945.5	85.1
Scalopus aquaticus eastern mole	6	1	0.1	1.0	0.2
Sylvilagus spp. rabbits	14	4	0.5	12.7	0.3
Sylvilagus cf. palustris marsh rabbit	1	(1)		1.9	0.05
Indeterminate rodent	2			0.4	0.01
Rattus norvegicus Norway rat	1	1	0.1	0.2	0.006
R. rattus black rat	3	1	0.1	0.5	0.01
Indeterminate carnivore	1			0.5	0.01
Procyon lotor raccoon	8	3	0.4	6.2	0.1
Ursus americanus black bear	1	1	0.1	60.5	1.1
cf. *Felis catus* possible domestic cat	1			0.7	0.02
Felis catus domestic cat	21	5	0.6	41.6	0.8
Indeterminate artiodactyl	333			2,023.6	24.9
Sus scrofa pig	193	14	1.7	1,441.7	18.3
Odocoileus virginianus white-tailed deer	80	11	1.3	1,076.4	14.1

Table A4.1 *(cont.)*

Taxa	NISP	MNI		Wt, g	Biomass, kg
		#	%		
Bos taurus cattle	202	13	1.6	7,309.9	79.0
Caprinae goat or sheep subfamily	18	3	0.4	312.3	4.6
Capra hircus goat	3	(1)		15.5	0.3
Indeterminate bird	145			67.2	0.9
Colinus virginianus bobwhite quail	4	3	0.4	1.7	0.03
Gallus gallus chicken	62	10	1.2	76.5	1.06
Meleagris gallopavo turkey	11	4	0.5	43.8	0.6
Anatidae duck family	21	7	0.8	12.5	0.2
Nycticorax nycticorax black-crowned night-heron	1	1	0.1	0.2	0.005
Eudocimus albus white ibis	5	4	0.5	9.9	0.2
Accipteridae hawk family	1	1	0.1	0.04	0.009
Scolopacidae sandpiper family	1			0.4	0.009
Gallinago gallinago common snipe	2	1	0.1	0.2	0.005
Himantopus mexicanus black-necked stilt	2	1	0.1	1.0	0.02
Burhinus bistriatus double-striped thick-knee	1	1	0.1	1.0	0.02
Larus sp. gull	1	1	0.1	0.7	0.02
Passeriformes perching birds	4			1.3	0.03
Corvus ossifragus fish crow	1	1	0.1	0.3	0.007

(cont.)

Table A4.1 *(cont.)*

Taxa	NISP	MNI		Wt, g	Biomass, kg
		#	%		
Turdidae	1	1	0.1	0.4	0.009
thrush family					
Quiscalus quiscula	1	1	0.1	0.1	0.003
common grackle					
Indeterminate turtle	84			48.9	0.4
Cheloniidae	1	1	0.1	1.2	0.04
sea turtle family					
Emydidae	8			4.8	0.09
water/box turtle family					
Malaclemys terrapin	2	2	0.2	3.0	0.07
diamondback terrapin					
Gopherus polyphemus	47	5	0.6	116.8	0.8
gopher tortoise					
Indeterminate snake	1			0.2	0.003
Viperidae	50	1	0.1	1.0	0.01
pit viper family					
Indeterminate amphibian	4			0.4	0.003
Rana/Bufo spp.	6			1.1	0.007
frogs or toads					
Bufo spp.	38	2	0.2	6.2	0.04
toads					
Carcharodon carcharias	1	(fossil tooth)			
white shark					
Carcharhinidae	6			3.2	0.3
requiem shark family					
Carcharhinus sp.	5	1	0.1	6.7	0.7
requiem shark					
Galeocerdo cuvier	2	1	0.1	0.6	0.08
tiger shark					
Sphyrna spp.	26	6	0.7	16.7	1.4
hammerhead sharks					
Indeterminate fish	1,345			381.0	3.6
Elops saurus	1	1	0.1	0.2	0.008
ladyfish					
Clupeidae	52	2	0.2	0.3	0.01
herring family					
Ariidae	217			41.8	0.7
sea catfish family					
Ariopsis felis	249	19	2.3	74.9	1.2
hardhead catfish					

Table A4.1 *(cont.)*

Taxa	NISP	MNI #	MNI %	Wt, g	Biomass, kg
Bagre marinus gafftopsail catfish	11	5	0.6	3.5	0.07
Mugil spp. mullets	981	53	6.4	111.6	1.4
Cyprinodontidae killifish family	4	1	0.1	0.04	0.002
Centropristis sp. sea bass	1	1	0.1	0.5	0.009
cf. *Epinephelus* sp. possible grouper	1	1	0.1	2.8	0.06
Lutjanus sp. snapper	1	1	0.1	0.1	0.004
Archosargus probatocephalus sheepshead	6	1	0.1	1.2	0.02
Sciaenidae drum family	395			93.6	1.1
Bairdiella chrysoura silver perch	7	3	0.4	0.6	0.027
Cynoscion spp. seatrouts	6	4	0.5	2.0	0.07
Leiostomus xanthurus spot	1	1	0.1	0.3	0.02
Menticirrhus spp. kingfishes	81	3	0.4	7.1	0.2
Micropogonias undulatus Atlantic croaker	4	4	0.5	1.0	0.04
Pogonias cromis black drum	26	5	0.6	40.5	0.6
Sciaenops ocellatus red drum	40	12	1.4	36.2	0.6
Paralichthys spp. flounders	23	5	0.6	8.3	0.2
Indeterminate vertebrate				462.9	
Indeterminate mollusc				46,116.92	
Mytilidae mussel family	91			42.5	0.013

(cont.)

Table A4.1 *(cont.)*

Taxa	NISP	MNI		Wt, g	Biomass, kg
		#	%		
Crassostrea virginica eastern oyster	800	240	29.0	13,749.75	1.754
Tagelus plebeius stout tagelus	100	39	4.7	222.7	0.411
Mercenaria spp. quahogs	18	10	1.2	1,126.42	0.123
Littorina irrorata marsh periwinkle	36	36	4.3	1.36	0.0006
Crepidula sp. slippersnail	9	9	1.1	3.06	0.002
Neverita duplicata shark eye	9	9	1.1	5.78	0.006
Nassarius obsoletus eastern mudsnail	27	27	3.3	39.78	0.018
Boonia impressa impressed odostome	147	147	17.7	7.82	
Polygyridae terrestrial snails	9	9	1.1	0.34	
Balanus spp. barnacles	309	44	5.3	108.8	
Decapoda crabs	573			142.8	
Callinectes spp. swimming crabs	200	24	2.9	131.24	
Indeterminate invertebrate				15,006.92	
Total	20,292	829		98,655.77	248.244

Table A4.2. *Hypothetical Collection: Number of specimens with modifications*

Taxa	Gnawed		Cut	Hacked	Sawed	Clean-cut	Burned	Worked
	Rodent	Carnivore						
Indeterminate mammal	9	4	61	3			3	1
Rabbit							1	
Indeterminate rodent							1	
Indeterminate artiodactyl	1		3		2	1		
Pig			12	4			1	
Deer			12	3	1			
Cattle			33	10	10			
Caprinae			1					
Indeterminate bird							6	
Chicken		1	5					
Indeterminate turtle				1			28	
Diamondback terrapin			1					
Gopher tortoise			1				22	
Requiem shark			1				1	
Indeterminate fish			2				76	
Sea catfish family							6	
Hardhead catfish			2				18	
Gafftopsail catfish							5	
Mullet							12	
Seatrout			1				1	
Black drum							11	
Total	10	5	135	21	13	1	192	1

Table A4.3. *Hypothetical Collection: Specimen distribution worksheet for white-tailed deer* (Odocoileus virginianus)

Element	Unfused			Fused			Indeterminate			Total
	rt	lt	ind	rt	lt	ind	rt	lt	ind	
Head:										
Antler/horn									1	1
Skull fragments										
Occipital			1							1
Bulla										
Maxilla										
Mandible				1	1		1	1		4
Indeterminate teeth			1							1
Axial:										
Indeterminate vertebra									1	1
Atlas										
Axis										
Cervical			1							1
Thoracic										
Lumbar									2	2
Caudal										
Rib										
Sternum										
Forequarter:										
Scapula		1		1	1		1	1		5
Humerus, proximal										
Humerus, shaft							2			2
Humerus, distal				2	3					5
Radius, proximal		1 pfdunf		1 pfdf	4					6
Radius, shaft							1			1
Radius, distal	2				1					3
Ulna, proximal					2					2
Ulna, shaft		1 punf					2	1		4
Ulna, distal										
Hindquarter:										
Sacrum										
Innominate										
Ilium		1					1	1		3
Ischium							3			3
Pubis										

Table A4.3 *(cont.)*

Element	Unfused			Fused			Indeterminate			Total
	rt	lt	ind	rt	lt	ind	rt	lt	ind	
Acetabulum					1					1
Femur, proximal					1					1
Femur, shaft							1	1		2
Femur, distal	1			2			1			4
Patella										
Tibia, proximal		1		1	2					4
Tibia, shaft										
Tibia, distal	1			2	1					4
Forefoot:										
Indeterminate carpal										
Radial carpal								1		1
Intermediate carpal								2		2
Ulnar carpal								1		1
Accessory carpal										
1st carpal										
2nd carpal										
3rd carpal										
4th carpal										
Magnum										
Metacarpus, proximal						1				1
Metacarpus, shaft										
Metacarpus, distal										
Hindfoot:										
Indeterminate tarsal										
Astragalus							2	2		4
Calcaneus				1	1					2
Os malleolare							1			1
Navicular										
1st tarsal										
2nd tarsal										
3rd tarsal										
Cuboid										

(cont.)

Table A4.3 *(cont.)*

Element	Unfused			Fused			Indeterminate			Total
	rt	lt	ind	rt	lt	ind	rt	lt	ind	
Cubonavicular										
Metatarsus, proximal						1				1
Metatarsus, shaft										
Metatarsus, distal										
Foot:										
Sesamoid										
Carpal/tarsal										
Metapodium, proximal										
Metapodium, shaft										
Metapodium, distal						2				2
Indeterminate phalanx										
1st phalanx						2				2
2nd phalanx						1				1
3rd phalanx									1	1
Total	4	5	3	11	18	7	16	11	5	80

Note: The following symbols are used to denote fusion for shaft fragments: p = proximal, d = distal, unf = unfused, f = fused. This is necessary because proximal and distal ends of many elements fuse at different times as an individual matures.

Table A4.4. *Hypothetical Collection: Fusion worksheet for white-tailed deer* (Odocoileus virginianus)

	Unfused	Fused	Total
Early-fusing specimens:			
Scapula, distal	1	2	3
Humerus, distal		5	5
Radius, proximal		6	6
Acetabulum	1	1	2
Metapodium, proximal		2	2
1st/2nd phalanx, proximal		3	3
Middle-fusing specimens:			
Tibia, distal	1	3	4
Calcaneus, proximal		2	2
Metapodium, distal		2	2
Late-fusing specimens:			
Humerus, proximal			
Radius, distal	3	2	5
Ulna, proximal	1	2	3
Ulna, distal			
Femur, proximal		1	1
Femur, distal	1	2	3
Tibia, proximal	1	3	4
Total	9	36	45

Table A4.5. *Measurements from the Hypothetical Collection and other collections used in examples*

Taxa	Element	Dimension	Measurement, mm
Rattus norvegicus	Mandible	Dh	4.3, 5.3
		Dl	7.0, 8.5
		H	6.5, 7.9
Rattus rattus	Mandible	Dh	3.8, 3.9
		Dl	5.3, 5.8
		H	5.1, 5.7
Odocoileus virginianus	Humerus, fused	Bp	41.0, 44.8, 46.9
		Bd	30.0, 33.7, 33.9, 34.5, 34.8, 34.8, 35.0, 35.0, 35.7, 36.0, 36.2, 36.9, 37.5, 37.8, 38.2, 38.5, 38.7, 38.8, 40.0, 40.3
	Radius, fused	Bp	30.5, 30.9, 31.5, 31.6, 31.6, 32.2, 33.0, 33.5, 33.5, 33.8, 34.0, 35.0, 35.7, 36.3, 36.5
		Bd	27.3, 27.6, 28.7, 28.8, 29.0, 29.0, 29.5, 29.5, 31.0, 31.7, 32.0, 33.2, 33.3, 38.2, 40.0
	Ulna, unfused	BPC	18.0
	Ulna, fused	BPC	22.0
	Ulna, fusion unknown	BPC	18.0, 19.0
	Metacarpus, fused	Bp	23.5, 23.7, 24.0, 24.0, 24.2, 25.4, 26.1
		Bd	24.0, 25.5, 30.4, 30.7
	Femur, fused	Bp	47.2, 48.0, 49.1, 52.8
		Bd	46.7, 48.4, 48.5, 51.1, 51.5
		DC	23.3
	Tibia, unfused epiphysis	Bp	50.0
	Tibia, fused	Bp	48.9, 52.4, 53.5, 53.7, 54.3
		Bd	27.8, 28.5, 28.5, 28.9, 29.0, 29.6, 29.9, 30.0, 30.6, 30.9, 31.0, 31.1, 32.0, 32.2, 32.3, 32.5, 32.7, 33.1, 33.4, 33.9, 34.7

Table A4.5 *(cont.)*

Taxa	Element	Dimension	Measurement, mm
	Astragalus	GLl	31.7, 32.7, 33.3, 33.8, 36.6, 36.7, 37.5, 37.6
		GLm	31.4, 32.1, 32.5, 33.9, 34.4, 35.3, 35.5
		Bd	19.3, 19.7, 21.6, 22.0, 22.3, 22.5, 22.9, 23.0, 23.5
	Calcaneus, fused	GL	69.2, 71.0, 72.2, 77.5, 82.1, 89.0
Bos taurus	Horn core	46	30.7, 41.1, 43.7, 53.9, 56.1, 57.9, 64.4
		47	125.0, 190.0, 330.0
Gallus gallus	Humerus	Bd	12.0, 12.0, 12.4, 13.0, 13.0, 14.0, 14.0, 14.0, 14.0, 14.0, 14.0, 14.0, 14.0, 14.0, 14.3, 14.4, 14.6, 14.6, 14.7, 14.8, 15.0, 15.0, 15.0, 15.0, 15.0, 15.0, 15.2, 15.3, 15.5, 15.8, 16.9, 17.2, 17.2, 17.7, 19.6
Ariidae	Otolith	Length	7.3, 8.1, 8.8, 9.5, 10.5, 10.8, 11.4, 11.5, 12.0, 12.4, 12.6, 13.4, 14.3
Mugil spp.	Atlas	Width	1.8, 1.9, 2.1, 2.4, 2.4, 2.6, 2.8, 3.0, 3.0, 3.0, 3.0, 3.1, 3.2, 3.4, 3.4, 3.4, 3.4, 3.6, 3.6, 3.6, 3.7, 3.7, 3.8, 3.8, 3.9, 4.0, 4.0, 4.2, 4.5, 4.5, 4.5, 4.7, 5.1, 5.2, 6.2, 6.3, 6.3, 6.4, 6.5, 6.6, 6.7, 6.7, 6.9, 7.2, 7.2, 7.4, 7.8, 8.2
Bairdiella chrysoura	Sagitta	Length	5.6, 6.8
	Lapillus	Length	5.0, 6.7, 7.0
	Atlas	Width	1.2, 2.3
Sciaenops ocellatus	Atlas	Width	4.3, 9.1, 17.6

Note: Rat mandible measurements follow Armitage et al. (1984); fish otolith measurements are the greatest length; and fish atlas measurements are the greatest width of the anterior centrum. All other measurements follow Driesch (1976).

BIBLIOGRAPHY

Abbott, R. T. 1974. *American seashells*. New York: Van Nostrand Reinhold.

Abele, L. G. (Ed.). 1982. *The biology of crustacea: 1. Systematics, the fossil record, and biogeography*. New York: Academic Press.

Akazawa, T. 1988. Variability in the types of fishing adaptation of the later Jomon hunter-gatherers, c. 2500 to 300 bc. In G. Bailey and J. Parkington (Eds.), *The archaeology of prehistoric coastlines*. Cambridge, UK: Cambridge University Press, pp. 78–92.

Albarella, U. (Ed.). 2001. *Environmental archaeology: Meaning and purpose*. Dordrecht: Kluwer.

Albarella, U., and Davis, S. M. D. 1996. Mammals and birds from Launceston Castle, Cornwall: Decline in status and the rise of agriculture. *Circaea* 12(1):1–156.

Albarella, U., Davis, S. J. M., Detry, C., and Rowley-Conwy, P. 2005. Pigs in the "Far West": The biometry of *Sus* from archaeological sites in Portugal. *Anthropozoologica* 40(2):27–44.

Albarella, U., Dobney, K., and Rowley-Conwy, P. 2006. The domestication of the pig (*Sus scrofa*): New challenges and approaches. In M. A. Zeder, D. G. Bradley, E. Emshwiller, and B. D. Smith (Eds.), *Documenting domestication: New genetics and archaeological paradigms*. Berkeley: University of California Press, pp. 209–27.

Albarella, U., and Serjeantson, D. 2002. A passion for pork: Meat consumption at the British Late Neolithic site of Durrington Wells. In P. Miracle and N. Milner (Eds.), *Consuming passions and patterns of consumption*. Cambridge, UK: McDonald Institute Monographs, pp. 33–49.

Alcorn, J. B. 1981. Huastec noncrop resource management: Implications for prehistoric rain forest management. *Human Ecology* 9(4):395–417.

Alen, A., and Ervynck, A. 2005. The large scale and specialised late medieval urban craft of marrow extraction: Archaeological and historical evidence from Malines (Belgium), confronted with experimental work. In J. Mulville and A. K. Outram (Eds.), *The archaeology of fats, oils, milk and dairying: An introduction and overview*. Oxford: Oxbow Books, pp. 193–200.

Alexander, R. McNeill. 1994. *Bones: The unity of form and function*. New York: Macmillan.

Alhaique, F. 2003. The role of small carnivores in the accumulation of bones in archaeological deposits: The case of the Fucino Basin sites (Central Italy). *Archaeofauna* 12:61–71.

Alhaique, F., and Cerilli, E. 2003. Handicraft, diet, and cult practices in the late Antique *villa rustica* of Brega (Rosà, Vicenza, NE Italy). *Archaeofauna* 12:95–111.

Allen, M. S. 2002. Resolving long-term change in Polynesian marine fisheries. *Asian Perspectives* 41(2):195–212.

Altuna, J. 1983. On the relationship between archaeofaunas and parietal art in the caves of the Cantabrian region. In J. Clutton-Brock and C. Grigson (Eds.), *Animals and archaeology: 1. Hunters and their prey.* Oxford: British Archaeological Reports International Series 163, pp. 227–38.

Alvard, M. S. 1993. Testing the "ecologically noble savage" hypothesis: Interspecific prey choice by Piro hunters of Amazonian Peru. *Human Ecology 21*(4):355–87.

Ambrose, S. H. 1993. Isotopic analysis of paleodiets: Methodological and interpretive considerations. In M. K. Sandford (Ed.), *Investigations of ancient human tissue: Chemical analyses in anthropology.* Philadelphia: Gordon and Breach Science Publishers, pp. 59–130.

Ambrose, S. H., and Norr, L. 1993. Experimental evidence for the relationship of the carbon isotope ratios of whole diet and dietary protein to those of bone collagen and carbonate. In J. B. Lambert and G. Grupe (Eds.), *Prehistoric human bone: Archaeology at the molecular level.* Berlin: Springer Verlag, pp. 1–37.

American Ornithologists' Union. 1983. *Check-list of North American birds.* (6th ed). Lawrence, KS: Allen Press.

Amorosi. T., McGovern, T., and Perdikaris, S. 1994. Bioarchaeology and cod fisheries: A new source of evidence. In J. Jakobson, Ó. S. Ástthórsson, R. J. H. Beverton, B. Björnsson, N. Daan, K. T. Frank, J. B. Rothschild, S. Sundby, and S. Tilseth (Eds.), *Cod and climate change I Copenhagen, Denmark. International Council for the Exploration of the Sea (ICES) Marine Science Symposium Series 198*:31–48.

Amorosi, T., Woollett, J., Perdikaris, S., and McGovern, T. 1996. Regional zooarchaeology and global change: Problems and potentials. *World Archaeology 28*(1):126–57.

Anderson, A. 1983. The prehistoric hunting of moa (Aves: Dinornithidae) in the high country of southern New Zealand. In C. Grigson and J. Clutton-Brock (Eds.), *Animals and archaeology: 2. Shell middens, fishes, and birds.* Oxford: British Archaeological Reports International Series 183, pp. 33–52.

———. 1988. Coastal subsistence economies in prehistoric southern New Zealand. In G. Bailey and J. Parkington (Eds.), *The archaeology of prehistoric coastlines.* Cambridge, UK: Cambridge University Press, pp. 93–101.

———. 1989. Mechanics of overkill in the extinction of New Zealand moas. *Journal of Archaeological Science 16*(2):137–51.

Anderson, R. M. 1965. *Methods of collecting and preserving vertebrate animals.* Ottawa: National Museum of Canada Bulletin 69, Biological Series 18.

Anderson, S., and Boyle, K. 1996. *Ritual treatment of human and animal remains.* Oxford: Oxbow Books.

Andrews, P. 1995. Experiments in taphonomy. *Journal of Archaeological Science 22*(2):147–53.

Andrus, C. F. T., and Crowe, D. E. 2000. Geochemical analysis of *Crassostrea virginica* as a method to determine season of capture. *Journal of Archaeological Science 27*:33–42.

Andrus, C. F. T., and Crowe, D. E. 2002. Alteration of otolith aragonite: Effects of prehistoric cooking methods on otolith chemistry. *Journal of Archaeological Science 29*:291–9.

Andrus, C. F. T., Crowe, D. E., and Romanek, C. S. 2002a. Oxygen isotope record of the 1997–1998 El Niño in Peruvian sea catfish (*Galeichthys peruvianus*) otoliths. *Paleoceanography 17*(5):1053–60.

Andrus, C. F. T., Crowe, D. E., Sandweiss, D. H., Reitz, E. J., and Romanek, C. S. 2002b. Otolith $\delta^{18}O$ record of Mid-Holocene sea surface temperatures in Peru. *Science 295*:1508–11.

Angress, S., and Reed, C. A. 1962. *An annotated bibliography on the origin and descent of domestic mammals: 1900–1955*. Chicago: Chicago Museum of Natural History, Fieldiana: *Anthropology* 54(1): 13–143.

Anthony, D. W. 1990. Migration in archaeology: The baby and the bathwater. *American Anthropologist* 92(4):895–914.

Anthony, D. W., and Brown, D. R. 1989. Looking a gift horse in the mouth: Identification of the earliest bitted equids and the microscopic analysis of wear. In P. J. Crabtree, D. Campana, and K. Ryan (eds.), *Early animal domestication and its cultural context*. Philadelphia: University of Pennsylvania, Museum of Archaeology and Anthropology Research Papers in Science and Archaeology, MASCA Special Supplement to vol. 6, pp. 99–116.

Arbogast, R.-M., Pétrequin, P, Pétrequin A.-M., Maréchal, D., and Viellet, A. 2003. Instances of animal traction in the Neolithic village of Chalain (Jura, France). End of the 31 st century B.C.. *Archaeofauna* 12:175–81.

Arbuckle, B., and Bowen, J. 2004. Zooarchaeology and agricultural colonization: An example from the colonial Chesapeake. In M. Mondini, S. Muñoz, and S. Wickler (Eds.), *Colonisation, migration and marginal areas: A zooarchaeological approach*. Oxford: Oxbow Books, pp. 20–7.

Armelagos, G. J. 1994. "You are what you eat." In K. D. Sobolik (Ed.), *Paleonutrition: The diet and health of prehistoric Americans*. Carbondale: Southern Illinois University at Carbondale Center for Archaeological Investigations Occasional Paper 22, pp. 235–44.

Armitage, P. L. 1982. A system for ageing and sexing the horn cores of cattle from British post-medieval sites (17th to early 18th century) with special reference to unimproved British longhorn cattle. In B. Wilson, C. Grigson, and S. Payne (Eds.), *Ageing and sexing animal bones from archaeological sites*. Oxford: British Archaeological Reports British Series 109, pp. 37–54.

⸻. 1986. Domestication of animals. In D. J. A. Cole and G. C. Brander (Eds.), *Bioindustrial ecosystems*. Amsterdam: Elsevier Science Publishers, pp. 5–30.

⸻. 1989a. Gazetteer of sites with animal bones used as building material. In D. Serjeantson and T. Waldron (Eds.), *Diet and crafts in towns: The evidence of animal remains from the Roman to the post-medieval periods*. Oxford: British Archaeological Reports British Series 199, pp. 201–23.

⸻. 1989b. The use of animal bones as building material in post-medieval Britain. In D. Serjeantson and T. Waldron (Eds.), *Diet and crafts in towns: The evidence of animal remains from the Roman to the post-medieval periods*. Oxford: British Archaeological Reports British Series 199, pp. 147–60.

⸻. 1993. Commensal rats in the New World, 1492–1992. *The Biologist* 40(4):174–8.

Armitage, P. L., and Clutton-Brock, J. 1976. A system for classification and description of the horn cores of cattle from archaeological sites. *Journal of Archaeological Science* 3(3):329–48.

Armitage, P. L., and West, B. 1985. Faunal evidence from a late medieval garden well of the Greyfriars, London. *Transactions of the London and Middlesex Archaeology Society* 36:107–36.

Armitage, P. L., West, B., and Steedman, K. 1984. New evidence of black rat in Roman London. *London Archaeologist* 4(14):375–83.

Arndt, A., Van Neer, W., Hellemans, B., Robben, J., Volckaert, F., and Waelkens, M. 2003. Roman trade relationships at Sagalassos (Turkey) elucidated by ancient DNA of fish remains. *Journal of Archaeological Science* 30:1095–105.

Arnold, E. R., and Greenfield, H. J. 2004. A zooarchaeological perspective on the origins of vertical transhumant pastoralism and the colonization of marginal habitats in temperate southeastern

Europe. In M. Mondini, S. Muñoz, and S. Wickler (Eds.), *Colonisation, migration and marginal areas: A zooarchaeological approach.* Oxford: Oxbow Books, pp. 96–117.

Audoin-Rouzeau, F. 1991. La taille du bœuf domestique en Europe de l'antiquité aux temps modernes. *Fiches d'ostéologie animale pour l'archéologie: Série B. Mammifères* 2. Juan-les-Pins, France: Centre de Recherches Archéologiques du CNRS, APDCA.

Auffenberg, W. 1981. *The behavioral ecology of the Komodo monitor.* Gainesville, FL: University Presses of Florida.

Austin, O. L. 1971. *Families of birds.* New York: Golden Press.

Avebury, Lord (John Lubbock). 1865. *Prehistoric times as illustrated by ancient remains and the manners and customs of modern savages.* London: Williams and Norgate.

Avery, D. M. 1987. Late Pleistocene coastal environment of the southern Cape Province of South Africa: Micromammals from the Klasies River mouth. *Journal of Archaeological Science* 14(4):405–21.

———. 2004. Size variation in the common mole rat *Cryptomys hottentotus* from southern Africa and its potential for palaeoenvironmental reconstruction. *Journal of Archaeological Science* 31:273–82.

Avery, G. 1985. Late Holocene use of penguin skins: Evidence from a coastal shell midden at Steenbras Bay, Lüderitz Peninsula, South West Africa-Namibia. *Annals of the South African Museum* 96(3):55–65.

Badenhorst, S., and Plug, I. 2003. The archaeozoology of goats, *Capra hircus* (Linnaeus, 1758): Their size variation during the last two millennia in southern Africa (*Mammalia: Artiodactyla: Caprini*). *Annals of the Transvaal Museum* 40:91–121.

———. 2004. Archaeozoology, law enforcement, and nature conservation in the Republic of South Africa: Perspectives from the Transvaal Museum, Pretoria. In R. C. G. M. Lauwerier and I. Plug (Eds.), *The future from the past: Archaeozoology in wildlife conservation and heritage management.* Oxford: Oxbow Books, pp. 117–21.

Bailey, G., King, G., and Manighetti, I. 2000. Tectonics, volcanism, landscape structure, and human evolution in the African Rift. In G. Bailey, R. Charles, and N. Winder (Eds.), *Human ecodynamics.* Oxford: Oxbow Books, pp. 31–46.

Bailey, V. 1931. *Mammals of New Mexico.* Washington, DC: United States Department of Agriculture, Bureau of Biological Survey, North American Fauna 53.

Bain, A. 2001. *Archaeoentomological and archaeoparasitological reconstructions at Ilot Hunt (CeEt-110): New perspectives in historical archaeology.* British Archaeological Reports International Series 973. Oxford: Archaeopress.

Baird, S. F. 1857. *Explorations and surveys for a railroad route from the Mississippi River to the Pacific Ocean: Mammals.* Made under the direction of the Secretary of War, Washington, DC.

Baker, F. C. 1923. The use of molluscan shells by the Cahokia mound builders. *Transactions of the Illinois State Academy of Science.* 16:328–34.

———. 1931. Additional notes on animal life associated with the mound builders of Illinois. *Transactions of the Illinois State Academy of Science* 23(3):231–5.

———. 1941. A study of ethnozoology of the prehistoric Indians of Illinois. *Transactions of the American Philosophical Society* 32(1):51–77.

Baker, J., and Brothwell, D. 1980. *Animal diseases in archaeology.* London: Academic Press.

Balasse, M., and Ambrose, S. H. 2005. Distinguishing sheep and goats using dental morphology and stable carbon isotopes in C_4 grassland environments. *Journal of Archaeological Science* 32:691–702.

Balasse, M., Ambrose, S. H., Smith, A. B., and Price, T. D. 2002. The seasonal mobility model for prehistoric herders in the south-western Cape of South Africa assessed by isotopic analysis of sheep tooth enamel. *Journal of Archaeological Science* 29:917–32.

Balasse, M., Smith, A. B., Ambrose, S. H., and Leigh, S. R. 2003. Determining sheep birth seasonality by analysis of tooth enamel oxygen isotope ratios: The Late Stone Age site of Kasteelberg (South Africa). *Journal of Archaeological Science* 30:205–15.

Balasse, M., and Tresset, A. 2002. Early weaning of Neolithic domestic cattle (Bercy, France) revealed in intra-tooth variation in nitrogen isotope ratios. *Journal of Archaeological Science* 29:853–9.

Balkwell, D. McCuaig, and Cumbaa, S. L. 1992. *A guide to the identification of postcranial bones of* Bos taurus *and* Bison bison. Ottawa: Canadian Museum of Nature Syllogeus No. 71.

Ballbè, E. G. 2005. Shell middens on the Caribbean coast of Nicaragua: Prehistoric patterns of mollusc collection and consumption. In D. E. Bar-Yosef Mayer (Ed.), *Archaeomalacology: Molluscs in former environments of human behaviour*. Oxford: Oxbow Books, pp. 40–53.

Banerjee, M., and Brown, T. A. 2004. Non-random DNA damage resulting from heat treatment: Implications for sequence analysis of ancient DNA. *Journal of Archaeological Science* 31:59–63.

Banfield, A. W. F. 1960. The use of caribou antler pedicels for age determination. *Journal of Wildlife Management* 24(1):99–102.

Barger, L. E. 1985. Age and growth of Atlantic croakers in the northern Gulf of Mexico, based on otolith sections. *Transactions of the American Fisheries Society* 114:847–50.

Barker, G. 1985. *Prehistoric farming in Europe*. Cambridge, UK: Cambridge University Press.

———. 1987. Prehistoric subsistence and economy in northern Italy: The contribution of archaeozoology. *ArchaeoZoologia* 1(2):103–14.

Barker, G., and Gamble, C. 1985. Beyond domestication: A strategy for investigating the process and consequences of social complexity. In G. Barker and C. Gamble (Eds.), *Beyond domestication in prehistoric Europe*. London: Academic Press, pp. 1–31.

Barnes, I., and Young, J. P. W. 2000. DNA-based identification of goose species from two archaeological sites in Lincolnshire. *Journal of Archaeological Science* 27:91–100.

Barone, R. 1976. *Anatomie comparée des mammifères domestiques:* 1. *Ostéologie*. Paris: Laboratoire d'Anatomie, Ecole Nationale Vétérinaire.

Bar-Oz, G., Dayan, T., Kaufman, D, and Weinstein-Evron, M. 2004. The Natufian economy at el-Wad Terrace with special reference to gazelle exploitation patterns. *Journal of Archaeological Science* 31:217–31.

Barrett, J. H. 1993. Bone weight, meat yield estimates and cod (*Gadus morhua*): A preliminary study of the weight method. *International Journal of Osteoarchaeology* 3:1–18.

Bartosiewicz, L. 1987. Metacarpal measurements and carcass weight of moose in central Sweden. *Journal of Wildlife Management* 51(2):356–7.

———. 1988. Biometrics at an early medieval butchering site in Hungary. In E. A. Slater and J. O. Tate (Eds.), *Science and Archaeology, Glasgow 1987: Proceedings of a conference on the application of scientific techniques to archaeology, Glasgow, September 1987*. Oxford: British Archaeological Reports British Series 196, pp. 361–7.

————. 1995a. Animal remains from the Avar Period cemetery of Budakalász-Dunapart. *Acta Archaeologica Academiae Scientiarum Hungaricae* 47:241–55.

————. 1995b. *Animals in the urban landscape in the wake of the Middle Ages: A case study from Vác, Hungary.* Oxford: British Archaeological Reports International Series 609.

Bartosiewicz, L., and Bartosiewicz, G. 2002. "Bamboo spine" in a Migration Period horse from Hungary. *Journal of Archaeological Science* 29:819–30.

Bartram, L. E., Jr. 1993. Perspectives on skeletal part profiles and utility curves from Eastern Kalahari ethnoarchaeology. In J. Hudson (Ed.), *From bones to behavior: Ethnoarchaeological and experimental contributions to the interpretation of faunal remains.* Carbondale: Southern Illinois University at Carbondale Center for Archaeological Investigations Occasional Paper 21, pp. 115–37.

Bartram, L. E., Jr., Kroll, E. M., and Bunn, H. T. 1991. Variability in camp structure and bone food refuse patterning at Kua San camps. In E. M. Kroll and T. D. Price (Eds.), *The interpretation of archaeological spatial patterning.* New York: Plnum Press, pp. 77–148.

Bassett, E. 2004. Reconsidering evidence of Tasmanian fishing. *Environmental Archaeology* 9:135–42.

Bate, D. M. A. 1937. Palaeontology: The fossil fauna of the Wady el-Mughara Caves. In D. A. E. Garrod and D. M. A. Bates (Eds.), *The Stone Age of Mount Carmel: Excavations at the Wady El-Mughara* (Vol. 1, part 2). Oxford: Clarendon Press, pp. 137–240.

Bates, D. G., and Lees, S. H. (Eds.). 1996. *Case studies in human ecology.* New York: Plenum Press.

Bathurst, R. R., 2005. Archaeological evidence of intestinal parasites from coastal shell middens. *Journal of Archaeological Science* 32:115–23.

Bathurst, R. R., and Barta, J. L. 2004. Molecular evidence of tuberculosis induced hypertrophic osteopathy in a 16th-century Iroquoian dog. *Journal of Archaeological Science* 31:917–25.

Baxter, I. L., and Hamilton-Dyer, S. 2003. Foxy in furs? A note on evidence for the probable commercial exploitation of the red fox (*Vulpes vulpes* L.) and other fur bearing mammals in Saxo-Norman (10th–12th century AD) Hertford, Hertfordshire, U.K. *Archaeofauna* 12:87–94.

Béarez, P. 2000. Archaic fishing at Quebrada de los Burros, southern coast of Peru, reconstruction of fish size using otoliths. *Archaeofauna* 9:29–34.

Beck, C. W. 1996. Comments on a supposed Clovis "mastic." *Journal of Archaeological Science* 23(3):459–60.

Begon, M., Harper, J. L., and Townsend, C. R. 1986. *Ecology: Individuals, populations and communities.* Oxford: Blackwell Scientific Publications.

Behrensmeyer, A. K. 1978. Taphonomic and ecologic information from bone weathering. *Paleobiology* 4(2):150–62.

Behrensmeyer, A. K., Gordon, K. D., and Yanagi, G. T. 1986. Trampling as a cause of bone surface damage and pseudo-cutmarks. *Nature* 319(6056):768–71.

————. 1989. Nonhuman bone modification in Miocene fossils from Pakistan. In R. Bonnichsen and M. H. Sorg (Eds.), *Bone modification.* Orono: University of Maine, Institute for Quaternary Studies, Center for the Study of the First Americans, pp. 99–120.

Behrensmeyer, A. K., and Hill, A. P. (Eds.). 1980. *Fossils in the making: Vertebrate taphonomy and paleoecology.* Chicago: University of Chicago Press.

Behrensmeyer, A. K., Western, D., and Dechant-Boaz, D. E. 1979. New perspective in vertebrate paleoecology from a recent bone assemblage. *Paleobiology* 5(1):12–21.

Beja-Pereira, A., England, P. R., Ferrand, N., Jordan, S., Bakhiet, A. O., Abdalla, M. A., Mashkour, M., Jordana, J., Taberlet, P., and Luikart, G. 2004. African origins of domestic donkey. *Science* 304:1781.

Belcher, W. R. 1994. Butchery practices and the ethnoarchaeology of South Asian fisherfolk. In W. Van Neer (Ed.), *Fish exploitation in the past*. Tervuren, Belgium: Annales du Musée Royal de l'Afrique Centrale, Sciences Zoologiques 274, pp. 171–6.

Bellairs, A. 1970. *The life of reptiles*. New York: Universe Books.

Bellwood, P. 2005. *First farmers: The origins of agricultural societies*. Malden, MA: Blackwell Publishing.

Benecke, N. 1987. Studies on early dog remains from northern Europe. *Journal of Archaeological Science* 14(1):31–49.

———. 1994. *Der Mensch und seine Haustiere: Die Geschichte einer Jahrtausendenalten Beziehung*. Stuttgart: Theiss.

Benedict, C. R., Wong, W. W. L., and Wong, J. H. H. 1980. Fractionation of the stable isotopes of inorganic carbon by seagrasses. *Plant Physiology* 65(1):512–17.

Benfer, R. A. 1990. The Preceramic Period site of Paloma, Peru: Bioindications of improving adaptation to sedentism. *Latin American Antiquity* 1(4):284–318.

Berlin, B. 1992. *Ethnobiological classification: Principles of categorization of plants and animals in traditional societies*. Princeton: Princeton University Press.

Bentley, R. A., Price, D. T., and Stephan, E. 2004. Determining the "local" ^{87}SR/^{86}Sr range for archaeological skeletons: A case study from Neolithic Europe. *Journal of Archaeological Science* 31:365–75.

Bettinger, R. L. 1991. *Hunter-gatherers: Archaeological and evolutionary theory*. New York: Plenum Press.

Bicchieri, M. G. (Ed.). 1972. *Hunters and gatherers today: A socioeconomic study of eleven such cultures in the twentieth century*. New York: Holt, Rinehart, and Winston.

Binford, L. R. 1964. A consideration of archaeological research design. *American Antiquity* 29(4):425–41.

———. 1977. General introduction. In L. R. Binford (Ed.), *For theory building in archaeology: Essays on faunal remains, aquatic resources, spatial analysis, and systematic modeling*. New York: Academic Press, pp. 1–10.

———. 1978. *Nunamiut ethnoarchaeology*. New York: Academic Press.

———. 1980. Willow smoke and dogs' tails: Hunter-gatherer settlement systems and archaeological site formation. *American Antiquity* 45(1):4–20.

———. 1984. *Faunal remains from Klasies River Mouth*. New York: Academic Press.

Binford, L. R., and Bertram, J. B. 1977. Bone frequencies and attritional processes. In L. R. Binford (Ed.), *For theory building in archaeology: Essays on faunal remains, aquatic resources, spatial-analysis, and systematic modeling*. New York: Academic Press, pp. 77–153.

Bird, D. W., Richardson, J. L., Veth, P. M., and Barham, A. J. 2002. Explaining shellfish variability in middens on the Meriam Islands, Torres Strait, Australia. *Journal of Archaeological Science* 29:457–69.

Blumenschine, R. J., and Caro, T. M. 1986. Unit flesh weights of some East African bovids. *African Journal of Ecology* 24:273–86.

Bobrowsky, P. T. 1982a. An examination of Casteel's MNI behavior analysis: A reductionist approach. *Midcontinental Journal of Archaeology* 7(2):171–84.

————. 1982b. Olsen and Olsen's identity crisis in faunal studies. *American Antiquity* 47(1): 180–3.

Bobrowsky, P. T., and Gatus, T. W. 1984. Archaeomalacological significance of the Hall Shelter, Perry County, Kentucky. *North American Archaeologist* 5(2):89–110.

Bocheński, Z. M., and Tomek, T. 2000. Identification of bones of galliform hybrids. *Journal of Archaeological Science* 27:691–8.

Bocherens, H., Mashkour, M., and Billiou, D. 2000. Paleoenvironmental and archaeological implications of isotopic analysis (^{13}C, ^{15}N) from Neolithic to Present in Qazvin Plain (Iran). *Environmental Archaeology* 5:1–19.

Boekelman, H. J. 1936. Shell trumpet from Arizona. *American Antiquity* 2(1):27–31.

————. 1937. Two probable shell trumpets from Ontario. *American Antiquity* 2(4):295–6.

Boessneck, J. 1969. Osteological differences between sheep (*Ovis aries* Linné) and goat (*Capra hircus* Linné). In E. Brothwell and E. Higgs (Eds.), *Science in archaeology: A survey of progress and research.* (2nd ed.) New York: Praeger Publishing, pp. 331–58.

Boessneck, J., Müller, H.-H., and Teichert, M. 1964. Osteologische Unterscheidungsmerkmale zwischen Schaf (*Ovis aries* Linné) und Ziege (*Capra hircus* Linné). *Kühn-Archiv* 78:1–129.

Bogan, A. E., and Robison, N. D. 1987. The zooarchaeology of eastern North America: History, method and theory, and bibliography. Knoxville, TN: Tennessee Anthropological Association Miscellaneous Papers 12.

Bogert, C. M. 1943. Dentitional phenomena in cobras and other elapids with notes on adaptive modifications of fangs. New York: Bulletin of the American Museum of Natural History 81: pp. 285–360.

Bogucki, P. 1988. *Forest farmers and stockherders.* Cambridge, UK: Cambridge University Press.

Böhlke, J. E., and Chaplin, C. C. G. 1968. *Fishes of the Bahamas and adjacent tropical waters.* Wynnewood, PA: Livingston Publishing.

Bökönyi, S. 1970. A new method for the determination of the number of individuals in animal bone material. *American Journal of Archaeology* 74:291–2.

Bolin, R. L. 1935. A method of preparing skeletons of small vertebrates. *Science* 82(2132):446.

Bonnaterre, P. J. 1788. Tableau encyclopédique et méthodique des trois régnes de la nature. *Ichthyologie* 1:96.

Bonnichsen, R., Hodges, L., Ream, W., Field, K. G., Kirner, D. L., Selsor, K., and Taylor, R. E. 2001. Methods for the study of ancient hair: Radiocarbon dates and gene sequences from individual hairs. *Journal of Archaeological Science* 28:775–85.

Borella, F. 2003. Aplicación de criterios tafonómicos en la evaluación del consumo de cetáceos en sitios arqueológicos de la costa meridional patagónica. *Archaeofauna* 12:143–55.

Bottema, S. 1975. The use of gastroliths in archaeology. In A. T. Clason (Ed.), *Archaeozoological studies.* Amsterdam: North-Holland Publishing Company, pp. 397–406.

Bourque, B. J. (Ed.). 1995. *Diversity and complexity in prehistoric maritime societies: A Gulf of Maine perspective.* New York: Plenum Press.

Boutton, T. W., Klein, P. D., Lynott, M. J., Price, J. E., and Tieszen, L. L. 1984. Stable carbon isotope ratios as indicators of prehistoric human diet. In J. F. Turnland and P. E. Johnson (Eds.), *Stable isotopes in nutrition: Based on a symposium sponsored by the Division of Agriculture and Food Chemistry at the 186th meeting of the American Chemical Society, Washington, DC, August 28–September 2, 1983.* Washington, DC: American Chemical Society, pp. 191–204.

Bowen, J. 1988. Seasonality: An agricultural construct. In M. C. Beaudry (Ed.), *Documentary archaeology in the New World*. Cambridge, UK: Cambridge University Press, pp. 161–71.

———. 1992. Faunal remains and urban household subsistence in New England. In A. E. Yentsch and M. C. Beaudry (Eds.), *The art and mystery of historical archaeology: Essays in honor of James Deetz*. Boca Raton, FL: CRC Press, pp. 267–81.

———. 1996. Foodways in the 18th-century Chesapeake. In T. R. Reinhard (Ed.), *The archaeology of 18th-century Virginia*. Richmond: Archeological Society of Virginia, pp. 87–130.

Boyle, K. V. 2005. Late Neolithic seal hunting in southern Brittany: A zooarchaeological study of the site of Er Yoh (Morbihan). In G. G. Monks (Ed.), *The exploitation and cultural importance of sea mammals*. Oxford: Oxbow Press, pp. 77–94.

Bradley, D. G. 2000. Mitochondrial DNA diversity and origins of domestic livestock. In C. Renfrew and K. Boyle (Eds.), *Archaeogenetics: DNA and the population of prehistory Europe*. Cambridge, Uk: McDonald Institute for Archaeological Research, pp. 315–20.

———. 2006. Documenting domestication: Reading animal genetic texts. In M. A. Zeder, D. G. Bradley, E., Emshwiller, and B. D. Smith (Eds.), *Documenting domestication: New genetics and archaeological paradigms*. Berkeley: University of California Press, pp. 273–93.

Bradley, D. G., MacHugh, D. E., Cunningham, P., and Loftus, R. T. 1996. Mitachondrial diversity and the origins of African and European cattle. *Proceedings of the National Academy of Sciences* 93:5131–5.

Bradley, D. G., and Magee, D. A. 2006. Genetics and the origins of domestic cattle. In M. A. Zeder, D. G. Bradley, E., Emshwiller, and B. D. Smith (Eds.), *Documenting domestication: New genetics and archaeological paradigms*. Berkeley: University of California Press, pp. 317–28.

Braidwood, L. S., and Braidwood, R. J. (Eds.). 1982. *Prehistoric village archaeology in south-eastern Turkey: The eighth millennium B.C. site at Çayönü: Its chipped and ground stone industries and faunal remains*. Oxford: British Archaeological Reports International Series 138.

Braidwood, R. J., and Howe, B. (Eds.). 1960. *Prehistoric investigations in Iraqi Kurdistan*. Chicago: The Oriental Institute of the University of Chicago Studies in Ancient Oriental Civilization 31, University of Chicago Press.

Brain, C. K. 1969. The contribution of Namib Desert Hottentots to an understanding of Australopithecine bone accumulations. *Scientific Papers of the Namib Desert Research Station* 39: 13–22.

———. 1981. *The hunters or the hunted? An introduction to African cave taphonomy*. Chicago: University of Chicago Press.

Branch, N., Canti, M., Clark, P., and Turney, C. 2005. *Environmental archaeology: Theoretical and practical approaches*. London: Hodder Arnold.

Brand, D. D. 1938. Aboriginal trade routes for sea shells in the southwest. *Yearbook of the Association of Pacific Coast Geographers* 4:3–10.

Brewer, D. J. 1987. Seasonality in the prehistoric Faiyum based on the incremental growth structures of the Nile catfish (Pisces: *Clarias*). *Journal of Archaeological Science* 14(5): 459–72.

———. 1992. Zooarchaeology, method, theory, and goals. In M. B. Schiffer (Ed.), *Archaeological method and theory* (vol. 4). Tucson: University of Arizona Press, pp. 195–244.

Brink, J. W. 1997. Fat content in leg bones of *Bison bison*, and applications to archaeology. *Journal of Archaeological Science* 24(3):259–74.

Brinkhuizen, D. C. 1994. Some notes on fish remains from the late 16th-century merchant vessel Scheurrak SO1. In W. Van Neer (Ed.), *Fish exploitation in the past.* Tervuren, Belgium: Annales du Musée Royal de l'Afrique Centrale, Sciences Zoologiques 274, pp. 197–205.

Brooks, A. S., Helgren, D. M., Cramer, J. S., Franklin, A., Hornyak, W., Keating, J. M., Klein, R. G., Rink, W. J., Schwarcz, H., Smith, J. N. L., Stewart, K., Todd, N. E., Verniers, J., and Yellen, J. E. 1995. Dating and context of three Middle Stone Age sites with bone points in the Upper Semliki Valley, Zaire. *Science 268*(5210):548–53.

Brothwell, D. 1976. Further evidence of bone chewing by ungulates: The sheep of North Ronaldsay, Orkney. *Journal of Archaeological Science 3*(2):179–82.

———. 2000. On the complex nature of microbial ecodynamics in relation to earlier human paleoecology. In G. Bailey, R. Charles, and N. Winder (Eds.), *Human ecodynamics.* Oxford: Oxbow Books, pp. 10–14.

Broughton, J. M. 1999. *Resource depression and intensification during the Late Holocene, San Francisco Bay: Evidence from the Emeryville Shellmound vertebrate fauna.* Berkeley: University of California Publications, Anthropological Records 32, University of California Press.

———. 2004. Pristine benchmarks and indigenous conservation? Implications from California zooarchaeology. In R. C. G. M. Lauwerier and I. Plug (Eds.), *The future from the past: Archaeozoology in wildlife conservation and heritage management.* Oxford: Oxbow Books, pp. 6–18.

Brown, L. D., and Heron, C. 2005. Presence or absence: A preliminary study into the detection of fish oils in ceramics. In J. Mulville and A. K. Outram (Eds.), *The archaeology of fats, oils, milk and dairying: An introduction and overview.* Oxford: Oxbow Books, pp. 67–76.

Brown, R. D. (Ed.). 1983. *Antler development in Cervidae.* Kingsville, Texas: Caesar Klebery Wildlife Research Institute.

Brumfiel, E. M., and Earle, T. K. 1987. Specialization, exchange, and complex societies: An introduction. In E. M. Brumfiel and T. K. Earle (Eds.), *Specialization, exchange, and complex societies.* Cambridge, UK: Cambridge University Press, pp. 1–9.

Brusca, R. C., and Brusca, G. J. 1990. *Invertebrates.* Sunderland, MA: Sinauer Associates.

Brush, S. B. 1976. Introduction to cultural adaptations to mountain ecosystems. *Human Ecology 4*(2):125–33.

Buikstra, J. E., Konigsberg, L. W., and Bullington, J. 1986. Fertility and the development of agriculture in the prehistoric Midwest. *American Antiquity 51*(3):528–46.

Buikstra, J. E., and Mielke, J. H. 1985. Demography, diet, and health. In R. I. Gilbert, Jr. and J. H. Mielke (Eds.), *The analysis of prehistoric diets.* New York: Academic Press, pp. 359–422.

Buikstra, J. E., and Milner, G. R. 1991. Isotopic and archaeological interpretations of diet in the Central Mississippi Valley. *Journal of Archaeological Science 18*(3):319–29.

Buikstra, J. E., and Swegle, M. 1989. Bone modification due to burning: Experimental evidence. In R. Bonnichsen and M. H. Sorg (Eds.), *Bone modification.* Orono: University of Maine, Institute for Quaternary Studies, Center for the Study of the First Americans, pp. 247–58.

Builth, H. 2006. Gunditjmara environmental management: The development of a fisher-gatherer-hunter society in temperate Australia. In C. Grier, J. Kim, and J. Uchiyama (Eds.), *Beyond affluent foragers: Rethinking hunter-gatherer complexity.* Oxford: Oxbow Books, pp. 4–23.

Bunn, H. T. 1986. Patterns of skeletal representation and hominid subsistence activities at Olduvai Gorge, Tanzania, and Koobi Fora, Kenya. *Journal of Human Evolution 15*:673–90.

————. 1993. Bone assemblages at base camps: A further consideration of carcass transport and bone destruction by the Hadza. In J. Hudson (Ed.), *From bones to behavior: Ethnoarchaeological and experimental contributions to the interpretation of faunal remains.* Carbondale: Southern Illinois University at Carbondale Center for Archaeological Investigations Occasional Paper 21, pp. 156–68.

Bunn, H. T., Bartram, L. E., and Kroll, E. M. 1988. Variability in bone assemblage formation from Hadza hunting, scavenging, and carcass processing. *Journal of Anthropological Archaeology* 7:412–57.

Bunn, H. T., and Kroll, E. M. 1986. Systematic butchery by Plio/Pleistocene hominids at Olduvai Gorge, Tanzania. *Current Anthropology* 27(5):431–52.

————. 1988. Reply to Binford: "Fact and fiction about the Zinjanthropus floor: Data, arguments, and interpretations." *Current Anthropology* 29(1):135–49.

Burke, A. 2000. Seasonality and human mobility during the Upper Palaeolithic in southwestern France. In P. Rowley-Conwy (Ed.), *Animal bones, human societies.* Oxford: Oxbow Books, pp. 28–35.

Burke, A., and Castanet, J. 1995. Histological observations of cementum growth in horse teeth and their application to archaeology. *Journal of Archaeological Science* 22:479–93.

Burt, W. H., and Grossenheider, R. P. 1964. *A field guide to the mammals: Field marks of all species found north of the Mexican border.* Boston: Houghton-Mifflin.

Burton, J. H., and Price, T. D. 1990. The ratio of barium to strontium as a paleodietary-indicator of consumption of marine resources. *Journal of Archaeological Science* 17(5):547–57.

Butler, V. L. 1993. Natural versus cultural salmonid remains: Origin of the Dalles Roadcut bones, Columbia River, Oregon, U.S.A. *Journal of Archaeological Science* 20(1):1–24.

————. 2001. Changing fish use on Mangaia, Southern Cook Islands: Resource depression and the prey choice model. *International Journal of Osteoarchaeology* 11(1–2):88–100.

Butler, V. L., and Campbell, S. K. 2004. Resource intensification and resource depression in the Pacific Northwest of North America: A zooarchaeological review. *Journal of World Prehistory* 18(4):327–405.

Butler, V. L., and O'Connor, J. E. 2004. 9000 years of salmon fishing on the Columbia River, North America. *Quaternary Research* 62:1–8.

Butzer, K. W. 1971. *Environment and archaeology: An ecological approach to prehistory.* Chicago: Aldine.

————. 1990. A human ecosystem framework for archaeology. In E. F. Moran (Ed.), *The ecosystem approach in anthropology: From concept to practice.* Ann Arbor: University of Michigan Press, pp. 91–130.

Byers, D. S. 1951. On the interpretation of faunal remains. *American Antiquity* 16(3):262–3.

Byers, D. S. (Ed.). 1967. *The prehistory of the Tehuacan Valley: Environment and subsistence* (Vol. 1.) Austin: University of Texas Press.

Byers, D. A., Smith, C. S., and Broughton, J. M. 2005. Holocene artiodactyl population histories and large game hunting in the Wyoming Basin, USA. *Journal of Archaeological Science* 32:125–42.

Cabral, J. P., and da Silva, A. C. F. 2003. Morphometric analysis of limpets from an Iron-Age shell midden found in northwest Portugal. *Journal of Archaeological Science* 30:817–29.

Cachel, S. 2000. Subsistence among Arctic peoples and the reconstruction of social organization from prehistoric human diet. In P. Rowley-Conwy (Ed.), *Animal bones, human societies.* Oxford: Oxbow Books, pp. 39–48.

Cailliet, G. M., Love, M. S., and Ebeling, A. W. 1986. *Fishes: A field and laboratory manual on their structure, identification, and natural history.* Belmont, CA: Wadsworth Publishing Company.

Cailliet, G. M., Radtke, R. L., and Welden, B. A. 1986. Elasmobranch age determination and verification: A review. In T. Uyeno, R. Arai, T. Taniuchi, and K. Matsuura (Eds.), *Indo-Pacific fish biology: Proceedings of the second International Conference on Indo-Pacific Fishes.* Tokyo: Ichthyological Society of Japan, pp. 345–60.

Cane, S. 1996. Australian Aboriginal subsistence in the Western Desert. In D. G. Bates and S. H. Lees (Eds.), *Case studies in human ecology.* New York: Plenum Press, pp. 17–53.

Cannon, A. 2000. Faunal remains as economic indicators on the Pacific Northwest Coast. In P. Rowley-Conwy (Ed.), *Animal bones, human societies.* Oxford: Oxbow Books, pp. 49–57.

Cannon, D. Y. 1987. *Marine fish osteology: A manual for archaeologists.* Burnaby, British Columbia: Department of Archaeology, Simon Fraser University Publication 18.

Carey, G. 1982. Ageing and sexing domestic bird bones from some late medieval deposits at Baynard's Castle, City of London. In B. Wilson, C. Grigson, and S. Payne (Eds.), *Ageing and sexing animal bones from archaeological sites.* Oxford: British Archaeological Reports British Series 109, pp. 263–8.

Carleton, M. D., and Musser, G. G. 1989. Systematic studies of Oryzomyine rodents (Muridae, Sigmodontinae): A synopsis of Microryzomys. New York: *Bulletin of the American Museum of Natural History* 191: 1–83.

Carr, A. F. 1986. *The sea turtle: So excellent a fishe.* Austin: University of Texas Press.

Carroll, R. L. 1987. *Vertebrate paleontology and evolution.* New York: W. H. Freeman and Company.

Carter, G. F. 1971. Pre-Columbian chickens in America. In C. L. Riley, J. C. Kelly, C. W. Pennington, and R. L. Rands (Eds.), *Man across the sea.* Austin: University of Texas Press, pp. 178–218.

Carter, H. H. 1975. A guide to rates of tooth wear in English lowland sheep. *Journal of Archaeological Science* 2(3):231–3.

Casteel, R. W. 1974. A method for estimation of live weight of fish from the size of skeletal elements. *American Antiquity* 39(1):94–8.

———. 1976. A comparison of methods for back-calculation of fish size from the size of scales found in archaeological sites. *Ossa* 3/4:129–39.

———. 1977. Characterization of faunal assemblages and the minimum number of individuals determined from paired elements: Continuing problems in archaeology. *Journal of Archaeological Science* 4(2):125–34.

———. 1978. Faunal assemblages and the "wiegemethode" or weight method. *Journal of Field Archaeology* 5(1):71–7.

Casteel, R. W., and Grayson, D. K. 1977. Terminological problems in quantitative faunal analysis. *World Archaeology* 9(2):235–42.

Cerón-Carrasco, R. 1994. The investigation of fish remains from an Orkney farm mound. In W. Van Neer (Ed.), *Fish exploitation in the past.* Tervuren, Belgium: Annales du Musée Royal de l'Afrique Centrale, Sciences Zoologiques 274, pp. 207–10.

Chaplin, R. E. 1965. Animals in archaeology. *Antiquity* 39:204–11.

————. 1971. *The study of animal bones from archaeological sites.* New York: Seminar Press.

Chaplin, R. E., and White, R. W. G. 1969. The use of tooth eruption and wear, body weight and antler characteristics in the age estimation of male wild and park fallow deer (*Dama dama*). *Journal of Zoology, London* 157:125–32.

Chauchat, C. 1992. *Préhistoire de la côte nord du Pérou: Le Paijanien de Cupisnique.* Bordeaux: Centre National de la Recherche Scientifique, Cahiers du Quaternaire 18.

Chilardi, S., Guzzardi, L., Iovino, M. R., and Rivoli, A. 2005. The evidence of *Spondylus* ornamental objects in the central Mediterranean Sea. Two case studies: Sicily and Malta. In D. E. Bar-Yosef Mayer (Ed.), *Archaeomalacology: Molluscs in former environments of human behaviour.* Oxford: Oxbow Books, pp. 82–90.

Chinzei, K., Koike, H., Oba, T., Matsushima, Y., and Kitazato, H. 1987. Secular changes in the oxygen isotope ratios of mollusc shells during the Holocene of Central Japan. *Palaeogeography, Palaeoclimatology, Palaeoecology* 61(1/2):155–66.

Chow, B.-S. 1984. Animal domestication in Neolithic China. In J. Clutton-Brock and C. Grigson (Eds.), *Animals and archaeology: 3. Early herders and their flocks.* Oxford: British Archaeological Reports International Series 202, pp. 363–9.

Choyke, A. M. 1987. The exploitation of red deer in the Hungarian Bronze Age. *ArchaeoZoologia* 1(1):109–16.

————. 2004. Archaeozoology and the transition from socialism to capitalism: The case of Roman Aquincum. In R. C. G. M. Lauwerier and I. Plug (Eds.), *The future from the past: Archaeozoology in wildlife conservation and heritage management.* Oxford: Oxbow Books, pp. 141–8.

Choyke, A. M., and Bartosiewicz, L. 1994. Angling with bones. In W. Van Neer (Ed.), *Fish exploitation in the past.* Tervuren, Belgium: Annales du Musée Royal de l'Afrique Centrale, Sciences Zoologiques 274, pp. 117–82.

Choyke, A. M., Vretemark, M., and Sten, S. 2004. Levels of social identity expressed in the refuse and worked bone from Middle Bronze Age Száhalombatta-Földvár, Vatya culture, Hungary. In S. J. O'Day, W. Van Neer, and A. Ervynck (Eds.), *Behaviour behind bones: The zooarchaeology of ritual, religion, status and identity.* Oxford: Oxbow Books, pp. 177–89.

Claassen, C. 1998. *Shells.* Cambridge, UK: University of Cambridge Press.

Clark, Gillian 1987. Faunal remains and economic complexity. *ArchaeoZoologia* 1(1):183–94.

Clark, J., and Keitze, K. K. 1967. Paleoecology of the Lower Nodular Zone, Brule Formation in the Big Badlands of South Dakota. In J. Clark, J. R. Beerbower, and K. K. Keitze (Eds.), *Oligocene sedimentation, stratigraphy, and paleoclimatology in the Big Badlands of South Dakota.* Chicago: Chicago Museum of Natural History, Fieldiana: *Geology Memoir* 5, pp. 111–37.

Clark, J. G. D. 1954. *Excavations at Star Carr, an early Mesolithic site at Seamer near Scarborough, Yorkshire.* Cambridge, UK: Cambridge University Press.

————. 1972. Foreword. In E. S. Higgs (Ed.), *Papers in economic prehistory.* Cambridge, UK: Cambridge University Press, pp. vii–x.

Clarke, D. L. 1968. *Analytical archaeology.* London: Methuen.

————. 1972. Models and paradigms in contemporary archaeology. In D. L. Clarke (Ed.), *Models in archaeology.* London: Methuen, pp. 1–60.

Clason, A. T. 1972. Some remarks on the use and presentation of archaeozoological data. *Helinium* 12(2):139–53.

————. 1973. A short survey of the history and development of archaeozoology in the Low Countries, especially in the Netherlands. In W. A. van Esea (Ed.), *Archeologie en historie*. Bussum, The Netherlands: Fibula-van Dishoeck, pp. 469–76.

————. 1983. A. E. van Giffen as archaeozoologist. *Palaeohistoria* 25:1–6.

————. 1986. Fish and archaeology. In D. C. Brinkhuizen and A. T. Clason (Eds.), *Fish and archaeology: Studies in osteometry, taphonomy, seasonality and fishing methods*. Oxford: British Archaeological Reports International Series 294, pp. 1–8.

Clastres, P. 1972. The Guayaki. In M. G. Bicchieri (Ed.), *Hunters and gatherers today: A socio-economic study of eleven such cultures in the twentieth century*. New York: Holt, Rinehart, and Winston, pp. 138–74.

Cleland, C. E. 1966. *The prehistoric animal ecology and ethnozoology of the Upper Great Lakes region*. Ann Arbor: University of Michigan Museum of Anthropology Anthropological Papers 29.

————. 1976. The focal-diffuse model: An evolutionary perspective on the prehistoric cultural adaptations of the eastern United States. *Midcontinental Journal of Archaeology* 1(1): 59–76.

Clermont, N. 1994. Edouard Lartet and the fine recovery of faunal samples. *ArchaeoZoologia* 7(1):73–6.

Clutton-Brock, J. 1984. Dog. In I. L. Mason (Ed.), *Evolution of domesticated animals*. London: Longman, pp. 198–211.

————. 1995. Origins of the dog: Domestication and early history. In J. Serpell (Ed.), *The domestic dog: Its evolution, behavior, and interactions with people*. Cambridge, UK: Cambridge University Press, pp. 8–20.

————. 1999. *A natural history of domesticated mammals* (2nd ed.). Cambridge, UK: Cambridge University Press/The Natural History Museum.

Clutton-Brock, J. (Ed.). 1989. *The walking larder: Patterns of domestication, pastoralism, and predation*. London: Unwin Hyman.

Clutton-Brock, J. (Ed.). 2002. *Mammals*. New York: Dorling Kindersley.

Clutton-Brock, J., Dennis-Bryan, K., Armitage, P. L., and Jewell, P. A. 1990. *Osteology of Soay sheep*. London: Bulletin of the British Museum (Natural History) 56(1), pp. 1–56.

Coe, M. D., and Flannery, K. 1964. Microenvironments and Mesoamerican prehistory. *Science* 143(3607):650–4.

Colburn, M. L., Kelly, L., and Snider, J. 1991. Redear sunfish in the Late Holocene of Illinois. In J. R. Purdue, W. E. Klippel, and B. W. Styles (Eds.), *Beamers, bobwhites, and blue-points: Tributes to the career of Paul W. Parmalee*. Springfield: Illinois State Museum Scientific Papers 23, pp. 67–79.

Colley, S. M. 1990. The analysis and interpretation of archaeological fish remains. In M. B. Schiffer (Ed.), *Archaeological method and theory* (Vol. 2). Tucson: University of Arizona Press, pp. 207–53.

Colley, S. M., and Spennemann, D. H. R. 1987. Some methods of preparing fish skeletons in the tropics. *Journal of Field Archaeology* 14(1): 117–19.

Collins, P. W. 1991. Interaction between island foxes (*Urocyon littoralis*) and Indians on islands off the coast of Southern California: I. Morphological and archaeological evidence of human assisted dispersal. *Journal of Ethnobiology* 11(1):51–81.

Conklin, H. C. 1972. *Folk classification: A topically arranged bibliography of contemporary and background references through 1971.* New Haven: Yale University, Department of Anthropology.

Cook, S. F., and Treganza, A. E. 1947. The quantitative investigation of aboriginal sites: Comparative physical and chemical analysis of two California Indian mounds. *American Antiquity* 13(2):135–41.

———. 1950. The quantitative investigation of Indian mounds. *University of California Publications in American Archaeology and Ethnology* 40:223–62.

Cooke, R. G. 1992. Prehistoric nearshore and littoral fishing in the eastern tropical Pacific: An ichthyological evaluation. *Journal of World Prehistory* 6(1):1–49.

———. 1993. Animal icons and pre-Colombian society: The Felidae, with special reference to Panama. In M. M. Graham (Ed.), *Reinterpreting prehistory of Central America.* Niwot: University Press of Colorado, pp. 169–208.

———. 2004. Observations on the religious content of the animal imagery of the "Gran Coclé" semiotic tradition of pre-Columbian Panama. In S. J. O'Day, W. Van Neer, and A. Ervynck (Eds.), *Behaviour behind bones: The zooarchaeology of ritual, religion, status, and identity.* Oxford: Oxbow Books, pp. 114–27.

Cooke, R. G., and Rodríguez, G. T. 1994. Marine and freshwater fish amphidromy in a small tropical river on the Pacific coast of Panama: A preliminary evaluation based on gill-net and hook-and-line captures. In W. Van Neer (Ed.), *Fish exploitation in the past.* Tervuren, Belgium: Annales du Musée Royal de l'Afrique Centrale, Sciences Zoologiques 274, pp. 99–106.

Coombs, G. 1980. Decision theory and subsistence strategies: Some theoretical considerations. In T. K. Earle and A. L. Christenson (Eds.), *Modeling change in prehistoric subsistence economies.* New York: Academic Press, pp. 187–208.

Cope, C. 2004. The butchering patterns of Gamla and Yodefat: Beginning the search for *kosher* practices. In S. J. O'Day, W. Van Neer, and A. Ervynck (Eds.), *Behaviour behind bones: The zooarchaeology of ritual, religion, status and identity.* Oxford: Oxbow Books, pp. 25–33.

Copley, M. S., Berstan, R., Dudd, S. N., Straker, V., Payne, S., and Evershed, R. P. 2005. Dairying in antiquity. I. Evidence from absorbed lipid residues dating to the British Iron Age. *Journal of Archaeological Science* 32:485–503.

Copley, M. S., Jim, S., Jones, V., Rose, P., Clapham, A., Edwards, D. N., Horton, M., Rowley-Conwy, P., and Evershed, R. P. 2004. Short- and long-term foraging and foddering strategies of domesticated animals from Qasr Ibrim, Egypt. *Journal of Archaeological Science* 31:1273–86.

Corbet, G. B., and Clutton-Brock, J. 1984. Appendix: Taxonomy and nomenclature. In I. L. Mason (Ed.), *Evolution of domesticated animals.* London: Longman, pp. 434–8.

Cornwall, I. W. 1956. *Bones for the archaeologist.* New York: Macmillan.

Cossette, É., and Horard-Herbin, M.-P. 2003. A contribution to the morphometrical study of cattle in colonial North America. *Journal of Archaeological Science* 30:263–74.

Costamagno, S., Beauval, C., Lange-Badré, B., Vandermeersch, B., Mann, A., and Maureille, B. 2005. Homme ou canivores? protocol d'étude d'ensembles osseux mixtes: l'exemple du gisement moustérien des Pradelles (Marillac-le-Franc, Charente). *Archaeofauna* 14:43–68.

Costamagno, S., Théry-Parisot, Brugel, J.-P., and Guibert, R. 2005. Taphonomic consequences of the use of bones as fuel. Experimental data and archaeological applications. In T. O'Connor (Ed.), *Biosphere to lithosphere: New studies in vertebrate taphonomy.* Oxford: Oxbow Books, pp. 51–62.

Courtemanche, M., and Legendre, V. 1985. *Os des poissons: Nomenclature cofifiée, noms français et anglais*. Gouvernement du Québec, Ministère du Loisir, de la Chasse, et de la Pêche, Rapport Technique 06–38.

Coutts, P. J. F. 1970. Bivalve-growth patterning as a method for seasonal dating in archaeology. *Nature* 226(5248):874.

———. 1975. Marine fishing in archaeological perspective: Techniques for determining fishing strategies. In R. W. Casteel and G. I. Quimby (Eds.), *Maritime adaptations of the Pacific*. The Hague: Mouton Publishers, pp. 265–306.

Coutts, P. J. F., and Higham, C. 1971. The seasonal factor in prehistoric New Zealand. *World Archaeology* 2(3):266–77.

Coutts, P. J. F., and Jones, K. L. 1974. A proposed method for deriving seasonal data from the echinoid, *Evechinus chloroticus* (Val.), in archaeological deposits. *American Antiquity* 39(1):98–102.

Cox, C. B., Healey, I. N., and Moore. P. D. 1976. *Biogeography: An ecological and evolutionary approach*. (2nd ed.) New York: John Wiley and Sons.

Cox, M., and Mays, S. (Eds.). 2000. *Human osteology in archaeology and forensic science*. London: Greenwich Medical Media.

Coy, J. P. 1975. Iron Age cookery. In A. T. Clason (Ed.), *Archaeozoological studies*. Amsterdam: North-Holland Publishing Company, pp. 426–30.

———. 1978. Comparative collections for zooarchaeology. In D. R. Brothwell, K. D. Thomas, and J. Clutton-Brock (Eds.), *Research problems in zooarchaeology*. London: University of London, Institute of Archaeology Occasional Publication 3, pp. 143–5.

———. 1979. The place of archaeozoology in rescue excavation in Britain. In M. Kubasiewicz (Ed.), *Archaeozoology*. Szczecin: Agricultural Academy, pp. 23–34.

———. 1996. Medieval records versus excavation results – Examples from southern England. *Archaeofauna* 5:55–63.

Coy, J. P., Jones, R. T., and Turner, K. A. 1982. Absolute ageing of cattle from tooth sections and its relevance to archaeology. In B. Wilson, C. Grigson, and S. Payne (Eds.), *Ageing and sexing animal bones from archaeological sites*. Oxford: British Archaeological Reports British Series 109, pp. 127–40.

Crabtree, P. J. 1989. *West Stow, Suffolk: Early Anglo-Saxon animal husbandry*. Suffolk County Planning Department: East Anglian Archaeology Report 47.

———. 1990. Zooarchaeology and complex societies: Some uses of faunal analysis for the study of trade, social status, and ethnicity. In M. B. Schiffer (Ed.), *Archaeological method and theory* (vol. 2). Tucson: University of Arizona Press, pp. 155–205.

———. 1991. Roman Britain to Anglo-Saxon England: The zooarchaeological evidence. In P. J. Crabtree and K. Ryan (Eds.), *Animal use and culture change*. Philadelphia: University of Pennsylvania, Museum of Archaeology and Anthropology Research Papers in Science and Archaeology, MASCA 8, pp. 32–8.

———. 1995. The symbolic role of animals in Anglo-Saxon England: Evidence from burials and cremations. In K. Ryan and P. J. Crabtree (Eds.), *The symbolic role of animals in archaeology*. Philadelphia: University of Pennsylvania, Museum of Archaeology and Anthropology Research Papers in Science and Archaeology, MASCA 12, pp. 20–6.

———. 2004. Ritual feasting in the Irish Iron Age: Re-examining the fauna from Dún Ailinne in light of contemporary archaeology theory. In S. J. O'Day, W. Van Neer, and A. Ervynck (Eds.),

Behaviour behind bones: The zooarchaeology of ritual, religion, status and identity. Oxford: Oxbow Books, pp. 62–5.

Crabtree, P. J., Campana, D., and Ryan, K. (Eds.). 1989. *Early animal domestication and its cultural context.* Philadelphia: University of Pennsylvania, Museum of Archaeology and Anthropology Research Papers in Science and Archaeology, MASCA Special Supplement to Volume 6.

Craig, O. E., Taylor, G., Mulville, J., Collins, M. J., and Pearson, M. P. 2005. The identification of prehistoric dairying activities in the West Isles of Scotland: An integrated biomolecular approach. *Journal of Archaeological Science* 32:91–103.

Cram, C. L. 2004. The hundred years rule – A century of curating archaeological animal bones in Britain. In R. C. G. M. Lauwerier and I. Plug (Eds.), *The future from the past: Archaeozoology in wildlife conservation and heritage management.* Oxford: Oxbow Books, pp. 159–66.

Crook, M. R., Jr. 1992. Oyster sources and their prehistoric use on the Georgia coast. *Journal of Archaeological Science* 19(5):483–96.

Crosby, A. W. 1986. *Ecological imperialism: The biological expansion of Europe, 900–1900.* Cambridge, UK: Cambridge University Press.

_____. 1994. *Germs, seeds, and animals: Studies in ecological history.* Armonk, New York: M. E. Sharpe.

Crumley, C. L. 1979. Three locational models: An epistemological assessment for anthropology and archaeology. In M. B. Schiffer (Ed.), *Advances in archaeological method and theory* (Vol. 2). New York: Academic Press, pp. 141–73.

_____. 1994. Historical ecology: A multidisciplinary ecological orientation. In C. L. Crumley (Ed.), *Historical ecology: Cultural knowledge and changing landscapes.* Santa Fe, NM: School of American Research Press, pp. 1–16.

Cruz, I. 2005. La representación de partes esqueléticas de aves. patrones naturales e interpretación arqueológica. *Archaeofauna* 14:69–81.

Cruz, I., and Elkin, D. 2003. Structural bone density of the Lesser Rhea (*Pterocnemia pennata*) (Aves: Rheidae). Taphonomic and archaeological implications. *Journal of Archaeological Science* 30:37–44.

Dahl, G., and Hjort, A. 1976. *Having herds: Pastoral herd growth and household economy.* Stockholm: Department of Social Anthropology, University of Stockholm, Stockholm Studies in Social Anthropology 2.

Dall, W. H. 1877. *On succession in the shell-heaps of the Aleutian Islands.* U.S. Geological and Geographic Service, Washington, DC: Contributions to North American Ethnology 1, pp. 41–91.

Daly, P. 1969. Approaches to faunal analysis in archaeology. *American Antiquity* 34(2):146–53.

Daniel, G. E. 1981. *A short history of archaeology.* London: Thames and Hudson.

Dalzell, P. 1998. The role of archaeological and cultural-historical records in long range coastal resource fisheries management strategies and policies in Pacific Islands. *Ocean and Coastal Management* 40:237–52.

Dark, P. 2003. Dogs, a crane (not duck) and diet at Star Carr: A response to Schulting and Richards. *Journal of Archaeological Science* 30:1353–6.

Dart, R. A. 1957. *The osteodontokeratic culture of Australopithecus prometheus.* Pretoria, South Africa: Transvaal Museum Memoir 10.

Daróczi-Szabó, L. 2004. Animal bones as indicators of *kosher* food refuse from 14th-century A.D. Buda, Hungary. In S. J. O'Day, W. Van Neer, and A. Ervynck (Eds.), *Behaviour behind bones: The zooarchaeology of ritual, religion, status and identity.* Oxford: Oxbow Books, pp. 101–13.

Darwent, C. M. 2004. The highs and lows of high Arctic mammals: Temporal change and regional variability in Paleoeskimo subsistence. In M. Mondini, S. Muñoz, and S. Wickler (Eds.), *Colonisation, migration and marginal areas: A zooarchaeological approach.* Oxford: Oxbow Books, pp. 62–73.

Daugherty, R. D. 1988. Problems and responsibilities in the excavation of wet sites. In B. A. Purdy (Ed.), *Wet site archaeology.* Caldwell, NJ: Telford Press, pp. 15–29.

Davidson, I. 1983. Site variability and prehistoric economy in Levante. In G. Bailey (Ed.), *Hunter-gatherer economy in prehistory: A European perspective.* Cambridge, UK: Cambridge University Press, pp. 79–95.

Davies, J., Fabiš, M., Mainland, I., Richards, M., and Thomas, R. (Eds.) 2005. *Diet and health in past animal populations: Current research and future directions.* Oxford: Oxbow Books.

Davis, S. J. M. 1987. *The archaeology of animals.* New Haven: Yale University Press.

———. 2000. The effect of castration and age on the development of the Shetland sheep skeleton and a metric comparison between bones of males, females, and castrates. *Journal of Archaeological Science* 27:373–90.

———. 2005. Why domesticate food animals? Some zoo-archaeological evidence from the Levant. *Journal of Archaeological Science* 31:1408–16.

Davis S. J. M., and Payne, S. 2003. 101 modos de tratar un erizo muerto: Notas sobre la preparación de esqueletos desarticulados para uso zooarqueológico. *Archaeofauna* 12:203–11.

Davis, S. J. M., and Valla, F. R. 1978. Evidence for domestication of the dog 12,000 years ago in the Natufian of Israel. *Nature* 276(5688):608–10.

De Boyrie Moya, E., Krestensen, M. K., and Goggin, J. M. 1957. *Zamia* starch in Santo Domingo: A contribution to the ethnobotany of the Dominican Republic. *Florida Anthropologist* 10(3/4): 17–40.

De Cupere, B., Van Neer, W., Monchot, H., Rijmenants, E., Udrescu, M., and Waelkens, M. 2005. Ancient breeds of domestic fowl (*Gallus gallus* f. domestica) distinguished on the basis of traditional observations combined with mixture analysis. *Journal of Archaeological Science* 32:1587–97.

d'Errico, F., and Vanhaeren, M. 2002. Criteria for identifying red deer (*Cervus elaphus*) age and sex from their canines. Application to the study of Upper Palaeolithic and Mesolithic ornaments. *Journal of Archaeological Science* 29:211–32.

Deevey, E. S., Jr. 1947. Life tables for natural populations of animals. *Quarterly Review of Biology* 22:283–314.

deFrance, S. D. 2006. The sixth toe: The modern culinary role of the guinea pig in southern Peru. *Food and Foodways* 14:3–34.

deFrance, S. D., Keefer, D. K., Richardson, J. B., and Alvarez, A. U. 2001. Late Paleo-Indian coastal foragers: Specialized extractive behavior at Quebrada Tacahuay, Peru. *Latin American Antiquity* 12(4):413–26.

Deith, M. R. 1983a. Molluscan calendars: The use of growth-line analysis to establish seasonality of shellfish collection at the Mesolithic site of Morton, Fife. *Journal of Archaeological Science* 10(5):423–40.

———. 1983b. Seasonality of shell collecting determined by oxygen isotope analysis of marine shells from Asturian sites in Cantabria. In C. Grigson and J. Clutton-Brock (Eds.), *Animals and archaeology: 2. Shell middens, fishes, and birds.* Oxford: British Archaeological Reports International Series 183, pp. 67–76.

Deith, M. R., and Shackleton, J. C. 1988. The contribution of shells to site interpretation: Approaches to shell material from Franchthi Cave. In J. L. Bintliff, D. A. Davidson, and E. G. Grant (Eds.), *Conceptual issues in environmental archaeology.* Edinburgh: Edinburgh University Press, pp. 49–58.

de la Vega, Garcilaso 1961 [1604]. *The Incas: The royal commentaries of the Inca,* translated by Maria Jolas, edited by A. Gheerbrant. New York: Orion Press.

De Nigris, M. E. 2004. Guanaco and huemel in Patagonian hunter-gatherers diet. In G. L. Mengoni Goñalons (Ed.), *Zooarchaeology of South America.* British Archaeological Reports International Series 1298. Oxford: Archaeopress, pp. 11–37.

De Nigris, M. E., and Mengoni Goñalons, G. L. 2005. The guanaco as a source of meat and fat in the southern Andes. In J. Mulville and A. K. Outram (Eds.), *The archaeology of fats, oils, milk and dairying: An introduction and overview.* Oxford: Oxbow Books, pp. 160–6.

Deniz, E., and Payne, S. 1982. Eruption and wear in the mandibular dentition as a guide to ageing Turkish angora goats. In B. Wilson, C. Grigson, and S. Payne (Eds.), *Ageing and sexing animal bones from archaeological sites.* Oxford: British Archaeological Reports British Series 109, pp. 155–205.

Dennell, R. W. 1979. Prehistoric diet and nutrition: Some food for thought. *World Archaeology* 11(2):121–35.

Derevenski, J. S. 2001. Is human osteology environmental archaeology? In U. Albarella (Ed.), *Environmental archaeology: Meaning and purpose.* Kluwer: Dordrecht, pp. 113–33.

Deshpande-Mukherjee, A. 2005. Marine shell utilisation by the Chalcolithic societies of the western Deccan region of India. In D. E. Bar-Yosef Mayer (Ed.), *Archaeomalacology: Molluscs in former environments of human behaviour.* Oxford: Oxbow Books, pp. 174–84.

Desse, J., and Desse-Berset, N. (Eds.). 1987–1996. *Fiches d'ostéologie animale pour l'archéologie.* Juan-les-Pins: Centre de Recherches Archéologiques du CNRS, APDCA.

———. 1994. Osteometry and fishing strategies at Cape Andreas Kastros (Cyprus, 8th millennium BP). In W. van Neer (Ed.), *Fish exploitation in the past.* Tervuren, Belgium: Annales du Musée Royal de l'Afrique Centrale, Sciences Zoologiques 274, pp. 69–79.

———. 1996. On the boundaries of osteometry applied to fish. *Archaeofauna* 5:171–9.

Desse-Berset, N. 1994. Sturgeons of the Rhône during protohistory in Arles (6th–2nd century BC). In W. Van Neer (Ed.), *Fish exploitation in the past.* Tervuren, Belgium: Annales du Musée Royal de l'Afrique Centrale, Sciences Zoologiques 274, pp. 81–90.

de Wet, E., Robertson, P., and Plug, I. 1990. Some techniques for cleaning and degreasing bones and a method for evaluating the long-term effects of these techniques. In E. M. Herholdt (Ed.), *Natural history collections: Their management and value.* Pretoria, South Africa: Transvaal Museum Special Publication 1, pp. 37–41.

Diamond, J. M. 1966. Zoological classification system of a primitive people. *Science* 151(3714): 1102–4.

———. 1989. Historic extinctions: A Rosetta Stone for understanding prehistoric extinctions. In P. S. Martin and R. G. Klein (Eds.), *Quaternary extinctions: A prehistoric revolution.* Tucson: University of Arizona Press, pp. 824–62.

———. 1990a. Biological effects of ghosts. *Nature* 345(6278):769–70.

———. 1990b. Bob Dylan and moas' ghosts. *Natural History* 99(10):26–31.

————. 1991. The earliest horsemen. *Nature* 350(6316):275–6.

————. 1994a. Spacious skies and tilted axes. *Natural History* 103(5):16–23.

————. 1994b. Zebras and the Anna Karenina principle. *Natural History* 103(9):4–10.

Dickinson, E. C. (Ed.). 2003. *The Howard and Moore complete checklist of the birds of the world* (3rd ed.). Princeton: Princeton University Press.

Dietler, M., and Hayden, B. 2001. Digesting the feast: Good to eat, good to drink, Good to think. In M. Dietler and B. Hayden (Eds.), *Feasts: Archaeological and ethnographic perspectives on food, politics, and power*. Washington, DC: Smithsonian Institution Press, pp. 1–20.

Dimbleby, G. W. 1967. *Plants and archaeology*. London: Humanities Press.

Dincauze, D. F. 1976. *The Neville site: 8,000 years at Amoskeag, Manchester, New Hampshire*. Cambridge, MA: Harvard University, Peabody Museum Monographs 4.

Dirrigl, F. J., Jr. 2001. Bone mineral density of wild turkey (*Meleagris gallopavo*) skeletal elements and its effect on differential survivorship. *Journal of Archaeological Science* 28:817–32.

Dobney, K., and Ervynck A. 2000. Interpreting developmental stress in archaeological pigs: The chronology of linear enamel hypoplasia. *Journal of Archaeological Science* 27:597–607.

Dobney, K., and Rielly, K. 1988. A method for recording archaeological animal bones: The use of diagnostic zones. *Circaea* 5(2):79–96.

Dodson, P., and Wexlar, D. 1979. Taphonomic investigations of owl pellets. *Paleobiology* 5(3):275–84.

Doetschman, W. H. 1947. An acarian infestation of dermestid larvae. *Journal of Mammalogy* 28(3):299.

Donnan, C. B. 1976. *Moche art and iconography*. Los Angeles: University of California Latin American Center Publications.

Douglas, M. 1975. Deciphering a meal. In M. Douglas (Ed.), *Implicit meanings: Essays in anthropology*. Boston: Routledge and Kegan Paul, pp. 249–75.

Driesch, A. von den. 1976. *A guide to the measurement of animal bones from archaeological sites*. Cambridge, MA: Harvard University, Peabody Museum of Archaeology and Ethnology Bulletin 1.

————. 1991. Joachim Boessneck. *ArchaeoZoologia* 4(1):9–10.

————. 1993. Faunal remains from Habuba Kabira in Syria. In H. Buitenhuis and A. T. Clason (Eds.), *Archaeozoology of the Near East*. Leiden, The Netherlands: Universal Book Services, pp. 52–9.

————. 1994. Hyperostosis in fish. In W. Van Neer (Ed.), *Fish exploitation in the past*. Tervuren, Belgium: Annales du Musée Royal de l'Afrique Centrale, Sciences Zoologiques 274, pp. 37–45.

Driver, J. C. 1982. Medullary bone as an indicator of sex in bird remains from archaeological sites. In B. Wilson, C. Grigson, and S. Payne (Eds.), *Ageing and sexing animal bones from archaeological sites*. Oxford: British Archaeological Reports British Series 109, pp. 251–4.

————. 1985. *Zooarchaeology of six prehistoric sites in the Sierra Blanca region, New Mexico*. Ann Arbor: University of Michigan Museum of Anthropology Technical Reports 17.

————. 1990. Meat in due season: The timing of communal hunts. In L. B. Davis and B. O. K. Reeves (Eds.), *Hunters of the recent past*. London: Unwin Hyman, pp. 11–33.

————. 1992. Identification, classification, and zooarchaeology. *Circaea* 9(1):35–47.

————. 1993. Zooarchaeology in British Columbia. BC *Studies* 99:77–105.

Driver, J. C., and Hobson, K. A. 1992. A 10,500-year sequence of bird remains from the southern boreal forest region of western Canada. *Arctic* 45(2):105–10.

Dudd, S. N., and Evershed, R. P. 1999. Evidence for varying patterns of exploitation of animal products in different prehistoric pottery traditions based on lipids preserved in surface and absorbed residues. *Journal of Archaeological Science* 26:1473–82.

Dufour, D. L. 1983. Nutrition in the northwest Amazon: Household dietary intake and time-energy expenditure. In R. B. Hames and W. T. Vickers (Eds.), *Adaptive responses of native Amazonians*. New York: Academic Press, pp. 329–55.

———. 1994. Diet and nutritional status of Amazonian peoples. In A. Roosevelt (Ed.), *Amazonian Indians from prehistory to the present*. Tucson: University of Arizona Press, pp. 151–75.

Dunnell, R. C. 1986. Five decades of American archaeology. In D. J. Meltzer, D. D. Fowler, and J. A. Sabloff (Eds.), *American archaeology past and future: A celebration of the Society for American Archaeology 1935–1985*. Washington, DC: Smithsonian Institution Press, pp. 23–49.

Dupras, T. L., and Schwarcz, H. P. 2001. Strangers in a strange land: Stable isotope evidence for human migration in the Dakhleh Oasis, Egypt. *Journal of Archaeological Science* 28:1199–208.

Dwyer, P. D., and Minnegal, M. 1991. Hunting in lowland, tropical rain forest: Towards a model of non-agricultural subsistence. *Human Ecology* 19(2):187–212.

Earle, T. K. 1980. A model of subsistence change. In T. K. Earle and A. L. Christenson (Eds.), *Modeling change in prehistoric subsistence economies*. New York: Academic Press, pp. 1–29.

———. 1982. Prehistoric economics and the archaeology of exchange. In J. E. Ericson and T. K. Earle (Eds.). *Contexts for prehistoric exchange*. New York: Academic Press, pp. 1–12.

Earle, T. K., and Christenson, A. L. (Eds.). 1980. *Modeling change in prehistoric subsistence economies*. New York: Academic Press.

Eastham, A. 1988. The season or the symbol: The evidence of swallows in the Palaeolithic of western Europe. *ArchaeoZoologia* 2(1/2):243–52.

Eaton, G. F. 1898. The prehistoric fauna of Block Island, as indicated by its ancient shell-heaps. *American Journal of Science* 156:137–59.

Eddy, S., and Jenks, A. E. 1935. A kitchen middens [*sic*] with bones of extinct animals in the Upper Lakes Area. *Science* 81(2109):535.

Edmund, A. G. 1969. Dentition. In C. Gans, A. d'A. Bellairs, and T. S. Parsons (Eds.), *Biology of the Reptilia: Morphology A* (Vol. 1). London: Academic Press, pp. 117–200.

Edwards, C. J., MacHugh, D. E., Dobney, K. M., Martin, L., Russell, N., Horwitz, L. K., McIntosh, S. K., Macdonald, K. C., Helmer, D., Tresset, A., Vigne, J.-D., and Bradley, D. G. 2004. Ancient DNA analysis of 101 cattle remains: Limits and prospects. *Journal of Archaeological Science* 31:695–710.

Edwards, J. K., Marchinton, R. L., and Smith, G. F. 1982. Pelvic girdle criteria for sex determination of white-tailed deer. *Journal of Wildlife Management* 46(2):544–7.

Edwards, K. J., Whittington, G., and Ritchie, W. 2005. The possible role of humans in the early stages of machair evolution: Paleoenvironmental investigations in the Outer Hebrides, Scotland. *Journal of Archaeological Science* 32:435–49.

Efremov, I. A. 1940. Taphonomy: A new branch of paleontology. *Pan-American Geologist* 74(2):81–93.

Eisenberg, J. F. 1981. *The mammalian radiations: An analysis of trends in evolution, adaptation, and behavior*. Chicago: University of Chicago Press.

———. 1989. *Mammals of the neotropics: The northern neotropics* (Vol. 1). Chicago: University of Chicago Press.

Elkin, D. C. 1995. Volume density of South American camelid skeletal parts. *International Journal of Osteoarchaeology* 5:29–37.

Ellen, R. 1982. *Environment, subsistence, and system: The ecology of small-scale social formations.* Cambridge, UK: Cambridge University Press.

Emerson, A. M. 1993. The role of body part utility in small-scale hunting under two strategies of carcass recovery. In J. Hudson (Ed.), *From bones to behavior: Ethnoarchaeological and experimental contributions to the interpretation of faunal remains.* Carbondale: Southern Illinois University at Carbondale Center for Archaeological Investigations Occasional Paper 21, pp. 138–55.

Emery, K. F. 2004a. Animals from the Maya underworld: Reconstructing elite Maya ritual at the Cueva de los Quetzales, Guatemala. In S. J. O'Day, W. Van Neer, and A. Ervynck (Eds.), *Behaviour behind bones: The zooarchaeology of ritual, religion, status, and identity.* Oxford: Oxbow Books, pp. 101–13.

———. 2004b. In search of the "Maya Diet": Is regional comparison possible in the Maya tropics? *Archaeofauna* 13:37–56.

Emery, K. F., Wright, L. E., and Schwarcz, H. 2000. Isotopic analysis of ancient deer bone: Biotic stability in Collapse Period Maya land-use. *Journal of Archaeological Science* 27:537–50.

Enghoff, I. B. 1983. Size distribution of cod (*Gadus morhua* L.) and whiting (*Merlangius merlangus* L.) (Pisces, Gadidae) from a Mesolithic settlement at Vedbæk, North Zealand, Denmark. *Videnskabelige Meddelelser fra Dansk Naturhistorisk Forening* 144:83–97.

Enloe, J. G. 1993. Ethnoarchaeology of marrow cracking: Implications for the recognition of prehistoric subsistence organization. In J. Hudson (Ed.), *From bones to behavior: Ethnoarchaeological and experimental contributions to the interpretation of faunal remains.* Carbondale: Southern Illinois University at Carbondale Center for Archaeological Investigations Occasional Paper 21, pp. 82–97.

Enlow, D. H., and Brown, S. O. 1956. A comparative histological study of fossil and recent bone tissue. *Texas Journal of Science* 8:405–43.

———. 1957. A comparative histological study of fossil and recent bone tissue. *Texas Journal of Science* 9:186–214.

———. 1958. A comparative histological study of fossil and recent bone tissue. *Texas Journal of Science* 10:187–230.

Epstein, H. 1971. *The origin of the domestic animals of Africa.* New York: Africana Publishing Corporation.

Erickson, D. L., Smith, B. D., Clarke, A. C., Sandweiss, D. H., and Tuross, N. 2005. An Asian origin for a 10,000-year-old domesticated plant in the Americas. *Proceedings of the National Academies of Sciences* 102(51):18315–20.

Erlandson, J. M. 1994. *Early hunter-gatherers of the California Coast.* New York: Plenum Press.

Evans, J. G. 1972. *Land snails in archaeology: With special reference to the British Isles.* London: Seminar Press.

———. 2003. *Environmental archaeology and the social order.* London: Routledge.

Evans, J., and O'Connor, T. 2001. *Environmental archaeology: Principles and methods.* Stroud: Sutton.

Ewel, J. J. 1990. Introduction. In R. L. Myers and J. J. Ewel (Eds.), *Ecosystems of Florida*. Orlando: University of Central Florida Press, pp. 3–10.

Ezzo, J. A. 1994. Putting the "chemistry" back into archaeological bone chemistry analysis: Modeling potential paleodietary indicators. *Journal of Anthropological Archaeology* 13:1–34.

Fandén, A. 2005. Ageing the beaver (*Castor fiber* L.): A skeletal development and life history calendar based on epiphyseal fusion. *Archaeofauna* 14:199–213.

Farb, P., and Armelagos, G. 1980. *Consuming passions: The anthropology of eating*. New York: Washington Square Press.

Felger, R. S., Cliffton, K., and Regal, P. J. 1976. Winter dormancy in sea turtles: Independent discovery and exploitation in the Gulf of California by two local cultures. *Science* 191(4224): 283–5.

Fernández, H., Taberlet, P., Mashkour, M., Vigne, J.-D., and Luikart, G. 2005. New archaeozoological approaches to trace the first steps of animal domestication: General presentation, reflections and proposals. In J.-D. Vigne, J. Peters, and D. Helmer (Eds.), *First steps of animal domestication: New archaeozoological approaches*. Oxford: Oxbow Books, pp. 50–4.

Fewkes, J. W. 1896. Pacific coast shell from prehistoric Tusayan Pueblos. *American Anthropologist* 9(11):359–67.

Fieller, N. R. J., and Turner, A. 1982. Number estimation in vertebrate samples. *Journal of Archaeological Science* 9(1):49–62.

Fiorillo, A. R. 1989. An experimental study of trampling: Implications for the fossil record. In R. Bonnichsen and M. H. Sorg (Eds.), *Bone modification*. Orono: University of Maine, Institute for Quaternary Studies, Center for the Study of the First Americans, pp. 61–71.

Fischer, W. 1978. *FAO species identification sheets for fishery purposes: Western Central Atlantic (Fishing Area 31)*. Rome: Food and Agriculture Organization of the United Nations.

Fisher, J. W., Jr. 1995. Bone surface modifications in zooarchaeology. *Journal of Archaeological Method and Theory* 2(1):7–68.

Flannery, K. V. 1967. Vertebrate fauna and hunting patterns. In D. S. Byers (Ed.), *The prehistory of the Tehuacan Valley* (Vol. 1). Austin: University of Texas Press, pp. 132–77.

———. 1968. Archaeological systems theory and early Mesoamerica. In B. Meggers (Ed.), *Anthropological archeology in the Americas*. Washington, DC: Anthropological Society of Washington, pp. 67–87.

Flannery, K. V., Marcus, J., and Reynolds, R. G. 1989. *The flocks of the Wamani: A study of llama herders on the punas of Ayacucho, Peru*. San Diego, CA: Academic Press.

Flannery, T. F. 1990. Pleistocene faunal loss: Implications of the aftershock for Australia's past and future. *Archaeology in Oceania* 25:45–87.

Flannery, T. F., and White, J. P. 1991. Animal translocation. *National Geographic Research and Exploration* 7(1):96–113.

Forbes, J. 2002. Prudent producers and concerned consumers: Ethnographic and historical observations on staple storage and urban consumer behaviour. In P. Miracle and N. Milner (Eds.), *Consuming passions and patterns of consumption*. Cambridge, UK: McDonald Institute Monographs, pp. 97–111.

Ford, P. J. 1990. Antelope, deer, bighorn sheep and mountain goats: A guide to the carpals. *Journal of Ethnobiology* 10(2):169–81.

Foster, J. B. 1964. Evolution of mammals on islands. *Nature* 202(4929):234–5.

Fowler, A. J. 1995. Annulus formation in otoliths of coral reef fish – A review. In D. H. Secor, J. M. Dean, and S. E. Campana (Eds.), *Recent developments in fish otolith research*. Columbia: University of South Carolina Press, pp. 45–63.

Fowler, C. S. 2007. Historical perspectives on Timbisha Shoshone land management practices, Death Valley, California. In E. J. Reitz, C. M. Scarry, and S. J. Scudder (Eds.), *Case studies in environmental archaeology*. (2nd ed.). London: Springer, pp. 43–57.

Fraser, K. L. 2001. Variation in tuna fish catches in Pacific prehistory. *International Journal of Osteoarchaeology* 11 (1–2):127–35.

Frazier, J. 2004. Marine turtles of the past: A vision for the future? In R. C. G. M. Lauwerier and I. Plug (Eds.), *The future from the past: Archaeozoology in wildlife conservation and heritage management*. Oxford: Oxbow Books. pp. 103–16.

Friesen, T. M., and Betts, M. W. 2006. Archaeofaunas and architecture: Zooarchaeological variability in an Inuit semi-subterranean house, Arctic Canada. In M. Maltby, M. (Ed.), *Integrating zooarchaeology*. Oxford: Oxbow Books, pp. 64–75.

Froese, R. and Pauly, D. (Eds.). 1998. *FishBase 98:Concepts, design, and data sources*. Kakati City, Philippines: The International Center for Living Resources Management.

Fry, G. F. 1985. Analysis of fecal material. In R. I. Gilbert, Jr. and J. H. Mielke (Eds.), *The analysis of prehistoric diets*. New York: Academic Press, pp. 127–54.

Gade, D. W. 1967. The guinea pig in Andean folk culture. *Geographical Review* 57(2):213–24.

———. 1977. Animal/man relationships of Neotropical vertebrate fauna in Amazonia. *National Geographic Society Research Reports, 1977 Projects* 18:321–6.

Gamble, C. 1984. Regional variation in hunter-gatherer strategy in the Upper Pleistocene of Europe. In R. Foley (Ed.), *Hominid evolution and community ecology: Prehistoric human adaptation in biological perspective*. London: Academic Press, pp. 237–60.

Garcia, M. M., and Rackham, J. 2000. Context level interpretation of animal bones through statistical analysis. In J. P. Huntley and S. Stallibrass (Eds.), *Taphonomy and interpretation*. Oxford: Oxbow Books, pp. 97–101.

Garvie-Lok, S. J., Varney, T. L., and Katzenberg, M. A. 2004. Preparation of bone carbonate for stable isotope analysis: The effects of treatment time and acid concentration. *Journal of Archaeological Science* 31:763–76.

Gautier, A. 1993. "What's in a name?" A short history of the Latin and other labels proposed for domestic animals. In A. Clason, S. Payne, and H.-P. Uerpmann (Eds.), *Skeletons in her cupboard*. Oxford: Oxbow Books Monograph 34, pp. 91–8.

———. 2005. Animal mummies and remains from the Necropolis of Elkab (Upper Egypt). *Archaeofauna* 14:139–70.

Geertz, C. 1963. *Agricultural involution: The processes of ecological change in Indonesia*. Berkeley: University of California Press.

Geffen, A., and Nash, R. D. M. 1995. Periodicity of otolith check formation in juvenile plaice *Pleuronectes platessa* L. In D. H. Secor, J. M. Dean, and S. E. Campana (Eds.), *Recent developments in fish otolith research*. Columbia: University of South Carolina Press, pp. 65–73.

Gejvall, N. G. 1969. *Lerna, a pre-classical site in Argolid: 1. The fauna*. Princeton: American School of Classical Studies at Athens.

Geigl, E.-M. 2005. Why ancient DNA research needs taphonomy. In T. O'Connor (Ed.), *Biosphere to lithosphere: New studies in vertebrate taphonomy*. Oxford: Oxbow Books, pp. 79–86.

Geigl, E.-M., and Pruvost, M. 2004. Plea for a multidisciplinary approach to the study of Neolithic migrations: The analysis of biological witnesses and the input of palaeogenetics. In M. Mondini, S. Muñoz, and S. Wickler (Eds.), *Colonisation, migration and marginal areas: A zooarchaeological approach.* Oxford: Oxbow Books, pp. 10–9.

Gentry, A., Clutton-Brock, J., and Groves, C. P. 1996. Proposed conservation of usage of 15 mammal specific names based on wild species which are antedated by or contemporary with those based on domestic animals. *Bulletin of Zoological Nomenclature 53*(1):28–37.

―――. 2004. The naming of wild animal species and their domestic derivatives. *Journal of Archaeological Science* 31:645–51.

Getty, R. 1975. *Sisson and Grossman's The anatomy of the domestic animals.* Philadelphia: Saunders.

Gidney, L. 2000. Economic trends, craft specialisation and social status: Bone assemblages from Leicester. In P. Rowley-Conwy (Ed.), *Animal bones, human societies.* Oxford: Oxbow Books, pp. 170–8.

Gifford, D. P. 1978. Ethnoarchaeological observations on natural processes affecting cultural materials. In R. A. Gould (Ed.), *Exploration in ethnoarchaeology.* Albuquerque: University of New Mexico Press, pp. 77–101.

―――. 1980. Ethnoarcheological contributions to the taphonomy of human sites. In A. K. Behrensmeyer and A. P. Hill (Eds.), *Fossils in the making: Vertebrate taphonomy and paleoecology.* Chicago: University of Chicago Press, pp. 94–107.

―――. 1981. Taphonomy and paleoecology: A critical review of archaeology's sister disciplines. In M. B. Schiffer (Ed.), *Advances in archaeological method and theory* (Vol. 4). New York: Academic Press, pp. 365–438.

Gifford, D. P., and Crader, D. C. 1977. A computer coding system for archaeological faunal remains. *American Antiquity* 42(2):225–38.

Gifford, D. P., Isaac, G. L., and Nelson, C. M. 1981. Evidence for predation and pastoralism at Prolonged Drift: A pastoral Neolithic site in Kenya. *Azania* 15:57–108.

Gifford-Gonzalez, D. 1989. Ethnographic analogues for interpreting modified bones: Some cases from East Africa. In R. Bonnichsen and M. H. Sorg (Eds.), *Bone modification.* Orono: University of Maine, Institute for Quaternary Studies, Center for the Study of the First Americans, pp. 179–246.

―――. 1991. Bones are not enough: Analogues, knowledge, and interpretative strategies in zooarchaeology. *Journal of Anthropological Archaeology* 10:215–54.

―――. 1993. Gaps in zooarchaeological analysis of butchery: Is gender an issue? In J. Hudson (Ed.), *From bones to behavior: Ethnoarchaeological and experimental contributions to the interpretation of faunal remains.* Carbondale: Southern Illinois University at Carbondale Center for Archaeological Investigations Occasional Paper 21, pp. 181–99.

Gilbert, A. S., and Singer, B. H. 1982. Reassessing zooarchaeological quantification. *World Archaeology* 14(1):21–40.

Gilbert, A. S., and Steinfeld, P. 1977. Faunal remains from Dinkha Tepe, Northwestern Iran. *Journal of Field Archaeology* 4(3):329–51.

Gilbert, B. M. 1980. *Mammalian osteology.* Laramie, WY: Modern Printing Company.

Gilbert, B. M., Martin, L. D., and Savage, H. G. 1981. *Avian osteology.* Laramie, WY: Modern Printing Company.

Gilmore, R. M. 1946. To facilitate cooperation in the identification of mammal bones from archaeological sites. *American Antiquity* 12(1):49–50.

———. 1947. Report on a collection of mammal bones from archeologic cave sites in Coahuilla, Mexico. *Journal of Mammalogy 28*(2):147–65.

———. 1949. The identification and value of mammal bones from archeologic excavations. *Journal of Mammalogy 30*(2):163–8.

Glassow, M. A. 2005. Prehistoric dolphin hunting on Santa Cruz Island, California. In G. G. Monks (Ed.), *The exploitation and cultural importance of sea mammals*. Oxford: Oxbow Press, pp. 107–20.

Goody, J. 1982. *Cooking, cuisine, and class: A study in comparative sociology*. Cambridge, UK: Cambridge University Press.

Gordon, B. C. 1988. *Of men and reindeer herds in French Magdalenian prehistory*. Oxford: British Archaeological Reports International Series 390.

Gordon, C. C., and Buikstra, J. E. 1981. Soil pH, bone preservation, and sampling bias at mortuary sites. *American Antiquity 46*(3):566–71.

Goss, R. J. 1983. *Deer antlers: Regeneration, function, evolution*. New York: Academic Press.

Gould, R. A. (Ed.). 1978. *Explorations in ethnoarchaeology*. Albuquerque: University of New Mexico Press.

Gould, S. J. 1986. The egg-a-day barrier. *Natural History 95*(7):16–24.

Gragson, T. L. 1992a. Fishing the waters of Amazonia: Native subsistence economies in a tropical rain forest. *American Anthropologist 94*:428–40.

———. 1992b. Strategic procurement of fish by the Pumé: A South American "fishing culture." *Human Ecology 20*(1):109–30.

———. 1993. Subsistence ecology of the Pumé in a tropical wet savanna: The allocation of time to food search and procurement. In J. L. Lanata (Ed.), *Explotación de recursos faunisticos en sistemas adaptativos Americanos. Arqueologia Contemporánea 4*:75–84.

Graham, R. W., Haynes, C. V., Johnson, D. L., and Kay, M. 1981. Kimmswick: A Clovis–mastodon association in eastern Missouri. *Science 213*(4512):1115–6.

Grant, A. 1978. Variation in dental attrition in mammals and its relevance to age estimation. In D. R. Brothwell, K. D. Thomas, and J. Clutton-Brock (Eds.), *Research problems in zooarchaeology*. London: University of London, Institute of Archaeology Occasional Publication 3, pp. 103–6.

———. 1982. The use of tooth wear as a guide to the age of domestic ungulates. In B. Wilson, C. Grigson, and S. Payne (Eds.), *Ageing and sexing animal bones from archaeological sites*. Oxford: British Archaeological Reports British Series 109, pp. 91–108.

———. 2002. Food, status and social hierarchy. In P. Miracle and N. Milner (Eds.), *Consuming passions and patterns of consumption*. Cambridge, UK: McDonald Institute Monographs, pp. 17–23.

Grant, E. M. 1982. *Guide to fishes: Queensland*. Queensland, Australia: Wilke Printers.

Grantham, B. 1995. Dinner in Buquata: The symbolic nature of food animals and meal sharing in a Druze village. In K. Ryan and P. J. Crabtree (Eds.), *The symbolic role of animals in archaeology*. Philadelphia: University of Pennsylvania, Museum of Archaeology and Anthropology Research Papers in Science and Archaeology, MASCA 12, pp. 73–8.

Grayson, D. K. 1973. On the methodology of faunal analysis. *American Antiquity 38*(4):432–9.

———. 1978. Minimum numbers and sample size in vertebrate faunal analysis. *American Antiquity 43*(1):53–65.

_____. 1979. On the quantification of vertebrate archaeofaunas. In M. B. Schiffer (Ed.), *Advances in archaeological method and theory* (Vol. 2). New York: Academic Press, pp. 199–237.

_____. 1981. The effects of sample size on some derived measures in vertebrate faunal analysis. *Journal of Archaeological Science* 8(1):77–88.

_____. 1984. *Quantitative zooarchaeology: Topics in the analysis of archaeological faunas.* Orlando, FL: Academic Press.

_____. 1986. Eoliths, archaeological ambiguity, and the generation of "middle-range" research. In D. J. Meltzer, D. D. Fowler, and J. A. Sabloff (Eds.), *American archaeology, past and future: A celebration of the Society for American Archaeology.* Washington, DC: Smithsonian Institution Press, pp. 77–133.

_____. 1989a. Bone transport, bone destruction, and reverse utility curves. *Journal of Archaeological Science* 16(6):643–52.

_____. 1989b. Explaining Pleistocene extinctions: Thoughts on the structure of a debate. In P. S. Martin and R. G. Klein (Eds.), *Quaternary extinctions: A prehistoric revolution.* Tucson: University of Arizona Press, pp. 807–23.

Grayson, D. K., and Delpech, F. 1998. Changing diet breadth in the early Upper Palaeolithic of southwestern France. *Journal of Archaeological Science* 25:1119–29.

Grayson, D. K., and Maser, C. 1978. An efficient, inexpensive dermestid colony for skeleton preparation. *Journal of Field Archaeology* 5(2):246–7.

Grayson, D. K., and Meltzer, D. J. 2003. A requiem for North American overkill. *Journal of Archaeological Science* 30:585–93.

Greenfield, H. J. 1999. The origins of metallurgy: Distinguishing stone from metal cut-marks on bones from archaeological sites. *Journal of Archaeological Science* 26:797–808.

_____. 2005. A reconsideration of the secondary products revolution in south-eastern Europe: On the origins and use of domestic animals for milk, wool and traction in the central Balkans. In J. Mulville and A. K. Outram (Eds.), *The zooarchaeology of fats, oils, milk and dairying.* Oxford: Oxbow Books, pp. 14–31.

_____. 2006. Sexing fragmentary ungulate acetabulae. In D. Ruscillo (Eds.), *Recent advances in ageing and sexing animal bones.* Oxford: Oxbow Books, pp. 68–86.

Gregory, W. K. 1933. Fish skulls: A study of the evolution of natural mechanisms. *Transactions of the American Philosophical Society* 23(2):75–481.

Grier, C., Kim, J., and Uchiyama, J. (Eds.). 2006. *Beyond affluent foragers: Rethinking hunter-gatherer complexity.* Oxford: Oxbow Books.

Grigson, C. 1974. The craniology and relationships of four species of *Bos.* 1. Basic craniology: *Bos taurus* L. and its absolute size. *Journal of Archaeological Science* 1(4):353–79.

_____. 1975. The craniology and relationships of four species of *Bos.* II. Basic craniology: *Bos taurus* L. proportions and angles. *Journal of Archaeological Science* 2(2):109–28.

_____. 1976. The craniology and relationships of four species of *Bos.* 3. Basic craniology: *Bos taurus* L. sagittal profiles and other non-measurable characters. *Journal of Archaeological Science* 3(2):115–36.

_____. 1978. Towards a blueprint for animal bone reports in archaeology. In D. R. Brothwell, K. D. Thomas, and J. Clutton-Brock (Eds.), *Research problems in zooarchaeology.* London: University of London, Institute of Archaeology Occasional Publication 3, pp. 121–8.

_____. 1982a. Sex and age determination of some bones and teeth of domestic cattle: A review of the literature. In B. Wilson, C. Grigson, and S. Payne (Eds.), *Ageing and sexing animal bones from archaeological sites*. Oxford: British Archaeological Reports British Series 109, pp. 7–23.

_____. 1982b. Sexing Neolithic domestic cattle skulls and horncores. In B. Wilson, C. Grigson, and S. Payne (Eds.), *Ageing and sexing animal bones from archaeological sites*. Oxford: British Archaeological Reports British Series 109, pp. 25–35.

Groenman-van Waateringe, W. 1994. The menu of different classes in Dutch medieval society. In A. R. Hall and H. K. Kenward (Eds.), *Urban-rural connexions: Perspectives from environmental archaeology*. Oxford: Oxbow Books Monograph 47, pp. 147–69.

Grouard, S. 2001. Faunal remains associated with Late Saladoid and post–Saladoid occupations at Anse a la Gourde, Guadeloupe, West Indies: Preliminary results. *Archaeofauna* 10:71–98.

Groube, L. 1989. The taming of the rain forest: A model for Late Pleistocene forest exploitation in New Guinea. In D. R. Harris and G. C. Hillman (Eds.), *Foraging and farming: The evolution of plant exploitation*. London, Unwin Hyman, pp. 292–304.

Groves, C. P. 1989. Feral mammals of the Mediterranean islands: Documents of early domestication. In J. Clutton-Brock (Ed.), *The walking larder: Patterns of domestication, pastoralism, and predation*. London: Unwin Hyman, pp. 46–58.

_____. 1995. On the nomenclature of domestic animals. *Bulletin of Zoological Nomenclature* 52(2):137–41.

Guilday, J. E., Parmalee, P. W., and Tanner, D. P. 1962. Aboriginal butchering techniques at the Eschelman Site (36La12) Lancaster Co., Pa. *Pennsylvania Archaeologist* 32(2):59–83.

Gust, S. M. 1983. Problems and prospects in nineteenth century California Zooarchaeology. In A. E. Ward (Ed.), *Forgotten places and things: Archaeological perspectives*. Albuquerque, NM: Center for Anthropological Studies, Contributions to Anthropological Studies 3, pp. 341–8.

Guzmán, A. F., and Polaco, O. J. 2003. A comparative analysis of fish remains from some Mexica offerings. *Archaeofauna* 12:7–20.

Haag, W. G. 1948. An osteometric analysis of some aboriginal dogs. *University of Kentucky Reports in Anthropology* 7(3):107–264.

Haak, W., Forster, P., Bramanti, B., Matsumura, S., Brandt, G., Tänzer, M., Villems, R., Renfrew, C., Gronenborn, D., Alt, K. W., and Burger, J. 2005. Ancient DNA from the first European farmers in 7,500-year-old Neolithic sites. *Science* 310:1016–8.

Haber, A., and Dayan, T. 2004. Analyzing the process of domestication: Hagoshrim as a case study. *Journal of Archaeological Science* 31:1587–601.

Hadlock, W. S. 1943. Bone implements from shell heaps around Frenchman's Bay, Maine. *American Antiquity* 8(4):341–53.

Hales, L. S., Jr., and Reitz, E. J. 1992. Historical changes in age and growth of Atlantic croaker, *Micropogonias undulatus* (Perciformes: Sciaenidae). *Journal of Archaeological Science* 19(1):73–99.

Hall, A. R., and Kenward, H. K. 1990. *Environmental evidence from the Colonia: General Accident and Rougier Street*. York, UK: York Archaeological Trust, Volume 14.

Hall, A. R., and Kenward, H. K. (Eds.). 1994. *Urban-rural connexions: Perspectives from environmental archaeology*. Oxford: Oxbow Monograph 47.

Halstead, P., Collins, P., and Isaakidou, V. 2002. Sorting the sheep from the goats: Morphological distinctions between the mandibles and mandibular teeth of adult *Ovis* and *Capra*. *Journal of Archaeological Science* 29:545–53.

Hames, R. B. 1983. The settlement pattern of a Yanomamo population bloc: A behavioral ecological interpretation. In R. B. Hames and W. T. Vickers (Eds.), *Adaptive responses of native Amazonians*. New York: Academic Press, pp. 393–427.

Hardesty, D. L. 1977. *Ecological anthropology*. New York: John Wiley and Sons.

Hargrave, L. L. 1938. A plea for more careful preservation of all biological material from prehistoric sites. *Southwestern Lore* 4(3):47–51.

———. 1970. Mexican macaws. *Anthropological Papers of the University of Arizona* 20:1–67.

Harris, M. 1968. *The rise of anthropological theory: A history of theories of culture*. New York: Crowell.

———. 1974. *Cows, pigs, wars and witches: The riddles of culture*. New York: Random House.

Hatting, T. 1975. The influence of castration on sheep horns. In A. T. Clason (Ed.), *Archaeozoological studies*. Amsterdam: North-Holland Publishing Company, pp. 345–51.

———. 1995. Sex-related characters in the pelvic bone of domestic sheep (*Ovis aries* L.). *Archaeofauna* 4:71–6.

Hawkes, K., and O'Connell, J. 1981. Affluent hunter? Some comments in light of the Alyawara case. *American Anthropologist* 83(3):622–6.

Hay, O. P. 1902. On the finding of the bones of the great auk (*Plautus impennis*) in Florida. *The Auk* 19:255–8.

Hayden, B. 2001. Fabulous feasts: A prolegomenon to the importance of feasting. In M. Dietler and B. Hayden (Eds.), *Feasts: Archaeological and ethnographic perspectives on food, politics, and power*. Washington, DC: Smithsonian Institution Press, pp. 23–64.

Haynes, G. 1980. Evidence of carnivore gnawing on Pleistocene and Recent mammalian bones. *Paleobiology* 6(3):341–51.

———. 1983. Frequencies of spiral and green-bone fractures on ungulate limb bones in modern surface assemblages. *American Antiquity* 48(1):102–14.

———. 1987. Proboscidean die-offs and die-outs: Age profiles in fossil collections. *Journal of Archaeological Science* 14(6):659–68.

———. 1988a. Longitudinal studies of African Elephant death and bone deposits. *Journal of Archaeological Science* 15(2):131–57.

———. 1988b. Mass deaths and serial predation: Comparative taphonomic studies of modern large mammal death sites. *Journal of Archaeological Science* 15(3):219–35.

Haynes, S., Searle, J. B., Bretman, A., and Dobney, K. M. 2002. Bone preservation and ancient DNA: The application of screening methods for predicting DNA survival. *Journal of Archaeological Science* 29:585–92.

Heaney, L. R. 1978. Island area and body size of insular mammals: Evidence from the tri-colored squirrel (*Callosciurus prevosti*) of southeast Asia. *Evolution* 32(1):29–44.

Hedges, R. E. M., and van Klinken, G.-J. (Eds.). 1995. Special issue on bone diagenesis. *Journal of Archaeological Science* 22(2):145–340.

Heinrich, D. 1994. Fish remains of two medieval castles and of an urban context – A comparison. In W. Van Neer (Ed.), *Fish exploitation in the past*. Tervuren, Belgium: Annales du Musée Royal de l'Afrique Centrale, Sciences Zoologiques 274, pp. 211–6.

Heiser, C. B., Jr. 1989. Domestication of Cucurbitaceae: *Cucurbita* and *Lagenaria*. In D. R. Harris and G. C. Hillman (Eds.), *Foraging and farming: The evolution of plant exploitation*. London: Unwin Hyman, pp. 471–80.

Helmer, D. 1987. Fiches descriptives pour les relèves d'ensembles osseux animaux. *Fiches d'ostéologie animale pour l'archéologie: Série B: Mammifères 1*. Juan-les-Pins, France: Centre de Recherches Archéologiques du CNRS, APDCA.

Helmer, D., and Rocheteau, M. 1994. Atlas de squelette appendiculaire des principaux genres Holocènes de petits ruminants du nord de la Méditerranée et du Proche-Orient (*Capra, Ovis, Rupicapra, Capreolus, Gazella*). *Fiches d'ostéologie animale pour l'archéologie: Série B: Mammifères 1*. Juan-les-Pins, France: Centre de Recherches Archéologiques du CNRS, APDCA.

Hemmer, H. 1990. *Domestication: The decline of environmental appreciation*. Cambridge, UK: Cambridge University Press.

Henrikson, L. S. 2004. Frozen bison and fur-trapper's journals: Building a prey-choice model for Idaho's Snake River Plain. *Journal of Archaeological Science* 31:903–16.

Henry, E. (Ed.) 1991. *Guide to the curation of archaeozoological collections*. Florida Museum of Natural History, Gainesville, Proceedings of the Curation Workshop held at the Smithsonian Institution.

Hernández C. F. 1992. Some comments on the introduction of domestic fowl in Iberia. *Archaeofauna* 1:45–53.

Hernández C. F., Martin, M., and Rando, J. C. 1993. Estudio osteologico comparado de dos subespecies de *Corvus corax* (Aves: Passeriformes). *Archaeofauna* 2:181–90.

Herre, W., and Röhrs, M. 1973. *Haustiere zoologisch Gesehen*. Stuttgart: Gustav Fischer Verlag.

Hershkovitz, P. 1962. *Evolution of neotropical Cricetine rodents* (Muridae). Chicago: Chicago Museum of Natural History, Fieldiana: *Zoology* 46.

Herz, N. 1990. Stable isotope geochemistry applied to archaeology. In N. P. Lasca and J. Donahue (Eds.), *Archaeological geology of North America*. Boulder, Colorado: Geological Society of America, Centennial Special vol. 4, pp. 585–95.

Hess, K. 1981. *Martha Washington's booke of cookery: And booke of sweetmeats, being a family manuscript, curiously copied by an unknown hand sometime in the seventeenth century*. New York: Columbia University Press.

Hesse, B. 1995. Husbandry, dietary taboos and the bones of the ancient Near East: Zooarchaeology in the post-processual world. In D. B. Small (Ed.), *Methods in the Mediterranean*. Leiden, The Netherlands: E. J. Brill, pp. 197–232.

Hesse, B., and Perkins, D., Jr. 1974. Faunal remains from Karatas-Semayük in southwest Anatolia: An interim report. *Journal of Field Archaeology* 1:149–60.

Hesse, B., and Wapnish, P. 1985. *Animal bone archeology: From objectives to analysis*. Washington, DC: Taraxacum Manuals on Archeology 5.

Higgins, J. 1999. Túnel: A case study of avian zooarchaeology and taphonomy. *Journal of Archaeological Science* 26:1449–57.

Higgs, E. S. (Ed.). 1975. *Palaeoeconomy*. Cambridge, UK: Cambridge University Press.

Higgs, E. S., and Jarman, M. R. 1972. Palaeoeconomy. In E. S. Higgs (Ed.), *Palaeoeconomy*. Cambridge, UK: Cambridge University Press, pp. 1–7.

Higgs, E. S., and Vita-Finzi, C. 1972. Prehistoric economies: A terrestrial approach. In E. S. Higgs (Ed.), *Papers in economic prehistory*. Cambridge, UK: Cambridge University Press, pp. 27–36.

Higgs, E. S., Vita-Finzi, C., Harris, D. R., and Fagg, A. E. 1967. The climate, environment and industries of Stone Age Greece: Part III. *Proceedings of the Prehistoric Society* 33:1–29.

Higham, C. F. W. 1969a. The metrical attributes of two samples of bovine limb bones. *Journal of Zoology, London* 157:63–74.

———. 1969b. Towards an economic prehistory of Europe. *Current Anthropology* 10:139–50.

Higham, T. F. G., and Horn, P. L. 2000. Seasonal dating using fish otoliths: Results from the Shag River Mouth site, New Zealand. *Journal of Archaeological Science* 27:439–48.

Hildebrand, M. 1982. *Analysis of vertebrate structure* (2nd ed.). New York: John Wiley and Sons.

Hill, A. P. 1989. Bone modification by modern spotted hyenas. In R. Bonnichsen and M. H. Sorg (Eds.), *Bone modification*. Orono: University of Maine, Institute for Quaternary Studies, Center for the Study of the First Americans, pp. 169–78.

Hill, F. C. 1975. Techniques for skeletonizing vertebrates. *American Antiquity* 40(2):215–19.

Hill, K., and Hawkes, K. 1983. Neotropical hunting among the Ache. In R. B. Hames and W. T. Vickers (Eds.), *Adaptive responses of native Amazonians*. New York: Academic Press, pp. 139–88.

Hillson, S. 2005. *Teeth* (2nd ed.). Cambridge, UK: Cambridge University Press.

Hodder, I. 1982. *Symbols in action: Ethnoarchaeological studies of material culture*. Cambridge, UK: Cambridge University Press.

———. 1990. *The domestication of Europe: Structure and contingency in Neolithic societies*. Oxford: Basil Blackwell.

Hodell, D. A., Quinn, R. L., Brenner, M., and Kamenov, G. 2004. Spatial variation of strontium isotopes (^{87}Sr/^{86}Sr) in the Maya region: A tool for tracking ancient human migration. *Journal of Archaeological Science* 31:585–601.

Hoffecker, J. F., Baryshnikov, G., and Potapova, O. 1991. Vertebrate remains from the Mousterian site of Il'skaya I (Northern Caucasus, U.S.S.R.): New analysis and interpretation. *Journal of Archaeological Science* 18(2):113–47.

Hoffman, B. W., Czederpiltz, J. M. C., and Partlow, M. A. 2000. Heads or tails: The zooarchaeology of Aleut salmon storage on Unimak Island, Alaska. *Journal of Archaeological Science* 27:699–708.

Hoffmann, R. C. 1994. Remains and verbal evidence of carp (*Cyprinus carpio*) in medieval Europe. In W. Van Neer (Ed.), *Fish exploitation in the past*. Tervuren, Belgium: Annales du Musée Royal de l'Afrique Centrale, Sciences Zoologiques 274, pp. 139–50.

Hoffstetter, R., and Gasc, J.-P. 1969. Vertebrae and ribs of modern reptiles. In C. Gans, A. d'A. Bellairs, and T. S. Parsons (Eds.), *Biology of the Reptilia: Morphology A* (Vol. 1). London: Academic Press, pp. 201–310.

Holdridge, L. R. 1967. *Life zone ecology*. San Jose, Costa Rica: Tropical Science Center.

Hole, F., Flannery, K. V., and Neely, J. A. 1969. *Prehistory and human ecology of the Deh Luran Plain: An early village sequence from Khuzistan, Iran*. Ann Arbor: University of Michigan Museum of Anthropology Memoirs 1.

Hollox, E. J., Poulter, M., and Swallow, D. M. 2006. Lactase haplotype diversity in the Old World. In M. A. Zeder, D. G. Bradley, E. Emshwiller, and B. D. Smith (Eds.), *Documenting domestication: New genetics and archaeological paradigms*. Berkeley: University of California Press, pp. 305–8.

Holman, J. A. 1995. *Pleistocene amphibians and reptiles of North America*. New York: Oxford University Press.

Holmberg, A. R. 1957. Lizard hunts on the north coast of Peru. Fieldiana: *Anthropology* 36(9):203–20.

Holt, R. D. 1993. Ecology at the mesoscale: The influence of regional processes on local communities. In R. E. Ricklefs and D. Schluter (Eds.), *Species diversity in ecological communities: Historical and geographical perspectives*. Chicago: University of Chicago Press, pp. 77–88.

Hong, S., Candelone, J.-P., Patterson, C. C., and Boutron, C. F. 1994. Greenland ice evidence of hemispheric lead pollution two millennia ago by Greek and Roman civilizations. *Science* 265(5180):1841–3.

———. 1996. History of ancient copper smelting pollution during Roman and Medieval times recorded in Greenland ice. *Science* 272(5259):246–9.

Hongo, H. 1993. Faunal remains from Kaman-Kalehöyük, Turkey: A preliminary analysis. In H. Buitenhuis and A. T. Clason (Eds.), *Archaeozoology of the Near East*. Leiden, The Netherlands: Universal Book Services, pp. 67–76.

Hoogewerff, J., Papesch, W., Kralik, M., Berner, M., Vroon, P., Miesbauer, H., Gaber, O., Künzel, K.-H., and Kleinjans, J. 2001. The last domicile of the iceman from Hauslabjoch: A geochemical approach using Sr, C and O isotopes and trace element signatures. *Journal of Archaeological Science* 28:983–9.

Hooper, E. T. 1952. *A systematic review of the harvest mice (genus* Reithrodontomys*) of Latin America*. Ann Arbor: University of Michigan Museum of Zoology Miscellaneous Publications 77.

Horrocks, N., Irwin, G. J., McGlone, M. S., Nichol, S. L., and Williams, L. J. 2003. Pollen, phytoliths and diatoms in prehistoric coprolites from Kohika, Bay of Plenty, New Zealand. *Journal of Archaeological Science* 30:13–20.

Horton, D. R. 1986. Archaeozoology in Australia: The tendency to regionalization. *ArchaeoZoologia Mélanges*:132–41.

Howard, H. 1929. The avifauna of Emeryville Shellmound. *University of California Publications in Zoology* 32(2):301–94.

Howard, M. M. 1963. The metrical determination of the metapodials and skulls of cattle. In A. E. Mourant and F. E. Levner (Eds.), *Man and cattle*. London: Royal Anthropological Institute Occasional Paper 18, pp. 91–100.

Howell, A. H. 1938. *Revision of the North American ground squirrels with a classification of the North American* Sciuridae. Washington, DC: United States Department of Agriculture, Bureau of Biological Survey, North American Fauna 56.

Hudson, J. (Ed.). 1993. *From bones to behavior: Ethnoarchaeological and experimental contributions to the interpretation of faunal remains*. Carbondale: Southern Illinois University at Carbondale Center for Archaeological Investigations Occasional Paper 21.

Humphrey, L. 2000. Growth studies of past populations: An overview and an example. In M. Cox and S. Mays (Eds.), *Human osteology in archaeology and forensic science*. London: Greenwich Medical Media, pp. 23–38.

Humphrey, S. R. (Ed.). 1992. *Rare and endangered biota of Florida: 1. Mammals*. Gainesville, FL: University Presses of Florida.

Huntley, J. P., and Stallibrass, S. (Eds.). 2000. *Taphonomy and interpretation*. Oxford: Oxbow Books.

Hurlbert, S. H. 1971. The nonconcept of species diversity: A critique and alternative parameters. *Ecology* 52(4):577–86.

Huss-Ashmore, R., Goodman, A. H., and Armelagos, G. J. 1982. Nutritional inference from paleopathology. In M. B. Schiffer (Ed.), *Advances in archaeological method and theory* (Vol. 5). New York: Academic Press, pp. 395–474.

Hyslop, J. 1984. *The Inka road system.* New York: Academic Press.

IJzereef, G. F. 1981. *Bronze Age animal bones from Bovenkarspel: The excavation at Het Valkje.* Amersfoort: Rijksdienst voor het Oudheidkundig Bodemonderzoek Nederlandse Oudheden 10.

———. 1988. Animal bones and social stratification: A preliminary analysis of the faunal remains from cess-pits in Amsterdam (1600–1850 A.D.). *ArchaeoZoologia* 2(1/2):283–92.

Ioannidou, E. 2003a. Taphonomy of animal bones: Species, sex, age, and breed variability of sheep, cattle, and pig bone density. *Journal of Archaeological Science* 30:355–65.

———. 2003b. The effect of dog scavenging on a modern cattle, pig, and sheep bone assemblage. *Archaeofauna* 12:47–59.

Iregren, E. 1988. Size of the brown bear (*Ursus arctos* L.) in northern Sweden during the last millennium. *ArchaeoZoologia* 2(1/2):165–78.

Irvinn, A. D., Cooper, J. E., and Hedges, S. R. 1972. Possible health hazards associated with the collection and handling of post-mortem zoological materials. *Mammal Review* 2(2):43–54.

Isaac, G. L. 1978. The food sharing behavior of protohuman hominids. *Scientific American* 238:90–108.

Izeta, A. D. 2005. South American camelid bone structural density: What are we measuring? Comments on data sets, values, their interpretation and application. *Journal of Archaeological Science* 32:1159–68.

Izumi, S., and Sono, T. 1963. *Andes 2: Excavations at Kotosh, Peru, 1960.* Tokyo: Kadokawa Publishing Company.

Izumi, S., and Terada, K. (Eds.). 1972. *Andes 4: Excavations at Kotosh, Peru, 1963 and 1966.* Tokyo: University of Tokyo Press.

Jablonski, D., Kaustov, R., and Valentine, J. W. 2006. Out of the tropics: Evolutionary dynamics of the latitudinal diversity gradient. *Science* 314:102–6.

Jackson, H. E. 1989. The trouble with transformations: Effects of sample size and sample composition on meat weight estimates based on skeletal mass allometry. *Journal of Archaeological Science* 16(6):601–10.

Jackson, H. E., and Scott, S. L. 2003. Patterns of elite faunal utilization at Moundville, Alabama. *American Antiquity* 68:552–72.

Jackson, J. B. C., Kirby, M. X., Berger, W. H., Bjorndal, K. A., Botsford, L. W., Bourque, B. J., Bradbury, R. H., Cooke, R., Erlandson, J., Estes, J. A., Hughes, T. P., Kidwell, S., Lange, C. B., Lenihan, H. S., Pandolfi, J. M., Peterson, C. H., Steneck, R. S., Tegner, M. J., and Warner, R. R. 2001. Historical overfishing and the recent collapse of coastal ecosystems. *Science* 293:629–38.

Jameson, R. 1987. Purity and power at the Victorian dinner party. In I. Hodder (Ed.), *The archaeology of contextual meaning.* Cambridge, UK: Cambridge University Press, pp. 54–65.

Janetski, J. C. 2005. Shifts in Epipaleolithic marine shell exploitation at Wadi Mataha, southern Jordan. In D. E. Bar-Yosef Mayer (Ed.), *Archaeomalacology: Molluscs in former environments of human behaviour.* Oxford: Oxbow Books, pp. 148–58.

Jannett, F. J., Jr., and Davies, J. G. 1989. An inexpensive apparatus for degreasing skulls. *Curator* 32(2):88–90.

Jans, M. M. E., Nielsen-Marsh, C. M., Smith, C. I., Collins, M. J., and Kars, H. 2004. Characterization of microbial attack on archaeological bone. *Journal of Archaeological Science 31*: 87–95.

Jochim, M. A. 1976. *Hunter-gatherer subsistence and settlement: A predictive model*. New York: Academic Press.

———. 1979. Breaking down the system; recent ecological approaches in archaeology. In M. B. Schiffer (Ed.), *Advances in archaeological method and theory* (Vol. 2). New York: Academic Press, pp. 77–117.

———. 1981. *Strategies for survival: Cultural behavior in an ecological context*. New York: Academic Press.

———. 2006. The implications of inter-group food exchange for hunter-gatherer affluence and complexity. In C. Grier, J. Kim, and J. Uchiyama (Eds.), *Beyond affluent foragers: Rethinking hunter-gatherer complexity*. Oxford: Oxbow Books, pp. 80–9.

Johannsen, N. N. 2006. Draught cattle and the south Scandinavian economies of the 4th millennium BC. *Environmental Archaeology 11*:35–48.

Johnson, E. 1985. Current developments in bone technology. In M. B. Schiffer (Ed.), *Advances in archaeological method and theory* (Vol. 8). New York: Academic Press, pp. 157–235.

Johnson, L. L. 2005. Aleut sea-mammal hunting: Ethnohistorical and archaeological evidence. In G. G. Monks (Ed.), *The exploitation and cultural importance of sea mammals*. Oxford: Oxbow Press, pp. 39–61.

Jones, D. S. 1980. Annual cycle of shell growth increment formation in two continental shelf bivalves and its paleoecological significance. *Paleobiology 6*(3):331–40.

———. 1983. Sclerochronology: Reading the record of the molluscan shell. *American Scientist 71*(4):384–91.

Jones, D. S., Arthur, S. M. A., and Allard, D. J. 1989. Sclerochronological records of temperature and growth from shells of *Mercenaria mercenaria* from Narragansett Bay, Rhode Island. *Marine Biology 102*(2):225–34.

Jones, D. S., and Quitmyer, I. R. 1996. Marking time with bivalve shells: Oxygen isotopes and season of annual increment formation. *Palaios 11*:340–6.

Jones, D. S., Quitmyer, I. R., Arnold, W. S., and Marelli, D. C. 1990. Annual shell banding, age, and growth rate of hard clams (*Mercenaria* spp.) from Florida. *Journal of Shellfish Research 9*(1):215–25.

Jones, D. S., Thompson, I., and Ambrose, W. 1978. Age and growth rate determinations for the Atlantic surf clam *Spisula solidissima* (Bivalvia: Mactracea), based on the internal growth lines in shell cross sections. *Marine Biology 47*(1):63–70.

Jones, E. L. 2004. Dietary evenness, prey choice, and human-environmental interactions. *Journal of Archaeological Science 31*:307–17.

Jones, J. S. 1991. Farming is in the blood. *Nature 351*(6322):97–8.

Jones, K. T., and Metcalfe, D. 1988. Bare bones archaeology: Bone marrow indices and efficiency. *Journal of Archaeological Science 15*(4):415–23.

Kansa, S. W., and Campbell, S. 2004. Feasting with the dead? – A ritual bone deposit at Domuztepe, south eastern Turkey (c. 5550 cal BC). In S. J. O'Day, W. Van Neer, and A. Ervynck (Eds.),

Behaviour behind bones: The zooarchaeology of ritual, religion, status and identity. Oxford: Oxbow Books, pp. 2–13.

Kardong, K. V. 1995. *Vertebrates: Comparative anatomy, function, evolution*. Dubuque, Iowa: Wm. C. Brown Publishers.

Karg, S., Baumeister, R., Robinson, D. E., and Schlichtherle, H. (Eds.) 2006. *Economic and environmental changes during the 4th and 3rd millennia BC. Environmental Archaeology* 11.

Katz, S. H., Hediger, M. L., and Valleroy, L. A. 1974. Traditional maize processing techniques in the New World. *Science 184*(4138):765–73.

Katzenberg, M. A. 2000. Stable isotope analysis: A tool for studying past diet, demography and life history. In M. A. Katzenberg and S. Saunders (Eds.), *Biological anthropology of the human skeleton*. New York: Wiley-Liss, pp. 305–27.

Katzenberg, M. A., and Saunders, S. R. (Eds.). 2000. *Biological anthropology of the human skeleton*. New York: Wiley-Liss.

Kaufman, D. 1995. Diversity of New World mammals: Universality of the latitudinal gradients of species and bauplans. *Journal of Mammalogy 76*(2):322–34.

Keene, A. S. 1981. *Prehistoric foraging in a temperate forest: A linear programming model*. New York: Academic Press.

Keepax, C. A. 1981. Avian egg-shell from archaeological sites. *Journal of Archaeological Science 8*(4):315–35.

Keigwin, L. D. 1996. The Little Ice Age and Medieval Warm Period in the Sargasso Sea. *Science 274*(5292):1504–8.

Kelly, L. S. 2001. A Case of Ritual Feasting at the Cahokia Site. In M. Dietler and B. Hayden (Eds.), *Feasts: Archaeological and Ethnographic Perspectives on Food, Politics, and Power*. Washington, DC: Smithsonian Institution Press, pp. 334–67.

Kennedy, G. E. 1986. The relationship between auditory exostoses and cold water: A latitudinal analysis. *American Journal of Physical Anthropology 71*(4):401–15.

Kennish, M. J., and Olsson, R. K. 1975. Effects of thermal discharges on the microstructural growth of *Mercenaria mercenaria. Environmental Geology* 1:41–64.

Kent, B. W. 1988. *Making dead oysters talk: Techniques for analyzing oysters from archaeological sites*. Crownsville, MD: Maryland Historical Trust, Historic St. Mary's City and Jefferson Pattern Park and Museum.

Kent, S. 1989. Cross-cultural perceptions of farmers as hunters and the value of meat. In S. Kent (Ed.), *Farmers as hunters: The implications of sedentism*. Cambridge, UK: Cambridge University Press, pp. 1–17.

⸻. 1993. Variability in faunal assemblages: The influence of hunting skill, sharing, dogs, and mode of cooking on faunal remains at a sedentary Kalahari community. *Journal of Anthropological Archaeology 12*(4):323–85.

Kent, S., and Vierich, H. 1989. The myth of ecological determinism – Anticipated mobility and site spatial organization. In S. Kent (Ed.), *Farmers as hunters: The implications of sedentism*. Cambridge, UK: Cambridge University Press, pp. 96–130.

Kenward, H. K. 1978. The value of insect remains as evidence of ecological conditions on archaeological sites. In D. R. Brothwell, K. D. Thomas, and J. Clutton-Brock (Eds.), *Research problems in zooarchaeology*. London: University of London, Institute of Archaeology Occasional Publication 3, pp. 25–38.

———. 2004. Do insect remains from historic-period archaeological occupation sites track climate change in northern England? *Environmental Archaeology* 9:47–59.

———. 2006. The visibility of past trees and woodland: Testing the value of insect remains. *Journal of Archaeological Science* 33:1368–80.

Kenward, H., and Carrott, J. 2006. Insect species associations characterise past occupation sites. *Journal of Archaeological Science* 33:1452–73.

Kidder, A. V. 1947. *The artifacts of Uaxactun, Guatemala.* Washington, DC: Carnegie Institution of Washington Publication 576.

Kim, J., and Grier, C. 2006. Beyond affluent foragers. In C. Grier, J. Kim, and J. Uchiyama (Eds.), *Beyond affluent foragers: Rethinking hunter-gatherer complexity.* Oxford: Oxbow Books, pp. 192–200.

Kimura, B., Brandt, S. A., Hardy, B. L., and Hauswirth, W. W. 2001. Analysis of DNA from ethnoarchaeological stone scrapers. *Journal of Archaeological Science* 28:45–53.

Kintigh, K. W. 1984. Measuring archaeological diversity by comparison with simulated assemblages. *American Antiquity* 49(1):44–54.

———. 1989. Sample size, significance, and measure of diversity. In R. D. Leonard and G. T. Jones (Eds.), *Quantifying diversity in archaeology.* Cambridge, UK: Cambridge University Press, pp. 25–36.

Kirch, P. V., Allen, M. S., Butler, V. L., and Hunt, T. L. 1987. Is there an early Far Western Lapita province? Sample size effects and new evidence from Eloaua Island. *Archaeology in Oceania* 22:123–7.

Kirch, P. V., Flenley, J. R., Steadman, D. W., and Lamont, F. 1992. Ancient environmental degradation. *National Geographic Research and Exploration* 8(2):166–79.

Kislev, M. E., Hartmann, A., and Galilli, E. 2004. Archaeobotanical and archaeoentomological evidence from a well at Atlit-Yam indicates colder, more humid climate on the Israeli coast during the PPNC period. *Journal of Archaeological Science* 31:1301–10.

Klein, R. G. 1981. Stone Age predation on small African bovids. *South African Archaeological Bulletin* 36(134):55–65.

———. 1982. Age (mortality) profiles as a means of distinguishing hunted species from scavenged ones in Stone Age archeological sites. *Paleobiology* 8(2):151–8.

———. 1989. Why does skeletal part representation differ between smaller and larger bovids at Klasies River Mouth and other archaeological sites? *Journal of Archaeological Science* 16(4):363–81.

Klein, R. G., Allwarden, K., and Wolf, C. 1983. The calculation and interpretation of ungulate age profiles from dental crown heights. In G. Bailey (Ed.), *Hunter-gatherer economy in prehistory: A European perspective.* Cambridge, UK: Cambridge University Press, pp. 47–57.

Klein, R. G., and Cruz-Uribe, K. 1983. The computation of ungulate age (mortality) profiles from dental crown heights. *Paleobiology* 9(1):70–8.

———. 1984. *The analysis of animal bones from archaeological sites.* Chicago: University of Chicago Press.

Klein, R. G., Cruz-Uribe, K., and Milo, R. G. 1999. Skeletal part representation in archaeofaunas: Comments on "Explaining the 'Klasies Pattern': Kua ethnoarchaeology, the Die Kelders Middle Stone Age Archaeofauna, long bone fragmentation and carnivore ravaging" by Bartram & Marean. *Journal of Archaeological Science* 26:1225–34.

Klein, R. G., Wolf, C., Freeman, L. G., and Allwarden, K. 1981. The use of dental crown heights for constructing age profiles of red deer and similar species in archaeological samples. *Journal of Archaeological Science* 8(1):1–31.

Klenck, J. D. 1995. Bedouin animal sacrifice practices: Case study in Israel. In K. Ryan and P. J. Crabtree (Eds.), *The symbolic role of animals in archaeology*. Philadelphia: University of Pennsylvania, Museum of Archaeology and Anthropology Research Papers in Science and Archaeology, MASCA 12, pp. 57–72.

Klevezal, G. A., and Shishlina, N. I. 2001. Assessment of the season of death of ancient human from cementum annual layers. *Journal of Archaeological Science* 28:481–6.

Klippel, W. E., Snyder, L. M., and Parmalee, P. W. 1987. Taphonomy and archaeologically recovered mammal bone from southeast Missouri. *Journal of Ethnobiology* 7(2):155–69.

Knight, J. V. 2001. Feasting and the emergence of platform mound ceremonialism in eastern North America. In M. Dietler and B. Hayden (Eds.), *Feasts: Archaeological and ethnographic perspectives on food, politics, and power*. Washington, DC: Smithsonian Institution Press, pp. 311–33.

Knüsel, C. J., and Outram, A. K. 2004. Fragmentation: The zonation method applied to fragmented human remains from archaeological and forensic contexts. *Environmental Archaeology* 9:85–97.

Koch, C. P. (Ed.). 1989. *Taphonomy: A bibliographic guide to the literature*. Orono: University of Maine, Institute of Quaternary Studies, Center for the Study of the First Americans.

Koch, T. 1973. *Anatomy of the chicken and domestic birds*. Ames: Iowa State University Press.

Koike, H. 1973. Daily growth lines of the clam, *Meretrix lusoria*: A basic study for the estimation of prehistoric seasonal gathering. *Journal of Anthropological Society of Nippon* 81:122–38.

———. 1975. The use of daily and annual growth lines of the clam *Meretrix lusoria* in estimating seasons of Jamon Period shell gathering. In R. P. Suggate and M. M. Cresswell (Eds.), *Quaternary Studies*. Wellington: The Royal Society of New Zealand, pp. 189–93.

———. 1979. Seasonal dating and the valve-pairing technique in shell midden analysis. *Journal of Archaeological Science* 6(1):63–74.

Koike, H., and Ohtaishi, N. 1987. Estimation of prehistoric hunting rates based on the age composition of Sika deer (*Cervus nippon*). *Journal of Archaeological Science* 14(3):251–69.

Kolb, C. C. 1987. *Marine shell trade and Classic Teotihuacan, Mexico*. Oxford: British Archaeological Reports International Series 364.

Korth, W. W. 1979. Taphonomy of microvertebrate fossil assemblages. *Annals of Carnegie Museum* 48:235–85.

Kozlov, A., and Lisitsyn, D. V. 2000. History of dairy cattle-breeding and distribution of LAC*R and LAC*P alleles among European populations. In C. Renfrew and K. Boyle (Eds.), *Archaeogenetics: DNA and the population of prehistory Europe*. Cambridge, UK: McDonald Institute for Archaeological Research, pp. 309–13.

Kozuch, L. 1993. *Sharks and shark products in prehistoric South Florida*. Gainesville, FL: Institute of Archaeology and Paleoenvironmental Studies Monograph 2.

Krantz, G. S. 1968. A new method of counting mammal bones. *American Journal of Archaeology* 72:286–8.

Krebs, C. J., Boutin, S., Boonstra, R., Sinclair, A. R. E., Smith, J. N. M., Dale, M. R. T., Martin, K., and Turkington, R. 1995. Impact of food and predation on the snowshoe hare cycle. *Science* 269(5227):1112–15.

Krebs, J. R. 1989. *Ecological methodology*. New York: Harper and Row.

Kreutzer, L. A. 1992. Bison and deer bone mineral densities: Comparisons and implications for the interpretation of archaeological faunas. *Journal of Archaeological Science 19*(3): 271–94.

Kroeber, A. L. 1939. *Cultural and natural areas of native North America*. Berkeley: University of California Publications in American Archaeology and Ethnology 38.

Kroll, E. M., and Price, T. D. (Eds.). 1991. *The interpretation of archaeological spatial patterning*. New York: Plenum Press.

Kubasiewicz, M. 1956. O metodyce badán wykopaliskowich szcz tków kostynch zwierze.cych. *Materialy Zachodnio-Pomorskie 2*:235–44.

Lam, Y. M., Pearson, O. M., Marean, C. W., and Chen, X. C. 2003. Bone density studies in zooarchaeology. *Journal of Archaeological Science 3 0*:1701–8.

Landes, K. K. 1966. A scrutiny of the abstract, II. *Bulletin of the American Association of Petroleum Geologists 5 0*(9):1992–9.

Landon, D. B. 1993. Testing a seasonal slaughter model for colonial New England using tooth cementum incremental analysis. *Journal of Archaeological Science 20*(4):439–55.

_____. 1996. Feeding colonial Boston: A zooarchaeological study. *Historical Archaeology 3 0*(1):1– 153.

_____. 2007. Seasonal slaughter cycles and urban food supply in the colonial Chesapeake. In E. J. Reitz, C. M. Scarry, and S. J. Scudder (Eds.), *Case studies in environmental archaeology* (2nd ed.). London: Springer, pp. 367–82.

Langemann, E. G. 2004. Zooarchaeological research in support of a reintroduction of bison to Banff National Park, Canada. In R. C. G. M. Lauwerier and I. Plug (Eds.), *The future from the past: Archaeozoology in wildlife conservation and heritage management*. Oxford: Oxbow Books, pp. 79–89.

Lapham, H. A. 2004. Zooarchaeological evidence for changing socioeconomic status within early historic Native American communities in Mid-Atlantic North America. In S. J. O'Day, W. Van Neer, and A. Ervynck (Eds.), *Behaviour behind bones: The zooarchaeology of ritual, religion, status and identity*. Oxford: Oxbow Books, pp. 293–303.

Larsen, C. S. 1997. *Bioarchaeology: Interpreting behavior from the human skeleton*. Cambridge, UK: Cambridge University Press.

Larsen, C. S., Kelly, R. L., Ruff, C. B., Schoeninger, M. J., Hutchinson, D. L. and Hemphill, B. E. 2007. Living on the margins: Biobehavioral adaptations in the western Great Basin. In E. J. Reitz, C. M. Scarry, and S. J. Scudder (Eds.), *Case studies in environmental archaeology* (2nd ed.). London: Springer, pp. 155–83.

Larsen, C. S., Schoeninger, M. J., van der Merwe, N. J., Moore, K. M., and Lee-Thorp, J. A. 1992. Carbon and nitrogen stable isotopic signatures of human dietary change in the Georgia Bight. *American Journal of Physical Anthropology 89*(2):197–214.

Larson, G., Dobney, K., Albarella, U., Fang, M., Matisso-Smith, E., Robins, J., Lowden, S., Finlayson, H., Brand, T., Willerslev, E., Rowley-Conwy, P., Andersson, L., and Cooper, A. 2005. Worldwide phylogeography of wild boar reveals multiple centers of pig domestication. *Science 3 07*:1618–21.

Lauwerier, R. C. G. M. 1983. Pigs, piglets and determining the season of slaughter. *Journal of Archaeological Science 10*(5):483–8.

_____. 1993a. Bird remains in Roman graves. *Archaeofauna* 2:75–82.

_____. 1993b. Twenty-eight bird briskets in a pot: Roman preserved food from Nijmegen. *Archaeofauna* 2:15–9.

Lauwerier, R. C. G. M., and de Vries, L. S. 2004. Lifting the iceberg – BoneInfo and the battle to save archaeological information. In R. C. G. M. Lauwerier and I. Plug (Eds.), *The future from the past: Archaeozoology in wildlife conservation and heritage management.* Oxford: Oxbow Books, pp. 167–75.

Lauwerier, R. C. G. M., and Zeiler, J. T. 2001. Wishful thinking and the introduction of rabbit to the Low Countries. *Environmental Archaeology* 6:87–90.

Lawrence, B. 1951. *Post-cranial skeletal characters of deer, pronghorn, and sheep-goat with notes on Bos and Bison, Part II.* Cambridge, MA: Harvard University, Papers of the Peabody Museum of Archaeology and Ethnology 35(3).

_____. 1957. Zoology. In W. W. Taylor (Ed.), *The identification of non-artifactual archaeological materials.* Washington, DC: National Academy of Science/Natural Resource Council Publication 565, pp. 41–2.

_____. 1973. Problems in the inter-site comparison of faunal remains. In J. Matolsci (Ed.), *Domestikationsforschung und Gerschichte der Haustiere.* Budapest: Kiadó, pp. 397–401.

Leach, B. F., and Anderson, A. J. 1979. Prehistoric exploitation of crayfish in New Zealand. In A. Anderson (Ed.), *Birds of a feather: Osteological and archaeological papers from the South Pacific in honour of R. J. Scarlett.* Oxford: British Archaeological Reports International Series 62, pp. 141–64.

Leach, B. F., Davidson, J. M., Horwood, L. M., and Anderson, A. J. 1996. The estimation of live fish size from archaeological cranial bones of the New Zealand barracouta *Thyrsites atun. Tuhinga Records of the Museum of New Zealand Te Papa Tongarewa* 6:1–25.

Leech, F. 2006. *Fishing in pre-European New Zealand. New Zealand Journal of Archaeology* Special Publication 15.

Legge, A. J. 1978. Archaeozoology – Or zooarchaeology? In D. R. Brothwell, K. D. Thomas, and J. Clutton-Brock (Eds.), *Research problems in zooarchaeology.* London: University of London, Institute of Archaeology Occasional Publication 3, pp. 129–32.

_____. 2000. Out of site, out of mind: Invisible earnings at Bronze Age Moncín, Spain. In P. Rowley-Conwy (Ed.), *Animal bones, human societies.* Oxford: Oxbow Books, pp. 106–14.

Legge, A. J., and Rowley-Conwy, P. A. 1987. Gazelle killing in Stone Age Syria. *Scientific American* 257(2):88–95.

_____. 1988. *Star Carr revisited.* University of London, Centre for Extra-Mural Studies.

Legge, A. J., Williams, J., and Williams, P. 2000. Lambs to the slaughter: Sacrifice at two Roman temples in southern England. In P. Rowley-Conwy (Ed.), *Animal bones, human societies.* Oxford: Oxbow Books, pp. 152–7.

Legge, T. 2005. Milk use in prehistory: The osteological evidence. In Mulville and A. K. Outram (Eds.), *The archaeology of fats, oils, milk and dairying: An introduction and overview.* Oxford: Oxbow Books, pp. 8–13.

Lentacker, A. 1994. Fish remains from Portugal: Preliminary analysis of the Mesolithic shellmidden sites of Cabeço da Amoreira and Cabeço da Arruda. In W. Van Neer (Ed.), *Fish exploitation in the past.* Tervuren, Belgium: Annales du Musée Royal de l'Afrique Centrale, Sciences Zoologiques 274, pp. 263–71.

Lentacker, A., Ervynck, A., and Van Neer, W. 2004. Gastronomy or religion? The animal remains from the *mithraeum* at Tienen (Belgium). In S. J. O'Day, W. Van Neer, and A. Ervynck (Eds.), *Behaviour behind bones: The zooarchaeology of ritual, religion, status and identity.* Oxford: Oxbow Books, pp. 77–94.

Leonard, J. A., Wayne, R. K., Wheeler, J., Valadez, R., Guillén, S., and Vilà, C. 2002. Ancient DNA evidence for Old World origin of New World dogs. *Science* 298:1613–6.

Leonard, R. D., and Jones, G. T. (Eds.). 1989. *Quantifying diversity in archaeology.* Cambridge, UK: Cambridge University Press, pp. 25–36.

Leone, M. P. 1972. Issues in anthropological archaeology. In M. P. Leone (Ed.), *Contemporary archaeology: A guide to theory and contributions.* Carbondale: Southern Illinois University Press, pp. 14–27.

Leone, M. P., and Potter, P. B. 1988. Introduction: Issues in historical archaeology. In M. Leone and P. Potter (Eds.), *The recovery of meaning: Historical archaeology in the eastern United States.* Washington, DC: Smithsonian Institution Press, pp. 1–22.

Lernau, O., Cotton, H., and Goren, Y. 1996. Salted fish and fish sauces from Masada. A preliminary report. *Archaeofauna* 5:35–41.

Levine, M. A., Bailey, G. N., Whitwell, K. E., and Jeffcott, L. B. 2000. Paleopathology and horse domestication: The case of some Iron Age horses from the Altai Mountains, Siberia. In G. Bailey, R. Charles, and N. Winder (Eds.), *Human ecodynamics.* Oxford: Oxbow Books, pp. 123–33.

Levitan, B. 1982. Errors in recording tooth wear in ovicaprid mandibles at different speeds. In B. Wilson, C. Grigson, and S. Payne (Eds.), *Ageing and sexing animal bones from archaeological sites.* Oxford: British Archaeological Reports British Series 109, pp. 207–14.

Lev-Tov, J. S. E. 2004. Implications of risk theory for understanding nineteenth century slave diets in the southern United States. In S. J. O'Day, W. Van Neer, and A. Ervynck (Eds.), *Behaviour behind bones: The zooarchaeology of ritual, religion, status and identity.* Oxford: Oxbow Books, pp. 304–17.

Levy, J. E. 1995. Animals good to think: Bronze Age Scandinavia and Ohio Hopewell. In K. Ryan and P. J. Crabtree (Eds.), *The symbolic role of animals in archaeology.* Philadelphia: University of Pennsylvania, Museum of Archaeology and Anthropology Research Papers in Science and Archaeology, MASCA 12, pp. 9–19.

Lewall, E. F., and Cowan, I. McT. 1963. Age determination in black-tail deer by degree of ossification of the epiphyseal plate in the long bones. *Canadian Journal of Zoology* 41(4):629–36.

Libois, R. M., and Hallet-Libois, C. 1988. Eléments pour l'identification des restes crâniens des poissons dulçaquicoles de Belgique et du nord de la France, 2. – Cypriniformes. *Fiches d'ostéologie animale pour l'archéologie: Série A: Poissons* 4. Juan-les-Pins: Centre de Recherches Archéologiques du CNRS, APDCA.

Libois, R. M., Hallet-Libois, C., and Rosoux, R. 1987. Eléments pour l'identification des restes crâniens des poissons dulçaquicoles de Belgique et du nord de la France, l – Anguilliformes, Gastérostéiformes, Cyprinodontiformes et Perciformes. *Fiches d'ostéologie animale pour l'archéologie: Série A: Poissons* 3. Juan-les-Pins: Centre de Recherches Archéologiques du CNRS, APDCA.

Lieberman, D. E. 1993a. Life history variables preserved in dental cementum microstructure. *Science* 261(5125):1162–4.

————. 1993b. The rise and fall of seasonal mobility among hunter-gatherers: The case of the Southern Levant. *Current Anthropology* 34(5):599–631.

————. 1994. The biological basis for seasonal increments in dental cementum and their application to archaeological research. *Journal of Archaeological Science* 21(4):525–39.

Lieberman, D. E., Deacon, T. W., and Meadow, R. H. 1990. Computer image enhancement and analysis of cementum increments as applied to teeth of *Gazella gazella*. *Journal of Archaeological Science* 17(5):519–33.

Liem, K. F., Bemis, W. E., Walker, W. F., and Grande, L. 2001. *Functional anatomy of the vertebrates: An evolutionary perspective* (3rd ed.). Orlando: Harcourt College Publishers.

Light, J. 2005. Marine mussel shells – Wear is the evidence. In D. E. Bar-Yosef Mayer (Ed.), *Archaeomalacology: Molluscs in former environments of human behaviour*. Oxford: Oxbow Books, pp. 56–62.

Linares, O. F. 1976. "Garden hunting" in the American tropics. *Human Ecology* 4(4):331–49.

Lindenbaum, S. 1987. Loaves and fishes in Bangladesh. In M. Harris and E. B. Ross (Eds.), *Food and evolution: Toward a theory of human food habits*. Philadelphia: Temple University Press, pp. 427–43.

Linnaeus, C. 1758. *Systema Naturae* (10th ed.). reformata. Stockholm: Tomus I, Laurentii Salvii, Holmiae.

Linse, A. R. 1992. Is bone safe in a shell midden? In J. K. Stein (Ed.), *Deciphering a shell midden*. San Diego: Academic Press, pp. 327–45.

Lloyd, A. T. 1986. Pussy cat, pussy cat, where have you been? *Natural History* 95(7):46–53.

Loomis, F. B., and Young, D. B. 1912. Shell heaps of Maine. *American Journal of Science* 34(199):17–42.

Loponte, D. M., and Acosta, A. 2004. Late Holocene hunter-gatherers from the Pampean Wetlands, Argentina. In G. L. Mengoni Goñalons (Ed.), *Zooarchaeology of South America*. British Archaeological Reports International Series 1298. Oxford: Archaeopress, pp. 39–57.

Loreille, O., Vigne, J.-D., Hardy, C., Callou, C., Treinen-Claustre, F., Dennebouy, N., and Monnerot, M. 1997. First distinction of sheep and goat archaeological bones by the means of their fossil mtDNA. *Journal of Archaeological Science* 24(1):33–7.

Lowe, V. P. W. 1967. Teeth as indicators of age with special reference to red deer (*Cervus elaphus*) of known age from Rhum. *Journal of Zoology, London* 152:137–53.

Lubinski, P. M., and O'Brien, C. J. 2001. Observations on seasonality and mortality from a recent catastrophic death assemblage. *Journal of Archaeological Science* 28:833–42.

Luff, R. 1994. Butchery at the workmen's village (WV), Tell-el-Amarna, Egypt. In R. Luff and P. Rowley-Conwy (Eds.), *Whither environmental archaeology?* Oxford: Oxbow Books Monograph 38, pp. 158–170.

Luff, R. M., and Bailey, G. N. 2000. Analysis of size changes and incremental growth structures in African catfish *Synodontis schall* (schall) from Tell el-Amarna, Middle Egypt. *Journal of Archaeological Science* 27:821–35.

Luikart, G., Fernández, H., Mashkour, M., England, P. R., and Taberlet, P. 2006. Origins and diffusion of domestic goats inferred from DNA markers: Example analyses of mtDNA, Y chromosome, and microsatellites. In M. A. Zeder, D. G. Bradley, E., Emshwiller, and B. D. Smith (Eds.), *Documenting domestication: New genetics and archaeological paradigms*. Berkeley: University of California Press, pp. 273–93.

Lupo, K. D., and O'Connell, J. F. 2002. Cut and tooth mark distributions on large animal bones: Ethnoarchaeological data from the Hazda and their implications for current ideas about early human carnivory. *Journal of Archaeological Science* 29:85–109.

Lyman, R. L. 1977. Analysis of historic faunal remains. *Historical Archaeology* 11:67–73.

———. 1979. Available meat from faunal remains: A consideration of techniques. *American Antiquity* 44(3):536–46.

———. 1982. Archaeofaunas and subsistence studies. In M. B. Schiffer (Ed.), *Advances in archaeological method and theory* (Vol. 5). New York: Academic Press, pp. 331–93.

———. 1984. Bone density and differential survivorship of fossil classes. *Journal of Anthropological Archaeology* 3(4):259–99.

———. 1985. Bone frequencies: Differential transport, in situ destruction, and the MGUI. *Journal of Archaeological Science* 12(3):221–36.

———. 1987. Zooarchaeology and taphonomy: A general consideration. *Journal of Ethnobiology* 7(1):93–117.

———. 1988. Was there a last supper at Last Supper Cave? *Danger Cave, Last Supper Cave, and Hanging Rock Shelter: The faunas.* New York: The American Museum of Natural History Anthropological Papers 66 (Part 1):81–104.

———. 1992. Anatomical considerations of utility curves in zooarchaeology. *Journal of Archaeological Science* 19(1):7–22.

———. 1994a. Quantitative units and terminology in zooarchaeology. *American Antiquity* 59(1):36–71.

———. 1994b. Relative abundances of skeletal specimens and taphonomic analysis of vertebrate remains. *Palaios* 9(3):288–98.

———. 1994c. *Vertebrate taphonomy.* Cambridge, UK: Cambridge University Press.

———. 1995. Determining when rare (zoo-)archaeological phenomena are truly absent. *Journal of Archaeological Method and Theory* 2:369–424.

———. 1996. Applied zooarchaeology: The relevance of faunal analysis to wildlife management. *World Archaeology* 28:110–25.

———. 2003. The influence of time averaging and space averaging on the application of foraging theory in zooarchaeology. *Journal of Archaeological Science* 30:595–610.

———. 2004. Late-Quaternary diminution and abundance of prehistoric bison (*Bison* sp.) in eastern Washington state, USA. *Quaternary Research* 62:76–85.

Lyman, R. L., Savelle, J. M., and Whitridge, P. 1992. Derivation and application of a food utility index for Phocid seals. *Journal of Archaeological Science* 19(5):531–56.

Lyon, P. J. 1970. Differential bone destruction: An ethnographic example. *American Antiquity* 35(2):213–15.

MacArthur, R. H. 1965. Patterns of species diversity. *Biological Review of the Cambridge Philosophical Society* 40(4):510–33.

McClane, A. J. 1978. *McClane's field guide to freshwater fishes of North America.* New York: Holt, Rinehart, and Winston.

McCormick, F. 1991. The effect of the Anglo-Norman settlement on Ireland's wild and domesticated fauna. In P. J. Crabtree and K. Ryan (Eds.), *Animal use and culture change.* Philadelphia: University of Pennsylvania, Museum of Archaeology and Anthropology Research Papers in Science and Archaeology, MASCA 8, pp. 41–52.

———. 2002. The distribution of meat in a hierarchical society: The Irish evidence. In P. Miracle and N. Milner (Eds.), *Consuming passions and patterns of consumption.* Cambridge, UK: McDonald Institute Monographs, pp. 25–31.

McCutcheon, P. T. 1992. Burned archaeological bone. In J. K. Stein (Ed.), *Deciphering a shell midden.* San Diego, California: Academic Press, pp. 347–70.

MacDonald, K. C. 1995. Why chickens? The centrality of the domestic fowl in West African ritual and magic. In K. Ryan and P. J. Crabtree (Eds.), *The symbolic role of animals in archaeology.* Philadelphia: University of Pennsylvania, Museum of Archaeology and Anthropology Research Papers in Science and Archaeology, MASCA 12, pp. 50–6.

MacDonald, R. H., MacDonald, K. C., and Ryan, K. 1993. Domestic geese from medieval Dublin. *Archaeofauna* 2:205–18.

McGovern, T. H. 1994. Management for extinction in Norse Greenland. In C. L. Crumley (Ed.), *Historical ecology: Cultural knowledge and changing landscapes.* Santa Fe, New Mexico: School of American Research Press, pp. 127–54.

McGowan, J. A., and Walker, P. W. 1993. Pelagic diversity patterns. In R. E. Ricklefs and D. Schluter (Eds.), *Species diversity in ecological communities: Historical and geographical perspectives.* Chicago: University of Chicago Press, pp. 203–14.

McGuire, K. R., and Hildebrandt, W. R. 2005. Re-thinking Great Basin foragers: Prestige hunting and costly signaling during the Middle Archaic Period. *American Antiquity* 70(4):695–712.

McKenna, M. C., and Bell, S. K. 1997. *Classification of mammals.* New York: Columbia University Press.

McLean, J. H. 1984. *Systematics of Fissurella in the Peruvian and Magellanic Faunal Provinces (Gastropoda: Prosobranchia).* Natural History Museum of Los Angeles County Contributions in Science 354.

McNiven, I., and Feldman, R. 2003. Ritually orchestrated seascapes: hunting magic and dugong bone mounds in Torres Strait, NE Australia. *Cambridge Archaeological Journal* 13:169–94.

Madsen, D. B., and Schmitt, D. N. 1998. Mass collecting and the diet breadth model: A Great Basin example. *Journal of Archaeological Science* 25:445–55.

Magnell, O. 2005. Harvesting wild boar – A study of prey choice by hunters during the Mesolithic in south Scandinavia by analysis of age and sex structures in faunal remains. *Archaeofauna* 14:27–41.

Mainland, I. 2006. Pastures lost? A dental microwear study of ovicaprine diet and management in Norse Greenland. *Journal of Archaeological Science* 33:238–52.

———. 2008. The uses of archaeofaunal remains in landscape archaeology. In B. David and J. Thomas (Eds.), *The handbook of landscape archaeology.* Walnut Creek, California: Left Coast Press, in press.

Makarewicz, C., and Tuross, N. 2006. Foddering by Mongolian pastoralists is recorded in the stable carbon (δ^{13}C) and nitrogen (δ^{15}N) isotopes of caprine dentinal collagen. *Journal of Archaeological Science* 33:862–70.

Maltby, J. M. 1979. *The animal bones from Exeter 1971–1975.* Sheffield: Sheffield University, Department of Prehistory and Archaeology, Exeter Archaeological Reports 2.

———. 1985. Patterns in faunal assemblage variability. In G. Barker and C. Gamble (Eds.), *Beyond domestication in prehistoric Europe: Investigations in subsistence archaeology and social complexity.* London: Academic Press, pp. 33–74.

———. 1989. Urban–rural variations in the butchering of cattle in Romano-British Hampshire. In D. Serjeantson and T. Waldron (Eds.), *Diet and crafts in towns: The evidence of animal remains from the Roman to the post-medieval periods*. Oxford: British Archaeological Reports British Series 199, pp. 75–106.

———. 1994. The meat supply in Roman Dorchester and Winchester. In A. R. Hall and H. K. Kenward (Eds.), *Urban–rural connexions: Perspectives from environmental archaeology*. Oxford: Oxbow Books Monograph 47, pp. 85–102.

Maltby, M. (Ed.). 2006. *Integrating zooarchaeology*. Oxford: Oxbow Books.

Mannino, M. A., Spiro, B. F., and Thomas, K. D. 2003. Sampling shells for seasonality: Oxygen isotope analysis on shell carbonates of the inter-tidal gastropod *Monodonta lineata* (da Costa) from populations across its modern range and from Mesolithic sites in southern Britain. *Journal of Archaeological Science* 30:667–79.

Mannino, M. A., and Thomas, K. D. 2001. Intensive Mesolithic exploitation of coastal resources? Evidence from a shell deposit on the Isle of Portland (southern England) for the impact of human foraging on populations of intertidal rocky shore molluscs. *Journal of Archaeological Science* 28:1101–14.

Marean, C. W. 1992. Hunter to herder: Large mammal remains from the hunter-gatherer occupation at Enkapune Ya Muto rockshelter, Central Rift, Kenya. *African Archaeological Review* 10:65–127.

Marean, C. W., and Spencer, L. M. 1991. Impact of carnivore ravaging on zooarchaeological measures of element abundance. *American Antiquity* 56(4):645–58.

Marean, C. W., Abe, Y., Nilssen, P. J., and Stone, E. C. 2001. Estimating the minimum number of skeletal elements (MNE) in zooarchaeology: A review and a new image-analysis GIS approach. *American Antiquity* 66:333–48.

Marelli, D. C., and Arnold, W. S. 2001. Shell morphologies of bay scallops, *Argopecten irradians*, from extant and prehistoric populations from the Florida Gulf Coast: Implications for the biology of past and present metapopulations. *Journal of Archaeological Science* 28:577–86.

Marks, S. A. 1976. *Large mammals and a brave people: Subsistence hunters in Zambia*. Seattle: University of Washington Press.

Marquardt, W. H. 1992. Shell artifacts from the Caloosahatchee Area. In W. H. Marquardt (Ed.), *Culture and environment in the domain of the Calusa*. Gainesville, FL: Institute of Archaeology and Paleoenvironmental Studies Monograph 1, pp. 191–227.

———. 1994. The role of archaeology in raising environmental consciousness: An example from southwest Florida. In C. L. Crumley (Ed.), *Historical ecology: Cultural knowledge and changing landscapes*. Santa Fe, New Mexico: School of American Research Press, pp. 203–21.

Marquardt, W. H., Montet-White, A., and Scholtz, S. C. 1982. Resolving the crisis in archaeological collections curation. *American Antiquity* 47(2):409–18.

Marshall, F. 1986. Implications of bone modification in a Neolithic faunal assemblage for the study of early hominid butchery and subsistence practices. *Journal of Human Evolution* 15(8):661–72.

———. 1990. Cattle herds and caprine flocks. In P. Robertshaw (Ed.), *Early pastoralists of southwestern Kenya*. Nairobi: British Institute in Eastern Africa, pp. 205–313.

Marshall, F., and Pilgram, T. 1991. Meat versus within-bone nutrients: Another look at the meaning of body part representation in archaeological sites. *Journal of Archaeological Science* 18(2):149–63.

Marshall, L. G. 1989. Bone modification and "the laws of burial." In R. Bonnichsen and M. H. Sorg (Eds.), *Bone modification*. Orono: University of Maine, Institute for Quaternary Studies, Center for the Study of the First Americans, pp. 7–24.

Marti-Grädel, E., Deschler-Erb, S., Hüster-Plogman, H., and Schibler, J. 2004. Early evidence of economic specialization or social differentiation: A case study from the Neolithic lake shore settlement "Arbon-Bleiche 3" (Switzerland). In S. J. O'Day, W. Van Neer, and A. Ervynck (Eds.), *Behaviour behind bones: The zooarchaeology of ritual, religion, status and identity*. Oxford: Oxbow Books, pp. 164–76.

Martin, P. S., and Klein, R. G. (Eds.). 1984. *Quaternary extinctions: A prehistoric revolution*. Tucson: University of Arizona Press.

Martin, P. S., and Stuart, A. J. 1995. Mammoth extinction: Two continents and Wrangel Island. *Radiocarbon 37*(1):7–10.

Mason, I. L. (Ed.). 1984. *Evolution of domesticated animals*. London: Longman.

Mateos, A. 2005. Meat and fat: Intensive exploitation strategies in the Upper Paleolithic approached from bone fracturing analysis. In J. Mulville and A. K. Outram (Eds.), *The archaeology of fats, oils, milk and dairying: An introduction and overview*. Oxford: Oxbow Books, pp. 150–9.

May, S. A. 1997. Carbon stable isotope ratios in mediaeval and later human skeletons from northern England. *Journal of Archaeological Science 24*(6):561–7.

Mayo, J., and Cooke, R. 2005. La industria prehispánica de conchas marinas en Gran Coclé, Panamá. Análisis tecnológico de los artefactos de concha del basurero-taller del Sitio Cerro Juan Díaz, Los Santos, Panamá. *Archaeofauna 14*:285–98.

Mayr, E. 1942. *Systematics and the origin of species from the viewpoint of a zoologist*. New York: Columbia University Press.

————. 1982. *The growth of biological thought: Diversity, evolution, and inheritance*. Cambridge, MA: Belknap Press.

Mayr, E., and Greenway, J. C., Jr. (Eds.). 1962. *Check-list of birds of the world: A continuation of the work of James L. Peters*. Cambridge, MA: Museum of Comparative Zoology 15.

Mayr, E., Linsley, E. G., and Usinger, R. L. 1953. *Methods and principles of systematic zoology*. New York: McGraw-Hill.

Mays, S. A. 2005. Tuberculosis as a zoonotic disease in antiquity. In J. Davies, M. Fabiš, I. Mainland, M. Richards, and R. Thomas (Eds.), *Diet and health in past animal populations: Current research and future directions*. Oxford: Oxbow Books, pp. 125–34.

Meadow, R. H. 1978a. "Bonecode" – System of numerical coding for faunal data from Middle Eastern sites. In R. H. Meadow and M. A. Zeder (Eds.), *Approaches to faunal analysis in the Middle East*. Cambridge, MA: Harvard University, Peabody Museum of Archaeology and Ethnology Bulletin 2, pp. 169–86.

————. 1978b. Effects of context on the interpretation of faunal remains: A case study. In R. H. Meadow and M. A. Zeder (Eds.), *Approaches to faunal analysis in the Middle East*. Cambridge, MA: Harvard University, Peabody Museum of Archaeology and Ethnology Bulletin 2, pp. 15–21.

————. 1984. Animal domestication in the Middle East: A view from the eastern margin. In J. Clutton-Brock and C. Grigson (Eds.), *Animals and archaeology: 3. Early herders and their flocks*. Oxford: British Archaeological Reports International Series 202, pp. 309–37.

Mech, L. D. 1979. Why some deer are safe from wolves. *Natural History 88*(1):70–7.

Meehan, B. 1982. *Shell bed to shell midden.* Canberra: Australian Institute of Aboriginal Studies.

Meighan, C. W., Pendergast, D. M., Swartz, B. K., Jr., and Wissler, M. D. 1958a. Ecological interpretation in archaeology, Part I. *American Antiquity* 24(1):1–23.

———. 1958b. Ecological interpretation in archaeology, Part II. *American Antiquity* 24(2): 131–50.

Mena, F., Velásquez, H., Trejo, V., and Torres-Mura, J. C. 2004. Aproximaciones zooarcqueológicas al pasado de Aisén continental (Patagonia Central Chilena). In G. L. Mengoni Goñalons (Ed.), *Zooarchaeology of South America.* British Archaeological Reports International Series 1298. Oxford: Archaeopress, pp. 99–121.

Mengoni Goñalons, G. L. 1986. Vizcacha (*Lagidium viscacia*) and taruca (*Hippocamelus* sp.) in early south Andean economies. *ArchaeoZoologia Mélanges*:63–71.

———. 1988. Analisis de materiales faunisticos de sitios arqueologicos. *Xama* 1:71–120. Mendoza, Argentina.

Mengoni Goñalons, G. L., and Yacobaccio, H. D. 2006. The domestication of South American camelids: A view from the south-central Andes. In M. A. Zeder, D. G. Bradley, E. Emshwiller, and B. D. Smith (Eds.), *Documenting domestication: New genetics and archaeological paradigms.* Berkeley: University of California Press, pp. 228–44.

Mercer, H. C. 1897. The finding of the remains of the fossil sloth at Big Bone Cave, Tennessee, in 1896. *Proceedings of the American Philosophical Society* 36:36–70.

Merriam, C. H. 1928. Why not more care in identification of animal remains? *American Anthropologist* 30(4):731–2.

Messineo, P. G. 2003. Análisis arqueofaunísticos en el sitio Laguna La Barrancosa 1 (Partido de Benito Juárez, Provincia de Buenos Aires, Argentina). *Archaeofauna* 12:73–86.

Metcalfe, D., and Jones, K. T. 1988. A reconsideration of animal body-part utility indices. *American Antiquity* 53(3):486–504.

Meunier, F. J., and Desse, J. 1994. Histological structure of hyperostotic cranial remains of *Pomadasys hasta* (Osteichthyes, Perciformes, Haemulidae) from archaeological sites of the Arabian Gulf and the Indian Ocean. In W. Van Neer (Ed.), *Fish exploitation in the past.* Tervuren, Belgium: Annales du Musée Royal de l'Afrique Centrale, Sciences Zoologiques 274, pp. 47–53.

Meyer de Schauensee, R. 1970. *A guide to the birds of South America.* Wynnewood, PA: Livingston Publishing Company.

Middleton, W. D., Feinman, G. M., and Nicholas, L. M. 2002. Domestic faunal assemblages from the Classic Period Valley of Oaxaca, Mexico: A perspective on the subsistence and craft economies. *Journal of Archaeological Science* 29:233–49.

Miller, G. H., M. L. Fogel, J. W. Magee, M. K. Gagan, S. J. Clarke, and B. J. Johnson. 2005. Ecosystem collapse in Pleistocene Australia and a human role in megafaunal extinction. *Science* 309:287–90.

Miller, G. J. 1975. A study of cuts, grooves, and other marks on recent and fossil bone: II. Weathering cracks, fractures, splinters, and other similar natural phenomena. In E. Swanson (Ed.), *Lithic technology, making and using stone tools.* The Hague: Mouton Publishers, pp. 211–26.

Miller, G. S., Jr. 1929a. *A second collection of mammals from caves near St. Michael, Haiti.* Washington, DC: Smithsonian Institution Miscellaneous Collections 81 (9).

———. 1929b. *Mammals eaten by Indians, owls, and Spaniards in the coast region of the Dominican Republic.* Washington, DC: Smithsonian Institution Miscellaneous Collections 82(5).

Miller, G. S., Jr., and Kellogg, R. 1955. *List of North American recent mammals.* Washington, DC: United States National Museum Bulletin 205.

Miller, M. E. 1968. *Anatomy of the dog.* Philadelphia: W.B. Saunders.

Mills, W. C. 1904. Explorations of the Gartner mound and village site. *Ohio State Archaeological and Historical Quarterly* 13:129–89.

———. 1906. Baum prehistoric village. *Ohio Archaeological and Historical Publications* 15: 45–136.

Milner, N. 2001. At the cutting edge: Using thin sectioning to determine season of death of the European oyster, *Ostra edulis. Journal of Archaeological Science* 28:861–73.

———. 2002. Oysters, cockles and kitchenmiddens: Changing practices at the Mesolithic/ Neolithic transition. In P. Miracle and N. Milner (Eds.), *Consuming passions and patterns of consumption.* Cambridge, UK: McDonald Institute Monographs, pp. 89–96.

Minc, L. D., and Smith, K. P. 1989. The spirit of survival: Cultural responses to resource variability in North Alaska. In P. Halstead and J. O'Shea (Eds.), *Bad year economics: Cultural responses to risk and uncertainty.* Cambridge, UK: Cambridge University Press, pp. 8–39.

Minnis, P. E., Whalen, M. E., Kelley, J. H., and Stewert, J. D. 1993. Prehistoric macaw breeding in the North American Southwest. *American Antiquity* 58(2):270–6.

Minniti, C. 2005. Shells at the Bronze Age settlement of Coppa Nevigata (Apulia, Italy). In D. E. Bar-Yosef Mayer (Ed.), *Archaeomalacology: Molluscs in former environments of human behaviour.* Oxford: Oxbow Books, pp. 71–81.

Minniti, C., and Peyronel, L. 2005. Symbolic or functional astragali from Tell Mardikh-Ebla (Syria). *Archaeofauna* 14:7–26.

Miracle, P., 2002. Mesolithic meals from Mesolithic middens. In P. Miracle and N. Milner (Eds.), *Consuming passions and patterns of consumption.* Cambridge, UK: McDonald Institute Monographs, pp. 65–88.

Miracle, P., and Milner, N. (Eds.). 2002. *Consuming passions and patterns of consumption.* Cambridge, UK: McDonald Institute Monographs.

Mitchell, P., and Charles, R. 2000. Later Stone Age hunter-gatherer adapations in the Lesotho Highlands, southern Africa. In G. Bailey, R. Charles, and N. Winder (Eds.), *Human ecodynamics.* Oxford: Oxbow Books, pp. 90–9.

Molleson, T., and Hodgson, D. 1993. A cart driver from Ur. *ArchaeoZoologia* 6(1):93–106.

Mondini, M. 2002. Carnivore taphonomy and the early human occupations in the Andes. *Journal of Archaeological Science* 29:791–801.

Mondini, M., Muñoz, S., and Wickler, S. (Eds.). 2004. *Colonisation, migration and marginal areas: A zooarchaeological approach.* Oxford: Oxbow Books.

Monks, G. G. 1981. Seasonality studies. In M. B. Schiffer (Ed.), *Advances in archaeological method and theory* (Vol. 4). New York: Academic Press, pp. 177–240.

———. 2005. An oil utility index for whale bones. In G. G. Monks (Ed.), *Exploitation and cultural importance of sea mammals.* Oxford: Oxbow Books, pp. 138–53.

Moore, O. K. 1969. Divination – New perspective. In A. P. Vayda (Ed.), *Environment and cultural behavior: Ecological studies in cultural anthropology.* New York: Natural History Press, pp. 121–9.

Morales, A., Cereijo, M. A., Brännstöm, P., and Liesau, C. 1994. The mammals. In E. Roselló and A. Morales (Eds.), *Castillo de Doña Blanca: Archaeo-environmental investigations in the Bay of Cádiz, Spain (750–500 B.C.)*. Oxford: British Archaeological Reports International Series 593, pp. 37–69.

Morales, A., and Rodríguez, J. 1997. Black rats (*Rattus rattus*) from medieval Mertola (Baixo Alentejo, Portugal). *Journal of Zoology, London* 241:623–42.

Morales, A., and Rosenlund, K. 1979. *Fish bone measurements: An attempt to standardize the measuring of fish bones from archaeological sites*. Copenhagen: Steenstrupia.

Morales, E. 1995. *The guinea pig: Healing, food and ritual in the Andes*. Tucson: University of Arizona Press.

Morales Muñiz, A. 1988. On the use of butchering as a paleocultural index: Proposal of a new methodology for the study of bone fracture from archaeological sites. *ArchaeoZoologia* 2(1/2):111–50.

———. 1993a. Ornithoarchaeology: The various aspects of the classification of bird remains from archaeological sites. *Archaeofauna* 2:1–13.

———. 1993b. Where are the tunas? Ancient Iberian fishing industries from an archaeozoological perspective. In A. Clason, S. Payne, and H.-P. Uerpmann (Eds.), *Skeletons in her cupboard: Festschrift for Juliet Clutton-Brock*. Oxford: Oxbow Books Monograph 34, pp. 135–41.

Morales Muñiz, L. C., and Morales Muñiz, A. 1995. The Spanish bullfight: Some historical aspects, traditional interpretations, and comments of archaeozoological interest for the study of the ritual slaughter. In K. Ryan and P. J. Crabtree (Eds.), *The symbolic role of animals in archaeology*. Philadelphia: University of Pennsylvania, Museum of Archaeology and Anthropology Research Papers in Science and Archaeology, MASCA 12, pp. 91–105.

Moran, E. F. 1979. *Human adaptability: An introduction to ecological anthropology*. North Scituate, MA: Duxbury Press.

———. 1990. Ecosystem ecology in biology and anthropology: A critical assessment. In E. F. Moran (Ed.), *The ecosystem approach in anthropology*. Ann Arbor: University of Michigan Press, pp. 3–40.

Moran, N. C., and O'Connor, T. P. 1994. Age attribution in domestic sheep by skeletal and dental maturation: A pilot study of available sources. *International Journal of Osteoarchaeology* 4:267–85.

Moreno-García, M. 2004. Hunting practices and consumption patterns in rural communities in the Rif mountains (Morocco) – Some ethno-zoological notes. In S. J. O'Day, W. Van Neer, and A. Ervynck (Eds.), *Behaviour behind bones: The zooarchaeology of ritual, religion, status and identity*. Oxford: Oxbow Books, pp. 327–34.

Morey, D. F. 1983. Archaeological assessment of seasonality from freshwater fish remains: A quantitative procedure. *Journal of Ethnobiology* 3(1):75–95.

———. 2006. Burying key evidence: The social bond between dogs and people. *Journal of Archaeological Science* 33:158–75.

Mori, J. L. 1970. Procedures for establishing a faunal collection to aid in archaeological analysis. *American Antiquity* 35(3):387–8.

Morlan, R. E. 1994. Oxbow bison procurement as seen from the Harder Site, Saskatchewan. *Journal of Archaeological Science* 21(6):797–807.

Morlot, A. von. 1861. *General views on archaeology*. Washington, DC: Annual Report of the Smithsonian Institution for 1860.

Morris, P. 1972. A review of mammalian age determination methods. *Mammal Review* 2(3):69–104.

———. 1978. The use of teeth for estimating the age of wild mammals. In P. M. Butler and K. A. Joysey (Eds.), *Development, function and evolution of teeth.* New York: Academic Press, pp. 483–94.

Morton, J. D., and Schwarcz, H. P. 2004. Paleodietary implications from stable isotopic analysis of residues on prehistoric Ontario ceramics. *Journal of Archaeological Science* 31:503–17.

Muir, R. J., and Driver, J. C. 2004. Identifying ritual use of animals in the northern American Southwest. In S. J. O'Day, W. Van Neer, and A. Ervynck (Eds.), *Behaviour behind bones: The zooarchaeology of ritual, religion, status and identity.* Oxford: Oxbow Books, pp. 128–43.

Mukherjee, A. J., Copley, M. S., Berstan, R., Clark, K. A., and Evershed, R. P. 2005. Interpretation of δ^{13} C values of fatty acids in relation to animal husbandry, food processing and consumption in prehistory. In J. Mulville and A. K. Outram (Eds.), *The archaeology of fats, oils, milk and dairying: An introduction and overview.* Oxford: Oxbow Books, pp. 77–93.

Müldner, G., and Richards, M. P. 2005. Fast or feast: Reconstructing diet in later medieval England by stable isotope analysis. *Journal of Archaeological Science* 32:39–48.

Müller, H.-H. 1982. *Bibliographie zur Archäo-zoologie und Geschichte der Haustiere (1980–1981).* Berlin: Akademie der Wissenschaften der DDR.

———. 1990. *Bibliographie zur Archäo-zoologie und Geschichte der Haustiere (1988–1989).* Berlin: Zentralinstitut für Alte Geschichte und Archäologie, Bereich Ur- und Frühgeschichte.

———. 1991. *Bibliographie zur Archäo-zoologie und Geschichte der Haustiere (1989–1990).* Berlin: Zentralinstitut für Alte Geschichte und Archäologie, Bereich Ur- und Frühgeschichte.

Mulville, J. 2005. A whale of a problem? The use of zooarchaeological evidence in modern whaling. In G. G. Monks (Ed.), *The exploitation and cultural importance of sea mammals.* Oxford: Oxbow Press, pp. 154–66.

Mulville, J., and Outram, A. K. (Eds.). 2005. *The zooarchaeology of fats, oils, milk and dairying.* Oxford: Oxbow Press.

Muñoz, A. S. 2004. Mammal exploitation in the insular environments of southern South America. In G. L. Mengoni Goñalons (Ed.), *Zooarchaeology of South America.* British Archaeological Reports International Series 1298. Oxford: Archaeopress, pp. 123–37.

Munro, N. D., and Bar-Oz, G. 2005. Gazelle bone fat processing in the Levantine Epipaleolithic. *Journal of Archaeological Science* 32:223–39.

Munson, P. J. 2000. Age-correlated differential destruction of bones and its effect on archaeological mortality profiles of domestic sheep and goats. *Journal of Archaeological Science* 27:391–407.

Munson, P. J., and Garniewicz, R. C. 2003. Age-mediated survivorship of ungulate mandibles and their teeth in canid-ravaged faunal assemblages. *Journal of Archaeological Science* 30:405–16.

Munson, P. J., Parmalee, P. W., and Yarnell, R. A. 1971. Subsistence ecology of Scovill, a Terminal Middle Woodland Village. *American Antiquity* 36(4):410–31.

Münzel, S. C. 1988. Quantitative analysis and archaeological site interpretation. *ArchaeoZoologia* 2(1/2):93–110.

Murphy, E. M. 2001. Medieval and Post-Medieval butchered dogs from Carrickfergus, Co. Antrim, Northern Ireland. *Environmental Archaeology* 6:13–22.

Murphy, P., Albarella, U., Germany, M., and Locker, A. 2000. Production, imports and status: Biological remains from a Late Roman farm at Great Holts Farm, Boreham, Essex, UK. *Environmental Archaeology* 5:35–48.

Murra, J. V. 1965. Herds and herders in the Inca state. In A. Leeds and A. P. Vayda (Eds.), *Man, culture, and animals: The role of animals in human ecological adjustments.* Washington, DC: American Association for the Advancement of Science Publication 78, pp. 185–215.

Murray, E., McCormick, F., and Plunkett, G. 2004. The food economies of Atlantic island monasteries: The documentary and archaeo-environmental evidence. *Environmental Archaeology* 9:179–88.

Mutundu, K. K. 2005. Domestic stock age profiles and herd management practices: Ethnoarchaeological implications from Maasai settlements in southern Kenya. *Archaeofauna* 14:83–92.

Nagaoka, L. 2002. Explaining subsistence change in southern New Zealand using foraging theory models. *World Archaeology* 34(1):84–102.

Nelson, J. S. 1984. *Fishes of the world* (2nd ed.). New York: John Wiley and Sons/Interscience Publishing.

Nelson, J. S., Crossman, E. J., Esponosa-Pérez, H., Findley, L. T., Gilbert, C. R., Lea, R. N., and Williams, J. D. 2004. *Common and scientific names of fishes from the United States, Canada, and Mexico.* Bethesda, MD: American Fisheries Society Special Publication 29.

Netting, R. McC. 1976. What alpine peasants have in common: Observations on communal tenure in a Swiss village. *Human Ecology* 4(2):135–46.

Neusius, S. W. 2007. Game procurement among temperate horticulturists: The case for garden hunting by the Dolores Anasazi. In E. J. Reitz, C. M. Scarry, and S. J. Scudder (Eds.), *Case studies in environmental archaeology* (2nd ed.). London: Springer, pp. 291–308.

Newman, M. E., Parboosingh, J. S., Bridge, P. J., and Ceri, H. 2002. Identification of archaeological animal bone by PCR/DNA analysis. *Journal of Archaeological Science* 29:77–84.

Newsom, L. A., and Wing, E. S. 2004. *On land and sea: Native American uses of biological resources in the West Indies.* Tuscaloosa: University of Alabama Press.

Newsome, S. D., Phillips, D. L., Culleton, B. J., Guilderson, T. P., and Koch, P. L. 2004. Dietary reconstruction of an early to middle Holocene human population from the central California coast: Insights from advanced stable isotope mixing models. *Journal of Archaeological Science* 31:1101–15.

Nichol, R. K., and Wild, C. J. 1984. "Numbers of individuals" in faunal analysis: The decay of fish bone in archaeological sites. *Journal of Archaeological Science* 11(1):35–51.

Nicholson, R. A. 1995. Out of the frying pan into the fire: What value are burnt fish bones to archaeology? *Archaeofauna* 4:47–64.

———. 2000. Otter (*Lutra lutra* L.) spraint: An investigation into possible sources of small fish bones. In J. P. Huntley and S. Stallibrass (Eds.), *Taphonomy and interpretation.* Oxford: Oxbow Books, pp. 55–64.

Nicholson, R. A., and O'Connor, T. P. (Eds.). 2000. *People as an agent of environmental change.* Oxford: Oxbow Books.

Nietschmann, B. 1973. *Between land and water: The subsistence ecology of the Miskito Indians, Eastern Nicaragua.* New York: Seminar Press.

Nishimura, A. 1975. Cultural and social change in the modes of ownership of stone tidal weirs. In R. W. Casteel and G. I. Quimby (Eds.), *Maritime adaptations of the Pacific.* The Hague: Mouton Publishers, pp. 77–88.

Niven, L. B., Egeland, C. P., and Todd, L. C. 2004. An inter-site comparison of enamel hypoplasia in bison: Implications for paleoecology and modeling Late Plains Archaic subsistence. *Journal of Archaeological Science* 31:1783–94.

Noddle, B. A. 1974. Ages of epiphyseal closure in feral and domestic goats and ages of dental eruption. *Journal of Archaeological Science* 1(2):195–204.

――――. 1994. The under-rated goat. In A. R. Hall and H. K. Kenward (Eds.), *Urban-rural connexions: Perspectives from environmental archaeology*. Oxford: Oxbow Books Monograph 47, pp. 117–28.

Noe-Nygaard, N. 1975. Bone injuries caused by human weapons in Mesolithic Denmark. In A. T. Clason (Ed.), *Archaeozoological studies*. Amsterdam: North-Holland Publishing Company, pp. 151–9.

――――. 1977. Butchering and marrow fracturing as a taphonomic factor in archaeological deposits. *Paleobiology* 3(2):218–37.

――――. 1988a. δ^{13}C-values of dog bones reveal the nature of changes in man's food resources at the Mesolithic–Neolithic transition, Denmark. *Chemical Geology (Isotope Geoscience Section)* 73(1):87–96.

――――. 1988b. Taphonomy in archaeology with special emphasis on man as a biasing factor. *Journal of Danish Archaeology* 6(1987):7–52.

――――. 1989. Man-made trace fossils in bones. *Human Evolution* 4(6):461–91.

Noe-Nygaard, N., Price, T. D., and Hede, S. U. 2005. Diet of aurochs and early cattle in southern Scandinavia: evidence from ^{15}N and ^{13}C stable isotopes. *Journal of Archaeological Science* 32:855–71.

Noe-Nygaard, N., and Richter, J. 1990. Seventeen wild boar mandibles from Sludegårds Sømose – Offal or sacrifice? In D. E. Robinson (Ed.), *Experimentation and reconstruction in environmental archaeology*. Oxford: Oxbow Books, pp. 175–89.

Nogueira de Queiroz, A. 2004. Étude des vertébrés du site archéologique Rs-Tq-58, Montenegro, RS, Brésil: aspects archéozoologiques et taphonomiques. In G. L. Mengoni Goñalons (Ed.), *Zooarchaeology of South America*. British Archaeological Reports International Series 1298. Oxford: Archaeopress, pp. 153–61.

Noonan, J. P., Hofreiter, M., Smith, D., Priest, J. R., Rohland, N., Rabeder, G., Krause, J., Detter, J. C., Pääbo, S., and Rubin, E. M. 2005. Genetic sequencing of Pleistocene cave bears. *Science* 309:597–600.

Nowak, R. M. 1991. *Walker's mammals of the world* (5th ed.). Baltimore: Johns Hopkins University Press.

Nyerges, E. A. 2004. Ethnic traditions in meat consumption and herding at a 16th-century Cumanian settlement in the Great Hungarian Plain. In S. J. O'Day, W. Van Neer, and A. Ervynck (Eds.), *Behaviour behind bones: The zooarchaeology of ritual, religion, status, and identity*, Oxford: Oxbow Books, pp. 262–70.

O'Connell, J., Hawkes, K., and Blurton-Jones, N. 1988. Hadza hunting, butchering, and bone transport and their archaeological implications. *Journal of Anthropological Research* 44: 112–62.

――――. 1990. Reanalysis of large mammal body part transport among the Hadza. *Journal of Archaeological Science* 17(3):301–16.

O'Connell, J. F., and Marshall, B. 1989. Analysis of kangaroo body part transport among the Alyawara of central Australia. *Journal of Archaeological Science* 16(4):393–405.

O'Connell, T. C., Hedges, R. E. M., Healey, M. A., and Simpson, A. H. R. W. 2001. Isotopic comparison of hair, nail and bone: Modern analyses. *Journal of Archaeological Science* 28: 1247–55.

O'Connor, T. (Ed.). 2005. *Biosphere to lithosphere: New studies in vertebrate taphonomy*. Oxford: Oxbow Books.

O'Connor, T. P. 1984. Selected groups of bones from Skeldergate and Walmgate. *The Archaeology of York*, London: Council for British Archaeology, 15 (1):1–60.

———. 1988. Bones from the General Accident Site, Tanner Row. *The Archaeology of York*, London: Council for British Archaeology, 15 (2):1–136.

———. 1996. A critical overview of archaeological animal bone studies. *World Archaeology* 28(1):5–19.

———. 2000a. Human refuse as a major ecological factor in Medieval urban vertebrate communities. In G. Bailey, R. Charles, and N. Winder (Eds.), *Human ecodynamics*. Oxford: Oxbow Books, pp. 15–20.

———. 2000b. *The archaeology of animal bones*. London: Sutton Publishing.

O'Day, S. J. 2004. Past and present perspectives on secular ritual: Food and the fisherwomen of the Lau Islands, Fiji. In S. J. O'Day, W. Van Neer, and A. Ervynck (Eds.), *Behaviour behind bones: The zooarchaeology of ritual, religion, status and identity*. Oxford: Oxbow Books, pp. 153–61.

O'Day, S. J., Van Neer, W., and Ervynck, A. (Eds.). 2004. *Behaviour behind bones: The zooarchaeology of ritual, religion, status, and identity*. Oxford: Oxbow Books.

Odum, E., and Barrett, G. W. 2005. *Fundamentals of ecology* (5th ed.). Belmont, CA: Thomson Brooks/Cole.

Odum, H. T. 1983. *Systems ecology: An introduction*. New York: John Wiley and Sons/Interscience.

Odum, W. E., and McIvor, C. C. 1990. Mangroves. In R. L. Myers and J. J. Ewel (Eds.), *Ecosystems of Florida*. Orlando: University of Central Florida Press, pp. 517–48.

Oelrich, T. M. 1956. *The anatomy of the head of Ctenosaura pectinata* (Iguanidae). Ann Arbor: University of Michigan Museum of Zoology Miscellaneous Publications 94, pp. 1–122.

Olsen, Sandra L. 1987. Magdalenian reindeer exploitation at the Grotte des Eyzies, southwest France. *ArchaeoZoologia* 1(1):171–82.

———. 1989. On distinguishing natural from cultural damage on archaeological antler. *Journal of Archaeological Science* 16:125–35.

———. 1994. Exploitation of mammals at the Early Bronze Age site of West Row Fen (Mildenhall 165), Suffolk, England. *Annals of Carnegie Museum* 63 (2):115–53.

———. 2006. Early horse domestication on the Eurasian steppe. In M. A. Zeder, D. G. Bradley, E. Emshwiller, and B. D. Smith (Eds.), *Documenting domestication: New genetics and archaeological paradigms*. Berkeley: University of California Press, pp. 245–69.

Olsen, S. L., and Olsen, J. W. 1981. A comment on nomenclature in faunal studies. *American Antiquity* 46(1):192–4.

Olsen, Stanley J. 1960. *Post-cranial skeletal characters of Bison and Bos*. Cambridge, MA: Harvard University, Papers of the Peabody Museum of Archaeology and Ethnology 35 (4).

———. 1964. *Mammal remains from archaeological sites: I. Southeastern and Southwestern United States*. Cambridge, MA: Harvard University, Papers of the Peabody Museum of Archaeology and Ethnology 56(1).

———. 1968. *Fish, amphibian and reptile remains from archaeological sites.* Cambridge, MA: Harvard University, Papers of the Peabody Museum of Archaeology and Ethnology 56(2).

———. 1972. *Osteology for the archaeologist: No. 3: The American mastodon and the wooly mammoth; No. 4: North American birds: Skulls and mandibles.* Cambridge, MA: Harvard University, Papers of the Peabody Museum of Archaeology and Ethnology 56(3/4).

———. 1985. *Origins of the domestic dog: The fossil record.* Tucson: University of Arizona Press.

Osborne, J. S., Johnson, A. S., Hale, P. E., Marchinton, R. L., Vansant, C. V., and Wentworth, J. M. 1992. *Population ecology of the Blackbird Island white-tailed deer.* Tallahassee: Bulletin of Tall Timbers Research 26.

Oswalt, W. H. 1973. *Habitat and technology: The evolution of hunting.* New York: Holt, Rinehart, and Winston.

———. 1976. *An anthropological analysis of food-getting technology.* New York: John Wiley and Sons/Interscience.

Outram, A. K. 2001. A new approach to identifying bone marrow and grease exploitation: Why the "indeterminate" fragments should not be ignored. *Journal of Archaeological Science* 28:401–10.

———. 2002. Bone fracture and within-bone nutrients: An experimentally based method for investigating levels of marrow extraction. In P. Miracle and N. Milner (Eds.), *Consuming passions and patterns of consumption.* Cambridge, UK: McDonald Institute Monographs, pp. 51–63.

———. 2004. Identifying dietary stress in marginal environments: Bone fats, optimal foraging theory and the seasonal round. In M. Mondini, S. Muñoz, and S. Wickler (Eds.), *Colonisation, migration and marginal areas: A zooarchaeological approach.* Oxford: Oxbow Books, pp. 74–85.

———. 2005. Distinguishing bone fat exploitation from other taphonomic processes: What caused the high level of bone fragmentation at the Middle Neolithic site of Ajvide, Gotland? In J. Mulville and A. K. Outram (Eds.), *The archaeology of fats, oils, milk and dairying: An introduction and overview.* Oxford: Oxbow Books, pp. 32–43.

Outram, A. K., Knüsel, C. J., Knight, S., and Harding, A. F. 2005. Understanding complex fragmented assemblages of human and animal remains: A fully integrated approach. *Journal of Archaeological Science* 32:1699–710.

Paine, R. T. 1966. Food web complexity and species diversity. *American Naturalist* 100(910):65–75.

Panagiotakopula, E. 2004. Dipterous remains and archaeological interpretations. *Journal of Archaeological Science* 31:1675–84.

Pannella, G. 1980. Growth patterns in fish sagittae. In D. C. Rhoads and R. A. Lutz (Eds.), *Skeletal growth of aquatic organisms: Biological records of environmental change.* New York: Plenum Press, pp. 519–90.

Parmalee, P. W. 1957a. Vertebrate remains from the Cahokia site, Illinois. *Transactions of the Illinois State Academy of Science* 50:235–42.

———. 1957b. Zoology. In W. W. Taylor (Ed.), *The identification of non-artifactual archaeological materials.* Washington, DC: National Academies of Sciences, Natural Resource Council Publication 565, pp. 45–6.

———. 1965. The food economy of the vertebrate fauna from Cahokia. *Illinois Archaeological Survey Bulletin* 10:137–55.

———. 1985. Identification and interpretation of archaeologically derived animal remains. In R. I. Gilbert, Jr. and J. H. Mielke (Eds.), *The analysis of prehistoric diets.* New York: Academic Press, pp. 61–95.

Parmalee, P. W., and Klippel, W. E. 1974. Freshwater mussels as a prehistoric food resource. *American Antiquity* 39(3):421–34.

Passmore, R., and Durnin, J. V. G. A. 1955. Human energy expenditure. *Physiological Reviews* 35:801–40.

Patton, M. 2000. Blitzkrieg or Sitzkrieg? The extinction of endemic faunas in Mediterranean island prehistory. In R. A. Nicholson and T. P. O'Connor (Eds.), *People as an agent of environmental change.* Oxford: Oxbow Books, pp. 117–24.

Pauly, D., and Christensen, V. 1995. Primary production required to sustain global fisheries. *Nature* 374:255–7.

Pauly, D., Christensen, V., Dalsgaard, J., Froese, R., and Torres, F., Jr. 1998. Fishing down marine food webs. *Science* 279:860–3.

Pauly, D., Christensen, V., Froese, R., and Palomares, M. L. 2000. Fishing down aquatic food webs. *American Scientist* 88(1):46–51.

Pauketat, T. R., Kelly, L. S., Fritz, G. J., Lopinot, N. H., Elias, S., and Hargrave, E. 2002. The residues of feasting and public ritual at Early Cahokia. *American Antiquity* 67(2):257–79.

Pavao, B., and Stahl, P. W. 1999. Structural density assays of leporid skeletal elements with implications for taphonomic, actualistic, and archaeological research. *Journal of Archaeological Science* 26:53–66.

Payne, S. B. 1972a. On the interpretation of bone samples from archaeological sites. In E. S. Higgs (Ed.), *Papers in economic prehistory.* Cambridge, UK: Cambridge University Press, pp. 65–81.

————. 1972b. Partial recovery and sample bias: The results of some sieving experiments. In E. S. Higgs (Ed.), *Papers in economic prehistory.* Cambridge, UK: Cambridge University Press, pp. 49–64.

————. 1973. Kill-off patterns in sheep and goats: The mandibles from Asvan Kale. *Anatolian Studies* 23:281–303.

————. 1975. Partial recovery and sample bias. In A. T. Clason (Ed.), *Archaeozoological studies.* Amsterdam: North-Holland Publishing Company, pp. 7–17.

————. 1985a. Morphological distinctions between the mandibular teeth of young sheep, *Ovis,* and goats, *Capra. Journal of Archaeological Science* 12(2):139–47.

————. 1985b. Zoo-archaeology in Greece: A reader's guide. In N. C. Wilkie and W. D. E. Coulson (Eds.), *Contributions to Aegean archaeology: Studies in honor of William H. McDonald.* Dubuque, IA: Kendall/Hunt Publishing Company, pp. 211–44.

————. 1987. Reference codes for wear states in the mandibular cheek teeth of sheep and goats. *Journal of Archaeological Science* 14(6):609–14.

————. 1992. Some notes on sampling and sieving for animal bones. *Ancient Monuments Laboratory Report* 55/92. London: English Heritage.

Payne, S., and Bull, G. 1988. Components of variation in measurements of pig bones and teeth, and the use of measurements to distinguish wild from domestic pig remains. *ArchaeoZoologia* 2(1/2):27–66.

Payne, S., and Munson, P. J. 1985. Ruby and how many squirrels? The destruction of bones by dogs. In N. R. J. Fieller, D. D. Gilbertson, and N. G. A. Ralph (Eds.), *Paleobiological investigations: Research design, methods, and data analysis.* Oxford: British Archaeological Reports International Series 266, pp. 31–40.

Peacock, E. 1998. Historical and applied perspectives on prehistoric land use in eastern North America. *Environment and History* 4:1–29.

Peacock, E., Rafferty, J., and Hogue, S. H. 2005. Land snails, artifacts and faunal remains: Understanding site formation processes at Prehistoric/Protohistoric sites in the southeastern United States. In D. E. Bar-Yosef Mayer (Ed.), *Archaeomalacology: Molluscs in former environments of human behaviour.* Oxford: Oxbow Books, pp. 6–17.

Pearce, J., and Luff, R. 1994. The taphonomy of cooked bone. In R. Luff and P. Rowley-Conwy (Eds.), *Whither environmental archaeology?* Oxford: Oxbow Books Monograph 38, pp. 51–56.

Pearsall, D. M. 2000. *Paleothnobotany: A handbook of procedures* (2nd ed.). San Diego: Academic Press.

Pechenkina, E. A., Ambrose, S. H., Xiaolin, M., and Benfer, R. A., Jr. 2005. Reconstructing northern Chinese Neolithic subsistence practices by isotopic analysis. *Journal of Archaeological Science* 32:1176–89.

Peet, R. K. 1974. The measurement of species diversity. *Annual Review of Ecology and Systematics* 5:285–307.

Perdikaris, S. 1996. Scaly heads and tales: Detecting commercialization in early fisheries. *Archaeofauna* 5:21–33.

Perkins, D. 1973. A critique on the methods of quantifying faunal remains from archaeological sites. In J. Matolcsi (Ed.), *Domestikationsforschung und Geschichte der Haustiere.* Budapest: Akadémiai Kiadó, pp. 367–9.

Perkins, D., Jr., and Daly, P. 1968. A hunter's village in Neolithic Turkey. *Scientific American* 219(5):96–106.

Perlman, S. M. 1980. An optimum diet model, coastal variability, and hunter-gatherer behavior. In M. B. Schiffer (Ed.), *Advances in archaeological method and theory* (Vol. 3). New York: Academic Press, pp. 257–310.

Peters, C. R., and Vogel, J. C. 2005. Africa's wild C_4 plant foods and possible early hominid diets. *Journal of Human Evolution* 48:219–36.

Peters, J. 1986. A revision of the faunal remains from two Central Sudanese sites: Kartoum Hospital and Esh Shaheinab. *ArchaeoZoologia, Mélanges:* 11–33.

———. 1993. Archaic Milet: Daily life and religious customs from an archaeozoological perspective. In H. Buitenhuis and A. T. Clason (Eds.), *Archaeozoology of the Near East.* Leiden, The Netherlands: Universal Book Services, pp. 88–96.

Peters, J., Dreisch, A von den, and Helmer, D. 2005. The upper Euphrates-Tigris basin: cradle of agro-pastoralism? In J.-D. Vigne, J. Peters, and D. Helmer (Eds.), *First steps of animal domestication: New archaeozoological approaches.* Oxford: Oxbow Books, pp. 96–124.

Peters, J., and Pöllath, N. 2004. Holocene faunas of the eastern Sahara: Zoogeographical and palaeoecological aspects. In R. C. G. M. Lauwerier and I. Plug (Eds.), *The future from the past: Archaeozoology in wildlife conservation and heritage management.* Oxford: Oxbow Books, pp. 34–50.

Phoca-Cosmetatou, N. 2004. A zooarchaeological reassessment of the habitat and ecology of the ibex (*Capra ibex*). In R. C. G. M. Lauwerier and I. Plug (Eds.), *The future from the past: archaeozoology in wildlife conservation and heritage management.* Oxford: Oxbow Books, pp. 64–78.

Piana, E. L. 2005. Cetaceans and human beings at the uttermost part of America: A lasting relationship in Tierra del Fuego. In G. G. Monks (Ed.), *Exploitation and cultural importance of sea mammals*. Oxford: Oxbow Books, pp. 121–37.

Pickering, T. R., Marean, C. W., and Dominguez-Rodrigo, M. 2003. Importance of limb bone-shaft fragments in zooarchaeology: A response to "On *in situ* attrition and vertebrate body part profiles" (2002), by M. C. Stiner. *Journal of Archaeological Science* 30:1469–82.

Pickersgill, B., and Heiser, C. 1977. Origin and distribution of plants domesticated in the New World tropics. In C. A. Reed (Ed.), *Origins of agriculture*. The Hague: Mouton Publishers, pp. 803–35.

Pielou, E. C. 1966. Shannon's formula as a measure of specific diversity: Its uses and misuses. *American Naturalist* 100(914):463–5.

Pike, R. L., and Brown, M. L. 1975. *Nutrition: An integrated approach*. New York: John Wiley and Sons.

Pike-Tay, A. 1991. *Red deer hunting and the Upper Paleolithic of south-west France: A study in seasonality*. Oxford: British Archaeological Reports International Series 569.

———. 1995. Variability and synchrony of seasonal indicators in dental cementum microstructure of the Kaminuriak caribou population. *Archaeofauna* 4:273–84.

Pike-Tay, A. (Ed.) 2001. *Innovations in assessing season of capture, age and sex of archaeofaunas*. *ArchaeoZoologia* 11(1/ 2):15–238.

Plug, C., and Plug, I. 1990. MNI counts as estimates of species abundance. *South African Archaeological Bulletin* 45 (151):53–7.

Plug, I. 1987a. An analysis of witchdoctor divining sets. *Research by the National Cultural History and Open-Air Museum* 1(3):49–67.

———. 1987b. Iron Age subsistence strategies in the Kruger National Park (KNP), South Africa. *ArchaeoZoologia* 1(1):117–25.

———. 1989. Aspects of life in the Kruger National Park during the Early Iron Age. *South African Archaeological Society Goodwin Series* 6:62–8.

———. 2005. Osteomorphological differences between some skeletal elements of *Labeobarbus kimberleyensis, Labeobarbus aeneus* and *Labeo capensis* (Pisces: Cyprinidae). *Annals of the Transvaal Museum* 42:5–17.

Plug, I., and Lauwerier, R. C. G. M. 2004. Zooarchaeology in nature conservation and heritage management. In R. C. G. M. Lauwerier and I. Plug (Eds.), *The future from the past: Archaeozoology in wildlife conservation and heritage management*. Oxford: Oxbow Books, pp. 1–5.

Plug, I., and Voight, E. A. 1985. Archaeozoological studies of Iron Age communities in southern Africa. *Advances in World Archaeology* 4:189–238.

Polanyi, K. 1957. The economy as instituted process. In K. Polanyi, C. M. Arensberg, and H. W. Pearson (Eds.), *Trade and market in the Early Empires*. Glencoe, IL: Free Press, pp. 243–70.

Politis, G. G, and Saunders, N. J. 2002. Archaeological correlates of ideological activity: Food taboos and spirit-animals in an Amazonian hunter-gatherer society. In P. Miracle and N. Milner (Eds.), *Consuming passions and patterns of consumption*. Cambridge, UK: McDonald Institute Monographs, pp. 113–30.

Poll, S., Wagenstaller, J., Schweissing, M. M., Driesch, A. von den, Grupe, G., and Peters, J. 2005. Sr isotopes in horn cores provide information on early modern cattle trade. *Archaeofauna* 14:243–51.

Potter, J. M. 2000. Pots, parties, and politics: Communal feasting in the American southwest. *American Antiquity* 65(3):471–82.

Pough, F. H., Andrews, R. M., Cadle, J. E., Crump, M. L., Savitsky, A. H., and Wells, K. D. 2004. *Herpetology* (3rd ed.). Upper Saddle Creek, NJ: Pearson Prentice Hall.

Powers, L. W., and Bliss, D. E. 1983. Terrestrial adaptations. In D. E. Bliss (Ed.), *The biology of Crustacea* (Vol. 8). Orlando, FL: Academic Press, pp. 271–333.

Prange, H. D., Anderson, J. F., and Rahn, H. 1979. Scaling of skeletal mass to body mass in birds and mammals. *American Naturalist* 113(1):103–22.

Price, C. R. 1985. Patterns of cultural behavior and intra-site distributions of faunal remains at the Widow Harris site. *Historical Archaeology* 19(2):40–56.

Price, T. D. 2000. Immigration and the ancient city of Teotihuacan in Mexico: A study using strontium isotope ratios in human bone and teeth. *Journal of Archaeological Science* 27:903–13.

Price, T. D., Blitz, J., Burton, J., and Ezzo, J. A. 1992. Diagenesis in prehistoric bone: Problems and solutions. *Journal of Archaeological Science* 19(5):513–29.

Price, T. D., Connor, M., and Parsen, J. D. 1985. Bone chemistry and the reconstruction of diet: Strontium discrimination in white-tailed deer. *Journal of Archaeological Science* 12(6):419–42.

Privat, K. L., O'Connell, T. C., and Richards, M. P. 2002. Stable isotope analysis of human and faunal remains from the Anglo-Saxon cemetery at Berinsfield, Oxfordshire: Dietary and social implications. *Journal of Archaeological Science* 29:779–90.

Proctor, N. S., and Lynch, P. J. 1993. *Manual of ornithology: Avian structure and function.* New Haven: Yale University Press.

Prowse, T., Schwarcz, H. P., Saunders, S., Macchiarelli, R., and Bondioli, L. 2004. Isotopic paleodiet studies of skeletons from the Imperial Roman-age cemetery of Isola Sacra, Rome, Italy. *Journal of Archaeological Science* 31:259–72.

Prummel, W. 1987a. Atlas for identification of foetal skeletal elements of cattle, horse, sheep and pig. Part 1. *ArchaeoZoologia* 1(1):23–30.

―――. 1987b. Atlas for identification of foetal skeletal elements of cattle, horse, sheep and pig. Part 2. *ArchaeoZoologia* 1(2):11–42.

―――. 1988. Atlas for identification of foetal skeletal elements of cattle, horse, sheep and pig. Part 3. *ArchaeoZoologia* 2(1/2):13–26.

―――. 1989. Appendix to atlas for identification of foetal skeletal elements of cattle, horse, sheep and pig. *ArchaeoZoologia* 3(1/2):71–8.

―――. 2001. The significance of animals to the early Medieval Frisians in the northern coastal area of the Netherlands: Archaeozoological, iconographic, historical and literary evidence. *Environmental Archaeology* 6:73–86.

―――. 2005. Molluscs from a Middle Bronze Age site and two Hellenistic sites in Thessaly, Greece. In D. E. Bar-Yosef Mayer (Ed.), *Archaeomalacology: Molluscs in former environments of human behaviour.* Oxford: Oxbow Books, pp. 107–21.

Prummel, W., and Frisch, H.-J. 1986. A guide for the distinction of species, sex, and body side in bones of sheep and goat. *Journal of Archaeological Science* 13(6):567–77.

Pruvost, M., and Geigl, E.-M. 2004. Real-time quantitative PCR to assess the authenticity of ancient DNA amplification. *Journal of Archaeological Science* 31:1191–7.

Purdue, J. R. 1980. Clinal variation of some mammals during the Holocene in Missouri. *Quaternary Research* 13:242–58.

————. 1983. Epiphyseal closure in white-tailed deer. *Journal of Wildlife Management* 47(4):1207–13.

————. 1987. Estimation of body weight of white-tailed deer (*Odocoileus virginianus*) from bone size. *Journal of Ethnobiology* 7(1):1–12.

Purdue, J. R., and Reitz, E. J. 1993. Decrease in body size of white-tailed deer (*Odocoileus virginianus*) during the Late Holocene of South Carolina and Georgia. In R. A. Martin and A. D. Barnosky (Eds.), *Morphological change in Quaternary mammals of North America*. Cambridge, UK: Cambridge University Press, pp. 281–98.

Purdue, J. R., Styles, B. W., and Masulis, M. C. 1989. Faunal remains and white-tailed deer exploitation from a late Woodland upland encampment: The Boschert site (23SC609), St. Charles County, Missouri. *Midcontinental Journal of Archaeology* 14(2):146–54.

Purdy, B. A. (Ed.) 1988. *Wet site archaeology*. Caldwell, NJ: The Telford Press.

Quilter, J., Ojeda, E. B., Pearsall, D. M., Sandweiss, D. H., Jones, J. G., and Wing, E. S. 1991. Subsistence economy of El Paraíso, an early Peruvian site. *Science* 251(4991):277–83.

Quintana, C. A. 2005. Despiece de microroedores en el Holoceno Tardío de las Sierras de Tandilia (Argentina). *Archaeofauna* 14:227–41.

Quitmyer, I. R. 1985. Zooarchaeological methods for the analysis of shell middens at Kings Bay. In W. H. Adams (Ed.), *Aboriginal subsistence and settlement archaeology of the Kings Bay locality*. Gainesville: University of Florida, Department of Anthropology Reports of Investigations 2, pp. 33–48.

————. 1990. *Zooarchaeological analysis of British Period food remains from the Ribera Gardens Well, St. Augustine, Florida*. Manuscript on file. Gainesville, FL: Florida Museum of Natural History.

Quitmyer, I. R., Hale, H. S., and Jones, D. S. 1985. Paleoseasonality determination based on incremental shell growth in the hard clam, *Mercenaria mercenaria*, and its implications for the analysis of three southeast Georgia coastal shell middens. *Southeastern Archaeology* 4(1):27–40.

Quitmyer, I. R., and Jones, D. S. 1992. Calendars of the coast: Coastal seasonal growth increment patterns in shells of modern and archaeological southern quahogs, *Mercenaria campechiensis*, from Charlotte Harbor, Florida. In W. H. Marquardt (Ed.), *Culture and environment in the domain of the Calusa*. Gainesville, FL: Institute of Archaeology and Paleoenvironmental Studies Monograph 1, pp. 247–64.

————. 1997. The over-exploitation of Atlantic rangia clams (*Rangia cuneata*) and hard clam (*Mercenaria* spp.) from six archaeological sites in the southeastern United States. *Journal of Ethnobiology* 17(1):127.

Quitmyer, I. R., Jones, D. S., and Andrus, C. F. T. 2005. Seasonal collection of coquina clam (*Donax variabilis* Say, 1822) during the Archaic and St. Johns Periods in coastal northeast Florida. In D. E. Bar-Yosef Mayer (Ed.), *Archaeomalacology: Molluscs in former environments of human behaviour*. Oxford: Oxbow Books, pp. 18–28.

Quitmyer, I. R., Jones, D. S., and Arnold, W. S. 1997. The sclerochronology of hard clams, *Mercenaria* spp., from the south-eastern U.S.A.: A method of elucidating the zooarchaeological records of seasonal resource procurement and seasonality in prehistoric shell middens. *Journal of Archaeological Science* 24(9):825–40.

Quitmyer, I. R., and Reitz, E. J. 2006. Marine trophic levels targeted between AD 300 and 1500 on the Georgia coast, USA. *Journal of Archaeological Science* 33:806–22.

Raab, L. M., and Goodyear, A. C. 1984. Middle-range theory in archaeology: A critical review of origins and applications. *American Antiquity* 49(2):255–68.

Rabett, R. J. 2004. The ones that come ready made: The identification and use of *Sus* tusks as tools in prehistoric cave sites in Malaysia. *Archaeofauna* 13:131–43.

Rabinovich, J. E., Capurro, A. F., and Pessina, L. L. 1991. Vicuña use and the bioeconomics of an Andean peasant community in Catamarca, Argentina. In J. G. Robinson and K. H. Redford (Eds.), *Neotropical wildlife use and conservation.* Chicago: University of Chicago Press, pp. 337–58.

Rackham, D. J. 1994. *Animal bones.* Berkeley: University of California Press.

Randsborg, K. 1985. Subsistence and settlement in northern temperate Europe in the First Millennium A.D. In G. Barker and C. Gamble (Eds.), *Beyond domestication in prehistoric Europe: Investigations in subsistence archaeology and social complexity.* New York: Academic Press, pp. 233–65.

Rappaport, R. A. 1967. *Pigs for the ancestors: Ritual in the ecology of a New Guinea people.* New Haven: Yale University Press.

Rathje, W. L. 1979. Modern material culture studies. In M. B. Schiffer (Ed.), *Advances in archaeological method and theory* (Vol. 2). New York: Academic Press, pp. 1–37.

Rau, C. 1884. *Prehistoric fishing in Europe and North America.* Washington, DC: Smithsonian Institution Contributions to Knowledge 509.

Rea, A. M. 1986. Verification and reverification: Problems in archaeofaunal studies. *Journal of Ethnobiology* 6(1):9–18.

Redding, R. W. 1991. The role of pig in the subsistence system of ancient Egypt: A parable on the potential of faunal data. In P. J. Crabtree and K. Ryan (Eds.), *Animal use and culture change.* Philadelphia: University of Pennsylvania, Museum of Archaeology and Anthropology Research Papers in Science and Archaeology, MASCA 8, pp. 20–30.

Redding, R. W., Wheeler Pires-Ferreira, J., and Zeder, M. A. 1975. A proposed system for computer analysis of identifiable faunal material from archaeological sites. *Paleorient* 3:191–205.

Redding, R. W., Zeder, M. A., and McArdle, J. 1978. "Bonesort II" – A system for the computer processing of identifiable faunal material. In R. H. Meadow and M. A. Zeder (Eds.), *Approaches to faunal analysis in the Middle East.* Cambridge, MA: Harvard University, Peabody Museum of Archaeology and Ethnology Bulletin 2, pp. 135–47.

Redford, K. H., and Eisenberg, J. F. 1992. *Mammals of The neotropics: The southern cone* (Vol. 2). Chicago: University of Chicago Press.

Redford, K. H., and Robinson, J. G. 1991. Subsistence and commercial uses of wildlife in Latin America. In J. G. Robinson and K. H. Redford (Eds.), *Neotropical wildlife use and conservation.* Chicago: University of Chicago Press, pp. 6–23.

Redman, C. L. 1999. *Human impact on ancient environments.* Tucson: University of Arizona Press.

Reed, C. A. 1963. Osteoarchaeology. In D. Brothwell and E. S. Higgs (Eds.), *Science in archaeology* (1st ed.). New York: Basic Books, pp. 204–16.

———. 1977. A model for the origin of agriculture in the Near East. In C. A. Reed (Ed.), *The origins of agriculture.* The Hague: Mouton Publishers, pp. 543–67.

———. 1978. Foreword. In R. H. Meadow and M. A. Zeder (Eds.), *Approaches to faunal analysis in the Middle East.* Cambridge MA: Harvard University, Peabody Museum of Archaeology and Ethnology Bulletin 2, pp. ix–xi.

Reese, D. S. 1980. Industrial exploitation of murex shells: Purple-dye and lime production at Sidi Khrebish, Benghazi (Berenice). *Libyan Studies* 1979–1980(11):79–93.

Reidhead, V. A. 1979. Linear programming models in archaeology. *Annual Review of Anthropology* 8:543–78.

———. 1980. The economics of subsistence change: A test of an optimization model. In T. K. Earle and A. L. Christenson (Eds.), *Modeling change in prehistoric subsistence economies*. New York: Academic Press, pp. 141–86.

Reinhard, K. J. 2007. Pathoecology of two Ancestral Pueblo villages. In E. J. Reitz, C. M. Scarry, and S. J. Scudder (Eds.), *Case studies in environmental archaeology* (2nd ed.). London: Springer, pp. 185–203.

Reitz, E. J. 1987. Urban/rural contrasts in vertebrate fauna from the southern Atlantic coastal plain. *Historical Archaeology* 20(2):47–58.

———. 1992. The Spanish colonial experience and domestic animals. *Historical Archaeology* 26(1):84–91.

———. 1994a. The wells of Spanish Florida: Using taphonomy to identify site history. *Journal of Ethnobiology* 14(2):141–60.

———. 1994b. Zooarchaeological analysis of a free African community: Gracia Real de Santa Teresa de Mose. *Historical Archaeology* 28(1):23–40.

———. 2001. Fishing in Peru between 10000 and 3750 BP. *International Journal of Osteoarchaeology* 11:163–71.

———. 2004a. "Fishing down the food web": A case study from St. Augustine, Florida, USA, *American Antiquity* 69:63–83.

———. 2004b. The use of archaeofaunal data in fish management. In R. C. G. M. Lauwerier and I. Plug (Eds.), *The future from the past: Archaeozoology in wildlife conservation and heritage management*. Oxford: Oxbow Books, pp. 19–33.

Reitz, E. J., Andrus, C. F. T., and Sandweiss, D. H. 2008. Ancient fisheries and marine ecology of coastal Perú. In T. C. Rick and J. M. Erlandson (Eds.), *Human impacts on ancient marine ecosystems: Regional case studies and global perspectives*. Berkeley: University of California Press, in press.

Reitz, E. J., and Cordier, D. 1983. Use of allometry in zooarchaeological analysis. In J. Clutton-Brock and C. Grigson (Eds.), *Animals and archaeology: 2. Shell middens, fishes, and birds*. Oxford: British Archaeological Reports International Series 183, pp. 237–52.

Reitz, E. J., and Cumbaa, S. L. 1983. Diet and foodways of eighteenth century Spanish St. Augustine. In K. A. Deagan (Ed.), *Spanish St. Augustine: The historical archaeology of a colonial community*. New York: Academic Press, pp. 151–85.

Reitz, E. J., and McEwan, B. G. 1995. Animals, environment, and the Spanish diet at Puerto Real. In K. Deagan (Ed.), *Puerto Real: The archaeology of a sixteenth-century Spanish town in Hispaniola*. Gainesville: University Press of Florida, pp. 287–334.

Reitz, E. J., and Masucci, M. A. 2004. *Guangala Fishers and Farmers: A Case Study of Animal Use at El Azúcar, Southwestern Ecuador; Pescadores y Agricultores Guangala: Un Estudio de Caso de Uso Animal en El Azúcar, Suroeste de Ecuador*. Pittsburgh, PA: University of Pittsburgh Memoirs in Latin American Archaeology 14.

Reitz, E. J., and Quitmyer, I. R. 1988. Faunal remains from two coastal Georgia Swift Creek sites. *Southeastern Archaeology* 7(2):95–108.

Reitz, E. J., Quitmyer, I. R., Hale, H. S., Scudder, S. J., and Wing, E. S. 1987. Application of allometry to zooarchaeology. *American Antiquity* 52(2):304–17.

Reitz, E. J., and Ruff, B. 1994. Morphometric data for cattle from North America and the Caribbean prior to the 1850s. *Journal of Archaeological Science* 21(5):699–713.

Reitz, E. J., Ruff, B. L., and Zierden, M. A. 2006. Pigs in Charleston, South Carolina: Using specimen count to consider status. *Historical Archaeology* 40:104–24.

Reitz, E. J., and Scarry, C. M. 1985. *Reconstructing historic subsistence, with an example from sixteenth-century Spanish Florida*. Ann Arbor, MN: The Society for Historical Archaeology Special Publication 3.

Reitz, E. J., and Zierden, M. 1991. Cattle bones and status from Charleston, South Carolina. In J. R. Purdue, W. E. Klippel, and B. W. Styles (Eds.), *Beamers, bobwhites, and blue-points: Tributes to the career of Paul W. Parmalee*. Springfield: Illinois State Museum Scientific Papers 23, pp. 395–407.

Renberg, I., Persson, M. W., and Emteryd, O. 1994. Pre-industrial atmospheric lead contamination detected in Swedish lake sediments. *Nature* 68(6469):323–6.

Renfrew, C. 2000. Archaeogenetics: Towards a population prehistory of Europe. In C. Renfrew and K. Boyle (Eds.), *Archaeogenetics: DNA and the population of prehistory Europe*. Cambridge, UK: McDonald Institute for Archaeological Research, pp. 3–11.

Renfrew, C., and Bahn, P. 2004. *Archaeology: Theories, methods, and practice* (4th ed.). New York: Thames & Hudson.

Renkonen, O. 1938. Statistisch-okologische Untersuchungen uber die Terrestiche Kaferwelt der Finnischen Bruchmoore. *Annals of the Zoological Society, Botany of Finland Vanamo* 6:1–231.

Reynolds, T. E., Koopman, K. F., and Williams, E. E. 1953. A cave faunule from western Puerto Rico with a discussion of the genus *Isolobodon*. *Breviora* 12:1–8.

Rhoads, D. C., and Lutz, R. A. (Eds.). 1980. *Skeletal growth of aquatic organisms*. New York: Plenum Press.

Rhode, D. 2003. Coprolites from Hidden Cave, revisited: Evidence for site occupation history, diet and sex of occupants. *Journal of Archaeological Science* 30:909–22.

Richards, M. P., Pearson, J. A., Molleson, T. I., Russell, N., and Martin, L. 2003. Stable isotope evidence of diet at Neolithic Çatalhöyük, Turkey. *Journal of Archaeological Science* 30:67–76.

Rick, A. M. 1975. Bird medullary bone: A seasonal dating technique for faunal analysts. *Bulletin of the Canadian Archaeological Association* 7:183–90.

Rick, T. C., Erlandson, J. M., Glassow, M. A., and Moss, M. L. 2002. Evaluating the economic significance of sharks, skates, and rays (Elasmobranchs) in prehistoric economies. *Journal of Archaeological Science* 29:111–22.

Ricklefs, R. E. 1973. *Ecology*. Newton, MA: Chiron Press.

Ricklefs, R. E., and Schluter, D. (Eds.). 1993. *Species diversity in ecological communities: Historical and ecological perspectives*. Chicago: University of Chicago Press.

Rindos, D. 1984. *The origins of agriculture: An evolutionary perspective*. San Diego, CA: Academic Press.

Ringrose, T. J. 1993. Bone counts and statistics: A critique. *Journal of Archaeological Science* 20(2):121–57.

Roberts, N. 1998. *The Holocene: An environmental history*. Oxford: Blackwell Publishers.

Rofes, J. 2004. Prehistoric guinea pig sacrifices in southern Perú, the case of El Yaral. In S. J. O'Day, W. Van Neer, and A. Ervynck (Eds.), *Behaviour behind bones: The zooarchaeology of ritual, religion, status and identity.* Oxford: Oxbow Books, pp. 95–100.

Rolett, B. V., and Chiu, M. 1994. Age estimation of prehistoric pigs (*Sus scrofa*) by molar eruption and attrition. *Journal of Archaeological Science 21*(3):377–86.

Romer, A. S. 1955. *Vertebrate paleontology.* Chicago: University of Chicago Press.

———. 1956. *Osteology of the reptiles.* Chicago: University of Chicago Press.

Romer, A. S., and Parsons, T. S. 1977. *The vertebrate body* (5th ed.). Philadelphia: Saunders.

Roper, D. C. 1979. The method and theory of site catchment analysis: A review. In M. B. Schiffer (Ed.), *Advances in archaeological method and theory* (Vol. 2). New York: Academic Press, pp. 119–40.

Rose, J. J. 1983. A replication technique for scanning electron microscopy: Applications for anthropologists. *American Journal of Physical Anthropology 62*(3):255–61.

Roselló Izquierdo, E. 1986. *Contribución al atlas osteológico de los teleósteos Ibéricos 1. Dentario y articular.* Madrid: Ediciones de la Universidad Autónoma de Madrid Colección Estudios 14.

Roselló Izquierdo, E., and Morales Muñiz, A. 1994. The fishes. In E. Roselló and A. Morales (Eds.), *Castillo de Doña Blanca: Archaeo-environmental investigations in the Bay of Cádiz, Spain (750–500 B.C.).* Oxford: British Archaeological Reports International Series 593, pp. 91–142.

Roskams, S. 2001. *Excavations.* Cambridge, UK: Cambridge University Press.

Rostlund, E. 1952. *Freshwater fish and fishing in native North America.* Berkeley: University of California Publications in Geography 9.

Roth, W. E. 1970 [1924]. *An introductory study of the arts, crafts, and customs of the Guiana Indians.* New York: Johnson Reprint Company.

Rothschild, N. A. 1989. The effect of urbanization on faunal diversity: A comparison between New York City and St. Augustine, Florida, in the sixteenth to eighteenth centuries. In R. D. Leonard and G. T. Jones (Eds.), *Quantifying diversity in archaeology.* Cambridge, UK: Cambridge University Press, pp. 92–9.

Rouse, J. E. 1973. *World cattle* (Vol. 3). Norman: University of Oklahoma Press.

Rowley-Conwy, P. 2000. Milking caprines, hunting pigs: The Neolithic economy of Arene Candide in its West Mediterranean context. In P. Rowley-Conwy (Ed.), *Animal bones, human societies.* Oxford: Oxbow Books, pp. 124–32.

Royle, S. A. 2004. Human interference on Ascension Island. *Environmental Archaeology 9:*127–34.

Ruscillo, D. 2005. Reconstructing *Murex* royal purple and biblical blue in the Aegean. In D. E. Bar-Yosef Mayer (Ed.), *Archaeomalacology: Molluscs in former environments of human behaviour.* Oxford: Oxbow Books, pp. 99–106.

Ruscillo, D. (Ed.). 2006. *Recent advances in ageing and sexing animal bones.* Oxford: Oxbow Books.

Russo, M. 1991a. A method for the measurement of season and duration of oyster collection: Two case studies from the prehistoric south-east U.S. coast. *Journal of Archaeological Science 18*(2):205–21.

———. 1991b. Archaic sedentism on the Florida coast: A case study from Horr's Island. Ph.D. dissertation, University of Florida. Ann Arbor: University Microfilms.

Russo, M., and Quitmyer, I. R. 2007. Developing models of settlement for the Florida Gulf Coast. In E. J. Reitz, C. M. Scarry, and S. J. Scudder (Eds.), *Case studies in environmental archaeology.* (2nd ed.). London: Springer, pp. 229–48.

Ryan, K. 2005. Facilitating milk let-down in traditional cattle herding systems: East Africa and beyond. In J. Mulville and A. K. Outram (Eds.), *The archaeology of fats, oils, milk and dairying: An introduction and overview*. Oxford: Oxbow Books, pp. 96–106.

Ryan, K., and Crabtree, P. J. (Eds.). 1995. *The symbolic role of animals in archaeology*. Philadelphia: University of Pennsylvania, Museum of Archaeology and Anthropology Research Papers in Science and Archaeology, MASCA 12.

Saavedra, B., and Simonetti, J. A. 1998. Small mammal taphonomy: Intraspecific bone assemblage comparisons between South and North American barn owl, *Tyto alba*, populations. *Journal of Archaeological Science* 25:165–70.

Sadek-Kooros, H. 1975. Intentional fracturing of bone: Description of criteria. In A. T. Clason (Ed.), *Archaeozoological studies*. Amsterdam: North-Holland Publishing Company, pp. 139–50.

Sale, P. F. (Ed.). 1991. *The ecology of fishes on coral reefs*. San Diego, CA: Academic Press.

Salls, R. A. 1989. To catch a fish: Some limitations on prehistoric fishing in southern California with special reference to native plant fiber fishing line. *Journal of Ethnobiology* 9(2):173–206.

Sampson, C. G. 2000. Taphonomy of tortoises deposited by birds and Bushmen. *Journal of Archaeological Science* 27:779–88.

———. 2003. Amphibians from the Acheulean site at Duinefontein 2 (Western Cape, South Africa). *Journal of Archaeological Science* 30:547–57.

Sanderson, S. L., and Wassersug, R. 1993. Convergent and alternative designs for vertebrate suspension feeding. In J. Hanken and B. K. Hall (Eds.), *The skull: Functional and evolutionary mechanisms* (Vol. 3). Chicago: University of Chicago Press, pp. 37–112.

Sandford, M. K. (Ed.). 1993. *Investigations of ancient human tissue: Chemical analyses in anthropology*. Philadelphia: Gordon and Breach Science Publishers.

Sandweiss, D. H. 1996. Environmental change and its consequences for human society on the central Andean coast: A malacological perspective. In E. J. Reitz, L. A. Newsom, and S. J. Scudder (Eds.), *Case studies in environmental archaeology* (1st ed.). New York: Plenum Press, pp. 127–47.

Sandweiss, D. H., Maasch, K. A., Chai, F. Andrus, C. F. T., and Reitz, E. J. 2004. Geoarchaeological evidence for multidecadal natural climatic variability and ancient Peruvian fisheries. *Quaternary Research* 61:330–34.

Sandweiss, D. H., and Wing, E. S. 1997. Ritual rodents: The guinea pigs of Chincha, Peru. *Journal of Field Archaeology* 24(1):47–58.

Sathe, V. 2000. Enamel ultrastructure of cattle from the Quaternary Period in India. *Environmental Archaeology* 5:107–15.

Sauer, C. O. 1966. *The early Spanish Main*. Berkeley: University of California Press.

Saunders, J. W., Mandel, R. D., Sampson, C. G., Allen, C. M., Allen, E. T., Bush, D. A., Feathers, J. K., Gremillion, K. J., Hallmark, C. T., Jackson, H. E., Johnson, J. K., Jones, R., Saucier, R. T., Stringer, G. L., and Vidrine, M. F. 2005, Wilson Brake, a Middle Archaic mound complex in northeast Louisiana. *American Antiquity* 70(4):631–68.

Savanti, F., Bourlot, T., and Aragone, A. 2005. Zooarqueología y uso del espacio en Lago Cardiel, Provincia de Santa Cruz, Patagonia Argentina. *Archaeofauna* 14:111–27.

Savolainen, P., Zhang, Y., Luo, J., Lundeberg, J., and Leitner, T. 2002. Genetic evidence for an East Asian origin of domestic dogs. *Science* 298:1610–3.

Schallmayer, E. 1994. Die Verarbeitung von Knochen in Römischer Zeit. In M. Kokabi, B. Schlenker, and J. Wahl (Eds.), *"Knochenarbeit": Artefakte aus tierischen Rohstoffen im Wandel der Ziet.* Stuttgart: Landesdenkmalamt Baden-Württemberg Archäologische Informationen aus Baden-Württemberg 27, pp. 71–82.

Schelvis, J., Van Thuyne, T., and Waelkens, M. 2005. Late Holocene environmental changes indicated by fossil remains of mites (Arthropoda: Acari) in the Marsh of Gravgaz, southwest Turkey. *Archaeofauna* 14:215–25.

Scheuer, L., and Black, S. 2004. *The juvenile skeleton.* San Diego: Academic Press.

Schibler, J. 2004. Bones as a key for reconstructing the environment, nutrition and economy of the lake-dwelling societies. In F. Menotti (Ed.), *Living on the lake in prehistoric Europe: 150 years of lake-dwelling research.* London: Routledge, pp. 144–61.

Schibler, J., and Chaix, L. 1994. In memoriam Prof. Dr. Elisabeth Schmid. *ArchaeoZoologia* 7(1):77–8.

Schiffer, M. B. 1976. *Behavioral archaeology.* New York: Academic Press.

———. 1983. Toward the identification of formation processes. *American Antiquity* 48(4):675–706.

Schluter, D., and Ricklefs, R. E. 1993. Species diversity: An introduction to the problem. In R. E. Ricklefs and D. Schluter (Eds.), *Species diversity in ecological communities: Historical and geographical perspectives.* Chicago: University of Chicago Press, pp. 1–10.

Schmid, E. 1972. *Atlas of animal bones for prehistorians, archaeologists, and Quaternary geologists.* Amsterdam: Elsevier Science Publishers.

Schmidt, E. 2006. Remains of fly puparia as indicators of Neolithic cattle farming. *Environmental Archaeology* 11:143–4.

Schmidt-Nielsen, K. 1984. *Scaling: Why is animal size so important?* Cambridge, UK: Cambridge University Press.

Schmitt, D. N., Madsen, D. B., and Lupo, K. D. 2004. The worst of times, the best of times: Jackrabbit hunting by Middle Holocene human foragers in the Bonneville Basin of western North America. In M. Mondini, S. Muñoz, and S. Wickler (Eds.), *Colonisation, migration and marginal areas: A zooarchaeological approach.* Oxford: Oxbow Books, pp. 86–95.

Schnurrenberger, P. R., and Hubbert, W. T. (Eds.). 1981. *An outline of the zoonoses.* Ames: Iowa State University Press.

Schoeninger. M. J. 1995. Stable isotope studies in human evolution. *Evolutionary Anthropology* 4(3):83–98.

Schoeninger, M. J., and Moore, K. 1992. Bone stable isotope studies in archaeology. *Journal of World Prehistory* 6(2):247–96.

Schulting, R., and Richards, M. P. 2002. Dogs, ducks, deer and diet: New stable isotope evidence on early Mesolithic dogs from the Vale of Pickering, north-east England. *Journal of Archaeological Science* 29:327–33.

Schulting, R., Tresset, A., and Dupont, C. 2004. From harvesting the sea to stock rearing along the Atlantic façade of north-west Europe. *Environmental Archaeology* 9:143–54.

Schultz, L. P. 1958. *Review of the parrotfishes Family Scaridae.* Washington, DC: United States National Museum Bulletin 214.

Schulz, P. D., and Gust, S. M. 1983. Faunal remains and social status in 19th-century Sacramento. *Historical Archaeology* 17(1):44–53.

Schwartz, C. W., and Schwartz, E. R. 1959. *The wild mammals of Missouri.* Columbia: University of Missouri Press.

Scott, E. M. 2001. Food and social relations at Nina Plantation. *American Anthropologist* 10:671–91.

———. 2007. Who ate what? Archaeological food remains and cultural diversity. In E. J. Reitz, C. M. Scarry, and S. J. Scudder (Eds.), *Case studies in environmental archaeology.* (2nd ed.). London: Springer, pp. 349–66.

Scott, S. L., and Jackson, H. E. 1995. Mississippian homestead and village subsistence organization: Contrasts in large-mammal remains from two sites in the Tombigbee Valley. In J. D. Rogers and B. D. Smith (Eds.), *Mississippian communities and households.* Tuscaloosa: University of Alabama Press, pp. 181–200.

Scudder, S. J. 1993. *Human influence on pedogenesis: Midden soils on a southwest Florida Pleistocene dune island.* Masters thesis, Department of Soil and Water Science, University of Florida, Gainesville.

Scudder, S. J., Foss, J. E., and Collins, M. E. 1996. Soil science and archaeology. *Advances in Agronomy* 57:1–75.

Scudder, S. J., Harris, W. G., and Collins, M. E. 1993. Clay-size mineral composition of anthropogenic and native soils on a southwest Florida Pleistocene dune island. In J. E. Foss, M. E. Timpson, and M. W. Morris (Eds.), *Proceedings of the First International Conference on Pedo-Archaeology.* Knoxville: University of Tennessee Agricultural Experiment Station, pp. 161–74.

Scudder, S. J., and Quitmyer, I. R. 1998. Evaluation of evidence for pre-columbian human occupation at Great Cave, Cayman Brac, Cayman Islands. *Caribbean Journal of Science* 34(1–2):41–9.

Sealy, J. C., and van der Merwe, N. J. 1988. Social, spatial and chronological patterning in marine food use as determined by ^{13}C measurements of Holocene human skeletons from the southwestern Cape, South Africa. *World Archaeology* 20(1):87–102.

Sealy, J. C., van der Merwe, N. J., Sillen, A., Kruger, F. J., and Krueger, H. W. 1991. ^{87}Sr/^{86}Sr as a dietary indicator in modern and archaeological bone. *Journal of Archaeological Science* 18(3):399–416.

Seaman, W., Jr. (Ed.). 1985. *Florida aquatic habitat and fishery resources.* Gainesville, FL: Chapter of the American Fisheries Society.

Selvaggio, M. M., and Wilder, J. 2001. Identifying the involvement of multiple carnivore taxa with archaeological bone assemblages. *Journal of Archaeological Science* 28:465–70.

Serjeantson, D. 1988. Archaeological and ethnographic evidence for seabird exploitation in Scotland. *ArchaeoZoologia* 2(1/2):209–24.

———. 1990. The introduction of mammals to the Outer Hebrides and the role of boats in stock management. *Anthropozoologica* 13:7–18.

———. 2000. Good to eat *and* good to think with: Classifying animals from complex sites. In P. Rowley-Conwy (Ed.), *Animal bones, human societies.* Oxford: Oxbow Books, pp. 179–89.

Serjeantson, D., Waldron, T., and McCracken, S. 1986. Veal and calfskin in eighteenth century Kingston? *London Archaeologist* 5 (9):227–32.

Serpell, J. 1986. *In the company of animals.* Oxford: Basil Blackwell.

———. 1989. Pet-keeping and animal domestication: A reappraisal. In J. Clutton-Brock (Ed.), *The walking larder: Patterns of domestication, pastoralism, and predation.* London: Unwin Hyman, pp. 10–21.

Serrand, N., and Bonnissent, D. 2005. Pre-columbian preceramic shellfish consumption and shell tool production: Shell remains from Orient Bay, Saint-Martin, Northern Lesser Antilles. In D. E. Bar-Yosef Mayer (Ed.), *Archaeomalacology: Molluscs in former environments of human behaviour.* Oxford: Oxbow Books, pp. 29–39.

Serrand, N., Vigne, J.-D., and Guilaine, J. 2005. Early Preceramic Neolithic marine shells from Shillourokambos, Cyprus (late 9th–8th mill. cal BC): A mainly-ornamental set with similarities to mainland PPNB. In D. E. Bar-Yosef Mayer (Ed.), *Archaeomalacology: Molluscs in former environments of human behaviour.* Oxford: Oxbow Books, pp. 122–9.

Severinghaus, C. W. 1949. Tooth development and wear as criteria of age in white-tailed deer. *Journal of Wildlife Management* 13(2):195–216.

Shackleton, M. J. 1973. Oxygen isotope analysis as a means of determining season of occupation of prehistoric midden sites. *Archaeometry* 15:133–41.

Shackley, M. 1981. *Environmental archaeology.* London: Allen and Unwin.

Shafer, H. J. 1986. *Ancient Texas: Rock art and lifeways along the Lower Pecos.* Austin: Texas Monthly Press.

Shaffer, B. S., Nicholson, H. A., and Gardner, K. M. 1995. Possible Mimbres documentation of Pueblo snake ceremonies in the eleventh century. *North American Archaeologist* 16(1):17–32.

Shaffer, B. S., and Sanchez, J. L. J. 1994. Comparison of 1/8″ and 1/4″ mesh recovery of controlled samples of small-to-medium-sized mammals. *American Antiquity* 59(3):525–30.

Shanks, O. C., Bonnichsen, R., Vella, A. T., and Ream, W. 2001. Recovery of protein and DNA trapped in stone tool microcracks. *Journal of Archaeological Science* 28:965–72.

Shanks, O. C., Hodges, L., Tilley, L., Kornfeld, M., Larson, M. L., and Ream, W. 2005. DNA from ancient stone tools and bones excavated at Bugas-Holding, Wyoming. *Journal of Archaeological Science* 32:27–38.

Shannon, C. E., and Weaver, W. 1949. *The mathematical theory of communication.* Urbana: University of Illinois Press.

Shapiro, B., Drummond, A. J., Rambaut, A., Wilson, M. C., Matheus, P. E., Sher, A. V., Pybus, O. G., Gilbert, M. T. P., Barnes, I., Binladen, J., Willerslev, E., Hansen, A. J., Baryshnikov, G. F., Burns, J. A., Davydov, S., Driver, J. C., Froese, D. G., Harington, C. R., Keddie, G., Kosintsev, P., Kunz, M. L., Martin, L. D., Stephenson, R. O., Storer, J., Tedford, R., Zimov, S., and Cooper, A. 2004. Rise and fall of Beringian Steppe Bison. *Science* 306:1561–5.

Shawcross, W. 1967. An investigation of prehistoric diet and economy of a coastal site at Galatea Bay, New Zealand. *Proceedings of the Prehistoric Society* 33:107–31.

———. 1975. Some studies of the influences of prehistoric human predation on marine animal population dynamics. In R. W. Casteel and G. I. Quimby (Eds.), *Maritime adaptations of the Pacific.* The Hague: Mouton Publishers, pp. 39–66.

Sheldon, A. L. 1969. Equitability indices: Dependence on the species count. *Ecology* 50:466–7.

Shigehara, N. 1994. Morphological changes in Japanese ancient dogs. *ArchaeoZoologia* 6(2):79–94.

Shimada, M., and Shimada, I. 1985. Prehistoric llama breeding and herding on the north coast of Peru. *American Antiquity* 50(1):3–26.

Shipman, P. 1981. Applications of scanning electron microscopy to taphonomic problems. In A. M. E. Cantwell, J. B. Griffin, and N. A. Rothschild (Eds.), *The research potential of anthropological museum collections.* Annals of the New York Academy of Sciences 376, pp. 357–85.

Shipman, P., Bosler, W., and Davis, K. L. 1981. Butchering of giant geladas at an Acheulian site. *Current Anthropology* 22(3):257–68.

Shipman, P., Foster, G., and Schoeninger, M. 1984. Burnt bones and teeth: An experimental study of color, morphology, crystal structure and shrinkage. *Journal of Archaeological Science* 11(4):307–25.

Shipman, P., and Rose, J. J. 1983a. Early hominid hunting, butchering, and carcass-processing behaviors: Approaches to the fossil record. *Journal of Anthropological Archaeology* 2:57–98.

———. 1983b. Evidence of butchery and hominid activities at Torralba and Ambrona, an evaluation using microscopic techniques. *Journal of Archaeological Science* 10(5):465–74.

Shipman, P., and Walker, A. 1980. Bone-collecting by harvesting ants. *Paleobiology* 6(4):496–502.

Shotwell, J. A. 1955. An approach to the paleoecology of mammals. *Ecology* 36(2):327–37.

———. 1958. Inter-community relationships in Hemphillian (Mid-Pliocene) mammals. *Ecology* 39:271–82.

Sidell, E. J. 1993. *A methodology for the identification of archaeological eggshell.* Philadelphia: University of Pennsylvania, Museum of Archaeology and Anthropology Research Papers in Science and Archaeology, MASCA Special Supplement to Volume 10.

Sillen, A., and Sealy, J. C. 1995. Diagensis of strontium in fossil bones: A reconsideration of Nelson et al. (1986). *Journal of Archaeological Science* 22(2):313–20.

Sillen, A., Sealy, J. C., and van der Merwe, N. J. 1989. Chemistry and paleodietary research: No more easy answers. *American Antiquity* 54(3):504–12.

Silver, I. A. 1970. The ageing of domestic animals. In D. R. Brothwell and E. S. Higgs (Eds.), *Science in archaeology: A survey of progress and research* (2nd ed.). New York: Praeger Publishing, pp. 283–302.

Simkiss, K. 1967. *Calcium in reproductive physiology: A comparative study of vertebrates.* London: Chapman and Hall.

Simonetti, J. A., and Cornejo, L. E. 1991. Archaeological evidence of rodent consumption in central Chile. *Latin American Antiquity* 2(1):92–6.

Simpson, G. G. 1941. Large Pleistocene felines of North America. New York: *American Museum Novitates* 1136:1–27.

———. 1945. *The principles of classification and a classification of mammals.* New York: Bulletin of the American Museum of Natural History 85.

Simpson, G. G., Roe, A., and Lewontin, R. C. 1960. *Quantitative zoology.* New York: Harcourt, Brace, and Co.

Siracusano, G. 2006. Archaeozoo-ecological footprints: How sustainable was cattle raising and breeding? In M. Maltby, M. (Ed.), *Integrating zooarchaeology.* Oxford: Oxbow Books, pp. 41–50.

Smith, B. 1975a. *Middle Mississippi exploitation of animal populations.* Ann Arbor: University of Michigan Museum of Anthropology Anthropological Papers 57.

———. 1975b. Toward a more accurate estimation of meat yield of animal species at archaeological sites. In A. Clason (Ed.), *Archaeozoological studies.* Amsterdam: North-Holland Publishing Company, pp. 99–108.

———. 1976. "Twitching": A minor ailment affecting human paleoecological research. In C. E. Cleland (Ed.), *Cultural change and continuity: Essays in honor of James Bennett Griffin.* New York: Academic Press, pp. 275–92.

———. 1995. *The emergence of agriculture*. New York: Scientific American Library.

Smith, C. I., Craig, O. E., Prigodich, R. V., Nielsen-Marsh, C. M., Jans, M. M. E., Vermeer, C., and Collins, M. J. 2005. Diagenesis and survival of osteocalcin in archaeological bone. *Journal of Archaeological Science* 32:105–13.

Smith, D. N., and Howard, A. J. 2004. Identifying changing fluvial conditions in low gradient alluvial archaeological landscapes: Can coleoptera provide insights into changing discharge rates and floodplain evolution? *Journal of Archaeological Science* 31:109–20.

Smith, E. A., and Winterhalder, B. (Eds.) 1992. *Evolutionary ecology and human behavior*. New York: Aldine.

Smith, F. A., Betancourt, J. L., and Brown, J. H. 1995. Evolution of body size in the woodrat over the past 25,000 years of climate change. *Science* 270(5244):2012–4.

Smith, R. E. 1937. *A study of Structure A-I complex at Uaxactun, Peten, Guatemala*. Washington, DC: Carnegie Institution of Washington Publication 456(19).

Smith-Vaniz, W. F., Kaufman, L. S., and Glowacki, J. 1995. Species-specific patterns of hyperostosis in marine teleost fishes. *Marine Biology* 121(4):573–80.

Smuts, M. M. S., and Bezuidenhout, A. J. 1987. *Anatomy of the dromedary*. Oxford: Clarendon Press.

Sobolik, K. D. 1993. Direct evidence for the importance of small animals to prehistoric diets: A review of coprolite studies. *North American Archaeologist* 14(3):227–44.

———. 2007. Nutritional constraints and mobility patterns of hunter-gatherers in the northern Chihuahuan desert. In E. J. Reitz, C. M. Scarry, and S. J. Scudder (Eds.), *Case studies in environmental archaeology* (2nd ed.). London: Springer, pp. 205–27.

Sobolik, K. D., Gremillion, K. J., Whitten, P. L., and Watson, P. J. 1996. Technical note: Sex determination of prehistoric human paleofeces. *American Journal of Physical Anthropology* 101:283–90.

Sobolik, K. D., and Steele, D. G. 1996. *A turtle atlas to facilitate archaeological identifications*. Rapid City: Mammoth Site of Hot Springs, South Dakota, Inc.

Sokal, R. R., Oden, N. L., and Wilson, C. 1991. Genetic evidence for the spread of agriculture in Europe by demic diffusion. *Nature* 351(6322):143–5.

Sokal, R. R., and Rohlf, F. J. 1969. *Biometry: The principles and practice of statistics in biological research*. San Francisco: W. H. Freeman.

Sommer, J. G., and Anderson, S. 1974. Cleaning skeletons with dermestid beetles – Two refinements in method. *Curator* 17(4):290–8.

South, S. 1977. *Method and theory in historical archaeology*. New York: Academic Press.

Southwood, T. R. E. 1987. Species–time relationships in human parasites. *Evolutionary Ecology* 1:245–6.

Speth, J. D. 1983. *Bison kills and bone counts: Decision making by ancient hunters*. Chicago: University of Chicago Press.

Spier, R. F. G. 1970. *From the hand of man: Primitive and preindustrial technologies*. Boston: Houghton Mifflin.

Spiess, A. E., and Lewis, R. A. 1995. Features and activity areas: The spatial analysis of faunal remains. In B. J. Bourque (Ed.), *Diversity and complexity in prehistoric maritime societies: A Gulf of Maine perspective*. New York: Plenum Press, pp. 337–73.

Spinage, C. A. 1973. A review of the age determination of mammals by means of teeth, with especial reference to Africa. *East African Wildlife Journal* 11(2):165–87.

Stahl, P. W. 1995. Differential preservation histories affecting the mammalian zooarchaeological record from the forested neotropical lowlands. In P. W. Stahl (Ed.), *Archaeology in the lowland American tropics: Current analytical methods and recent applications.* Cambridge, UK: Cambridge University Press, pp. 154–80.

———. 1999. Structural density of domesticated South American camelid skeletal elements and the archaeological investigation of prehistoric Andean ch'arki. *Journal of Archaeological Science* 26:1347–68.

———. 2005. An exploratory osteological study of the muscovy duck (*Cairina moschata*) (Aves: Anatidae) with implications for neotropical archaeology. *Journal of Archaeological Science* 32:915–29.

Stahl, P. W., and Norton, P. 1987. Precolumbian animal domesticates from Salango, Ecuador. *American Antiquity* 52(2):382–91.

Stallibrass, S. 1982. The use of cement layers for absolute ageing of mammalian teeth. In B. Wilson, C. Grigson, and S. Payne (Eds.), *Ageing and sexing animal bones from archaeological sites.* Oxford: British Archaeological Reports British Series 109, pp. 109–26.

———. 2000. Dead dogs, dead horses: Site formation processes at Ribchester Roman fort. In P. Rowley-Conwy (Ed.), *Animal bones, human societies.* Oxford: Oxbow Books, pp. 158–65.

Stampfli, H. R., and Schibler, J. 1991. *Bibliography of archaeozoology.* Basel, Switzerland: Institut für prähistorische und naturwissenschaftliche Archäologie (IPNA).

Steadman, D. W. 1980. A review of the osteology and paleontology of turkeys (Aves: Meleagridinae). In K. E. Campbell, Jr. (Ed.), *Papers in avian paleontology honoring Hildegarde Howard.* Natural History Museum of Los Angeles Contributions in Science 330, pp. 131–207.

———. 1995. Prehistoric extinctions of Pacific Island birds: Biodiversity meets zooarchaeology. *Science* 267(5201):1123–31.

Steadman, D. W., and Jones, S. 2006. Long-term trends in prehistoric fishing and hunting on Tobago, West Indies. *Latin American Antiquity* 17:316–34.

Steadman, D. W., Plourde, A., and Burley, D. V. 2002. Prehistoric butchery and consumption of birds in the Kingdom of Tonga, South Pacific. *Journal of Archaeological Science* 29:571–84.

Steele, D. G., and Bramblett, C. A. 1988. *The anatomy and biology of the human skeleton.* College Station: Texas A&M University Press.

Steele, D. G., and Parama, W. D. 1981. Frequencies of dental anomalies and their potential effect on determining MNI counts. *Plains Anthropologist* 26(91):51–4.

Stein, G. J. 1987. Regional economic integration in early state societies: Third Millennium B.C. pastoral production at Gritille, southern Turkey. *Paléorient* 13(2):101–11.

Steinbock, R. T. 1976. *Paleopathological diagnosis and interpretation: Bone diseases in ancient human populations.* Springfield, IL: Charles C. Thomas.

Sternberg, M. 1992. Ostéologie du loup *Dicentrarchus labrax* (Linnaeus, 1758) = *Labrax lupus* (Cuvier, 1828). *Fiches d'ostéologie animale pour l'archéologie 7.* Juan-les-Pins, France: Centre de Recherches Archéologiques du CNRS, APDCA.

Stevenson, J. R. 1985. Dynamics of the integument. In D. E. Bliss and L. H. Mintel (Eds.), *The biology of crustacea* (Vol. 9). New York: Academic Press, pp. 1–42.

Steward, J. H. 1955. *Theory of culture change: The methodology of multilinear evolution.* Urbana: University of Illinois Press.

Stewart, F. L., and Stahl, P. W. 1977. Cautionary note on edible meat poundage figures. *American Antiquity* 42(2):267–70.

Stewart, H. 1977. *Indian fishing: Early methods on the Northwest coast.* Seattle: University of Washington Press.

Stewart, K. M. 1994. Early hominid utilisation of fish resources and implications for seasonality and behavior. *Journal of Human Evolution* 27:229–45.

Stiner, M. C. 1991. Food procurement and transport by human and non-human predators. *Journal of Archaeological Science* 18:455–82.

_____. 1994. *Honor among thieves: A zooarchaeological study of Neanderthal ecology.* Princeton, NJ: Princeton University Press.

_____. 2002. On *in situ* attrition and vertebrate body part profiles. *Journal of Archaeological Science* 29:979–91.

Stiner, M. C., Kuhn, S. L., Weiner, S., and Bar-Yosef, O. 1995. Differential burning, recrystallisation, and fragmentation of archaeological bone. *Journal of Archaeological Science* 22:223–7.

Stock, C. 1929. A census of the Pleistocene mammals of Rancho La Brea, based on the collections of the Los Angeles Museum. *Journal of Mammalogy* 10(4):281–9.

Stokes, P. 2000a. A cut above the rest? Officers and men at South Shields Roman fort. In P. Rowley-Conwy (Ed.), *Animal bones, human societies.* Oxford: Oxbow Books, pp. 145–51.

Stokes, P. R. G. 2000b. The butcher, the cook, and the archaeologist. In J. P. Huntley and S. Stallibrass (Eds.), *Taphonomy and interpretation.* Oxford: Oxbow Books, pp. 65–70.

Stone, R. 1995. Taking a new look at life through a functional lens. *Science* 269(5222):316–7.

Storå, J., and Lõugas, L. 2005. Human exploitation and history of seals in the Baltic during the late Holocene. In G. G. Monks (Ed.), *The exploitation and cultural importance of sea mammals.* Oxford: Oxbow Press, pp. 95–106.

Storey, A. A., Ramírez, J. M., Quiroz, D., Burley, D. V., Addison, D. J., Walter R., Anderson, A. J., Hunt, T. L., Athens, J. S., Huynen, L., and Matisoo-Smith, E. A. 2007. Radiocarbon and DNA evidence for a pre-Columbian introduction of Polynesian chickens to Chile. *Proceedings of the National Academy of Sciences* 104:10335–9.

Studer, J. 1994. Roman fish sauce in Petra, Jordan. In W. Van Neer (Ed.), *Fish exploitation in the past.* Tervuren, Belgium: Annales du Musée Royal de l'Afrique Centrale, Sciences Zoologiques 274, pp. 191–6.

Stutz, A. J. 2002. Polarizing microscopy identification of chemical diagenesis in archaeological cementum. *Journal of Archaeological Science* 29:1327–47.

Styles, B. W. 1981. *Faunal exploitation and resource selection: Early Late Woodland subsistence in the lower Illinois valley.* Evanston, IL: Northwestern University Archeological Program Scientific Papers 3.

Styles, B. W., and Klippel, W. E. 1996. Mid-Holocene faunal exploitation in the Southeastern United States. In K. E. Sassaman and D. G. Anderson (Eds.), *Archaeology of the Mid-Holocene Southeast.* Gainesville, FL: University Press of Florida, pp. 115–33.

Styles, B. W., and Purdue, J. R. 1991. Ritual and secular use of fauna by Middle Woodland peoples in western Illinois. In J. R. Purdue, W. E. Klippel, and B. W. Styles (Eds.), *Beamers, bobwhites, and blue-points: Tributes to the career of Paul W. Parmalee.* Springfield: Illinois State Museum Scientific Papers 23, pp. 421–36.

Subías, S. M. 2002. Cooking in zooarchaeology: Is this issue still raw? In P. Miracle and N. Milner (Eds.), *Consuming passions and patterns of consumption.* Cambridge, UK: McDonald Institute Monographs, pp. 7–15.

Sutcliffe, A. J. 1970. Spotted hyaena: Crusher, gnawer, digester and collector of bones. *Nature* 227(5263):1110–3.

———. 1973. Similarity of bones and antlers gnawed by deer to human artifacts. *Nature* 246(5433):428–30.

Sutherland, W. J. 1990. Evolution and fisheries. *Nature 344*(6269):814–15.

Sutton, M. Q. 1995. Archaeological aspects of insect use. *Journal of Archaeological Method and Theory* 2(3):253–98.

Swanton, J. R. 1979[1946]. *The Indians of the Southeastern United States*. Washington, DC: Smithsonian Institution Press, Bureau of American Ethnology Bulletin 137.

Sykes, B., and Renfrew, C. 2000. Concepts in molecular genetics. In C. Renfrew and K. Boyle (Eds.), *Archaeogenetics: DNA and the Population of Prehistory Europe*. Cambridge, UK: McDonald Institute for Archaeological Research, pp. 13–21.

Sykes, N. 2004. The introduction of fallow deer to Britain: A zooarchaeological perspective. *Environmental Archaeology 9*(1):75–83.

Symmons, R. 2004. Digital photodensitometry: A reliable and accessible method for measuring bone density. *Journal of Archaeological Science 31*:711–9.

———. 2005. Bone density variation between similar animals and density variation in early life: Implications for future taphonomic analysis. In T. O'Connor (Ed.), *Biosphere to lithosphere: New studies in vertebrate taphonomy*. Oxford: Oxbow Books, pp. 86–93.

Szuter, C. R. 1988. Small animal exploitation among desert horticulturalists in North America. *ArchaeoZoologia 2*(1/2):191–200.

———. 1991. A faunal analysis of home butchering and meat consumption at the Hubbel Trading Post, Ganado, Arizona. In P. J. Crabtree and K. Ryan (Eds.), *Animal use and culture change*. Philadelphia: University of Pennsylvania, Museum of Archaeology and Anthropology Research Papers in Science and Archaeology, MASCA 8, pp. 79–89.

———. 1994. Nutrition, small mammals, and agriculture. In K. D. Sobolik (Ed.), *Paleonutrition: The diet and health of prehistoric Americans*. Carbondale: Southern Illinois University at Carbondale, Center for Archaeological Investigations Occasional Paper 22, pp. 55–65.

Szuter, C. R., and Bayham, F. E. 1989. Sedentism and prehistoric animal procurement among desert horticulturalists of the North American Southwest. In S. Kent (Ed.), *Farmers as hunters: The implications of sedentism*. Cambridge, UK: Cambridge University Press, pp. 80–95.

Tanner, A. 1979. *Bringing home animals: Religious ideology and mode of production of the Mistassini Cree hunters*. New York: St. Martin's Press.

Tappen, N. C. 1969. The relationship of weathering cracks to split-line orientation in bone. *American Journal of Physical Anthropology 31*:191–8.

———. 1976. Advanced weathering cracks as an improvement on split-line preparations for analysis of structural orientation in compact bone. *American Journal of Physical Anthropology 44*:375–80.

Tappen, N. C., and Peske, G. R. 1970. Weathering cracks and split-line patterns in archaeological bone. *American Antiquity 35*(3):383–6.

Taylor, W. W. 1948. *A study of archeology*. Washington, DC: Memoirs of the American Anthropological Association 69.

———. 1972. Old wine and new skins: A contemporary parable. In M. P. Leone (Ed.), *Contemporary archaeology: A guide to theory and contributions*. Carbondale: Southern Illinois University Press, pp. 28–33.

Taylor, W. W. (Ed.). 1957. The identification of non-artifactual archaeological materials. Washington, DC: *National Academy of Science–National Resource Council Publication* 565:1–64.

Tchernov, E. 1992a. Evolution of complexities, exploitation of the biosphere and zooarchaeology.
ArchaeoZoologia 5(1):9–42.

———. 1992b. From sedentism to domestication – A preliminary review for the southern Levant.
In A. Clason, S. Payne, and H.-P. Uerpmann (Eds.), *Skeletons in her cupboard: Festschrift for
Juliet Clutton-Brock*. Oxford: Oxbow Books Monograph 34, pp. 189–233.

———. 1993. Exploitation of birds during the Natufian and Early Neolithic of the southern
Levant. *Archaeofauna* 2:121–43.

Tchernov, E., and Horwitz, L. K. 1991. Body size diminution under domestication: Unconscious
selection in primeval domesticates. *Journal of Anthropological Archaeology* 10:54–75.

Teegen, W.-R. 2005. Linear enamel hypoplasia in Medieval pigs from Germany. In J. Davies,
M. Fabiš, I. Mainland, M. Richards, and R. Thomas (Eds.), *Diet and health in past animal
populations: Current research and future directions*. Oxford: Oxbow Books, pp. 89–92.

Teeter, W. C., and Chase, A. F. 2004. Adding flesh to bones: Using zooarchaeology research to
answer the big-picture questions. *Archaeofauna* 13:155–72.

Teta, P., Andrade, A., and Pardiñas, U. F. J. 2005. Micromamíferos (Didelphimorphia y Rodentia)
y paleoambientes del Holoceno tardío en la Patagonia noroccidental extra-andina (Argentina).
Archaeofauna 14:183–97.

Théry-Parisot, I. 2002. Fuel management (bone and wood) during the Lower Aurignacian in the
Pataud Rock Shelter (Lower Palaeolithic, Les Eyzies de Tayac, Dordogne, France). Contribution
of experimentation. *Journal of Archaeological Science* 29:1415–21.

Théry-Parisot, I., Costamagno, S., Brugal, J. P., Fosse, P., and Guilbert, R. 2005. The use of bone as
fuel during the Palaeolithic, experimental study of bone combustible properties. In J. Mulville
and A. K. Outram (Eds.), *The archaeology of fats, oils, milk and dairying: An introduction and
overview*. Oxford: Oxbow Books, pp. 50–9.

Thomas, D. H. 1969. Great Basin hunting patterns: A quantitative method for treating faunal
remains. *American Antiquity* 34(4):392–401.

———. 1971. On distinguishing natural from cultural bone in archaeological sites. *American
Antiquity* 36(3):366–71.

———. 1986. Contemporary hunter-gatherer archaeology in America. In D. J. Meltzer, D. D.
Fowler, and J. A. Sabloff (Eds.), *American archaeology past and future: A celebration of
the Society for American Archaeology*. Washington, DC: Smithsonian Institution Press,
pp. 237–74.

Thomas, D. H., and Mayer, D. 1983. Behavioral faunal analysis of selected horizons. In D. H.
Thomas (Ed.), *The archaeology of Monitor Valley: 2. Gatecliff Shelter*. New York: American
Museum of Natural History Anthropological Papers 59, pp. 353–90.

Thomas, R., and Locock, M. 2000. Food for dogs? The consumption of horseflesh at Dudley
Castle in the Eighteenth Century. *Environmental Archaeology* 5:83–91.

Thomas, R., and Mainland, I. L. 2005. Introduction: Animal diet and health – Current perspectives
and future directions. In J. Davies, M. Fabiš, I. Mainland, M. Richards, and R. Thomas (Eds.),
Diet and health in past animal populations: Current research and future directions. Oxford:
Oxbow Books, pp. 1–7.

Thompson, I., Jones, D. S., and Dreibelbis, D. 1980. Annual internal growth banding and life
history of the ocean quahog *Artica islandica* (Mollusca: Bivalvia). *Marine Biology* 57:25–34.

Thomson, A. L. 1964. *A new dictionary of birds.* New York: McGraw-Hill.

Titcomb, M. 1969. *Dog and man in the ancient Pacific with special attention to Hawaii.* Honolulu, HI: Bernice P. Bishop Museum Special Publication 59.

Todd, L. C., and Rapson, D. J. 1988. Long bone fragmentation and interpretation of faunal assemblages: Approaches to comparative analysis. *Journal of Archaeological Science* 15(3):307–25.

Tomé, C., and Vigne, J.-D. 2003. Roe deer (*Capreolus capreolus*) age at death estimates: New methods and modern reference data for tooth eruption and wear, and for epiphyseal fusion. *Archaeofauna* 12:157–73.

Toussaint-Samat, M. 1992. *History of food.* Translated by A. Bell. Cambridge, MA: Blackwell Research.

Travis, D. F. 1960. Matrix and mineral deposition in skeletal structures of the Decapod Crustacea (Phylum Arthropoda). In R. F. Sognnaes (Ed.), *Classification in biological systems.* Washington, DC: American Association for the Advancement of Science, pp. 57–116.

Trippel, E. A. 1995. Age at maturity as a stress indicator in fisheries. *BioScience* 45(11):759–71.

Trotter, M. M., and McCulloch, B. 1989. Moas, men, and middens. In P. S. Martin and R. G. Klein (Eds.), *Quaternary extinctions: A prehistoric revolution.* Tucson: University of Arizona Press, pp. 708–27.

Troy, C., MacHugh, D. E., Bailey, J. F., Magee, D. A., Loftus, R. T., Cunningham, P., Chamberlain, A. T., Sykes, B. C., and Bradley, D. G. 2001. Genetic evidence for Near-Eastern origins of European cattle. *Nature* 410:1088–91.

Trueman, C. N. G., Behrensmeyer, A. K., Tuross, N., and Weiner, S. 2004. Mineralogical and compositional changes in bone exposed on soil surfaces in Amboseli National Park, Kenya: Diagenetic mechanisms and the role of sediment pore fluids. *Journal of Archaeological Science* 31:721–39.

Turgeon, D. D., Quinn, J. F., Bogan, A. E., Coan, E. V. Hochberg, F. G., Lyons, W. G., Mikkelsen, P. M., Neves, R. J., Roper, C. F. E., Rosenberg, G., Roth, B., Schetema, A., Thompson, F. G., Vecchione, M., Williams, J. D. 1998. *Common and scientific names of aquatic invertebrates from the United States and Canada: Mollusks* (2nd ed.). Bethesda, MD: American Fisheries Society Special Publication 26.

Turner, J. C. 1977. Cemental annulations as an age criterion in North American sheep. *Journal of Wildlife Management* 41(2):211–17.

Tveskov, M. A., and Erlandson, J. M. 2003. The Haynes Inlet weirs: Estuarine fishing and archaeological site visibility on the southern Cascadia coast. *Journal of Archaeological Science* 30:1023–35.

Tyzzer, E. E. 1943. Animal tooth implements from shell heaps of Maine. *American Antiquity* 8(4):354–62.

Ubelaker, D. H. 2000. Methodological considerations in the forensic applications of human skeletal biology. In M. A. Katzenberg and S. Saunders (Eds.), *Biological anthropology of the human skeleton.* New York: Wiley-Liss, pp. 41–102.

Uchiyama, J., 2006. The environmental troublemaker's burden? Jomon perspectives on foraging land use change. In C. Grier, J. Kim, and J. Uchiyama (Eds.), *Beyond affluent foragers: Rethinking hunter-gatherer complexity.* Oxford: Oxbow Books, pp. 136–67.

Uerpmann, H.-P. 1973. Animal bone finds and economic archaeology: A critical study of "osteoarchaeological" method. *World Archaeology* 4(3):307–22.

_____. 1978. The "Knocod" system for processing data on animal bones from archaeological sites. In R. H. Meadow and M. A. Zeder (Eds.), *Approaches to faunal analysis in the Middle East.* Cambridge, MA: Harvard University, Peabody Museum of Archaeology and Ethnology Bulletin 2, pp. 149–67.

Uerpmann, M. 1993. Animal remains from Qala'at Al-Bahrain, a preliminary report. In H. Buitenhuis and A. T. Clason (Eds.), *Archaeozoology of the Near East.* Leiden, The Netherlands: Universal Book Services, pp. 60–6.

Ugan, A., and Bright, J. 2001. Measuring foraging effiency with archaeological faunas: The relationship between relative abundance indices and foraging returns. *Journal of Archaeological Science 28*:1309–21.

Van de Noort, R., and Fletcher, W. 2000. Bronze Age human ecodynamics in the Humber Estuary. In G. Bailey, R. Charles, and N. Winder (Eds.), *Human ecodynamics.* Oxford: Oxbow Books, pp. 47–54.

van der Merwe, N. J., Lee-Thorp, J. A., and Raymond, J. S. 1993. Light, stable isotopes and the subsistence base of Formative cultures at Valdivia, Ecuador. In J. B. Lambert and G. Grupe (Eds.), *Prehistoric human bone: Archaeology at the molecular level.* Berlin: Springer Verlag, pp. 61–97.

van Gennep, A. 1960. *The rites of passage.* Chicago: University of Chicago Press.

Vanhaeren, M., d'Errioc, F., Billy, I., and Grousset, F. 2004. Tracing the source of Upper Paleolithic shell beads by strontium isotope dating. *Journal of Archaeological Science 31*:1481–88.

Van Neer, W., and Ervynck, A. 1994. New data on fish remains from Belgian archaeological sites. In W. Van Neer (Ed.), *Fish exploitation in the past.* Tervuren, Belgium: Annales du Musée Royal de l'Afrique Centrale, Sciences Zoologiques 274, pp. 217–29.

_____. 2004. Remains of traded fish in archaeological sites: Indicators of status, or bulk food? In S. J. O'Day, W. Van Neer, and A. Ervynck (Eds.), *Behaviour behind bones: The zooarchaeology of ritual, religion, status and identity.* Oxford: Oxbow Books, pp. 203–14.

Van Neer, W., and Gautier, A. 1993. Preliminary report on the faunal remains from the coastal site of ed-Dur, 1 st–4th century A.D. Umm al-Quwain, United Arab Emirates. In H. Buitenhuis and A. T. Clason (Eds.), *Archaeozoology of the Near East.* Leiden, The Netherlands: Universal Book Services, pp. 110–8.

Van Neer, W., and Lentacker, A. 1994. New archaeozoological evidence for the consumption of locally-produced fish sauce in the Northern Provinces of the Roman Empire. *Archaeofauna 3*:53–62.

Van Neer, W., Wouters, W., Ervynck, A., and Maes, J. 2005. New evidence from a Roman context in Belgium for fish sauce locally produced in northern Gaul. *Archaeofauna 14*:171–82.

Van Valkenburgh, B. 1994. Ecomorphological analysis of fossil vertebrates and their paleocommunities. In P. C. Wainwright and S. M. Reilly (Eds.), *Ecological morphology: Integrative organismal biology.* Chicago: University of Chicago Press, pp. 140–66.

Vartanyan, S. L., Garutt, V. E., and Sher, A. V. 1993. Holocene dwarf mammoths from Wrangel Island in the Siberian Arctic. *Nature 362*(6418):337–40.

Vaught, K. C. 1989. *A classification of the living Mollusca.* Melbourne, FL: American Malacologists, Inc.

Vayda, A. P., and Rappaport, R. A. 1968. Ecology, cultural and noncultural. In J. A. Clifton (Ed.), *Introduction to cultural anthropology: Essays in the scope and methods of the science of man.* Boston: Houghton-Mifflin, pp. 477–97.

Vehik, S. C. 1977. Bone fragments and bone grease manufacturing: A review of their archaeological use and potential. *Plains Anthropologist* 22(75):169–82.

Vermeij, G. J. 1977. Patterns in crab claw size: The geography of crushing. *Systematic Zoology* 26(2):138–51.

———. 1987. *Evolution and escalation: An ecological history of life.* Princeton: Princeton University Press.

———. 1993. *A natural history of shells.* Princeton: Princeton University Press.

Vigne, J.-D. 1992. Zooarchaeology and the biogeographical history of the mammals of Corsica and Sardinia since the last Ice Age. *Mammal Review* 22(2):87–96.

Vigne, J.-D., Peters, J., and Helmer, D. 2005. New archaeozoological approaches to trace the first steps of animal domestication: General presentation, reflections and proposals. In J.-D. Vigne, J. Peters, and D. Helmer (Eds.), *First steps of animal domestication: New archaeozoological approaches.* Oxford: Oxbow Books, pp. 1–16.

Vilà, C., Leonard, J. A., Götherström, A., Marklund, S., Sandberg, K., Lidén, K., Wayne, R. K., and Ellegren, H. 2001. Widespread origins of domestic horse lineages. *Science* 291:474–7.

Vilà, C., Savolainen, P., Maldonado, J. E., Amorim, I. R., Rice, J. E., Honeycutt, R. L., Crandall, K. A., Lundeberg, J., and Wayne, R. K. 1997. Multiple and ancient origins of the domestic dog. *Science* 276(5319):1687–9.

Vita-Finzi, C., and Higgs, E. S. 1970. Prehistoric economy in the Mount Carmel area of Palestine: Site catchment analysis. *Proceedings of the Prehistoric Society* 36:1–37.

Voigt, E. A. 1975. Studies of marine mollusca from archaeological sites: Dietary preferences, environmental reconstructions and ethnographic parallels. In A. T. Clason (Ed.), *Archaeozoological studies.* Amsterdam: North-Holland Publishing Company, pp. 87–98.

———. 1987. The dispersion of domestic stock into Southern Africa. *ArchaeoZoologia* 1(1):149–59.

Voorhies, M. R. 1969. *Taphonomy and population dynamics of an early Pliocene vertebrate fauna, Knox County, Nebraska.* Laramie: University of Wyoming Contributions to Geology Special Paper 1.

Wagner, G. E. 2007. What seasonal diet at a For Ancient community reveals about coping mechanisms. In E. J. Reitz, C. M. Scarry, and S. J. Scudder (Eds.), *Case studies in environmental archaeology* (2nd ed.). London: Springer, pp. 271–90.

Walker, K. J. 1992a. Bone artifacts from Josslyn Island, Buck Key Shell Midden, and Cash Mound: A preliminary assessment for the Caloosahatchee Area. In W. H. Marquardt (Ed.), *Culture and environment in the domain of the Calusa.* Gainesville, FL: Institute of Archaeology and Paleoenvironmental Studies Monograph 1, pp. 229–46.

———. 1992b. The zooarchaeology of Charlotte Harbor's prehistoric maritime adaptation: Spatial and temporal perspectives. In W. H. Marquardt (Ed.), *Culture and environment in the domain of the Calusa.* Gainesville, FL: Institute of Archaeology and Paleoenvironmental Studies Monograph 1, pp. 265–366.

Walker, K. J., Stapor, F. W., Jr., and Marquardt, W. H. 1995. Archaeological evidence for a 1750–1450 BP higher-than-present sea level along Florida's Gulf Coast. *Holocene cycles: Climate, sea levels, and sedimentation. Journal of Coastal Research Special Issue* 17:205–18.

Walker, P. L. 2000. Bioarchaeological ethics: A historical perspective on the value of human remains. In M. A. Katzenberg and S. Saunders (Eds.), *Biological anthropology of the human skeleton.* New York: Wiley-Liss, pp. 3–39.

Walker, P. L., and Long, J. C. 1977. An experimental study of the morphological characteristics of tool marks. *American Antiquity* 42(4):605–16.

Walker, R. 1985. *A guide to post-cranial bones of East African animals: Mrs. Walker's bone book.* Norwich, England: Hylochoerus Press.

Walker, W. F., Jr. 1987. *Functional anatomy of the vertebrates: An evolutionary perspective.* Philadelphia: Saunders.

Walsh, R. 1996. Barnacles in butter sauce. *Natural History* 105(11):80–3.

Walters, I. 1984. Gone to the dogs: A study of bone attrition at a central Australian campsite. *Mankind* 14(5):389–400.

———. 1985. Bone loss: One explicit quantitative guess. *Current Anthropology* 26(5):642–3.

Wapnish, P., and Hesse, B. 1991. Faunal remains from Tel Dan: Perspectives on animal production at a village, urban and ritual center. *ArchaeoZoologia* 4(2):9–86.

Ware, D. M., and Thomson, R. E. 2005. Bottom-up ecosystem trophic dynamics determine fish production in the Northeast Pacific. *Science* 308:1280–4.

Warner, W. L., and Lunt, P. S. 1941. *The social life of a modern community.* New Haven: Yale University Press.

Watson, J. P. N. 1972. Fragmentation analysis of animal bone samples from archaeological sites. *Archaeometry* 14(2):221–8.

———. 1978. The interpretation of epiphyseal fusion data. In D. R. Brothwell, K. D. Thomas, and J. Clutton-Brock (Eds.), *Research problems in zooarchaeology.* London: University of London, Institute of Archaeology Occasional Publication 3, pp. 97–101.

———. 1979. The estimation of the relative frequencies of mammalian species: Khirokitia 1972. *Journal of Archaeological Science* 6(2):127–37.

Wayne, R. K., Leonard, J. A., and Vilà, C. 2006. Genetic analysis of dog domestication. In M. A. Zeder, D. G. Bradley, E. Emshwiller, and B. D. Smith (Eds.), *Documenting domestication: New genetics and archaeological paradigms.* Berkeley: University of California Press, pp. 279–93.

Webb, C. H. 1959. *The Belcher Mound: A stratified Caddoan site in Caddo Parish, Louisiana.* Washington, DC: Memoirs of the Society for American Archaeology 16.

Webb, W. S. 1928. A prehistoric village site in Greenup County, Kentucky. *American Anthropologist* 30(2):268–81.

Weigelt, J. 1989[1927]. *Recent vertebrate carcasses and their paleobiological implications,* translated by Judith Schaefer. Chicago: University of Chicago Press.

Weinstock, J. 2000. Osteometry as a source of refined demographic information: Sex-ratios of reindeer, hunting strategies, and herd control in the Late Glacial site of Stellmoor, Northern Germany. *Journal of Archaeological Science* 27:1187–95.

———. 2002. Reindeer hunting in the Upper Palaeolithic: Sex ratios as a reflection of different procurement strategies. *Journal of Archaeological Science* 29:365–77.

Weir, G. H., Benfer, R. A., and Jones, J. G. 1988. Preceramic to Early Formative subsistence on the central coast. In E. S. Wing and J. C. Wheeler (Eds.), *Economic prehistory of the Central Andes.* Oxford: British Archaeological Reports International Series 427, pp. 56–97.

Weir, J. T., and Schluter, D. 2007. The latitudinal gradient in recent speciation and extinction rates of mammals and birds. *Science* 315:1574–6.

Weissbrod, L., and Bar-Oz, G. 2004. Caprines and toads: Taphonomic patterning of animal offering practices in a Late Bronze Age burial assemblage. In S. J. O'Day, W. Van Neer, and

A. Ervynck (Eds.), *Behaviour behind bones: The zooarchaeology of ritual, religion, status and identity.* Oxford: Oxbow Books, pp. 20–4.

Weissbrod, L., Dayan, T., Kaufman, D., and Weinstein-Evron, M. 2005. Micromammal taphonomy of el-Wad Terrace, Mount Carmel, Israel: distinguishing cultural from natural depositional agents in the Late Natufian. *Journal of Archaeological Science* 32:1–17.

Welch, P. D., and Scarry, C. M. 1995. Status-related variation in foodways in the Moundville chiefdom. *American Antiquity* 60(3):397–419.

Wendrich, W. Z., and Van Neer, W. 1994. Preliminary notes on fishing gear and fish at the late Roman fort at 'Abu Sha'ar (Egyptian Red Sea coast). In W. Van Neer (Ed.), *Fish exploitation in the past.* Tervuren, Belgium: Annales du Musée Royal de l'Afrique Centrale, Sciences Zoologiques 274, pp. 183–9.

West, B. 1982. Spur development: Recognizing caponized fowl in archaeological material. In B. Wilson, C. Grigson, and S. Payne (Eds.), *Ageing and sexing animal bones from archaeological sites.* Oxford: British Archaeological Reports British Series 109, pp. 255–60.

West, B., and Zhou, B.-X. 1988. Did chickens go north? New evidence for domestication. *Journal of Archaeological Science* 15(5):515–33.

Wheat, J. B. 1972. The Olsen-Chubbuck site: A PaleoIndian bison kill. *American Antiquity Memoirs* 26, 37(1):1–180.

Wheeler, A., and Jones, K. G. 1989. *Fishes.* Cambridge, UK: Cambridge University Press.

Wheeler, J. C. 1984. On the origin and early development of camelid pastoralism in the Andes. In J. Clutton-Brock and C. Grigson (Eds.), *Animals and archaeology: 3. Early herders and their flocks.* Oxford: British Archaeological Reports International Series 202, pp. 395–410.

———. 1985. De la chasse à l'élevage. In Lavallée, D. (Ed.), *Telarmachay: chasseurs et pasteurs préhistoriques des Andes-I.* Paris: Institut Français d'études Andines Editions Recherche sur les Civilisations, pp. 63–79.

Wheeler, J. C., and Reitz, E. J. 1987. Allometric prediction of live weight in the alpaca (*Lama pacos* L.). *ArchaeoZoologia* 1(1):31–46.

Wheeler, J. C., Russel, A. J. F., and Redden, H. 1995. Llamas and alpacas: Pre-conquest breeds and post-conquest hybrids. *Journal of Archaeological Science* 22(6):833–40.

White, C. D. 1993. Isotopic determination of seasonality in diet and death from Nubian mummy hair. *Journal of Archaeological Science* 20(6):657–66.

———. 2004. Stable isotopes and the human-animal interface in Maya biosocial and environmental systems. *Archaeofauna* 13:183–98.

White, C. D., Pohl, M., Schwarcz, H. P., and Longstaffe, F. J. 2001. Isotopic evidence for Maya patterns of deer and dog use at Preclassic Colha. *Journal of Archaeological Science* 28:89–107.

White, T. D., and Folkens, P. A. 1991. *Human osteology.* San Diego, California: Academic Press.

———. 2005. *The human bone manual.* Amsterdam: Elsevier Academic Press.

White, T. E. 1952. Observations on the butchering techniques of some aboriginal peoples: 1. *American Antiquity* 17(4):337–8.

———. 1953a. A method of calculating the dietary percentage of various food animals utilized by aboriginal peoples. *American Antiquity* 18(4):396–8.

———. 1953b. Observations on the butchering techniques of some aboriginal peoples no. 2. *American Antiquity* 19(2):160–4.

————. 1954. Observations on the butchering techniques of some aboriginal peoples, nos. 3, 4, 5, and 6. *American Antiquity* 19(3):254–64.

————. 1955. Observations on the butchering techniques of some aboriginal peoples, nos 7, 8, and 9. *American Antiquity* 21(2):170–8.

————. 1956. The study of osteological materials in the Plains. *American Antiquity* 21(4):401–4.

Whitehouse, N. J., and Smith, D. N. 2004. "Islands" in Holocene forests: Implications for forest openness, landscape clearance and "culture-steppe" species. *Environmental Archaeology* 9:199–208.

Whitney, E. N., and Rolfes, S. R. 2008. *Understanding nutrition* (11th ed.). Belmont, CA: Wadsworth.

Whittaker, R. H. 1975. *Communities and ecosystems* (2nd ed.). New York: Macmillan.

Wickler, S. 2004. Modelling colonisation and migration in Micronesia from a zooarchaeological perspective. In M. Mondini, S. Muñoz, and S. Wickler (Eds.), *Colonisation, migration and marginal areas: A zooarchaeological approach.* Oxford: Oxbow Books, pp. 28–40.

Wijngaarden-Bakker, L. H. van 1984. Faunal analysis and historical record: Meat preservation and the faunal remains at Smeerenburg, Spitsbergen. In C. Grigson and J. Clutton-Brock (Eds.), *Animals and archaeology: 4. Husbandry in Europe.* Oxford: British Archaeological Reports International Series 227, pp. 195–204.

————. 2000. Experimental taphonomy. In J. P. Huntley and S. Stallibrass (Eds.), *Taphonomy and interpretation.* Oxford: Oxbow Books, pp. 85–9.

Wijngaarden-Bakker, L. H. van, and Bergström, P. L. 1988. Estimation of the shoulder height of cattle. *ArchaeoZoologia* 2(1/2):67–82.

Wijngaarden-Bakker, L. H. van, and Pals, J. P. 1981. Life and work in Smeerenburg: The bioarchaeological aspects. In A. G. F. van Holk, H. K. s'Jacob, and A. A. H. T. Temmingh (Eds.), *Early European exploitation of the northern Atlantic 800–1700.* Groningen, The Netherlands: Arctic Centre, University of Groningen, pp. 133–51.

Wilkinson, K., and Stevens, C. 2003. *Environmental archaeology: Approaches, techniques, and applications.* Stroud: Tempus.

Willey, G. R., and Sabloff, J. A. 1974. *A history of American archaeology.* London: Thames and Hudson.

Williams, A. B., Abele, L. G., Felder, D. L., Hobbs, H. H., Jr., Manning, R. B., McLaughlin, P. A., and Pérez Farfante, I. 1989. *Common and scientific names of aquatic invertebrates from the United States and Canada: Decapod crustaceans.* Bethesda: American Fisheries Society Special Publications 17.

Wilson, B. 1989. Fresh and old table refuse. The recognition and location of domestic activity at archaeological sites in the Upper Thames Valley, England. *ArchaeoZoologia* 3(1/2):237–60.

————. 1994. Mortality patterns, animal husbandry and marketing in and around medieval and postmedieval Oxford. In A. R. Hall and H. K. Kenward (Eds.), *Urban–rural connexions: Perspectives from environmental archaeology.* Oxford: Oxbow Books Monograph 47, pp. 103–15.

Wilson, B., Grigson, C., and Payne, S. (Eds.). 1982. *Ageing and sexing animal bones from archaeological sites.* Oxford: British Archaeological Reports British Series 109.

Wilson, D. E., and Reeder, D. A. M. (Ed.) 2005. *Mammal species of the world: a taxonomic and geographic reference* (2nd ed.). Baltimore, MD: Johns Hopkins University Press.

Wilson, E. O., and Bossert, W. H. 1971. *A primer of population biology.* Sunderland, MA: Sinauer Associates.

Wilson, J. P. N. 1978. The interpretation of epiphyseal fusion data. In D. R. Brothwell, K. D. Thomas, and J. Clutton-Brock (Eds.), *Research problems in zooarchaeology.* London: University of London, Institute of Archaeology Occasional Publication 3, pp. 97–101.

Wing, E. S. 1972. Utilization of animal resources in the Peruvian Andes. In S. Izumi and K. Terada (Eds.), *Andes 4: Excavations at Kotosh, Peru. 1963 and 1966.* Tokyo: University of Tokyo Press, pp. 327–51.

_____. 1978. Use of dogs for food: An adaptation to the coastal environment. In B. L. Stark and B. Voorhies (Eds.), *Prehistoric coastal adaptations: The economy and ecology of maritime Middle America.* New York: Academic Press, pp. 29–41.

_____. 1980. Human–Animal relationships. In M. D. Coe and R. A. Diehl (Eds.), *In the land of the Olmec* (Vol. 2). Austin: University of Texas Press, pp. 97–123.

_____. 1986. Domestication of Andean mammals. In F. Vuilleumier and M. Monasterio (Eds.), *High altitude tropical biogeography.* Oxford: Oxford University Press, pp. 246–64.

_____. 1988. *Dusicyon sechurae,* en contextos arqueológicos tempranos. In K. E. Stothert (Ed.), *La prehistoria temprana de la Península de Santa Elena, Ecuador: Cultura Las Vegas.* Guayaquil: Museos del Banco Central del Ecuador Miscelánea Antropológica Ecuatoriana Serie Monográfica 10, 179–85.

_____. 1989. Human exploitation of animal resources in the Caribbean. In C. A. Woods (Ed.), *Biogeography of the West Indies: Past, present, and future.* Gainesville, FL: Sandhill Crane Press, pp. 137–52.

_____. 1991. Dog remains from the Sorcé site on Vieques Island, Puerto Rico. In J. R. Purdue, W. E. Klippel, and B. W. Styles (Eds.), *Beamers, bobwhites, and blue-points: Tributes to the career of Paul W. Parmalee.* Springfield: Illinois State Museum Scientific Papers 23, pp. 379–86.

_____. 2001. The sustainability of resource use by Native Americans on four Caribbean islands, *International Journal of Osteoarchaeology* 11:112–26.

_____. 2007. Pets and camp followers in the West Indies. In E. J. Reitz, C. M. Scarry, and S. J. Scudder (Eds.), *Case studies in environmental archaeology* (2nd ed.). London: Springer, pp. 397–416.

Wing, E. S., and Brown, A. 1979. *Paleonutrition: Method and theory in prehistoric foodways.* New York: Academic Press.

Wing, E. S., and Quitmyer, I. R. 1992. A modern midden experiment. In W. H. Marquardt (Ed.), *Culture and environment in the domain of the Calusa.* Gainesville, FL: Institute of Archaeology and Paleoenvironmental Studies Monograph Number 1, pp. 367–73.

Wing, S. R., and Wing, E. S. 2001. Prehistoric fisheries in the Caribbean. *Coral Reefs* 20:1–8.

Winn, H. E., and Bardach, J. E. 1957. Behavior, sexual dichromatism, and species of parrot fishes. *Science 125* (3253):885–6.

Wintemberg, W. J. 1919. Archaeology as an aid to zoology. *Canadian Field Naturalist 33* (4):63–72.

Winterhalder, B. P. 1981. Optimal foraging strategies and hunter-gatherer research in anthropology: Theory and models. In B. P. Winterhalder and E. A. Smith (Eds.), *Hunter-gatherer foraging strategies: Ethnographic and archeological analyses.* Chicago: University of Chicago Press, pp. 13–35.

———. 1987. The analysis of hunter-gatherer diets: Stalking an optimal foraging model. In M. Harris and E. B. Ross (Eds.), *Food and evolution: Toward a theory of human food habits.* Philadelphia: Temple University Press, pp. 311–39.

———. 1994. Concepts in historical ecology: The view from evolutionary theory. In C. L. Crumley (Ed.), *Historical ecology: Cultural knowledge and changing landscapes.* Santa Fe, NM: School of American Research Press, pp. 17–41.

Winterhalder, B. P., Baillargeon, W., Cappelletto, F., Daniel, I. R., Jr., and Prescott, C. 1988. The population ecology of hunter-gatherers and their prey. *Journal of Anthropological Archaeology* 7(4):289–328.

Winterhalder, B. P., and Smith, E. A. 1992. Evolutionary ecology and the social sciences. In E. A. Smith and B. P. Winterhalder (Eds.), *Evolutionary ecology and human behavior.* New York: Aldine, pp. 3–23.

Wolff, R. G. 1973. Hydrodynamic sorting and ecology of a Pleistocene mammalian assemblage from California (U.S.A.). *Palaeogeography, Palaeoclimatology, Palaeoecology* 13:91–101.

———. 1991. *Functional chordate anatomy.* Lexington, MA: D.C. Heath and Company.

Wright, H. T., Redding, R. W., and Pollock, S. M. 1989. Monitoring interannual variability: An example from the period of early state development in southwestern Iran. In P. Halstead, and J. O'Shea (Eds.), *Bad year economics: Cultural responses to risk and uncertainty.* Cambridge, UK: Cambridge University Press, pp. 106–13.

Wylie, A. 1985. The reaction against analogy. In M. B. Schiffer (Ed.), *Advances in archaeological method and theory* (Vol. 8). Orlando, FL: Academic Press, pp. 63–111.

Wyman, J. 1868a. An account of some kjoekkenmoeddings, or shell-heaps, in Maine and Massachusetts. *American Naturalist* 1(11):561–84.

———. 1868b. On the fresh-water shell-heaps of the St. Johns River, East Florida. *American Naturalist* 2(8):393–403.

———. 1875. Fresh-water shell mounds of the St. Johns River, Florida. *Memoirs of the Peabody Academy of Science* 4:3–94.

Yalden, D. W., and Carthy, R. I. 2004. The archaeological record of birds in Britain and Ireland compared: Extinctions or failures to arrive? *Environmental Archaeology* 9:123–6.

Yang, D. Y., Cannon, A., and Saunders, S. R. 2004. DNA species identification of archaeological salmon bone from the Pacific Northwest Coast of North America. *Journal of Archaeological Science* 31:619–31.

Yang, D. Y., Woiderski, J. R., and Driver, J. C. 2005. DNA analysis of archaeological rabbit remains from the American Southwest. *Journal of Archaeological Science* 32:567–78.

Yellen, J. E. 1977a. *Archaeological approaches to the present: Models for reconstructing the past.* New York: Academic Press.

———. 1977b. Cultural patterning in faunal remains: Evidence from the !Kung Bushmen. In D. Ingersoll, J. Yellen, and W. Macdonald (Eds.), *Experimental archeology.* New York: Columbia, pp. 271–331.

Yen, D. E. 1989. The domestication of environment. In D. R. Harris and G. C. Hillmand (Eds.), *Foraging and farming: The evolution of plant exploitation.* London: Unwin Hyman, pp. 55–75.

Yerkes, R. W. 2005. Bone chemistry, body parts, and growth marks: Evaluating Ohio Hopewell and Cahokia Mississippian seasonality, subsistence, ritual, and feasting. *American Antiquity* 70(20):241–65.

Yodzis, P. 1993. Environment and trophodiversity. In R. E. Ricklefs and D. Schluter (Eds.), *Species diversity in ecological communities: Historical and geographical perspectives.* Chicago: University of Chicago Press, pp. 26–38.

Yohe, R. M., II, Newman, M. E., and Schneider, J. S. 1991. Immunological identification of small-mammal proteins on aboriginal milling equipment. *American Antiquity* 56(4):659–66.

Yoneda, M., Suzuki, R., Shibata, Y., Morita, M., Sukegawa, T., Shigehara, N., and Akazawa, T. 2004. Isotopic evidence of inland-water fishing by a Jomon population excavated from the Boji site, Nagano, Japan. *Journal of Archaeological Science* 31:97–107.

Yoneda, M., Tanaka, A., Shibata, Y., Morita, M., Uzawa, K., Hirota, M., and Uchida, M. 2002. Radiocarbon marine reservoir effect in human remains from the Kitakogane site, Hokkaido, Japan. *Journal of Archaeological Science* 29:529–36.

Zangerl, R. 1969. The turtle shell. In C. Gans, A. d'A. Bellairs, and T. S. Parsons (Eds.), *Biology of the Reptilia: Morphology A* (Vol. 1). London: Academic Press, pp. 311–39.

Zeder, M. A. 1991. *Feeding cities: Specialized animal economy in the ancient Near East.* Washington, DC: Smithsonian Institution Press.

———. 1994. After the revolution: Post-Neolithic subsistence in northern Mesopotamia. *American Anthropologist* 96(1):97–126.

———. 2001. A metrical analysis of modern goats (*Capra hircus aegargus* and *C. h. hircus*) from Iran and Iraq: Implications for the study of caprine domestication. *Journal of Archaeological Science* 28:61–79.

———. 2006a. A critical assessment of markers of initial domestication in goats (*Capra hircus*). In M. A. Zeder, D. G. Bradley, E. Emshwiller, and B. D. Smith (Eds.), *Documenting domestication: New genetics and archaeological paradigms* Berkeley: University of California Press, pp. 181–227.

———. 2006b. Reconciling rates of long bone fusion and tooth eruption and wear in sheep (*Ovis*) and goat (*Capra*). In D. Ruscillo (Eds.), *Recent advances in ageing and sexing animal bones.* Oxford: Oxbow Books, pp. 87–118.

Zeder, M. A., and Arter, S. A. 2007. Meat consumption and bone use in a Mississippian village. In E. J. Reitz, C. M. Scarry, and S. J. Scudder (Eds.), *Case studies in environmental archaeology* (2nd ed.). London: Springer, pp. 329–47.

Zeder, M. A., Bradley, D. G., Emshwiller, E., and Smith, B. D. (Eds.). 2006. *Documenting domestication: New genetics and archaeological paradigms.* Berkeley: University of California Press.

Zeder, M. A., Emshwiller, E., Smith, B. D. and Bradley, D. G. 2006. Documenting domestication: The intersection of genetics and archaeology. *Trends in Genetics* 22:119–82.

Zeder, M. A., and Hesse, B. 2000. The initial domestication of goats (*Capra hircus*) in the Zagros Mountains 10,000 years ago. *Science* 287:2254–7.

Zeiler, J. T. 2004. Private investigations – Working in a commercial setting. In R. C. G. M. Lauwerier and I. Plug (Eds.), *The future from the past: Archaeozoology in wildlife conservation and heritage management.* Oxford: Oxbow Books, pp. 149–52.

Zeuner, F. E. 1963. *A history of domesticated animals.* New York: Harper and Row.

Ziegler, A. C. 1973. *Inference from prehistoric faunal remains.* Reading, MA: Addison-Wesley Module in Anthropology 43.

Zohar, I., Dayan, T., Galili, E., and Spanier, E. 2001. Fish processing during the Early Holocene: A taphonomic case study from coastal Israel. *Journal of Archaeological Science* 28:1041–53.

Zohar, I., Dayan, T., Spanier, E., Galili, E., and Lernau, O. 1994. Exploitation of grey triggerfish (*Balistes carolinensis*) by the prehistoric inhabitants of Atlit-Yam, Israel: A preliminary report. In W. Van Neer (Ed.), *Fish exploitation in the past*. Tervuren, Belgium: Annales du Musée Royal de l'Afrique Centrale, Sciences Zoologiques 274, pp. 231–7.

Zusi, R. L. 1993. Patterns of diversity in the avian skull. In J. Hanken and B. K. Hall (Eds.), *The skull* (Vol. 2). Chicago: University of Chicago Press, pp. 391–437.

Zvelebil, M. 1985. Iron Age transformations in northern Russia and the northeast Baltic. In G. Barker and C. Gamble (Eds.), *Beyond domestication in prehistoric Europe: Investigations in subsistence archaeology and social complexity*. London: Academic Press, pp. 147–80.

Zvelebil, M., and Dolukhanov, P. 1991. The transition to farming in Eastern and Northern Europe. *Journal of World Prehistory* 5(3):233–78.

SYSTEMATIC INDEX

Page references to figures and tables are italicized.

TOPICAL INDEX

Page references to figures and tables are italicized.

DNA (deoxyribonucleic acid), 5, 34, 80–82,
144, 274–275, 386
ancient DNA (aDNA), 81–82, 118, 182,
288–289
mitochondrial DNA (mtDNA), 81–82,
288–289, 294
nuclear DNA (nDNA), 80–82, 289
see also archaeogenetics; genetics; genome
document, *see* written record
domestic animal, 2, 7, 16, 17, 28, 100, 115, *115*,
290, 293, 344
barnyard, 293, 295, 296–297
breed, 36, 65, 73, 189, 201–202, *291*
free-ranging, 193
herd, 255, 293, 295–296, 330–331
house, 293, 295, 296–297
introduction and spread of, 28, 87, 302–303,
310–311, 325, 331, 348
pet, 7, 216, 281, 300, 301
see also animal husbandry; pathology;
Systematic Index
domestication, 287–288, *291–292*
behavioral features, 268, 287–288, 290,
301–302, 304
capture and control, 298–299
castration, 73, 201–202, 268, 304, 306, 307,
312
centers of, 293, 302–303
change in faunal composition, 311
change in proportion, 302–305, 312
and coat color, 287, 298, 305–306
confinement, 243, 302–303, 311–312
and conformation, 183, 186, 202, 297, 302,
304–305, 331
control of breeding, 73, 289, 290, 299, 301,
302–306
demographic change, 303, 306–310, 311
diet, 243, 290
and environment, 293, 296, 330–331, 349–350
and environmental reconstruction, 313–314,
317, 325
evidence for, 184, 189–190, 215, 297, 302–314
features of age and sex, 72–73, 172, 192
and genetics, 81–82, 288–289, 305–306
and health, 28, 243, 311–312
history of, 1, 28, 29, *291–292*, 293, 303, 305,
310–311
impact on culture, 295–296, 348

inbreeding, 312
and isotopes, 83
major domestic species, *291–292*, 301
methods of study, 297–310
and modifications, 243–244
morphology, 288, 289, 290, 297, 302, 311
phenotypic features of, *3 05*
physiological features of, 73, 301–302
and plant cultivation, 293, 298, 310, 311, 314,
330–331
polling, 268, 305, 312
process of, 290, 297–307
range extension, 299–300
and site-catchment analysis, 24
slaughter schedule, 103
and subsistence strategies, 260
and taming, 299–301
taxonomy of, 290, *291–292*
timing of, 293, 303
unintentional, 298–299
and zooarchaeological research, 5
see also Systematic Index; taxonomy
Driver, J. C., 161

Eaton, G. F., 16
ecofact, 5
ecological analogy, 143, 182–183, 266, 320–322,
343
ecology, 13–14, 21, 29, 31, 251, 297, 332
definition, 88–89
methods, 113–115
see also community ecology; population
ecology
economies
and behavior, 253–255
and domestic animals, 311
and environmental change, 319
and isotopes, 82
and social organization, 252, 276, 280
and social systems, 254–255
and zooarchaeological research, 1, 4, 5, 13,
24, 27–28, 169, 213, 344, 348
ecosystem, 8, 84, 86, 90, *105*, 106, *108*, 109, 110,
115–116, 316, 330, 347, 349
aquatic, 104, 106, 109
definition, 104
estuary, 104, *105*, 106
island, 303, 310, 324–325

recent, 170
root-etching, 139, 142
saw, 130, 170, 172, 243
saw, metal, 130, 243
saw, non-metal, 130
sawtoothed, *169*
scrape, 128, *130*, 170, 243
skinning, 126–127, 242–243
slaughter, 125–126
slice, 128
spiral fracture, 127, 136, 142, 169–170, 383, 384
spiral, irregular, *169*
spiral, regular, *169*
splintered, 169, *169*
stepped, 169, *169*
trample, 124, 138–139, 141, 143, 170, 243
transverse, 169
transverse, irregular, *169*
transverse, regular, *169*
weathering, 142, 170, 384
worked, 28, 133–134, *169*, 285, 300, 386
see also food preparation; pathology; tools
moisture, 109, 140, 260
mollusc valve
color, 32
and environmental reconstruction, 320
increments in, 176
length, 186, 198
and MNI, 207
morphology, *40*, *41*, 45
as raw material, 133
seasonal growth, 74, *75–79*
shape, 164
and site-formation processes, 141
weight, 65, 239
see also increments
molt (ecdysis), 62
Mongolia, *291–292*
Morlot, A. von, 2
morphology, 17, 31, 32, 297, *see also* anatomy
mortality rate, 101–102
mutualism, 103, 306, 315

Nagaoka, L., 328
nail, 41, 61
Native American Graves Protection and Repatriation Act (NAGPRA), 390

Native Americans, 311
natural area, 13
Near East, *291–292*
neoteny, 304
Netherlands Antilles (West Indies), *3*, 300
Netherlands, The, 17
Neusius, S. W., 298
New Britain (Melanesia), *3*, 300
New England (USA), 78, 313
New Guinea, *3*, 33, 277, 296, 329
New Ireland (Melanesia), *3*, 300
Newsom, L. A., 328
New Zealand, 49, 100, 328
niche, 39, 318
    breadth, 14, 24, 28, 182, 245–246
    definition, 89
NMI, 206
Noddle, B. A., 73
Noe-Nygaard, N., 125, 127
normal distribution, 113
North America, 32, 90, 144, 145, 275, 320, 328–330, 331
northwest Pacific Coast (North America), *3*, 262, 267, *269*, *271*, 277
notochord, 42
nucleus, 81
number of identified specimens (NISP)
    and age, *195*, *197*
    and estimates of dietary contribution, 233
    and MNI, 206, 208
    observed to expected ratios, 222, *223*
    and niche breadth, 245
    and recovery methods, *149*
    and relative frequency of taxa, 212–213
    and skeletal portions, 216–217, 230–232
    and specimen weight, 211
    and utility indices, 226, 227
    as primary data, 158, 167–168
    as secondary data, 202–205
    see also minimum number of individuals; modifications; quantification; specimen weight
number of remains (NR), 167
Nunamiut, 225
nursery ground, 64, 323
nutrients, 22, 106, 109
    amino acid, 96, 349
    calories, 24, 95